Infonomics for Distributed Business and Decision-Making Environments:
Creating Information System Ecology

Malgorzata Pankowska
Karol Adamiecki University of Economics in Katowice, Poland

BUSINESS SCIENCE REFERENCE
Hershey · New York

Director of Editorial Content: Kristin Klinger
Senior Managing Editor: Jamie Snavely
Assistant Managing Editor: Michael Brehm
Publishing Assistant: Sean Woznicki
Typesetter: Sean Woznicki, Jamie Snavely
Cover Design: Lisa Tosheff
Printed at: Yurchak Printing Inc.

Published in the United States of America by
Business Science Reference (an imprint of IGI Global)
701 E. Chocolate Avenue
Hershey PA 17033
Tel: 717-533-8845
Fax: 717-533-8661
E-mail: cust@igi-global.com
Web site: http://www.igi-global.com/reference

Library of Congress Cataloging-in-Publication Data

Infonomics for distributed business and decision-making environments : creating information system ecology / Malgorzata Pankowska, editor.
p. cm.
Includes bibliographical references and index.
Summary: "In this book, The authors focus on the development of new approaches to the management of information, addressing several topics i.e. information evaluation and ecology of information, agent technology for information management, ethics of information, infological interpretation of information in distributed business environment, and business models in information economy"--Provided by publisher.
ISBN 978-1-60566-890-1 (hbk.) -- ISBN 978-1-60566-891-8 (ebook) 1. Information technology--Management. 2. Information resources management. 3. Information networks. I. Pankowska, Malgorzata. II. Title.

HD30.2.I523 2010
658.4'038--dc22

2009018417

British Cataloguing in Publication Data
A Cataloguing in Publication record for this book is available from the British Library.

List of Reviewers

Dimitris Kanellopoulos, *University of Patras, Greece*
El Hassan Bezzazi, *University de Lille 2, France*
Judit Olah, *University of Wyoming, USA*
Brane Semolic, *University of Maribor, Slovenia*
Bo Sundgren, *Senior Adviser to the Director General of Statistics, Sweden*
Claus-Peter Rueckemann, *RRZN/Leibniz Universitaet Hannover, Germany*
Chiang Lichun, *National Cheng Kung University, Taiwan*
Adriana Schiopoiu Burlea, *University of Craiova, Romania*
Wita Wojtkowski, *Boise State University, USA*
Ole Axvig, *Environmental Services Cheyenne, USA*
Vassiliki Andronikou, *National Technical University of Athens, Greece*
Henry Linger, *Monash University, Australia*
Michael Mackert, *The University of Texas at Austin, USA*

Table of Contents

Section 2
Information Management Progress

Section 3
Information Valuation

Detailed Table of Contents

Section 1
Information Interpretation and Modeling

Defining data, information, knowledge and their relationships is mainly a point of view matter. Indeed, the same entity may be related to any of these concepts depending on the use of it. This is true, at least as long as the entity is communicable through some means (text, voice, gesture, signal, object, or media, for example). By restricting our attention to symbolic entities and to the World Wide Web in particular, we can learn much about these concepts, their interconnections, the functions that apply on them and their values.

This chapter is focused on state-of-the art issues in the area of ontology-based autonomic communications and it considers how ontologies can be useful for network management as a way to achieve semantic interoperability among different network management models. In addition, it presents the autonomic communications paradigm as a possible solution to the ever-growing complexity of commercial networks due to the increasing complexity of individual network elements, the need for intelligent network and communication services and the heterogeneity of connected equipment. Finally, the chapter analyses how ontologies can be used to combine data correlation and inference technologies in autonomic networks. Such technologies are used as core components to build autonomic networks.

This chapter gives a comprehensive overview of the current status of accounting and billing for up-to-date computing environments. Accounting is the key for the management of information system resources. At this stage of evolution of accounting systems it is adequate not to separate computing environments into High Performance Computing and Grid Computing environments for allowing a "holistic" view showing the different approaches and the state of the art for integrated accounting and billing in distributed computing environments. Requirements resulting from a public survey within all communities of the German Grid infrastructure, as well as from computing centres and resource providers of High Performance Computing resources like HLRN, and ZIVGrid, within the German e-Science framework, have been considered as well as requirements resulting from various information systems and the virtualisation of organisations and resources. Additionally, conceptual, technical, economical, and legal questions also had to be taken into consideration. After the requirements have been consolidated and implementations have been done over one year ago, now the overall results and conclusions are presented in the following sections showing a case study based on the GISIG framework and the Grid-GIS framework. The focus is on how an integrated architecture can be built and used in heterogeneous environments. A prototypical implementation is outlined that is able to manage and visualise relevant accounting and billing information based on suitable monitoring data in a virtual organisation specific way regarding basic business, economic, and security issues.

The main purpose of this chapter is the comparison of differences between results of three methods used for quality evaluation of individual e-banking services. The comparison has been conducted for selected sixteen banks in Poland. The author uses three types of research: traditional expert scoring method, AHP (Analytic Hierarchy Process) method and conversion method. After a general introduction, a detailed report of the results arising from this research is presented and analyzed. Finally, the author draws general conclusions from the analysis. He also discusses the future research regarding this topic.

Researchers are currently challenged to document the economic aspects of information across an array of contexts. While some lessons can be applied generally, certain contexts present unique challenges for researchers interested in the acquisition, management, and use of information. Health is one such field currently undergoing a revolution driven by new applications of information-based technologies and services. This chapter provides background on health informatics and current issues as health informatics impacts the provision of health in doctors' offices, shifts the provision of healthcare services into patients' homes, and presents new opportunities to address public health concerns. An outline of a

Preface

The field of information resources management is broad and encompasses many facets of information technology research and practice as well as business and organizational processes. Because information technology changes at an incredible rate, it is essential for all who use, teach or research information management to have access to the most current data and research and keep up with emerging trends. This publication is aimed at providing a greater understanding of issues, challenges, trends and technologies effecting the overall utilization and management of information in modern organizations around the world.

The chapters in this book address the emerging issues in information resources economics and its application. Information modeling, information management, governance and valuation, collaborative networks development, ethical issues in distributed information environments are topics relevant to business people and academics. Additionally, the chapters provide concrete ways for academics to broaden their research and case study examples, which enable business people to better interpret the text and to avoid the pitfalls discussed in the book.

The phenomenon where an organization extends outside its traditional boundaries is commonly described as an extended enterprise, a virtual enterprise, or even a virtually integrated enterprise. As the diversity of the e-business environment proliferates, the real benefits for an organization will be attained by those entities that endorse and embrace this extended enterprise concept and adapt to best fit the environment in which they operate. In an extended enterprise, the core focus replaces a centralized one, and there is a shift to shared services, cosourcing and outsourcing, extending out to partners, suppliers and customers to accomplish the objectives more effectively.

For many years, economics of information was developed in closed and hierarchical organizations; now organizations are connected together in open networks and in extended enterprises, so the approach to economics of information (or infonomics) must be changed. The question is to what degree the traditional methods of information valuation are still valid and what new methods of information valuation, cost and benefits estimation are developed and must be implemented.

The book is designed to detail the main concepts of infonomics, how the issues transcend beyond the physical boundaries of an enterprise, how it has extended out into entities' customers, trading partners and suppliers, and the interdependencies that have been created. It provides new ideas and ways to think, utilizing concepts that are familiar and accepted by business and governmental entities. Although infonomics may be a familiar concept, applying it outside the physical boundaries of an organization is a relatively new idea, and certainly one that is not yet well accepted in the marketplace.

The advent of the Internet, and the technologies related to it, has created the opportunity and the need to seize the advantages of operating in the extended enterprise. Globalization and worldwide communications have overridden traditional boundaries. In many markets, these global interdependencies (governmental, political and business) are now so interconnected that they must be considered with almost any decision being made. Additionally, information technology (IT) has moved from being an enabler of organization strategy to a key element of it. The central hypothesis of this book is that the implementation of information technology in organizations has entered a new stage.

Authors have endeavored to take a global view and draw on the experiences of leading analysts, IT experts, technologists and organizations around the world. They have included case studies and interviews with influential businesses and business leaders to illustrate how management theory, new business practices and cutting-edge technology can help companies achieve IT benefits in distributed business environments.

Most importantly, we have tried to take a pragmatic and real life approach to the subjects. The book aims to provide a practical and useful guide for business and IT professionals to help you address the issues of today and the future.

The authors hope you find it both enlightening and useful, and look forward to featuring some of your organizations in future success stories!

STRUCTURE OF THE BOOK

The book's 18 chapters are organized into four parts that address four issues of the information economics: These are:

Section 1: Information Interpretations and Modeling, Chapters 1 to 4.
Section 2: Information Management Progress, Chapters 5 to 8.
Section 3: Information Valuation, Chapters 9 to 13.
Section 4: Collaboration in Networks, Chapters 14 to 18.

Section 1 outlines the fundamental principles that emerged as important premises and pervasive themes of the book. We urge readers to start here as these ideas underlie all the chapters that follow. The first section's chapters address the information modeling. Through four chapters, Section 1 contains a discussion on the actual approaches to information modeling.

Chapter 1 presents a discussion on information and knowledge concepts and functions. The author assumes that the defining data, information, knowledge and their relationships is mainly a point of view matter. He argues that the same entity may be related to any of these concepts depending on the use of it. This is true, at least as long as the entity is communicable through some means (text, voice, gesture, signal, object, and media for example). By restricting our attention to symbolic entities and to the World Wide Web in particular, we can learn much about these concepts, their interconnections, the functions that apply on them and their values.

In this chapter, the author discusses issues related to the concept of data, information and knowledge. He first observes that very often the same functions apply to these concepts and few functions are specific to one or another of these concepts. Secondly, he discusses the concept of meaning as being a relation between pieces of information. In the last two sections, he restricts our attention to the context of the World Wide Web by considering information flow from Web to user and from user to Web. The first flow is mainly the outcome of a search process. The second one results from user personal data being collected by first or third parties with or without his knowledge when surfing the Web. In these particular contexts, information is not a concept which is restricted to human minds. Indeed, applications like Web services may act on behalf of the user or third parties to achieve some intelligent research or data processing.

Chapter 2 focuses on state-of-the art issues in the area of ontology-based autonomic communications and it considers how ontologies can be useful for network management as a way to achieve semantic interoperability among different network management models. In addition, it presents the autonomic communications paradigm as a possible solution to the ever-growing complexity of commercial networks due to the increasing complexity of individual network elements, the need for intelligent network and communication services and the heterogeneity of connected equipment. Finally, the chapter analyzes how ontologies can be used to combine data correlation and inference technologies in autonomic networks. Such technologies are used as core components to build autonomic networks.

Chapter 3 presents a proposition of so-called infological interpretation of information. The concept was formulated by Bo Sundgren (1973) in his publication devoted to databases. Sundgren developed a consistent theory of a model of database based on the concept of message as a specific set of data. The model inspires not only for a new interpretation of information but also is a good base for manifold analysis of the concept. In the chapter, among others, the following basic concepts are discussed: properties of information, diversity of information, and information space.

Chapter 4 provides a method supporting the information modeling. Authors argue that various models and methods are used to support information system development process, but still after many years of practice, projects still continue to fail. One of the reasons is that the conventional modeling approaches do not provide efficient support for learning and communication among stakeholders. Authors believe that lack of an integrated method for systematic analysis, design and evolution of static and dynamic structures of information system architectures is the core of frustration in various companies. Semantic problems of communication between business analysis and design experts lead to ambiguous and incomplete system requirement specifications. The traditional modeling approaches do not view business data and process as a whole.

The objective of this chapter is to present a comprehensive review of fundamental theoretical assumptions concerning communication and learning as well as to present some basic problems in traditional modeling approaches for analysis and design of information systems in this perspective. The analysis done provides assumptions that should be taken into consideration while constructing models and methods to support communication and learning during the information system development process. The chapter shortly presents a method that enables system analysts and designers to reason about pragmatic, semantic and syntactic aspects of the system in an integrated way, which is necessary to understand the system as a whole. The service-oriented approach was presented as a solution to integration of static and dynamic parts of the system using one modeling notation. The presented solutions are motivated by taking into account theoretical ideas concerning communication, understanding and learning.

Section 2 addresses information management progress. It confronts and redefines the problems of information management. Whereas most literature on management addresses the problem of information management, the authors treat this from different business and technological perspectives. The next four chapters cast familiar scenery in a new light as authors discuss new technical and managerial approaches to successfully deal with information in a distributed business environment. This section contains four chapters.

Chapter 5 concerns the expanding of the strategic role of information interaction in the enterprise environment. The authors propose an integrated model, which was developed using the results of an empirical study. The model puts a user-centered focus on business process model building by mapping all information interactions surrounding the business processes (i.e. creation, storage, management, retrieval of documents/contents as well as information and data). The model characterizes the business processes by types of information interaction, analyzes process phases by those interactions and evaluates actual locations of information content extractions.

Chapter 6 introduces the information management in a Grid-based e-health business environment. In this chapter, the authors analyze the technical and business requirements of the e-healthcare collaborative environment. The authors argue that, given the nature, variety, volume and importance of the information in the e-healthcare collaborative environment as well as the complexity of the information flows, current techniques applied within this domain prove to be obsolete or inadequate. With efficient, reliable and privacy-aware data management and interoperability climbing the highest stairs in the hierarchy of the technical and business requirements, the integration of Grid technologies followed by the implementation of the HL-7 (Health Level Seven) specifications paves the way towards the successful realization of a large-scale international e-healthcare collaborative environment allowing for the continuous, timely and reliable communication of medical and administrative information across organizational boundaries. The SWOT (Strengths Weaknesses Opportunities Threats) analysis presented shows that the potential of this integration is promising, although quite a few barriers need to be overcome; reluctance in the adoption of new technology and the transformation of the currently followed operations, data privacy concerns, current technological insufficiency in meeting the strict requirements for efficient, reliable, privacy-aware data management and interoperability. However, these deterring factors can be translated into interesting research fields that require feverish work and a multidisciplinary approach.

Chapter 7 explains the usage of intelligent agents in business process modeling and business process management systems. The basic notions of agent-based systems and their architectures are given. Multi-agent systems as sets of multiple interacting software agents, as well as frameworks and methodologies of their development are a valuable solution to cope with information overload problems. Generally, they can be applied for information filtering, searching, gathering and administration. In this chapter, three kinds of architectures of agent-based systems – holons, multi-agent systems and aspect-oriented architecture are described. Examples of already implemented agent-based systems in logistics, transportation and supply chain management are given. The chapter gives an insight into recent business process management systems and their architectures, and highlights several issues and challenges which underpin the necessity for agent-based business process management. Methodologies and implementation of agent-based business process management systems are discussed and directions of future research in this area are outlined.

Chapter 8 concerns information governance in distributed business environments (i.e. virtual heterarchies). The authors assume that corporate governance models are needed to concentrate on changes of existing rules, customs, practices and rights as the subject matter of governance to be influenced. Governance models must recognize the limitations of the overburdened state and the consequent need to take advantage of existing institutions and structures that promote sustainability. The differences between governance and management are presented in the chapter as well as the fundamental characteristics of corporate governance, information technology governance and information governance. The authors noticed that an increasing number of companies are moving into new forms of competition which can be described as information-based competition, knowledge-based competition, technology-based competition and ICT (Information Communication Technology) relationship-based competition. However, an unlimited supply of information from Internet and other sources, easiness to register and transfer the information, and reduced prices of ICT devices results in theincrease of information processing and its overload. Therefore, the information governance model proposed in the chapter seems to be a pattern to deal with information in contemporary common organizations (i.e. virtual heterarchical organizations) where access to information is democratically permitted. The proposed model aims to ensure sustainable governance of information (i.e. balance, stability and progress of information processing).

Section 3 examines the most basic work in infonomics: information valuation. Information, its value and valuation processes were the subject of many research works for many years. Information technology development encourages researchers to look for new definitions. In distributed business environments and in Internet business organizations, information is perceived in different ways. Therefore, the authors of the Section 3 chapters are involved in redefining and reevaluating information processes as well as information sectors. This section contains five chapters.

Chapter 9 deals with the analysis of the value of information in distributed decision support systems. It characterizes the basic measures of the value of information, with the stress put on the utility function, the effect of the knowledge discovery techniques in databases, on the value of information and multicriteria methods of decision support. In the chapter, a multi-agent system is presented, which is an example of a distributed decision support system. In the last part of the chapter, the choice methods and consensus methods for increasing the value of information through eliminating contradiction of information within the system are discussed.

Chapter 10 gives a comprehensive overview of the current status of accounting and billing for up-to-date computing environments. Accounting is the key for the management of information system resources. At this stage of evolution of accounting systems it is adequate not to separate computing environments into High Performance Computing and Grid Computing environments for allowing a "holistic" view showing different approaches to integrated accounting and billing in distributed computing environments. Requirements resulting from a public survey within all communities of the German Grid infrastructure, as well as from computing centers and resource providers of High Performance Computing resources like HLRN, and ZIVGrid, within the German e-science framework, have been considered as well as requirements resulting from various information systems and the virtualization of organizations and resources. Additionally, conceptual, technical, economical, and legal questions also had to be taken into consideration. After the requirements have been consolidated and implementations have been done over one year ago, now the overall results and conclusions are presented in the following sections showing a case study based on the GISIG framework and the Grid-GIS framework. The focus is on how an integrated architecture can be built and used in heterogeneous environments. A prototypical implementation is outlined that is able to manage and visualize accounting and billing relevant information based on suitable monitoring data in a way specific for virtual organizations regarding basic business, economic, and security issues.

Chapter 11 concerns a very specific approach to information valuation. The author focuses on e-banking services and analyzes the application of three methods of quality evaluation. The main purpose of this chapter is the comparison of differences between results of three methods used for quality evaluation of individual e-banking services. The comparison has been conducted for 16 selected banks in Poland. The author uses three types of research: traditional expert scoring method, AHP (Analytic Hierarchy Process) method and conversion method. After a general introduction, a detailed report of the results arising from this research is presented and analyzed. Finally, the author draws general conclusions from the analysis. He also discusses the future research regarding this topic.

Chapter 12 provides background on health informatics and current issues as health informatics impacts the provision of health in doctors' offices, shifts the provision of healthcare services into patients' homes, and presents new opportunities to address public health concerns. An outline of a future research agenda in health informatics and a look at the prospect of health informatics applications provides the necessary foundation for focused work on the economic impact of this information-driven transformation in healthcare delivery.

Chapter 13 introduces the concept of the information sector and provides a new sense of the problems and opportunities. Here, the author focuses on analyses of the information sector in the economy, ensures the method of the classification of the economic sectors, presents the information sector in the Polish economy and in economies of selected countries, and eventually considers the value of the information sector in the economy.

Section 4 concerns collaboration in networks. We start with the more conventional view – designing infrastructure – and then propose more work on new organizational forms development as well as on business ethics in distributed business environment. This section contains five chapters.

Chapter 14 describes the approach to the design of collaborative infrastructures. The author argues that collaboration is playing an increasing role in business especially given an increase in business networking. Such networks are formed to gain business advantage by combining expertise from many businesses or organizational units to quickly create new and competitive products and services. Most processes in business networks now consist of a number of activities whose processes must be coordinated to reach enterprise goals. The chapter addresses ways of supporting such activities using technology and proposes a collaboration infrastructure that encourages collaboration and sharing of knowledge across activities.

Chapter 15 covers considerations on virtual network development. The authors discuss issues of the governance of virtual organizations and living laboratories. They describe the managerial processes inside virtual organizations and living laboratories, focusing particularly on the architecture design for living laboratories. The chapter presents the findings of research regarding the state of development and application of a laser living laboratory management and governance system in Toolmakers Cluster of Slovenia.

Chapter 16 concerns the new forms of work created because of the globalization in the software development domain. The authors argue that globalization in software development introduced significant changes in the way organizations operate today. Software is now produced by team members from geographically, temporally and culturally remote sites. Organizations seek benefits that the global market offers and face new challenges. Naturally resistant to change, these organizations often do not realize the necessity for tailoring existing methods for distributed collaboration. The authors' empirical investigation shows a great variety in the ways organizations distribute responsibilities across remote sites and conclude that these can be divided into two main categories: joint collaboration that requires investments in team building and independent collaboration that requires investments in knowledge management and transfer. Finally, they discuss practices that are applied in industry to overcome these challenges and emphasize the necessity to fully understand the pros and cons of different ways to organize distributed software projects before starting one in this new environment.

In the final two chapters, authors shift from information economics to information ethics issues in business environment.

Chapter 17 aims to understand the perceptions of employee information ethics using a company within the Environmental Protection Science Park in the southern part of Taiwan. The two purposes of this research are (1) to understand the environments of employees who understand information ethics, and (2) to clarify variables regarding information ethics which could provide a framework for policy controlling information ethics for businesses related to information technology. The findings of this study show that respondents understand the concept of unethical or illegal use of IT. All respondents perceived unauthorized behaviors, such as illegal downloads and reading other IT accounts without permission as unethical behaviors.

Chapter 18 offers an examination of some issues of ethics related to information in distributed business environment, *DBE*. The ethical issue of what is moral to do in order to optimize the use of information in *DBE* is dealt with. The varied ways of integrating and putting into the practice information in *DBE* are discussed as well as the great variety of ethical approaches. The author argues that in the field of ethics of information in *DBE* we are no longer confronted with a "policy vacuum," so she is facing the *dissipation of ethical responsibility* (*DER)* and this phenomenon leads to difficult and usually late locating and solving ethical dilemmas within the system.

TARGET AUDIENCES

This book will appeal most to university students and researchers inclined not just to manage information and IT, but to understand it as well – not only to gain knowledge for its own sake but because they realize that a better understanding of infonomics leads to governing better. This, in turn, circles back to deeper understanding.

This book is expected to be read by academics (i.e. teachers, researchers and students), technology solutions developers and enterprise managers (including top-level managers).

The book should give incentives for and guide the creation of indispensable information environments, as well as the information valuation as a particular one proposed in the book.

Looking from a future perspective and more advanced social needs, this book ought to guide the creation of the interorganizational, cross-functionalities structures (or infrastructures) as a part of the paradigm shift in organizational sciences.

This book draws on the diverse experience of the authors – an academic with broad practical experience drawn from business organizations around the world in improving their people, processes and systems.

The text will assist readers in becoming familiar with the critical issues of concern related to information economics, and doing it with world-class excellence in the new environment called the business distributed environment. It has often been stated that information is the grease that allows an enterprise to run efficiently. This statement, when related to extended enterprises, can mean the difference between success and failure and profit or loss.

Both academics and practitioners have spent considerable efforts during the last years to establish ICT support for the handling of knowledge. Not surprisingly, the solution is still not there and many businesses trying to implement the technologies have been frustrated by the fact that the technologies certainly could not live up to the overly high expectations. However, there are still numerous projects in organizations that try to tackle the fundamental challenge of how to increase productivity of information work.

This book is also expected to raise awareness of information management needs for supporting environments. The book provides a base for further study and research definition as well as solution development. The authors hope that the book will contribute to the diffusion of infonomics concepts all over the world. The authors will be grateful to the readers for any constructive criticisms and indication of omissions or misinterpretations.

Acknowledgment

Putting together this book would not have been possible without the assistance and cooperation of many academics, practitioners, freelancers and other people whose insights proved highly valuable and beneficial for our project. First of all, I would like to thank the authors for submitting their contributions and their assistance during the process. Most of the authors also served as referees for the chapters. I want to express my gratitude to those who provided critical, constructive and comprehensive reviews. In particular, I want to thank Dr. Dimitris Kanellopoulos from University of Patras, Prof. El Hassan Bezzazi from University de Lille 2, Prof. Judit Olah from University of Wyoming, Dr Brane Semolic from University of Maribor, Dr. rer. nat. Claus-Peter Rueckemann from University in Hannover, Prof. Chiang Lichun from National Cheng Kung University, Prof. Adriana Schiopoiu Burlea from University of Craiova, Ole Axvig from Environmental Services Cheyenne, Wyoming, Dr. Vassiliki Andronikou from National Technical University of Athens, and Prof. Michael Mackert from the University of Texas at Austin.

I'm the beneficiary of wise counsel from others as well: special thanks go to Prof. Bo Sundgren, senior adviser to the Director General of Statistics Sweden and professor of Informatics at Mid Sweden University, Prof. Wita Wojtkowski from the College of Business and Economics at Boise State University and Prof. Henry Linger from the School of Information Management and Systems at Monash University in Australia for reading the chapters and providing intelligent suggestions.

I would also like also to thank the team at IGI Global, in particular to Jan Travers, Kristin M. Klinger, Rebecca Beistline, and Christine Bufton for their tolerance and patience, for their invaluable support and advice without which the book would have remained just a good idea.

It should be added that the publication of this volume does not mean the end of our work. Many ideas were proposed for further chapters, many concepts have yet to be properly nailed down, and many issues need to be further explored.

Our thinking developed considerably through the discussions and debates. We hope this publication is a way of launching the continuing discussion in a wider field.

Organizational Infonomics has a vital role to play in the post-industrial agency, which has information as its key resource. At present we have well-developed disciplines concerned with the hard and soft extremes of the information fields.

Thank you.

Malgorzata Pankowska
editor
Katowice, April 2009

Section 1
Information Interpretation and Modeling

Chapter 1
Information and Knowledge: Concepts and Functions

El Hassan Bezzazi
CERAPS, Université de Lille 2, France

ABSTRACT

Defining data, information, knowledge and their relationships is mainly a point of view matter. Indeed, the same entity may be related to any of these concepts depending on the use of it. This is true, at least as long as the entity is communicable through some means (text, voice, gesture, signal, object, or media, for example). By restricting our attention to symbolic entities and to the World Wide Web in particular, we can learn much about these concepts, their interconnections, the functions that apply on them and their values.

INTRODUCTION

Defining data, information, knowledge and their relationships is mainly a point of view matter. Indeed, the same entity may be related to any of these concepts depending on the use of it. This is true, at least as long as the entity is communicable through some means (text, voice, gesture, signal, object, media for example). In the free online encyclopedia Wikipedia, the page about the "Monty Hall problem", a probabilistic puzzle, represents at the same time data, information and knowledge. It is simple data when seen as a file downloaded to be interpreted and displayed in the web browser. The reading of the page reveals information about the problem and the solution. This web page will also be a source of knowledge for the reader who managed understanding the counterintuitive solution. On the other hand, this knowledge may help him for example, as valuable information for some reasoning by analogy, if he is asked to give an answer to the similar "three prisoners' problem". By restricting our attention to symbolic entities and to the World Wide Web in particular, we can learn much about these concepts, their interconnections and their values. It is a fact that symbols are used beyond a self-contained meaning as keywords to annotate other entities of different nature like documents,

DOI: 10.4018/978-1-60566-890-1.ch001

images and videos to allow relevant classification and search. By this, textual symbols play an important role in expressing and interpreting various things but also in pointing out information in order to catch attention to the object they are annotating.

By symbolic entities we mean any type of data in the sense of databases (like numeric, text, date, image or logical). In knowledge bases they are called facts or literals when we deal with rule bases, instances when we deal with ontologies and cases when we deal with case based reasoning systems. Composed data like records or sets of literals, instances or cases represent specific information. We think that it will be of great interest to propose a unifying framework for investigating information functions with respect to both the quantity of information and its quality or value. This would be the main contribution of this paper together with a clarification of the concepts of information and knowledge with respect to each other and the functions that operate on them. Many definitions have been proposed for the concept of information and other related concepts such as data, knowledge and sometimes meaning. A comprehensive summary of some of these definitions is given in (Stenmark, 2002). In (Chaim, 2007), the author investigates these concepts on the basis of definitions proposed by a panel composed by information science experts. Five models based on universal or subjective domains were identified for defining the data, information and knowledge concepts. The study is limited to inferential propositional knowledge, the two other kinds of knowledge, practical knowledge and knowledge by acquaintance being considered not relevant within the field of information science. In our opinion, the two latter kinds of knowledge do exist in the electronic documents world on which we shall focus. Indeed some of the practical knowledge can be codified into documentation. Consider for example websites aimed to help repair engines, build origami, learn programming, or teach healthy behavior. Undoubtedly, these websites are means for successfully transferring at various degrees skills and practical knowledge. As to the knowledge by acquaintance, it is also at work since one can feel, as an immediate sensation, that a given website is esthetically well designed or that the content of some document may be highly relevant for him, he might also identify an anonymous forum member as being an acquaintance of his, based on his posts.

We discuss in this chapter issues related to the concept of data, information and knowledge. We shall first see that very often the same functions apply to these concepts and few functions are specific to one or another of these concepts. Secondly we shall discuss the concept of meaning as being a relation between informations. In the two last sections, we restrict our attention to the context of the World Wide Web by considering information flow from web to user and from user to web. The first flow is mainly the outcome of a search process. The second one results from user personal data being collected by first or third parties with or without his knowledge when surfing the web. In these particular contexts, information is not a concept which is restricted to human minds. Indeed, applications like Web Services may act on behalf of the user or third parties to achieve some intelligent research or data processing.

INFORMATION FUNCTIONS

The processing of the information uses **information functions** which come either from human minds or from database management systems, reasoners or inference engines. The application of these functions yields other informations which might be used in their turn as input for the other information functions along the classical information acquisition/processing/feedback scheme. Such functions are used to obtain explicit information from implicit information or discover new information, for example in the case of large databases through data mining.

From a common point of view, databases are information systems allowing functions like selection, aggregation and sorting. Their fields values represent data and a record represent an information which may gain the statute of knowledge depending on its content or instead contribute in building a piece of knowledge when it comes to be put in relation with other records in the relational database. Linking information in the web and decrypting a message are examples for operations producing inferential propositional knowledge. There are also functions designed to protect the user's anonymity in the web. These are real information functions with anonymity as a result and this anonymity can be measured as information can be (Diaz & al 2002). Other information functions deal with incomplete information and allow inferring new plausible information which may be canceled later in the light of new evidence. Incompleteness is one of the parameters that may define the value of the information. Another parameter which might be relevant is information consistency. Unlike inconsistent logics formulas, inconsistent information generally contains some coherent parts thanks to their meaning. Therefore inconsistency is only local and would not absolutely make the whole information uninteresting. The sentence "Lina participated in the conference of 2/29/2007" is inconsistent since there is no 2/29/2007 but nevertheless informs us of Lina's participation in the conference possibly on late February.

Actually, there is an ambiguous relationship which exists between the concepts of data, information and knowledge. This ambiguity is not necessarily located between data and information on one hand and between information and knowledge on the other hand. These confusions are present in the vocabulary used for some "polymorphic" functions such as: collecting, organizing, representing, analyzing, transferring and sharing which may apply to either data, information or knowledge. However some functions prove to be more concept-specific. For example mining, searching and revision are functions which application is more appropriate to respectively data, information and knowledge. Even with this kind of functions the other concepts are often present. The outcome of data mining is new information. One searches for information to enrich his knowledge and one may also revise his knowledge in the light of new information. Another source of confusion for these concepts is the tacit transformation of one concept to another by applying to the first concept a function defined for the second concept. If the web is primarily considered as a huge information resource, it is at the same time a fertile ground for data mining to make new information emerge. Therefore, in this context the web is rather considered as a precious resource for data.

The transformations from one concept to another are "point of view issues" and can be formalized as follows: We distinguish two kinds of knowledge, simple knowledge and complex knowledge. Simple knowledge is merely a qualification we shall give to an information that a person may consider relevant in a given situation. Complex knowledge is the association of pieces of simple knowledge in order to solve a problem, a sort of answer to a how-to-do question. Solving a puzzle and planning are examples of complex knowledge. The judge and the doctor use complex knowledge to make their decisions. In the first case the complex knowledge is built from simple knowledge such as facts, rules of law and case law. In the second case simple knowledge comes from symptoms, analysis results and medication. Some of this knowledge may be explicit and therefore codified. The codification could be done syntactically in a way that it transforms knowledge into data that can be processed by some inference engine to produce new information.

MEANING AND KNOWLEDGE

It is a fact that, traditionally, logical systems are related to knowledge in a narrow way as long as they focus on the truth value of assertions. When it comes to information, its value doesn't coincide solely with the truth value if ever there is one. We argue that some elementary informational system could be formally defined just like logical systems are defined. In (Bezzazi, 2007) the author considers a variant for the input output logic of Makinson (Makinson & Van Der Torre, 2000) as a relevant starting point for defining norms. Input output logic singles out some natural inference steps which are not "logically correct" but "informationally correct". However the classical consequence inference is still present in its formal definition and the system proposed in (Bezzazi[2], 2007) is based on a syntactical non-monotonic inference instead. Within this informational system the author investigates the concept of norms and their effects, legal information being used as the running example.

The issue of information might be considered from different fields' point of views like psychology, sociology or logics. Our approach to this issue is a pragmatic one and can be linked to the definitions in (Quigley & Debons, 1999). Information is seen as data that answers the questions who, when, what or where and where knowledge, when codified, is seen as data that answers the questions why and how. Precisely, we consider **knowledge** as the ability to use specific information or instructions to achieve some goal. For example, justified decision making on the basis of available information or building a website following given instructions are two forms of knowledge.

We believe that **meaning** is some information we might attach to some other basic information. Such information constitutes in general some knowledge and depends for the same basic information on the informee, the agent being informed. The information "light is red" carries the meaning "cars should stop" for the motorist and "you may walk" for the pedestrian when the same signal is used both for pedestrians and motorists. It may happen that the "light remains abnormally red". This constitutes basic information. New information which comes at the same time as a meaning and as a knowledge emerges for the motorist "the light is out of work" leading him to consider the information "he may drive on". In law there are many concepts which are given legal definitions. However, in the global environment, within the cyberspace, issues related to the meaning of these concepts as they might be defined in the different legal systems rise. Copyright, privacy and freedom of expression are typical issues. For example, Europe experienced a tough dispute with United States, where data privacy is much less regulated, on the famous Passenger Name Record.

Both knowledge and meaning are based on information. As we have seen, knowledge may be a complex construction whereas the meaning is in general an information "ready-to-use" attached to some basic information. The semantic web is based on the annotation of words by their meaning. However, to attach some information as a meaning to some other information might be the result of different processes involving observation, experience, reasoning and learning for example. The bee dance and its meaning or simply words and their meaning are examples. Another distinction among meanings might be done on the past or future aspect of the event described by the basic information.

Let I be the set of informations. A meaning is a couple (i,m) in IxI. Terms and their synonyms or their definitions are simple examples of meanings. However, attaching a meaning to some information may prove to be a non trivial cognitive process. Consider law domain where basic information consists in the written norms, already resolved cases and the case at hand. Facing a given case, the judge and the lawyer will try to give a meaning to the available information of the case to support their usually conflicting reasoning. The search for a meaning does not restrict to case informations but may also concern the norms of the law in their interpretation to decide whether they should apply or not.

As for the knowledge we define it as some set K of tokens called knowledges. Relevant knowledges for a rational agent with respect to an activity A are singled out with a function $\kappa(a,A) \subset K$. Knowledge $\kappa(a,A)$ is used by agent a in the activity A. An activity can be finite or infinite and we shall assume that as long as knowledge is involved in its achievement, an activity has an objective o(A). Note that activities do not depend on agents but on the knowledge they use and that based on this knowledge the objective may be reached or not. This means also that we are assuming that knowledge is interchangeable between agents in equal conditions. If agent a reaches objective o(A) with knowledge $\kappa(a,A)$ then we can have agent b reach the same objective using the same knowledge when the same means used by agent a are made available for agent b.

INFORMATION AND KNOWLEDGE FROM WEBSITES

The web provides an abundance of information contained in web pages of personal or professional websites, forums, blogs and other wikis. The author of a published content in the web aims to share with others information about some subject. This information may evolve to knowledge or fuel it. This is the case with tutorial websites. Many people have learned a programming language or improved their knowledge on the matter by gleaning the web. The quality of the information or the knowledge acquired this way depends both on the content quality and on the reader's willingness. If the reader's willingness seems to be more of a subjective matter, information quality can be measured in a variety of ways based on its nature and properties like accuracy, understandability and relevance.

The internet user has potential access to all of the unprotected web pages. As a matter of fact the user has mainly access to pages which have been indexed by search engines or to pages returned by search portals like online phone directories. The search engine response to the user request on some given subject is a possibly empty ordered set of pages. Among these pages, only a few will catch her attention. In this particular context, the quality of the information may be defined through indicators like:

- The kind of subject being asked on: like news, science, or some person.
- The formulation of the request: The choice of keywords and the use of search operators.
- The search engine ordering method: This could be ranking, votes or site notoriety for example.
- The willingness and satisfaction of the requester: This is mainly a subjective indicator.
- The reliability of the source: Site notoriety and its specialization on a given subject.

In general, the information provided by the selected pages will generate more information for the reader based on his knowledge. Note that the aggregated information might prove to be inconsistent and therefore the resulting confusion might lead the informee to further research. The information contained in a web page P is denoted by p. In general this information is defined in terms of textual, audio, video content immediately accessible on the page on one hand and on the other hand in terms of information contained in other linked pages. This could be denoted by c $p_1 \dots p_{n\rightarrow}$ p with $p_i \neq p$ for any p_i. Examples of such definitions are $_\rightarrow$ p; an empty page, c $_\rightarrow$ p, a page with non-empty content and no links and $p_1 \dots p_{n\rightarrow}$ p, a page with only links. The definition c $p_1 \dots p_{i\rightarrow}$ p is to be read as "to know (information of) p we need to know c $p_1 \dots p_i$". The definition of a web page is unique. Let I be a set of definitions. The importance or the relevance of information p is measured by some function R: (p,I) $_\rightarrow$ v. For example v may be the number of times it appears in the left part of a page definition possibly weighed by values according to the importance of their sources. Other measures may be based on experimental methods such as the number of visits or the number of votes a page receives. These methods aim to build a model for the user's intention and offer a tool for building dynamically links related to the topic the user is interested in, implementing thus a kind of serendipity process.

INFORMATION AND KNOWLEDGE FOR THE WEBSITES, PERSONAL DATA AND IDENTIFICATION

When surfing the web, the internet user happens to deliver information about himself and maybe about other people as well. The user may be aware at various degrees or not at all of the trails he leaves behind him and which are very often persistent. The information sent to the visited website by the browser comes as a set of data used by the http protocol or encapsulated in cookies. Collecting and linking this kind of information may lead to produce a more or less accurate profile of the user and in some cases to his identification. Identification proves in this case to be a form of inferential propositional knowledge. It is important to notice that law makes use of the concepts of data, information, knowledge and meaning either explicitly or implicitly. For example, the Data Protection Directive (EU Directive 95/46/EC) defines personal data as follows:

"personal data" shall mean any information relating to an identified or identifiable natural person ("data subject"); an identifiable person is one who can be identified, directly or indirectly, in particular by reference to an identification number or to one or more factors specific to his physical, physiological, mental, economic, cultural or social identity.

This article assigns a meaning to the information "personal data" as being any information related to the data subject. Knowledge is implicitly attached to the individual who can identify the data subject. In (Hogben & al., 2003) the concept of identification is defined through a formal ontology. In what follows we shall fit the concept of identification to the definitions above.

Let I(x) be the set of informations on person x and let Id(x) be the subset of I(x) which elements are informations that identify x. Let D(x) be a subset of I(x)-Id(x), D(x) is said to be an identifier of x for agent a if the relevant knowledge κ(a,I) of agent a to perform the identification activity I is not sufficient to allow a identify x but when information D(x) is provided, a identifies x:

$\kappa(a,I) \,_{\rightarrow}\, i(x)$ for any $i(x) \in Id(x)$,

$\kappa(a,I) \cup D(x) \,_{\rightarrow}\, i(x)$ for some $i(x) \in Id(x)$,

$\kappa(a,I) \cup D(x) \,_{\rightarrow}\, i(y)$ when $i(y) \in Id(y)$ for $x \neq y$.

The symbol $_{\rightarrow}$ denotes some general inference which may use deductive, inductive or abductive reasoning steps. In this case, **identification** is the activity and i(x), the identity of x, is the objective. This activity may fail to reach its objective in that the identification ends up either with no i(x) or with more than one candidate for x, i.e. D(x) is true for more than one x. Note that this process is not infallible since the agent a may identify a person x on the basis of κ(a,I) and that this knowledge is not sufficient to allow a notice that other individuals than x satisfy D(x). This is typically the case in default reasoning where κ(a,I) may be built over incomplete information and may be revised later with new knowledge.

The identification activity may take two forms:

- Agent a starts from D(x) to find x. The use of logs to identify an internet user is an example of such an activity.

- Agent a knows the person x and seeks to find her by trying different $D(x)$. For example agent a uses a search engine to locate an old acquaintance thanks to possible linkable informations available in the web.

A huge amount of information that was first attached to an anonymous person turn into disclosed personal data as soon as the person is identified. This was the unfortunate experience of an internet user chosen randomly on the web by another internet user who portrayed him by giving a number of personal details collected from the web using Google and from social websites. The resulting biography was published in a magazine (Meltz, 2009) to warn people that much of the data they leave in the web and which they think is private is or may easily become public. This is also an example of how the aggregation of information provides knowledge.

CONCLUSION

By considering two cases where information is the main motivation, we have pointed out an approach to define the concepts of information, knowledge and meaning. It follows that information is the input a rational agent receives and that helps him perform some activity in order to achieve some goal. However, such a distinction remains fundamentally a matter of point of view and depending on the epistemic level we adopt an information can be qualified as being a knowledge and conversely a knowledge ca turn into information. Based on the definitions we have proposed, the web is seen as not only an information resource but also as a knowledge resource as long as real knowledge is codified tutorial and other "do it yourself" websites. We also pointed out that the internet users happen to supply information into the web that produces identification as a typical process of "knowing". Future work will focus on the issue of economic value that comes with knowledge asymmetry. Information asymmetry is well known and deals with transactions where there is an imbalance between parties relevant information on the object of transaction. Based on what have been said above, knowledge asymmetry occurs when a party has better knowledge or is more skilled to use the common available information without having more or better information than the second party.

REFERENCES

Bezzazi, E.-H. (2007). On some inferences based on stratified forward chaining: An application to e-Government. *Advances in Information Systems Development* (Vol. 1). Springer Verlag.

Bezzazi, E.-H. (2007, November). *Identité numérique et anonymat: concepts et mise en oeuvre*. Paper presented at the Colloque International sur la sécurité de l'individu numérisé, Paris, France.

Chaim, Z. (2007). Conceptual approaches for defining data, information, and knowledge. *Journal of the American Society for Information Science and Technology*, *58*, 335–350. doi:10.1002/asi.20507

Diaz, c., Seys, S., Claessens, J., & Preneel, B. (2002). Towards measuring anonymity (LNCS 2482).

Hogben, G., Wilikens, M., & Vakalis, I. (2003). On the ontology of digital identification (LNCS 2889).

Makinson, D., & Van Der Torre, L. (2000). Input-output logics. *Journal of Philosophical Logic*, *29*, 383–408. doi:10.1023/A:1004748624537

Meltz, R. (2009). Marc L***. *Le tigre, 28* (nov.-déc. 2008). Retrieved February 15, 2009, from http://www.le-tigre.net/Marc-L.html

Quigley, E. J., & Debons, A. (1999). Interrogative theory of information and knowledge. In [ACM Press.]. *Proceedings of SIGCPR, 99*, 4–10. doi:10.1145/299513.299602

Stenmark, D. (2002). Information vs. knowledge: The role of intranets in knowledge management. In *Proceedings of HICSS-35*. Hawaii, January 7-10, 2002.

KEY TERMS AND DEFINITIONS

Data: Any electronic artifact which could be part of the input of a computer program. Numbers, texts, images, web pages but also programs are data.

Information: Any data that answers the questions who, when, what or where.

Knowledge: The ability to use specific information to achieve some goal.

Codified Knowledge: Any data that answers the questions why and how.

Meaning: Information that makes understandable some other information.

Information Function: A function that apply to information. It comes from verbs like to share, to search, to disclose, to collect and to interpret. Such functions may also apply to data and knowledge as well.

Identification: The process that comes out with naming uniquely an individual.

Chapter 2
Ontology-Based Network Management for Autonomic Communications

Dimitris Kanellopoulos
University of Patras, Greece

ABSTRACT

This chapter is focused on state-of-the art issues in the area of ontology-based autonomic communications and it considers how ontologies can be useful for network management as a way to achieve semantic interoperability among different network management models. In addition, it presents the autonomic communications paradigm as a possible solution to the ever-growing complexity of commercial networks due to the increasing complexity of individual network elements, the need for intelligent network and communication services and the heterogeneity of connected equipment. Finally, the chapter analyses how ontologies can be used to combine data correlation and inference technologies in autonomic networks. Such technologies are used as core components to build autonomic networks.

INTRODUCTION

Nowadays multimedia information is transmitted under the control of different protocols through various physical devices manufactured and operated by different vendors. Many integrated network management models use different technologies for resource management. Such network management frameworks include SNMP (Simple Network Management Protocol), OSI-SM (Open Systems Interconnection-Systems Management), CMIP (Common Management Information Protocol), DMI (Desktop Management Interface) and WBEM (Web-based Enterprise Management). As different management technologies are used for the same-networked system, semantic interoperability is required among all different network management models in order to provide a unified view of the whole managed system (López de Vergara et al., 2003). Such a semantic interoperability is achieved using ontologies, which could allow machine-supported network management data interpretation and integration.

DOI: 10.4018/978-1-60566-890-1.ch002

From another perspective, there is an increasing network complexity due to the increasing complexity of individual network elements, the need for intelligent network and communication services and the heterogeneity of connected equipment. The ever-growing size and complexity of commercial networks impose new intelligent techniques to manage their operation and communications. The central problem in system and network management is the critical human intervention that is time-consuming, expensive, and error-prone. Many systems management tasks such as system configuration, performance analysis, performance tuning, error handling, and availability management are often performed manually. This work can be time-consuming and error-prone, and it requires a growing number of highly skilled personnel, making IT systems costly. It has been estimated that companies have to spend 33–50% of their total cost of ownership recovering from or preparing against failures (Patterson et al., 2002). Autonomic computing will decline this complexity crisis of commercial networks and automate all the above system management tasks. A high level of autonomy characterizes autonomic systems, while human intervention is only foreseen in the definition of business goals. Autonomic communications improve the ability of network and services to cope with unpredicted change, including changes in topology, load, task, the physical and logical characteristics of the networks that can be accessed, and so forth (Dobson et. al, 2006). Autonomic communications seek to simplify the management of complex communications structures and reduce the need for manual intervention and management. Autonomic communication is more oriented towards distributed systems and services and to the management of network resources at both the infrastructure and the user levels. On the contrary, autonomic computing is more directly oriented towards application software and management of computing resources (Quitadamo and Zambonelli, 2007).

It is worth noting that autonomic communication treats the Internet as an ecosystem (the Internet Ecosystem) and adopts a methodology of using context-awareness and distributed policy-based control to achieve efficiency, resilience, immunity and evolvability in large-scale heterogeneous communication infrastructures. Autonomic communication enables an evolving network platform for sensing, communicating, decision-making, and reacting, with high degree of autonomy to easy human efforts. It draws on a number of existing disciplines including protocol design, network management, artificial intelligence, pervasive computing, control theory, game theory, semantics, biology, context-aware systems, sensor networks, trust, and security. Research in autonomic network management focuses on the development of highly distributed algorithms that seek to optimize one or more aspects of network operation and/or performance, in essence aiming to provide various self-management capabilities. In this context, many researchers are investigating the potential use of biologically-inspired algorithms and processes (Bicocchi & Zambonelli, 2007).

This chapter explores ontology-based autonomic communication issues and how ontologies can be useful for network management as a way to achieve semantic interoperability among different network management models. In addition, it presents how ontologies can be used to combine data correlation and inference technologies in autonomic networks.

BACKGROUND

An ontology is a set of knowledge terms including the vocabulary, the semantic interconnections, and some simple rules of inference and logic for some particular topic (Brewster et al., 2004). An ontology is made up of three parts:

- *Classes and instances* used to model elements.
- *Properties* which establish relationships between the concepts of an ontology.

Figure 1. An ontology for matching travelling preferences to airline seat offers

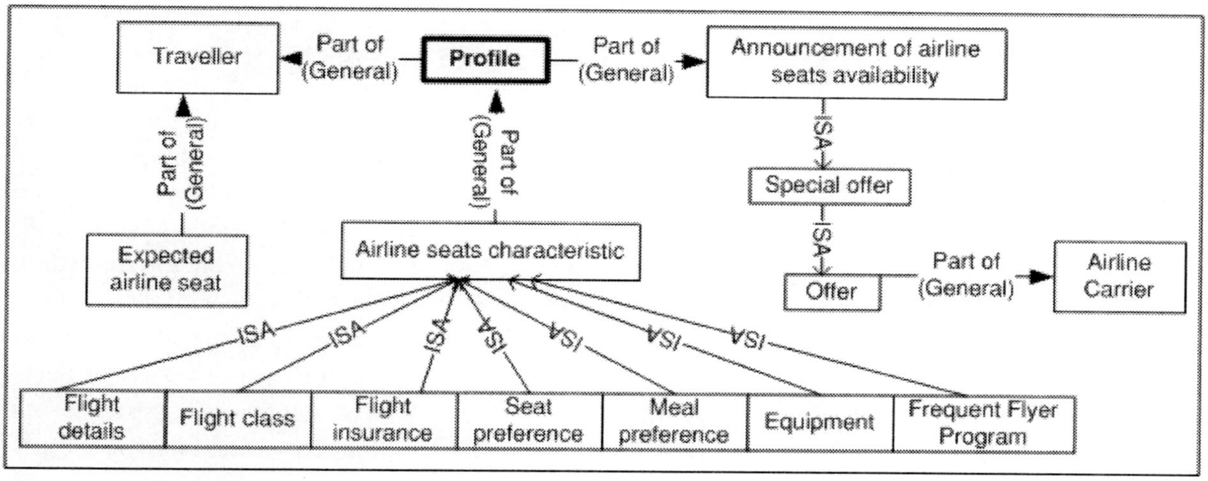

- *Rules* which model logical sentences that are always true (Chandrasekaran et al., 1999).

Figure 1 depicts an example ontology which is used for matching travelling preferences to airline seat offers.

Maedche et al. (2003) analyzed how ontologies can be used for implementing enterprise knowledge management tasks. However, the use of ontologies to represent information related to the network management scope has been addressed to a significant extent in recent research (López de Vergara et al., 2003; López de Vergara et al., 2004a; Quirolgico et al., 2004; Guerrero et al., 2005; Wong et al., 2005; Keeney et al., 2006).

The envisaged goal of autonomic computing (Kephart and Chess, 2003) is the production of systems that are self-managing in four main respects: *self-configuring, self-healing, self-protecting* and *self-optimizing*. In the self-healing context, one or more detectors can detect software failure; and then one or more failure analyzers analyze failures. An analyzer, to discover the relationships among these failures and help better characterize these failures, might analyze more than one failure and their underlying root causes. A failure analyzer also predicts and/or determines the risk raised by the failure(s). A number of software failure classifications are defined in the reliability engineering literature. Some of them simply classify failures into different types based on their risk levels, while others focus on the causes of the failures. The self-healing capability is already met in ZFS file system (http://en.wikipedia.org/wiki/ZFS) developed by Sun Microsystems, Inc for the Solaris Operating System. ZFS can heal itself, while its heal time depends on amount of stored information, not the disk size. A ZFS file system is built on top of virtual storage pools called *zpools*. A *zpool* is constructed of virtual devices, which are themselves constructed of block devices (e.g., files, hard disk partition, or entire drives). ZFS supports end-to-end data integrity - all data and metadata undergoes checksum operations using one of several available algorithms (e.g., SHA256). This allows detecting with very high probability silent data corruptions caused by any defect in disk, controller, cable, driver, or firmware. ZFS metadata are always checksummed using SHA256 algorithm.

An autonomic system manages resources in order to provide management services to its users while meeting the operational and business goals of those responsible for the resources and the provision of the services. The autonomic vision includes zero touch, self-sensing, context-aware, dynamic, self-programming and evolvable networks. Some of the prerequisites for autonomic computing include: complete visibility of the managed platform, complete control of that platform without undesirable side effects, and complete knowledge of how to relate visible situations to concrete actions (Sterritt et al., 2005). Most significantly is the ability to capture and represent both enterprise and personal policy (rules). Besides, the management unit of an autonomic system performs security tasks, which are governed by the element's and the system's policies, of which security policies are a subset (Chess et al., 2003). In terms of autonomizing legacy systems, software agents could be utilized to add capabilities without requiring direct alterations to the legacy code (Haas et al., 2003).

Autonomic networks manage themselves and will largely decrease the above discussed complexity crisis of the commercial networks. The autonomic communications paradigm involves moving more decision-making down into the systems to enable them to self-manage their activity, including self-healing. To fabricate autonomic networks requires the co-operation of the industry to develop open standards to evolve from the current network elements to *autonomic network elements*. Certainly, autonomic communication is dependant on a successful *autonomic networking* infrastructure. The basic building blocks of any autonomic system architecture include sensors and effectors (Ganek and Corbi, 2003). By monitoring behavior through sensors, comparing this with expectations (historical and current data, rules and beliefs), planning what action is necessary (if any) and then executing that action through effectors, creates a *control loop* (IBM, 2001). The control loop is the fundamental management unit in any autonomic computing architecture. The elements of this control loop are responsible for monitoring the managed elements and other relevant data about the managed elements and the environment in which they are operating. Those data are analyzed and a specific action is taken if a state of a managed entity and/or system is changed to an undesirable (failed) state. In particular, an autonomic system forms a feedback loop (Figure 2) and collects information from a variety of sources including traditional network sensors and reporting streams but also including higher-level device and user context.

In autonomic communications, highly decentralized algorithms are used. These algorithms have desirable emergent properties and retain both a high level of global predictability and a close integration with cognitive and other contextual goals. Besides, a high degree of self-management and self-optimization exists in autonomic communications. To give self-management and optimization capabilities, it is required to investigate the context-aware approach to improve networking properties. In order to collect context information related to the location, the presence, the identity, and the profile of users and services, it is necessary to use network components, software entities, and software agents. As Dobson et al. (2006, p.234) state: "*A typical context use involves locating services and users, calling-up services according to user behavior, providing information for service composition, facilitating ad hoc communication mechanisms between users, and adaptation of the qualities of service to changes in the environment as a result of user and service mobility (Coutaz et al., 2005)*". Moreover, two types of context-aware infrastructure can be proposed: *passive context-aware infrastructure*, and *active context-aware infrastructure*. A context model can consistently inform autonomic decision-making process and this leads to self-optimization. It provides an explicit representation of concerns from a number of different semantic levels. Moreover, it provides a helpful approach for open-adaptive behavior, a collaboration using standard protocols and formats. It is worth noting that ontology-based context models can support

Figure 2. Autonomic control loop. Adapted from (Dobson et al., 2006)

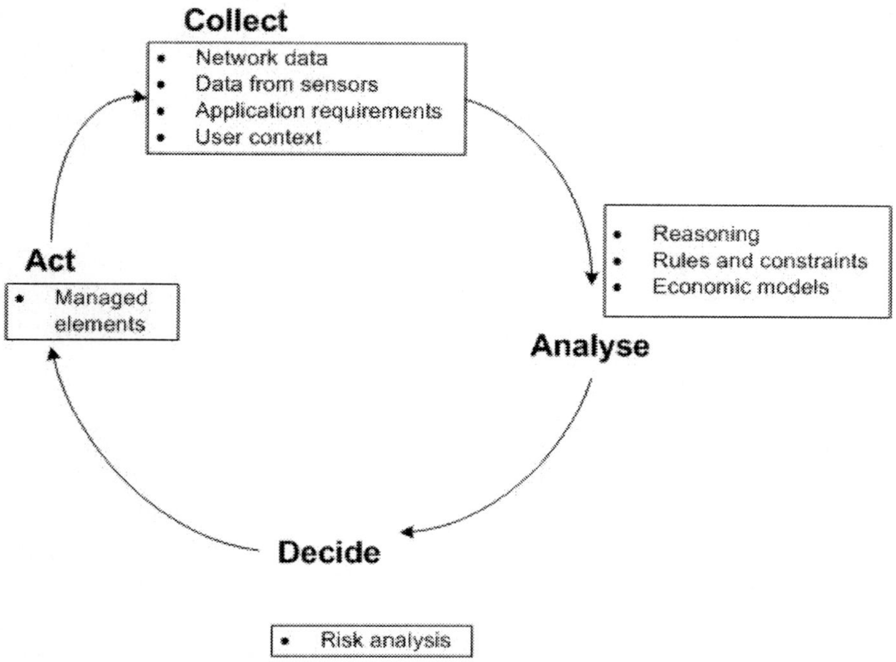

context reasoning and context management for adaptive multimedia systems (Kanellopoulos, 2009). In the *Autonomic Network Architecture* (ANA) project (http://www.ana-project.org/) a few participating Universities and research institutes designed and developed a novel autonomic networking architecture that enables flexible, dynamic, and fully autonomous formation of network nodes as well as whole networks. Another project called ANEMA (Derbel et al., 2009) defined an autonomic network management architecture that implements a set of policy concepts to achieve autonomic behavior in network equipment, while ensuring that the network behavior as a whole is satisfying the high-level requirements of the human administrators as well as the users. Jennings et al. (2007) introduced the FOCALE autonomic network management architecture, which gives emphasis on the use of business goals (codified as policy rules) to determine how resources in the network should be collectively utilized to best deliver services to users. The FOCALE architecture adopts a novel combination of information and data modeling, augmented by ontological data, to enable the system to 'learn' and 'reason' about itself and its environment. In addition, context-aware policy management processes (to adapt the management control loops) are used to ensure that system functionality adapts to meet changing user requirements, business goals, and environmental conditions. Finally, the AutoMate architecture (Liu and Parashar, 2006) is a materialization of the autonomic –element based information model to enable autonomic grid applications. In AutoMate, each autonomic element encapsulates rules, constraints, and mechanisms for self-management, where three classes of ports are defined for interactions with other autonomic elements: the *functional port* defining the computational behavior of the element, the *control port* exporting the sensors and effectors to the element manager, and the *operational port* defining the interfaces to inject and manage policy rules. Cheng et al. (2006) presented the *Autonomic Service Architec-*

ture (ASA), a uniform framework for automated management of both Internet services and their underlying network resources. ASA ensures the delivery of services according to specific service level agreements (SLAs) between customers and service providers.

Autonomic communications rely mainly on cross-layer architectures. Cross-layering shares information amongst different layers, which can be used as input for algorithms, for decision processes, and adaptations. Information in cross-layer architectures (e.g., POEM) is exchanged between non-adjacent layers of the protocol stack, typically using a broader and more open data format, and end-to-end performance is optimized by adapting to this information at each protocol layer. Razzaque et al. (2007) explored the possible use of cross-layering architectures in autonomic communications. The example of self-healing using cross-layering shows the potential of such approaches to realize the goals of autonomic communications. This also motivates new cross-layer architectures with a hybrid local and global view for autonomic communications.

INTEROPERABILITY OF MANAGEMENT MODELS AND AUTONOMIC COMMUNICATIONS

Interoperability of Network Management Models

Networks are made up of many different devices which have different programming models and provide different management data, describing the same or similar concepts (e.g., the concept of the router). Therefore, it is imperative to harness information models and ontologies to abstract away vendor-specific funtionality to facilitate a standard way of reconfiguring that functionality. Resource models for management purposes have been extensively standardized in the form of management information bases (MIBs) that conform to the successful manager-agent paradigm. Bodies such as IETF, the Telecommunication Standardization Sector of the International Telecomunications Union (ITU-T) and the Distributed Management Task Force (DMTF) developed large MIBs for a large proportion of network and system equipment.

In the domain of network management, tangible and intangible network objects, and management operations comprise the concepts that can be modeled in a network ontology. Between these concepts, semantic relationshps far more complex than 'is-a' relationship exist. For example, the concept 'gateway configuration command' can be semantically expressed as the state transition of network object, while a single semantic relationship can be represented using slots.

Wong et al. (2005) proposed a semantic interoperability approach for solving the semantic heterogeneity problem and illustrated it with heterogeneous router configuration management. In order to develop interoperability standards for an autonomic system, all of the boundary elements, namely resources, services, context and goals/policies should be addressed within the same framework. In particular, to achieve semantic interoperability of different network management models three steps are required:

- *Describing the management information with ontology languages.* Management information must be described using an ontology language with high semantic expressiveness. Ontology languages, such as OWL (Web Ontology Language), which allow the definition of classes and properties can be valid to define management information. However, as López de Vergara et al. (2004b, p.1010) state "*it is possible that some information get lost if these languages do not have the suitable facets or a mechanism to define them*". OWL (Dean & Schreiber, 2004) is the dominant ontology language for representing network management information because it allows the definition of classes as well as of properties, which can have different facets such as the type or cardinality constraint. The cardinality constraint restricts the maximum and minimum number of values of an attribute. López de Vergara et al. (2003) analyzed and compared different languages usually applied for the definition of management information for networks and systems. Such languages are: GDMO (Guidance for the Definition of Managed Objects), MIF (Managed Information Format), IDL (Interface Definition Language), MOF (Managed Object Format) which is used for Common Information Model (CIM), and SMI (Structure and Management Information) Next Generation which has been proposed by the Internet Research Task Force (IRTF) Network Management Research Group.

- *Merging and mapping the management information using the techniques used for ontologies*. In order to integrate management information models semantically, an ontology merging and mapping management information process must be completed. Ontology merging defines the act of bringing together two conceptually divergent ontologies or the instance data associated to two ontologies. This merging process can be performed in a number of ways, manually, semi automatically, or automatically. Manual ontology merging although ideal is extremely labour intensive and current research attempts to find semi or entirely automated techniques to merge ontologies. These techniques are statistically driven often taking into account similarity of concepts and raw similarity of instances through textual string metrics and semantic knowledge. On the other hand, ontology mapping is a search procedure of finding the highest similarity match between concepts belonging to the mapped ontologies. López de Vergara et al. (2004a), based on the work of Noy and Musen (1999), defined such a process.
- *Adding constraints to the obtained common management model*. Adding a set of constraints to the obtained common management model allows the description of the behavior related to the information contained in this model. And managers can check this behavior. Two types of constraints can be included in the information:
    1. *Implicit constraints* which refer to the information that must be true in a correct operation state. Implicit constraints are typical constraints upon the properties and classes of the managed objects. SWRL (Semantic Web Rule Language) (Horrocks et al., 2004) allows the representation of behavior restrictions that can be expressed in a natural language as conditional clauses (if…then…). For example, this includes values that depend on other values, state-machine behavior, temporal behavior or composite functions. Hereafter, we present an example of implicit constraints in SNMP MIB and how SWRL can be used to formally define these implicit constraints. *Example*: A definition from SNMP's MIB II restricts the value of the mask for route entries in the routing table:

```
ipRouteMask OBJECT-TYPE
SYNTAX IpAddress
ACCESS read-write
STATUS mandatory
DESCRIPTION
```

"... If the value of the ipRouteDest is 0.0.0.0 (a default route), then the mask value is also 0.0.0.0 ..."

::= { ipRouteEntry 11 }If the MIB II has been mapped and integrated in the management information base in OWL, then the SWRL rule to define this example restriction would be the following:

ipRouteEntry(IR?) ∧ swrlb:equal (ipRouteDest(IR?), "0.0.0.0")

⇒ swrlb:equal(ipRouteMask(IR?),"0.0.0.0")
where ipRouteDest and ipRouteMask are properties of the class ipRouteEntry.

2. *Explicit constraints* which follow a concrete policy, and they are defined by managers to specify the behavior of the network resources. If certain conditions are met on the network or the managed systems, the behavior of the manager can also be specified by means of conditional rules such as:

If condition then action. For example,

If connection=video then connection.bandwidth ≥ 100 Mbps

In SWRL, such conditional rule is expressed as: condition set ⇒ action set.

Executing an action can be interpreted as 'calling a service' that executes an action and it is possible to define that action as an OWL-Schema (OWL-S) process, and then instantiate an object of the class Perform, with such process as its argument: perform(MyProcess). The class perform is an auxiliary class used in OWL-S (www.w3.org/Submission/OWL-S/) to represent the execution of atomic processes inside a composite process. For example, using the class CIM_SystemDevice from the CIM schema, with two instances which are port devices. With this SWRL rule, the manager will activate the second port, if the first port is not working, i.e.: If LogicalPort #1 is "Operatively Down", then enable LogicalPort #2

In SWRL:

CIM_SystemDevice(LP1?) ∧ swrlb:equal(deviceName(LP1?)," Lport1") ∧ CIM_SystemDevice(LP2?) ∧ swrlb:equal(deviceName(LP2?), "Lport2") ∧

swrlb:equal(StatusInfo(LP1?), "OPERATIVELY_DOWN")

⇒ Perform(SetAdminAvailability(LP2?, "ENABLE"))

In this case, the rule is applied upon certain instances of a class, not upon all elements of the class.

Ontology-Based Correlation Engines in Autonomic Networks

Ontology-based semantics will bring benefits to the management of future autonomic services. Lewis et al. (2006) examined the role of ontology modeling for the modeling of services, policies, context, management information and semantic mappings.

- ***Modeling services***: There are a few languages for expressing and manipulating semantic web services. Semantic web service languages introduce the modeling of conditional expressions detailing the state of the world in which the service is executed, before and after the services invocation. Applying ontology-based semantics to web service descriptions exploits automated reasoning using off-the-shelf logic engines to assist in service discovery and service composition. OWL-S supports the automated discovery, invocation, composition and management of web services. On the other hand, WSMO (Web Service Modeling Ontology) is a conceptual model for relevant aspects related to semantic web services. It provides an ontology based framework, which supports the deployment and interoperability of semantic web services. WSMO (www.wsmo.org/) includes the modeling of goals of a service user, against which service offering are matched. WSMO also includes a range of mediation types that can be used in binding semantic expressions between services, goals, ontologies, and groundings.

- ***Modeling policies:*** *Rei* (Kagal et al., 2003) is a policy specification language which allows user to express and represent the concepts of rights, prohibitions, obligations, and dispensations. The Rei engine reasons over Rei policies and domain knowledge in OWL to provide answers about the current permissions and obligations of an entity, which are used to guide the entity's behavior.
- ***Modeling management information***: López de Vergara et al. (2004a) have demonstrated directly the value of modeling management information in OWL, and how this can can be used to ease the interoperation between management models which are represented in different MIB languages (e.g., SMI, CIM).
- ***Modeling of context.*** Ontology-based models for context management exploit formal models of context to express concepts and relations between them. A representative ontology-based model is SOUPA (Chen et al., 2005).
- ***Modeling semantic mapping.*** Mappings between elements in ontologies are usually expressed as pairs of related entities in some mapping expression. The MAFRA (Maedche et al., 2002) system includes a formal representation to specify such mappings. Another example is the OntoMerge system (Dou et al, 2004) which uses bridging axioms written in the first order logic (FOL) language to express the translation rules beteen the concepts in the ontologies, and then it runs a theorem prover optimized for ontology translation over the ontologies and the axioms.

As it was previously mentioned, autonomic communications aim to improve the ability of network and services to cope with unpredicted change, including changes in load, topology, task, the physical and logical characteristics of the networks that can be accessed. To provide broad-ranging autonomic solutions, network designers have to take into account many issues such as: network and contextual modelling, decentralised algorithms, trust acquisition, and maintenance. Dobson et al. (2006) survey the current state of autonomic communications research and identify significant emerging trends and techniques. But now let us be more descriptive. Problems and failures in the network are unavoidable but quick detection and identification of their source is essential to ensure robustness. Figure 3 depicts IBM's view of the necessary components within an autonomic manager.

An autonomic manager is responsible for a managed element within a self-contained autonomic element. The *monitor* and *analyze* parts of the structure process information from the sensors to provide both self-awareness and an awareness of the external environment. The *plan* and *execute* parts decide on the necessary self-management behavior that will be executed through the effectors. The simple correlators in the monitor part and the rules engines in the *analyze* part use correlations, rules, beliefs, expectations, histories and other information known to the autonomic element, or available to it. The introduction of autonomic principles requires the monitoring of individual system components through sensors and the ability of those components to respond to requests through effectors. Monitoring involves the correlation of several related pieces of information (Figure 3). Due to the complexity the situation has arisen, a large number of uncorrelated alarm event messages may reside on a network at any one time. Correlation is important in both self-assessment (self-awareness) and in the assessment of a component's operating environment (environment awareness). This helps in deciding when action is required and what should be done. A correlation engine captures and selects important events. It

Figure 3. Necessary components within the autonomic manager (IBM, 2001)

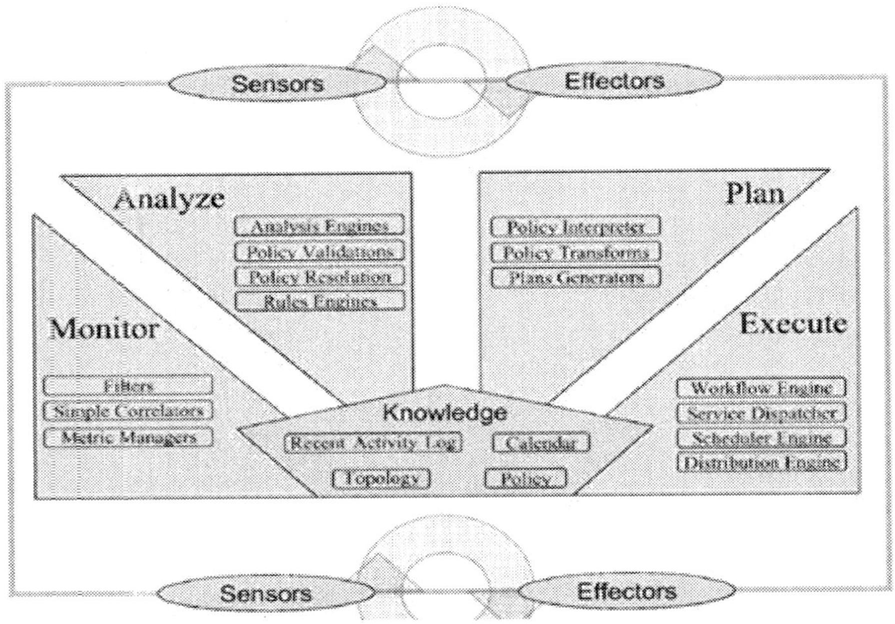

detects changes or problems based on knowledge of state changes, and initiates actions to correct any behavior not in line with a desired goal. Figure 4 depicts a reference model for correlation engines, which condense the received events into a single event directly indicating a problem (i.e., a situation event) in the managed system. According to Stojanovic et al. (2004a) correlation rules can be divided in two types:

- *Stateless rules* consider events in isolation; they operate on a single current event. For example, a specific stateless rule detects a system failure, when a file system has crashed or a IP adrees has failed.
- *State-based rules* allow the same or repeating events over time. They rely on a history of events and are critical of analyzing events, regardless of the frequency

Figure 4. Reference model for correlation engines

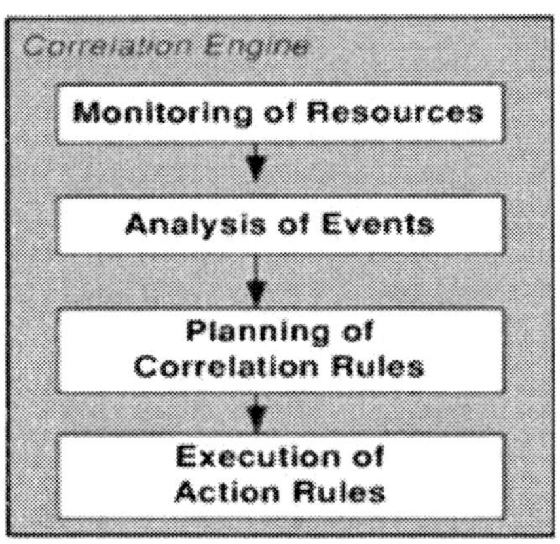

of occurence. For example, a state-based rule might require that the administrator be alerted if an IP address is involved in four separate attacks on the network gateway over a five months period.

Actions rules are used to reduce a system administrator's work by trigering automatic remedy actions; and by gathering additional monitoring data to achieve a detailed view of the current expectional state of resource. However, additional inference rules and designated actions should be required to automate corrective actions. For example, in the case of a problematic hub funtionality/operation, action rules can be used to reset the hub or to inform the administrator about the hub funtionality. Additional inference rules or designated acttions are needed in this case to automate corrective actions.

The correlation of alarm event messages is an important part of the *Root Cause Analysis* (RCA) (Jackobson and Weissman, 1993). RCA is a class of problem solving methods aimed at identifying the root causes of problems or events. The practice of RCA is predicated on the belief that problems are best solved by attempting to correct or eliminate root causes, as opposed to merely addressing the immediately obvious symptoms. By directing corrective measures at root causes, it is hoped that the likelihood of problem recurrence will be minimized. However, it is recognized that complete prevention of recurrence by a single intervention is not always possible. Thus, RCA is often considered to be an iterative process, and is frequently viewed as a tool of continuous improvement. RCA in complex systems is key to achieving autonomics. The ability to automatically determine the root cause of any event is clearly an enabler to opening new autonomic options that will assist in attaining higher levels of autonomic maturity within the systems.

The major telecommunication equipment manufacturers deal with event correlation through alarm monitoring, filtering and masking as specified by ITU-T (ITU-T, 2000). Resulting rule type diagnostic systems provide assistance to the operator whose expertise is then used to determine the underlying fault (or faults) from the filtered set of alarms reported. Event correlation is a conceptual interpretation of multiple events, giving them a collective meaning. This produces a new higher-order compound event that helps determine what action is required. The principle aim of event correlation is the interpretation of the events involved. The event signals or messages represent symptoms. Rules and beliefs identify which events to correlate and how they should be transformed. Machine learning, data mining and other artificial intelligence techniques can assist in the discovery of correlation rules and beliefs (Sterritt, 2002).

IBM states that effect complexity in problem determination is diluting the effectiveness of computing in the corporate environment (IBM, 2003). The same can be said for communications and networks. The IBM's white paper highlights the multitude of ways that different parts of a system report events, conditions, errors and alerts as a major factor contributing to the complexity in problem determination. IBM proposes a common format for log/trace information, called the *common base event* (CBE) *format*, to create consistency across systems and ease cross-product problem determination and heterogeneity. It is worth noting that Sterritt (2004) considered the self-healing and problem determination aspects of autonomic communications with particular focus on the analysis of alarm events in the telecommunication-distributed systems. Figure 5 depicts the process of a correlation algorithm which is based on semantic knowledge.

As it is shown in Figure 5, a semantic knowledge-based correlation model includes Event templates which standardize the event description form. The formalizing process is a process of instantiation of all the event parameters. A network management unit receives unformatted alarm events and puts them to the set EventF.

Figure 5. The process of a correlation algorithm. Adapted from (Xilin and Jianxin, 2007)

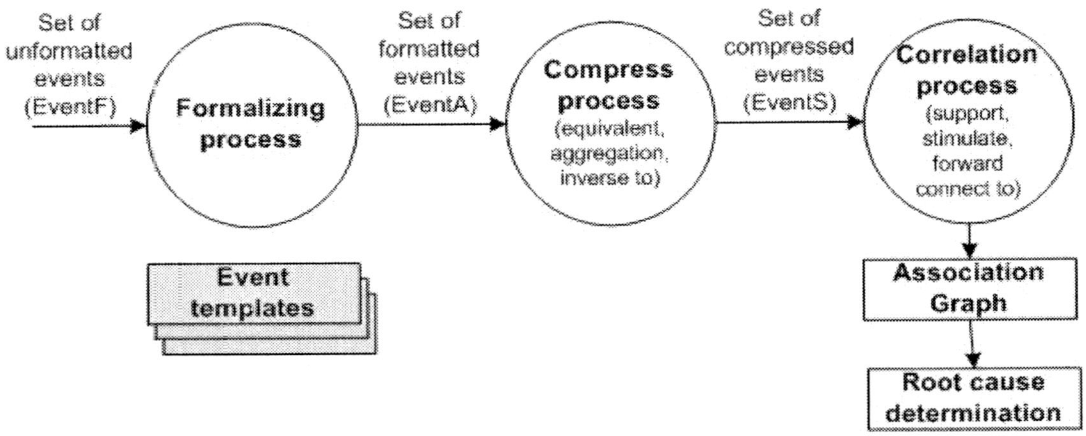

EventA is a set of fomarlized events. The compress process performs a compression operation to EventA. All events with the same interpretation in EventA will be merged into one event. Finally, the correlation process associates all elements in EventS generating a set of association graphs, and a set of association matrix. The relationships 'A_Equivalent_B', 'A_Aggregation_B' and 'A_Inverse_B' are incorporated in the compress process, while the relationships 'A_Support_B', 'A_Stimulate_B', 'A_Forward_connect_to_B' are incorporated in the correlation process (Figure 5). A simple explanation of these relationships follows:

- 'A_Equivalent_B': under interpretation, A is a set of events that have the same interpretation with event A.
- 'A_Aggregation_B': under interpretation, event B is the aggregation of all elements in the set A. Event B has the same interpretation with set A.
- 'A_Inverse_B': under interpretation, A is a set of events that has the contrary interpretation with event A.
- 'A_Support_B': under interpretation, B is a set of events that are supported by the event A.
- 'A_Stimulate_B': under interpretation, A is a set of events that probably serve as reasons of the event B.
- 'A_Forward_connect_to_B': under interpretation, A is a set of events that indirectly are supported by the event B, and it connects to B in the association graph.

Ontologies can make a 'problematic event' domain's assumptions explicit. It is very beneficial to make explicit domain assumptions underlying an implementation because we can change easily these assumptions, if our knowledge about the 'problematic event' domain changes. Using ontologies, we can also separate domain knowledge from the operational knowledge. For example, we can describe a task of reasoning (algorithm) to a required specification and implement a software agent that executes this task independent of the domain knowledge (i.e. knowledge terms). Computational processes and software agents can interpret semantic content and derive consequences from the system and network information they collect. Semantic annotation of network and system information could enable the deployment of intelligent applications in the 'problematic event' domain that could reason over system and network metadata. And the models of various correlation engines can be transformed into special ontologies. Hidden knowledge embedded in a correlation engine can be translated into a set of rules in the corresponding ontology and used in distinctive inferencing tasks. Lanfranchi et al. (2003) applied reasoning mechanisms across not only the entities of the autonomic computing model, bus also the resource model. Stojanovic et al. (2004a) introduced a reference model for correlation engines that consists of three layers: a) the resource layer, b) the event layer, and c) the rule layer. Resource can be a real-world entity (e.g., CPU) or a virtual entity (e.g., a business application). An event represents a significant change in the state of a resource. Events are generated to provide changes or problems. Correlation rules or action rules may trigger an automated response to an event. Correlation rules try to discover a problem, for example by translating several dependent events into one meaningful event. Actions rules trigger actions to resolve a problem, for example by executing a special program. According to Stojanovic et al. (2004a) the advantages of ontology-based correlation engines are distinguished in two categories:

- *Modeling benefits* (reusability, extensibility, applicability, verification, integration, evolution, visualization, and open standards). This means that ontology-based correlation engines can be reusable, extensible, and applicable; reasoning tasks can verify their models. The heterogeneous models of correlation engines can be integrated, evolution capable, well visualised, and exchanged between different systems with minimal loss of knowledge in the translation process.
- *Runtime benefits* (justification, ranking, and gap analysis). Justification refers to the generation of human-understandable descriptions of the inference process (i.e., how a result was inferred). An explanation of the reasons for suggesting a certain corrective action can be presented to administrators for their information or to a software agent that is responsible for recovering from errors. Ranking involves determination of results when many results were inferred. More breadth indicates significant support for that particular result; more depth indicates less confidence in the result (Stojanovic et al., 2003). Gap analysis is related to the discovery of problems or deficiencies in domain knowledge when no result is retrieved. For example, in the case we have MS Excel and MS PowerPoint applications running, and the MS PowerPoint application is not responding. We have a 'gap analysis', although we have two rules for monitoring the MS Excel application:
    - ***Rule 1:***IF (application.type= "MS Excel" and application.time>15 min and application.size>25MB and application application.status="failure) THEN there is a problem in RAM
    - ***Rule 2:***IF (application.type= "MS Excel" and application.time>15 min and application.lastAction="Save" and application.status="failure) THEN there is a HARD-DISK problem

and the following resources' attributes for the MS PowerPoint:

- ***Resources' state:***

application.type="MS PowerPoint"
application.time=30 mins
application.size=29MB
application.status="failure"

Table 1.

• Berkeley University: OceanStore • Berkeley University: Recovery-Oriented Computing • Carnegie Mellon University: Self-securing Storage • Columbia University: Autonomizing Legacy Systems • Cornell University: Astrolabe • Georgia Institute of Technology: Qfabric	• IBM: Discovering Dynamic Dependencies in Enterprise Environments for Problem Determination • IBM: Dynamic Surge Protection: An Approach to Handling Unexpected Workload Surges With Resource Actions That Have Dead Times • IBM: Eos: An Approach of Using Behavior Implications for Policy-based Self-management • IBM: Dynamic Surge Protection: An Approach to Handling Unexpected Workload Surges With Resource Actions That Have Dead Times • IBM: Generic Online Optimization of Multiple Configuration Parameters With Application to a Database Server • IBM: LEO -- DB2's Learning Optimizer • IBM: Policy-Based, Autonomic Storage Allocation Manager • IBM: Storage Tank

FUTURE RESEARCH DIRECTIONS

Ontology-based correlation engines (Stojanovic et al., 2004b) could combine information about an inference with information about the usage of a number of entities in the network and system management domain in order to discover corrupted resources or problematic situations. In the light of this evidence, we can develop proactive autonomic computing systems. Such systems will use predictive methods to eliminate problems. Proactive systems can diagnose themselves and plan repairs before, but can also eliminate problems before they arise (Curran et al., 2007). In our opinion, in the near future many special ontologies modeling software and hardware components will be proposed, and their semantic heterogeneity will be solved using aligning, merging and mapping techniques. In addition, a few special ontology languages will be written. Such ontology languages will be used for making system and network management agents acting as inference machines. One of them, under in-depth consideration, will become a W3C standard language for representing the behavior of autonomic communication systems. Standardization and integration play a significant role in the evolution of automated network and system management. Actually, formality can push the development of machine-aware automatic executions for managing system and network devices. In addition, automation (as a goal) requires many technologies and thus it presupposes proper technologies (e.g., ontologies, agents, etc.) that achieve integration. It is worth noting that IBM, Berkeley University, Carnegie Mellon Univerity, Columbia University, Cornell University, and Georgia Institute of Technology are working intensively in the area of autonomic computing. The names of their related projects are shown below (http://www.research.ibm.com/autonomic/research/projects.html).

CONCLUSION

Many examples of network device management and configuration are based on vendor-specific snapshots of static data. Existing management data does not inform the user/administrator why a problematic event is occuring. In autonomic communication, this information must be inferred using these and other data, and retained for future investigation (reference). Thus, intelligent learning and reasoning algorithms should be incorporated into autonomic network management systems. In order to develop interoperability standards for an autonomic system, all of the boundary elements, namely resources, services, context and goals/policies should be addressed and modeled within the same framework. Certainly, an ontology-based autonomic network requires the ontology-based modeling of the services, policies, context, management information and semantic mappings. In the area of domain modelling, ontologies facilitate interoperability between correlation engines by providing shared understanding of a 'problematic event' domain. In particular, ontology-based correlation engines can interoperate between them as they share a common understanding for the domain, which is machine processable. Ontology-based correlation engines can also achieve semantic integration and will provide novel services in autonomic communications. As a result, such correlation engines can improve the performance of autonomic communication systems drastically. To illustrate these benefits, special system and network management ontologies have to be proposed by the research community. Moreover, a few case studies must be applied to existing ontology-based correlation engines and evaluated such as to demonstrate their novelty. In addition, it must be examined how to benchmark ontology-based systems; what is the performance of ontology-based reasoners for communications intense environments; how can ontology mappings bridge management information heterogeneity; and how to integrate policy-based directives into semantic web services using current language features.

REFERENCES

Bicocchi, N., & Zambonelli, F. (2007). Autonomic communication learns from nature. *IEEE Potentials*, *26*(6), 42–46. doi:10.1109/MPOT.2007.906119

Brewster, C., O'Hara, K., Fuller, S., Wilks, Y., Franconi, E., & Musen, M. A. (2004). Knowledge representation with ontologies: The present and future. *IEEE Intelligent Systems*, *19*(1), 72–81. doi:10.1109/MIS.2004.1265889

Chandrasekaran, B., Johnson, T.R., & Benjamins, V.R. (1999). Ontologies: What are they? Why do we need them?. *IEEE Intelligent Systems and their Applications*, *14*(1), 20-26.

Chen, H., Finin, T., & Joshi, A. (2005). The SOUPA ontology for pervasive computing. *Whitestein Series in Software Agent Technologies* (pp. 233-254).

Cheng, Y., Farha, R., Kim, M. S., Leon-Garcia, A., & Won-Ki Hong, J. (2006). A generic architecture for autonomic service and network management. *Computer Communications*, *29*(18), 3691–3709. doi:10.1016/j.comcom.2006.06.017

Chess, D. M., Palmer, C. C., & White, S. R. (2003). Security in an autonomic computing environment. *IBM Systems Journal*, *42*(1), 107–118.

Coutaz, J., Crowley, J., Dobson, S., & Garlan, D. (2005). Context is key. *Communications of the ACM*, *48*(3), 49–53. doi:10.1145/1047671.1047703

Curran, K., Mulvenna, M., Nugant, C., & Galis, A. (2007). Challenges and research directions in autonomic communications. *Int. J. Internet Protocol Technology*, *2*(1), 3–17. doi:10.1504/IJIPT.2007.011593

Dean, M., & Schreiber, G. (Eds.). (2004). *OWL Web ontology language reference* (W3C recommendation).

Derbel, A., Agoulmine, N., & Salaun, M. (2009). ANEMA: Autonomic network management architecture to support self-configuration and self-optimization in IP networks. *Computer Networks*, *53*, 418–530. doi:10.1016/j.comnet.2008.10.022

Dobson, S., Denazis, S., Fernandez, A., Gaiti, D., Gelenbe, E., & Massacci, F. (2006). A survey of autonomic communications. *ACM Transactions on Autonomous and Adaptive Systems*, *1*(2), 223–259. doi:10.1145/1186778.1186782

Dou, D., McDermott, D., & Qi, P. (2004). Ontology translation on the Semantic Web. *Journal on Data Semantics II*, (. *LNCS*, *3360*, 35–57.

Ganek, A. G., & Corbi, T. A. (2003). The dawning of the autonomic computing era. *IBM Systems Journal*, *42*(1), 5–18.

Guerrero, A., Villagrá, V.A., López de Vergara, J.E., & Berrocal. J. (2005). Ontology-based integration of management behaviour and information definitions using SWRL and OWL. *DSOM'2005* (LNCS 3775, pp.12-23).

Haas, R., Droz, P., & Stiller, B. (2003). Autonomic service deployment in networks. *IBM Systems Journal*, *42*(1), 150–165.

Horrocks, I., Patel-Schneider, P.F., Boley, H., Tabet, S., Grosof, B., & Dean, M. (2004). *SWRL: A Semantic Web rule language combining OWL and RuleML*. W3C Member submission (21 May 2004).

IBM (2001). *Autonomic computing concepts* [IBM White paper].

IBM (2003). *An architectural blueprint for autonomic computing*. April, revised October.

ITU-T (2000). *M.3010 principles for a telecommunications management network*. ITU-T Recommendations, February.

Jackobson, G., & Weissman, M. D. (1993). Alarm correlation. *IEEE Network*, *7*(6), 52–59. doi:10.1109/65.244794

Jennings, B., van der Meer, S., Balasubramaniam, S., Botvich, D., & Foghlú, Ó, M., & Donnelly, W. (2007). Towards autonomic management of communications networks. *IEEE Communications Magazine*, *45*(10), 112–121. doi:10.1109/MCOM.2007.4342833

Kagal, L., Finin, T., & Joshi, A. (2003). A policy language for a pervasive computing environment. *IEEE 4th International Workshop on Policies for Distributed Systems and Networks* (pp.63-74).

Kanellopoulos, D. (2009). Adaptive multimedia systems based on intelligent context management. *Int. J. Adaptive and Innovative Systems*, *1*(1), 30–43. doi:10.1504/IJAIS.2009.022001

Keeney, J., & Lewis, D. O'Sullivan, D., Roelens, A., Boran, A., & Richardson, R. (2006, April). Runtime semantic interoperability for gathering ontology-based network context. In *Proc. 10th IFIP/IEEE Network Operations and Management Symposium (NOMS'2006),* Vancouver, Canada.

Kephart, J. O., & Chess, D. M. (2003). The vision of autonomic computing. *IEEE Computer*, *36*(1), 41–50.

Lanfranchi, G., Della Peruta, P., Perrone, A., & Calvanese, D. (2003). Toward a new landscape of system management in an autonomic computing environment. *IBM Systems Journal*, *42*(1), 119–129.

Lewis, D., O'Sullivan, D., Feeney, K., Keeney, J., & Power, R. (2006). Ontology-based engineering for self-managing communications. *1st IEEE International Workshop on Modeling Autonomic Communications.*

Liu, H., & Parashar, M. (2006). Acoord: A programming framework for autonomic applications. *IEEE Transactions on Systems, Man and Cybernetics. Part C, Applications and Reviews*, *36*, 341–352. doi:10.1109/TSMCC.2006.871577

López de Vergara, J. E., Villagrá, V. A., Asensio, J. I., & Berrocal, J. (2003). Ontologies: Giving semantics to network management models. *IEEE Network*, *17*(3), 15–21. doi:10.1109/MNET.2003.1201472

López de Vergara, J. E., Villagrá, V. A., & Berrocal, J. (2004a). Applying the Web ontology language to management information definitions. *IEEE Communications Magazine*, *42*(7), 68–74. doi:10.1109/MCOM.2004.1316535

López de Vergara, J.E., Villagrá, V.A, & Berrocal J. (2004b). Benefits of using ontologies in the management of high speed networks (LNCS 3079, pp.1007-1018).

Maedche, A., Motik, B., Silva, N., & Volz, R. (2002). MAFRA—A MApping FRAmework for Distributed Ontologies. *Knowledge engineering and knowledge management: Ontologies and the Semantic Web* (LNCS 2473, pp. 69-75).

Maedche, A., Motik, B., Stojanovic, L., Studer, R., & Volz, R. (2003). Ontologies for enterprise knowledge management. *IEEE Intelligent Systems*, *18*(2), 26–33. doi:10.1109/MIS.2003.1193654

Noy, N., & Musen, M. (1999, July). An algorithm for merging and aligning ontologies: Automation and tool support. In *Proceedings of the Workshop on Ontology Management. Sixteen National Conference on Artificial Intelligence*. Orlando, Florida, USA.

Patterson, D.A., Brown, A., Broadwell, P., Candea, G., Chen, M., Cutler, J., Enriquez, P., Fox, A., Kiciman, E., Merzbacher, M., Oppenhiemer, D., Sastry, N., Tetzlaff, W., Traupman, J., & Treuhaft, N. (2002, 15 March). *Recovery-oriented computing (ROC): Motivation, definition, techniques, and case studies* (UC Berkeley Computer Science Technical Report, UCB//CSD-02-1175). University of California, Berkeley.

Quirolgico, S., Assis, P., Westerinen, A., Baskey, M., & Stokes, E. (2004). Toward a formal Common Information Model ontology. *WISE'2004* (. *LNCS*, *3307*, 11–21.

Quitadamo, R., & Zambonelli, F. (2007). Autonomic communication services: A new challenge for software agents. *Autonomous Agents and Multi-Agent Systems*, *17*(3), 457–475. doi:10.1007/s10458-008-9054-9

Razzaque, M. A., Dobson, S., & Nixon, P. (2007). Cross-layer architectures for autonomic communications. *Journal of Network and Systems Management*, *15*(1), 13–27. doi:10.1007/s10922-006-9051-8

Sterritt, R. (2002). Facing fault management as it is, aiming for what you would like it to be. In D.W. Bustard, W. Liu, R. Sterritt Ceds (Eds.), *Soft Ware: First International Conference on Computing in an Imperfect World* (LNCS 2311, pp. 31-45).

Sterritt, R. (2004). Autonomic networks: engineering the self-healing property. *Engineering Applications of Artificial Intelligence*, *17*, 727–739. doi:10.1016/S0952-1976(04)00111-3

Sterritt, R., Parashar, M., Tianfield, H., & Unland, R. (2005). A concise introduction to autonomic computing. *Advanced Engineering Informatics*, *19*, 181–187. doi:10.1016/j.aei.2005.05.012

Stojanovic, L., Abecker, A., Stojanovic, N., & Studer, R. (2004b). Ontology-based correlation engines. *International Conference on Autonomic Computing* (pp. 304-305).

Stojanovic, L., Schneider, J., Maedche, A., Libischer, S., Studer, R., & Lumpp, T. (2004a). The role of ontologies in autonomic computing systems. *IBM Systems Journal*, *43*(3), 598–616.

Stojanovic, N., Studer, R., & Stojanovic, L. (2003). An approach for the ranking of query results in the Semantic Web. In *Proceedings of the 2nd International Semantic Web Conference (ISWC2003)* (LNCS 2870, pp. 500-516).

Wong, A. K. Y., Ray, P., Parameswaran, N., & Strassner, J. (2005). Ontology mapping for the interoperability problem in network management. *IEEE Journal on Selected Areas in Communications, 23*(10), 2058–2068. doi:10.1109/JSAC.2005.854130

Xilin, J., & Jianxin, W. (2007). Applying semantic knowledge for event correlation in network fault management. *2007 Int. Conf. on Convergence Information Technology* (pp.715-720).

KEY TERMS AND DEFINITIONS

Autonomic Communication Forum (ACF): The ACF (http://www.autonomic-communication.org) was established at the end of 2004 following an initiative by the EU-funded Autonomic Communication Accompanying Action Project. ACF aims to define an autonomic reference framework and a set of baseline compliance statements to guarantee interoperability.

Autonomic Networking: It is an initiative started at 2001 by the IBM, which aims to create self-managing networks to overcome the rapidly growing complexity of the Internet and other networks.

Configuration Management: It is responsible for the interaction with network elements and interfaces. It includes an accounting capability with historical perspective that provides for the tracking of configurations over time. It interoperates with all of the other sub-systems including: autognostics (receives direction for and validation of changes), policy management (implements policy models through mapping to underlying resources), security (applies access and authorization constraints for particular policy targets) and autodefense (receives direction for changes).

Management Information Base (MIB): A MIB stem from the OSI/ISO Network management model and is a type of database used to manage the devices in a communications network. It comprises a collection of objects in a (virtual) database used to manage entities (such as routers and switches) in a network.

Network Compartmentalization: Network compartments implement the operational rules and administrative policies for a given communication context. Instead of a layering approach, autonomic networking targets a more flexible structure called compartmentalization.

Policy Management: It includes policy specification, deployement, reasoning over policies, updating and maintaining policies, and enforcement. It is required for: a) constraining different kinds of behavior including security, privacy, resources access, and collaboration; b) configuaration management; c) defining business processes and defining performance; and d) defining role and relationship, and establishing trust and reputation.

Root Cause Analysis (RCA): It is a class of problem solving methods aimed at identifying the root causes of problems or events. It is defined as the action of interpreting a set of symptoms/events and pinpointing the source that caused those symptoms/events, and then finding out the proper neans to solve this problem.

Chapter 3
On the Infological Interpretation of Information

Bogdan Stefanowicz
Warsaw School of Economics, Chair of the Business Informatics, Poland

ABSTRACT

In the chapter, a proposition of so-called infological interpretation of information is presented. The concept was formulated by Bo Sundgren (1973) in his publication devoted to data bases. Sundgren developed a consistent theory of a model of data base based on the concept of message as a specific set of data. The model inspires not only a new interpretation of information but also is a good base for manifold analysis of the concept. In the chapter, the following basic concepts are disused: properties of information, diversity of information, and information space.

INTRODUCTION

Information is one of the most fascinating concepts present in theoretical discussions and practical projects. There are different proposals of its definition and interpretation. As an example one can mention the following concepts:

- **Claud Shannon's** theory of information (Shannon 1948).
- Non-probabilistic theory of **Andriej N. Kolmogorov** (1969).
- The theory of **Ralph L. Hartley** (1928) describing the information quantity in a set.

And among the Polish authors:

- Quality theory of information by **Marian Mazur** (1970).
- Pragmatic theory of information by **Klemens Szaniawski** (1971).
- Semantic interpretation of information proposed by **Józef Olenski** (2001).

DOI: 10.4018/978-1-60566-890-1.ch003

A common character of these approaches is the fact that all of them actually describe some selected aspects of information (e.g. its quantity) and don't explain what **information** is. One can find a long list of proposals in this area but all of them are biased with the field of interested of the authors. To prove this, we cite two known definitions of information:

- (**NorbertWiener**, 1954, p. 17): "**Information** is a name for the content of what is exchanged with the outer world as we adjust to it, and makes our adjustment felt upon it".
- (**GlynnHarmon**, 1984, p. 193): "(...) **information** as *metaenergy* – a very minute amount of energy that regulates larger amounts of energy in and among various kinds of biological or physical systems".

This is why, still there is a need of looking for a satisfactory definition of this concept. In this chapter, a proposition of so-called **infological interpretation of information** is presented. The concept was formulated by **Bo Sundgren** (1973) in his publication devoted to data bases. Sundgren developed a consistent theory of a model of data base based on the concept of **message** as a specific set of data.

The model inspires to look for a new interpretation of information, and is a good source of manifold analysis of the concept.

INFOLOGICAL CONCEPT OF INFORMATION

An interesting and forward-thinking attempt of defining the term **information** was presented by **Bo Sundgren** (1973) and **Börje Langefors** (1980). The essence of this approach is as follows.

Let us assume that observer *U* focuses on a certain segment of reality **R**. Analysis of **R** means separating certain objects *O* within it, their attributes *X* and relations between them. Generally – according to Sundgren (1973, p. 92) – a description of object *O* can be presented as:

$$M := \langle O, P, t \rangle \qquad [1]$$

Where:

O – object belonging to the analysed reality **R**;

P – predicate determining the value of attribute *X* of object *O* or its relation with other objects also belonging to **R**;

t – time, in which object *O* is considered with regard to *P*.

Expression [1] enables one to describe object *O* in terms of both its state and relations with other objects as well. This allows distinguishing two specific variants of [1]:

(a) Description of object *O* in terms of its attributes characterising the state of *O*:

$$M := (O, P(X = x), t, \mathbf{v}), \qquad [1a]$$

Where:

O – analysed object.

X – attribute of object *O*.

x – value of attribute *X*.

t – time in which object *O* takes value *x* of attribute *X*.

v – vector of additional characteristics related to object *O*, attribute *X* and its value *x* and time *t*.

Expressions *M* defined according to [1a] can be interpreted as the following sentence: "object *O* *has* value *x* of attribute *X* in time *t* with additional characteristics **v**". The word *has* distinguished in italic stresses the special kind of relation between elements of [1a]: it emphasises that object *O* is characterised by attribute *X*, which *has* value *x*.

We have added an additional **vector v** to [1a], which is not present in [1]. Its task is to make the contents provided by *M* more precise: to indicate the measure unit which has already been referred to, the source of x, the method how x has been registered, etc. Without these additional characteristics, the disambiguity of the contents delivered by M might be dubious and – what is even worse – the recipient of the contents might read it in a different way than the sender of the information intended. In particular, **vector v** may play a significant role in analysis of coherence and other desired attributes of **information**. This statement is proved by the accident relating to Mars Climate Orbiter probe crash in 1999: British measure units were not converted into metric ones and as a result, NASA specialists were unable of correct troubleshooting and controlling the probe.

(b) M takes a different form than in [1a], where object O is described in terms of its relations with other objects:

$$M := \langle O, P(O'), t, \mathbf{v} \rangle \qquad [1b]$$

Where $P(O')$ represents relation of object O with another object O'.

[1b] should be interpreted as: „object O is connected with object O' by means of relation P in time t providing that conditions **v** exist". In this way, formula M can be used for representing mutual relations between various elements belonging to **R**.

In [1b] we have retained the **vector v** in order to keep both structures: [1a] and [1b] uniform and also to enable representation of a number of significant parameters of M: the strength of relation between O and O', possible variation of this relation in time, probability of its coming into existence, and others.

In a general case the relation connecting elements of M may describe various dependencies between them: it may indicate existence of hierarchical, cause and effect, co-existential, purposefulness and other dependencies between O and O'. It may also describe the location of object O, indicate affiliation of O to a certain group or category or show its other characteristics.

Generalizing [1a] and [1b], we shall introduce a general formula of object O description, arranged in the order of sequence of its elements:

$$M := p(O, A, t, \mathbf{v}) \qquad [2]$$

Where p stands for **predicate** describing object O, while A is an argument of **predicate p**, specifying the selected aspect of this description. This may be some attribute X characterising the state of the object together with its value x ($X = x$), some other time – another object O', with which O is connected in a certain manner (p identifies the manner) or a place where O is situated, etc.

M defined by [2] can be analysed in two ways:

(a) Structurally – in terms of its elements. In this context it is called ***amessage***.
(b) Semantically, as a description (picture) of the object O with regard to argument A and relation p in time t with additional characteristics **v.** In this context, M is a carrier of ***information***.

Message *M*, connecting certain elements in one entity according to formula [2], gives some sense (meaning) to them, binding them by means of relation p. We shall call this relation an ***informational relation***. To put it another way, ***information*** is a **relation** defined on elements of **message *M*** according to [2]. This is the contents, Wiener refers to as a referent identified by the term ***information***. Sundgren calls it ***information at the datalogical level*** or otherwise – *at the**objective level***. We shall denote information at this level as $I(M)$. Symbol I stands for information delivered by M irrespective of recipient U. Some authors, **Wieslaw Flakiewicz** (1990) for example, define it as *informational function* on message M.

Infological approach to information $I(M)$, proposed by Sundgren, is not in contradiction to other specialists' view on the matter of information, for example:

1. The conformity of this concept with Wiener's approach results from the assumption that information is a relation on message elements belonging to **R**, i.e. this is contents originating in Wiener's "external world".
2. The conformity of **infological interpretation** with views of Harmon results from analysis of the functions of information.

It comes from formulas [1] and [2] that **information *I(M)*** appears as relation objectively at the **datalogical level** and it does not depend on the recipient – user *U*. Distinguishing the datalogical level enables one to use the term *information* in conditions when it is difficult to talk of any interpretation of the contents of message *M*. This take place for example in commonly available information systems, intended for gathering, storing, processing and making available information which is intended for not entirely identified individual recipients, before it is subjected to interpretation processes by a concrete person. It also enables one to use the concept of *biological information* or *genetic information*, which is encoded in genes of a living organism – it is difficult to assume that any process of interpretation takes place in this case in the sense that can be ascribed to this concept in statements assuming that information is the same as interpreted data.

The **datalogical level** makes it possible to look at *I(M)* as ***potential information***, which can be used by someone someday to clarify and solve some problem. **Langefors** (1995) states that we are not always able to identify unambiguously the information a particular sentence carries.

The pragmatic aspect of information requires taking the process of *I(M)* reception by the user *U* into consideration. We shall write this fact down as *I(M,U, Q)*, where *I* stands for information contained in *M* and received by *U* in the context of solving task *Q*. In this, i.e. pragmatic sense, information becomes subjective, dependent on *U*; this is *information in infological meaning of the word*. Information in this sense is an equivalent of ***active information*** distinguished in psychology as information accepted by a concrete recipient. The outcomes of this human interpretation depend on individual's thesaurus of concepts and his/her psychological determinants and intelligence.

Let us add that Langefors stresses that **information at the infological level** the user is able to read in **message *M*** depends on the time he/she has at his/her disposal to analyse the information, his/her knowledge (the thesaurus of concepts; Langefors uses the term *pre-knowledge* here).

One may state that information at the infological level, i.e. information *I(M,U,Q)* the recipient of a certain **message *M*** is able to realise, depends on such factors as:

- The time to think the matter over – this time can be restricted by e.g. the necessity of making an urgent decision based on *I(M)* and then subjective information *I(M,U, Q)* may turn out to be poorer than information some user might derive from *I(M)* having more time for reflection and analysis at his/her disposal.
- Knowledge possessed so far – *pre-knowledge*. Since this knowledge differs from user to user, their conclusions concerning the subjective contents of message *M* will differ, i.e. subjective information *I(M,U,Q)* derived by various recipients will vary.
- The context, i.e. problem *Q*, which has a significant impact on starting the human processes of thinking when receiving, interpreting and evaluating information.
- The user's emotional state.
- The circumstances of information reception: information *I(M)* is analysed differently when the message is received through technical means and differently when it is received in direct, personal contact: subjective interpretation of the contents of **message *M*** is influenced by the way how *M* is presented and by additional accompanying factors, such as sender's facial expression, intonation, gestures, etc.

One may encounter an opinion sometimes that a message may carry no information at all. As **Ireneusz Ihnatowicz** (1989) stresses, in some periods and circles such expressions as: "your humble servant!" or "I would be delighted" were very popular, although no one was humble nor was the delight so obvious.

On the other hand, **Marian Mazur** (1970, p.25) writes that many seemingly meaningless statements may contain a concrete message. For example, a statement: "The green freedom is pursuing the thinking house" may contain a confidential information: "The rebel peasantry combat the disregarding government". Such method of hiding the real contents underlies various ciphers. Sometimes our inability to understand the information does not mean that there is no information at all there. Each foreign language we do not know is a carrier of various contents, but we do not understand it. Quipu – Inca's "talking knots" can be given as a meaningful example here – it has not been deciphered so far, which does not mean that it contains no information.

Distinguishing **information in datalogical (objective) sense** and **infological (subjective) sense** enables one to explain the seeming contradiction between the assumption that each **message *M*** provides information and the opinion expressed by Ihnatowicz that **"empty" messages** with no contents may appear sometimes. If some object *O* is distinguished in a message (e.g. the lady someone was a humble servant of and the humble servant himself), this is an objective fact and an adequate sentence as message *M* provides information *I(M)* at the datalogical level. But interpretation of this information by a concrete recipient *U*, i.e. information *I(M,U,Q)* at the infological level – subjective information – may contribute no new contents. In this case message *M* provides no new information indeed – but this is an „empty" message to a concrete recipient only. And the same message may carry significant information to other users, describing for example how people communicated in certain circles and ages.

Thus, symbols *I(M)* and *I(M,U,Q)* emphasise the **dual nature of information** – its existence in both objective and subjective sense. Psychology takes heed of this fact, distinguishing **potential information**, useful „to anyone" and **active information**, useful to a concrete user. Seidler (1983, p. 72) writes that information is of a *potential* nature, i.e. that it "(…) may, but does not always have to be used for more efficient purposeful acting".

Some researchers assume that the message does not deliver any information to the user if its contents is already known to him/her. But in many problem situations (e.g. in business or military matters), the user strives for confirming if the information is true and tries to obtain analogical information from other sources. In a case like this, the message delivering information which has already been known is not an "empty" message – it delivers information which confirms the knowledge.

Thus, one needs to be careful when assessing messages *M* in terms of information value. One might formulate a thesis that each of them – providing that it satisfies the assumptions of [2] – carries some contents at the datalogical level, but we are not always able to decipher it at the infological level.

Message *M* as an information carrier has two essential **properties**:

1. The set of elements listed in [2] is the minimum sufficient set of data ensuring the unambiguity of elementary information *I(M)* at the level of object *O*, its characteristics *A*, predicate *p*, and time *t*. If any element in *M* – including *t* and **v**, is omitted, the message is not a source of unambiguous information any longer. The exception occurs in case of deliberate omission of some element in the message when it may be identified explicitly as a default element and is omitted for the sake of notation economy. This is how time *t* can be omitted in a set of messages for example, if *t* stands for the same time in

all these messages and it has been specified clearly separately. But such an abbreviated formula of *M* does not mean that some element (*t* for example) is eliminated in terms of the message contents – this is only our acceptance of a more economic notation.

On the other hand, one should also take notice of a case when the absence of some element or even several elements (even all – in theory) also carries some information. Such an incomplete as compared with [2] structure can be construed as a message containing a question about elements missing from the message.

Assuming for example that element *O* is missing from the given message *M'*, predicate

$$M' := p(?, A, t, \mathbf{v}) \qquad [2a]$$

can be regarded as a question about an object characterised by attribute *A* in time *t*, with additional parameters included in vector **v**.

The absence of **predicate *p*** determining the relation of object *O* with another object *O'* is a special case of message [2a]:

$$M' := ?(O, A, t, \mathbf{v}) \qquad [2b]$$

This absence can be interpreted as the user's question about the relation between *O* and *A*, directed to a certain source, e.g. a database.

2. Supplementing *M* with additional elements that have not been indicated in [2] may translate into redundancy (surplus) of notation and therefore make reception of information more difficult. One should remember, however, that sometimes such additional elements are necessary to make the contents of *M* more precise. This is why we have introduced **vector v** to formula [2] – its task is to make description of *O* more specific.

DIVERSITY OF INFORMATION

One of the interesting features of information is its **diversity**. We shall analyse this aspect of information at the datalogical level. Due to multitude of objects *O* and their attributes *A* **messages *M*** carry various informational contents. Thus, in objective sense, information can be differentiated and grouped according to various criteria based on elements included in message *M*.

With regard to time *t* the following can be distinguished:

- *Retrospective information*, when *t* applies to the past in relation to time regarded as the current time. This type of information includes all information from records or files. Historical information also represents this type.
- *Current information*, when *t* indicates the current time. One should stress here that the concept of the "current time" is a relative one: as a rule it means some accepted range of time considered to be the „present" time („now").
- *Prospective information*, when *t* applies to the future in advance – it stands for time ahead of the current time. This group of information includes all forecasts and plans, all fortune telling, predictions and intentions.

The greatest **diversity of information** can be noticed when analysing the contents of argument *A*: sometimes this attribute describes the state of object *O*, sometimes – processes in *O* and sometimes – conditions in which *O* functions. Therefore, the following types of information can be distinguished with regard of this contents:

(a) *Fact-collecting* – describing the state of object *O* by means of indicating some specific attribute *X* and its value *x* in a certain time *t*:

$M{:}= p(O, X = x, t, \mathbf{v})$.

Fact-collecting information enables one to answer such questions as: *what is object O like in terms of attribute X, what is its condition in terms of this attribute*. **Predicate *p*** is usually interpreted as verb *has*. This information is delivered by messages where attribute X describes object O in terms of its situation (real or hypothetical) in time t, giving the concrete value x of this attribute. These are basic information resources of data-recording systems, management information systems, databases, business intelligence agencies, data warehouses.

(b) *Comparative* – showing the state of object O as compared with something: with its state in some other moment t' or in comparison with the state of another object O':

$M{:}= p\_c(O,O',t,\mathbf{v})$

Where p_c stands for relation between O and O'. Information of this type answers such questions as: *what is better* or *worse*, *what is larger* or *smaller*, *more* or *less expensive*, etc. In this case, **predicate *p*** stands for such relation as *larger, smaller, better, worse, more distant*, etc., while O' indicates the object with which O is being compared.

(c) *Semantic*, determining the meaning (semantics) assigned to object O:

$M{:}= p\_s(O,A,t,\mathbf{v})$

Where p_s stands for predicate *is* or *means*. **Semantic information** enables one to obtain an answer to the question: *what O means, how O should be understood and construed*. Definitions and interpretation of concepts described in this chapter are examples of semantic information. The weight of information of this type grows along with the necessity of giving an unambiguous statement, as it happens in case of science, in descriptions of economic, social or political reality. It is included in all types of dictionaries explaining the meaning of words and terms listed there.

(d) *Procedural*, sometimes referred to as operational, describing how the subject – object O in this case – works. Semantic and fact-collecting information, including comparative information, constitutes an important factor in decision making and as a component of the general human knowledge. Nevertheless, it does not answer the questions about how the state of object O can be altered, how planned undertakings should be performed or what needs to (should) be done to achieve the planned goal.

Answers to such questions are given in ***procedural* information**, included in messages (sometimes compound messages), where A stands for the procedure:

$M{:}= p\_a(O,A,t,\mathbf{v})$

Where p_a stands for predicate of the *performs* type, while argument A indicates the procedure performed by object O. Information of this type gives also answers to questions “why”, “in what circumstances”, “what will happen if...”, etc..

Procedural information is included in various regulations and instructions, mathematical formulas and models, computer programs, bases of expert systems models. It constitutes a basis of technologies and technological processes. This type of information is looked for in „know-how” entries.

(e) *Normative*. Information of this type specifies norms (standards) imposed on O or conditions of its functioning:

$M{:}= p\_n(O,A,t,\mathbf{v})$

Where p_n is a predicate of the type *is_limited by* or *subject to* and it emphasises that object O is subject to a standard specified as A. In this case argument A specifies the condition which has to be satisfied by object O. Information of this type is presented for example in statements containing such predicate – also with "does not" negation – as: "should", "has to", "may", etc. Examples of such standards can be found in Decalogue, but also in various regulations, such as traffic regulations for example, or rules in games. These are also system communication regulations and rules and data transmission protocols in computer networks. This group includes also orders, commands, decrees, bans and warnings. They can be divided into *de facto* standards (customs for example), *de jure* standards (resulting from the law) or *internal* standards – set according to internal assumptions of object O.

(f) *Classifying* (taxonomic), constituting criteria for recognising the class object O belongs to or recognising O among other objects within the given set:

$M{:}= p\_g(O,A,t,\mathbf{v})$

Where p_g stands for predicate *belongs_to* or a similar one. It answers such questions as: *what class (category, type) object O belongs to.* Its importance grows along with the drive for higher degree of coherence (harmony) of various information systems. This is where increased interest of various institutions in working out international classification systems in many fields can be observed: in production, types of business activities, natural environment protection, health care, education and other.

(g) *Structural*, describing the structure of object O and answering such questions as: *„what is O structure, what elements does it consist of and how are they inter-related*":

$M{:}= p\_h(O,A,t,\mathbf{v})$

Where p_h can be interpreted as: predicate *has_structure*. In this case A stands for structure of object O. Information of this type constitute a measure of the object organisation (order) O. It is worth noting that contemporary information technologies give us many methods of presenting the structure of objects: traditional sign records (texts), schemes and graphic pictures. This expands the possibilities of using computer technology for collecting structural information and making it available in various forms in information systems supported with information technologies.

(h) *Spatial*, describing object O location in space:

$M{:}= p\_r(O,A,t,\mathbf{v})$

Where p_r is a predicate of *is_in, heads_towards* type, etc. Space-related information answers such questions as *where, where from, where to* – where is object O situated, where does it come from or where is it heading towards. Argument A stands for address (in broad meaning of the word). This may be a traditional mailing address, e-mail address, geographic coordinates or any other way of indicating the position of O in the given space.

(i) *Imperative*, bearing contents of the ordering nature in sentences containing such expressions as *should, must* or verbs in the imperative mode. In this case, the predicate (let us use symbol $p\_!$) stands for the verb, while A indicates, what O is supposed to do.

(j) *Queries*, including information contained in messages-questions. Such messages are characterised by predicates ($p\_?$) consisting of such particles and pronouns as *if, who, what, which,* or *how many, how much,* combined with adequate verbs, like for example *has, is, possesses*. This type of information should be red as facts expressing the user's intention to explore circumstances, situations or events unknown to him/her and concerning object *O* with regard of attribute *A*. They appear in social talk in such expressions as: "*have you heard?*", "*do you know that?*". Sometimes none of the particles or pronouns listed above does not appear explicitly, but the statement itself indicates the question clearly.

PROPERTIES OF INFORMATION

Discovering and exploring **properties of information** is necessary in activities relating to organisation and performance of any information-related processes. Knowledge of these properties is the only thing enabling one to avoid excessive costs of such processes and unreasonable demands, that are impossible to satisfy. Such properties include:

1. **Infological interpretation of information** enables one to regard it as a relation determined by formula [2]. This opens the possibility of analysing this concept and exploring its properties in terms of relations.
2. Information *I(M)* – i.e. **information at the datalogical level** – about object *O* mentioned in **message *M*** exists independently on subject *U* receiving it, as object *O* exists independently on *U*. In this sense, *I(M)* is an objective information. This property complies in particular with the view expressed by Ursul (1971) that information reflects the diversity of object *O*.
3. The same pieces of information *I(M)* mean different things to various recipients (users), depending on their information-related needs resulting from varying interests, tasks being solved and their knowledge. What is more, the same piece of information means different things to one and the same user, depending on the problem he/she is dealing with at the moment. Thus, this feature depends on time: it alters under the influence of problems being solved, available methods and *U*'s changing knowledge. To stress this fact, Sundgren has introduced the concept of information at the infological, i.e. subjective level, [this substantiates introduction of symbol *I(M,U,Q)*]. Though, the particular user's subjective reception of information is secondary to the objective existence of information, even when no one notices it (information).

Thus, information shows the **property of duality**: it is objective and it can be subjective at the same time.

4. Any unit information *I(M)* reflects only some attribute *A* of object *O* or, to put it differently – it is some fragmentary description (informational model) of this object in terms of this attribute. This means that none unit information *I(M)* or even some selected sub-set **I(M)** can not be regarded as exhaustive characteristics of this object (**M** stands for a selected sub-set of messages delivering collective information **I**). Creating a universal, exhaustive picture of an object like this is impossible in both theory and practice as well, due to unlimited and inexhaustible diversity of its characteristics. Such a complete description is a rare thing and it may take place in some extremely trivial cases, for example as regards formal objects defined in mathematics, computer science or other much formalised fields. In practice, we have only a certain sub-set of fragmentary characteristics at our disposal. As a matter of fact, the thing is not to deliver "complete" information to the user, but to provide a set of pieces of information the user will find sufficient.
5. Information shows the feature of synergy, i.e. it strengthens the effect resulting from

the process of concurrent use of two or more units of information. This means that effect $e(i_1 \cup i_2)$, resulting from the process of thinking, where two independent pieces of information are taken into consideration: i_1 and i_2, is greater than the total (in the logical sense) of effects $e(i_1)$ and $e(i_2)$, that can be achieved considering the same pieces of information – i_1 and i_2 – separately:

$$e(i_1 \cup i_2) > e(i_1) + e(i_2)$$

Let us take examining oneself in the mirror as an example here: if we have several mirrors at our disposal and examine ourselves in each of them in turn, we may become uncertain how we really look like. But if we manage to arrange these mirrors in a system showing ourselves from various sides at a time, the synergy of fragmentary reflections will result in a more complete picture.

6. In the opinion of some specialists (see Harmon 1984), information at the datalogical level, i.e. $I(M)$, can be regarded as a physical quantity, similarly as electric energy for example, because:
   - it exists objectively, as we have stated earlier,
   - its quantity can be measured (for example, with Shannon or Hartley measure).
7. The **diversity of information** is its important property resulting from variety and diversity of objects, sources (senders) of information and from users' subjective interpretation.
8. Information can be duplicated and transferred in time and space. Unfortunately, it can be distorted in this process, due to various disturbing factors (noises). The life proves that gossips, fabrications and so-called "press facts" (i.e. pseudo-, para- and disinformation) spread fast, similarly as various sensational news, especially those containing some elements of truth.
9. Information can be processed: based on messages M_{in}, delivering initial information $I_{in}(M_{in})$, one can generate other messages M_{out} in order to obtain new, derivative information $I_{out}(M_{out})$ without destroying M_{in}. Certainly, it happens sometimes that initial information is destroyed deliberately or unknowingly. But this effect does not result from the nature of information.
10. Information constitutes inexhaustible resources. The feature of inexhaustibility means that an infinite set of undiscovered, unrevealed information exists. It has been computed that a human receives 10 billion bites of information and during all life he/she accepts some 10^{16} bites, most of them remaining unrealised and not passing to the semantic level (Ursul 1971, p.190). We do not imagine how many various unnoticed and unrealised pieces of information reach us every day. Human eyes and ears keep filtering stimuli, causing that only a small part of them is recorded by the senses of sight and hearing, to be thereafter analysed by the brain. The rest is ignored according to the rule of living organisms' defence against an excessive amount of stimuli attacking it (someone might say today: this is a *spam*).
11. Information costs: to gain it and thereafter store, process, transfer and make available to the recipient, one needs to engage specialists, devote someone's time, use adequate resources – one needs to incur costs in terms of finance, time and people. The developing information society brushes aside – to the future – the opinion that water and information cost nothing and can be taken up without any negative consequences, limitations or costs.
12. Information distribution is asymmetric: information is unequally available to various recipients. This property can not be eliminated. There are many various reasons to this situation: depending on the source of

information, its costs, priority in ascertaining the facts (in case of a discovery for example). This asymmetry causes various effects relating to the multitude of information functions. From the social point of view, the asymmetry of information determines the social structure. Once, a student has written that if the information distribution had been symmetric in the society, Shakespeare would have had no reason to kill Romeo and Juliet – their parents would have known their love and they would have prevented the tragedy.

THE SPACE OF MESSAGES. THE INFORMATION SPACE

The definition of information as the contents of messages described by formula [2] at both the datalogical and the infological level tempt one to look for a synthetic way of showing the concept as some particular, compound being. This can be interpreted as a certain space set up on axes that constitute components of these messages.

Thus, set **O** of objects *O*, together with set **A** of their attributes *A* analysed within the time interval **T** determine a certain **space M of messages *M***. This space can be defined as Cartesian product:

$$\mathbf{M} = \mathbf{O} \times \mathbf{A} \times \mathbf{T} \qquad [3]$$

The following can be considered as attributes of space **M**:

1. Each point of this space constitutes a certain message $M = p(O, A, t)$, whose elements belong to sets **O**, **A** and **T**, respectively. To make it simpler, let us skip vector **v**.
2. **M** is an non-continuous, grainy space consisting of points (messages) *M*. This results from the fact that time axis (**T**) is the only continuous axis, arranged in chronological order in **M**. Both the set of objects – axis **O** and axis **A** (the set of attributes) consist of elements independent one on another, clearly identifiable at the level of language which has been used to describe them.
3. **M** is a non-metric space. This means that in a general case the position of any message *M* within it does not involve any sort of privilege towards other messages. There is no ground for distinguishing any point (message) determining its beginning within this space.
4. With the known number N_o of objects *O* in set **O**, known number N_a of attributes *A* in set **A** and number N_t of points of the time axis **T** based on [3] one may determine the number *N* of messages belonging to **M**:

$$N = N_o \times N_a \times N_t \qquad [4]$$

This number can serve as a ***measure of datalogical capacity of space* M.**

5. Each element of space **M**, i.e. each message *M* delivers a particular piece of information *I(M)*, which is a unit (elementary) information. Thus, space **M** constitutes a set delivering a number of unit pieces of information *I(M)*, which form set **I** together. We shall call set **I** the ***information space***. Similarly as **M**, space **I** is a grainy space, this resulting from the assumption that information is the contents of the message. Number *N* determined by [4] is a measure of informational capacity of space **I.**
6. Distribution of messages *M* within space **M**, and in consequence – distribution of information *I(M)* within **I**, is uneven: some its areas may remain empty (there can be no messages there), while some other are thickly packed with messages *K* situated side by side. The density of filling **M** with messages depends on the real logical relationships between objects on axis **O**, attributes on axis **A** and time axis **T**. These dependencies result in their turn from the segment of reality **R** being

analysed. Therefore, previously named number N of messages theoretically acceptable in **M**, and consequently – the number of unit pieces of information $I(M)$ in **I**, is the upper limit of this **space capacity**. In practice, due to the absence of relations between some objects and attributes, the number of real messages in **M**, and in consequence – the set of fragmentary pieces of information in **I**, in terms of the analysed segment of reality **R**, is smaller.

7. Since both set **O**, and set **A** may contain elements (O and A respectively) showing various degrees of complexity and forming sometimes a hierarchic structure, space **I** should be regarded as a hierarchic structure, where subsets entering various mutually subordinated subspaces appear.

Structure of **space M** becomes more complex, when values of attributes A and elements of **vector v** are taken into consideration. In this case any additional characteristics recorded in this vector introduces a new dimension of space **M**.

Thus, in a general case, **M**, and consequently – also space **I**, is a multi-dimensional space, where the number of dimensions depends on the number of elements included in messages M. Properties of this space listed before still remain valid.

Some operations can be defined in the **space of messages** and consequently – in the **information space**. The operations are based on the concept of ***semantic field*** $\pi(O)$ of object O defined as a set of objects semantically connected with O.

Semantic Total of Information Pieces

Let us assume that two messages with the common **predicate** ***p*** are given:

$M_1 := p\,(O_1, A_1, t_1, \mathbf{v}_1)$

$M_2 := p\,(O_2, A_2, t_2, \mathbf{v}_2)$

The **semantic total** of these messages will be represented by the resultant message M_s defined as:

$$M_s := M_1 + M_2 = p\,(O_s, A_s, t_s, \mathbf{v}_s) \qquad [5]$$

Where:

- Sign „+" stands for the **semantic total of messages** M_1 and M_2.
- Object O_s is a semantic compound of objects O_1 and O_2:

$O_s := O_1 \cup O_2$.

The semantic compound (**semantic total**) of objects O_1 and O_2 means defining a new object O_s in a manner, where its contents (its semantic field) includes the contents (semantic fields) of both input objects: $\pi(O_s) = \pi(O_1) \cup \pi(O_2)$, where $\pi(O_s)$ is a semantic field of object O_s, $\pi(O_1)$ is a semantic field of object O_1 and $\pi(O_2)$ is a semantic field of object O_2.

Object O_s will be identical with O_1 and O_2 – its semantic field will conform to the semantic field of both O_1 and O_2: $\pi(O_s) = \pi(O_1) = \pi(O_2)$ if:

1. The same object has been named in both messages M_1 and M_2 (although formally O_1 and O_2 may appear in the form of some other given value). Otherwise, the resultant object O_s is a semantic extension (its semantic field is extended) of the objects analysed so far – it is a new object which differs semantically from both O_1 and O_2 as well.
2. Argument A_s is a semantic compound (semantic total) of arguments A_1 and A_2: $A_s := A_1 \cup A_2$. The semantic compound of arguments A_1 and A_2 means defining a new argument with the contents of arguments A_1 and A_2 taken into account. This means that semantic field $\pi(A_s)$ of argument A_s is a logic total of semantic fields $\pi(A_1)$ and

$\pi(A_2)$ of argument A_1 and argument A_2: $\pi(A_s) = \pi(A_1) \cup \pi(A_2)$. If A_1 and A_2 are identical in terms of the contents {their semantic fields are equal: $\pi(A_1) = \pi(A_2)$} in input messages, the compound $A_1 \cup A_2$ does not bring any new component of the resultant message in. Otherwise, a new element is received (new given value) – A_s, and in consequence – new informational contents in message M_s.

3. Time t_s is a logical compound (semantic total) of time t_1 and t_2, which in case of any difference between them leads to consideration of object O_s in a different, wider time perspective.
4. Vector $\boldsymbol{v}_s$ is a semantic compound {semantic total – compound of semantic fields $\pi(\boldsymbol{v}_1)$ and $\pi(\boldsymbol{v}_2)$} of vectors $\boldsymbol{v}_1$ and $\boldsymbol{v}_2$. The semantic compound of vectors $\boldsymbol{v}_1$ and $\boldsymbol{v}_2$ implies totalling respective semantic fields of these vectors, i.e. defining new elements in $\boldsymbol{v}_s$, where contents of individual elements belonging to $\boldsymbol{v}_1$ and $\boldsymbol{v}_2$ are included. If components of these vectors are respectively equal (i.e. $\boldsymbol{v}_1$ and $\boldsymbol{v}_2$ are semantically identical), the resultant vector $\boldsymbol{v}_s$ is semantically identical with $\boldsymbol{v}_1$ and $\boldsymbol{v}_2$.

If at least one component of message M_s is a new given value added to the values forming input messages M_1 and M_2, then M_s differs from the two previous messages. The new message brings a new informational contents in – a new piece of information.

The following should be considered as properties of semantic total of messages:

1. The operation of **semantic totalling of messages** is at the same time definition of semantic compound (semantic total) of pieces of information delivered by two various input messages.
2. The operation of totalling messages can be extended with any number of messages.
3. The **semantic total of messages** does not depend on the sequence of elements:

$$M_s = M_1 + M_2 = M_2 + M_1$$

Semantic Difference of Information

Let us assume that two messages with the same predicates p are given:

$$M_1 := p\ (O_1, A_1, t_1, \mathbf{v}_1)$$

$$M_2 := p\ (O_2, A_2, t_2, \mathbf{v}_2)$$

The **semantic difference** of these predicates will be the resultant message M_r defined as follows:

$$M_r := M_1 - M_2 = p\ (O_r, A_r, t_r \boldsymbol{v}_r) \qquad [6]$$

Where:

1. Object O_r is a semantic difference of objects O_1 and O_2. The term *semantic difference of objects O_1 and O_2* stands here for such object O_r, the semantic field $\pi(O_r)$ of which is a logical difference of semantic fields $\pi(O_1)$ and $\pi(O_2)$ of objects O_1 and O_2. This difference consists of a set of elements belonging to $\pi(O_1)$ and not belonging to $\pi(O_2)$. If in both messages M_1 *and* M_2 the same object O has been mentioned, the semantic difference O_1 - O_2 stands for an object with an empty semantic field. This object will be identified as $O°$.
2. Argument A_r is a semantic difference of arguments A_1 and A_2. This term should be understood as such resultant argument A_r, the semantic field $\pi(A_r)$ of which is a logical difference of semantic fields $\pi(A_1)$ and $\pi(A_2)$ of arguments A_1 and A_2. This difference consists of a set of elements belonging to $\pi(A_1)$ and not belonging to $\pi(A_2)$. If A_1 and

A_2 are identical in both messages M_1 and M_2 then the difference $A_r = A_1 - A_2$ is an empty argument and its semantic field $\pi(A_r)$ is an empty field. We shall identify an argument like this as $A°$.

3. Time t_r is a logical difference between time t_1 and t_2. In case when $t_1 \neq t_2$, the time perspective in which both input messages are analysed is narrowed. In case when both these times are identical ($t_1 = t_2$), the resultant object O_r will be analysed in „zero" time, i.e. without any time taken into consideration as a matter of fact. We shall identify this "zero" time as $t°$.
4. Vector $\boldsymbol{v}_r$ is a logical difference of vectors $\boldsymbol{v}_1$ and $\boldsymbol{v}_2$, i.e. a logical difference of respective semantic fields of these vectors components. If elements of these vectors are respectively equal, the resultant vector $\boldsymbol{v}_r$ does not bring any new contents to message M_r. A vector like this is an empty vector; we shall identify it as $\boldsymbol{v}°$. But if at least one element of this vector does not have an equivalent element in the second vector then $\boldsymbol{v}_r$ constitutes a new given value.

The following should be considered as properties of **semantic difference** of messages:

1. Semantic difference of messages M_1 and M_2 is not symmetric:

$$\mathrm{M}_1 - \mathrm{M}_2 \neq \mathrm{M}_2 - \mathrm{M}_1.$$

2. If at least one of the elements of message M_r is a new given value added to given values forming input vectors M_1 and M_2 then this message differs from the two previous messages. The new message brings a new informational content in – a new piece of information. Thus, the presented definition of the semantic difference of messages is at the same time a definition of the **semantic difference of pieces of information** included in two various messages.
3. If all elements of message M_r are zero elements, i.e.:

$$M_r = M°_r = p\,(O°, A°, t°, \boldsymbol{v}°),$$

then there is no semantic difference between messages $I(M_1)$ and $I(M_2)$: $I(M_1)$ and $I(M_2)$ is the same information. We shall say that messages M_1 and M_2 are equivalent. One of messages belonging to the pair of equivalent messages contains pseudo-information. This does not mean however that it does not make any sense to possess both these messages: in some circumstances information confirming knowledge one already has can be valuable.

4. If at least one of the elements of the resultant message M_r is not zero, then a semantic difference occurs between information $I(M_1)$ and $I(M_2)$. The more elements of message M_r are not zero messages, the greater the difference is. This number can serve as a *measure of* ***semantic distance*** *from between* $I(M_2)$ and $I(M_1)$. In general, the semantic difference of message M_1 from M_2 is different than the analogical distance of M_2 from M_1.

Semantic difference M_r of two messages may constitute a basis for evaluating the degree of coherence of messages M_1 and M_2, based on which it has been computed. If message M_r is a zero message ($M_r = M°_r$), i.e. if all its components are zero elements – including elements vector $\boldsymbol{v}°$ consists of – in the sense specified above then these messages are coherent in terms of data appearing in them. But if any of the elements message M_r consists of is not a zero element then coherence of M_r and M_2 is not complete: it applies to zero elements only. If there is no zero element in M_r, then messages M_1 and M_2 are not mutually coherent.

Semantic Product of Information

Let us assume that two messages with any predicates have been given:

$M_1 := p_1 (O_1, A_1, t_1, \mathbf{v}_1)$

$M_2 := p_2 (O_2, A_2, t_2, \mathbf{v}_2)$

Let us build Cartesian product $\boldsymbol{M}_k$ on elements (data) of these messages:

$$\boldsymbol{M}_k := \times X(\boldsymbol{p}, \boldsymbol{O}, \boldsymbol{A}, \boldsymbol{t}_i) \quad [7]$$

Where "×" stands for Cartesian product on elements:

$$\boldsymbol{p} := \{ p_1, p_2\}, \boldsymbol{O} := \{O_1, O_2\}, \boldsymbol{A} := \{ A_1, A_2\}, \boldsymbol{t} := \{ t_1, t_2\}. \quad [8]$$

Each element $M \in \boldsymbol{M}_k$ is a message constructed of data belonging to messages M_1 and M_2 after one element is selected from each of the sets: $\boldsymbol{p}$, $\boldsymbol{O}$, $\boldsymbol{A}$, and $\boldsymbol{t}$. Each of messages M constructed in this way delivers certain contents, i.e. it is a carrier of a certain piece of information. As we do not impose any semantic restrictions on elements (data) messages M_1 and M_2 consist of, some of messages $M \in M_k$ may not deliver any contents that can be interpreted in terms of reasonable information. We shall refer to such messages as to *messages with information noises*. We shall identify the set of such messages as $\boldsymbol{M}_{noise}$.

Pairs of some messages $M \in M_k$ can be equivalent in terms of informational contents included in them. We shall identify this set as $\boldsymbol{M}_e$. Having eliminated from this set one element of each pair of equivalent messages, we shall have set $\boldsymbol{M'}_e$. We shall call eliminated equivalent messages redundant. Each redundant message carries pseudo-information.

Having eliminated from $\boldsymbol{M}_k$ messages with noise and redundant messages, i.e. having created set $\boldsymbol{M}$ [$\boldsymbol{M} = \boldsymbol{M}_k - (\boldsymbol{M}_{noise}, \cup \boldsymbol{M'}_e)$], where „-" stands for logical difference between set $\boldsymbol{M}_k$ and the logical total of sets $\boldsymbol{M}_{noise}$, and $\boldsymbol{M'}_e$, we shall obtain a **semantic product of messages**M_1 and M_2.

We have omitted vectors $\boldsymbol{v}_1$ and $\boldsymbol{v}_2$ in this definition. This results from the assumption that elements of these vectors only supplement (make more precise) the informational contents of messages and depend on the remaining elements each concrete message consists of. This is why their introduction to resultant messages should occur after individual analysis of each of them in terms of informational contents.

The following should be considered as properties of the semantic product of messages:

1. A product like this may include any number of input messages.
2. Each of messages $M \in \boldsymbol{M}$ brings a new informational contents in – a new piece of information. Thus, the definition of the semantic product of messages presented above is at the same time a definition of the semantic product of pieces of information two various messages contain.
3. The product of message M and itself does not bring any new information in. Each of sets $p := \{p_1, p_2\}$, $\boldsymbol{O} := \{O_1, O_2\}$, $\boldsymbol{A} := \{A_1, A_2\}$, $\boldsymbol{t} := \{t_1, t_2\}$ contains two semantically equivalent elements: the semantic fields of both elements these sets consist of are the same. Thus, redundant messages will appear in two various messages $M_1 \in \boldsymbol{M}$ and $K_2 \in \boldsymbol{M}$ belonging to semantic product of $\boldsymbol{M}$. Gradual and consistent elimination of such messages will lead to the situation when only one message is left in $\boldsymbol{M}$ – message M.
4. Number n of messages $M \in \boldsymbol{M}$ determines the power of this set. This is the number of new messages that can be generated based on two given input messages. As each message like this brings a certain new piece of

information in at the datalogical level, the number n can be regarded as a measure of growth of information resources resulting from the operation of semantic product on the given input messages

CONCLUSION

The presented study does not exhaust the conclusions resulting from **infological interpretation of information** by any means. Just the opposite – it encourages the reader to develop the work towards building the ***infological theory of information*** with his/her own terminology and research apparatus.

REFERENCES

Flakiewicz, W. (1990). *Informacyjne systemy zarządzania* (*Management Information Systems*). Warsaw, Poland: Polskie Wydawnictwo Ekonomiczne.

Harmon, G. (1984). The measurement of information. *Information Processing & Management, 1-2*, 193–198. doi:10.1016/0306-4573(84)90049-9

Hartley, R. W. L. (1928). Transmission of Information. *The Bell System Technical Journal*, 7(3), 535–563.

Ihnatowicz, I. (1989). *Człowiek. Informacja. Społeczeństwo (Man, Information, Society*). Warsaw, Poland: Czytelnik.

Kolmogorov, A. N. (1969). K logiczeskim osnovam teorii informacii i tieorii vierojatnosti (On the Logical Principles of the Theory of Information and the Theory of Probability). *Problemy Peredaczi informacii* (Problems of information transmission).

Langefors, B. (1980). Infological models and information users view. *Information Systems, 5*, 17–32. doi:10.1016/0306-4379(80)90065-4

Langefors, B. (1995). *Essays on infology – Summing up and planning for the future*. Lund, Studentlitteratur.

Mazur, M. (1970). *Jakościowa teoria informacji* (*A Quality Theory of Information*). Warsaw, Poland: Wydawnictwo Naukowo-Techniczne.

Olenski, J. (2001). *Ekonomika informacji* (*Information Economics*). Warsaw, Poland: Polskie Wydawnictwo Ekonomiczne.

Seidler, J. (1983). *Nauka o informacji* (*Science of Information*). Warsaw, Poland: Wydawnictwo Naukowo-Techniczne.

Shannon, C. E. (1948). A mathematical theory of communication. *Bell System Techn. Journal, 27*(3-4).

Sundgren, B. (1973). *An infological approach to data bases*. Stockholm: Skriftserie Statistika Centralbyran.

Szaniawski, K. (1971). Pragmatyczna wartość informacji (Pragmatic Theory of Information). In: J. Kozielecki (Ed.), *Problemy psychologii matematycznej* (*Problems of the Mathematical Psychology*) (pp. 325-347). Warsaw, Poland: Polish Scientific Publishing House.

Ursul, A. D. (1971). *Informacija*. Moscow: Nauka.

Wiener, N. (1954). *The human use of human beings – Cybernetics and society* (2nd ed). New York: Doubleday Anchor Books, Doubleday & Company, Inc.

KEY TERMS AND DEFINITIONS

Message: A set of data having a meaningful content.

Infological Interpretation of Information: Content of message.

Properties of Information: Information features independent of the user's view.

Information Space: Cartesian product on the set O of objects O, together with the set A of their attributes A, and the time interval T.

Semantic Field: A set of objects semantically connected with the given object.

Semantic Operations: Logical operations on semantic fields.

Chapter 4
How Models and Methods for Analysis and Design of Information Systems can be Improved to Better Support Communication and Learning

Prima Gustienė
Karlstad University, Sweden

Sten Carlsson
Karlstad University, Sweden

ABSTRACT

Various models and methods are used to support information system development process, but after many years of practice, projects still continue to fail. One of the reasons is that the conventional modeling approaches do not provide efficient support for learning and communication among stakeholders. Lack of an integrated method for systematic analysis, design and evolution of static and dynamic structures of information system architectures is the core of frustration in various companies. Semantic problems of communication between business analysis and design experts lead to ambiguous and incomplete system requirement specifications. The traditional modeling approaches do not view business data and process as a whole. Our goal is to propose a method, which would help system designers to reason about the pragmatic, semantic and syntactic aspects of a system in a communication and learning perspective. Service-oriented paradigm was shortly presented as one of the possible solutions to the problems of integration.

INTRODUCTION

Changes in market, global competition and distributed environments force companies to produce their products and services with better quality and more flexibly, which results in necessity for introduction of new technological solutions. Information systems, as support for realization of business processes become of great importance. It

DOI: 10.4018/978-1-60566-890-1.ch004

demands a better understanding and integration of organizational and technical components. If goals stated by business experts should fit with the outputs from implementation, it is necessary that all partners involved in system development process have a common understanding of both organizational and technical aspects.

Information systems are developed to support information exchange among people and to perform businesses more effectively. Information system development is the way in which information systems are conceived, analyzed, designed and implemented (Avison & Fitzgerald, 2006). The analysis and design of information systems is based on understanding of the organizational objectives, structure and processes as well as how to exploit information technology for advantage. It is the process consisting of many phases, necessary to overcome to get a final result, which should be consistent with the user requirements. Information systems analysis and design is a complex process involving different stakeholders with different views, purposes and backgrounds that develop and maintain information systems. Mutual understanding and agreement among all these stakeholders is crucial in this process. Communication is the basis of understanding. It is the prerequisite for successful communication. Semantic problems of communication among different stakeholders are reasons for ambiguous, and incomplete system requirements that contribute to the failures of system development projects (Yoo, Catanio, Paul, & Bieber, 2004). Distributed environments of information system makes communication and learning more difficult and complex. To obtain the improvement of understanding in use and development of these systems, this ability also has to be supported during the development process.

The quality of system specifications and successful communication between business people and system developers lies not in amount of methods, models and diagrams. To come to consensus and understanding it is necessary to have integrated models and methods. An integrated method will help systematically identify semantic conflicts that arise during development process as well as it guide how to achieve the complete picture of the system, while showing the way how to link and check consistency between pragmatic, semantic and syntactic levels of system specifications. An integrated method for analysis and design can contribute to complete, consistent and unambiguous system understanding as well as guide systematic development process (Avison & Fitzgerald, 2006). The models should be useful in many perspectives (Fowler, 1997); from having semantic power to express the necessary 'domain entities' and relationships among them, have ability to clarify the meaning of ambiguous terms and ensues that no different interpretations of concepts occur. Having this semantic power models and methods would support communication and learning among people.

Many methodologies with different techniques and tools are used to support the information development process. Already in the early sixties when computers more regularly were used in different companies it was realized that something should be done concerning the development process (Langefors, 1995). The failures flagged among other things to the developers that the methods for this process have to be better. There are two important issues concerning models and methods used as a means of communication during information system development process a) Methods should provide integrated guidelines for the whole information system development process. Such graphical representations should have a reasonable pedagogical capacity that promotes learning and communication among different partners involved and facilitates understanding of information systems architectures b) Architectures should be built in such a way that they have enough semantic power to represent communicational aspects of the information systems. Common to them all is that these methods and models in some way or another should support communication and learning during the system development process to specify the system requirements.

One reason for failures is usually to be found in an inaccurate process of communication and learning when the system analysts, designers and business users communicate the prerequisites for the system. The problems of understanding the communication and learning about the system are reciprocal. Developers need to use a pedagogical language about the models in communicating them with the users and vice versa, the users have to teach the developers how they want the system to be used. These languages should have such semantic power that enables communication of models on different levels of abstraction to present proposed solutions at different levels of details (Maciaszek, 2001). Further more models should have a reasonable pedagogical capacity that promotes the learner's way of learning and communication among different partners involved with the aim to facilitate understanding of the information systems contents.

We start our discussion about learning and communication from the fact that different methods, models with different graphical motivation is used in information system development to visualize, specify, construct and document them, do not support communication and learning among stakeholders. The questions we therefore raise here are: Is there something wrong with the models for information system development concerning learning and communication? Are they not good enough to describe the enterprise services and information that is needed for them? Are they not good enough as the means of communication among different actors involved? All these questions result to other questions which are as following:

- How do different fundamental theoretical linguistic ideas influence the assumptions concerning understanding and communication?
- How do different fundamental ideas for learning influence understandability of models?
- How can methods and models of information system development be improved to better support communication and learning?

The objective of this chapter is to present a comprehensive review of fundamental theoretical assumptions concerning communication and learning as well as to present some basic problems in traditional modeling approaches for analysis and design of information systems in this perspective. The analysis done provides assumptions that should be taken into considerations while constructing models and methods to support communication and learning during information system development process. The chapter shortly presents a method that enables system analysts and designers to reason about pragmatic, semantic and syntactic aspects of the system in an integrated way, which is necessary to understand the system as a whole. Service-oriented approach was shortly presented as a solution to integration of static and dynamic parts of the system using one modeling notation. The presented solutions are motivated taking into account theoretical ideas concerning communication, understand and learning.

SOME THEORETICAL LINGUISTIC ASSUMPTIONS CONCERNING UNDERSTANDING AND COMMUNICATION

What is important to realize is that different theoretical assumption about what understandable communication is and what has to be fulfilled in communication to be understandable also influence our ideas when constructing methods and models for communication. The aim of this part is make clear a couple linguistic theories which one definitely can find hidden behind what is assumed about improvement of communication in information system development.

The first idea we call the rationalistic standpoint. According to this standpoint we can figure out two central ways for obtaining intersubjective understanding in communication (Apel, 1972).

The first one is traditional empirism by means of causal explanations. The second one, semantic empirism, which we will say is more common in systems development than the first one. According to semantic empirism we assume that language is intersubjective by itself by means of being objective and universal. This means what Winograd and Flores (Winograd & Flores, 1986) call the reproducing traditional view on the relationship between language and the world. They write as follows about this view:

- Sentences say things about the world, and can be either true or false.
- What a sentence says about the world is a function of the words it contains and the structures into which these are combined.
- The content words of a sentence (such as nouns, verbs and adjectives) can be taken as denoting (in the world) objects, properties, relationships or sets of these. (p. 17)

If we use these ideas as a starting point for our methodical constructions there will no problem to understand the communication. The words mean the same thing for everyone and as these words are related as something true about the world. So the only mismatch in communication will depend on saying something which is false, you cannot hear or you do not know the word (Linell, 1994). In the perspective of models these linguistic assumptions will mean that the models you construct say true things about the world which is a function of the parts and the structure of the model. The process of human communication is often summed up in two transformations, consisting of the following four phases:

- The sender must make clear for himself, exactly what to communicate.
- The sender must choose symbols which externalize the internal content (The first transformation).
- The receiver must assimilate symbols. It means to hear the transmission and know the language.
- The receiver must thereafter integrate all received symbols and transform them into an internal content (The second transformation).

These assumptions about communication are built on that cognition is some sort of manipulation of words in the brain (Linell, 1989). According to Linell (1989) communication is more like a mediation of input from the sender to the receiver who interpret the symbols by means of his or her linguistic code in the brain. If we instead choose another linguistic origin, a more relational and constitutional world view on language and communication then Ricoeur (1976) asserts that "the sentence is not a larger or complex word, it is a new entity. A sentence is a whole irreducible to the sum of the parts. It is made up of words, but is not a derivative function of its words" (p.7). In this sense interpretation is not a sort of deciphering of the words and how they are combined in the sentence. The meaning of the sentence is instead a synthesis of what the sentence means for him or her who told it. For constructing models this means that they do not contain any meaning by themselves. That is the drawer of the model who just knows what the model means synthetically until he or she has told someone else about that meaning. If the models do not contain any meaning by themselves why should we use them?

As we do not accept that the models factually mean something that can objectively be interpreted by someone without any comments from someone else we must suggest another way of using the models in order support communication and learning. According to our view and relational theory of language model always has to be explained using natural language. The models can help us to sharp up the dialogue to be sure that we are talking about the same thing which is most fundamental for avoiding ambiguity. Ambiguity is one of the deficiencies of the natural and system modeling languages. It causes misunderstanding among system developers. Ambiguity of concepts in system modeling may occur because a formal expression or natural language sentence has more than one meaning (Dori, 2002), or because of incompleteness or inconsistency of conceptual models. Natural language being a means of communication can not hinder unambiguous interpretation, which is essential for precise understanding of engineering tasks in system development (Dori, 2002).

The way to sharp up what we are talking about is one very important prerequisite for obtaining intersubjectivity about what we mean by what we are saying and drawing in models. But to obtain this mutuality, communication has to be performed in an open minded dialogue in which the listener is as much important as the speaker for the understanding the contents.

DIFFERENT THEORETICAL ASSUMPTIONS OF LEARNING INFLUENCING UNDERSTANDABILITY OF MODELS

It is often told in conferences and in literature on systems development that methods and models should support learning. Consequently these methods and models must be built on a theory of learning which is assumed be successful. The problem is however that there are much talks a little substance according to these assertions in the books. Sometimes very surface recommendations are suggested, like thumb rules as what Coad and Yourdon (1991) suggest for the designer "ask them to talk about the problem domain" (p.59). Another idea is to suggest different assumptions about peoples thinking. Coad and Yourdon (1991) wrote that "people use association to tie together certain things that happen at some point in time or under similar circumstance" (p.15). Proposing some idea about people thinking as something important for learning, might be a good idea, as didactical and theoretical claims very often are correlated to human thinking. But the problem is however that Coad and Yordons assertions are not supported by theoretical outlines. Otherwise the proposals will be of no value. So what is important in order to increase learning in relation to information systems methods and models is to start by discussing learning in a theoretical perspective.

The theoretical foundations for gaining knowledge have been put into question since Plato. One idea has been that knowledge is descended from inside a person's brain quite separated from happens outside (Marton & Booth, 1997). Marton and Booth (1997) claim that knowledge just comes from outside, from the world around us according to the empiricist tradition. The third suggestion that Marton and Booth (1997) propose is that knowledge is gained both from inside and outside not constructed but constituted as an internal relation between inside and outside by people experiencing the world as such. If we now put these ideas in relation to methods and models the result will be like this. According to the first idea we can sit at home alone and construct methods and models without discussing them with someone. What we learn always happens inside our heads so therefore we do not need to ask anyone else about something if we want to construct a good method or good model. That we can do just by thinking. The second idea gives us another problem. When everything always comes from outside the problem is what we are able to learn just from outside. If we do not know anything about something, how do we then know what we should learn from outside especially if we do not know what it is. This second assumption about learning would be of any help only if there is something in the head before and just then it can help you to gain the right things in order to learn more. But the spokesmen for these assumptions have never explained what that something is and has got into your head in the first place (Linell, 1989). If we want to use these assumptions to help us for constructing methods and models, we also have to explain what we need in our heads before we construct these methods and models. Using the starting point that knowledge is gained both from outside and inside than we have to gain knowledge about system development methods and models both from outside and inside. Making these methods and models just logically from inside will never lead to any success. Marton and Booth (1997) states that:

"One should not, and we do not, consider person and world as being separate. One should not resort to hypothetical mental structures divorced from the world and we have no intention of doing so, nor should one resort to the social, cultural world as seen by the researcher only. People live in a world which they – and not only researchers – experience. They are affected by what affects them, and not what affects the researches. What this boils down to – as far as learning of the kind to be dealt with in this book is concerned – is taking the experiences of people seriously and exploring the physical, social and cultural world as they experience" (pp.12-13).

This means, if learning is related to how methods and models should be developed for information systems development we have to do it together with the users of the information system during the development process or at least test them in that context. Otherwise we will never know if the methods or models will be better. There are no differences between this type of learning compared with any other type of learning and what is experienced in terms of learning during this process concerns the user as much as the researcher. Therefore if we ignore this we do not take the user's experiences as something important for how methods and models supporting learning should be developed and nothing else but failures will be the result. A very strong didactic devise is, to be precise, that strategies of learning always should start from what the learner is thinking about the content that should be learned (Kroksmark & Marton, 1987; Marton, 1986). The system users, as well the system developers, are the learners in systems development, therefore the methods and models have to be comprehensible for all stakeholders involved.

IMPORTANT ASSUMPTIONS CONCERNING COMMUNICATION AND LEARNING FOR MODELS AND METHODS USED IN INFORMATION SYSTEM DEVELOPMENT

The former suggested theoretical grounds of communication and learning should be integrated into system development process. Communication and didactical ideas for supporting learning should be joined into one unit. You cannot talk during systems development process without thinking of what your talk means to them who are the learners. You cannot either use didactical ideas without thinking of how to present them by means of your talk.

One important theoretical rule earlier mentioned is that in order to support learning it is necessary to choose the didactical strategy from how the learner is thinking about the contents that should be learned. Then we must ask ourselves: who is the learner in systems development and what are the contents? The contents in systems development are what the participants are talking about the system in the development process. The roles of learners are relative; all stakeholders involved play the role of learners at some point of development process. The solutions taken much depends how system users and system developers perceive and agree upon the contents.

An important remark about this thinking has to be done concerning the contents of activities. The contents of today and that for tomorrow are not similar because of the contents change. Regarding to the contents of the routines system users have the answers and are able to tell the system designer as a learner what they do, why and how. But there is a special problem of understanding what concerns the projected new routines. As the new routines are projected to be used in the future no one has the answer from the beginning what the contents would be (Schutz & Luckmann, 1974). The system designer perhaps might have experiences from other design contexts, but they cannot however be sure of if the suggested routines are right before the designer has performed a methodical deep dialog together with the end-user when testing the suggested solutions. Agreement and mutual understanding can be achieved just in a close dialogue among different stakeholders.

A further principal of human thinking is when we are interpreting something in order to understand it. In that case the peoples thinking swing to and fro the part and the whole. What the part means depends on what wholeness you interpret is against. If the participants in systems development interpret the part in different ways of understanding the wholeness, the result of interpretation of the part will consequently not be comparable. This is called the hermeneutical circle in interpretation theory (Palmer, 1969). In order to apply the question of the hermeneutical circle in methods and models we suggest that the wholeness, which the part in focus concerns, always is presented together with the part by means of the model. By doing this, the models help up the situation to be able to know that people discuss and understand the same thing from the same circumstance, because what we talk about is represented in the model.

A second further principal of thinking is when we think of an object either *present-at- hand* or *ready-to-hand* (Winograd & Flores, 1986). If you think of a hammer present-at-hand, a famous example which Winograd and Flores have got from Heidegger, you can tell how the hammer looks like. But if you are in the mood of using the hammer ready-to-hand you instead is thinking of the hammering and not at all how it looks like. This you do until there is a break down in your hammering, when you perhaps hit you thumb or the handle breaks. After the break down, you will be aware of the hammer again being a thing, present-at-hand. In order to understand an object ready-to-hand you must according to (Heidegger, 1962) have a pre-understanding of how the object is used ready-to-hand. If you don't know how to use it, than it is almost impossible to realize that by looking at the object present-at-hand. When therefore a person is unfamiliar with something used ready-to-hand talking to the designer, who presumably knows that very well, the end-user has big difficulties to understand what is communicated. In this situation it is very important that if the design models concern different types of ready-to-hand situations in the context, it is necessary to find out how you can show the design problem presented in the model ready to hand.

From former suggested theoretical grounds of communication and learning we can conclude the following assumptions that should be taken into consideration when constructing and using methods and models for designing information systems to better support communication and learning:

- Intersubjectivity as mutual understanding can be achieved in a close dialogue between different actors involved in the development process.
- The models should represent both the part and the whole according to the hermeneutical circle.
- The models should support a presentation of the objects ready-to-hand situation.

In the following part of the chapter we will present some problems in traditional modeling approaches that causes difficulties in communication and learning.

PROBLEMS IN TRADITIONAL MODELING APPROACHES FOR INFORMATION SYSTEMS DEVELOPMENT CONCERNING COMMUNICATION AND LEARNING

There are many attempts in solving modeling problems by introducing new modeling approaches such as DEMO method (Dietz, 2001), object-process methodology (Dori, 2002), the BPEL4People (Dubray, 2007), Business Process Execution Language for People adds additional information to the standard BPEL process context (Kloppmann et al., 2005), ArchiMate, an architectural language for enterprise architecture (Lankhorst, 2004), Functional and Object-Oriented Methodology for analysis and design (Shoval & Kabeli-Shani, 2008), which take advantage of implementation independent business process representations trying to combine static and dynamic aspects. Such models are technology neutral descriptions of organizational architectures that supposed to provide integrating principles for isolated diagrams. The weakness in applying such methodologies is in lack of systematic guidance and clearly defined linkage between implementation-dependent graphical representations and business process models that are typically defined on a higher level of abstraction.

The fundamental problem in conventional information system development methods for system analysis and design is that conventional approaches do not take into account some important interdependencies that are crucial to glue organizational and technical system descriptions (Gustas & Gustienė, 2004). It results in difficulties to integrate views of two subcultures: business people and system designers. The organizational and technical requirements need to be captured, visualized and agreed upon (Gustas & Gustienė, 2002). This may be regarded as one of the main reasons of misunderstandings between business users and system designers (Gustienė, 2003). Generally, information system requirement specifications are not easy to validate for the simple reason that they are spanning across organizational and technical system boundaries, and these boundaries are not always clear as they are changing over time. The integrated enterprise modeling foundation (Gustas, 2000) is necessary to facilitate reasoning and fitness of enterprise architectures across organizational and technical system boundaries.

One of the problems with conventional information system development modeling approaches is the lack of integrated models of static and dynamic aspects of business processes across organizational and technical system boundaries (Gustas & Gustienė 2007; Gustas & Gustienė, 2008; Gustiene & Gustas, 2008).Static aspects define the structural part of the system, it defines "what" is changing and transforming. The behavioral aspects of the system defines "how" the objects in a system cooperates to achieve broader results (Blaha & Rumbaugh, 2005). Usually traditional methodologies are centered on modeling separate aspects of the system either static aspects or dynamic ones and uses different diagrams to represent these aspects. For instance, database design languages are centered on modeling of the static aspects, which represent business data (the "what" dimension). On the contrary, the Business Process Modeling Notation (White, 2004) is restricted to a business process modeling (the "how" dimension), which excludes the static aspects. Interdependencies among models and perspectives that specify information system can not be analyzed in isolation because there is always an overlapping in different perspectives to some degree, because they are defining the same artifact. Likewise, there are intersecting elements, which are represented in different dimensions. For instance, the concept of operation in UML is represented in a class diagram (the "what" dimension), activity diagram (the "how"), sequence diagram (the "where") and state-transition diagram (the "when" dimension). Furthermore, the atomic operations are typically aggregated into the higher granularity operations that are represented as the elements of a use case diagram (the "who" dimension). At the highest level of abstraction, some use case functionality can be interpreted as a goal that belongs to the "why" dimension (Moor, 2005; Singh, 2002).

Object-oriented approach uses the Unified Modeling Language (UML) (Booch, Rumbaugh, & Jacobsson, 1999) approved by the Object Management Group (OMG) as an industry standard for visual modeling. It provides twelve standard diagram types to analyze a technical system solution at various layers of abstraction. These diagrams are divided into three categories. The first category comprises static diagrams, the second category comprises the dynamic diagrams and the third category represents the diagrams that help to organize and manage applications. Still the problem of integrity between static and behavioral aspects exists. Semantics of individual UML diagram types is quite clear, but integrated semantics among models is missing (Gustas & Gustienė 2007). UML grows in size and becomes more complex, difficult to understand and of less use as a standard (Avison & Fitzgerald, 2006). Complexity of the diagrams and increasing number of graphical symbols does not solve the problems. It just adds more semantically unsolved issues that deepen misunderstanding and confusion.

To have a systematic view of the whole system, it is necessary to take into account three levels of enterprise engineering: pragmatic, semantic and syntactic level (Gustas & Gustienė, 2004). Semantic consistency between levels is crucial for checking validity of system requirements.

Semantic inconsistency between system specifications on different levels of abstraction decreases the quality of enterprise engineering, which is essential for understanding of the organizational and technical system fitness. The semantic quality is essential when engineering artifact intends to serve for effective communication of various architectural solutions among system designers and system users.

Another problem is that conventional modeling approaches used at analysis and design level are heavily centered on implementation issues, they usually follow the principle of "bottom up" identification, trying to analyze requirements identifying computerized information items (Dori, 2002). Most computer languages are not suitable for business modeling, because they are implementation dependent and enforce implementation details that are not relevant at early analysis stage (Blaha & Rumbaugh, 2005). A good model should capture just crucial aspects of problem domain. Conceptual models must follow the basic conceptualization principles (Griethuisen, 1982) in representing aspects that are not influenced by possible implementation solutions. According to Fowler (Fowler, 1997) analysis techniques used intend to be independent of technology as this independence would prevent technology from hindering an understanding of the problem domain. It is difficult for business people to understand computation specific models, because they have no or very little technical knowledge.

SOLUTIONS AND RECOMMENDATIONS

The study of theoretical ideas concerning communication and learning as well as the problems in traditional modeling approaches for information system development pose the question '*How can models and methods be improved to better support communication and learning?*' The outcomes from theoretical review done made it clear that intersubjectivity or mutual understanding among stakeholders is one of the critical points in the system development process. Another important issue that contributes to understanding (according the hermeneutical circle) is that to comprehend the system as a whole, the models should have enough semantic power to represent both the part and the whole in an integrated way. Analysis of the problems in traditional modeling approaches showed that these issues are not taken into consideration while constructing the graphical representations. Such models and methods do not support communication and learning during the system development process. The theoretical analysis done, help us to come to the following challenges:

- The necessity of computation independent modeling at the analysis level. The same implementation-oriented foundations can not be applied for system analysis, because they cause communication problems among business people, who are not technical experts.
- Communication can be seen as a process of information transition governed by three levels of semiotic rules (Morris, 1938): syntactic, pragmatic and semantic. These rules together contribute to success of communication. To describe a holistic view of the whole system, it is necessary to take into consideration pragmatic, semantic and syntactic aspects of an enterprise. Integration model of three aspects is crucial for validation and verification of system specifications.
- It is necessary to have one model that enables to combine intersubjective and objective perspectives in one graphical representation. Such model enables integration of static and dynamic aspects of the system. Such way of modeling reduces complexity of diagrams and from pedagogical point of view increases learning capacity.

The proposed modeling approach, shortly presented further in the chapter, is a new modeling approach based on service-oriented way of modeling. This approach shows the way how the challenges mentioned above, and which are motivated on the basis of theoretical analysis done, can be fulfilled. This approach provides the way of modeling that combines intersubjective and objective perspectives in one modeling notation and enables to integrate static and dynamic parts. Such integration facilitates to maintain the holistic representation of the enterprise which is necessary for systematic analysis of service architectures. The framework of three levels and integrated modeling method provides with a new modeling way for semantic traceability via three levels and the guidelines for interplay business and technical solutions. Implementation independent modeling done at pragmatic and semantic levels is more understandable for business people. It contributes to a better learning and communication capabilities.

The solution to the first and the second challenges can be seen through integrated way of modeling on three levels as well as dividing the modeling process into computation independent and computation dependent. This way of modeling is done using different semantic dependencies at every level. Figure 1 presents the architectural framework for computation independent and computation dependent modeling. Three interrelated levels provide a natural view to understand the modeling artifact as a whole.

As stakeholders with different backgrounds are involved in information system development process, it should be divided into Computation Independent Modeling (CIM) and Computation Dependent Modeling (CDM) (Miller & Mukerji, 2003). Computation independent models define the system from the computation independent viewpoint, which is necessary for bridging the gap between domain and design experts. Computation independent models should be established before any implementation specific decisions are taken. Fitness between two ways of modeling is crucial for the success of the final implemented product. It means that implemented product should fit with the goals stated by business people. The quality of the information system depends on consistency between computation independent and computation dependent models.

To understand why a technical system is useful and how it fits and supports the overall business

Figure 1. Architectural framework for IS modeling at CIM and CDM levels

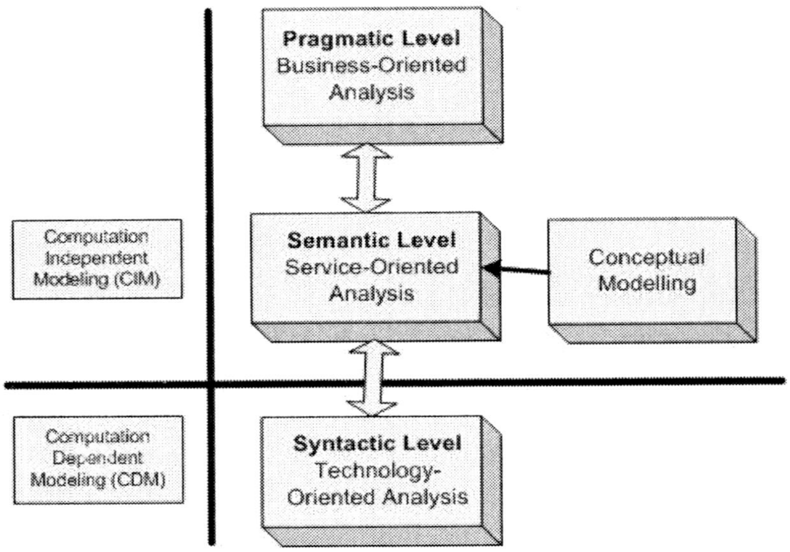

strategy of organizational system, three levels are necessary for change management: pragmatic, semantic and syntactic. Computation Independent Modeling is done by using pragmatic and semantic dependencies.

Pragmatic level is the most abstract one where strategy-oriented business analysis is made. This level is important because it supposed to give definition of a "why"- a long term intentions under information system development. It is fundamental for understanding and provides motivations behind new business solutions in terms of problems, goals and opportunities. As business processes in organization can be seen as a service or composition of services, the analysis at this level can be made looking at services from the different points of pragmatic entities (Gustas & Gustiene, 2008).

Semantic level must have capacity to describe clearly static and dynamic structures of business processes as services across organizational and technical system boundaries. At this level semantic dependencies are used for conceptual modeling, which are of two kinds static and dynamic, provide capacity to identify and overcome inconsistency. Service-oriented modeling at semantic level will be explained further in the chapter.

Output from semantic level should provide input to implementation dependent modeling which will be done at syntactic or technology-oriented level. This level should define implementation details, which explain the data processing needs of a specific application or software component. Some examples of possible syntactic elements for implementation (Gustas & Gustiené, 2002) are represented in figure 2.

Syntactic level defines how the enterprise model is going to be implemented. It means that syntactic dependencies should be consistent with semantic and pragmatic model. Such way of enterprise engineering can be used as a unified basis of reasoning about modeling quality on all three levels. It provides possibilities for verification and validation of system specifications on different levels. Such systematic and integrated method has strong pedagogical capacity as it bridges a gap between analysis and design experts.

The solution to the third challenge concerning integration of static and dynamic aspects can be reached using service-oriented modeling. Service

Figure 2. Syntactic elements

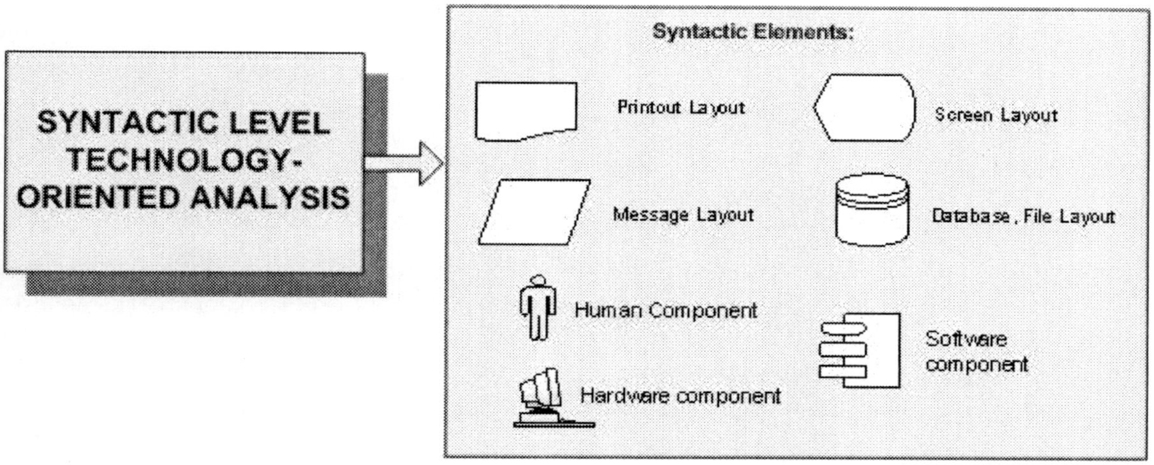

orientation is a new approach for computation independent modeling of business processes. It is an implementation-agnostic paradigm that can be realized with any suitable technology platform (Feuerlicht, 2006). One of the advantages of service concept is that it could be applied both to organizational and technical system components. The service concept is well understood in different domains, and that is why it can be used as a mutually understandable 'language' which facilitates to a better understanding and communication between business and information technology people. The concept of service is not explicitly used in system analysis and design phases. It is almost always related to technological or implementation dependent issues. But the very nature of the concept service has nothing to do with technology. The definition of the service concept provides itself the way of acting, which is very similar to communication and interaction principles. Longman lexicon of Contemporary English (McArthur, 1981), defines 'service' as " something done by one person for another" (p.194).

The definition clearly emphases the necessity of interaction between actors, that can be viewed as service requester and service provider to reach the goal. If one of the actors is missing then we can not call the concept 'service'. As the notion of communication implies the process of conveying information from a sender to a receiver, we can say that communication and service has much in common both needs four elements; service requester, service provider, service request and service response (provision). As it was stated before, mutual understanding (intersubjectivity) is achieved just in an open dialogical relationship. It means that there should be a close loop between one who asks for the service and one who provides it. Otherwise, the communication is not successful. Every communication action is goal - driven. Actors involved in a communication action have commitments and responsibilities to follow, in order to fulfill the goals. It means that interaction loop should be complete. With complete is meant that two interaction dependencies into opposite directions between the agent (service requester) and recipient (service provider) should take place. Break down in interaction loops causes discontinuity in business processes that results in the problems of inconsistency and incompleteness. Service as a closed interaction loop is presented in figure 3.

Business interaction is a collaboration performed by two or more actors that can play different business roles, and could be not just

Figure 3. Service as a closed interaction loop

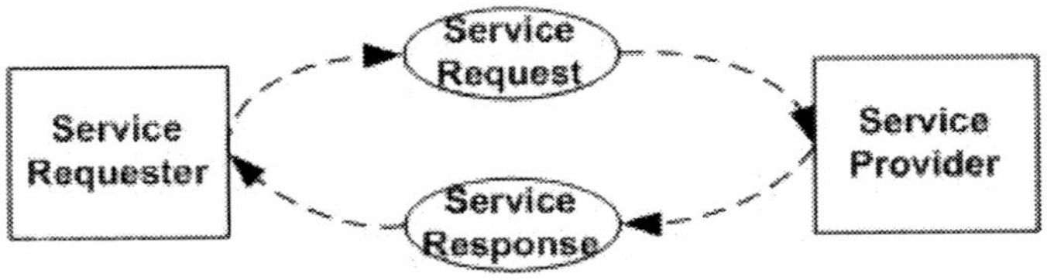

humans but also technical components. Interplay between organizational and technical components are crucial for understanding the overall business behavior and structure. Service-orientated analysis approach (Gustas & Gustienė 2009) is based on the assumption that business process models are composed of loosely coupled components, which are viewed as service requestors and service providers. From ontological point of view (Bunge, 1979; Dietz, 2006), every enterprise system could be seen as a composition of organizational and technical system components that could be viewed as enterprise actors, related by different semantic links. There are two important orthogonal perspectives of a communication action: intersubjective and objective. Synergy of two aspects of communication action is very important as it indicates actors' dependency on each other. Intersubjective perspective is usually distinguished by physical, information or decision flow between actors involved in interaction.

Objective perspective defines the changes of objects during the communication action. These changes are usually specified by transition from one object class to another. In information system development it implies data necessary for processing information. Objective part of the communication is the part that concerns the concepts (objects) from the universe of discourse, the content of communication. From objective stand point a request and respond actions change business data from one consistent state to another. These two perspectives combined in one model provide the complete view of the service as a business process. Service request and service response are viewed as communication actions. Every action results in some changes in objective part. The cohesion of two perspectives in one notation allows us to represent static and dynamic aspects in one graphical representation. Unified notation of integrated model is represented in figure 4.

In traditional modeling approaches these two aspects are represented using different models. Using separate diagrams for representation of static and dynamic aspects of a business process, makes difficulties for quality control of system specifications. Having one modeling notation, that facilitates integration of static and dynamic aspects, provides possibility for reasoning and control of semantic completeness, consistency and continuity of information system design. A simple example of employment service loop is presented in figure 5.

The starting point of service-oriented modeling is definition of interaction flows between actors. In this example just one interaction loop is illustrated. The interaction takes place between the Person as service requester and Organization as service provider. Intersubjective perspective is defined by information flows in two directions. Person (service requester) applied for the job by sending application (Application Data as flow) to Organization. If it is decided to employ the Person, Organization as service provider sends Employment Data to the Person. Intersublective perspective also prescribes the responsibilities for the actors involved in the interaction loop. If service requester sends the request to servicer provider, service provider should react to request by responding. Otherwise the loop will not be

Figure 4. Integrated model for objective and intersubjective perspectives

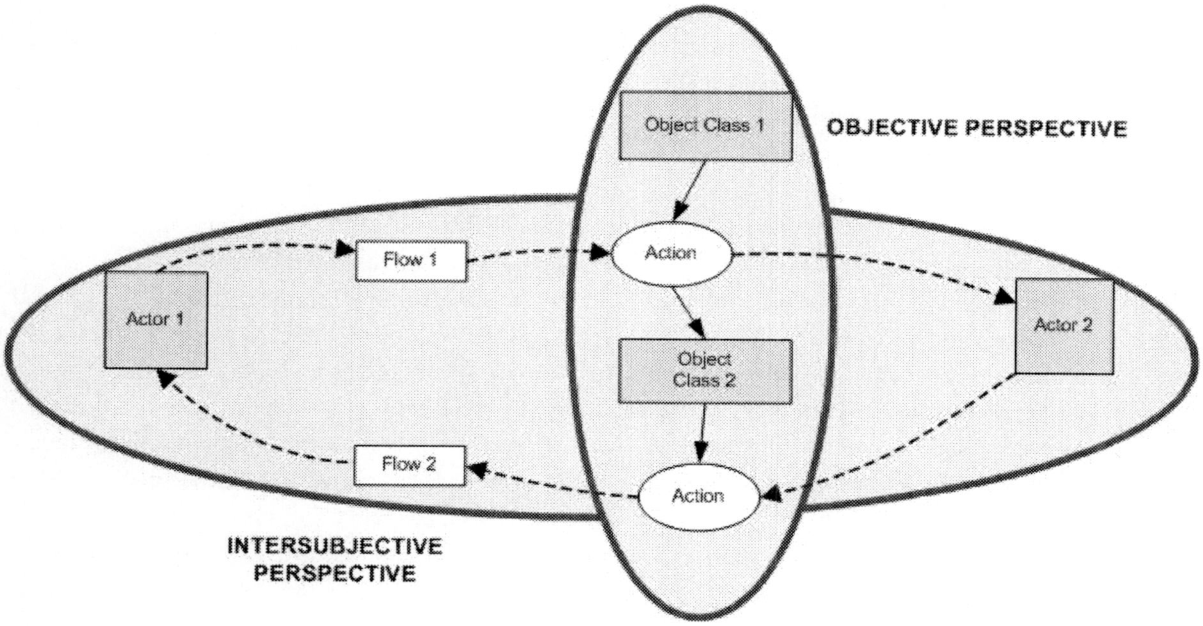

complete, that result in unsuccessful communication and the goal of service requester was not achieved.

The objective perspective in this example is defined showing what changes take place with the objects. When the application was send the Applicant object was created. When the organization employs the Applicant, he becomes an Employee. Applicant will be reclassified into Employee. From the internal system's point of view, the object of Applicant will be deleted and a new object of Employee will be created. In this example the objective aspect is not complete, because of the space limitation we are not showing attribute dependencies that are very important to indicate semantic difference between concepts (Gustas & Gustiené 2009).

Modeling of data and process can not be done separately. Coherence of static and dynamic

Figure 5. Service as an interaction loop combining intersubjective and objective perspectives

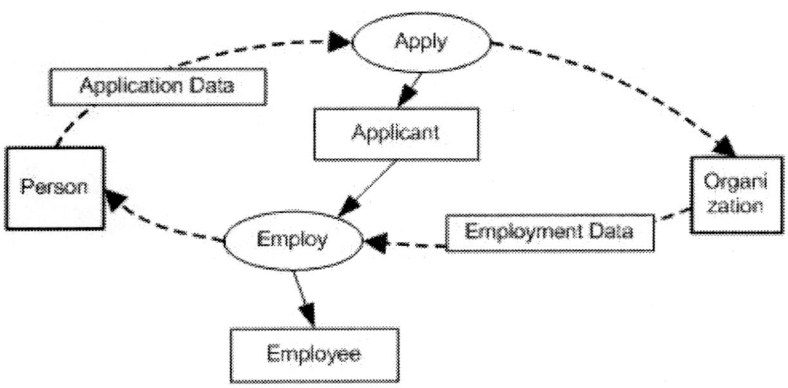

aspects is critical for defining and reasoning the holistic understanding of enterprise architecture. The main outcome of our proposed solution is an integrated method used through three levels and service-oriented approach for analysis and design at semantic level. Such approach has semantic power to conceptualize organizational and technical system components, by distinguishing intersubjective and objective perspectives that facilitates integration of static and dynamic aspects. Such integrated way of modeling could be seen as a big help for business people as well as system designers as it provides the guidelines and techniques to follow the modeling process and understand the system as a whole.

CONCLUSION

One of the aims of the models used is to promote understanding between stakeholders involved in system development process as well as to have a reasonable pedagogical capacity in learning process. Still after many years information system projects fail. The central argument of this paper is that semantic problems of communication among stakeholders and restricted learning possibilities in system development process contribute to failures in system development projects. At the same time it was noted, that as models are used as a means of communication, to reach mutual understanding among all the partners involved in the system development process the models and methods used should be constructed taking into account the theoretical assumptions concerning understanding, communication and learning. Analysis of the problems in conventional modeling approaches resulted in the conclusions that these assumptions are not taken into account. The conventional approaches do not view business data and processes as a whole. The consequence is inability to integrate the static and dynamic parts of system specifications in one graphical representation. Another problem is that traditional methods and models are heavily centered on implementation issues. Computation-oriented models are more complex. It restricts learning capacity and creates difficulties for stakeholders with little technical expertise to understand information system architectures. The main problem is the lack of a systematic method to describe, visualize and reason about the pragmatic, semantic and syntactic aspects of specifications across organizational and technical system boundaries.

The foundation of the presented service-oriented approach is based on theoretical assumptions concerning understanding and communication. We can see, therefore, this way of modeling as a solution to the problems mentioned in the chapter. This modeling approach has ability to combine business data and business process dimensions and to integrate static and dynamic aspects in one type of diagram type. A new modeling method through three levels of abstraction provides integrated guidelines for business people as well as for system designers to validate and verify their solutions. It helps to comprehend the system as a whole. The advantages of service-oriented approach are as follows:

- Service orientation combines intersubjective and objective perspectives in one modeling notation, which facilitates understanding and reasoning about service architectures across organizational and technical system boundaries.
- The notion of service can be equally applied both to organizational and technical system components, which are viewed as service requesters and service providers.
- Service-orientated analysis is computation neutral. Service-oriented way of thinking is based on the foundations of communication. This way is more comprehensible from pedagogical point of view and facilitates the learning process. It also facilitates involvement of stakeholders without deep technical knowledge in the area of information systems and therefore can contribute to bridge a gap between

enterprise business architects and system designers.

Such conceptualizations of enterprise architectures facilitate system designers to identity discontinuities in technical system specifications. It helps to reason about semantic quality of system specifications by identifying semantic inconsistencies and ambiguities of specifications. A new approach helps to check consistency of pragmatic (business-oriented analysis), semantic (service-oriented analysis) and syntactic (technology-oriented analysis) issues. This integrated way of modeling has reasonable pedagogic capacity. Service-oriented way of thinking is implementation independent; therefore it facilitates human understanding and learning. The contribution of this chapter to the main topic of the book is that modeling and integration of technical and organizational components are very important for enterprise interoperability. It describes the process by which enterprise interacts with other enterprises, or business units regardless of where on the globe they are.

REFERENCES

Apel, K. O. (1972). The priori of communication and the foundation of the humanities. *Man and World/an international philosophical review, 5*(1), 3-37.

Avison, D., & Fitzgerald, G. (2006). *Information system development: Methodologies, techniques and tools* (4th ed.). McGraw-Hill Education.

Blaha, M., & Rumbaugh, J. (2005). *Object-oriented modeling and design with UML* (Second ed.). Pearson Education Inc.

Booch, G., Rumbaugh, J., & Jacobsson, I. (1999). *The Unified Modelling Language user guide*. MA: Addison Wesley Longman, Inc.

Bunge, M. (1979). *Treatise on basic philosophy: A world of systems* (Vol. 4, Ontology II). Dordrecht, Holland: D.Reidel Publishing Company.

Coad, P., & Yourdon, E. (1991). *Object-oriented analysis*. London: Prentice-Hall, Inc.

Dietz, J. L. G. (2001). DEMO: Towards a discipline of organisation engineering. *European Journal of Operational Research, 128*, 351–363. doi:10.1016/S0377-2217(00)00077-1

Dietz, J. L. G. (2006). *Enterprise ontology theory and methodology*. Berlin/Heidelberg: Springer-Verlag.

Dori, D. (2002). *Object-process methodology*. Berlin/Heidelberg: Springer-Verlag.

Dubray, J. J. (2007). The Seven fallacies of business process execution [Electronic Version]. Retrieved September 23, 2008, from http://www.infoq.com/articles/seven-fallacies-of-bpmhttp://www.infoq.com/articles/seven-fallacies-of-bpm

Feuerlicht, G. (2006). *System development life-cycle support for service-oriented applications*. Quebec, Ont., Canada.

Fowler, M. (1997). *Analysis patterns: Reusable object models*. Addison-Westley Longman, Inc.

Griethuisen, J. J. (1982). *Concepts and terminology for the conceptual schema and information base* (No. 695).

Gustas, R. (2000). Integrated approach for information system analysis at the enterprise level. In J. Filipe (Ed.), *Enterprise information systems* (pp. 81-88). Kluwer Academic Publishers.

Gustas, R., & Gustiené, P. (2002). Extending Lyee methodology using the enterprise modelling approach. In H. Fujita & P. Johannesson (Eds.), *New trends in software methodologies, tools and techniques. Proceedings of Lyee_Wo2* (Vol. 1, pp. p. 273-288). Frontiers in Artificial Intelligence and Applications. Amsterdam: IOS Press.

Gustas, R., & Gustiené, P. (2004). Towards the enterprise engineering approach for information system modelling across organisational and technical boundaries. In *Enterprise Information Systems* (pp. 235-252). Netherlands: Kluwer Academic Publisher.

Gustas, R., & Gustiene, P. (2008). Pragmatic-driven approach for service-oriented analysis and design. In P. Johannesson & E. Söderström (Eds.), *Information systems engineering: From data analysis to process networks* (pp. 97-128). Hershey, PA: IGI Global.

Gustas, R., & Gustiené, P. (2008). *A New method for conceptual modelling of information systems*. Paper presented at the the 17th International Conference on Information System Development (ISD2008), Paphos, Cyprus.

Gustas, R., & Gustiené, P. (2009). Service-oriented foundation and analysis patterns for conceptual modellling of information systems. In C. Barry, K. Conboy, M. Lang, G. Wojtkowski & W. Wojtkowski (Eds.), *Information system development: Challenges in practice, theory and education. Proceedings of the 16th International Conference on Information System Development (ISD2007)* (Vol. 1, pp. 249-265). Springer Science+Business Media, LLC.

Gustiené, P. (2003). On desirable qualities of information system specifications. In J. Cha, R. Jardim-Goncalves & A. Steiger-Garcao (Eds.), *Concurrent Engineering: The Vision for the Future Generation in Research and Applications. Proceedings of the 10th ISPE International conference on concurrent engineering: Research and applications* (Vol. 1, pp. 1279-1287). The Netherlands: Swets & Zeitlinger B.V.

Gustiene, P., & Gustas, R. (2008). Introducing service-orientation into system analysis and design. In J. Cordeiro & J. Filipe (Eds.), *ICEIS 2008 Proceedings of the Tenth International Conference on Enterprise Information Systems* (Vol. ISAS-2, pp. 189-194). Barcelona, Spain-June 12-16 INSTICC-Institute for Systems and Technologies of Information, Control and Communication.

Heidegger, M. (1962). *Being and time*. New York: Harper and Row.

Kloppmann, M., Koenig, D., Leymann, F., Pfau, G., Rickayzen, A., von Riegen, C., et al. (2005, July). *WS-BPEL Extention for people-BPEL4People* [Electronic Version, *A* Joint White Paper by IBM and SAP].

Kroksmark, T., & Marton, F. (1987). Läran om undervisning. *Forskning om utbildning, 3*, 14-26.

Langefors, B. (1995). *Essays on infology. Summing up and planning for the future*. Lund: Studentlitteratur.

Lankhorst, M. (2004). *ArchiMate Language Primer*: Telematica Institute/Archimate Consortium.

Linell, P. (1989). *Computer technology and human projects: Theoretical aspects and empirical studies of socio-cultural practices of cognition and communication.* Linköping: Universitet.

Linell, P. (1994). *Approaching dialogue: On monological and dialogical models of talk and interaction*. University of Linköping: Department of Communication Studies

Maciaszek, L. (2001). *Requirements analysis and system design: Developing information systems with UML*: Pearson Education Limited.

Marton, F. (Ed.). (1986). *Vad är fackdidaktik?* (Vol. 1). Lund: Studentlitteratur.

Marton, F., & Booth, S. (1997). *Learning and awareness*. New Jersey: Lawrence Erlbaum Association.

McArthur, T. (1981). *Longman lexicon of contemporary English*. Longman Group Limited.

Miller, J., & Mukerji, J. (2003). MDA Guide, version 1.0.1, [Electronic Version]. *OMG Architectural Board*. Retrieved March 12, 2007 from http://www.omg.org/docs/omg/03-06-01.pdf

Moor, A. (2005). *Patterns for the pragmatic Web.* Paper presented at the 13th International Conference on Conceptual Structures (ICCS), Kassel, Germany.

Morris, C. W. (1938). *Foundations of the theory of signs.* Chicago, IL: University of Chicago Press.

Palmer, E. R. (1969). *Hermeneutics.* Evanston: Northwestern University Press.

Ricoeur, P. (1976). *Interpretation theory: Discourse and the surplus of meaning.* Texas: Texas Christian University Press.

Schutz, A., & Luckmann, T. (1974). *The structures of the life-world.* London: Heinemann.

Shoval, P., & Kabeli-Shani, J. (2008). *Designing class methods from dataflow diagrams.* Paper presented at the 17th International Conference on Information System Development (ISD), Paphos, Cyprus.

Singh, M. P. (2002). *The pragmatic Web: Preliminary thoughts.* Paper presented at the NSF-EU Workshop on Database and Information Systems Research for Semantic Web and Enterprises, Amicalolo Falls and State Park, Georgia.

White, S. A. (2004). Process modelling notations and workflow patterns. *IBM Corp.* Retrieved June 9, 2005 from http://www.bpmn.org

Winograd, T., & Flores, F. (1986). *Understanding computers and cognition: A new foundation for design.* Norwood: Ablex Publishing Corporation.

Yoo, J., Catanio, J., Paul, R., & Bieber, M. (2004). Relationship analysis in requirements engineering [Electronic Version]. *Requirements Engineering,* 1–19.

KEY TERMS AND DEFINITIONS

Learning: A process of acquiring new knowledge, behavior, skills, values and understanding

Communication: A process by which we assign and convey meaning in an attempt to create mutual understanding.

Didactics: The theory of education.

Hermeneutic Circle: It describes the process of understanding a text hermeneutically. It refers to the idea that understanding of the text as a whole is established by reference to the individual parts and understanding of each individual part by reference to the whole.

Modeling: The process that helps the development team to visualize, specify, construct and document the structure and behavior of system architecture

Information System Analysis and Design: A process that a team of business and systems professionals uses to develop and maintain computer-based information systems.

Intersubjective Perspective: It represents how different enterprise actors are mutually related to each other by interaction dependency link.

Objective Perspective: It represents how states of different enterprise object change when the action takes place during interaction.

Section 2
Information Management Process

Chapter 5
Expanding the Strategic Role of Information Interactions in the Enterprise Environment:
Developing an Integrated Model

Judit Olah
University of Wisconsin, Madison, USA

Ole Axvig
Consultant, USA

ABSTRACT

In a modern enterprise environment, many information resources are available to people working to produce valuable output. Due to technology proliferation, remote work access, and multiple geographical locations generating their own solutions for local infrastructure challenges, as well as the fact that modern professionals are tasked to make decisions autonomously, it is not self-evident what types of information resources could or should be accessed in what order in order to move processes towards the desired product outcome. Our integrated model was developed using the results of an empirical study. The model puts a user-centered focus on business process model building by mapping all information interactions surrounding the business processes (i.e. creation, storage, management, retrieval of documents/contents as well as information and data). The model characterizes the business processes by types of information interaction, analyzes process phases by those interactions and evaluates actual locations of information content extractions.

INTRODUCTION

Enterprise information management research has long wrestled with the problems of optimizing information usage and of describing and leveraging enterprise knowledge. Earlier research in this area placed a strong emphasis on various aspects of access/retrieval efficiencies, as well as injecting rigor into enterprise content and document management policies as required by regulatory and enterprise policy frameworks. Business process management research has turned renewed attention on the information assets facilitating organizational business processes, attempting to ground the organizational

DOI: 10.4018/978-1-60566-890-1.ch005

decision-making processes into the larger context of the organizational information environment.

Our approach, presented in the chapter, examines the historic research trends of these two connecting areas, pushing their boundaries towards an interdisciplinary solution.

This is not a philosophical overview of theoretical works, but a pragmatic and operational discussion of our empirical experience and the model that was developed and tested in an organization environment. Our model offers a comprehensive interpretation of efficiency measures, much needed in today's business environments, by offering a method of evaluation of information management and process management components. The model bridges a gap between management and information interactions that are traditionally examined in isolation. While focusing on the process efficiencies that became a regularly assumed path to address enterprise efficiency issues in the 1990s, information management is typically looked at from a software application management point of view.

Recently, an increasing body of literature examined the cost-benefit approach to various IT and IS functions, as those ameliorate or prohibit effective communication of information. We strongly feel that looking beyond information technology will be a critical element in contemporary enterprise management for evaluating how information is captured, managed, stored, retrieved, validated, authenticated, confirmed and delivered to the most relevant and efficient point of organizational use, as identified by business process analysis. The model presented here was developed on empirical data and has been tested on internal and outside projects.

INFORMATION MANAGEMENT IN ENTERPRISE MANAGEMENT

During the 1990s organizational management and the surrounding research have witnessed two key areas of revolutionary change: the realization of the central role of enterprise information asset management, and the renewed appreciation of the benefits of business process analysis (Teng, 1995). During the course of the last decade, there has been a dramatically marked shift in recognizing the importance of information sources and valuing those for their strategic role in enterprise management.

There has been much debate and discussion in the professional literature amongst theoreticians as well as practicing professionals as to what constitutes corporate information assets, how best to define those, and what are the direct and indirect values that can be attributed to those assets. These discussions inherently convey an important shift in perspective, and demarcate a new era of enterprise research; by stating that there is a critical relationship between information asset management and the overall success of enterprise management. While in the past most authors might have implied that any improvement in the efficiency of corporate information asset management could have resulted in improved overall corporate performance, the new research would draw a closer and more direct causal relationship between the two. Yet attaching values to these assets has appeared to be challenging and often cumbersome. Financial planning, prompted by increased attention to information assets as part of the enterprise, often continues to rely on technical measures of asset management such as data storage capacity and network throughput. Potential financial gains to be made through the improved efficiency of quick, reliable access to correct information remain elusive because they are hard to measure and report. Our model was developed in part to offer a way of measuring the use of information as an integral part of business processes.

Theoreticians and professionals alike continue to wrestle with how best to define the relationship between the fundamental elements of information assets: data, information, and knowledge, and how best to describe their impact on one another (Buchanan, 2007). Data, the basic and most concrete unit in this hierarchy, along with its closest derivative, the information, seem to be easier to measure, as 'information products' or 'inputs /outputs'.

Corporate knowledge, either in explicit or in tacit forms, is more elusive. This is particularly so when attempts are made to define knowledge elements as quantifiable items of operations. Tacit knowledge, while we seem to understand intuitively what the term intends to convey, is even more difficult to grasp in measurable qualifiers describing people skills, on the job experiences, and situational trainings in specific business environments. Understandably, with the great degrees of ambiguity surrounding these fundamental concepts, researchers most typically narrow their focus to the more tangible, thus quantifiable, 'documented' knowledge formats (Zack, 1999).

Inherent in these discussions is the newly appreciated understanding that business management should not only include the efficient management of information sources, but also incorporate the enterprise wide derivatives of interacting with them. Here the discussions become increasingly fuzzy; while some researchers try to maintain their focus on the optimal management of the tangible, and recorded, organizational information assets, others put their investigative focus on the impact and consequences of interacting with them. Truthfully, there are significant overlaps in the target of investigation here; below, we highlight studies that focus on recorded or documented forms of resource management that also explore the challenge of placing those within the context of various organizational functions.

Abecker et al. developed two experimental models (VirtualOffice and KnowMore) to explore the benefits of using a proactive document delivery system that connects documents to the appropriate decision making points of a workflow (Abecker, 2000). Interestingly, the authors chose to pursue their investigation in a very traditional environment, where most workflow decisions are supported by delivering hardcopy documents, that is, a tangible information environment. In their approach, a workflow analysis is conducted to acquire a better grasp of document context, e. g. indexing incoming business letters. The authors developed a document analysis and understanding (DAU) approach to improve the organizational document representation method; yet, by bridging 'knowledge' to business knowledge, and creating a working definition in the model that equates knowledge to 'information made actionable', they also lose ground in making their experimental models readily implementable in an operational environment. The model is designed with the recognition that the content analysis and representation of a document (hard copy document in this specific case) does not end by handing it over to a corresponding workflow. The workflow may frequently have additional information needs from a given document after this document has already been assigned to it. Abecker et al. envision a dynamic interaction that evolves and changes as the workflow context changes in a naturally observed situation. The model does not only deliver an electronic image of a hard copy document, but also retrieves previous analysis results as called by other workflows.

The authors strongly recommend adopting a just-in-time knowledge delivery approach that identifies what information is needed and where, by identifying the workflow states that are characteristically document (and knowledge) intensive activities (Abecker, 2000).

A theoretical model of document engineering was developed by Glushko and McGrath (Glushko, 2005). Document engineering examines document transactions as packages of information utilized to carry out business transactions in order to identify reusable (and thus engineerable) patterns that can be readily implemented across business service networks. As the authors noted, "processes produce and consume documents, which are a static snapshot or a tangible result of process activity." (Glushko, 2005). Further, that "there is no single correct way to create models of business processes and their documents. Task analysis and document analysis are closely related; document analysis reveals candidate information components and task analysis reveals rules about their intent and usage. Task analysis is especially important when few documents or information sources exist, because human problems or errors can suggest that important information is missing. Documents analysis tends to start from analysis of document instances. These techniques extract or disentangle the presentational, structural, and content components of documents or other information sources. Data analysis (or object analysis) techniques often start from a conceptual perspective about a domain and yield an abstract view of the information components revealed by document analysis." (Glushko, 2005).

The model presented in this study treats information objects and information inputs/outputs not as static entities but as dynamic components of the enterprise information interaction. These dynamic components constitute the cornerstone of the corporate knowledge base in our model, and the foundation for the development of corporate learning practices.

The important realization that the fundamental structure of an organization's information base and its business processes are closely interconnected, and that those need to be mapped against one another in order to facilitate any reasonable support for organizational decision making, led to the birth of a new research area that became known as information architecture. (Brancheau, 1986). In the course of the study, Brancheau noted that users preferred developing their own information applications without going through the 'official' organizational channels, storing not only redundant, but conflicting information. Eventually those 'shortcuts' were mimicked by enterprise applications development, resulting in applications that support ultimately faulty decisions, developed for and reinforcing the misuse and the misinterpretation of information.

Teng and Kettinger furthered this work by exploring the inherent relationship between business process modeling and information architecture (Teng, 1995). The authors particularly suggested three areas of investigations: how does information architecture support business process redesign; how does the lack of information architecture hinder business process redesign; and what new approach to information architecture can facilitate business process redesign? The authors challenged the surprisingly small body of research examining the relationship between these two areas in depth; and in particular, they noted the critical lack of empirical studies evaluating the relationship between the two areas (Teng, 1995).

The strategic role of organizational information resource research and utility exploration peaked in a new area of interest frequently identified as knowledge management. While a particularly unfortunate choice of terms, knowledge management originated in the need to reflect the intellectual values and consequently information assets created by understanding the nature, extent, and patterns of consumptions of the large volumes of data and information created by organizations. While pronouncedly ironic questions were articulated under raised eyebrows (how should one manage knowledge?) the meaning behind the coined phrase indicated a very real need albeit a not very well articulated intent: intellectual capital is produced by organizations; and an organizational asset value must be assigned to them in order to operationalize their management. It is worthwhile to also point to Zimmerman's reference to a study by T.D. Wilson in 2002 of American business schools and their course descriptions of knowledge management, where, in general, knowledge is interpreted as information (Zimmerman, 2006). The study presented here in no way attempts to provide and overview or critique of the rapidly developing field of knowledge management; the few references included were cited to illustrate examples where knowledge management has been equated to information management. In our view, knowledge management has more to do with the intellectual value-added transformation of information assets when they are manipulated in the course of enterprise activities. As noted earlier, the concept of the enterprise knowledge base is a component of our model, and continues to be part of our research; this study, however, focuses on the pragmatics of an integrated approach to capturing process details and information interactions.

There has also been a widening circle of criticism recognizing the disconnect between theoretical research calling for the increased operationalization of information assets and the lagging practice offering means and measures to assist operations management. Zack called for making knowledge strategies (developed according to local organizational knowledge management principles) into the foundations of business strategies. He also noted that the "link between knowledge management and business strategies, while often talked about, has been widely ignored in practice." (Zack, 1999). Abecker found that today's standard workflow management systems do not adequately address the information space and information context aspects of those processes (Abecker, 2000). Vaast found and documented strong connections between information management and improved business practices in a study focusing on the implementation and use of knowledge management systems by members of a network within the bureaucratic environment of a public administration (Vaast, 2007).

Research interest in organizational management and business process modeling has grown significantly in the last 10 years; along with it came the realization among theoreticians as well as among practicing professionals that we need to seek pragmatic avenues to make information asset management an organically inherent part of the process analysis.

NEW AVENUES IN BUSINESS PROCESS MODELING RESEARCH

As noted earlier, business process research has seen changes in the last decade, as a new round of efforts has been made to expand the traditional scope of business process modeling in order to make it more directly relevant, and more importantly, directly applicable to operations management and business-wide implementations. Business process modeling has traditionally been interested in the analytical study of business processes with the objective of implementing efficiency measures across the enterprise. A reliable and consistent representation of activities and tasks that comprise a business process is a deceptively complex challenge. While there is a vast and diverse body of research concerning business process modeling, we focus in this study on the issue of increasing the clarity and practicality of process modeling by incorporating within the model explicit representations of information interactions. We do not include the considerable body of research dealing with automated business process modeling/reengineering, or with that directly surrounding the manifesto of Hammer and Champy (Hammer and Champy, 2001).

Gibb noted that processes are one of the key capabilities of an enterprise (Gibb, 2006).

In order to respond to and successfully meet any challenge, to stay competent as well as competitive, the organization needs to understand its business processes, needs to comprehend how to modify them, and needs to understand what degree those changes are constrained by technical, technological, and human skills factors. Yet, as also noted by Gibb, a key element of the need for the analysis is to create metrics against which the processes can be tested and benchmarked, even when we aim at measuring such organizational qualities as 'responsiveness', 'capability', and 'usability'. (Gibb, 2006).

More recent models respond to this need by including additional elements of the enterprise processes. Tsalgatidou stated that a business process model should encapsulate information as IT relates to organizational activities: resources, including personnel, documents, data; control or trigger elements prompting the execution of an activity following another; the flow or direction of the process; and the organizational structures (Tsalgatidou, 1996). Koubarakis experimented with building on the information architecture work done in previous decades and created an enterprise model comprised of five interconnected submodels: organizational; objectives and goals; process; concepts (or non-intentional entities); and finally, a constraints submodel (factors of limitations of the enterprise). (Koubarakis, 2001).

Gibb's model of the enterprise system includes corporate strategies, and information strategies, along with business processes. Gibb further suggested that a dynamic view of the enterprise-as- process, can strongly benefit management to analyze and connect functions in increase efficiencies in designing, implementing and managing enterprise functions. (Gibb, 2006). Note that the model transformed information strategies, indicated at the high level, into information resources, which is a significant leap in association in this theoretical model. Further, the fundamental goal of creating the integrated model was to explore means of raising efficiency levels in business/ service management. (Gibb, 2006). Jackson, while exploring the impact of transactive memory systems in organizations, also implements the method of exploring corporate decision making hierarchies as those are mirrored in enterprise knowledge directories (Jackson, 2008). As the authors state, "an organization can be seen as a transactive memory system and make a strong case for including the studies of information systems which are intended to support TMS to be a component within the complex and multi-dimensional information retrieval ecology." A number of researchers have experimented with expanding their models to include either 'information' or 'document' input / output products in order to create a more comprehensive analysis of business processes. (Gibb, 2006, Wierzbicki, 2007, Chen, 2008, Glassey, 2008, Wang, 2006).

What seems to be evident from the array of solutions pushing against the constraints of the traditional context of business process modeling is the growing awareness that decision making activities are better understood, analyzed and evaluated within the context of their information environments. Further, any meaningful suggestions to alter elements of business processes that directly translate into operationally manageable change initiatives (including personnel, budgetary, planning, and all other aspects of implementation) will necessarily include both the information resource and the business process components. This is the point where the most recent results in interactive information retrieval research can deliver their greatest benefits to management information systems that so greatly depend on the value, trustworthiness, timeliness, accuracy, etc. of the delivered data, information, and knowledge.

MODELING INFORMATION INTERACTIONS IN BUSINESS ENVIRONMENTS

In recent years information science research has been dedicating increasing attention to the role and impact of information interactions in business environments. Unfortunately, these investigations have been carried out with very little interdisciplinary impact between the two disciplines and the interest in the areas continues to be maintained independently.

Recent studies focused on collective information behavior in the work environment. Building on patterns of cognitive human information behavior, researchers explored Cognitive Work Analysis as means of studying collective information behavior within the corporate environment (Fidel, 2004). The model uses a gradually rising spiral of analyses that explores and analyzes numerous dimensions within the work environment: macro environment, work domain, organizational unit, task analysis in domain terms, task analysis in decision making terms, applied strategies, and actors' [users'] resources and skills (Fidel, 2004). Xie further built upon Fidel's model by researching models of integrated human-work domain interactions (Xie, 2006). Human-information system interaction was the primary focus of Veronneau. With the purpose of optimizing operations resource management, the author evaluated the elements of human-computer interactions from an operations management perspective (Veronneau, 2007).

The field of information science, and interactive information retrieval in particular, is able to share significant results with enterprise information management. Both areas seem to have isolated special research focus on questions that are very similar in nature. In this sense, an interdisciplinary communication may genuinely benefit both contributing discipline areas; offering benefits to information science by expanding its areas of investigation to information interactions mediated by enterprise constraints, and offering benefits to enterprise management by delivering results of user studies, user modeling, and user behavior analysis that directly relate to the business concerns of information asset management. We note three such key areas:

1. User focus in information interaction.

One of the key realizations of modern information retrieval research is that observing and analyzing the user's information behavior in order to understand his information needs is key to any efforts of improving the success of the interaction. While there has been a relatively long history in optimizing the organization and representation of document contents, modern interactive information retrieval research made significant headways in designing more efficient information systems since user studies assumed such a focal role in the discipline.

From a business process model perspective it may appear quite straightforward to make suggestions towards delivering the right set of information to the appropriate group of employees at the appropriate point of task execution as suggested by Buchanan and many others in business process modeling (Buchanan, 2007). Yet, as Catarci noted, "anticipating the users will not work" (Catarci, 2000). Revere warned about the "elusive" nature of the users' information needs in modern corporate environments (Revere, 2007). From a managerial perspective, large-scale user studies can appear prohibitively expensive, and call for a reasonable estimate of the gains to be realized from anticipated increases in user efficiency.

Some authors described the initiator of a business task by using the analogy of a "knowledge gap" (Zack, 1999) or an information/strategy gap. These concepts are very close to the notion of knowledge gap long researched in information science since the original publication of Belkin's notion of the anomalous state of knowledge (Belkin, 1995). Information gap discussions all point to the complexities of expecting the user or the operations manager to present a well-defined information need that then can be successfully addressed by adjusting business processes. Yet, as supported by a substantial body of literature across both areas, such user needs are extremely difficult to articulate or to capture in the first place.

2. Context of the interaction.

Often, as noted by Petrelli (Petrelli, 2008), studies capture the human- system interaction, analyze that interaction from qualitative or quantitative point of view, but "fail to capture much of the context, the system, the user, or the environment, respectively".

The impact of context has been of traditional interest to interactive information retrieval research (Kelly, 2006, Brier, 2004). Cool and Spink identified four levels of context to information seeking and retrieving as established by empirical studies: information environment; information seeking; interaction; and query levels (Cool, 2002). Our study utilizes the top three levels of interactions: at the top level, by examining the business function as context for the interaction (business functions defined at the macro level as impacted by internal and external policies, e. g. state and federal legislative policies); at the second level are the specific goals and tasks defined by the expectations of the business function; the third interaction level is interpreted somewhat differently by our study, by looking at individual interactive sessions from the perspective of information content, frequency of retrieval of a particular content, as well as groups of users of interacting with identical content.

3. Dynamic nature of interactions.

This is one of the key benefits that an information interaction analysis will be able to deliver. In a modern enterprise environment, one of which was captured by our empirical study, a multitude of resources are available to employees working towards a value output product. Due to technology, remote work access, and multiple geographical locations, users generate their own solutions for local infrastructure challenges. Modern professionals are tasked with making decisions autonomously, and it is not self-evident or prescribed what type of resources could or should be accessed in what order to complete a task. Notably, our analysis has demonstrated that while the ultimate outcome maybe identical, employees chose to pursue quite different paths in reaching that outcome.

The Integrated Model

Business functions are analyzed in process models at various levels of detail depending on the scope, definition, and complexity of functions they describe. The level of detail, i.e. the granularity of the model, is determined along a dual set of objectives: 1. to provide analytical information by enumerating each task executed within a business function; 2. to provide measures of evaluation to identify efficiency breakdowns existence of redundancies, anomalies, gaps, bottlenecks in execution, etc. in the function. The objectives and the degrees to which they impact the model are driven by the ad hoc project management needs and determined by the priorities of operations management.

Within the context of our study, the business objectives of the organization are realized by accomplishing business goals. Business goals are satisfied by completing functions. Functions are comprised of tasks and executed by business units. Tasks and the information interactions surrounding them are modeled for business functions.

We define information interaction as a task-driven activity that incorporates simple transactions of information objects, e. g. receiving original data from outside sources such as e-mailed spreadsheets of outside data. Information interactions also include the activities of database querying and searching the corporate electronic repository.

The two fundamental challenges in the modeling process are: the highly intuitive nature of defining a single step in the sequence, mostly relying on a 'common sense' approach; and the breaking down of high level business steps into more analytical sub-steps. The level of specificity in representing a single step is highly intuitive as well: in one of our examples we accepted the sequence established by our initial interviews: 1. receive project data; 2. data entry and verification 3. prepare permit maps. Yet we could have very easily established the following sequence: 1. request project data; 2. receive project data; 3. verify data via internal and external information resources; 4. data entry; 5. prepare permit maps.

Our integrated model enumerates tasks contributing to the execution of a business function, and the tasks are segmented by elemental units of information interactions. From a business process perspective 'enter permit data into permit data da-

Figure 1. Task level representation of a business function

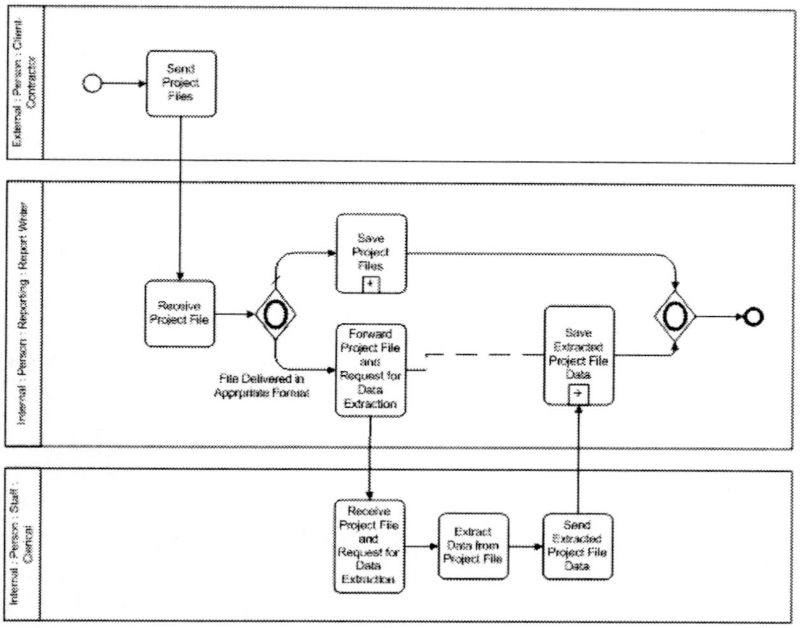

tabase' is a single step in the process of generating a new permit. In the traditional model of information object shadowing there would be no document outfall, as the employee interacts directly with a database, simply updating its contents.

Field Study and Empirical Model

Our findings are based on an empirical model developed as well as tested in a for-profit corporate environment during the course of 2008. It evolved from a bottom-up investigation of enterprise information management practices at an environmental consulting company based in the Rocky Mountain region. The company employs about 100 consultants, working in four primary geographic locations, spread across two states. Some consultants telecommute from remote locations.

The project was originally created and framed in the traditional context of enterprise information management. The unique challenges of that project prompted us to carry on the investigation with a wider scope, ultimately leading to the realization of our need to create an integrated model of business process modeling and information interaction. As we progressed with gathering information towards our business model, we learned about the variances in internal information management practices that lead to significantly different information interactions conducted by individuals working in the same business unit. This was plainly obvious and traceable in the corporate content management system. Further complexities originated from the co-existence of multiple knowledge domains, as well as from various regulatory and other information existing essentially as a collection of micro digital repositories stored in various islands within the content management system. The complexities quickly turned into tangible retrieval constraints, resulting in a situation where an increasing proportion of the enterprise knowledge base resided outside the reach of many individual users, further resulting in information / content / and knowledge duplication efforts on one hand, and large portions of unused corporate contents on the other.

METHODOLOGY OF DATA COLLECTION AND ANALYSIS

The completion of our first integrated model, including data collection and data analysis, took four months. Based on the success of that model, three further models are currently being completed targeting other important organizational functions. A total of twelve users were interviewed for the first model. The interviews included everyone involved in the task performances, regardless of their length of time at their current position, levels of experience, or any other discriminating factor. As long as a user was involved in the functions, they were asked to participate in the interview.

The interviews were conducted by multiple interviewers, two or three, depending on staff schedules, and commentary notes were synchronized following each interview. The interviews were highly iterative in nature, as all narratives went through repeated cycles of verifications. Questions focused on three areas: detailed steps in business functions; the description of all information, data, documents searched, queried, needed to achieve a set of objectives; and system sources consulted in for finding those. We also included all in-house and outside online databases used to complete a task. The user interacted with multiple document repositories, in-house and outside contracted databases. Users maintain and search multiple document repositories that are maintained separately by organizational units.

In addition to the interviews, we validated the narratives by on-site observations, when researchers directly observed users as they searched and accessed information needed in various task phases. Both the interviews and the direct observations covered the function as a whole. We also consulted earlier process diagrams, and physically examined information resources typically accessed during task performance.

RESULTS AND DISCUSSION

We prepared traditional business models showing the sequence of tasks that comprised a function of a particular business unit. Figure 1 shows an example for a task level representation of a business function. This function is comprised of 108 tasks. Following that we shadowed that traditional task by adding the dimension of information interactions by users, which allowed us to understand what information was used at given point of a task, and what exactly the nature of that use was: a query, a search, retrieval, new data entry, new record creation, etc. Figure 2 shows an example for a multitude of interactions surrounding a single task element: 127 file repository interactions and 43 database queries. In Figure 2 we see the user's task is to enter types, objects and descriptions into the internal reporting application. This is a single task in a sequence of tasks in order complete a project. In order to accomplish this single step, the user queried an outside online database, as well as queried the in-house data system files; further the user searched the in-house content management system to locate three different types of contents. The user then integrated all information gathered from the five sources, and entered up-to-date information into a form handled by the reporting application.

Figure 1 and Figure 2 also show that a single component of the process model, a task, is connected to six corresponding information interactions. We also totaled the number of tasks it took to execute the function; and also totaled the total number of information interactions that supported the task. Figure 3 shows the graphical interpretation of those figures. We gained an analytical understanding of the volume of tasks and volumes

Figure 2. Information interaction representation of a business task

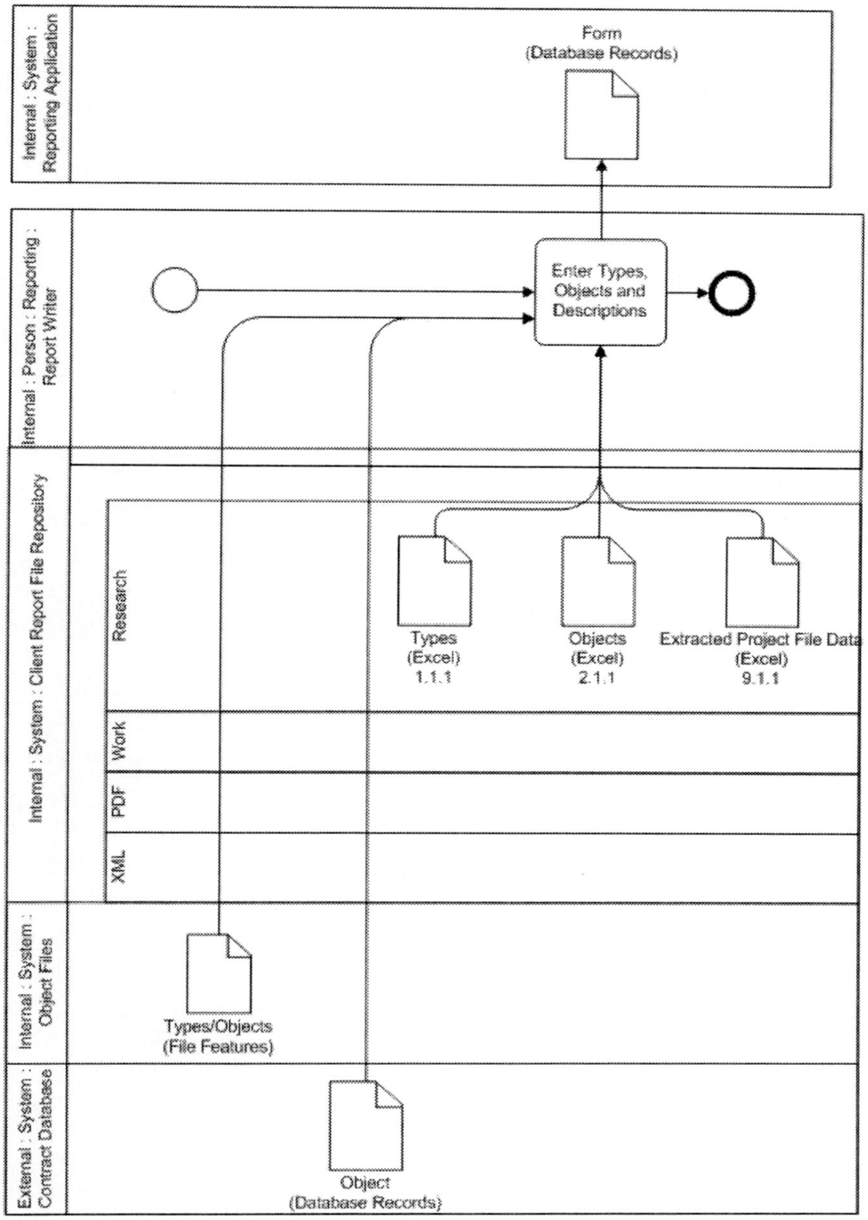

of information interaction it takes to complete a function, as well as the information-heavy and information-poor task elements comprising the full function.

Figure 3 is a representation of observed business and information activities by task. It highlights the pressure points of the function indicating when a single task may require high information activities. One benefit of the process/interaction model is that it helps us to understand the details of interactions, moving us away from the anecdotal levels of discussion: we can draw conclusions

Figure 3. Information interactions per task

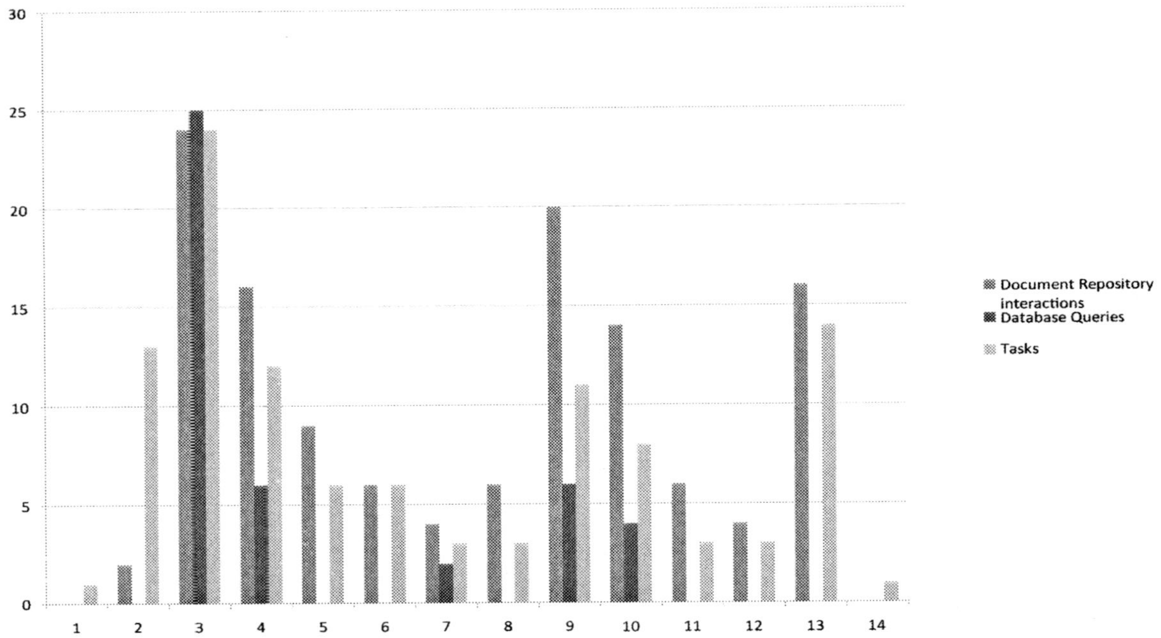

about system demand, data traffic, and task load allocations adjustments by simply understanding users moving through their task sequences.

The graphical representation of an entire modeled process reveals intriguing questions, notably concerning ambiguities in the uses of repositories versus databases; multiple quasi-equivalent repositories maintained by multiple functional units; the contrasts of information-intensive and information-poor tasks and their ordering in the processes as a whole.

We learned that the users rely on the document repository to a much greater extent than they rely on the database. That prompts us to investigate two separate issues: one is the relationship between the information values – in terms of currency and accuracy – of the document repositories and the enterprise database; second, is the significantly large number of interactions linked to certain tasks.

In the first case, the significant under-utilization of the database throughout the second part of the process is to be examined and should be challenged. At the minimum, there is a notable disconnect between database use and documentary repository activities, which do not appear to be saved in the enterprise database at all. The graph allows us to ask the more fundamental question whether this is an adequate process to accomplish the business goal that was set. If the answer is negative, then clearly the process needs to be reengineered. If the answer is affirmative, than any efficiency measures should be focused on bettering the document repository system, by making it faster and more robust, because the database system is underutilized as is.

In the second case, the large volumes of repository activities connected to relatively small number of task sequences may suggest a bureaucratization of the process. At minimum, the nature of these interactions needs to be evaluated for unnecessary redundancies. These concerns can be the key indicators of the problems noted above, in Section 3, when domains of the enterprise knowledge base are outside the reach of certain user groups, yet certain sub-domains are heavily duplicated.

By examining a single task and the information interactions it encompasses, operations management can address the quality, source, and validation of information sources to be used by employees. Management may address efficiency problems related to task, repository use, or systems use: e. g. whether the appropriate number of correctly trained and skilled employees is delegated to a particular task execution, and whether all relevant information is available for any given task (simplifying the assignment of system permissions). For example, it is from the integrated model that we learn that a given database is updated by a second tier of employees not because there is a second tier of verification justified by the process, but because the original set of users interacting with the database have not been granted access rights to modify/enter data at that level. Further, using the same example, a certain group of users accessing the database is procedurally conditioned to wait for the data to be provided by a different user group, instead of running a query directly.

As we pursue disentangling interactions and processes, we aim to understand the multiple user contexts accessing overlapping or identical information contents. The highly situational nature of enterprise information retrieval interactions can only be successfully improved if we trace the very basic, triangular model of information interaction (the interaction of users and systems within an information environment) and attempt to examine the enterprise information interactions within the multitude of contexts hosting them.

Knowledge management research continues to maintain a 'repository' approach in evaluating enterprise practices, whether it is investigating the representation, the management, or the retrieval aspects of enterprise information assets. The traditional approach continues to be hindered by a conceptual view of information as entity. Our results point towards the further exploration of the information-as-process perspective, which has served as the foundation for numerous theoretical models of information retrieval interactions (Saracevic, 1996, Belkin, 1995, Ingversen, 1996).

Collaborative information behavior at the enterprise level sustains two opposing dynamics: the frequent need to access relatively stable information content in a highly situational retrieval environment, impacted by a multitude of parameters (co-existing knowledge domains, multiple project and task phases) as well as macro-level changes in the regulatory environment impacting business policy as a whole.

THE BUSINESS – INFORMATION INTERACTION – PROCESS MODEL OF ENTERPRISE PROCESSES

The model shown in Figure 4 was developed by the authors based on the cumulative results of our empirical study. It is a high-level model synthesized from the results of the processes modeled in Figure 1 and Figure 2. The model has been tested and applied in corporate environments and has proved invaluable for operationalizing new enterprise management situations.

The key benefit of this model is that it conveys the high-level integration and the dynamics of business operations. The several facets comprising our model also allow for an analytical evaluation of the elements composing those operations. These facets are:

1. Information assets

The first facet represents data, content, and the information base supporting all processes (I – IV). The information is either provided by outside organizations (I.)(client data shared with the enterprise), or other outside source queried (e.g. online sources of current regulatory material). Alternatively, the organization may need to generate its own input information, e. g. conducting a primary data gathering project (II.).

Figure 4. Integrated process and interaction model

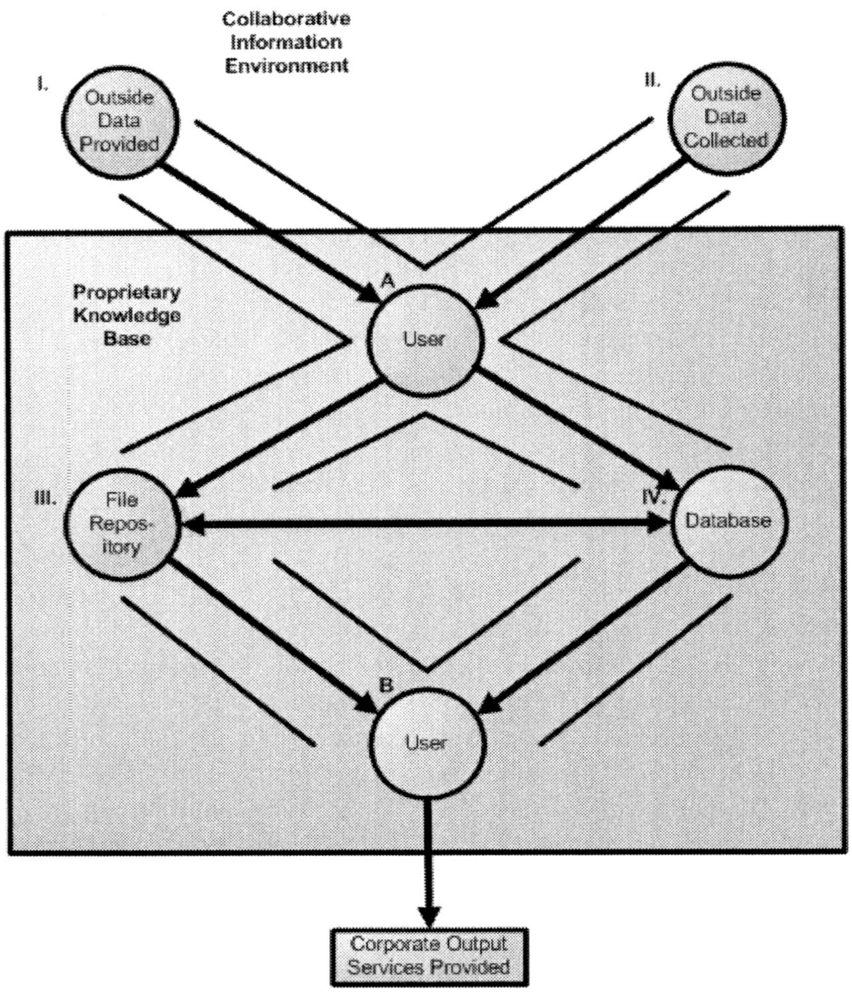

We distinguish and differentiate, for reasons of knowledge management, regulatory compliance, and legal reasons, whether the input data has been provided and created by an outside entity or by the organization. In the same facet we track which information is stored in the enterprise file repository (III.), or in the enterprise database (IV.). At this stage we are not validating usage patterns and preferences; we are describing information interactions without making any judgments as to their accuracy, redundancy, or relevance. Finally, the corporate intellectual output and services provided are indicated.

From the perspective of information resource management, the model allows us to follow the lifecycles of information objects as they move through the processes, offering a means for managing the content verification, authentication, etc. needs of business management.

2. Users

The second facet indicates the groups of users interacting with the information assets. This second facet allows us to manage a highly collaborative information environment, track all users who interact with a particular information source, and trace preferred and non-preferred sources for certain business processes. Although two user groups are shown in the model, the representation says nothing specific about whether or not groups A and B have the same members, have different members, or overlapping sets of members. Again, no judgments are made as to whether the users mapped are the appropriate ones from an operational perspective; the mapping represents the actual operational situation.

3. Business process functions

This facet provides the scope and framework for the function as a whole, indicating the dynamics and the direction of the task sequences, as well as the required, necessary, or recommended user groups and sources that should interact for the process to be completed in an optimal fashion.

Return on Investment

While the benefits of developing business process models are significant, the cost and time spent developing them, in dedicating economic and human resources, often challenge the immediacy of their usefulness from a management/operations point of view. Because the details of business processes are often not well understood or well documented, descriptions of inefficiencies in them usually remain at an anecdotal level, where there is little impetus to make concrete improvements. Change at the process level will usually require sponsorship from upper management if it is to succeed, and there will inevitably be a need to quantify the benefits that will result from the process modeling that will be necessary to direct improvements. One of the simplest and most widely accepted quantification methods is return on investment (ROI).

ROI has traditionally been discussed in the framework of manufacturing enterprises, where the logic of the investment decision is based on units of goods produced. Roughly speaking, one estimates the increase in production (and/or the reduction in defective product) over the projected useful life of the new equipment or facility under consideration and multiplies that by price per unit to obtain a revenue estimate. One then compares this revenue estimate with the project cost, and if the percent return on the investment is greater than the projected cost of capital over the life of the project, then the project has, at this level, been justified. The details of the calculations and assumptions for determining ROI are outside the scope of this study (Walsh, 2002; Hayes et al., 2005). For our purposes, the important difficulties reside at the level of transferring this logic to the activities of an information-driven service enterprise. The same lack of detailed analysis that will hinder a process change initiative at the organizational development level will make it all but impossible to adapt the manufacturing-based ROI model to information-based service tasks, where there is no obvious counterpart to the manufacturing of sub-assemblies that comprise a finished product. The methodology outlined here allows explicit costs to be associated with process tasks that have anomalously large numbers of information interactions and allows those costs to be ultimately assigned to inter- and intradepartmental process bottlenecks.

By examining Figure 3 in our example we can see immediately that Task 3 requires a very large number of both document repository and database interactions, and that both Task 9 and Task 13 require large numbers of data repository interactions. The direct labor costs associated with the time spent in these interactions (to say nothing of the implied time spent working with their results) could be quite significant over time. Identifying unnecessary interactions (e.g. redundant data pulls, redundant verifications, multiple files accessed due to poor file content structure and resulting information fragmentation) and summing their occurrences over the course of a year can give a very good first approximation of direct cost savings that can be used to offset the cost of process modeling. More accurate estimates of the direct costs can be had by adding the effects of increased file system and database server equipment needs and subsequent expansion of the enterprise IT support staff.

Indirect costs include time spent by professional level employees correcting errors resulting from the poor management of data, time spent by database administrators addressing issues of data reliability, data verification/authentication, and data access, and managerial time spent attempting to achieve better control over enterprise intellectual ownership and improved protection of proprietary data. By their nature, indirect costs are hard to quantify; however, if they can be tied to specific business functions, our method of analysis will allow them to be associated to specific tasks. These costs can then be added to the direct costs to give a fairly accurate picture of the overall inefficiency cost burden per task and per function. A comprehensive enterprise-wide assessment of these costs will allow operations and business unit managers to make rational decisions concerning the placement, timing, and duration of process improvement initiatives.

FUTURE RESEARCH

Future evaluations will focus on refining the three facets of our model, evaluating the transaction descriptions and the impacts of information lifecycles, users, and business task contexts. Efforts will be made to use the integrated model as a guide for producing consistent sets of process-information interaction models which, when complete, will offer a comprehensive enterprise knowledge base.

CONCLUSION

Our empirical study developed an integrated model of enterprise business processes and enterprise information interaction activities. Our model includes the facets of information assets, users interacting with and managing those assets, and business processes that provide the objective and determine the scope of those interactions. The model enabled us to prepare a comprehensive analysis of all facets, and resulted in pragmatic recommendations in improving efficiencies by all three facets.

The model facilitates the development of comprehensive solutions for improving organizational performance by tying business tasks and information sources together in a dynamic process via recognizing the realistic information needs and information activities of the users. With this new perspective, the model is built on the theoretical work done in the fields of business process modeling and interactive information retrieval, by not only recognizing but also successfully integrating the dynamic processes into linking chains of organic interactions defining the competitiveness of the organization.

REFERENCES

Abecker, A. (2000). Information supply for business processes: Coupling workflow with document analysis and information retrieval. *Knowledge-Based Systems*, *13*, 271–284. doi:10.1016/S0950-7051(00)00087-3

Allen, D. (2007). Cost/benefit analysis for implementing ECM, BPM systems. *The Information Management Journal*, May-June, 34-41.

Belkin, N. J. (1995). Cases, scripts, and information-seeking strategies: On the design of interactive information retrieval systems. *Expert Systems with Applications*, *9*(3), 379–395. doi:10.1016/0957-4174(95)00011-W

Brancheau, J. C., & Wetherbe, J. C. (1986). Information architecture: Methods and practices. *Information Processing & Management, 22*(6), 45–463. doi:10.1016/0306-4573(86)90096-8

Brier, S. (2004). Cybersemiotics and the problems of the information-processing paradigm as a candidate for a unified science of information behind library information science. *Library Trends, 52*(3), 629–657.

Buchanan, S., & Gibb, F. (2007). The information audit: Role and scope. *International Journal of Information Management, 27*, 159–172. doi:10.1016/j.ijinfomgt.2007.01.002

Catarci, T. (2000). What happened when database researchers met usability. *Information Systems, 25*(3), 177–212. doi:10.1016/S0306-4379(00)00015-6

Chen, Y.-J., & Chen, Y.-M. (2008). On technology for functional requirement-based reference design retrieval in engineering knowledge management. *Decision Support Systems, 44*, 798–816.

Cool, C., & Spink, A. (2002). Issues of context in information retrieval. (IR): An introduction to the special issue. *Information Processing & Management, 38*, 605–611. doi:10.1016/S0306-4573(01)00054-1

Fidel, R. (2004). A multidimensional approach to the study of human information interaction: A case study of collaborative information retrieval. *Journal of the American Society for Information Science American Society for Information Science, 55*(11), 939–953.

Gibb, F., Buchanan, S., & Shah, S. (2006). An integrated approach to process and service management. *International Journal of Information Management, 26*, 44–58. doi:10.1016/j.ijinfomgt.2005.10.007

Glassey, O. (2008). A case study on process modelling – Three questions and three techniques. *Decision Support Systems, 44*, 842–853. doi:10.1016/j.dss.2007.10.004

Glushko, R. J., & McGrtah, T. (2005). Document engineering: analyzing and designing the semantics of business service networks. In *Proceedings of the IEEE EEE05 International Workshop on Business Services Networks*.

Hammer, M., & Champy, J. (2001). *Reengineering the corporation: A manifesto for business revolution.* New York: Harper Business.

Hayes, R., Pisano, G., Upton, D., & Wheelwright, S. (2005). *Operations, strategy, and technology: Pursuing the competitive edge*. Hoboken, NJ: John Wiley & Sons.

Ingwersen, P. (1996). Cognitive perspectives of information retrieval interaction: Elements of a cognitive IR theory. *The Journal of Documentation, 52*(1), 3–50. doi:10.1108/eb026960

Jackson, P., & Klobas, J. (2008). Transactive memory systems in organizations: Implications for knowledge directories. *Decision Support Systems, 44*, 409–424. doi:10.1016/j.dss.2007.05.001

Kelly, D. (2006). Measuring online information seeking context, Part 1: Background and method. *Journal of the American Society for Information Science American Society for Information Science, 57*(13), 1729–1939.

Kelly, D. (2006). Measuring online information seeking context, Part 2: Findings and discussion. *Journal of the American Society for Information Science American Society for Information Science, 57*(14), 1862–1874.

Koubarakis, M., & Plexousakis, D. (2001). A formal framework for business process modeling and design. *Information Systems, 27*, 299–319. doi:10.1016/S0306-4379(01)00055-2

Perotti, V. J., & Pray, T. F. (2002). Integrating visualization into the modeling of business simulations. *Simulation & Gaming, 33*(4), 409–424. doi:10.1177/1046878102238605

Petrelli, D. (2008). On the role of user-centred evaluation in the advancement of interactive information retrieval. *Information Processing & Management, 44*, 23–38. doi:10.1016/j.ipm.2007.01.024

Revere, D. (2007). Understanding the information needs of public health practitioners: A literature review to inform design of an interactive digital knowledge management system. *Journal of Biomedical Informatics, 40*, 410–421. doi:10.1016/j.jbi.2006.12.008

Saracevic, T. (1996). Interactive models in information retrieval (IR): A review and proposal. In *Proceedings of the 59th Annual Meeting of the American Society for Information Science,* 33, 3-9.

Teng, J. T. C., & Kettinger, W. J. (1995). Business process redesign and information architecture: Exploring the relationships. *Data Base Advances, 26*(1), 30–42.

Tsalgatidou, A. (1996). Multilevel Petri Nets for modeling and simulating organizational dynamic behavior. *Simulation & Gaming, 27*(2), 484–506. doi:10.1177/1046878196274005

Vaast, E. (2007). What goes online comes offline: Knowledge management system use in a soft bureaucracy. *Organization Studies, 28*(3), 283–306. doi:10.1177/0170840607075997

Veronneau, S., & Cimon, Y. (2007). Maintaining robust decision capabilities: An integrative human-systems approach. *Decision Support Systems, 43*, 127–140. doi:10.1016/j.dss.2006.08.003

Walsh, C. (2002). *Key management ratios*. London: Financial Times/Prentice Hall.

Wang, M., & Wang, H. (2006). From process logic to business logic – A cognitive approach to business process management. *Information & Management, 43*, 179–193. doi:10.1016/j.im.2005.06.001

Wierzbicki, A. P. (2007). Modeling as a way of organizing knowledge. *European Journal of Operational Research, 176*, 610–635. doi:10.1016/j.ejor.2005.08.018

Xie, H. (2006). Understanding human-work domain interaction: Implications for the design of a corporate digital library. *Journal of the American Society for Information Science and Technology, 57*(1), 128–143. doi:10.1002/asi.20261

Zack, M. H. (1999). Developing a knowledge strategy. *California Management Review, 41*(3), 125–145.

Zimmermann, H.-J. (2006). Knowledge management, knowledge discovery, and intelligent data mining. *Cybernetics and Systems: An International Journal, 37*, 509–531. doi:10.1080/01969720600734412

KEY TERMS AND DEFINITIONS

Enterprise Information Management: The oversight and facilitation of enterprise information interactions.

Enterprise Information Interactions: The manipulations of all information assets necessary for the completion of business functions.

Business Process Model: Any combination of graphical and verbal descriptions of, at the minimum, task sequences that comprise business activities.

Knowledge Management: The intellectual value-added transformation of information assets when they are manipulated in the course of enterprise activities.

Chapter 6
Information Management in a Grid-Based E-Health Business Environment:
A Technical-Business Analysis

Vassiliki Andronikou
National Technical University of Athens, Greece

Gabriel Sideras
National Technical University of Athens, Greece

Dimitrios Halkos
National Technical University of Athens, Greece

Michael Firopoulos
Intracom IT Services, Greece

Theodora Varvarigou
National Technical University of Athens, Greece

ABSTRACT

E-business today has moved focus to information sharing and integration across organisational boundaries in an effort to transform business processes throughout the value chain and standardize collaboration among communicating entities. Healthcare comprises a strongly collaborative distributed business environment in which information value plays a strategic role and informational privacy comprises a great concern. This new era in e-business, however, is followed by a series of issues that need to be addressed both at application and infrastructural level, such as information heterogeneity, system interoperability, security and privacy. The Grid as a technology enables sharing, selection, and aggregation of a wide variety of distributed resources comes to fill these gaps. In this chapter, the communication of information among healthcare organisations operating over a Grid infrastructure will be presented and analysed both from a technical and a business perspective.

DOI: 10.4018/978-1-60566-890-1.ch006

INTRODUCTION

Healthcare provision organisations (hospitals, clinics, etc), pharmacies as well as insurance organisations typically perform their operations from keeping and tracking patients' records and billing records to exchanging and retrieving e-health information through various computer systems. The efficient, reliable and effective operation of these intra- and inter-organisational collaborations requires the communication of these trusted systems. In fact, in such a strongly collaborative distributed business environment information comprises a valuable resource that requires cost-effective and efficient management. Yet, the variety of the systems and the data and message formats involved in such collaborations lead to serious interoperability and standardisation problems concerning the exchange, integration, sharing and retrieval of e-health information. Moreover, great differences are met across these entities in terms of data collected, database and file structures, software systems, politics, payment structures, business models; in other words each entity and even each department of theirs (such as doctor's office, out-patient clinics, imaging center, microbiological laboratories and so on) has specific requirements related to data queried and collected and interaction with patients. These issues combined with the reluctance of organisations to share their data due to lack of trust and/or security concerns lead to limitations to the successful operation of the collaborations. Moreover, given the nature of the data exchanged crucial privacy issues rise that pose even stricter requirements for prudent management of information flows, access and storage within the collaborations.

From a technical point of view these interoperability and performance issues in the healthcare environment can be distinguished into infrastructure-related and application-related. In the infrastructural level, organisations in the extended healthcare environment, including not only hospitals, clinics and doctors but also insurance organisations and pharmacies among others, use a variety of computers, networks, topologies, operating systems, configurations and data management systems offering and supporting various levels of reliability, performance, availability and security depending on their needs, budget and management policies. The existing systems improve internal processes of organisations but are not robust and secure enough to efficiently support the load of information and transactions and enable the efficient and effective cooperation, communication and sharing of information across organisational borders among the participating entities in the collaborative healthcare environment from start to finish.

At the application level, current limitations of health information systems to a specific department or healthcare organisation in the environment comprise an important obstacle to the interoperability of these systems beyond organisational boundaries. The lack of a universally accepted encoding for representing information about drugs, diseases and Electronic Health Records (EHRs) and a globally adopted message protocol for the exchange and sharing of information among the different entities in the collaborative healthcare environment pose serious restrictions to the interoperability of their systems and the efficient communication of information among them. Significant delays of information communication, when the latter is required, are posed and more importantly great inconsistencies in the EHR of the patient across healthcare providers are met leading to significant implications in care provisioning, quality of treatment and related costs.

BACKGROUND

There are several ongoing development efforts on health care standards globally aiming at information sharing and processing among healthcare stakeholders in a uniform and consistent manner. An important effort towards the treatment of the interoperability and standardisation issues mentioned above is HL7 (Health Level Seven) (HL7 Organisation, 2009), which provides messaging standards that improve care delivery, optimize workflow, reduce ambiguity and enhance knowledge transfer among stakeholders and collaborates with other standards development organisations both in the healthcare and the information systems domain so that compatible standards are produced and promoted. However, the financial cost and the great technical effort related to the transition of the currently used message mechanisms to HL7-based ones, as well as the rather slow adoption rate which stems from the reluctance of the various entities in adopting new technology and changing their perennially followed processes pose tremendous obstacles towards the adoption of the standard.

In the meanwhile, as mentioned in the previous paragraphs, the distributed nature of the intra- and inter- organisational collaborations in healthcare and the strategic role of information in these environments pose strict infrastructural requirements as well. In fact, in many cases real or 'near' real-time data integration and delivery across heterogeneous data sources as well as real-time analysis of business data and fast end-user access to key business data for decision-making acceleration are required. And what is more, issues of data consistency and privacy as well as system flexibility and robustness need to be dealt with in a cost-effective way – with security, reliability, interoperability and scalability climbing the higher stairs in the hierarchy. Such advanced infrastructural requirements combined with the innate business goal for lowering costs have driven key business sectors such as healthcare towards adopting Grid solutions into their business.

Although initially designed to cover the computational needs of high performance applications, Grid (Foster, 2002) technology of nowadays aims at providing the infrastructure for the general business domain. In fact, Data Grids (Chervenak, Foster, Kesselman, Salisbury, & Tuecke, 2001) – as a specialisation and extension of the Grid - are regarded to be the next generation inter-organisational data management systems for coordinated sharing and exchange of data as well as distributed, heterogeneous storage resources among organisations. Thus, a well-defined Grid-based solution combined with evolving international standardization efforts in healthcare comprises a new approach to information economics and can eliminate the myth of most weaknesses mentioned above and this will be the main focus of the respective paragraph.

THE MEDICAL INFORMATICS BUSINESS ENVIRONMENT

E-Health Scenario

Overview

Nowadays, e-health management and administration systems are mainly tailored to the needs and focus of the healthcare institution and the insurance organisation they serve. However, recent advances in infrastructure technologies combined with the general tendency of the population for mobility and the need for and the proven value of minimisation of communication overhead among collaborating entities within the broad healthcare domain bring to front a new era; *collaborative e-health*. A scenario of a futuristic collaborative e-health environment will be presented in this section aiming to provide the basis for analysing the technical requirements of such an environment in which inter-organisational communication is supported.

Entities and Roles

In this collaborative e-health scenario the main entities and roles involved include:

- **Healthcare Provider:** the term encapsulates hospitals, clinics, private doctors registered to the collaboration. Provision of healthcare services may be offered by public, private and non-public health care institutions. The roles interacting with this collaborative environment include doctors, nurses, the logistics department, among others.
- **Health Insurance Organisation:** it may be a government-sponsored social insurance organisation or a private insurance company. The covered individual pays (directly themselves or through stoppages) premiums or taxes to the Health Insurance Organisation it has registered to in order to help avoid high or unexpected healthcare expenses. Health Insurance Organisations closely cooperate with the Healthcare Providers in order to proceed with transaction clearing of the healthcare-related expenses of the covered individual. Quite often this process does not only involve the communication of the receipts and the appropriate supporting documents but also a negotiation process between the two parties due to their conflicting interests, leading to slow cycles of information exchange.
- **Pharmacy:** it provides the prescribed medication to the patient and based on the Health Insurance Organisation the patient is registered to as well as the related policies requests for a specific percentage of the total amount of money or even the whole sum.
- **Patient:** it involved every insured person visiting a Healthcare Provider. The individual may be covered by a public or a private health insurance, whereas it is not unusual that the person may have both types of health insurance and thus be registered to more than one Health Insurance Organisations (one public and one private).

Scenario Description

Patient X insured at Insurance Organisation A in Greece is traveling quite often in his country for business purposes. After a long meeting at his enterprise headquarters in Salonica he felt intense discomfort and took his heart pills. However, the pills didn't manage to ease his pain and based on his doctor's advice he took after calling him, he went to Hospital B that his insurance organisation cooperates with in Salonica to be examined. The doctor at Hospital B requests for the patient's e-health record (EHR) from the system. He gets information about his medical history, examination reports and list of medication he receives or has taken in the past as well as his allergy list. After examining him, he decides to proceed with the admission of the patient to the hospital for one day in order to monitor carefully the status of the patient.

After the patient is officially admitted to the hospital, his e-health record is updated with the admission information (hour, hospital section, floor, room, supervising doctor, cause for admission, expected duration of staying). After the results of the cardiogram, the doctor decides to increase for a few days the dosage of his medication and orders the nurse to give him another pill that will relax him and ease the pain on his chest. The next day the patient is ready to leave the hospital. The doctor prescribes him another set of pills, while he advices him not to forget to increase for a few days the dosage of his previous medication. The doctor proceeds with updating the patient's e-health record with the examination performed and the results as well as the temporary change in the patient's medication. Patient X goes to the accounting department where they access his e-health record to proceed with the final billing of his exams. The employee is able to view the list of examinations the patient took only that day at the specific Healthcare Provider as well as the related cost. The information displayed concerns the patient's exams performed within

Hospital B followed by their cost. Patient X is worried about his health status after this episode and decides to visit his personal doctor in Athens. For this reason, he calls him and arranges an appointment with him for the following day. The doctor's secretary updates the patient EHR with the upcoming appointment.

The patient gets a receipt for these exams and pays 20% of the total cost based on his insurance organisation policy. The list of pending operations for Insurance organisation A that patient X is insured at is updated with the current examinations the patient took. The insurance organisation accesses the billing record and the list of examinations the patient took as well as the patient's demographic information and the Hospital B information. In the meanwhile, patient X will be soon out of pills after the increase in his medication dosage and thus goes to a pharmacy the doctor at Hospital B suggested based on the list of cooperating pharmacies with his insurance organisation. The patient pays 25% of the total cost of the pills while his EHR is updated with this information. The insurance organisation receives the request through the system and is displayed with the medication the patient bought followed by the justification and the related billing information as well as the pharmacy's details. In the meanwhile, the Statistics company S is performing an anonymous resource management survey on European Hospitals and requests data from the EHR system including examination records per hospital and city.

Technical Requirements

Based on the scenario described above a set of technical requirements can be identified:

- As the information managed through such a system contains *sensitive data*, enhanced *data protection mechanisms* need to be established. In fact, *dataprivacy* and *security* constitute important issues that need to be carefully dealt with. Different levels of access to e-health medical records need to be defined and developed, secure data storage and transfer must be offered, advanced identity management needs to be supported, traceability, end-to-end message security and message integrity checks must be offered, identity theft occurrences need to be predicted and eliminated, whereas the content of the e-health medical record must be relevant, accurate but not excessive.
- Given that information comprises the most valuable resource within a collaborative e-health environment, the cost deriving from information loss (due to system attacks or network, application or hardware problems or even due to the human factor) can have great impact on the proper and successful operation of the system as well as the relations among collaborating parties (e.g., loss of medical subscription or patient history medical data) and thus a reliable and robust infrastructure is required. For this reason, *fault-tolerant mechanisms* need to be integrated to the system with the main priority being on *data reliability*.
- *Scalability* comprises an important non-functional requirement as the system must be able to serve a continuously growing number of users who are geographically dispersed.
- It should be noted that fluctuating factors affect the e-health environment, such as epidemic and a new flue among others. Hence, *efficient load balancing* techniques are required combined with enhanced dynamic data replication mechanisms must be supported by the underlying infrastructure so that the system is able to operate efficiently during rush hours and increased seasonal demand.
- In such a collaborative data-oriented system, strong needs for *efficient and real-time data management* are posed. Information is continuously updated, data

may be heterogeneous, distributed to many sites and each requiring different levels of authorisation.

- Given the current state in the e-health sector, information exchange focusing not only on e-health medical records but also on financial and billing information is required in order for non-affiliated healthcare organisations to be able to interact and exchange information. In other words, *interoperability* comprises one of the most important issues that need extensive work to be done. The IEEE (Institute of Electrical and Electronics Engineers, 1990) defines interoperability as follows: the ability of two or more systems or components to exchange information and to use the information that has been exchanged. In other words, interoperability is a term that refers both to the functional level regarding the exchange of messages and information, i.e., the physical communication among components and systems and to semantic level, i.e., interpreting operations, messages and information with a common language. In this example, interoperability issues rise due to the different encodings each healthcare actor may have adopted (regarding encoding for drugs, diseases, EHR, etc) as well the messages exchanged (e.g., different versions of HL7, etc) as it can be easily seen in figure 1.
- As already mentioned security, privacy and trust are of paramount importance. Moreover, as it can be easily deduced from the scenario described in the previous section, *effective and flexible SLA (Service Level Agreement) mechanisms* need to be established among the collaborating parties within the e-health environment monitoring and evaluating different SLAs established between the varying parties in the collaboration and handling unexpected occurrences during operation.

TECHNICAL ANALYSIS OF THE MEDICAL INFORMATICS BUSINESS ENVIRONMENT

As it can be easily deduced from the analysis of the technical requirements of an e-health collaborative environment presented above, secure, dynamic, privacy-preserving, *efficient and reliable information management* as well as interoperability comprise two of the major challenges and poses string infrastructural requirements. In the following paragraphs, it is presented how Grid technologies and the HL-7 initiative aim at addressing these issues respectively.

Information Management and the Grid

The Grid infrastructure comes to offer dynamic, on-demand provisioning of resources (storage, data, applications, processing units, bandwidth, etc) and interoperability. For this reason the use of Grid technology in this environment for sharing and integrating heterogeneous resources seems more than beneficial and gives the opportunity for meeting the demands of such a dynamic and complex collaborative environment.

As it has been mentioned, Data Grids comprise an extension of the Grid and aim to be the next generation inter-organisational data management systems for coordinated sharing and exchange of data as well as distributed, heterogeneous storage resources among organisations. Chervenak et al (2001) identify four main principles for the Data Grid architecture: mechanism, neutrality, policy neutrality, compatibility with Grid infrastructure and uniformity of information infrastructure. Mechanism neutrality refers to the independence of the architecture from the underlying low-level mechanisms which are used for data management, such as storing, transfering, etc. With the term policy neutrality they point out that apart from the basic operations, the implementation of the policies should be via high-level procedures so that the end user can adjust them to their needs. The third principle denotes that Data Grid must be an extension of the Grid inheriting the mechanisms relating to authentication, resource management, and so on. Uniformity of information infrastructure refers to using a common data model and interface to the data.

Based on this brief analysis of the Data Grid concept, applying the Data Grid mechanisms within the e-healthcare collaborative environment (i.e., *Grid-enabling*) can enable the sharing of information across organisational boundaries through an extended list of operations and services it offers. Among others, data state information including audit trails, file versions, validation data (size, checksum, validation date), locks, can be managed as well as interactions with storage systems, metadata can be assigned, efficient data replication techniques can be applied, owners to data and access controls can be assigned. Thus, what the Data Grid infrastructure offers is a set of mechanisms and technologies that provide efficient and reliable data management.

In an effort to enable trust among collaborating parties Service Level Agreements (SLAs) are established between them. An SLA (Wustenhoff, 2002) helps in the definition of the relationship between two parties by allowing the setting of the expectations between the *consumer* and the *provider*. In the case of the healthcare collaborative environment the main aim is to ensure that the overall need for timely, secure, efficient and reliable information communication is offered according to predefined Quality of Service (QoS) parameters. Thus, an SLA in this environment would for example include terms such as, the message broker service technical team will respond to service unavailability during rush hours (Monday to Friday) within 5 minutes and resolve the problem within 30 minutes or response time of 99% of drug database transactions from clinic A will be less than 1 second, with response time being the time interval between the time the user from clinic A sends the transaction request and the time he receives confirmation of successful transaction completion, whereas any deviation from these figures comprises a *violation*.

However, an SLA itself does not offer much to the participating parties if not managed appropriately. For this reason feverish research is taking place in Service Level Agreement Management (SLAM). In (Rosenberg and Juan, 2009), the authors present the SLA lifecycle including (i) SLA template specification, (ii) publication and discovery, (iii) negotiation, (iv) optimisation of resource selection, (v) monitoring, (vi) evaluation, (vii) re-negotiation and (viii) accounting. This way, after an SLA is defined and accepted by both parties (steps i-iv), the metrics (e.g., memory and disk space, transaction response time, network bandwidth, etc) related to the terms in the agreed-upon SLA are being monitored (v). The evaluation step (vi) includes the comparison of these terms with the metrics being monitored so that violations are detected and the respective pre-agreed action is taken by the system and upcoming violations of the term are prevented. Hence, for example, if more than 1% of the drug database transactions take more than 1 second, then this comprises a violation and specific action needs to be taken according to the pre-agreed policy (e.g., the technical support team needs to take action or requests are redirected automatically to another replica of the database).

The reliability aspects of data management within a Grid environment are mainly dealt with through data replication techniques. The major topics that the task of data replication covers include the replica creation, placement, relocation and retirement, replica consistency and replica access (Venugopal, Buyya, & Ramamohanarao, 2006). In real-world environments, constraints that the system imposes need to be taken into account such as available storage space, computational resources, network bandwidth, maintenance, access and storage costs, energy consumption, etc.

The Grid provides an environment suitable for solving the problem of storage and most importantly management of such data sets and for making them available over wide geographical areas. Data replication techniques that can be employed by the Grid imply the creation of exact copies of data sets. In other words a data set or just a part of it can be located at many different storage nodes at the same time, thus making possible the redirection of requests made for the data set by a client application to the most 'appropriate' storage node. When developing a data replication management set of services within the e-healthcare environment, certain features of the environment must be taken into account; the *great volume of information exchanged* on a daily basis, the *variety of roles* and the *various levels of authorization*, the *significant number of users* of the e-healthcare services, the *geographical dispersion* of the entities and resources in the e-healthcare environment, the need for *real-time operations* (especially related to the synchronization of the e-health records).

An important decision to make in such an environment is the number of replicas to be created as well as the location of these new replicas in order to meet a performance goal. In the e-healthcare environment, this decision strongly depends on the Quality of Service (QoS) requested (e.g., level of reliability the participating entity is willing to pay for or the law poses), whereas minimal infrastructure cost is targeted for from the Service Provider's side. In fact, in the case of the e-healthcare environment in which a significant portion of the data exchanged and stored comprises sensitive data, a perfect balance between achieving the desired QoS and reducing the number of instances of the data to the minimum so that the possibility of data abuse, disclosure and attack is reduced is required. Based on the replication scheme followed a replica persists until the authorised entity deletes it based on a predefined policy or its lifetime expires (static replication), or replicas are automatically created and deleted based on system or entity-related parameters (dynamic replication), such as current workload, network bandwidth, cost, expected demand. Though the latter incurs additional costs and network overhead, it allows for workload balancing, fault-tolerance and more efficient handling of the dynamicity of the Grid environment.

Concerning the user management and the authorisation assignment and monitoring aspects, Role-Based Access Control (RBAC) (Chakrabarti et al, 2008) and/or Process-Based Access Control (PBAC) mechanisms (GRIA, 2009) are used. The first one requires accurate directories of the healthcare provider's and health insurance organisation's staff based on their position in the respective organisations as well as careful listing and description of the different roles having access to the information and their authorisation levels. This process will actually form the privacy levels of the information in the environment. Thus, doctors will be granted access to different pieces of information (including historical data, medication, examinations, surgeries, allergies, symptoms, signs) of a patient's e-health record than the nurses or the logistic department within the same healthcare Organisation, whereas the information exposed to different roles in a health insurance organisation will involve a different perspective focusing on pending payments and thus including billing information linked to the specific healthcare provider's details as well as supporting documents related to the billing data. PBAC 2 comprises a dynamic access control mechanism. In brief, each web service has a list of operations that it can perform and PBAC determines which user can perform which actions in which context. The core component is a Policy Decision Point (PDP), which responds to the question "Can <this user> perform <this operation> on <this resource>?". The response depends on the roles the user belongs to that are bound with the resource and policy related to the resource. Although these mechanisms are met individually on various systems serving from healthcare to surveillance and defence, hybrid models also exist.

Figure 1. Conceptual View of Interoperability among healthcare domains

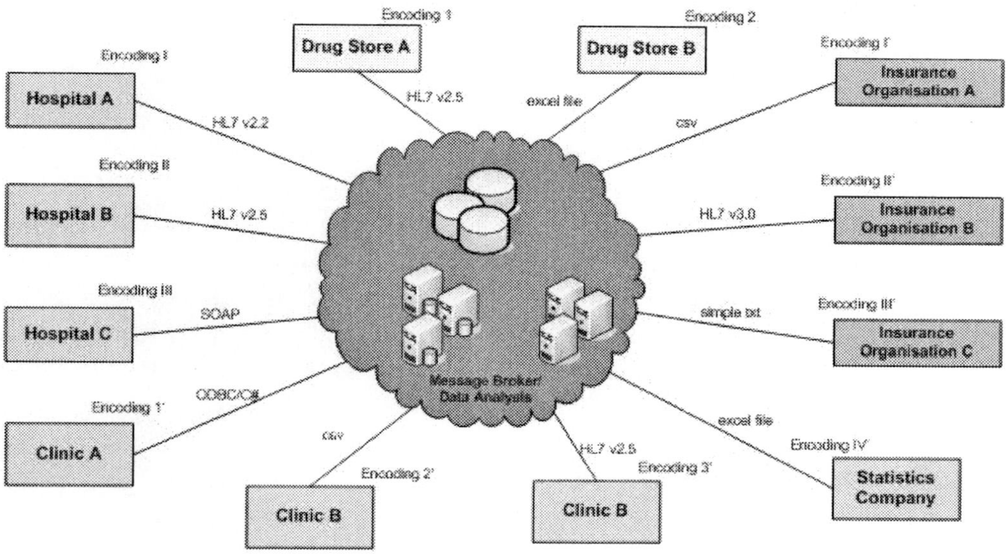

Application Interoperability: The HL7

Apart from the infrastructural demands at resource level, current limitations of health information systems to a specific department or healthcare organisation in the environment comprise an important obstacle to the interoperability of these systems beyond organisational boundaries. These interoperability issues mainly stem from the various encodings used by each healthcare organisation for describing information about drugs, diseases, EHR as well as the different messaging mechanisms used for the communication of information, including different versions of HL7, simple text files, CSV (Comma Separated Values) and so on (see Figure 1). This results in significant delays of communication when required and more importantly in great inconsistencies in the EHR of the patient across healthcare providers leading to significant implications in care provisioning, quality of treatment and related costs. Hence, application interoperability is also required; a need that is tightly coupled with standardisation of the terms and the interaction in the healthcare environment while maintaining flexibility and cost-effectiveness. The "Health Level-7" initiative aims at producing specifications for bringing these gaps, just like a common language gives the opportunity to people of different native tongues to communicate with each other.

What is unique about HL7 (HL7 Organisation, 2009) is the fact that it deals with specifying flexible standards and guidelines of the entire healthcare organisation and is not limited to specific departments and is continuously adjusted and extended in an effort to support the varying requirements and needs of the different users, roles and entities within the e-healthcare domain. By defining a set of rules allowing for information exchange and processing while achieving uniformity and consistency, HL-7 specification aims at enabling interoperability among different healthcare entities and thus minimising delays in the information flow as well as geographical isolation and great variations in medical care. Healthcare providers are thus given the opportunity to standardise their daily operations and procedures. Based on common events taking place in healthcare organisations with clear focus among others in the patient administration domain, the HL-7 initiative has been developing message structures, Web services among others, able to carry HL7 messages. An example comprises the HL7 ADT (Admission, Discharge and Transfer) set of messages for exchanging information about the patient's state and status of their demographic data (Spronk, 2008). Thus, using the patient data (e.g., demographic data, next of kin, diagnosis, insurance information and so on) collected by the ADT application and transmitted via the related messages, the healthcare providers' Patient Billing System (PBS) will then create a billing record for this patient. The analysis of the HL-7 specification goes beyond the scope of this book chapter.

The implementation of the e-healthcare collaborative environment can, thus, be realised in two ways: either through the wide adoption of an HL7-based messaging architecture able to use different messaging and transports, including web services over a Grid infrastructure or through the integration of a *message broker* able to "translate" the exchanged messages to the standard each organisation is currently using. There are ongoing efforts for achieving the wide adoption of HL7 as a messaging standard for communicating information within and across the various entities in the healthcare environment. According to Rowland (2007) until 2007 HL7 had already 27 recognised International Affiliates with negotiations with 5 other countries in process, whereas the latest list of HL7 Affiliates includes more than 30 countries worldwide (HL7Australia, 2009).

As already mentioned however, the realisation of these standards in the healthcare environment comprises a time-consuming process requiring tremendous effort. For this reason, during this transitional stage the incorporation of a message broker responsible for translating the messages from one entity using a specific messaging protocol to another entity using a different one can enable the interoperability among the various systems. As a prerequisite each collaborating entity should have registered in advance the message protocol as well as the encodings for drugs, diseases and EHR it is currently using to the message broker, whereas a mapping from one messaging protocol to other and from one encoding to the other will be required. Thus, for example if clinic A is using X-based messages for communication of information, Y-based encoding for EHR and Z-based encoding for drugs and wants to communicate with clinic B using H-based messages for information communication, T-based encoding for EHR and W-based encoding for drugs, then, when receiving a request from clinic A to clinic B, the message broker should "translate" the messages from clinic A to clinic B based on the pre-defined mapping { $X \leftrightarrow H$, $Y \leftrightarrow T$, $Z \leftrightarrow W$).

Use of standard web services makes the incorporation of the services into the different entities in the domain relatively easy and cost-efficient, whereas the Grid infrastructure, as a standard-based infrastructure offering security, reliability, policy definition and monitoring and efficient content management, proves to be the proper enabling technology. Currently efforts on Grid-enabling application within the healthcare domain have mainly focused on exploiting the computational capabilities of the Grid or Data Grid within the healthcare providers' domain. Jin et al (2006) presented MIGP (*Medical Image Grid Platform*) which performed information retrieval and integration in distributed medical information systems focusing on combining HL7 and Grid infrastructure into the WSRF-compliant HL7 (Health Level 7) Grid middleware to enable medical data and image retrieval within Healthcare Providers. Another approach for the medical information integration as well as content-based image diagnosis of emphysema disease based on the Grid infrastructure was presented by Zheng et al (2008). However, the presented medical informatics collaborative environment goes beyond the organisational boundaries integrating healthcare providers', health insurance organisations' and pharmacies' systems through the introduction of *a reliable and robust Grid infrastructure* enabling *message brokering, encoding mapping* and *data analysis and aggregation.*

BUSINESS ANALYSIS OF THE E-HEALTH BUSINESS ENVIRONMENT

The healthcare domain comprises one of the strongest business environments as it is tightly coupled with "inevitability" in people's life; health problems. During the latest national conference held some months ago in Florida USA, Senator Tom Coburn mentioned that "*administrative costs in account for $700 billion of the $2.3 trillion spent on health care annually in the U.S.*", indicating that about 30% of the healthcare budget is actually put on non-healthcare provision tasks. These figures lead to great cost concerns which make ICT-enabled information management and communication as well as interoperability and general infrastructural changes a crying need.

The presented scenario indicates the frequency of the interactions with the system as well as the complexity of the information flow. Currently however, it is quite often that even within a healthcare provider specialized systems serving different departments are not integrated, forcing staff in search of a patient's medical or administrative data to enter another department's system in order to obtain a full clinical picture. Given the lack of standardization and the resource-poor infrastructures which are unable to meet the overwhelming demands of these information flows ICT solutions climb the highest stairs of the next steps hierarchy within the e-healthcare collaborative environment. Through the integration of Grid technologies in the resource infrastructure level and the implementation of the HL7 specifications in the application infrastructure level significant steps towards the efficient and privacy-aware information management and exchange will be made. Taking a closer look to this collaborative environment these infrastructural changes allow for a set of benefits to be realized.

In the technical analysis of the proposed e-health collaborative environment HL7 is presented as a set of specifications working towards enabling interoperability in the healthcare domain through developing standards for the management and integration of e-healthcare information. Standards comprise the most efficient path towards enabling interoperability between systems in a cost-effective manner, allowing for the sharing of health-related information among healthcare providers as well as healthcare providers and pharmacies with health insurance organisations. In fact, through standardization waiting times across the transaction cycle within the full healthcare environment (including not only healthcare providers but also pharmacies and public and private health insurance organisations) are minimized, errors mainly due to the human factor are significantly reduced and the road to large-scale e-health realization can finally open. In other words, the quality of healthcare provision can improve significantly while the overall costs within the healthcare domain can in fact be lowered and/or transferred for the improvement of the healthcare services offered to the patients, such as better medical devices, lower queues to doctor's office and timely management and communication of information to the interested parties.

As it has been quite obvious from the previous analysis of the e-health collaborative environment information comprises the most valuable resource. Within this domain information can be distinguished between medical information and administrative data. Medical information includes symptoms, signs, medication, diagnoses, family history, surgeries, examinations (from blood measurement to amniocentesis and cervical smear test), whereas patient demographic information, health insurance, billing information, health plan are regarded administrative data. It is quite evident that within a large-scale e-healthcare collaborative environment constant updating of information is required in order to achieve information synchronization, the size of the information collected and continuously being updated is tremendous whereas the nature of much of this information requires proper handling and management since it encapsulates sensitive data.

Efficient organisation of information and timely communication of administrative data not only between the medical departments and the logistic department of a healthcare provider but also between healthcare providers and health insurance organisations (public or private) offers a significant reduction in the billing process. Nowadays, especially the lack of standardization in the communication between healthcare providers and health insurance organisations and of integration of the various systems (medical system, record system, billing system, etc) causes tremendous delays in the billing cycle. Many records are still in paper format whereas those electronically kept are still incompatible across systems – even within the same organisation. Before the finalisation of the process health insurance organisations quite often request for additional supporting documents from the healthcare providers and a negotiation process begins in order for both parties to meet their interests. More specifically, the first ones want to ensure that the amount of money claimed by the healthcare provider is not greater than the expected cost of the medical examinations, the treatment and facilities use due to possible admission, the medication provided and the equipment of materials used. At the same time, the second ones want to reassure the full settlement of their patient's billing. For this reason, it is a common phenomenon that people or healthcare providers – based on the policy of the health insurance organisation – experience long delays before the final financial settlement.

Efficient information sharing and communication along with interoperability among systems of these entities comes to make the billing process a less tedious task and a more accurate and cost-effective process.

Efficient privacy-aware information management through a scalable and interoperable infrastructure based on Grid technologies and HL7 specification leads the way towards the implementation of a large-scale multi-institutional international platform offering consistent and secure linking of e-health records and providing privacy-preserving access to the latter to different departments and organisations at the same time. Such an implementation offers a helping hand to doctors who frequently lack access to updated and complete patient medical information allowing for the improvement of the quality of patient treatment as well as the reduction of the duplication of examinations occurrences. In fact enabling inter-linked e-health records can accelerate the diagnosis and treatment processes and thus through its wealth of important – often critical - information proves to provide valuable input during the doctor's decision making process. However, apart from the personal treatment of patients, e-health records implemented and exposed within a large-scale e-healthcare collaborative environment, it also offers great benefits related to clinical trials. In fact, the collection and processing of medical information from e-health records while ensuring the anonymity of the patients, allows for researchers to exploit this informational wealth for examining the effects of medication on a certain disease, the relation of demographic data to a specific health problem, the regular progress of a certain illness and so on.

ISSUES, CONTROVERSIES, PROBLEMS

Following the business-technical analysis of the e-health collaborative environment this section presents the related concerns and challenges of the proposed Grid- and HL7-enabled environment as well the expected future trends. Initially a common SWOT (Strengths, Weaknesses, Opportunities and Threats) analysis for the proposed environment is presented in the following table.

Table 1. E-health collaborative environment SWOT analysis

Strengths	Weaknesses
• Reduced operating expenses • Operations performance improvement • Increased efficiency, availability and reliability of the offered services • Interoperability among the players within the e-health environment • More timely communication of information both among healthcare providers as well as between healthcare providers and health insurance organisations • Reduction of the delays related to the fulfillment of the transactions cycle among the involved entities and thus of the finalization of the payment procedure • Access to important, quite often critical information related to their e-health medical record by the healthcare provider serving them	• The different players are unfamiliar with Grid technology • Unwillingness of patients as well as healthcare providers and health insurance organisations to share their data externally • Ownership of e-health medical records • Aggregation of massive data requiring long-term preservation and maintenance
Opportunities	**Threats**
• Increasing market maturity • Generally accepted need for standardization and interoperability of e-health systems • International market • Growing and improved networks • Continuously advancing information technologies	• Security, profiling and privacy concerns for individual's confidential as well as sensitive data being exposed through an extended network of collaboration. • Reluctance of healthcare providers and health insurance organisations to proceed with the adoption of new technology • Vague presence of Grid applications in large-scale collaborative environments

Businesses are slow at and quite reluctant in adopting new ICT solutions. Especially when it comes to the healthcare domain in which traditional processes are more than commonly rooted within, the barriers for integrating new ICT solutions become greater. For this reason a significant transition period will be required starting from intra-organisational changes and followed by inter-organisations ICT-enabled collaborations establishment. The lack of successful implementation and operation of large-scale collaborative environments with quantifiable benefits poses even greater obstacles towards this direction.

Data privacy comprises also an important issue. Entities within the e-healthcare collaboration are really concerned about the exposure of the medical and administrative data to other parties over the network or even their disclosure to other parties. The Electronic Privacy Information Centre (EPIC) identifies 4 main concepts of privacy (Electronic Privacy Information Center, 2002): (1) bodily privacy, (2) territorial privacy, (3) information privacy and (4) informational privacy. Informational privacy which incorporates a more descriptive definition and constitutes the main privacy aspect within an e-healthcare collaborative environment, comprises the establishment of rules governing the collection and handling of personal data such as credit information, medical and government records (also known as "data protection") with any secondary uses of that information constituting violation of the person's right to control it (Banisar, 2000). In the e-healthcare domain, informational privacy is almost equal to medical privacy, with the latter referring to the right of the person to manage their medical records at their desire. Common concerns include disposal of medical information to their insurance company, their employer, the media or even their acquaintances for different reasons per occasion, such as financial, social or even personal ones.

From the legal perspective, apart from informational privacy, ownership of the e-health records comprises an important issue. In such a large-scale distributed medical informatics environment the most potential scenario would include a company serving e-health record preservation and maintenance. In this case, trust establishment through legal means as well as close watch by an appointed authority would be required to ensure proper data handling according to predefined policies and standards avoiding data disclosure or illegal processing, as well as provision in case of company closing down.

From the technological aspect, information within the e-healthcare collaborative environment currently is stored and exchanged in many different forms; printed, written on paper, electronically stored in different formats (such as files, databases), displayed with slides or films, spoken, sent by mail or through electronic means. In order for a Grid- and HL7-enabled solution to be applicable within this environment however the transformation of this information initially into an interoperable electronic form is required, which is a time-consuming and tedious task.

FUTURE RESEARCH DIRECTIONS

Grid technologies – although a set of technologies feverishly researched for years – still retain open issues that need to be tackled with. In fact, as they were initially inspired from and designed for enabling and improving computationally intensive applications, support for large-scale collaborative environments and their resulting shifting of non-functional requirements priorities from performance to reliability, scalability, trust and security poses stricter requirements related to efficient and cost-effective data management, informational privacy, dynamic SLA establishment and flexible user management. Taking into consideration the e-healthcare – and more specifically the medical informatics - sector-specific features, developing reliable, cost-effective, robust, privacy-aware data management techniques which address the heterogeneity, the dynamicity and the great volume of information is of great importance. When it comes to the privacy preservation aspect of the data management techniques, it should be noted that its successful development satisfying the strict requirement for informational privacy requires a *multidisciplinary* approach integrating considerations and joint effort from the legal, medical, technical and social domain. Hence, when implementing such a collaborative environment, the legal framework covering data protection (leading to data minimization and requiring special handling of *sensitive data*) along with the specific informational needs from each entity (doctors, hospital's billing department, different departments in insurance organization, etc) should be taken into account.

A great challenge also met concerns the maintenance of the Electronic Health Records. As the vision for the e-healthcare collaborative environment incorporates their long-term preservation, special provision needs to be made on the lifetime of the information stored so that information included is not out-dated while no obsolete or unnecessary information is kept in the system.

Aiming at providing an evolvable and flexible platform for the e-healthcare collaborative environment, mobility should also be taken into account. According to Litke et al (2004) Mobile Grid comprises a full inheritor of Grid with its additional trait being its ability to support mobile resources (with the latter serving either as a service provider or a service consumer) in a seamless, transparent, secure and efficient way. Hence, our environment can be extended providing m-health services through allowing for real-time access and update of the e-health record of a patient could by using 3G-enabled PDA devices in cases that the doctors perform examinations out of the healthcare providers premises, e.g., medical visit at the patients' home, if required. Moreover, mobile telemedicine can be integrated to the system allowing for real-time monitoring of patients health status, communication of information to their personal doctors and automatic updating of their e-health records.

CONCLUSION

This book chapter showed that it will not be long before e-healthcare collaborative environments become commonplace for the broader healthcare domain, including healthcare professionals, health insurance organisations, pharmacies, patients and citizens. Medical informatics comprises a rising interdisciplinary field that promises substantial benefits within the healthcare provision area. In this book chapter we analysed the technical and business requirements of the e-healthcare collaborative environment. Given the nature, the variety, the volume and the importance of the information in the e-healthcare collaborative environment as well as the complexity of the information flows current techniques applied within this domain prove to be obsolete or inadequate. With efficient, reliable and privacy-aware data management and interoperability climbing the highest stairs in the hierarchy of the technical and business requirements, the integration of Grid technologies followed by the implementation of the HL-7 specifications paves the way towards the successful realization of a large-scale international e-healthcare collaborative environment allowing for the continuous, timely and reliable communication of medical and administrative information across organisational boundaries. The SWOT analysis presented showed that the potential of this integration is promising although quite a few barriers need to be overcome; reluctance in the adoption of new technology and the transformation of the currently followed operations, data privacy concerns, current technological insufficiency in meeting the strict requirements for efficient, reliable, privacy-aware data management and interoperability. However, these deterring factors can be translated into interesting research fields that require feverish work and a multidisciplinary approach.

REFERENCES

Banisar, D. (2000). *Privacy and human rights: An international survey on privacy laws and developments*. Washington: Electronic Privacy Information Centre.

Chakrabarti, A., Damodaran, A., & Sengupta, S. (2008). Grid computing security: A taxonomy. *IEEE Security and Privacy*, *6*(1), 44–51. doi:10.1109/MSP.2008.12

Chervenak, A., Foster, I., Kesselman, C., Salisbury, C., & Tuecke, S. (2001). The data grid: Towards an architecture for the distributed management and analysis of large scientific datasets. *Journal of Network and Computer Applications*, *23*, 187–200. doi:10.1006/jnca.2000.0110

Electronic Privacy Information Center. (2002). *Privacy and human rights: An international survey of privacy laws and developments*. EPIC.org.

Foster, I. (2002). What is the Grid? A three point checklist. *GRID Today*.

GRIA. (2009). *GRIA - PBAC 2 Manual*. Retrieved February 10, 2009, from http://www.gria.org/documentation/5.1/manual/pbac-2-manual

HL7 Organisation. (2009). *Health Level 7*. Retrieved Februart 10, 2009, from http://www.hl7.org

HL7Australia. (2009). HL7 Affiliates Links. Retrieved February 10, 2009, from http://www.hl7.org.au/HL7-Links.htm

Institute of Electrical and Electronics Engineers. (1990). *IEEE standard computer dictionary: A compilation of IEEE standard computer glossaries*. New York.

Jin, H., Sun, A., Zhang, Q., Zheng, R., & He, R. (2006). MIGP: Medical Image Grid Platform based on HL7 Grid middleware. In *Advances in Information Systems* (pp. 254-263). Berlin/Heidelberg: Springer.

Litke, A., Skoutas, D., & Varvarigou, T. (2004). *Mobile Grid computing: Changes and challenges of resource management in a mobile Grid environment*. Access to Knowledge through Grid in a Mobile World, PAKM 2004 Conference. Vienna.

Report, K. D. H. P. Coverage & Access (2008, September 22). *U.S. residents cut back on health care spending as economy worsens*. Available at http://www.kaisernetwork.org/daily_reports/rep_index.cfm?DR_ID=54579

Rosenberg, I., & Juan, A. (2009). *Integrating an SLA architecture based on components* [BEinGRID White Paper].

Rowlands, D. (2007). *Report on the HL7 Working Group Meeting held in Cologne, Germany*. Retrieved February 10, 2009, from http://www.hl7.org.au/docs/HL7%20Mtg.%202007-04%20Koln%20-%20Combined%20WGM%20Report.pdf

Spronk, R. (2008, August 21). *HL7 ADT Messages*. Retrieved October 28, 2008, from http://www.ringholm.de/docs/00210_en_HL7_ADT_messages.htm

Venugopal, S., Buyya, R., & Ramamohanarao, K. (2006). A taxonomy of data Grids for distributed data sharing, management, and processing. *ACM Computing Surveys*, *38*(1). doi:10.1145/1132952.1132955

Wustenhoff, E. (2002). *Service level agreement in the data center*. Retrieved February 10, 2009, from http://www.sun.com/blueprints/0402/sla.pdf

Zheng, R., Jin, H., Zhang, Q., Liu, Y., & Chu, P. (2008). Heterogeneous medical data share and integration on Grid. *International Conference on BioMedical Engineering and Informatics. 1* (pp. 905-909). Sanya: IEEE.

KEY TERMS AND DEFINITIONS

Medical Informatics (or Health Informatics): A scientific field involving the collaboration of information and computer science with health care concerning the storage, retrieval, acquisition and use of biomedical and health information, data and knowldge for decision support and problem solving.

HL7: An ANSI (American National Standards Institute)-accredited set of standards for information exchange concerning clinical and administrative data in the healthcare industry; also the not-for-profit volunteer organization developing this set of standards

Data Grid: Specialization and extension of the Grid enabling efficient coordinated data exchange and sharing as well as distributed, heterogeneous storage resources among organizations

Infrastructure (in Computer Engineering): Involves the hardware, software and network elements supporting the flow and processing of information.

E-Health: Health services and information delivered and/or supported by electronic processes and communication

Chapter 7
Intelligent Agents for Business Process Management Systems

Janis Grundspenkis
Riga Technical University, Latvia

Antons Mislevics
Riga Technical University, Latvia

ABSTRACT

The chapter is focused on the usage of intelligent agents in business process modelling and business process management systems in particular. The basic notions of agent-based systems and their architectures are given. Multiagent systems as sets of multiple interacting software agents, as well as frameworks and methodologies of their development are discussed. Three kinds of architectures of agent-based systems – holons, multi-multi-agent systems and aspect-oriented architecture are described. Examples of already implemented agent-based systems in logistics, transportation and supply chain management are given. The chapter gives an insight into recent business process management systems and their architectures, and highlights several issues and challenges which underpin the necessity for agent-based business process management. Methodologies and implementation of agent-based business process management systems are discussed and directions of future research in this area are outlined.

INTRODUCTION

Recently business process management (BPM) systems are becoming more and more popular because only understanding and management of the whole set of business processes can provide success and competitiveness of organizations. The most characteristic feature of present time business processes is their change (they are not static), as well as organizations should adapt to changes in their environment. That is why organizations are focusing on formalization of their business processes and start to implement BPM systems. The goal of BPM system is not only to ensure that individual employees are performing specific tasks in the specific order but also to provide information which helps business analysts to improve the effectiveness of processes in organizations (Chang, 2005; Smith, 2003). This is why the architecture of modern BPM systems is becoming more and more

DOI: 10.4018/978-1-60566-890-1.ch007

complicated and the whole BPM system paradigm has changed. If the first systems were focusing on the software application itself, now the business process is the core.

A modern BPM system should not only provide tools for defining and executing processes, but also provide performance meter counters, management tools and support real time changes in processes (Chang, 2005). A BPM system should contain the whole set of tools to integrate with external systems through the variety of different protocols. Besides it should integrate with other BPM systems, and support cross-organization business processes (Smith, 2003). In addition, a modern BPM system should adapt to changes in the environment. This is where the intelligent agents can help. The use of agents in business settings does not have a long history. The most compelling applications of agent technologies are in business-to-business (B2B) domains. For example, during the week of 9-13 April 2007, some 31.7 percent of shares traded on the NYSE by volume were program-traded. Most of these will be trades undertaken by software agents (McBurney & Luck, 2007). This is one more B2B example from finance, in January 2007 Barclays Capital launched an automated, foreign-exchange currency fund, a software program that buys and sells forex automatically (McBurney & Luck, 2007). Another area where agent technologies are popular is transportation and logistics (Graudina & Grundspenkis, 2006). Intelligent agents represent organizations in logistics domain, model their logistics functions and expertise, and interactions with other organizations for solving such problems as coordination in supply chain management, dispatching of transportation orders, efficient management of container terminals, etc. Some publications (Belecheanu et al., 2006; Munroe et al., 2006) may be mentioned as related resources where commercial applications of agents are described. Several applications of different agent-based system architectures are discussed below. It is worth to stress that some results of research on agent-based business processes and their management are also published, for instance, (Jennings et al., 2000; Pang, 2000; Yuhong, Zakaria, & Weiming, 2001; Grundspenkis & Pozdnyakov, 2006). Components of the modern BPM system are shown in Figure 1.

Implementing the BPM system in the organization is an iterative process. The standard waterfall software development model cannot be used to implement a BPM system, because it is nearly impossible to analyze and document all business processes that exist in the organization. In addition, as mentioned above, in the modern world business processes are changing rapidly – at the time business analysts have documented a process A, and start documenting a process B, the process A probably has already changed (NEXUM Insurance Technologies, 2005; Chang, 2005). That is why the only correct strategy of implementing the BPM system is an iterative development. In addition, it allows start using (and gain benefits from) the BPM system much earlier. In case of the BPM system it is also a significant advantage, because typically 20% of the business processes in the organization produce 80% of income (NEXUM Insurance Technologies, 2005). This means, that if a company implements only 20% of core processes and starts using the BPM system it gets a solid boost in productiveness in a short time. Figure 2 shows a complete BPM lifecycle. It consists of 5 stages: design, execution, control, analysis and improvement. The first two stages ensure business process management, while the other three – business intelligence (NEXUM Insurance Technologies, 2005).

ARCHITECTURE OF BPM SYSTEMS

The purpose of the BPM system is to automate manual work, improve information exchange among employees involved in business processes, control existing business processes and assist implementation of business process reengineering.

Figure 1. Components of BPM system

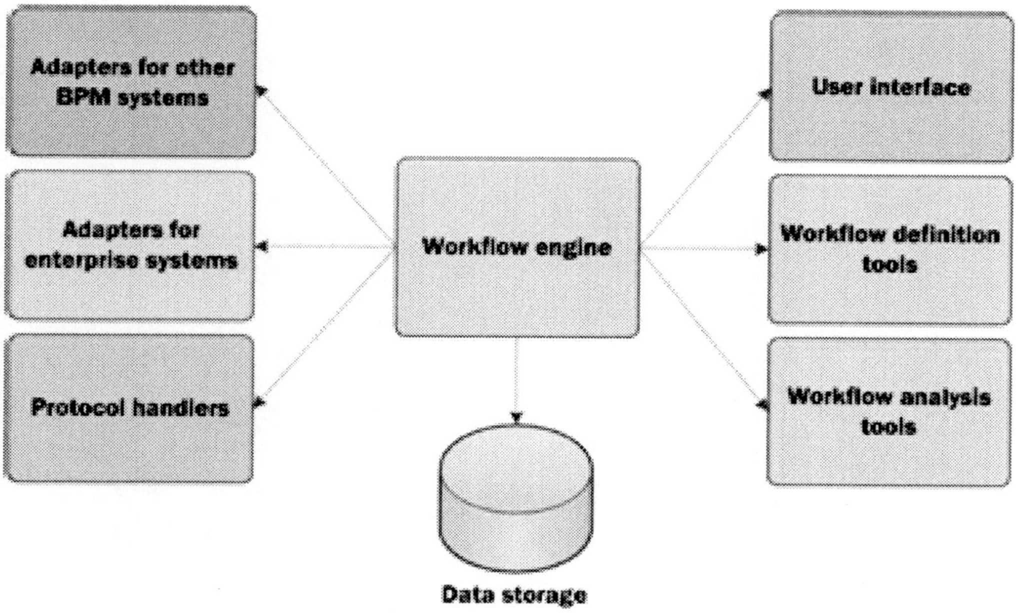

There are many approaches of implementing BPM in the field. The choice between these depends on multiple factors, like knowledge and skill level of the development team, specific requirements of business process and existing infrastructure and software. Workflow-Oriented BPM (WBPM) is the most common architecture for implementing BPM systems. WBPM is primary focusing on a workflow itself. BPM systems of this kind are also called centralized, because these systems have a single process which ensures the execution of all workflows. Workflow is the automation of a business process (Yuhong, Zakaria, & Weiming, 2001). A typical workflow consists of the following elements (Dejong, 2006):

- Messages – ensure communication between employees (e-mails, files, paper documents, etc.).
- Activities – tasks, which should be completed by employees after receiving a message.
- Business rules – logics of business processes.
- Flowcharts – specify the process flow in the organization.

Workflow building blocks in WBPM are activities. They are used to create flowcharts and define the flow of work in the organization. That is why developers of WBPM try to include as many different activities as possible, from simple task activities to complex calls to external Web services (providing possibilities to integrate with external BPM systems and thus ensure BPM across company boundaries) (Grundspenkis & Pozdnyakov, 2006; Pang, 2000). Figure 3 shows the architecture of a centralized BPM system.

WBPM systems are straightforward to implement, and due to this fact, also the most popular. Enterprises gain the following advantages by using WBPM systems (Yuhong, Zakaria, & Weiming, 2001):

- The system helps to define and formalize all business processes. It makes clear to everyone what is happening in the organization and what role each individual plays.

Figure 2. BPM lifecycle

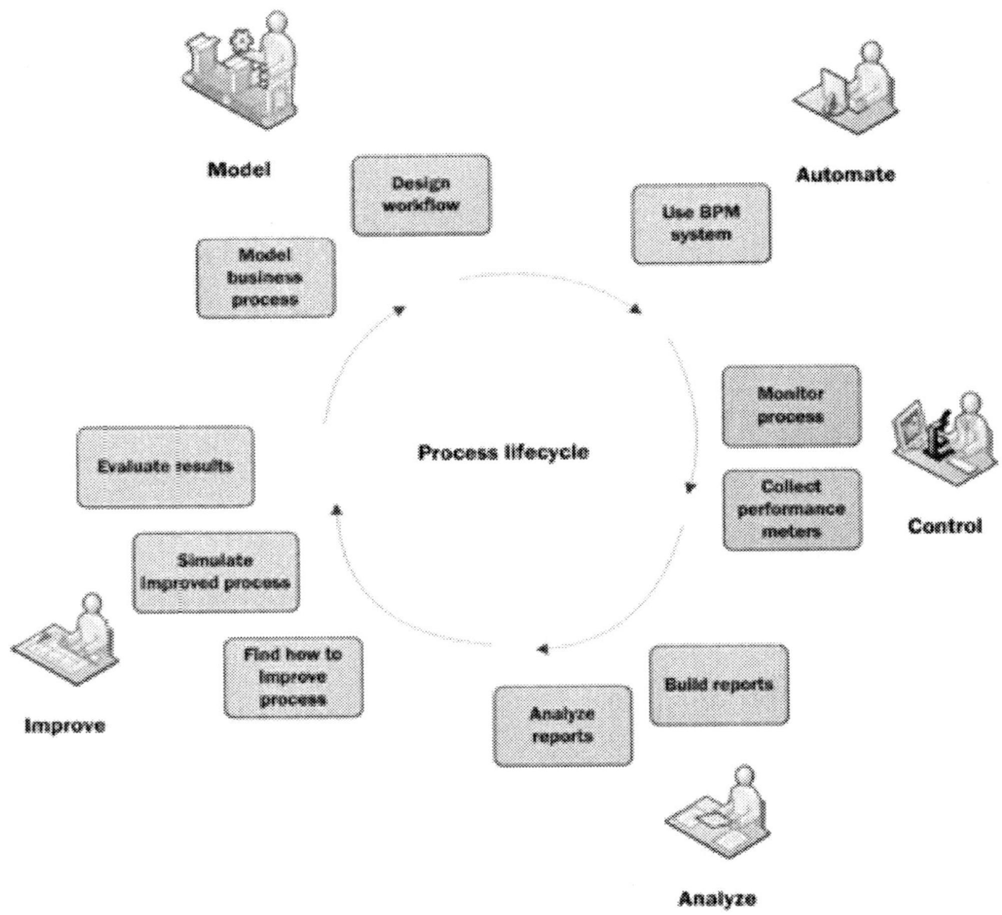

- It is easier to analyze and optimize processes when they are well defined.
- Complicated business processes are broken down to simpler parts. It is possible to analyze and improve each part separately.
- It helps to monitor daily operations.
- It integrates different applications (which may be even hosted on different platforms) in order to ensure the single business process.
- It provides personal workspace for each employee (typically, a personal workspace contains a list of actual tasks, and is supporting information – documents, reports, etc.).
- The system separates business logics of the process from actual work items. Each employee should not know each business process in detail. He should focus on his own tasks only.

These advantages are obvious and well describe why BPM systems are becoming more and more popular. But taking a closer look at organizations' business processes (especially at more complex ones), opens up the whole set of issues, with which WBPM systems cannot deal so well. These issues are as follows:

- The system is based upon the single central workflow server. It may be inappropriate

Figure 3. Centralized BPM system

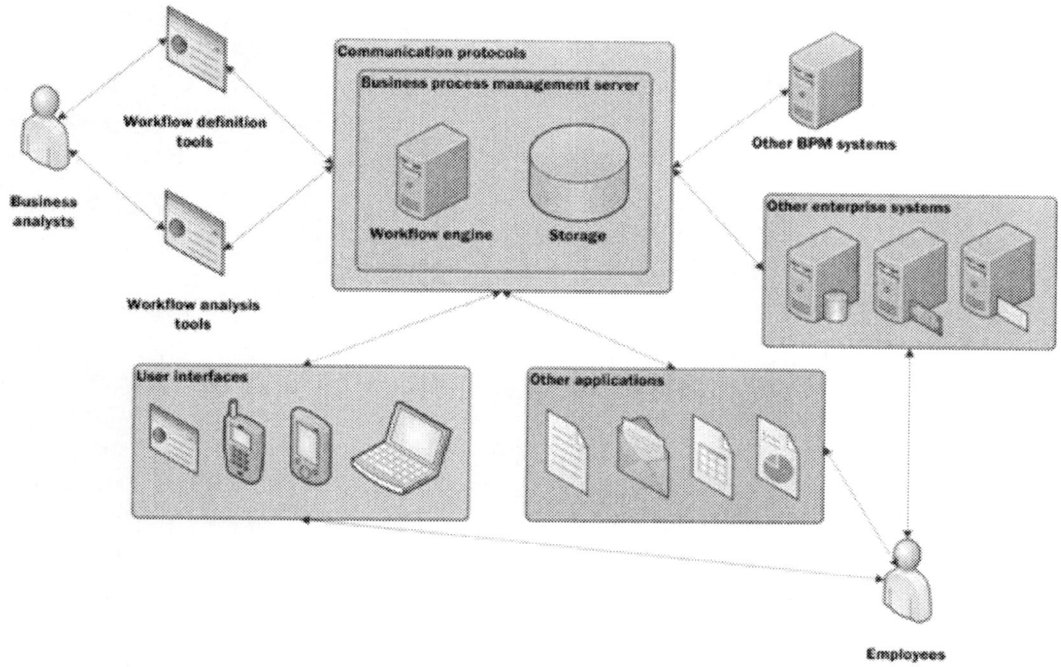

in scenarios, where a company has multiple branches in different offices, and each branch is managing its own business processes (Yuhong, Zakaria, & Weiming, 2001).

- Insufficient automation: a system describes the logics of the business process – a sequence of steps that should be performed to achieve the goal, but all tasks are processed by employees (Yuhong, Zakaria, & Weiming, 2001).
- The system is not flexible enough: the whole process with all branches should be defined (O'Brien & Wiegand, 1998; Trammel, 1996).
- No resource management: the system is not controlling whether all resources required to complete the task are available. It assumes that this was taken into consideration while planning the process. That is why the system is not adaptive enough (O'Brien & Wiegand, 1998; Trammel, 1996).
- No knowledge of process semantics: the system has lack of information about the business process itself. This information cannot be used to make situation appropriate decisions (O'Brien & Wiegand, 1998; Trammel, 1996).
- Lack of well defined protocols to exchange information among systems, and integrate different BPM systems to support cross-company workflows (O'Brien & Wiegand, 1998).
- Non trivial error handling: an error in each step results in an error in the process. Developers should predict possible errors and implement error handlers. Unhandled exceptions will result in aborting the whole process. Things are getting even worse, when the developers are dealing with parallelism and complex business logics (Pang, 2000).
- Users cannot control the workflow execution, thus in a non-standard situation a user cannot perform some action, which was

not specified while defining the workflow.

- Usually centralized systems have a lack of performance, scalability and reliability (Grundspenkis & Pozdnyakov, 2006).
- Complicated versioning and upgrade process.

The majority of these limitations are obvious and are caused by the design of centralized BPM systems. This justifies the necessity for a new approach in implementing BPM systems, and agent-based solutions bring new capabilities to this field because multiagent systems are distributed systems where each agent represents a specific part of business process, while collaboration between agents ensures the integrity of the whole process. Before description of agent-based solutions let's discuss basic notions and features of agents and multiagent systems.

AGENT-BASED SYSTEMS

Agent technologies are one of the most actively researched areas in the last two decades. As is to be expected from a rather young area of research, even such fundamental concept as "an agent" has not been defined in a single unified and widely accepted definition. The agent metaphor subsumes both natural and artificial systems. Several approaches were made attempting to define what may be considered as an agent (Murch & Johnson, 1999). If the most general approach is used then "an agent is anything that can be viewed as perceiving its environment through sensors and acting upon that environment through effectors" (Russell & Norvig, 2003, p. 32). An agent may be considered as a computer system that is situated in some environment and is capable of autonomous action in order to meet its design objectives (Wooldridge, 2002). A software agent approach, in its turn, emphasizes the significance of application independent high-level agent-to-agent communication in an agent communication language (Genesereth & Ketchpel, 1994). Other definitions state that a software agent is a computer program, which behaves in a similar way as a human-agent (Etzioni & Weld, 1995) or that a software agent is a software entity which functions continuously and autonomously in a particular environment, often inhabited by other agents and processes (Bradshaw, 1997).

From the software point of view agents are a natural progression from objects. There is an ontological distinction between agents and objects (Wagner, 2001). Only agents are active entities that can perceive events, perform actions, solve problems, communicate and make commitments. Objects are passive entities with no such capacities. Different authors take different view on basic properties of software agents. So, Padgham and Winikoff (2004) define an intelligent agent as a piece of software that is situated (exists in an environment), autonomous (independent, not controlled externally), reactive (responds in a timely manner to changes in its environment), proactive (persistently pursues goals), flexible (has multiple ways of achieving goals), robust (recovers from failure) and social (interacts with other agents). Moreover, intelligent agents should act rationally. Rationality means that for each possible percept sequence, an ideal rational agent should do whatever action is expected to maximize its performance measure, on the basis of the evidence provided by the percept sequence and whatever built-in knowledge the agent has in the memory (knowledge base) (Grundspenkis & Kirikova, 2005). Other agent features may be added, too. For example, Nwana (1996) combines agents' autonomy with their ability to collaborate among themselves, and with the agents' ability to learn, thus defining these three as the basic abilities. Instead of mentioning many features, which well-rounded intelligent agent should have, Wooldridge and Jennings (1995) define two notions, namely the weak notion (weak agency) and the strong notion (strong agency), where each notion contains a set of agent features. These definitions are shortly summarized by Tveit (2001). The weak notion of agency takes into account the following: agents have their own will (autonomy), they are able to interact with each other (social ability), they respond to stimulus (reactivity), and they take initiative (pro-activity). In the strong notion of agency the weak agency is preserved, and in addition agents can move around (mobility), they are truthful (veracity), they do what they are told to do (benevolence), and they will perform in an optimal manner to achieve goals (rationality). Besides, the strong agency also requires that agents are viewed as having mental attitudes such as beliefs (necessarily limited and possibly inaccurate knowledge about the world), desires (goals) and intentions (goals or subgoals the agent is currently engaged in pursuing) (Padgham & Winikoff, 2004). Bradshaw (1997) adds: 1) temporal continuity (the ability to maintain identity and state over longer periods of time), 2) personality (ability to show believable characteristics such as emotions) and 3) adaptability (ability to learn and improve by gaining new experience).

Many taxonomies of software agents have been developed taking into account their features and/or application purposes. So, Franklin and Graesser developed the taxonomy in which software agents are divided into three types: task-specific agents, entertainment agents and viruses (Bradshaw, 1997). Nwana (1996), taking into account three basic abilities mentioned above, classifies agents in the following way: collaborative agents, interface agents, reactive agents, information agents, hybrid agents, heterogeneous agent systems, smart agents and mobile agents. The analysis of agents from the knowledge worker perspective gives the following types of agents: 1) personal agents, such as search agents, filtering agents, assistant agents and workflow agents, 2) internal communication agents including collaborative agents, cooperative agents, team agents, messaging agents and communication facilitation agents, 3) external communication agents, for instance, network agents, network software distribution agents, communication and access agents, database agents and intelligent Web agents (Grundspenkis & Kirikova, 2005). The abovementioned are only a few examples of different software agent taxonomies.

From the structural point of view an agent is a program and architecture. The initial phase for an agent program is to understand and describe percepts, actions, goals and environment. The core of the agent program, the body of which consists of three functions, may be written as follows (Grundspenkis & Kirikova, 2005):

- Agent program
- Input: Percepts
- Update-Memory(memory, percept)
- Choose-Best-Action(memory)
- Update-Memory(memory, action)
- Output: Actions

Agent architecture specifies the decomposition of an agent to a set of modules and relationships between these modules. The architecture of agents besides the main components of intelligent systems, such as knowledge base and inference engine, includes additionally also sensors and effectors as it is shown in Figure 4. Such architecture realizes the intelligent agent program: sensors supply it with percepts, knowledge base and inference engine executes Update-Memory and Choose-Best-Action functions, and effectors apply actions to the environment. Several simple agent architectures are described in (Russell & Norvig, 2003), among which the more interesting from the business process management point of view are goal-based, utility-based and learning agent architectures. Agents that are able to search for solutions and to make plans are examples of goal-based agents. Decision-making agents are examples of utility-based agents. Learning agents are able to improve their actions in the future. Learning takes place as a result of interaction between the agent and the world, and from observations by the agent of its own decision-making processes. One of the advanced subtypes of learning agents is self-

Figure 4. Schematic diagram of a simple agent

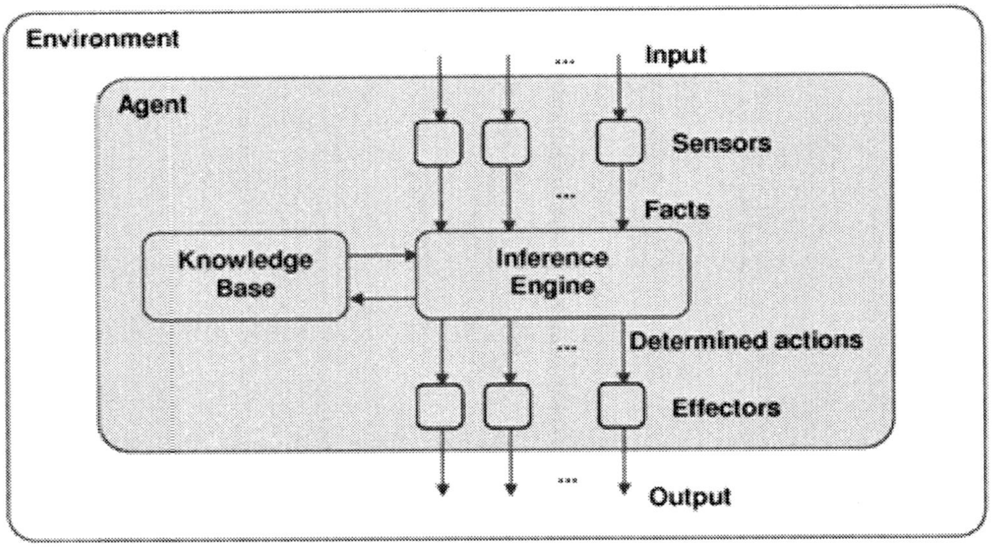

learning agents. These agents give the possibility for each user to adjust the agent's instructions. Instead of traditional programming, the agent is instructed through: 1) giving direct, unambiguous examples of needed functionality, 2) importing functionality from other agents, and 3) letting the agent observe the user's working processes and determine what it should do. It is quite obvious that learning agents have great perspectives for business process management. Speaking about agent architectures, at least two of them should also be mentioned. First, so called BDI architectures are based on belief-desire-intention qualities (Wooldridge, 1999). Second, there are mobile agents (Kotz & Gray, 1999). A mobile agent is an execution unit able to migrate in an autonomous way to another host, transporting along with itself its code and state, and resume its execution in this new environment before that installing its own code (Nwana, 1996; Lange & Oshima, 1999; Kotz, Gray, & Rus, 2002). However, there is surprisingly little overlap between the work on intelligent agents and the work on mobile agents because the latter is more of a system-level issue and associated issues in security (Padgham & Winikoff, 2004).

For distributed problem solving many ideas of mobile agents as well as agents as computational entities are developed under the rubric of distributed artificial intelligence (Huhns & Singh, 1998). The latest developments in this area are connected with so called Web Intelligence (Zhong, Liu, & Yao, 2003) which represents future trends such as intelligent agents and the semantic Web. Web intelligence is the most urgent direction of research and development that explores the fundamental roles and practical impacts on the next generation of Web-empowered products, systems, services and activities. Web services might be one of the most powerful uses of semantic Web techniques based on ontologies, and will be a key enabler for Web agents (Hendler, 2001). Creating machine-readable ontologies used by Web agents allows them to find Web services particularly those in supply chain management for B2B e-commerce, and automate their use. Single agents such as Web-indexing agent can turn documents into formal semantic Web-based knowledge which a personal Web agent may use to find possible ways to meet user needs and offer the user choices for their achievement, for instance, to give a list of several flights to take, to book tickets or hotel for holidays, etc.

All agents overviewed may be designated and implemented using different programming languages and environments because the theory of agents does not give software engineers enough ground to base their implementation decisions on. Lacking any backups from theory, software engineers made their own decisions based on pragmatic considerations (Dignum et al., 2007). As a consequence, it led to many different agent-programming platforms and languages. Agent programming languages usually have some common features, namely, some support for artificial intelligence and networking: easiness of distributing agents across a network and collecting information from networks, as well as make easy communication for agents. Usually such programming languages as Java, Smalltalk and Objective C are suggested, but also Tcl/Tk, Telescript Obliq, Limbo and Python are mentioned in literature. In (Knapik & Johnson, 1998) it is argued that Java and Smalltalk have a tremendous potential as agent languages however they are not yet ready to provide a standardized agent execution environment and architecture. The arguments in favour of Java are the following: it is a platform independent object-oriented language with an excellent network support. Practically Smalltalk and Objective C, which is an object-oriented subset of C with Smalltalk style message syntax, have the same features.

Because different aspects of the agent systems are emphasized, the platforms and languages also differ in many aspects and are hard to use together – let alone that a standard could be developed (Dignum et al., 2007). Two efforts to ease this problem were coming from DARPA through the CoABS (Control of Agents-Based Systems) project and from the Foundations for Intelligent Physical Agents (FIPA) through its efforts to standardize agent interfaces. While FIPA Agent Communication Language (ACL) has become a de facto standard for agent communication, the CoABS software is not used outside the US.

To be useful, any agent cannot be an isolated entity. An agent is an entity that can sense input data, reason using these data and built-in knowledge, and act according to its goals and beliefs. Both sensing and acting are forms of communication. As it is stated in (Russell & Norvig, 2003), communication is the intentional exchange of information brought about by the production and perception of signs drawn from a shared system of conventional signs. A shared, structured system of communications is a language (Knapik & Johnson, 1998). A particularly promising agent language is Agent Communication Language (ACL) which is based on Knowledge Sharing Effort (KSE) consortium essential approaches: dictionaries, ontologies, Knowledge Interchange Format (KIF), and Knowledge Query and Manipulation Language (KQML). One way agents can use the ACL is to communicate knowledge and actions about a particular application domain. The corresponding architecture is proposed by Genesereth (1995). KQML is being positioned as a linguistic layer above KIF which semantics are based on the first-order predicate logic. Such approach allows as part of an agent message to take into account context information, i.e., a sender, a receiver, a message time. Thus, ACL message is a KQML expression in which the arguments are terms or sentences in KIF formed from words in the ACL vocabulary. The KQML as an all-purpose widely used agent communication formalism is an advanced query protocol which allows diverse agents to communicate without forcing agents into a specific structure or implementation (Knapik & Johnson, 1998). Communication is being fostered by defining common dictionary and by using common ontologies, which define concepts of particular domain and relationships between them. Common ontology gives base for vocabularies to be used in agent communications.

In addition, common ontology is used to design conversation protocols, and, as a consequence, in such an open environment as Internet agents should not be forced to use one particular protocol (Zeng, Meng, & Zeng, 2005).

MULTIAGENT SYSTEMS

Communication and learning abilities concentrate in multiagent systems (MASs) that are the hot research topic of distributed artificial intelligence (AI) which brings together ideas, concepts and results from such disciplines as computer science, artificial intelligence, organization and management science, economics, philosophy and sociology. Distributed AI focuses on MASs, that is, systems in which interacting distributed autonomous agents engage in such kinds of social activities as cooperation, coordination, negotiation, and the like, and pursue some set of goals or perform some set of tasks (Weiss, 2000).

In MASs interaction is goal and/or task oriented coordination. Two basic, alternative activities of coordination are cooperation and competition. Cooperation takes place if agents work together using their knowledge and capabilities to achieve a common goal, while in case of competition agents work against each other because their goals are conflicting. Cooperating agents try to accomplish as a team what they as individuals cannot. Competitive agents try to maximize their own benefit at the expenses of others. It is quite obvious that for business process management inside one organization cooperation is crucially important but competition is undesirable.

The main issues in MASs are centered on the question of interaction, i.e., how to give agents the ability to determine what and when to communicate, and with whom. Interaction indicates that agents may have relationships with other agents or humans. Interaction can be indirect (agents observe each other or carry out actions that modify the environment state) or direct (agents use shared language to provide information and knowledge). So, agents must understand each other's communications. Understanding makes use of some language or protocol: a formal specification of syntax and semantics of a statement, a message or a knowledge unit. Direct communication is possible if communicating agents share the same internal knowledge representation scheme. If agents need to communicate having different knowledge representation schemes, they use more complex external languages. This may require parsing messages, performing syntactic, lexical and semantic analysis, and performing disambiguation – a technique used to diagnose or interpret a message in relation to a particular world model (Knapik & Johnson, 1998).

Today MASs may play an important role for business process management at least for two main reasons. First, modern organizational systems are distributed, complex and heterogeneous. Typically they perform in complex, open, dynamic and unpredictable environments. Moreover, they require processing of huge amounts of decentralized data, information and knowledge. It is straightforward that MASs, consisting of autonomous communicating agents that can join and leave the system at runtime, and where processing is distributed across multiple agents with each agent often running its own process concurrently with other agents, may be particularly suitable for business process management in modern organizations. Second, MASs may model interactivity in human societies forming organizational structures. Modelling allows better understanding of psychological and sociological foundations of interactive processes among humans that still are poorly understood.

In addition, Jennings, Sycara and Wooldridge (1998) identify the following characteristics of MASs: 1) each agent has incomplete information and is restricted in its capabilities, 2) communication is asynchronous, 3) data are decentralized, 4) system control is distributed. It is clear that these characteristics match organization's needs in case business process management system is implemented helping to overcome several abovementioned limitations of centralized BPM systems.

MASs can differ in agents themselves, the interactions among them, and environments in which agents perform their actions. MASs cover both types of distributed AI systems: systems where several agents coordinate their knowledge and activities, and reason about coordination processes, as well as distributed problem solving systems where the work is divided among a number of agents that divide and share knowledge about the problem and its solution. An extensive overview of multiagent systems is given in (Huhns & Singh, 1998; Wooldridge, 2002).

MASs are highly applicable in domains and problems where centralized approaches meet their limits because these systems have such features as parallelism, robustness and scalability. Moreover, multiagent based approaches suit for domains, which require integration and interaction of multiple actors and knowledge sources, resolution of interest and goal conflicts, or time bounded processing of data (Weiss, 1995). Therefore, these approaches allow distributed task modelling which make them very attractive for business process management.

Various MASs have been developed and applied due to the growing success of FIPA (Foundation for Intelligent Physical Agents) standardization (http://www.fipa.org/) for multiagent systems, increasing the availability of FIPA-compliant frameworks, such as JADE (http://jade.cselt.it/) or Zeus (Bergenti et al., 2001), and open service infrastructures, for instance, AgentCities (Stockheim et al., 2004; Nimis & Stockheim, 2004). From the implementation point of view, one of the most popular frameworks is JADE (Java Agent DEvelopment Framework) which is fully implemented in Java language. It simplifies the implementation of multiagent systems through a middle-ware that complies with the FIPA specifications, and through a set of graphical tools that supports debugging and deployment phases. The agent platform can be distributed across machines, which do not even need to share the same OS, and the configuration can be controlled via a remote GUI (graphical user interface). The configuration can be even changed at run-time by moving agents from one machine to another one, as and when required. All agent communication is performed through message passing, where FIPA ACL is the language to represent messages (Java agent development framework, n.d.). Zeus platform supports agent communication in KQML and ACL languages and is used for agent-based workflow and e-commerce development purposes.

A large number of agent-oriented methodologies have been proposed in recent years, part of which are described and compared in (Padgham & Winikoff, 2004). All methodologies may be divided into five classes:

1. Methodologies based on object-oriented approach. This is the largest class including such methodologies as Prometheus (Padgham & Winikoff, 2002), MESSAGE/UML (Caire et al., 2002; Massonet, Deville, & Neve, 2002), MaSE (DeLoach, 2001), AUML (Odell, Parunak, & Bauer, 2000; Bauer, Müller, & Odell, 2001), PASSI (Burrafato & Cossentino, 2002; Cossentino & Potts, 2002), OPEN process framework (Debenham & Henderson-Sellers, 2002), AORML (Wagner, 2002; Wagner, 2003), AOMT (Sturm & Shehory, 2002) and SODA (Omrichi, 2001).
2. Methodologies based on knowledge engineering such as Tropos (Bresciani et al., 2002; Giunchiglia, Mylopoulos, & Perini, 2002), MAS-CommonKADS (Iglesias et al., 1997) and CoMoMAS (Glasser, 1996).
3. Methodologies based on formal languages, for example, DESIRE (Brazier et al., 1997), and the use of Z for specifying agent systems (Luck, Griffiths, & d'Inverno, 1997; d'Inverno & Luck, 2001; d'Inverno et al., 1997).

4. Methodologies based on organizational design such as ARCHON (Varga, Jennings, & Cockburn, 1994), the method described in (Kendall, Malkoun, & Jiang, 1996), Styx (Bush, Cranefield, & Purvis, 2001) and Agent.Enterprise (Nimis & Stockheim, 2004).
5. Methodologies based on theoretical aspects of agents, for example, Gaia (Wooldridge, Jennings, & Kinny, 2000), Cassiopeia (Drogoul & Zucker, 1998), BDI agent modelling (Kinny, Georgeff, & Rao, 1996; Kinny & Georgeff, 1997), MASSIVE (Lind, 2000) and approach described in (Elammari & Lalonde, 1999).

Methodologies belonging to the first four classes in fact are inspired by already known methodologies. So, methodologies of the first class are either extensions of existing object-oriented methodologies or adaptation of object-oriented methodologies to the purposes of agent-oriented software engineering. Methodologies from the second till the fourth class adapt knowledge engineering and other techniques. Methodologies from the fifth class are anew developed for special purpose – design of agent-based systems. Unfortunately none of the already known methodologies can be used as a complete methodology for the development and implementation of the agent-based BPM systems. There are at least two reasons. First, only a few of known methodologies have significant tool support. Second, these methodologies do not offer some kind of framework for implementation of the agent-based BPM systems that takes into account all specific features of such systems.

ARCHITECTURES OF AGENT-BASED SYSTEMS

The recent advances in network-based software applications and the advent of ubiquitous computing are pushing towards a world of autonomous software architectures (Garcia & Lucena, 2008). This trend has stimulated revitalization of agent technologies as a complement to the object paradigm for a variety of modern application domains. Agents, like objects, provide services to their clients, but unlike objects, an agent is an autonomous entity that takes the initiative to achieve systems goals and represent software users (Bergenti, Gleizes, & Zambonelli, 2004; Bordini et al., 2005). Thus, agents are recognizably different from objects as seen from an architectural point of view (Bordini et al., 2005; Garcia, Lucena, & Cowan, 2004; Jennings, 2001). As a result, architects of software agents are faced with several concerns starting with basic concerns such as agent services that are made available to the clients, and ending with a number of additional concerns. The internal architecture of a single agent encompasses such properties as autonomy, interaction, adaptation, collaboration, learning and mobility. The internal architecture of distinct agent types differs from each other since they incorporate distinct properties of concerns that need to be guaranteed throughout all development phases (Jennings, 2001) and is a critical issue for the development of agent-based software systems (Garcia, Lucena, & Cowan, 2004; Ubayashi & Tamai, 2001). The applied architectural styles must enable the modularization of each agent concern for the reuse and maintenance of agent elements in other software projects. Agent-based applications require an architectural approach that is flexible enough to support adjustable composition of agent concerns and the construction of heterogeneous agent architectures according to the application demands (Garcia & Lucena, 2008).

Design of agent-based systems for transportation and logistics has created an architecture which is called a holonic agent or a holon (Bürckert, Fischer, & Vierke, 1999). A holon is composed of agents working together in order to reach a common goal. A holon interacts with its environment similarly as a single agent. In (Bürckert, Fischer,

& Vierke, 1999) three kinds of holonic structures are described. First a holon may be organized as a federation of autonomous agents (Figure 5a). This structure is one version of multiagent systems because all sub-holons are fully autonomous agents and a super-holon (composition of subordinate agents) is just a new conceptual instantiation of the same agent architecture. A super-holon is realized exclusively through cooperation among the sub-holons. Second, a holonic agent may be created as a union of all involved agents (Figure 5b). In this case agents merge into one agent completely giving up their autonomy. After super-holon is terminated, each agent may be reverted into its initial state. Third, a holon as a moderated group is a hybrid way of forming a holon because agents give up only part of their autonomy to a super-holon keeping their own plans, goals and communication facilities. A super-holon (a representative or a head of a holon) is one of the agents which coordinates resource allocation within a holon and controls communication with the rest of agent society (Figure 5c). The competence of a head of a holon ranges from pure administrative tasks to the authority of messaging directives to other agents.

In multiagent systems holonic structures occur when agents not only cooperate but also have to be combined in order to perform their tasks (Bürckert & Vierke, 1999). Autonomous agents may join others and form holons without losing their autonomy completely to leave a holon and act autonomously again, or to rearrange themselves as new holons. The most important requirements for a holonic agent are the structure and cooperation. This means, that a problem domain must be recursively decomposed and must have sufficient cooperative elements between the distinguished problem solvers. Moreover, holonic structures besides such characteristics as hierarchy, decomposability, communication and cooperation have the most important feature – an open architecture. This made the design of multiagent systems much easier because instead of monolith agents with all needed functionality the holonic architecture promotes the design of small units with limited functionality. These units may be added or deleted from the multiagent system without any impact on the rest of the system. All abovementioned characteristics have made the holonic approach quite popular first of all for problem solving in transportation and logistics. Several projects have been successfully implemented. The TELETRUCK system (Bürckert, Fischer, & Vierke, 1999) models basic transportation units (drivers, trucks, trailers, chassis, containers, etc.) of transportation domain explicitly by component agents that merge into a holon representing a vehicle for a transportation task. The agent society is implemented as a holonic agent system that acts in a corporate way. The purpose of TELETRUCK system is order scheduling using heterogeneous agents modelling different forms of vehicles. The extension of TELETRUCK – the TELETRUCK-CC (Bürckert & Vierke, 1999) allows several independent shipping companies to cooperatively optimise their fleet schedules. Later it was used as a base for the PLATFORM project. The PLATFORM (Gambardella, Rizzoli, & Funk, n.d.) architecture consists of the intermodal transport planner that manages planning of the whole intermodal transport chain, and the simulation system that simulates intermodal transport unit transportation process. The intermodal planning and execution units contacting specialized agents for planning, booking, reservation of the initial and final leg on the road, and the main leg by train plan the whole intermodal transport task. Forwarding agents (one for each forwarder) are responsible for planning the delivery of intermodal transport units to and their pick-up from terminals. Booking agents check for availability of places on scheduled trains, checking which bookings are possible, then choose the best and make reservation. More details about the holonic architecture, its applications in transportation and logistics, advantages and drawbacks are summarized in (Graudina & Grundspenkis, 2006; Grundspenkis, 2008).

Figure 5. Three kinds of holonic structure. Adapted from (Bürckert, Fischer, & Vierke, 1998)

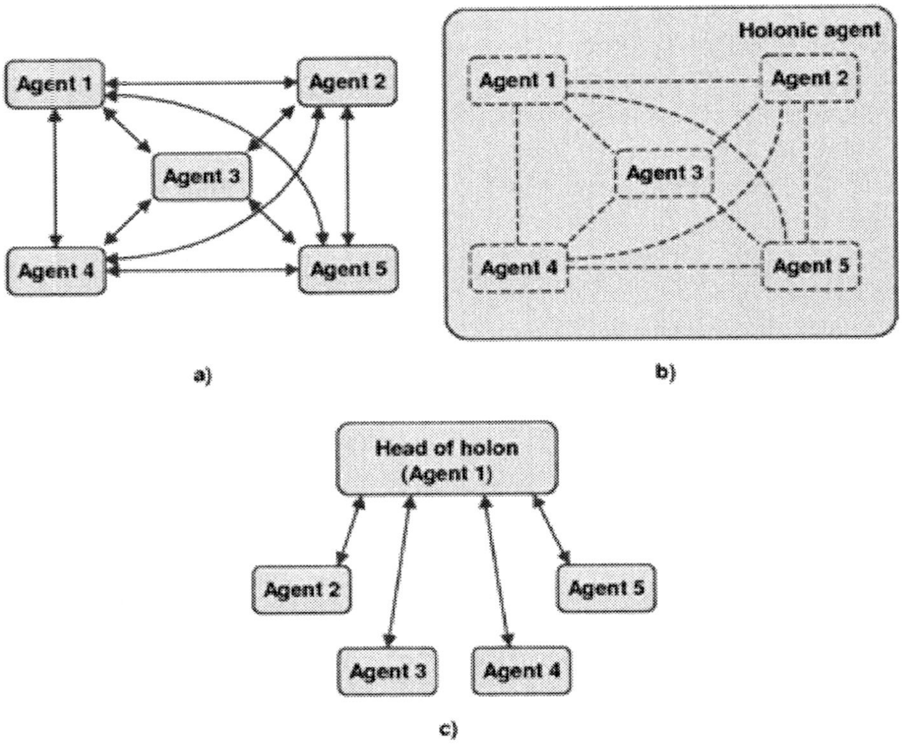

In the Casa ITN system (Gerber & Klusch, 2002) each member of the participant group (producers, buyers, retailers and logistic companies) is represented by an appropriate holonic agent. Holonic agents accomplish hierarchically decomposed tasks and resource allocations, as well as coordinate and control the activities and information flows of their sub-agents. This holonic technique lets personal assistants to act on behalf of corresponding human users even if they are offline. A corporation holon consists of several holonic agents each representing a special department and its tasks and services.

Another example of the use of the holonic architecture is described in (Grundspenkis & Lavendelis, 2006). This is the holonic system for auction simulation which is used as a test bed to investigate the influence of auction protocols on price, i.e., to find the answer to the question which auction gives the lowest price. The simulation tool consists of client's agents, logistics companies' agents and agents of each carrier. The system simulates delivery of goods from Asia to Europe using the following supply chain:

Deep sea port Shanghai (China) → deep sea shipping lines → deep sea port in Europe (Hamburg, Germany) → feeder shipping lines → Mediterranean and Baltic feeder ports (Greece, Finland, Lithuania, Latvia, Estonia) → trains → railway container terminals → customers in the EU and CIS countries.

There are known also other successful applications of holonic architecture such as scheduling of work in a production plan and coordination of business processes in a virtual enterprise. It is easy to see that there are many other business processes that meet all requirements for the holonic architecture. So, it may be foreseen that

Figure 6. Multi-multi-agent design concept. Adapted from (Nimis & Stockheim, 2004)

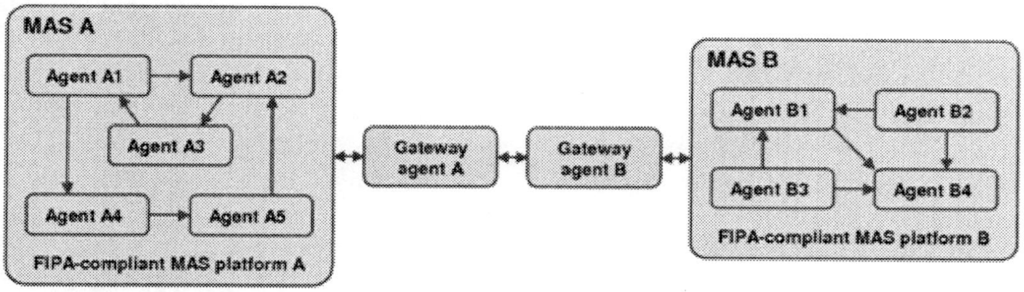

the holonic approach will be used in future more widely including business process management as well.

Integration of heterogeneous multiagent systems leads to the concept of multi-multi-agent systems (MMASs). Analysis, design and implementation of MMAS have resulted in the Agent. Enterprise system (Frey et al., 2003; Stockheim et al., 2004; Nimis & Stockheim, 2004). The Agent. Enterprise methodology focuses on a distributed and weakly coupled development process. The results of the analysis and design phases are consolidated in functionally restricted prototypes which constitute a test bed for components of MMASs. The project substitutes their prototypes with so-called gateway-agents in order to connect their applications to the common scenario. Details of MMAS development process are given in (Stockheim et al., 2004). In brief, the analysis phase includes the role definition and assignment step followed by the use case specific action. At the design phase two central design decisions are united in the gateway-agent concept as it is shown in Figure 6.

The use of FIPA-compliant platforms avoids many of communication-related obstacles connected with heterogeneity of knowledge representation and semantics in the individual MAS. The gateway-agent concept defines a virtual MAS where agents are scattered across a number of agent platforms such that ontology can specify semantics of conversations, and ontology expressions are used as means of communication. At the design phase every individual MAS to be integrated should be represented by a single agent that comprises all roles of the corresponding MAS and provides them to the resulting MMAS. The implementation phase starts with the implementation of functionally restricted prototypes. There are some advantages of the gateway-agent concept. Developers can focus on a single agent and only gateway-agents must be available during the operation. Moreover, the MMAS provides an integration of different agent platforms. On the other hand, the multi-multi-agent concept may be less flexible than the holonic agent approach because an individual MAS should be represented by a single agent with its full functionality.

A supply chain management is a subarea where different architectures of intelligent agent systems are intensively studied and implemented. MMASs and individual MASs become quite popular for this subarea covering services of supply chain scheduling, shop floor production planning and control, as well as pro-active tracking and tracing services. Individual MASs support distributed task modelling for supply chains which involve many different independent tasks (planning, execution and control of production, transportation and warehousing processes) (Nimis & Stockheim, 2004). In the supply chain these MASs depend on each other input and output, and therefore need to be integrated in heterogeneous systems. As a consequence, the MMAS provides reliability of overall supply chain processes which is practically tested in several implemented projects: DISPOWEB, KRASH, IntaPS, FABMAS and ATT/SCC (Stockheim et al., 2004).

From a logistics management perspective two generic meta-types of agents are needed. Management agents pursue goals with respect to their environment and their defined action space, whereas their contractors, the service agents solve well specified tasks autonomously (Henoch & Ulrich, 2000). The DIAL project (Satapathy, Kumara, & Moore, 1998), which is open system architecture, is based on the MAS framework where a customer's problem can be decomposed and assigned to one or more intelligent agents which together generate a logistics plan. Intelligent software agents are built on top of simulation models to communicate among themselves, and to generate a correct course of actions.

The new software architecture for managing the supply chain at tactical and operational levels with the purpose to improve its overall quality is worked out (Fox, Barbuceanu, & Teigen, 2000). This architecture is composed from a typical set of intelligent software agents, each of which is responsible for one or more activities in a supply chain and is interacting with other agents in planning and executing their responsibilities. A typical logistics scenario (Zhengping, Low, & Kumar, 2003) includes a variety of logistics service providers, manufacturers and suppliers whose actions must be coordinated. Generic roles in a typical supply chain are represented by the following types of agents: a distribution hub agent, a logistics coordinator agent, a manufacturer agent and a transporter agent. The architecture of agent-based logistics coordination has been designed using JADE agent platform. Each participant of a supply chain provides the agent platform with a set of agent instances. The agent platforms which include management agents and application agents are linked via Internet. More details about the usage of different intelligent agents for supply chain management in already developed projects can be found in (Graudina & Grundspenkis, 2006).

In (Garcia & Lucena, 2008) it is argued that the existing approaches to agent architectures do not scale up to support the separation of agent properties in heterogeneous architectures. Yet more, these approaches impose rigid connections on the architectural components, which make the construction of heterogeneous agent types difficult and not scalable to cope with the complexity of multiple interactive agent concerns. Garcia and Lucena (2008) propose to use the aspect-oriented approach for architecturing of software agents. The notion of aspects encourages modular descriptions of complex software by providing support through new composition mechanisms for cleanly separating the system functionality from its crosscutting concerns. Aspect-oriented software development is an evolving paradigm to modularize concerns that existing software engineering abstractions and mechanisms are not able to capture explicitly (Kiczales, 1997). In the context of heterogeneous agent architecture aspects and its new composition possibilities can be exploited at the architectural level to capture the multiple interacting agent concerns that are difficult to modularize with the existing architectural abstractions. Aspect-oriented agent architecture brings a new abstraction, the notion of architectural aspects, and new composition means for handling each crosscutting agent concern as an individual component. Each architectural aspect modularizes a typical agent property and separates it from the agent kernel. The key idea to enable adjustable composition is the notion of crosscutting interfaces, which are modularity abstractions attached to the architectural aspects. A crosscutting interface differs from a module which provides services to other components. Crosscutting interfaces provide services to the system, but also specify when and how an aspect affects other architectural components. They flexibly determine which external components and interfaces the architectural aspect of a software agent will be connected. Thus, each agent's architectural aspect can be more flexibly composed with the agent kernel and with any agent aspects depending on the requirements of the specific agent architecture. Each of the architectural aspects is related to more than one component representing the crosscutting nature of agent properties in complex architectures. An agent's architectural aspect can realize more than one crosscutting interface since it can crosscut multiple agent components in different ways.

There are several advantages of aspect-oriented approach (Garcia & Lucena, 2008). Firstly, this approach improves the composability of agent architecture concerns. Secondly, using this architecture the agent concerns are modularized and do not affect the definitions and interfaces of multiple architectural modules. Thirdly, the notion of crosscutting interfaces allows addressing tangling- and scattering-related problems usually found in the definition of heterogeneous agent architectures. This, in its turn, allows to make decisions about an agent property only looking at agent's description and interface with other concerns. Fourthly, at the implementation level this aspect-oriented architectural style helps to guarantee a smooth transition from the specification of heterogeneous agent architecture to their detailed design and implementation. At the same time drawbacks of aspect-oriented approach should not be ignored. First of all, unlike the holonic and the MMAS architectures at the moment there are not known real world projects in which this approach is successfully used. Besides, the implementation of aspect-oriented agent architecture requires using of aspect-oriented programming languages, such as AspectJ (AspectJ website, n.d.). AspectJ which extends the Java programming language is not a widespread language and not as popular as Java. So, considerable amount of work should be done before the aspect-oriented approach turns from a promising step forward to allow the construction of more flexible agent architectures and to foster enhanced quality of realistic multiagent systems into the common and widely used practical approach.

It is shown above that at the moment several architectures of multiagent systems are proposed and some of them are also successfully used. At the same time only few works are known which are devoted to agents for business process management (see the next section). So, it is too early to predict which architectures for these systems will be used in future.

ARCHITECTURE OF AGENT-BASED BPM

Agent-based business process management (ABPM) is a modern approach for the implementation of BPM systems. The ABPM system is a distributed system and has no central workflow processing engine. It is implemented as MAS, where each agent represents a specific part of a business process. Collaboration of agents ensures the complete process (Jennings et al., 2000).

The first step of developing an ABPM system is to split a business process into separate functions and operations. Then an intelligent agent for each function and operation is created. Putting all agents together will result in successful execution of the entire process. The agents may be different in implementation and reasoning complexity. For example, the simplest agent may address some task to an employee, wait for him to complete the task, and then depending on the outcome decide what to do next. This idea is depicted in Figure 7.

The key to success of the ABPM system is effective collaboration among agents. That is why developers should focus on how to establish effective communication, how agents will solve conflicts, how to share knowledge about business processes, specific workflow instances and environment in general (Jennings et al., 2000). In addition, the implementation of each agent is also a complex task: an intelligent agent should be autonomous, it should proactively try to improve

Figure 7. Multiagent business process management

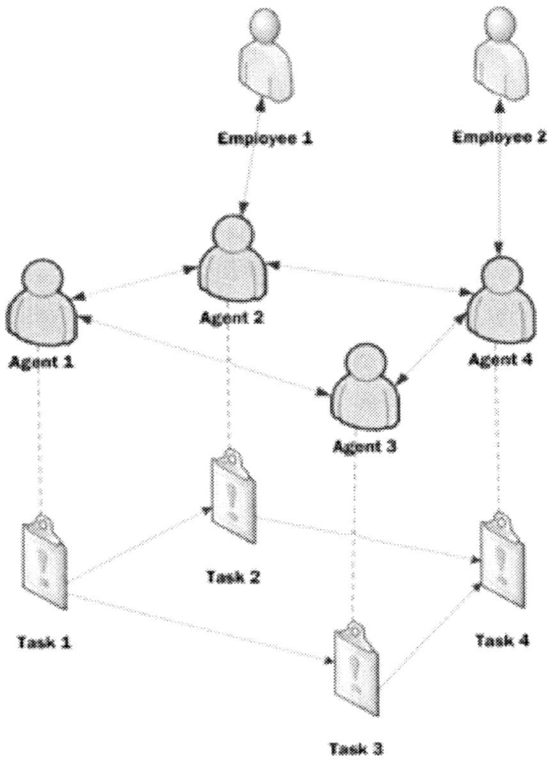

the effectiveness of itself and the whole business process (if possible), and it should monitor changes in the environment and adapt to them.

This entirely new vision on BPM affects the architecture of the system as well (Grundspenkis & Pozdnyakov, 2006). A complete architecture of the ABPM system is shown in Figure 8. ABPM systems enlarge the capabilities of BPM systems in comparison with the generally accepted centralized BPM systems. The principal advantages of this approach are, for instance, a distributed architecture which allows easily integrate different ABPM systems (across boundaries of organizations as well) (Yuhong et al., 2001). Also, autonomous agents can perform tasks without human interaction, thus process automation is achieved. Besides that, agents may represent resources, ensuring advanced resource management scenarios and they may determine changes in environment and adapt execution of the whole business process to them (here learning capabilities of intelligent agents become very important). Agents are heterogeneous. They can easily communicate with other agents, or systems, by using some predefined messaging protocol. Agents may learn over time, make better decisions and thus achieve their goals more effectively. They are focused not on executing all steps of the process, but on achieving some business goal. Agents may autonomously search for a better way to achieve the goal, thus automatically improving the effectiveness of the whole business process (Grundspenkis & Pozdnyakov, 2006). The BPM system becomes very dynamic and easily expandable. Separate agents can be modified, added or removed without affecting the system operation in general.

Despite the advantages, an agent-based paradigm leads also to a number of problems, which

Figure 8. Agent BPM system

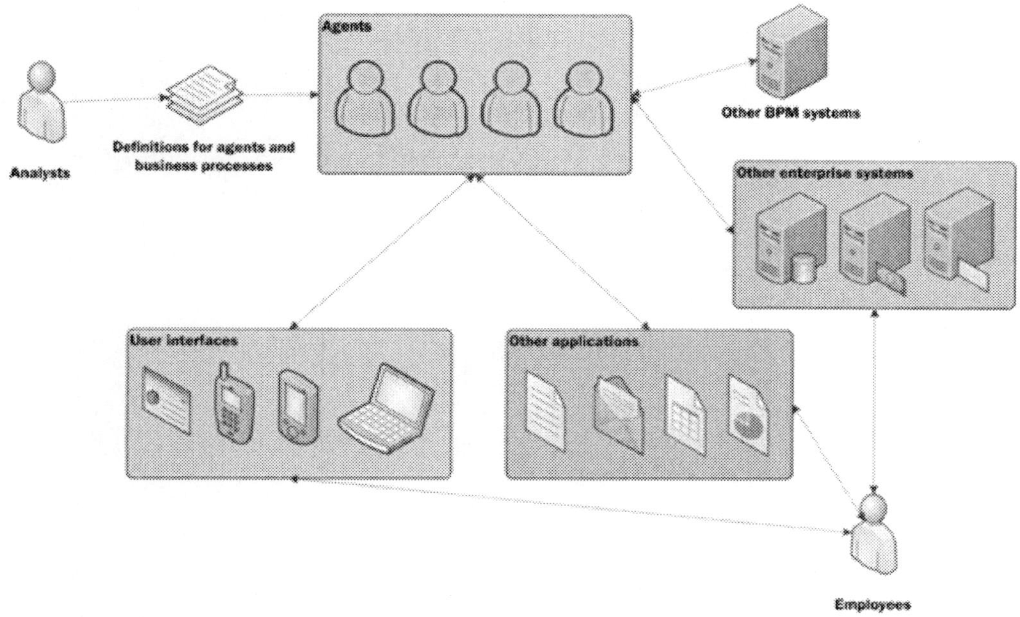

are common to distributed systems. These are the following:

- The system does not provide an overall view of the business processes. It is hard to analyze and optimize processes. Moreover, it is complicated even to verify that all business rules and constraints are applied.
- Typically the system has no central coordination mechanism, which makes it unstable and unsafe (Yuhong, Zakaria, & Weiming, 2001).
- Distributed systems have no overall system controller. That is why it is not the best way to manage processes with a large amount of global constraints, or real-time processes (Grundspenkis & Pozdnyakov, 2006).
- Agents in a distributed system cannot maintain global knowledge base. That is why they will never make optimal decisions, just because they will never have complete knowledge (Grundspenkis & Pozdnyakov, 2006).
- Human factor: it is typically hard for users to rely on intelligent agents. That is why they avoid delegating tasks to agents and meet the idea of agents managing business processes with a high degree of scepticism (Grundspenkis & Pozdnyakov, 2006).

Some of these issues are related to the distributed nature of agent-based systems. The impact of this may be minimized by implementing new agents and improving collaboration between them. That could add more centralization and coordination to the system.

METHODOLOGIES AND IMPLEMENTATION OF ABPM SYSTEMS

There are two scenarios, how agents can be used in business process management: agent-supported BPM and agent-driven BPM. In the first scenario intelligent agents support business processes, which are operated by the BPM system (for example, any classic centralized WBPM). In the second – the agents are driving the process, encapsulating the whole logic.

Typical roles of an agent in the first scenario could be (Yuhong, Zakaria, & Weiming, 2001):

- User interface: the agent helps the user to complete tasks assigned during a business process (for example, agent may filter e-mails, auto-response incoming e-mails, remind about upcoming events, etc.).
- Autonomous work item processing: the agent completes tasks without user interaction.
- Interface to external systems: the agent ensures communication between BPM system and external applications. This can help to manage cross-company business processes, to provide some information from BPM system to the external world, or to retrieve data from external systems, for which a specific BPM system has no adapter by default.

Figure 9 shows agents of different types in action. Agent A1 is a user interface, agents A2 and A3 autonomously process work items and agents A6 and A7 represent an interface to the external system.

In cross-organizational BPM scenarios, various heterogeneous BPM systems of different companies should be integrated. Many researchers propose a concept of Web service (WS) as a solution. From a business perspective, WSs can be viewed as the latest, dynamic stage in the e-business evolution, but also as a simple low cost enterprise application vehicle supporting the cross platform sharing of functions and data. WSs can be used for Business-to-Business (B2B) or Business-to-Consumer (B2C) applications. Usage scenarios cover both Human-to-Application (H2A) and Application-to-Application (A2A) situations (Rabaey, Vandijck, & Tromp, 2003). As the number of WSs available on the Internet exponentially grows, it is becoming more and more difficult to discover the right WS. Intelligent agents, that are able to evaluate the WS, may be used as the intermediary between the WS and its clients (a human or an application). The next logical step is that WS receives the same capabilities of searching, evaluating, selecting and invoking other WSs. Therefore WSs should be enriched with a semantic dialogue interface, so they can promote themselves what they are capable of doing (delivering what services) (Rabaey, Vandijck, & Tromp, 2003). In this case WSs are becoming business intelligent agents built on top of service oriented architecture. However, concerning more complex cooperation processes, the service model is limited for the following reasons (Fan & Lai, 2002):

1. Classic service model always has a service vendor and a service consumer, which means a job is done by just one of them simultaneously and no parallel task is taken in its consideration. That is why the service model cannot describe the enterprise cooperation pattern completely.
2. Service model helps to build a fine granular business services. However, this granularity makes it hard to understand the idea of complex business processes.
3. With a service vendor and a service consumer, the classic service is binate and is not fitted for the multi-sided cooperation scenarios.
4. Service model is not flexible enough, because most services are defined by one enterprise and opened to its cooperators.

Taking into consideration the limitations of prevailing "business service" model, Fan and Lai (2002) propose a new improved architecture for cross-organization business process management, based on business intelligent agents. It consists of three layers, which are the agreement management layer on the top, the service management layer in

Figure 9. Agent-supported BPM

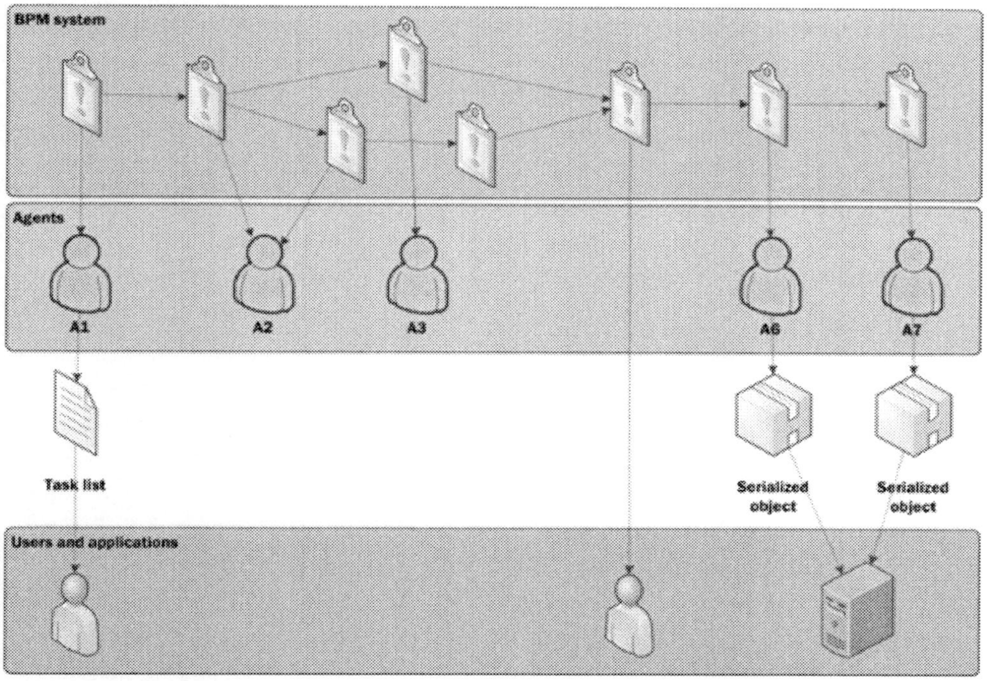

the middle and the local workflow management layer at the bottom. Communication with another co-operator is performed through a portal agent. In the agreement management layer the authors present a novel cooperation agreement model. In addition this layer hosts the shared main collaboration process. The service management layer takes charge of local service definition, enactment administration and remote service monitoring. It also provides the extend service model, which allows co-operators to actively participate in the execution of the business process. The local workflow management layer executes a business process and records its trail. Proposed architecture overcomes limitations of the "business service" model, and enables automation and management of the cross-organization processes in various types of cooperation scenarios. However, considering the implementation of this architecture, there is still a lot of work to do.

In agent-driven BPM approach agents are controlling a flow of the process. Each agent is responsible for one or multiple workflow steps, and communicating with other agents decides which step should be executed next (Yuhong, Zakaria, & Weiming, 2001). In order to complete a work item an agent may connect external systems or generate new tasks to users or other agents (see Figure 10). This scenario is the core of ABPM systems. It can be used with centralized BPM systems as well, thus ensuring that at some stage a business process is adapting to the changes in the environment. To implement this scenario, at a specific stage of the workflow it generates a task for the agent and waits for its completion. After receiving the task the agent takes control of the business process. It analyzes the state of environment and takes appropriate actions: generates other tasks, completes some work items, calls external Web services or other systems, etc. Thus, the adaptation of the workflow to the process is implemented. After completion of this part, the agent closes the task assigned to it, and the workflow engine continues the process in a centralized manner.

A good example of the multiagent approach of building business process management systems is ADEPT (Advanced Decision Environment for Process Tasks), which was successfully deployed in British Telecom (Jennings, Norman, & Faratin, 1998). The ADEPT multiagent architecture is composed of a number of autonomous agencies, which contain a single responsible agent, a set of subsidiary agencies (which may be empty), and a set of tasks that are under direct management of the responsible agent. In the ADEPT environment agents are autonomous: agents have control over the tasks that they may perform, the resources available to them and how they coordinate their activities with other agents. Therefore, negotiation is the only way in which such agents may cooperate in problem solving.

All ADEPT agents have the same basic internal architecture. An agent has a number of functional components concerned with each of its main activities: communication, service execution, situation assessment and interaction management. The agent architecture includes all these aspects (see Figure 11).

The agency consists of the following modules:

- Communication Module (CM) routes messages between an agent and both its agency and peers.
- Interaction Management Module (IMM) provisions services through negotiation. IMM generates initial proposals, evaluates incoming proposals, produces counter-proposals, and finally, accepts or rejects agreements for the provision of a service – Service Level Agreements or SLAs.
- Situation Assessment Module (SAM) is responsible for assessing and monitoring the agent's ability to meet the SLAs it has already agreed and any SLAs that it may agree in the future. This involves scheduling and exception handling.
- Service Execution Module (SEM) is responsible for managing services throughout their execution. This involves service execution management (start executing services as specified by the agent's SLAs), information management (routing information between tasks, services and other agents during execution), and exception

Figure 10. Agent-driven BPM

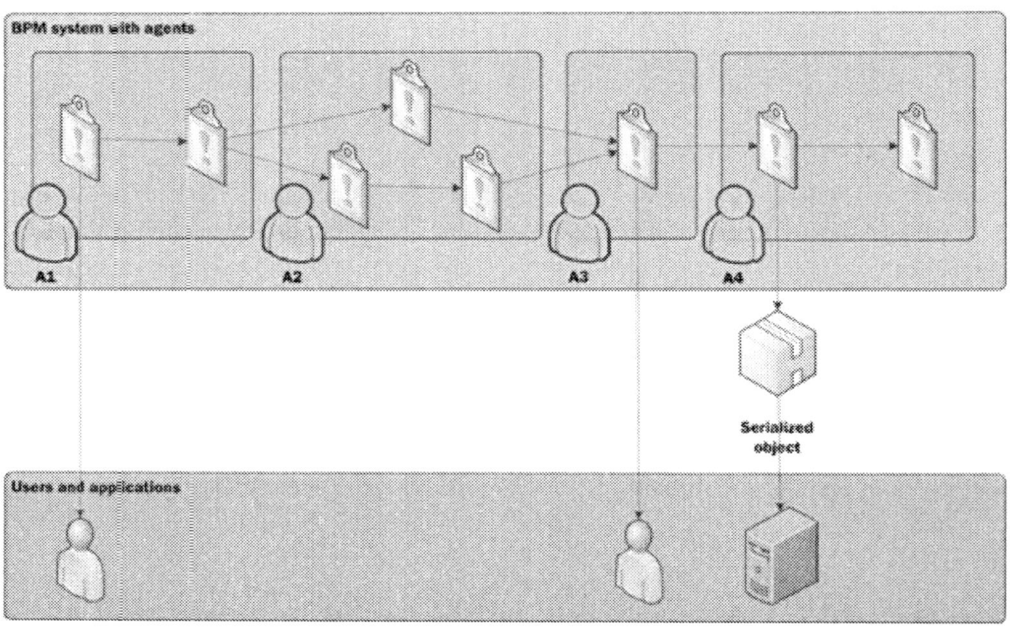

handling (monitoring the execution of tasks and services for unexpected events and then reacting appropriately).
- Acquaintance Model (AM) and Self Model (SM). Within the AM, the agent maintains a record of peers and subsidiaries which can provide services of interest. The SM is the primary storage site for SLAs to which the agent is committed, descriptions of the services the agent can provide, run time application/service specific information, and generic domain information.

Since agents in ADEPT are autonomous there are no control dependencies between them. Therefore, if an agent requires a service which is managed by another agent it cannot simply instruct it to start the service. The agents must come to a mutually acceptable agreement about the terms and conditions under which the desired service will be performed – an acceptable SLA must be instantiated. The mechanism for making SLAs is negotiation – a joint decision making process in which the parties verbalize their demands and then move towards agreement by a process of concession. There are three components of the ADEPT negotiation model: the communication protocol, the service level agreements and the reasoning model.

ADEPT implementation has become an example of how agent-driven BPM systems could be implemented. On the other hand, it has also

Figure 11. ADEPT architecture. Adapted from (Jennings, Norman, & Faratin, 1999)

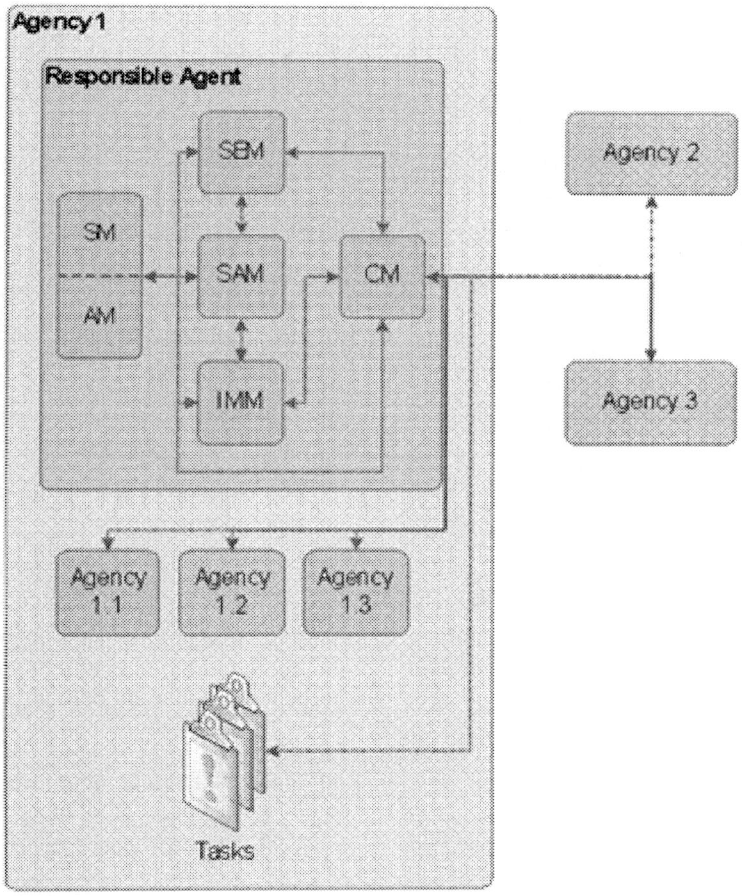

brought out some issues that arise in distributed environment, which were addressed in future researches. Thus, Reichert, Bauer and Dadam (1999) have covered a versioning issue. The authors offer a versioning mechanism that supports various types of modifications in distributed environment: updating workflow schema (template) and ad-hoc changes to a single instance. As a result of this research, the existing ADEPT concepts have been extended, especially in the area of process schema evolution. These modifications allowed automatic propagation of process type-specific changes to already running instances and were implemented in ADEPT2 (Reichert et al., 2005; Goser et al., 2006).

Analyzing the usage of ABPM in management of cross-organizational business processes, it is critical to understand what the main challenges of cross-organizational BPM are. Figure 12 shows the agent-driven business process between companies A and B.

As shown in Figure 12, each company has its own specific data, which contain organization structure and business rules. The organization structure defines roles, which are participating in business processes, and business rules describe how decisions are made. The ABPM environment consists of agents and workflows. Instances of specific workflows are created and operated by agents. Agents are using company data while making decisions. Workflow instances consist of history and actual data. As process flows across boundaries of companies, workflow instance should be transmitted from environment of one company to the other. This transmission occurs as a result of communication between agents. To make better decisions, agents should have information on history and data of the specific workflow instance, not only the description of the task that they should complete. That is why transmitting not only the task, but the whole instance is important. On the other hand, history and data may contain some business sensitive information, and should not be available to agents representing other companies.

Software evolution and progressive ideas of "cloud computing" and "Software as a Service" (SaaS) have also influenced the concept of BPM. Software vendors and their partners start providing hosted BPM solutions. This allows enterprises to start using BPM systems on demand with minimal initial costs. Figure 13 shows the idea of BPM in the cloud. Multiple vendors are providing hosted BPM services (BPM 1, BPM 2). Companies are free to choose the service that best matches their needs. Communication between different BPM systems is established through standard protocols (as REST, SOAP) and using standard process description languages (as BPEL). BPM system hosted in the cloud may be implemented in a centralized or agent-driven fashion, or even combining capabilities of both approaches. However, a couple of obvious limitations exist in this architecture. First of all, the company should have a very stable link to the cloud hosting BPM system: in case of connectivity problems, business process management in the organization will stop. This could be an issue for companies located in areas with low level of networking services. The second issue is related to the fact, that companies have business-related data in local networks. Complex infrastructure customizations may be required to connect external BPM system to this data. Transmitting this data to the cloud will also generate additional load on networks.

The authors see mobile agents as a possible solution addressing both of these issues. First of all, the mobile agent may be moved from BPM in the cloud to the local device (server, PC, laptop, or even PDA), to ensure process execution even if there is no network connection. In addition this would support BPM in dynamic environments, where employees are often travelling and have no stable connection to the cloud. Addressing the second issue, as mobile agents will be running on local machines, no special infrastructure

Figure 12. Cross-organizational ABPM

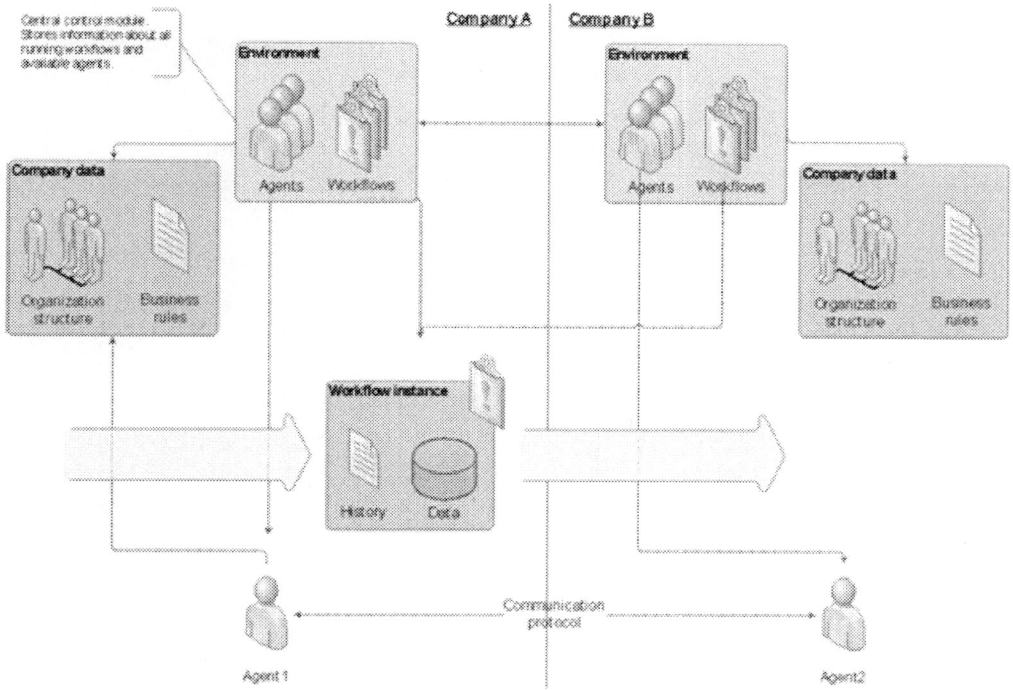

customizations are needed to use internal business data in BPM. In addition, this can possibly improve the overall performance of BPM system, because the amount of data transmitted through the network is greatly reduced. However, using mobile agents causes some other issues identified in the previous sections. The authors will address these in future research.

Future research will cover existing approaches of developing mobile agents, and analyze their strengths and weaknesses in BPM scenarios. The research will focus not only on architectures but

Figure 13. BPM in the cloud

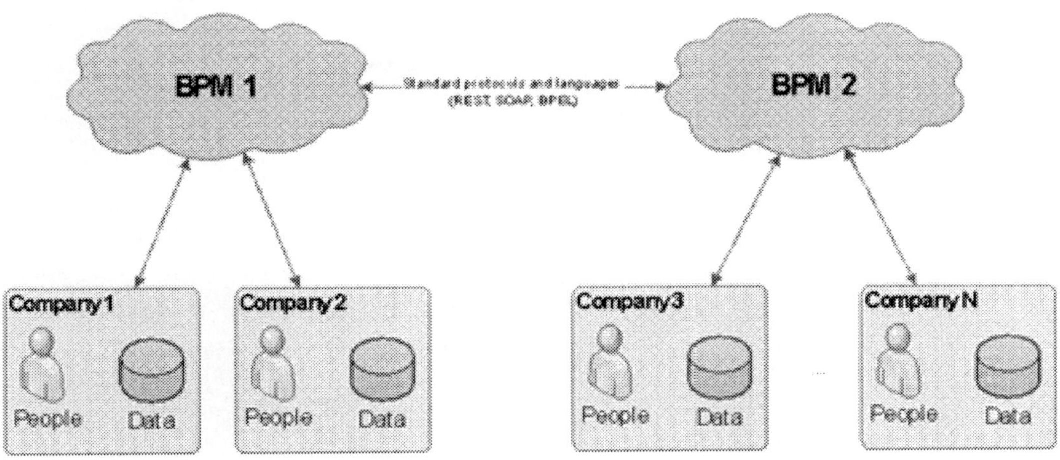

also on programming languages. Capabilities of different business process definition languages will be compared (BPEL, BPEL4People, XAML and others), also covering integration with existing BPM systems. Detailed architecture of BPM mobile agents will be provided as a result. The next step is implementing a proof of concept to validate how proposed mobile agents may improve BPM in practice.

CONCLUSION

Business process management (BPM) systems are becoming more and more popular providing success and competitiveness of organizations. A BPM system should contain the whole set of tools to integrate with other BPM systems and other external systems, support cross-organization business processes and adapt to changes in the environment. This is where agent-based technologies promise a real help. Agent technologies are one of the most actively researched areas of artificial intelligence in the last two decades. A plethora of intelligent agents is already developed. Integration of different individual agents has promoted emergence of multiagent systems. Multiagent based approaches allow distributed task modelling that makes them attractive for business process management.

Several multiagent system architectures have been developed. The most popular are the holonic architecture which is successfully applied for problem solving in transportation and logistics, and the multi-multi-agent systems which, in their turn, are effective for supply chain management. Recently a new, so called, aspect-oriented architecture is proposed which promises to be a step forward to allow the construction of more flexible agent architectures.

Agent-based BPM (ABPM) is a modern approach for the implementation of BPM systems. It is clear that due to their characteristics the ABPM is implemented as a multiagent system where each agent represents a specific part of a business process, and collaboration of agents ensures the complete process. This new vision of BPM affects the architecture of the system as well, but at the moment it is hard to predict which multiagent-based system architecture will be used in the ABPM because additional research is needed in this direction.

There are two scenarios, how agents can be used in business process management: agent-supported BPM and agent-driven BPM. In the first scenario intelligent agents support business processes, while in the second scenario they are driving the process encapsulating the whole business process logic. The analysis of cross-organizational business processes reveals the main problems for solution of which the cross-organizational ABPM conceptual model is proposed.

Progressive ideas of "cloud computing" and "Software as a Service" have also influenced the concept of BPM. In this case mobile agents may help to ensure closer integration between hosted BPM solution, and the existing infrastructure of the company. Mobile agents may also be a solution for managing business processes in situations, when employees are mainly on the move, thus do not have a stable connection to a BPM system.

A lot of work should be done to develop a framework for development and implementation of ABPM and mobile agents for business process management. This is the main direction of future research leading towards more flexible and qualitative business process management systems.

REFERENCES

AspectJ website. (n.d.). Retrieved from http://www.eclipse.org/aspectj/

Bauer, B., Müller, J. P., & Odell, J. (2001). Agent UML: A formalism for specifying multiagent software systems. In *Proceedings of the first international workshop on agent-oriented software engineering (AOSE-2000), Limerick, Ireland* (LNCS 1957, 91-104).

Belecheanu, R. A., et al. (2006). Commercial applications of agents: Lessons, experiences and challenges. In *Proceedings of the 5th international conference on autonomous agents and multiagent systems (AAMAS 06)*(pp. 1549-1555). ACM Press.

Bergenti, F. (2001). Deploying FIPA-compliant systems on handheld devices. *IEEE Internet Computing*, *5*(4), 20–25. doi:10.1109/4236.939446

Bergenti, F., Gleizes, M. P., & Zambonelli, F. (Eds.). (2004). *Methodologies and software engineering for agent systems: The agent-oriented software engineering handbook* (Vol. 11). Springer-Verlag.

Bordini, R., et al. (Eds.). (2005). *Multiagent programming languages, platforms and applications.* New York: Springer.

Bradshaw, J. (1997). *An introduction to software agents* (pp. 1-46). AAAI Press/The MIT Press. Retrieved from http://www.cs.umbc.edu/agents/introduction/01-Bradshaw.pdf

Brazier, F. M. T. (1997). DESIRE: Modelling multi-agent systems in a compositional formal framework. *International Journal of Cooperative Information Systems*, *6*(1), 67–94. doi:10.1142/S0218843097000069

Bresciani, P., et al. (2002). *TROPOS: An agent-oriented software development methodology* (Technical report DIT-02-015). Informatica e Telecomunicazioni, University of Trento, Italy.

Bürckert, H.-J., Fischer, K., & Vierke, G. (1998). Transportation scheduling with holonic MAS – The TELETRUCK approach. In H.S. Nwama & D.T. Ndumu (Eds.), *Proceedings of the third international conference on practical application of intelligent agents and multi-agent technology (PAAM'98).*

Bürckert, H.-J., Fischer, K., & Vierke, G. (1999). Holonic fleet scheduling with TELETRUCK. In *Proceedings of the second international conference on computing anticipatory systems (CASYS'98).*

Bürckert, H.-J., & Vierke, G. (1999). Simulated trading mechanismen für speditionsübergreifende transportplanung. In H. Kopfer & C. Bierwirth (Eds.), *Logistic management – intelligente I+K technologien.*Springer-Verlag.

Burrafato, P., & Cossentino, M. (2002). Designing a multi-agent solution for a bookstore with the PASSI methodology. In *Proceedings of the fourth international bi-conference workshop on agent-oriented information systems (AOIS-2002) at CAiSE'02, Toronto, Ontario, Canada.* Retrieved from http://www.pa.icar.cnr.it/cossentino/paper/AOIS02.pdf

Bush, G., Cranefield, S., & Purvis, M. (2001). *The Styx agent methodology.* The information science discussion papers series 2001/02. Department of Information Science, University of Otago, Otago, New Zealand. Retrieved from http://waitaki.otago.ac.nz/~martin/Documents/dp2001-02.pdf

Caire, G., et al. (2002). Agent oriented analysis using MESSAGE/UML. In *Proceedings of the agent-oriented software engineering II second international workshop (AOSE 2001), Montreal, Canada* (LNCS 2222, pp. 101-108).

Chang, J. F. (2005). *Business process management systems, strategy and implementation.* Boca Raton, FL: Auerbach Publications.

Cossentino, M., & Potts, M. (2002). A CASE tool supported methodology for the design of multi-agent systems. In *Proceedings of the 2002 international conference on software engineering research and practice (SERP'02), Las Vegas, USA.* Retrieved from http://www.pa.icar.cnr.it/cossentino/paper/SERP02.pdf

d'Inverno, M. (1997). A formal specification of dMARS. *Intelligent Agents IV (. LNAI, 1365,* 155–176.

d'Inverno, M., & Luck, M. (2001). *Understanding agent systems*. Berlin: Springer.

Debenham, J., & Henderson-Sellers, B. (2002). Full lifecycle methodologies for agent-oriented systems – The extended OPEN process framework. In *Proceedings of the workshop on agent oriented information systems (AOIS-2002) at CAiSE'02, Toronto, Canada.*

Dejong, P. (2006). Going with the flow. *ACM Queue; Tomorrow's Computing Today*, *4*(2), 24–32. doi:10.1145/1122674.1122686

DeLoach, S. (2001). Analysis and design using MaSE and agentTool. In *Proceedings of the 12th Midwest artificial intelligence and cognitive science conference (MAICS 2001), Oxford, OH, March 31-April 1, 2001* (pp. 1-7).

Dignum, F. (2007). The challenges of finding intelligent agents. *IEEE Intelligent Systems*, *22*(4), 3–7. doi:10.1109/MIS.2007.78

Drogoul, A., & Zucker, J.-D. (1998). *Methodological issues for designing multi-agent systems with machine learning techniques: Capitalizing experiences from the Robocup challenge* (Technical report LIP6 1998/041). Laboratoire d'Informatique de Paris 6.

Elammari, M., & Lalonde, W. (1999). An agent-oriented methodology: High-level and intermediate models. In *Proceedings of the 1st international workshop on agent-oriented information systems*.

Etzioni, O., & Weld, D. (1995). Intelligent agents on the Internet: Fact, fiction, and forecast. *IEEE Expert*, *10*(4), 44–49. doi:10.1109/64.403956

Fan, Y., & Lai, J. (2002). An architecture for cross-organization business process integration. In *Proceedings of the 5th international conference on managing innovations in manufacturing (MIM), Milwaukee, Wisconsin, USA, September 9-11, 2002* (pp. 125-134).

Fox, M. S., Barbuceanu, M., & Teigen, R. (2000). Agent-oriented supply-chain management. *International Journal of Flexible Manufacturing Systems*, *12*, 165–188. doi:10.1023/A:1008195614074

Frey, D., et al. (2003). Integrated multi-agent-based supply chain management. *Proceedings of the 1st international workshop on agent-based computing for enterprise collaboration*. Gambardella, L. M., Rizzoli, E., & Funk, P. (n.d.). Agent-based planning and simulation of combined rail/road transport. Retrieved from http://www.idsia.ch/~luca/simulation02.pdf

Garcia, A., & Lucena, C. (2008). Taming heterogeneous agent architectures. *Communications of the ACM*, *51*(5), 75–81. doi:10.1145/1342327.1342341

Garcia, A., Lucena, G., & Cowan, D. (2004). Agents in object-oriented software engineering. *Software, Practice & Experience*, *34*(5), 489–521. doi:10.1002/spe.578

Genesereth, M. R. (1995). Interoperability: An agent based framework. *AI Expert, March 1995*, 34-40.

Genesereth, M. R., & Ketchpel, S. P. (1994). Software agents. *Communications of the ACM*, *37*(7), 48–53. doi:10.1145/176789.176794

Gerber, A., & Klusch, M. (2002). Agent-based integrated services for timber production and sales. *IEEE Intelligent Systems*, *17*(1), 33–39. doi:10.1109/5254.988446

Giunchiglia, F., Mylopoulos, J., & Perini, A. (2002). The Tropos software development methodology: Processes, models and diagrams. In *Proceedings of the third international workshop on agent-oriented software engineering (*LNCS 2585, pp. 162-173).

Glasser, N. (1996). The CoMoMAS methodology and environment for multi-agent system development. *Multi-agent systems, methodologies and applications, Second Australian workshop on distributed artificial intelligence (. LNAI, 1286,* 1–16.

Goser, K., et al. (2006). Next-generation process management with ADEPT2. In M. Adams & S. Sadiq (Eds.), *Proceedings of the BPM demonstration program at the fifth international conference on business process management (BPM'07) Brisbane, Australia, 24-27 September 2007.*

Graudina, V., & Grundspenkis, J. (2006). Agent-based systems, their architecture and technologies from logistics perspective. *Scientific proceedings of Riga Technical University, Computer science, Applied computer systems, 5th Series, Vol. 26* (pp. 159-173). Riga: RTU Publishing House.

Grundspenkis, J. (2008). Intelligent agents in logistics: Some trends and solutions. In *Proceedings of the 11th international workshop on harbor maritime multimodal logistics modelling & simulation, September 17-19, 2008, Campora S. Giovanni, Italy, DIPTEM University of Genoa* (pp. 174-179).

Grundspenkis, J., & Kirikova, M. (2005). Impact of the intelligent agent paradigm on knowledge management. In C.T. Leondes (Ed.), *Intelligent knowledge-based systems: Business and technology in the new millennium* (Vol. 1, pp. 164-206). Boston: Kluwer Academic Publishers.

Grundspenkis, J., & Lavendelis, E. (2006). Multiagent based simulation tool for transportation and logistics decision support. In *Proceedings of the 3rd international workshop on computer supported activity coordination (CSAC 2006)* (pp. 45-54). Portugal: INSTICC Press.

Grundspenkis, J., & Pozdnyakov, D. (2006). An overview of the agent based systems for the business process management. In *Proceedings of the international conference on computer systems and technologies (CompSysTech'06), June 15-16, 2006, Veliko Tarnovo, Bulgaria,* II.13-1 - II.13-6.

Hendler, J. (2001). Agents and the semantic Web. *IEEE Intelligent Systems, 16*(2), 30–37. doi:10.1109/5254.920597

Henoch, J., & Ulrich, H. (2000). Agent-based management systems in logistics. In I.J. Timm et al. (Eds.), *14th European conference on artificial intelligence, Workshop notes, Agent technologies and their application scenarios in logistics* (pp. 11-15).

Huhns, M. N., & Singh, M. P. (1998). Agents and multiagent systems: Themes, approaches and challenges. In M.N. Huhns & M.P. Singh (Eds.), *Readings in agents* (pp. 1-23), San Francisco, CA: Morgan Kaufman.

Iglesias, C., et al. (1997). Analysis and design of multiagent systems using MAS-CommonKADS. In *Proceedings of the agent theories, architectures and languages workshop (ATAL 97)*. Java agent development framework. (n.d.). Retrieved from http://jade.cselt.it/

NEXUM Insurance Technologies. (2005). *Business process management (BPM) for insurance industry.*

Jennings, N. R. (2001). An agent-based approach for building complex software systems. *Communications of the ACM, 44*(4), 35–41. doi:10.1145/367211.367250

Jennings, N. R. (2000). Autonomous agents for business process management. *Applied Artificial Intelligence, 14*, 145189.

Jennings, N. R., Norman, T. J., & Faratin, P. (1998). ADEPT: An agent-based approach to business process management. *SIGMOD Record, 27*, 32–39. doi:10.1145/306101.306112

Jennings, N. R., Sycara, K., & Wooldridge, M. (1998). A roadmap of agent research and development. *Autonomous Agents and Multi-Agent Systems, 1*(1), 7–38. doi:10.1023/A:1010090405266

Kendall, E. A., Malkoun, M. T., & Jiang, C. H. (1996). A methodology for developing agent based systems. *Distributed artificial intelligence: Architecture and modelling, First Australian workshop on DAI, Canberra, ACT, Australia, November 13, 1995* (LNCS 1083).

Kiczales, G., et al. (1997). Aspect-oriented programming. In *Proceedings of the European conference on object-oriented programming (ECOOP '97)* (LNCS 1241, pp. 220-242).

Kinny, D., & Georgeff, M. (1997). Modeling and design of multi-agent systems. In *Proceedings of the agent theories, architectures, and languages workshop (ATAL 06)* (LNCS 1193).

Kinny, D., Georgeff, M., & Rao, A. (1996). A methodology and modelling technique for systems of BDI agents. *Agents breaking away, 7th European workshop on modelling autonomous agents in a multi-agent world, Eindhoven, The Netherlands* (. *LNCS, 1038*, 56–71.

Knapik, M., & Johnson, J. (1998). *Developing intelligent agents for distributed systems*. New York: McGraw-Hill.

Kotz, D., & Gray, R. (1999). Mobile agents and the future of the Internet. *ACM Operating Systems Review, 33*(3), 7–13. doi:10.1145/311124.311130

Kotz, D., Gray, R., & Rus, D. (2002). Future directions for mobile agent research. *IEEE Distributed Systems Online, 3*(8), 1-6. Retrieved from http://dsonline.computer.org/

Lange, D., & Oshima, M. (1999). Seven good reasons for mobile agents. *Communications of the ACM, 42*(3), 88–89. doi:10.1145/295685.298136

Lind, J. (2000). A development method for multiagent systems. *Cybernetics and systems: Proceedings of the 15th European meeting on cybernetics and systems research, Symposium: from agent theory to agent implementation.*

Luck, M., Griffiths, N., & d'Inverno, M. (1997). From agent theory to agent construction: A case study. *Intelligent agents III* (. *LNAI, 1193*, 49–64.

Massonet, P., Deville, Y., & Neve, C. (2002). From AOSE methodology to agent implementation. In *Proceedings of the first international joint conference on autonomous agents and multiagent systems, Bologna, Italy* (pp. 27-34).

McBurney, P., & Luck, M. (2007). The agents are all busy doing stuff. *IEEE Intelligent Systems, 22*(4), 6–7. doi:10.1109/MIS.2007.77

Munroe, S. (2006). Crossing the agent technologies chasm: Experiences and challenges in commercial applications of agents. *The Knowledge Engineering Review, 21*(4), 345–392. doi:10.1017/S0269888906001020

Murch, R., & Johnson, T. (1999). *Intelligent software agents*. NJ: Prentice Hall PTR.

Nimis, J., & Stockheim, T. (2004). The Agent. Enterprise multi-multi-agent system. *Special track on agent technology in business applications (ATeBa 04) at multi-conference on business information systems (MKWI 2004).*

Nwana, H. (1996). Software agents: An overview. [Retrieved from http://agents.umbc.edu/introduction/ao/]. *The Knowledge Engineering Review, 11*(3), 1–40. doi:10.1017/S026988890000789X

O'Brien, P. D., & Wiegand, M. E. (1998). Agent based process management: Applying intelligent agents to workflow. *The Knowledge Engineering Review, 13*(2), 161–174. doi:10.1017/S0269888998002070

Odell, J., Parunak, H. V. D., & Bauer, B. (2000). Extending UML for agents. In *Proceedings of the agent-oriented information systems workshop at the 17th national conference on artificial intelligence* (pp. 3-17).

Omrichi, A. (2001). SODA: Societies and infrastructure in the analysis and design of agent-based systems. In *Proceedings of the first international workshop of agent oriented software engineering (AOSE-2000)* (LNCS 1957, pp. 185-194).

Padgham, L., & Winikoff, M. (2002). Prometheus: A methodology for developing intelligent agents. In *Proceedings of the third international workshop on agent oriented software engineering at AAMAS 2002, Bologna, Italy.*

Padgham, L., & Winikoff, M. (2004). *Developing intelligent agent systems. A practical guide.* Chichester: John Wiley & Sons.

Pang, G. (2000). *Implementation of an agent-based business process* [Diploma thesis]. Institut für Informatik der Universität Zürich.

Rabaey, M., Vandijck, E., & Tromp, H. (2003). Business intelligent agents for enterprise application integration: The link between business process management and Web services. In *Proceedings of the 16th international conference on software & systems engineering and their applications, Paris, December 2-4, 2003.*

Reichert, M., et al. (2005). Adaptive process management with ADEPT2. In *Proceedings of the 21st international conference on data engineering (ICDE 2005).*

Reichert, M., Bauer, T., & Dadam, P. (1999). Enterprise-wide and cross-enterprise workflow management: Challenges and research issues for adaptive workflows. In *Proceedings of the Informatik'99 workshop: Enterprise-wide and cross-enterprise workflow management: concepts, systems, applications, Paderborn, Germany, 1999.*

Russell, S., & Norvig, P. (2003). *Artificial intelligence. A modern approach* (2nd ed.). NJ: Prentice Hall.

Satapathy, G., Kumara, S. R. T., & Moore, L. M. (1998). Distributed intelligent agents for logistics (DIAL). *Expert Systems with Applications, 14*(4), 409–424. doi:10.1016/S0957-4174(98)00001-3

Smith, H. (2003). *The third wave of business process management.* CSC Europe.

Stockheim, T., et al. (2004). How to build a multi-multi-agent system: The Agent.Enterprise approach. In *Proceedings of the 6th international conference on enterprise information systems (ICEIS 2004)* (pp.1-8).

Sturm, A., & Shehory, O. (2002). Towards industrially applicable modelling technique for agent-based systems. In *Proceedings of the first international joint conference on autonomous agents and multiagent systems (ADMAS 2002), Bologna, Italy* (pp. 39-40). ACM Press.

Trammel, K. (1996). Workflow without fear. *Byte, April 1996.*

Tveit, A. (2001). A survey of agent-oriented software engineering. In *Proceedings of the first NTNU computer science graduate student conference, Norwegian University of Science and Technology, May 2001.* Retrieved from http://amundtveit.info/publications/2001/aose.pdf

Ubayashi, N., & Tamai, T. (2001). Separation of concerns in mobile agent applications. In *Proceedings of the 3rd international conference Reflection 2001* (LNCS 2192, pp. 89-109).

Varga, L. Z., Jennings, N. R., & Cockburn, D. (1994). Integrating intelligent systems into a cooperating community for electricity distribution management. *International Journal of Expert Systems with Applications*, *7*(4), 563–579. doi:10.1016/0957-4174(94)90080-9

Wagner, G. (2001). Agent-oriented analysis and design of organizational information systems. In J. Barzdins & A. Caplinskas (Eds.), *Databases and information systems* (pp. 111-124). Kluwer Academic Publishers.

Wagner, G. (2002). A UML profile for external AOR models. In *Proceedings of the international workshop on agent-oriented software engineering (AOSE-2002), held at Autonomous agents & multi-agent systems (AAMAS 2002), Palazzo, Re Enzo, Bologna, Italy, July 15, 2002* (LNAI 2585).

Wagner, G. (2003). The agent-object-relationship metamodel: Towards a unified view of state and behaviour. [Retrieved from http://www.informatik.tu-cottbus.de/~gwagner/AORML/AOR.pdf]. *Information Systems*, *28*(5), 475–504. doi:10.1016/S0306-4379(02)00027-3

Weiss, G. (1995). Adaptation and learning in multi-agent systems: Some remarks and a bibliography. *Proceedings of the IJCAI'95 workshop on adaptation and learning in multi-agent systems* (LNAI 1042, 1-22).

Weiss, G. (Ed.). (2000). *Multiagent systems. A modern approach to distributed artificial intelligence*. Massachusetts: The MIT Press.

Wooldridge, M. (1999). *Intelligent agents* (pp. 1-51). The MIT Press. Retrieved from http://www.csc.liv.ac.uk/~mjw/pubs/mas99.pdf

Wooldridge, M. (2002). *An introduction to multi agent systems*. Chichester, UK: John Wiley & Sons. Retrieved from http://www.csc.liv.ac.uk/~mjw/pubs/imas/

Wooldridge, M., & Jennings, N. (1995). Intelligent agents: Theory and practice. *The Knowledge Engineering Review*, *10*(2), 1–46. doi:10.1017/S0269888900008122

Wooldridge, M., Jennings, N., & Kinny, D. (2000). The Gaia methodology for agent-oriented analysis and design. *Journal of Autonomous Agents and Multi-Agent Systems*, *3*(3), 285–312. doi:10.1023/A:1010071910869

Yuhong, Y., Zakaria, M., & Weiming, S. (2001). Integration of workflow and agent technology for business process management. *The sixth international conference on CSCW in design, July 12-14, 2001, London, Ontario, Canada* (pp. 420-426).

Zeng, Z., Meng, B., & Zeng, Y. (2005). An intelligent agent-based system in Internet commerce. *Proceedings of the fourth international conference on machine learning and cybernetics, Guangzhou, China, August 2005*, 18-21.

Zhengping, L., Low, M. Y. H., & Kumar, A. A. (2003). A framework for multi-agent system-based dynamic supply chain coordination. In *Proceedings of the workshop at the second international joint conference of autonomous agents and multiagent systems (AAMAS 2003).*

Zhong, N., Liu, J., & Yao, Y. (Eds.). (2003). *Web intelligence*. Berlin: Springer.

ADDITIONAL READING

Agent Oriented Software Group. (n.d.). Retrieved from http://www.agent-software.com/

Agentis Software. (n.d.). Retrieved from http://www.agentissoftware.com/

Alesso, H. P., & Smith, C. F. (2002). *The intelligent wireless Web*. Addison-Wesley.

Ankolekar, A., et al. (2001). DAML-S: Semantic markup for Web services. In I.F. Cruz et al. (Eds.), *Proceedings of the first semantic Web working symposium (SWWS'01), Stanford, July 2001* (pp. 411-430).

Ankolekar, A., et al. (2002). DAML-S: Web service description for the semantic Web. In *Proceedings of the first international semantic Web conference (ISWC), June 2002* (pp. 348-363).

Belecheanu, R. A., et al. (2006). Commercial applications of agents: Lessons, experiences and challenges. *Proceedings of the 5th international conference on autonomous agents and multiagent systems (AAMAS 06)* (pp. 1549-1555). ACM Press.

Berners-Lee, T., Hendler, J., & Lassila, O. (2001). The semantic Web. *Scientific American*, (May): 35–43.

Chang, J. F. (2006). *Business process management systems*. Auerbach Publications.

Christensen, E., et al. (2001). Web services description language (WSDL) 1.1. Retrieved from http://www.w3.org/TR/2001/NOTE-wsdl-20010315

Cyganiak, R., et al. (2008). Exposing large data sets with semantic sitemaps. In *Proceedings of the 5th European semantic Web conference* (LNCS 5021, 690-704).

Dean, J., & Ghemawat, S. (2004). MapReduce: Simplified data processing on large clusters. In *Proceedings of the 6th symposium on operating system design and implementation (OSDI 04)* (pp. 137-150). Usenix Association.

Dumas, M., et al. (2001). Towards a semantic framework for service description. In *Proceedings of the IFIP conference on database semantics, Hong Kong, April 2001*. Kluwer Academic Publishers.

Finkelstein, C. (2005). Business process management languages, part 1: BPEL. Retrieved from http://www.information-management.com/issues/20050201/1018124-1.html

Genesereth, M., et al. (n.d.). Knowledge interchange format version 3.0 reference manual. Retrieved from http://logic.stanford.edu/kif/Hypertext/kif-manual.html

Gerber, A., Vierke, G., & Zinnikus, I. (2000). Generic modeling of multi-agent solutions for transportation domains. In I.J. Timm et al. (Eds.), *Proceedings of the ECAI 2000 workshop 13 on agent technologies and their application scenarios in logistics* (pp. 29-33).

Gillot, J.-N. (2008). *The complete guide to business process management*. BookSurge Publishing.

Heflin, J., & Hendler, J. (2000). Dynamic ontologies on the Web. In *Proceedings of the 17th national conference on artificial intelligence (AAAI 2000)* (pp. 443-449). Cambridge: MIT Press.

Hendler, J. (2006). Introduction to the special issue: AI, agents, and the Web. *IEEE Intelligent Systems*, *21*(1), 11. doi:10.1109/MIS.2006.11

Hendler, J., & McGuinness, D. L. (2001). Darpa agent markup language. *IEEE Intelligent Systems*, *15*(6), 72–73.

Henesey, L. E. (2003). More than just piers: A multi-agent systems on defining organization in a seaport terminal management system. In *Proceedings of the 47th annual conference of the International Society for the Systems Sciences, Crete, Greece, 2003*.

Holmes, T., et al. (2008). Modeling human aspects of business processes – a view-based, model-driven approach. *Proceedings of the 4th European conference on model driven architecture – foundations and applications (ECMDA-FA 2008), Berlin, Germany, June 9-13, 2008* (pp. 246-261). Springer. Retrieved from http://research.taid.holmes.at/publications/conf/ecmdafa/2008/human_vbm.pdf

Holmes, T., Vasko, M., & Dustdar, S. (2008). VieBOP: Extending BPEL Engines with BPEL-4People. In *Proceedings of the 16th Euromicro international conference on parallel, distributed and network-based processing 2008* (pp. 547-555). Retrieved from http://research.taid.holmes.at/publications/conf/pdp/2008/VieBOP.pdf

Horrocks, I. (2002). DAML+OIL: A reasonable Web ontology language. In *Proceedings of the eighth conference on extending database technology (EDBT'02), March 2002.*

Hower, C. Z. (2005). Mobile agents – Software on the move. Retrieved from http://www.codeproject.com/KB/architecture/MobileAgents.aspx

Jeston, J., & Nelis, J. (2006). *Business process management: Practical guidelines to successful implementations*. Butterworth-Heinemann.

Lind, J. (2001). *Iterative software engineering for multi-agent systems: The MASSIVE method* (LNCS/LNAI 1997).

Liu, J., et al. (Eds.). (2001). *Agent engineering*. World Scientific.

Martin, D., Cheyer, A., & Moran, D. (1999). The open agent architecture: A framework for building distributed software systems. *Applied Artificial Intelligence*, *13*(1-2), 92–128.

Matlis, J. (2005). QuickStudy: Business process execution language (BPEL). Retrieved from http://www.computerworld.com/action/article.do?command=viewArticleBasic&articleId=102580&pageNumber=1

McIlraith, S. A., Son, T. C., & Zeng, H. (2001). Semantic Web services. *IEEE Intelligent Systems*, *16*(2), 46–53. doi:10.1109/5254.920599

Mika, P., & Tummarello, G. (2008). Web semantics in the clouds. *IEEE Intelligent Systems*, *23*(5), 82–87. doi:10.1109/MIS.2008.94

Munroe, S. (2006). Crossing the agent technology chasm: Experiences and challenges in commercial applications of agents. *The Knowledge Engineering Review*, *21*(4), 345–392. doi:10.1017/S0269888906001020

Noy, N. F., & Klein, M. C. A. (2004). Ontology evolution: Not the same as schema evolution. *Knowledge and Information Systems*, *6*(4), 428–440. doi:10.1007/s10115-003-0137-2

Object Management Group. (2008). Business process modeling notation, V1.1. Retrieved from http://www.omg.org/docs/formal/08-01-17.pdf

Oracle Corporation. (2004). Business process management in the finance sector. Retrieved from: http://www.oracle.com/industries/financial_services/BPM_WP_final.pdf

Payne, T. R. (2008). Web services from an agent perspective. *IEEE Intelligent Systems*, *23*(2), 12–14. doi:10.1109/MIS.2008.37

Perugini, D., et al. (2003). Agents in logistics planning – Experiences with the coalition agents experiment project. In *Proceedings of workshop at the second international joint conference on autonomous agents and multiagent systems (AAMAS 2003), Melbourne, Australia, July 2003.*

Roychowdhury, P., & Dasgupta, D. (2008). Take advantage of Web 2.0 for next-generation BPM 2.0. Retrieved from http://www.ibm.com/developerworks/webservices/library/ws-web2bpm2/index.html?ca=drs

Russell, N., & van der Aalst, W. M. P. (2007). Evaluation of the BPEL4People and WS-HumanTask extensions to WS-BPEL 2.0 using the workflow resource patterns. BPM Center report BPM-07-11, BPMcenter.org. Retrieved from http://is.tm.tue.nl/staff/wvdaalst/BPMcenter/reports/2007/BPM-07-10.pdf

SAP AG & IBM Corporation. (2005). WS-BPEL extension for people – BPEL4People. Retrieved from https://www.sdn.sap.com/irj/servlet/prt/portal/prtroot/docs/library/uuid/cfab6fdd-0501-0010-bc82-f5c2414080ed

Schoder, D., & Eymann, T. (2000). Technical opinions: The real challenges of mobile agents. *Communications of the ACM, 42*(6), 111–112. doi:10.1145/336460.336488

Sebastian, H.-J., & Nüßer, G. H. (2000). Introduction to Minitrack: Intelligent systems in traffic and transportation. In *Proceedings of the 33rd Hawaii international conference on systems science* (pp. 1-3).

Sensoy, M., & Yolum, P. (2008). A cooperation-based approach for evolution of service ontologies. *Proceedings of the 7th international conference on autonomous agents and multiagent systems (AAMAS 08)* (pp. 837-844). International Foundation for Multiagent Systems.

Skonnard, A. (n.d.). WCF and WF services in the. NET framework 4.0 and Dublin. Retrieved from http://msdn.microsoft.com/en-us/magazine/2009.01.net40.aspx

Smith, H., & Fingar, P. (2003). *Business process management: The third wave*. Meghan-Kiffer Press.

Tamma, V., & Payne, T. R. (2008). Is a semantic Web agent a knowledge-savvy agent? *IEEE Intelligent Systems, 23*(4), 82–85. doi:10.1109/MIS.2008.69

TechTarget. (2008). Business process execution language (BPEL) tutorial. Retrieved from http://searchsoa.techtarget.com/generic/0,295582,sid26_gci1330911,00.html

Trastour, D., Bartolini, C., & Gonzalez-Castillo, J. (2001). A semantic Web approach to service description for matchmaking services. In *Proceedings of the international semantic Web working symposium (SWWS)*.

Ye, Y., Liu, J., & Moukas, A. (2001). Agents in electronic commerce. *Electronic Commerce Research Journal, special issue on intelligent agents in electronic commerce*.

KEY TERMS AND DEFINITIONS

Agent-Based BPM System: An agent-based BPM system manages business processes through collaboration of intelligent agents.

Business Process Management: Business process management is the concept of shepherding work items through a multi-step process. The items are identified and tracked as they move through each step, with either specified people or applications processing the information.

Business Process: A business process is a collection of interrelated tasks, which accomplish a particular goal.

Holon (Holonic Agent): A holon is composed from agents working together in order to reach a common goal and interacting with its environment similarly as a single agent.

Intelligent Software Agent: An intelligent software agent is an entity which communicates correctly in an agent communication language.

Mobile Agent: A mobile agent is a composition of computer software and data which is able to migrate (move) from one computer to another autonomously and continue its execution on the destination computer.

Multiagent System: A multiagent system is composed of multiple interacting intelligent software agents.

Multi-Multi-Agent System: A multi-multi-agent system is composed from heterogeneous individual multiagent systems.

Chapter 8
Virtual Heterarchy: Information Governance Model

Malgorzata Pankowska
University of Economics, Katowice, Poland

Henryk Sroka
University of Economics, Katowice, Poland

ABSTRACT

The rapid development of information communication technology (ICT) encourages companies to compete. However, those competitive development goals should enable people to satisfy their own needs and enjoy a better quality of work and life without compromising the quality of life of other people and future generations. Corporate governance models are needed to concentrate on changes of existing rules, customs, practices and rights as the subject matter of governance to be influenced. Governance models must recognize the limitations of the overburdened state and the consequent need to take advantage of existing institutions and structures that promote sustainability. An increasing number of companies are moving into new forms of competition which can be described as information-based competition, knowledge-based competition, technology–based competition and ICT relationship-based competition. However, unlimited supply of information from Internet and other sources, easiness to register and transfer the information, reduced prices of ICT devices result in increase of information processing and its overload. Therefore, information governance model proposed in the chapter seems to be a pattern to deal with information in contemporary common organizations i.e. virtual heterarchical organizations where access to information is democratically permitted. The proposed model is to be an answer to ensure sustainable governance of information i.e. balance, stability and progress of information processing.

DOI: 10.4018/978-1-60566-890-1.ch008

INTRODUCTION – BUSINESS COMPUTING ENVIRONMENT

The information economy challenges business in many ways, information technologies and globalization lead to blurring the organizational boundaries. The creation of value for companies becomes more and more dependent on information assets. Business organizations are not interested in maximizing profits or minimizing costs, but pursue competitive advantage on the basis of innovation in products, processes, governance and business relationships' development.

Frequent exchange of messages in electronic communication networks supports shared mutual understanding – a collective way of organizing relevant knowledge. Having shared understanding enables people to anticipate and predict the behavior of their members, so that work can move forward without constant monitoring and consultation (Hinds & Weisband, 2003). Shared understanding can contribute to performance by increasing the satisfaction and motivation of business network members. Predictability, ability to implement agreed decision and motivation results from shared understanding and contributes to improved further performance. In the absence of mutual understanding negotiation, consulting and business exchange are difficult and time-consuming.

Nowadays, pervasive computing environment enables:

- Distributed, shared performance based on mutual understanding.
- Flexible process-oriented configuration and acting on the global scene.
- Autonomy of partners within organizational business networks.

Pluralistic, flexible, decentralized interorganizational networks are called heterarchies. The vision of heterarchy is an organizational form structuring its operation according to the requirements of the innovative processes, favoring cooperation. In heterarchies, organization members are connected together without excluding anybody from participation in decision-making. In agile heterarchical business networks coordination and cooperation patterns are developed according to the situational requirements. Operational compatibilities regarding partners' capabilities, the profitability of the relationships, and the trust and fair dealing are important factors for cooperation. Heterarchies are negotiable networks. Their coordination is reached through mutual understanding, mutual adjustment and participative management between organizational members. Heterarchies must combine autonomy with business integration to create flexible organizational configuration. Decision power in heterarchies is tied to situational expertise of organizational members. Reihlen argues that decision competences have to be negotiated according to democratic principles (1996).

In heterarchies, governing the innovative processes must be fulfilled by the people working together in the value creation processes. Heterarchies internally tolerate or even appreciate conflicts as a source of motivation to the partners' more intensive work. Heterarchies do not demand the acceptance of the other value system, but they require tolerance for others (Von Goldammer et al. 2003). Heterarchies are hidden in a broad range of distributed intelligence institutions, in collaborative structures, lateral coordination organizations which move from economies of scale and speed to economies of network externalities. An example of a heterarchical form of government is the democratic one, in which all votes count equally in representation of the whole governed body of partners.

Well known around the world Information Systems Audit and Control Association (ISACA, www.isaca.org/) is a heterarchical network of auditors from different countries. The network covers legally and economically autonomous partners and is controlled by committee structures. ISACA got its start in 1967, today, ISACA's membership – more than 86,000 strong worldwide – is characterized by its diversity. Members live and work in more than 160 countries and cover a variety of professional IT-related positions i.e. IS auditor, consultant, educator, IS security professional, regulator, chief information officer and internal auditor. They work in nearly all industry categories, including financial and banking, public accounting, government and the public sector, utilities and manufacturing. An illustrious ISACA's strength is its chapter network.

ISACA has more than 175 chapters established in over 70 countries worldwide and those chapters provide members education, resource sharing, advocacy, professional networking. Since its inception, ISACA has become a pace-setting global organization for information governance, control security and audit professionals. Its IS auditing and IS control standards are followed by practitioners worldwide. The evolution of large international audit firms i.e. Pricewaterhouse Coopers, Deloitte Touche Tohmatsu, Ernst &Young, KPMG was driven by the emergence of multinational audit standards, which are needed for auditing cross-national operations and specific legal regulations. Clients of audit firms often have subsidiaries in different countries around the world with different cultural, social and legal norms and rules e.g. accounting and tax laws. They need audit and consulting services with respect to their subsidiaries abroad (Lenz & James, 2007).

According to Stark, heterarchy represents a new mode of organizing that is neither market nor hierarchy, hierarchies involve relations of dependence and markets involve relations of independence, heterarchies demand relations of interdependence (2001). Collective intelligence in heterarchy emerges through the interaction of the partners - people consider for whom they are working. Success there depends on learning by mutual monitoring, but the question is who and where is the governor. Some people believe in self-organizing and self-controlling, but others assume that customer is the best governor. According to Rocha, a heterarchy is a self-organizing autopoietic system, which is not established structurally and where the centers of action are emergent in actions themselves (2001).

Within the heterarchical network the distributed authority is deliberated. Heterarchies demand distributed information systems (DISs) as collections of electronic networked information resources (e.g. the Internet, the World Wide Web, corporate intranets, databases, library information retrieval systems) in some kind of interaction with communities of users. Four characteristics of information on the Internet are critical to the discovery of new business hierarchy opportunities:

- All information on the Internet is digital.
- Information is costly to produce, but cheap to reproduce.
- Information needs to be sampled for people to fully appreciate its value and benefits.
- People that are using information benefit from intermediaries (i.e. human beings as well as software agents) (Hamilton, 2000).

The characteristics of information mean that digital products must be priced according to how much people will pay for them, rather than their cost of production. Since reproducing information products is cheap, they can be made available to people and companies at very low marginal costs, creating circumstances for information overload. Socioeconomic heterarchies are virtual when they are producing work deliverables across different locations, at different work cycles and across culture. They are also characterized by the temporality, intensity, reciprocity and multiplexity of the linkages in their networks (Powell, 1990). In this chapter, virtuality is considered as an ability of an organization to consistently obtain and coordinate critical competences through the design of value-adding business processes and governance mechanisms involving external and internal elements to deliver superior value to the community. Generally, a virtual organization can be hierarchical, heterarchical or federal. It is a set of individuals or institutions with some common purposes or interests and who need to share their information resources (on the Internet) to pursue their objectives. Lewis and Weigert say that the fundamentals (pillars) of virtual organizations comprise: 1) standardizing interactions, 2) standardizing meta-data 3) treating knowledge separately from the individual 4) abstracting information from operations (Lewis & Weigert, 1985).

Nowadays, an increasing number of governments has come to perceive decentralization and heterarchical organizations as more efficient than centrally delivered services and hierarchical pyramids (Mette Kjaer, 2004). When decision-making is concentrated at the level of central authority, it is believed to be too remote from the customer at the bottom and lacking information of real problems and preferences at the lowest level. When the functions and power are transferred to lower levels, decisions can be made that are more responsive to the needs of the local community. Decentralized and distributed decision–making requires intensive networking relations. Networks encourage information integration, coordination and resource sharing (Helaakoski et al, 2007).

Contemporary companies should be able to form the business linkages quickly and dissolve them rapidly. Agility is the ability of an organization to rapidly respond to changes in an uncertain and changing business environment. Dynamically reconfigurable virtual heterarchies can implement this more easily than hierarchical organizations. Business partners within heterarchical networks concentrate on their core competences and by networking complement their non-core activities. This specialization may result in improved efficiency and effectiveness (Lindstrom & Jeffries, 2003, Desouza, 2007).

Interoperability among business enterprise information systems is the key to achieving business agility, especially for partners operating within a collaborative heterarchical value creation network, as it largely determines their capacity to respond swiftly to changing market conditions and new collaboration opportunities. Schelp and Winter argue that agility is not aimed at creating change, but as a proactive means to support change (2007). Agility is the successful exploration of competitive bases (speed, flexibility, innovation, proactivity, quality and profitability) through the integration of reconfigurable resources and best practices in an information-rich environment to provide customer-driven products and services in a fast changing market environment (Schelp & Winter, 2007, p. 135). Agility gives enterprises the ability to sense and respond rapidly to unpredictable events and to take advantage of changes as opportunities. This means that the supporting information systems and their interoperability must be equally agile in order to achieve a close alignment between business and information systems. Governance is being created to ensure the agility of business organizations and management of uncertainty. Governance itself is a contestable concept, a hybrid in which logics of democracy and of managerial process is variably intertwined (Power, 2007).

BACKGROUND - GOVERNANCE VS. MANAGEMENT

Distinction has to be made between the governance of networks and management within them. Perri et al. explain that governance of a network is the steering from an external standpoint. That activity is designed to exercise control, regulation, inducement, incentives, or persuasive influence over the whole network (Perri et al., 2006). According to the authors, the purpose of such governance is to influence the structure of the network, the nature and range of ties between its members, its capacity for collective action, its openness to new members, its commitment to existing functions, or its ability or willingness to take new tasks. In contradiction to governance, the management within a network is an activity performed by individuals who are themselves members of the network. The objective of such management is to exercise control.

Jessop argues that literature on governance rejects the rigid polarization between the anarchy of the market and the hierarchy of imperative coordination in favor of the concept of heterarchy (1999). According to him, the key to success is to continue commitment to dialogue to generate and exchange more information, to reduce the bounded rationality.

Riemer and Klein assume that network governance comprises formal rules and norms as well as informal aspects such as culture and identity (2006). Institutional arrangements and governance structures are needed to deal with the complexity of the network relations and to ensure the implementation strategies. The structural arrangements have to reflect the network strategy and the constraints resulting from the fact that the network participants are autonomous organizations. They have to combine flexible institutional arrangements, limited power and commitment of the participants. Therefore, the basic questions concerning business network governance should be as follows: What formal rules and policies should be established to guide members in their network interactions? Who is in charge of network governance?

Governance mechanisms must ensure a framework in which business network partners can reach agreement over the problems mentioned above. Jessop noticed that, differently from the institutional approach, the mechanism of organizing governance of heterarchy is interactions, relations and communication (1999). That covers negotiations among different network members in order to find common aims, strategies and compromises.

In virtual heterarchy development process, there is a need to accept the assumption of Luhmann's system theory that an organization is not composed of individuals but rather of information flows. In virtual heterarchies communication i.e. message exchanges are based on agreements and partners comply with the negotiated agreements because they consider maximization of their own returns. So, the governance is a process of permanent negotiation, implementation and evaluation of decision-making consequences. Bruszt argues that heterarchy is a specific type of democracy that represents diverse associations of heterogeneous interests, prevents any of them from dominating and bases the making of decisions on compromises among business partners (2002). Saxton adds that in a heterarchy, similarly to TQM approach all members should equally participate in problem solving (2004).

Rosenau says that governance is not synonymous with government (2004). Both refer to purposive behavior, to goal-oriented social activities, to a system of rules, but government suggests activities that are stimulated by formal authority, whereas governance refers to activities realized by sharing goals that may or may not derive from legal and formally prescribed responsibilities. It can be added that the regulatory mechanisms required for effective governance need not to be centralized in order to maintain coordination among them.

There is a vital need for control and collaboration in heterarchical business networks. A control approach helps reduce human limitations through vigilance and discipline, while a collaborative approach develops individuals' aspiration via cooperation and empowerment (Sundaramurthy & Lewis, 2003). Virtual heterarchy members learn by monitoring and controlling their work as well as the communication process. Cognitive conflicts facilitate cooperation by aiming criticisms of task performance, not individuals. Multichannel communication should support conflict understandability. The explicit specification of responsibilities, clear task classification may reduce task complexity and aid systematic information processes.

To sum up, in heterarchical organizations governance is based on more than one decision-making centre and on shared leadership. Within the heterarchical network there is no sovereign authority, but network as a whole is having considerable autonomy.

GOVERNANCE ISSUES AND CONTROVERSIES

Governance structures are used in many disciplines. Naturally the topic suits to political science, where government of the citizens and organizations is a central subject. Economics is a natural place to study governance structures, and here it is very much about economizing exchange transactions. The most diverse and recent application area is management, including information systems management, where governance structures can be applied in many ways. On the contrary to the tradition in economics, in management governance structures are not just used for economizing purposes, but exchange relationships can be seen as tools for many organizational goals. The term "governance" derives from Latin and suggests the notion of steering. It refers to the use of institutions, structures of authority and even collaboration, to allocate resources and coordinate or control activities in societies or economies (Romero et al, 2007).

Corporate Governance

In corporate governance research the overwhelming emphasis has been on the efficiency of the various mechanisms available to protect shareholders from the self-interested executives (Daily et al., 2003). The dominant theoretical perspective applied in corporate governance studies is agency theory. Corporate governance is the system and processes put in place to direct and control an organization in order to increase performance and achieve sustainable shareholder value. It concerns the effectiveness of management structures, including the roles of directors, the sufficiency and reliability of corporate reporting, and the effectiveness of risk management systems (Fahy et al. 2005). The Sarbanes-Oxley Act (SOX) is the basis of corporate governance and has reset the responsibilities of organizational senior management and Boards of Directors, and the expectations of investors, regulators and external stakeholders. Compliance to regulatory issues is now one of the most dominant business challenges that corporations face today. SOX supports a simple premise: good corporate governance and ethical business practices are no longer optional (Bloem et.al., 2006). Chatterjee and Harrison assume that corporate governance deals with all the factors and forces, both internal and external to the organization, that work to harmonize the interests of managers and shareholders (2005). Effective corporate governance requires that organizations not only have the ability to monitor and measure historic performance on a monthly basis but they are also able to meet the more forward-looking direction setting needs of the firm. The Anglo-Saxon governance solution to the relational issues generally emphasizes well-specified contractual terms. Other governance systems, however, such as the Japanese, have historically relied on long-standing relationships between individuals in the respective companies and unwritten expectations of reciprocal actions (Kaen, 2003). Each form of governance, whether it is corporate, financial, or IT has a direct relationship of business-economic performance.

Information Technology Governance

The development of information technology (IT) governance and recognition of the information economy-driven convergence between business management and IT management are essential for executives and managers at all levels in organizations of all sizes to understand how decisions about information technology in business organizations should be made and monitored and how information security risks ought to be best dealt with (Calder & Watkins, 2006).

IT governance arrangement refers to the patterns of authority for the key IT activities in business organization, which include IT infrastructure management and IT use and project management. IT governance is specifying the framework for decision rights and accountabilities to encourage desirable behavior in the use of IT (Burton et al. 2008). According to Van Grembergen IT governance is the organizational capacity exercised by executive management and IT management to control the formulation and implementation of IT strategy and to ensure the fusion of business and IT (Van Grembergen, 2004). Contrary to the governance, IT management is focused on the internal effective supply of IT services and products and the management of present IT operations. There are two important components of IT governance: strategic alignment and the achievement of business value of IT (Van Grembergen, 2004, Strategie…2006, Zarys…2007).

The SOX is viewed as a turning point in the governance of organizations, especially in respect to the direct involvement of management and the use of information technology. For two reasons IT governance seems to be important:

- Business and IT have become extremely interwoven.
- Good IT governance practices are lacking in many companies (Bloem et al., 2006).

IT Governance Institute defines IT governance as a set of responsibilities and practices exercised by the board and executive management with the goal of providing strategic direction, ensuring that objectives are achieved, ascertaining that risks are managed appropriately and verifying that the enterprise's resources are used responsibly (Board .., 2003). IT Governance Institute recognizes the following works as essential for the information governance model in the virtual heterarchical organization:

- Balanced Scorecard as the help to translate vision and strategy into a coherent set of performance measures.
- Board Briefing on IT Governance as a document covering high-level guidance to Boards of Directors.
- Capability Maturity Model (CMM) as the model providing the principles and practices to ensure IT project maturity.
- COSO Enterprise Risk Management Framework as the conceptual framework providing integrated principles and implementation guidance to develop risk management processes.
- European Framework for Quality Management (EFQM).
- Malcolm Baldridge National Quality Framework as the framework covering leadership, strategic planning, customer and market focus, information and analysis, human resources focus, process management and business.
- OECD principles of corporate governance.
- Technical Reference Model as common vocabulary of IT terms.

In contemporary business organizations, information technology is fully incorporated into business processes and a lot of money is devoted for IT investment year by year. IT implemented solutions are more and more user-friendly and human-oriented, provided directly for the usage by employees, therefore, strong control as well as empowerment of the end user as well as a supervision of their behavior is needed.

Information Governance

Information governance is the ensuring that corporate information is where and when it is needed, and available only to those who have an authorized access. Information governance should be also about protecting information from destruction, degradation, manipulation and exploitation by an opponent. It is referred to ensuring information availability, integrity, authentication, confidentiality and non-repudiation.

Business information should be protected similarly as the other value-creating assets. The value of information is usually found to be inversely correlated with quantity and it itself cannot be guaranteed, but there are certain characteristics of information that must be present, if the information is to be useful. Information should be accurate, timely, complete, verifiable and consistent. Although, assuming that contemporary business organizations have got unlimited access to Internet information, for free or paying for it, however, the information utility measured by the relative satisfaction from its usage seems to be decreasing. Perhaps the diminishing marginal utility of information can be observed and known as information uselessness, overload or discomfort of usage. An increasing number of computers and input-output devices, and fax machines do not improve effectiveness and efficiency. The market becomes saturated and that is a normal case for products with unlimited supply.

Therefore, the particular tasks within information governance should cover:

- Information planning and information requirements specification.
- Information collecting.
- Information processing, transferring or disseminating.
- Information analysis to answer the decision-maker's questions.
- Producing the reports to answer the questions raised by decision-makers.
- Information security and integrity assurance.

The information systems of the past were inside the organization. Complex information could only be transmitted by means of costly personal contracts. Now, information systems are beginning to be extended beyond company boundaries and can thus establish close information ties with suppliers, distribution channels, and end users. The new economics of information is arising from universal connectivity. By redefining the way in which information can be transmitted, universal connectivity can have a significant impact on the economic structure and configuration of value-created systems, which are influenced by the economics of information.

RECOMMENDATION – MODEL OF INFORMATION GOVERNANCE

Ubiquitous computing plays a key role in the vision of the successful pervasive information environment. The governing principle for establishing a pervasive information environment is the access to one set of information anytime from anywhere through any device. Data integrity is critical, so the underlying data structures must be carefully conceived and implemented. One crucial issue is data format; incompatible data can prevent flexibility in the applications that access the data. The environment, in which data from heterogeneous and distributed sources can be readily combined and delivered, ought to be maintained. It requires the use of a certain information governance model to achieve compatibility between data sources and interoperability of hardware, software and information forms. The development of the information economy demands a complementary regulatory structure that allows greater commercial freedom for operators. Such changes are expected to stimulate increased investments in the information industry, induce innovations in terms of services and applications, lead directly to greater value being available to users. The ongoing evolution of the information economy depends upon the regulations across the following areas: accessibility, interconnectivity, interoperability, accountability, awareness of security, ethics, periodical reassessibility.

Information governance models refer to all the arrangements, by which power and authority are exercised involving formal and informal systems, public and private auspices, regulative and normative mechanisms. Governance should also comprise establishing policies, monitoring and reporting processes to ensure sustainability i.e. expectation of long-term results. In the context of information governance, governance structure is important, namely power relations arising from asymmetries of information, as well as information resources and capabilities that determine how information is distributed within the network and how activities are coordinated within the network and across firms.

Information governance can be defined as specifying decision rights and accountability framework to encourage desirable behavior in the use of information. Information governance covers structures and processes management that ensure that information really supports the organization's mission. The purpose information governance is to align information with the organization, maximize the benefits of information, use information resources responsibly and manage information risks, a structure of relationships and processes to direct and control the enterprise in order to achieve the enterprise's goals by adding value while balancing risk versus return over information processes. Information governance is the responsibility of the Board of Directors and executive management. It is an integral part of corporate governance and consists of the leadership and organizational structures and processes that ensure that the organization's information sustains and extends the organization's strategies and objectives. Information governance describes the distribution of decision-making rights and responsibilities among different stakeholders in the organization and the rules and procedures for making and monitoring decisions. Good information governance allows achieving a management paradox: simultaneously empowering and controlling. Information governance is critical to organizational learning and value network creation and it should cover answers to the following questions:

- For whom is information?
- In which interest is the information managed?
- Who should control the performance of information computing?
- Who should make the decision on information computing?
- Who is responsible and for what?
- Who has the rights to the information assets and profits?
- On what principles is the redistribution of the information profits based?

The information governance within heterarchical network is to be developed for coordination of the network. From a strategic perspective, the coordination of heterarchical network require some degree of centralization in order to ensure an efficient use of resources, rapid and agile decision-making and the mergence of a global vision driving the network. Therefore, the model proposed in this work for information governance is composed of four elements:

1. Information strategy.
2. Information architecture.
3. Interoperability.
4. Contracts and contractibility as a way to ensure reliability and agility of information systems of heterarchical networks (Figure 1).

The term "strategy" is derived from the Greek "strategia", meaning "the art of the general". A strategy is seen as something an organization needs or uses in order to win or establish its legitimacy in a world of rivalry (Coad, 2005). For Mintzberg

Figure 1. Information governance in heterarchical networks

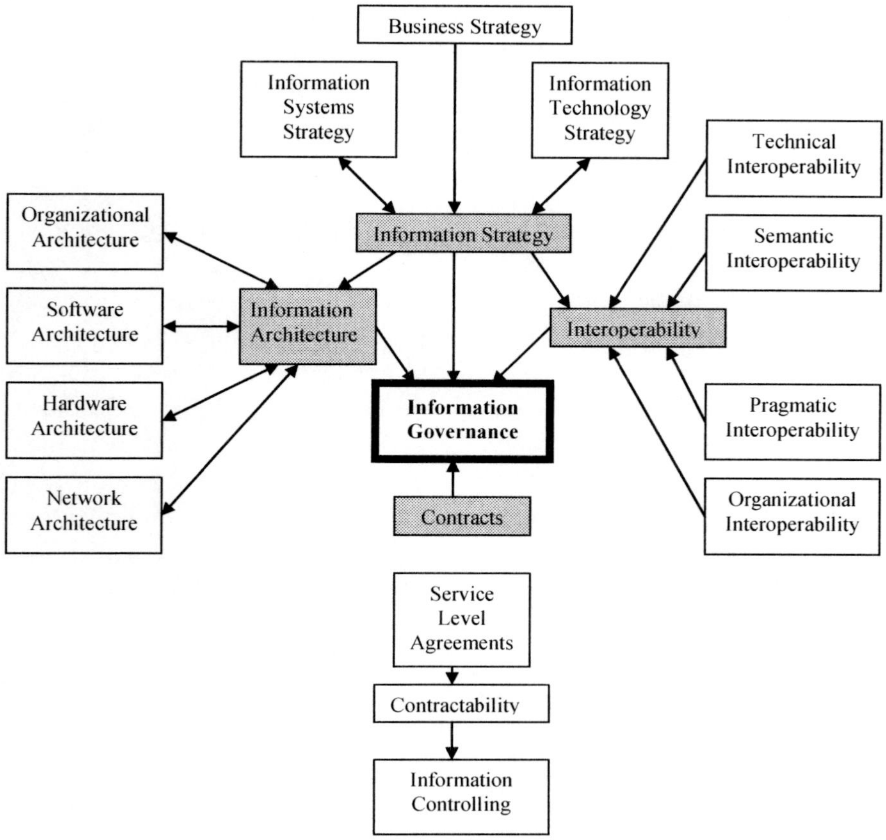

and Quinn, strategy refers to a plan, strategy can be a ploy, strategy is a pattern, a perspective and a position in the business environment (1991). Strategy formulation is a version of positional analysis, concerned with the status of an organization relative to competition and other aspects of its environment, such as customers, suppliers, investors, and the governments of the countries within which it operates. The term "collective strategy" is used by Astkey and Fombrun (1983) to describe the situation in which strategy formation is the result of a process of collaboration and negotiation between separate organizations acting in partnership.

Collective strategies have become increasingly popular because individual organizations do not always have the resources and competences needed to cope with increasingly complex environments. It may be more economically viable to obtain specific materials, skills, technologies, finance or access to markets by cooperating with other organizations rather than through individual acquisitions. The adoption of cooperative strategies requires reconstruction of governance and control approaches. Success in network partnership demands commitment, coordination, trust, the sharing of risks and information and participation and joint problem solving to reduce transaction and production costs. Strategy enables the organization to achieve long-term and sustainable competitive advantage in every business in which they participate.

The importance of strategy formulation for heterarchies development and their information governance was clarified in the analytical reports of projects funded within FP6 TP5 Food Quality and Safety for the knowledge development in such areas as genomics, medicine, information technologies, ethics, environmental, economic and social sciences (Food…, 2007). Generally, all the analyzed projects realized the common strategy named "From-fork-to-farm" and concerning development of rational habits in food consumption and food production to ensure human health and long life. Projects' stakeholders established virtual heterarchies covering project partners and outsiders for knowledge creation and dissemination, as it is in the following project cases:

1. GMO-COMPASS (www.gmo-compass.org) oriented towards creation of an Internet-based platform providing a venue for a broad and open discussion of genetically modified organisms (GMOs).
2. REPRO (www.repro-food.net) aimed at harnessing new techniques in bioprocesses and combining them with physical separation methods to extract useful products from food processing waste efficiently.
3. BIOPOP (www.biopop-eu.org) focused on the public debate surrounding genetically modified organisms (GMOs), biodiversity, cloning and ethics.
4. EADGENE (www.eadgene.info) as a Network of Excellence aimed to develop new or perfected therapeutics and vaccines, improved diagnostics and the breeding of farm animals for disease resistance.
5. EPIZONE (www.epizone-eu.net) aimed at improving research on preparedness, prevention, detection and control of epizootic diseases by collaboration of virtual institute partners, with clear rules and processes on knowledge creation and distribution.

A frequently used term, related to information strategy, is strategic information systems planning defined as the process of deciding on the objectives for organizational computing and identifying potential computer applications which the organization should implement (Smits et al., 1999). They view information strategy in a certain context, together with information technology strategy, information management strategy, management of change strategy, and human resources strategy. Here, information strategy is defined as a complex of implicit or explicit visions, goals, guidelines and plans with respect to the supply and the demand of formal information in an organization, sanctioned by management, intended to support the objectives of the organization in the long run, while being able to adjust to the environment. The linkages between information strategy and business strategy are presented in several ways: by looking at the attitudes of senior managers (as a part of the information strategy environment), by analyzing the information strategy process (with roles, methods and coordination), by analyzing the content of the strategy and by looking at how the effects are evaluated. One other important link is how previous strategy affects the actual environment, and how this again influences the strategy process and content. The information strategy process describes the way in which the information strategy is created and changed. The information strategy content describes the subject areas or issues for which the strategy is meant to provide solutions or directions. The main aspects of the content of the information strategy are scope, objectives, architectures, rules and plans.

The architecture can be divided into four parts: software (or applications), technical, network and organizational. The software architecture is sometimes equated to the information strategy and may indeed be the core of it. The technical architecture defines the hardware elements that support the information strategy, notably in the form of an infrastructure. The organizational architecture indicates the distribution of tasks and responsibilities for information technology and information systems. Business network architecture can be defined as a representation of a conceptual framework of components and their relationships at a point in time. The notion of architecture is used in a wide range of domains, from town planning to building and construction, and from computer hardware to information systems, each being characterised by the types of structures and systems being designed. The IEEE Standard 1471-2000 definition of architecture explains that the architecture is a fundamental organization of a system embodied in its components, their relationships to each other, and to the environment, and the principle guiding its design and evolution (Lankhorst, 2005). Business organization architecture is a coherent whole of principles, methods and models that are used in the design and realisation of an enterprise's organizational structures, business processes, information systems and infrastructure. Architecture is a process as well as a product. The product serves to guide managers in designing business processes and system developers in building applications in a way that is in line with business objectives and policies. The architecture process consists of the usual steps that take an initial idea through design and implementation phases to an operational system, and finally changing or replacing this system, closing the loop. Information architecture is a set of high-level models which complements the business plan in IT-related matters and serves as a tool for information system planning and a blueprint for information system plan implementation (Periasamy & Feeny, 1997, p.342). In the presented above model, information architecture covers logical information models, data and processes worked out in functions and data groups and possibly used applications. Brancheau and Wetherbe (1986) argue that an information architecture is explored as a fundamental building block underlying the development of effective information systems. An information architecture is a personnel-, organization-, and technology-independent profile of the major information categories used within an enterprise.

Business partners of heterarchical network can only work if they are able to communicate and work with other compatible information systems. This requirement is called interoperability and it can only be met if communication standards are applied. A standards-based technology platform allows partners to execute a traditional business function in a digitally enhanced way. In the context of information and communication systems compatibility is important, many different computer networks, operating systems, user interfaces, application systems have evolved in companies over a number of years. One of the major drawbacks of the heterogeneous legacy is the fact that there is no seamless integration of different data and applications. However, the common use of standards simplifies transactions carried out between business partners and eases the exchange of information between them. Using standards also has some disadvantages, such as the possible loss of uniqueness. But loss of uniqueness is not an inevitable result of using standards (Buxmann et al, 1999). Standards are important for information systems, e.g. SQL as a database language, standard software solutions as well as protocols such as TCP/IP or ATM, EDI standards for transfer of commercial documents. Communication protocol or natural languages set general rules for exchanging information regardless of the content to be transferred. Standard software solutions also define contents to be transferred. Furthermore, the use of a standard software solution determines rules for processing information e.g. the use of specific cost accounting systems.

Three basic forms of governance structure have emerged so far in the ICT industries. The first is the governance of compatibility standards by voluntary standards organization, the second is the explicit setting of standards for the international interoperability of telecommunication networks by intergovernmental organizations, and the third involves the emergence of coalitions of firms that sponsor standards. In the third case, the coalitions may represent the shared aims of virtually all producers to improve the market acceptance of new technologies or they may serve the interest of a group of firms aimed at strategic promotion of one standard over one or more alternatives (Steinmueller, 2007).

Standards increase the value and usability of governed information as well as enable interoperability, which (as the capability to ensure an effective collaboration in heterarchical networks) is necessary to mutually communicate information in order to exchange proposals, requests, results, and commitments. According to the Oxford Dictionary interoperable means "able to operate in conjunction". The word "interoperate" also implies that one system performs an operation on behalf of another system. From software engineering point of view, interoperability means that two cooperating systems can easily work together without a particular interfacing effort (Chen & Doumeingts, 2004). According to IEEE STD 610.12 Standard Glossary of Software Engineering Technology, published on May, 1990, interoperability is defined as the ability of two of more systems or components to exchange and use information (Hugoson et al, 2008). Interoperability requires standardization in five dimensions: technology, syntax, semantics, pragmatics and organizational. Technical interoperability concerns connectivity between the computational services, allowing messages to be transported from one application to another basing on technology standards for middleware, network protocols, security protocols and the like. Syntax interoperability means that the network organization has to agree on how to integrate heterogeneous applications based on the structure or language of the messages exchanged. Normally, commonly acceptable data structures are chosen to represent well-known constructs. Semantic interoperability means that the message content is understood in the same way by the senders and the receivers. This concerns both information representation and messaging sequences. Semantic interoperability constitutes agreements in extension to syntactic agreements on the meanings of the terms used for an information system to communicate with and understand the messages of another information system. For instance, consider the immense variety of components and parts in university didactic processes, for most of which many universities may have their own names and possibly different meanings. All these names must be standardized if the supply chain support is to be fully automated. Pragmatic interoperability captures the willingness of partners to perform the actions needed for the collaboration. This willingness to participate refers both to the capability of performing a requested action and to policies dictating whether it is preferable for the enterprise to allow that action to take place. Organizational interoperability concerns defining business goals, modeling business processes and bringing about the collaboration of administrations that wish to exchange information and may have different internal structures and processes. Interoperability is more than just the flow of information between agencies and the connection of information technology systems. It requires a collective mindset, an understanding of how each collaborating agency operates and the development of arrangements which effectively manage business processes that cut across organizational boundaries. Interoperability is not just a technical matter of connecting computer networks. It also embraces the sharing of information between networks and the redesign of business processes to deliver improved outcomes and efficiencies and to support the seamless government services.

Information governance can be defined as the institutional framework in which contracts are initiated, monitored, adapted and terminated. An exchange occurs between two organizations when information resources are transferred from one party to the other in return for resources controlled by the other party. The formulation of interorganizational exchanges has become of critical importance in today's business environment. Some scholars criticize the inadequacies of legal contracts as mechanisms for governing exchange, especially in the face of uncertainty and dependence. Other scholars argue that it is not the contracts per se but the social contexts in which they are embedded that determine their effectiveness. In heterarchical networks the contribution of the individual partners to the final products or services generated by the network may be impossible to distinguish. Every partner contributes to the final goal by concentrating on specific competences. The framework agreement is the strongest tool in the hands of the business partners. In heterarchical network, the principle of contracting allows partners to regulate their interactions in ways they deem best, thus leaving the least possible situation to chance. What heterarchical network partners can do is to reduce the margin of uncertainty as much as possible by signing carefully drawn framework agreements. A contract is a legally enforceable agreement in which two or more parties commit to certain obligations in return for certain rights. Contracts guarantee rights (protection) and impose obligations (demanding the requirements' fulfilment) concerning exchanged values i.e. knowledge, service, money, digital product (music, information, expert's report), material product (Power et al., 2006, Eggleston, 1996, Marcolin, 2006).

The contracting of information services has become an essential strategy for organizations in light of corporate downsizing and restructuring, volatile and competitive environments and rapid advances in information technology.

Interconnections on Internet or any other global network occur between many different types of networks at many different locations by many different firms (i.e. companies and users). There are four basic models of heterarchical interconnection agreements:

1. Main contractor model: all network partners are obliged to sign the contract with the main contractor mainly responsible for the network governance.
2. Process-oriented model: network partners sign contracts with one another as they are included in the value chain, they are responsible for the delivery of the whole value product, however, each of them should control their part.
3. Peer-to-peer model: Model adopted by many partners, if they are of approximately the same size, experience, technology and customer base. The network externalities are symmetric in the peer-to-peer bilateral agreement, direct connections are preferable, and the increase of indirect connections makes the indirect traffic susceptible to the reliability of the intermediary network. In customer-provider relations experience, technology and customer base and particularly the size of network are important, otherwise customers pay more for externalities. Experience and intensity of information exchanges are also critical since the parties entering the interconnection agreement must be able to trust each other.
4. The mixed model including various mixtures of the models mentioned above.

In heterarchical organization, all members have to agree upon the rules on how to allocate tasks in the value net that they create and consequently on how to share profits and losses, all for tax purposes in compliance with applicable regulations. As a general principle, partners regulate their relationships by agreements, but agreements cannot possibly cover each present and future tasks and interactions within heterarchical organization. They may be renewed or rewritten but not continuously – otherwise the stability of rules would be lost. Codes and law in force can be applied for what is not specifically provided for in the agreements. In the absence of a clear solution, each partner might be potentially subject to the law of every other particular business organization member which contributes to the same product or service and also to the law of every country in which products and services are provided.

Particularly in the IT sector, in its most basic form, a service level agreement (SLA) is a contract or agreement that formalizes a business relationship, a part of the relationship between two parties. Most often it takes the form of a negotiated contract made between an information service provider and an information service recipient and defines a price paid in exchange for an entitlement to a product to be delivered under certain terms, conditions and with certain financial guarantees. The roles most commonly given to SLAs can generally be grouped into six areas i.e. defining the roles and accountability as well as responsibility of information services of business partners, managing the expectations of information provider and its recipient, control implementation and execution of information transfer and computing services, providing the verification of quality of services, enabling the communication among business partners in heterarchy to better address their needs, expectations, performance relative to those expectations and progress on action items that may be undertaken to improve upon either the SLA itself or the service provider's performance, assessing the return on investment.

PROPOSED MODEL VIABILITY

Proposed above model is a certain abstract schema, however in practice, as it will be presented in the case study, information governance development without full acceptance of all the model core elements i.e. strategy, interoperability, contracts and architecture is leading to some threats and weaknesses. In the case study SEKAP – electronic communication system for public administration (http://www.sekap.pl) in Silesia, Poland is considered. The project of the local and regional authorities was realized in 2005-2007 with the objective to deliver easy access to information and public e-Services, which are a good way of implementing the information governance model. The information strategy within the project was quite well specified and concerns enabling access to public administration electronic services for citizens and transfer of electronic documents among municipal and regional public administration agencies in 54 towns in Silesia, Poland. Silesian Centre of Information Society (SCIS), sponsored by regional administration manages the SEKAP project. The main task of the SCIS is to ensure the further SEKAP system development. The SCIS is responsible for the cooperation with institutions participating in the project, as well as for reporting and monitoring project, for disposal of finances, for controlling and accountability in the project, for contracting with all project stakeholders, particularly with municipal offices and ICT services and software providers. The ICT architecture for SEKAP system is sufficiently well developed, including:

1. Software:
   a. Docflow and Workflow system integrated with the Public Information Bulletin.
   b. e-Forms Platform.
   c. Public Services Platform.
   d. Automatic Digital Signature Verification System.
   e. Security System.
   f. e-Payment system.
2. Hardware:
   a. SEKAP Data Centre Equipment.
   b. Individual infrastructure and digital signature equipment.
   c. Public administration processes engineering.

The project realization was divided into following stages:

- Electronic document circulation system.
- Security system.
- Electronic forms platform.
- Automatic verification of electronic signature system.

- Payment system.
- Public e-Services system.

A deficiency of clear and coherent legal framework concerning the term of e-Services and lack of organizational interoperability of public administration agencies still constitute big impediments encountered during the implementation of the project. The problems are solved in course of time when the national legislation evolved rendering the notion of e-Services clearer. The project is complex in its technical and organizational aspects, what caused some problems in the field of its management, since this was the first project of such a huge scope in the region. The problems are worked out gradually, when stakeholders involved in the project development process began to learn how to get over the impediments.

Institutional arrangements and governance structures are needed to deal with the complexity of the network relations and to ensure the implementation of the strategies. Traditionally, in hierarchical organizations a separate umbrella agency could be established to deal with the issues of network information governance, but in heterarchies the structural arrangements have to reflect the network strategy and the constraints resulting from the fact that the network participants are autonomous partners. In heterarchies, a challenge for information infrastructure is to support dynamic collaboration on the design, production and maintenance of products that are described in complex databases and data warehouses. The InteliGrid (http://inteligrid.eu-project.info/) project aims to ensure a flexible, secure, robust, and interoperable, pay-per-demand access to information, communication and processing infrastructure. The InteliGrid framework architecture includes four layers: a) problem domain layer b) various conceptual models and ontologies c) the software layer which includes applications and services d) the layer of basic hardware and software resources. The software architecture distinguishes between business applications, interoperability services, business services and grid middleware services. The concepts in the layer of models and ontologies are organized in the following ontologies: business ontology, organization ontology, service ontology and meta-ontology.

The InteliGrid document management system provides a generic, grid-based, ontology enabled document management solution that provided client as well as server side components with well-defined web services interface that enables remote access to the underlying document management services. Some of the main features of the system are:

- The system is generic and can support any domain specific ontology or taxonomy used in document annotation. Domain specific resources are treated as properties of a specific heterarchy.
- Actors (organizations, individuals, services) can specify different preferred settings e.g. storage resources, remote directories etc.
- Security is strictly enforced and all document transfers are encrypted.
- Several end-user client applications are provided for document annotations, document storing and retrieval etc.
- The system supports several different schemas for storing/uploading documents. Currently the system only fully supports manual and semi-automatic uploading the documents (based on a predefined local directory structure) (Dolenc et al., 2007).

CONCLUSION

Information value in the business network is seen in the opportunities of relationships and intensive information exchanges, in joint experiences and synergies creation because of information resources sharing. The larger a virtual heterarchy becomes the more value a product acquires as a relationships-enabling means. However, information users cannot believe that the more information the better. Eventually, information overload will cause the reduction of efficiency, because people will spend more time on communications instead of their individual work. The information governance is needed, as a certain equilibrium. Therefore, the first and the most important issue is to establish strategy of information, to answer question for what purpose and what information is needed, next, architecture and interoperability problems ought to be solved to ensure fluent transfer of messages and documents among network partners. Interoperability is to be a communication between software applications and the ability for anyone to use and act on the information in a useful way, the seamless and smart sharing and exchanging of information via integrated technical solutions. Virtual heterarchies are helpful in complex problem solving. Instead of work of one concrete organization, a network of business partners works on joint problem, so the synergy effects can be created. Although partners in heterarchy utilize their own information and IT resources, for all of them new IT infrastructure can be created, therefore they are able to share the risk of fluent data processing as well as commonly use and reuse created, within that network, knowledge. The last but not least are the contracts for controlling and reliability of realized information provision services.

REFERENCES

Astley, W. G., & Fombrun, C. J. (1983). Collective strategy, social ecology for organizational environments. *Academy of Management Review*, *8*(4), 476–587. doi:10.2307/258259

Bloem, J., Van Doorn, M., & Mittal, P. (2006). *Making IT governance work in a Sarbanes-Oxley World*. Hoboken, NJ: John Wiley & Sons.

Boisot, M. H. (1995). *Information space, A framework for learning in organizations, institutions and culture*. New York: Routledge.

Brancheau, J. C., & Wetherbe, J. C. (1986). Information architecture: Methods and practice. *Information Processing & Management*, *22*(6), 453–463. doi:10.1016/0306-4573(86)90096-8

Bruszt, L. (2002). Market making as state making: Constitutions and economic development in post-communist eastern Europe. *Constitutional Political Economy*, *13*, 53–72. doi:10.1023/A:1013687107792

Burton, R. M., Eriksen, B. H., & Hakonsson, D. D. Knudsen, T., & Snow, C.C. (2008). *Designing Organizations, 21st Century Approaches*. New York: Springer.

Buxmann, P., Wietzel, T., Westarp, F., & Konig, W. (1999). The standardization problem – An economic analysis of standards in information systems. In *Proceedings of the 1st IEEE Conference on Standardization and Innovation in Information Technology* (pp.157-162). SIIT'99, Aachen, Germany, Retrieved October 13, 2008, from http://www.nets.rwth-aachen.de/~jakobs/siit99/Proceedings.html

Calder, A., & Watkins, S. (2006) *International IT Governance: An executive guide to ISO17799/ ISO 27001*. London: Kogan Page.

Chatterjee, S., & Harrison, J. S. (2005). Corporate governance. In M.A. Hitt, R.E. Freeman, & J.S. Harrison (Eds.), *The Blackwell handbook of strategic management* (pp.543-564). Blackwell Publishing.

Chen, D., & Doumeingts, G. (2004). Basic concepts and approaches to develop interoperability of enterprise applications. In L.M. Camarinha-Matos & H., Afsarmanesh (Eds.), *Processes and foundations for virtual organizations* (pp. 323-330). Boston: Kluwer Academic Publishers.

Cliquet, G., Hendrikse, G., Tuunanen, M., & Windsperger, J. (Eds.). (2007). *Economics and management of networks, franchising, strategic alliances, and cooperatives.* Berlin: Springer.

Coad, A. (2005). Strategy and control. In A.J. Berry, J. Broadbent, & D. Otley (Eds.), *Management control, theories, issues and performance* (pp. 167-191). New York: Palgrave Macmillan.

Daily, C. M., Dalton, D. R., & Cannella, A. A. (2003). Corporate governance: Decades of dialogue and data. *Academy of Management Review, 28*(3), 371–382.

Desouza, K. C. (2007). Preface. In K.C. Desouza (Ed.), *Agile information systems, conceptualization, construction, and management* (pp. 11-18). Amsterdam: Elsevier.

Dolenc, M., Kurowski, K., Kulczewski, M., & Gehre, A. (2007). InteliGrid document management System: An overview. In M. Bubak, M. Turała, K. Wiatr (Eds.), *Cracow '06 Grid Workshop* (pp. 21-28), Cyfronet AGH Cracow.

Eggleston, B. (1996). *The new engineering contract.* London: Blackwell Science.

Fahy, M., Roche, J., & Weiner, A. (2005). *A beyond governance, creating corporate value through performance, conformance and responsibility.* Chichester: John Wiley & Sons.

Food Quality and Safety in Europe, Project Catalogue, European Commission, Brussels, December 2007, http://ec.europa.eu/research/biosociety/food_quality/download_en.html

Hamilton, S. (2000) Controlling risks. In D.A. Marchand (Ed.), *Competing with information, A Manager's guide to creating business value with information content* (pp. 209-230). Chichester: John Wiley & Sons.

Helaakoski, H., Iskanius, P., & Peltomaa, I. (2007). Agent-based architecture for virtual enterprise to support agility. In L.Camarinha-Matos, H.Afsarmanesh, P. Novais, & C. Analide (Eds.), *Establishing the foundation of collaborative networks* (pp. 299-306). Berlin: Springer.

Hinds, P. J., & Weisband, S. P. (2003). Knowledge sharing and shared understanding in virtual teams. In C.B. Gibson & S.G. Cohen (Eds.), *Virtual teams that work, creating conditions for virtual team effectiveness* (pp. 21-36). San Francisco: Jossey-Bass.

Hugoson, M.-A., Magoulas, T., & Pessi, K. (2008). Interoperability strategies for business agility. In J.L.G. Dietz, A. Albani & J. Barjis (Eds.), *Advances in enterprise engineering I* (pp.108-121). Berlin: Springer.

IT Governance Institute (2003, October). *Board Briefing on IT Governance* (2nd ed.). Rolling Meadows: Author..

Jessop, B. (1999). The dynamics of partnership and governance failure. *The new politics of local governance in Britain* (pp.11-32). Basingstoke: Macmillan.

Kaen, F. R. (2003). *A blueprint for corporate governance strategy, accountability and the preservation of shareholder value.* New York: Amacom American Management Association.

Lankhorst, M. (2005). *Enterprise architecture at work, modelling, communication and analysis.* Berlin: Springer.

Lenz, H., & James, M. L. (2007). International audit firms as strategic networks – The evolution of global professional service firms. In G. Cliquet, G. Hendrikse, M. Tuunanen & J. Windsperger (Eds.), *Economics and management of networks* (pp. 367-392). Heidelberg: Springer.

Lewis, J. D., & Weigert, A. (1985). Trust as a social reality. *Social Forces, 63*(4), 967–985. doi:10.2307/2578601

Lindstrom, L., & Jeffries, R. (2003). Extreme programming and agile software development methodologies. In C.V. Brown & H. Topi (Eds.), *IS management handbook* (pp. 511-530). London: Auerbach Publications.

Marcolin, B. L. (2006). Spiraling effects of IS outsourcing contract interpretations. In R. Hirschheim, A. Heinzl, & J. Dibbern (Eds.), *Information systems outsourcing* (pp. 223-256). Heidelberg/Berlin: Springer.

Mette, K. A. (2004). *Governance*. Cambridge: Polity.

Mintzberg, H., & Quinn, J. B. (1991). *The strategy process, concepts, contexts, cases*. Englewood Cliffs, NJ: Prentice Hall.

6P., Goodwin, N., Peck, E, & Freeman, T. (2006). *Managing networks of twenty–first century organizations*. London: Palgrave Macmillan.

Periasamy, K. P., & Feeny, D. F. (1997). Information architecture practice: Research–based recommendations for the practitioner. In L. Willcocks, D. Feeny, G.Islei (Eds.). *Managing IT as a strategic resource* (pp. 339-359). London: The McGraw-Hill Companies.

Powell, W. (1990). Neither market nor hierarchy: Network forms of organization. *Research in Organizational Behavior, 12*, 295–336.

Power, M. (2007). *Organized uncertainty: Designing a world of risk management*. Oxford University Press, Oxford.

Power, M. J., Desouza, K. C., & Bonifazi, C. (2006). *The Outsourcing handbook, how to implement a successful outsourcing process*. London: Kogan Page.

Reihlen, M. (1996). *The logic of heterarchies, making organizations competitive for knowledge-based competition*. Arbeitsbericht nr 91 / Working Paper No 91, Seminars fur Allgemeine Betruebswirtschaftslehre, Betriebswirtchaftliche Planung und Logistik, der Universitat zu Koln, University of Cologne, Germany. Retrieved October 13, 2008, from http://www.spl.uni-koeln.de/fileadmin/documents/arbeitsberichte/arbb-91.pdf

Riemer, K., & Klein, S. (2006). Network management framework. In S. Klein, & A. Poulymenakou (Eds.), *Managing dynamic networks* (pp. 17-68). Berlin: Springer.

Rocha, L. M. (2001). *Adaptive Webs for heterarchies with diverse communities of users*. Paper prepared for the Workshop from Intelligent Networks to the Global Brain: Evolutionary Social Organization through Knowledge Technology, Brussels, July, 3-5. Retrieved October 13, 2008, from http://www.ehealthstrategies.com/files/heterarchies_rocha.pdf

Romero, D., Giraldo, J., Galeano, N., & Molina, A. (2007). Towards governance rules and bylaws for virtual breeding environments. In L. Camarinha-Matos, H. Afsarmanesh, P. Novais, C. Analide, *Establishing the Foundation of Collaborative Networks* (pp. 93-102). Berlin: Springer.

Rosenau, J. N. (2004). Governing the ungovernable: The challenge of a global disaggregation of authority. In *Regulation & Governance* (pp. 88-97). Retrieved October 13, 2008, from http://www3.interscience.wiley.com/cgi-bin/fulltext/117994572/PDFSTART

Saxton, G. (2004). *The rise of participatory society: Challenges for the nonprofit sector*. 33rd Annual Conference of the Association for Research on Nonprofit Organizations and Voluntary Action, November 18-20, Los Angeles CA. Retrieved October 13, 2008, from http://www.itss.brockport.edu/~gsaxton/ participatorysociety_research.htm

Schelp, J., & Winter, R. (2007). Integration management for heterogeneous information systems. In K.C. Desouza (Ed.), *Agile information systems, conceptualization, construction, and management* (pp. 134-150). Amsterdam: Elsevier.

Smits, M. T., van der Poel, K. G., & Ribbers, P. M. A. (1999). Information strategy. In R.D. Galliers, D.E. Leidner & B.S.H. Baker (Eds.), *Strategic information management, challenges and strategies in managing information systems* (pp.61-85). Butteworth-Heinemann, Oxford.

Sroka, H. (Ed.). (2006). *Strategie i metodyka przekształcania organizacji w kierunku e-biznesu na podstawie technologii informacyjnej*. Wydawnictwo Akademii Ekonomicznej, Katowice.

Sroka, H. (Ed.). (2007). *Zarys koncepcji nowej teorii organizacji i zarzadzania dla przedsiebiorstw e-gospodarki.* Wydawnictwo Akademii Ekonomicznej, Katowice.

Stark, D. (2001). Ambiguous assets for uncertain environments: Heterarchy in postsocialist firms. In P. DiMaggio (Ed.), *The twenty-first-century firm: Changing economic organization in international perspective* (pp. 69-104). Princeton, NJ: Princeton University Press. Retrieved October 13, 2008, from http://www.colbud.hu/main/PubArchive/PL/PLo8-Stark.pdf

Steinmueller, W. E. (2007). The economics of ICTs: Building blocks and implications. In R. Mansell, Ch. Avgerou, D. Quanh, R. Silverstone (Eds.), *The Oxford handbook of information and communication technologies* (pp. 196-224). Oxford: Oxford University Press.

Sundaramurthy, Ch., & Lewis, M. (2003). Control and collaboration: paradoxes of governance. *Academy of Management Review*, *28*(3), 397–415.

Van Grembergen, W. (2004). *Strategies for information technology governance*. Hershey, PA: IGI Global.

Von Goldammer, E., Paul, J., & Newbury, J. (2003). *Heterarchy – Hierarchy, Two complementary categories of description.* Retrieved October 13, 2007, from http://www.vordenker.de /heterarchy/het_into_en.htm

KEY TERMS AND DEFINITIONS

Architecture: The fundamental organization of a system embodied in its components, their relationships to each other, and to the environment, and the principle guiding its design and evolution (IEEE Standard 1471-2000)

Contract: Legally enforceable agreement in which two or more parties commit to certain obligations in return for certain rights.

Governance: Act or manner of governing, or steering: the office or function of governing

Heterarchy: Organizational form, decentralized interorganizational network

Information Governance: Organizational or interorganizational activity to ensure information value creation through strategy, technology, architecture and agreements development

Information Management: Activities and policies which determine and ensure information mission, authority and responsibility

IT Governance: The organizational capacity to control the formulation and implementation of IT strategy and to ensure the fusion of business and IT (Van Grembergen, 2004)

Interoperability: The ability of two or more systems or components to exchange and use information (IEEE STD 610.12 Standard Glossary of Software Engineering Technology)

Strategy: Goals to be achieved in long time, as well as the path and the plan for the achievement

Section 3
Information Valuation

Chapter 9
Value of Information in Distributed Decision Support Systems

Jadwiga Sobieska-Karpińska
Wroclaw University of Economic, Poland

Marcin Hernes
Academy of Management in Lodz, Poland

ABSTRACT

This chapter deals with the analysis of the value of information in a distributed decision support systems. It characterises the basic measures of the value of information, with the stress put to the utility function, the effect of the knowledge discovery techniques in databases on the value of information and multicriteria methods of decisions support. In the chapter, a multi-agent system is presented, which is an example of a distributed decision support system. In the last part of the chapter, the choice methods and consensus methods for increasing the value of information through the eliminate contradiction of information within the system are presented.

INTRODUCTION

Nowadays information is a crucial element of an economic development of a society. Only base information that have a given value persons, who management different kind of organisations have to make correct decision. Information gains the particular meaning in the distributed decision support systems. These systems function as a set of computers joined in local and global networks (e.g. Internet) and assigned to the decision support. The value of information in these systems is measured through the application of the utility functions. An important problem is that the genuine utility of information is known only in the moment when the results of the decision made with its use are known.. The important attributes of information are its urgency and actuality because a correct decision may be only made when the system is able to get the up-to-date information, which is needed to make this decision, quickly. Other attributes of information are undeniability, intelligibility and credibility. Often the information is credible if it can be crosschecked. A correct determination of the value of information is very important in the process of decision making, because the correctness

DOI: 10.4018/978-1-60566-890-1.ch009

of the decision depends on that value. Thus, the problem with decision support systems is getting such information, which value is the greatest for solving the problem. If decision support system is distributed then the expectations for the value of information are even greater because the system can obtain the information from different sources. The sources of information of a distributed system can be placed in many different parts of the world and the value of information can differ. The information of the as greatest value is crucial for making proper decisions. This chapter make a suggestion to solve mentioned problems. Thus the fundamental measures of the value of information considering the distributed decision support system are presented. In distributed system situations that lower the value of information can occur. For example, if data replication occurs, it can happen, that the out-of-date data on one of the servers is the cause of the outdating of the information or can also be such, that one of the system nodes generate incorrect information (e.g. "byzantine" failure), which is entirely useless in the decision support process. An "information chaos' which often happens on the Internet is also a frequent problem. There is so much information in the network, that proper selection becomes a serious challenge for the system. There can also be situations, in which several different sources give contradictory information; determining which information is correct is a task for the distributed decision support system.

An essential problem are also different versions of information generated by different nodes of system (e.g. servers), which cause the intrasystem information contradiction. In this situation the system can present the user with several variants of decisions (which may also be contradictory) or it can analyze information and define one, the most satisfactory for the user (based on the criteria given by the user). This second solution is certainly better, because the user does not have to think about which decision to choose.

The chapter will also present solutions influencing the increase of the value of information in distributed decision support systems, such as data mining and their projecting on the utility of information. It also describes the multicriteria distributed decision support systems with the use of different sources of information.

In next part multi-agent distributed decision support systems are characterized. Agent, as an intelligent and mobile program, can not only execute commands, but also read signals from its environment and react accordingly. Thus multi-agent system can get and process information of the greatest value automatically.

To eliminate contradiction of information within the system, choice methods which allow to choose one of the examined decisions, and the consensus methods are presented. The difference between these two methods is, that in the latter the chosen decision does not have to be one of the existing decisions (generated by the system nodes); it can be a new decision, which will be the most approximate to those existing ones. In other words all of existing decision will be taken into consideration to certain extent. It certainly decreases the risk of the decision making.

The main purpose of the chapter is to determine the methods for the measurement of the value of information in the distributed decision support systems and to find the methods of increasing the value of information in this systems.

BACKGROUND

Decision making is a difficult and complex process. It must be noted that in current socioeconomic circumstances making a quick and right decision is becoming the basis of business competitiveness. Given the changing nature of economy, development of information technologies, globalization and unlimited flow of knowledge, organizations must promptly react to both internal and external changes. Solving the problems thus arising requires company management to make complex decisions of operational, tactical and above all strategic nature, which affects the future of the organization. Those who are responsible for decision making in companies most often act under risk and uncertainty because they cannot predict the outcomes of the decision made or can predict them with very little probability. Since the decision making process is so complex, it has been divided into several stages (Drucker, 1995; Kulikowski, Libura & Słomiński, 1998; Stanek, Sroka & Twardowski, 2003). In the first stage the situation needs to be analyzed. The decision-maker must be aware that the situation has occurred that requires certain decision to be made. If such a situation goes unnoticed, the opportunity to gain competitive advantage will be lost. At this stage, all the factors affecting the decision need to be defined. If such factors are independent from the decision – maker, they are called limiting conditions, if they depend on the decision-maker, they are called evaluation criteria. In the second stage the problem needs to be formulated. The decision-maker must precisely define which segment the problem concerns and which areas of business activity will be affected by the decision. The third stage consists in building a decision model, that is a theoretical reflection of the segment of reality which the problem concerns describing synthetically the decision problem. In the fourth stage, the model is used to determine acceptable decisions (that is those that meet all conditions determined by the decision-maker) and optimal decisions (that is the best ones in terms of the criteria established by the decision-maker). In the fifth stage, the final decision is made, which is a choice from optimal decisions.

In the last, sixths stage, the decision made is put into action. Thus, it can be seen that the decision making process is extremely complex. The decision –maker needs to collect and analyze a significant portion of information in order to make a final decision. Even if all the stages of the decision making process have been properly implemented, there is no guarantee that the decision will be good because it depends on the value of the information possessed by the decision-maker. It can be said that the decision making process depends on the availability of valuable information. Now, information is one of the most expensive goods on the market and it constitutes the main factor of the decision making process. It is considered to be a strategic factor enabling proper functioning of the business. Information enables correct assessment of the environment, condition or situation in which the organization is, it enables forecasting the condition or situation of the organization in the future, correct assessment of external and internal factors affecting business efficiency and above all it enables making correct decisions. It must be noted that decision making in business does not rely on random information. This information needs to have a proper value for the company. First of all, it needs to be accurate, reliable, up-to-date, timely, unambiguous, complete and credible.

A number of these qualities depend on the selection of a proper source of information. Generally, such sources can be divided into:

1. External, for example: press, radio, television, books, information leaflets, written documents, suppliers, agents, customers, market, Internet.
2. Internal, for example: company staff, processes taking place in the company, internal databases, procedures, internal regulations, reports.

Proper selection of information sources determines its value for the company. Now, the greatest source of information is the Internet. It must be emphasized, however, that on the web there is information of different value and its proper selection is of importance in obtaining information necessary for proper decision making. It must be noted that the value of a specific piece of information is subjective, i.e. the same piece of information may be of great value for one company and of no value for another.

Literature on this subject distinguishes four basic functions that valuable information needs to perform (Rojek, 2001):

1. Supporting the change process i.e. a sequence of decisions made the management.
2. Enabling communication by staff and management i.e. exchange of information.
3. Improvement of individual knowledge.
4. Enabling the establishment of relationships with environment.

Possession and skillful use of information that is of proper value for the company is one of the most important factors in achieving competitive advantage. Nowadays, information systems supporting decision making (Decision Support Systems) are used. Especially in the first four stages of decision making process. Such systems enable fast collection of up-to-date information, processing such information and presentation of suggested decisions (either acceptable or optimal, depending on the system configuration) to the decision-maker. The final decision, however, is taken by the decision- maker who bears responsibility for the outcomes. Decision support systems significantly shorten the time needed to take a decision because they select and process the information and can draw conclusions on the basis of the information possessed and in consequence they can suggest different solutions to the decision-maker.

The history of decision making support systems dates back to mid fifties of the last century when transactional systems were in use which enabled development of simple data sheets used for example in accounting or payrolls. They did not directly support the decision making process but only made it possible to obtain certain information needed to take a decision.

In the early seventies of the 20th century, Management Information Systems came into use. They were based on transactional systems but in addition they possessed complex data processing algorithms thanks to which synthetic information for the management was generated. By analyzing how these systems were used a problem with information structuring was revealed. It turned out that management information systems operated well only if the information was well structured. For poorly structured information these systems did not work. Structured information is the information which may be written down in the form of a structure, i.e. the arrangement of individual components and relationships between them which are typical of certain set as a whole. Poorly structured information is the information that cannot be written down in the form of structure; it is mainly information written in a natural language.

For the poorly structured information to be processed Decision Support Systems were developed which support decision-makers at medium and high levels. They are based on data bases and programmed decision making models. Such systems are characterized mainly by:

- ease of use,
- presentation of information in the form technology known to the user,
- selectiveness in providing information,
- support and not replacement of the decision-maker's thinking process,
- supporting decision-makers in processing poorly structured information.

The examples of Decision Support Systems are Interactive financial Planning System and Portfolio Management System. Decision Support Systems were addressed to individual decision-makers. It whas been noticed, however, that most often decisions are taken by a group of decision-makers in discussion, exchange of views, negotiations, brainstorming etc.

There has emerged a class of Group Decision Systems which make it possible to support parallel data processing, exchange of views by a group of decision –makers, presentation of the results of different alternative solutions. Such systems are for example STATISTICA Enterprise – wide Data Analysis System, Lotus Notes or Group Wise. The development of another class of decision support systems was connected with the development of artificial intelligence. There arose a need not only to process information but also to draw conclusions, which is a characteristic feature of intelligence. Thus, expert systems came into being which made use of the knowledge bases (that is a set of facts and rules governing these facts) and a conclusion drawing mechanism. It is worth mentioning that the knowledge base is separated from the conclusion drawing mechanism, in which way for the same data base different conclusion methods may be applied and vice versa. Such systems make it possible to store symbolic knowledge, i.e. facts and principles written down in the forms of symbols. The first implementation of such systems took place in medicine, now however, they are used in banking, insurance or commerce. Although numerous decision support systems met the expectations of decision makers, it turned out that they have difficulty in using them, especially while operating complex models and structures. Thus, Executive Information Systems have been developed which make it possible to quickly generate general or detailed analyses. The results presented in graphic form enable decision makers to improve their knowledge about a rapidly changing environment. The example of such a system is SIK Logotec Enterprise.

In the late nineties of the twentieth century Business Intelligence systems were developed which make it possible to integrate data, conduct multidimensional analyses, data mining and visualize them. Until then, much of the information had been lost because decision making support systems were unable to store historical data, unify them, aggregate or reveal the relations between them, in result of which the information provided to the decision- maker was not fully valuable. Business Intelligence Systems do offer such possibilities. The examples of such systems are SAP Business Suite, ESTEEM, Stottler Henke or CDN.

The development of computer networks has led to that nowadays Decision Support Systems are distributed, mainly on the Internet. Such systems make it possible to collect and process enormous quantities of information. Therefore, the value of information in distributed decision support systems is becoming a key component affecting the quality of the decisions determined by these systems and in consequence the quality of the decisions taken by the decision-maker. As has been mentioned earlier, if the decision-makers does not possess information of a proper value, they will not be able to make a good decision. Thus, the decision support system needs to possess the information of a proper values for the decision –maker to be able to make use of the results presented by such a system in order to make a final decision. This issue has been discussed by numerous authors. It has been stated for example (Olender-Skorek & Wydro, 2007) that information constitutes such an important resource that it is becoming a key component taken into account by decision-makers shaping social development. Information is a specific goods item, partly similar to public goods and partly possessing its unique properties. For example, it cannot be evaluated before it is obtained. It has also been stated that a proper measure of information in a broad sense is to which extent it simplifies or improves the process of goal achieving. In another work (Van Alsyne, 1999) it is said that because information possesses indirect utility known only after it has been used, direct measurement of its utility is hardly effective. However, attempts are often made to estimate potential or real value of this resource. It has been observed (Varian, 2002) that in the decision making process the quality of the decision success is measured by utility function which determines the relationships between the components affecting decision making and the outcomes of such a decision. In economics, utility function is an orderly set of preferences individually ascribed to particular individuals. Thus, if we arrange the information quantitatively, we can obtain a very useful decision making tool (Olender – Skorek & Wydro, 2007). In turn, each new piece of information introducing a specific change to the decision situation may be viewed as a useful piece of information for such a situation (Stefanowicz, 2004). Stefanowicz has also noted that the value of the information depends on a number of factors, such as:

- the information itself,
- the user,
- the intentions that affect the user's interpretation,
- the actions undertaken by the user,
- the outcomes achieved by the user.

According to some authors, the measures of the information value depend mainly on the area in which the information is used. In some works (Jaworski, 2002; McCann, 1994; Purczyński, 2003) the value of information in business activities has been characterized. Others (Morrison & Cohen, 2005) focus on the value of information in administrative and organizational area or in science and research, cultural, social and political activities (Tappenden, Chilcott, Eggington, Oakley, McCabe, 2004; Gudea, 2004) or geo-spatial activities (Alexander, 2003).

Certain item of information is often connected with numerous areas of activity, therefore it needs to be determined in which area the decision is to be made and to take this area into account while determining the value of this item of information. Vast literature on the subject matters does not deal with information value measures in a distributed decision support system. Now, thanks to the utilization of global computer networks (e.g. the Internet) distrbuted decision support systems are becoming more and more common and their specific nature creates a need to define new measures of information value that will be presented in the subsequent part of this paper.

MAJOR MEASURES VALUE OF INFORMATION

The information in distributed decision support systems has a crucial meaning. These systems function as sets of computers connected into local and global networks, which purpose is the decision support.

According to (Ahituv & Neumann, 1986) we specify three basic kinds of the measure of the value:

1. Normative, which requires determining of the unit, for which the value of different information can be related. This way of determining the value requires the assignment of general premises, which are the ground for setting the norms and estimations. Obviously, the system of norms should be minimal ("Ockham's razor"). Information is very diverse, it can describe everything what may be observed, so it is not possible to formulate such general premises. Normative measure can only be used with homogenous groups of information, although the feature of universality, which is necessary to mesure the value of information in distributed decision support system, is lost.
2. Realistic; it is based on estimating the result of the use of information, that is the consequence of making decision. It is an ex post method, what makes it impossible to use it to evaluate the content of information (Van Alsyne, 1999). Realistic methods could be used, if the values of all possible employments of information were known and categorized, as it is in case of many years experience in evaluation of the value of other resources. The value of information can usually be known after it was used, but it is possible that this method will be used in the future, when information civilization has more experience in this field.

3. Subjective; it takes into account factors of the dependence of the measure on the person and conditions in which it is used. A particular information may have a big value for one person and be valueless for another person. This kind of measure is the most useful in measuring the value of information. Potential users are those who evaluate the value of particular piece of information. That value creates the market and demand for information.

The value of information can be set in reference to the results caused by the choice of the target decision, in which forming this information was used. Setting of this value is not direct. The target decision is, in this case, based on the target hipothesis *C*, i.e. hypothesis concerned with the possibility of achieving the purpose while taking into consideration the piece of information, which evaluates the situation state, that has an immediate influence on the result of the target decision. (Olender-Skorek & Wydro, 2007).

The correctness of evaluation usually comes down to the evaluation of its probability. So, it is a probability formulation (Wierzbicki & Wydro K. B, 2006). Variable *C* is a random variable with possible values *c* belonging to *C*, and possible operations *d* (decisions) are represented by decision variable *D*. In formal wording, we say, that the states and operations (*C* i *D*) are domains of variables *c* and *d*. Each random variable is characterized by the probability distribution of its values, whereas the decision variable is the determined value, characterized by the decision maker. There are some values or utilities that can be ascribed to the action of the decision maker in given situation, which present the level of desireability. The levels of satisfaction with the achieved result can be described with a function of utility. In general, it can be accepted, that the influence of the factors of the target hypothesis, i.e. state c and the decision made d can be shown by the utility function *U(d,c)*. An optimal decision is taking up such operation, which maximises the expected value of *U(d,c)* at given reliability (known distribution function) of the situation, so making such decision is optimal which allows to maximise the value of utility. So, if the distribution of values *p*(*c*) and the random variable *C are* known, the value of the desired utility is defined:

$$OU(C) = \sum_{c \in C} p(c)U(d,c).$$

Maximising condition looks like this:

$$OU_{\max}(C) = \max_{d \in D} \sum_{c \in C} p(c)U(d,c).$$

In many cases, it is not possible to observe the state of situation *C* relating to the target hypothesis. Therefore, it is inevitable to conclude on the base of other observables, which can give the decision maker some knowledge referring to the target hypothesis. In this situation an index (an indicatory variable), i.e. an other value connected to the target hypothesis, must be used. This will be called I, its value will be *i*, and assuming that it is a random variable – its distribution of probablity will be *p*(*i*). Accepting, that the joint probability of the relationship of *I* and *C* is known, it is possible to define the distribution of probability of variable *I* and *C*, and condition probabilities *p*(*I*|*C*) i *p*(*C*|*I*). In distributed systems, the joint probability can be assigned effectively by Bayesian network of reliability; it is proper to mention, that there are algorithms which assign the estimation of such distribution of probability. The cost *KI* has to be taken into consideration in case of the index variable. It is necessary to make a subsidiary decision to make making the target decision possible. For making subsidiary decision it is necessary to define the value of information contributed by the indexes to the target hypothesis (Olender-Skorek & Wydro, 2007). Using such indexes and acquiring the knowledge about their state requires the incurring of cost *KI*. The value of information, which is used as an index variable can be defined as function showing the difference between the utilities gained from applying two strategies: the choice of the optimal action considering the index variable and the action without applying that piece of information. In the first situation the desired value optimal action looks like this:

$$OU_m(C \mid i) = \max_{d \in D} \sum_{c \in C} p(c \mid i) U(d, c).$$

The result of taking into account the index variable I is not known, thus it is necessary to calculate the desired value of utility by the averaging of all possible values of *I*. In the first situation, the desired value of the maximal utility in case of the first strategy is:

$$OU_m(C \mid i) = \sum_{c \in C} p(i) OU_m(C \mid i).$$

And in the second:

$$OU_m(C).$$

The value of information is defined:

$$WI(C \mid I) = OU_m(C \mid I) - OU_m(C).$$

Taking into consideration the cost of getting the index information, its net value is:

$$WI_K(C \mid I) = OU_m(C \mid I) - OU_m(C) - K_I$$

where: *KI* – cost of gotten information about state *I*.

In other form it is:

$$WI = \sum_{i=1}^{k} p(r_i) \max_{1 \le a \le l} \left[\sum_{j=1}^{Z} U_{a,j} p(\psi_j | r_i \right] - OU(d_a^*).$$

where: *ri* – the index variable (information), *Ua, j* – the utility function, *Ψj* – the environment state. The second part of the equation determines the value of utility achieved when the piece of information was not taken into account. The cost of getting the piece of information is also not taken into consideration. (Olender-Skorek & Wydro, 2007).

The use of the presented methods is limited in practice as they require a reasonable calculation of time and cost. The real form of the utility function is also a problem. In practice indexes are used, which allow comparing the intangible values in different organizations.

The information is an intangible and hard to measure asset and it is presented so in the economics. It is worth mentioning, that the intangible assets, as in opposition to the tangible ones, are more difficult to copy by competitors what allows to achieve a competitive superiority. An additional problem is, that the value of intangible assets is relative, for example a piece of information, which is valuable to one organization can be seen as useless for other organization. The intangible assets develop values when confronted with other assets. Moreover, they effect the financial result indirectly – they work as a chain of cause-and-effect relationship.

The problem of assigning the subjective value was researched empirically for many market and non-market goods. One interesting result of those researches is finding the difference between the willingness to pay (WTP) and the willingness to accept compensation (Willingness to Accept – WTA). WTA/WTP methodology can be used to assign the subjective value of information with the intention of determining the characteristics of information as the economic goods. This mechanism is compatible with the economical demand and supply laws, it is the mechanism of determining the price in the competitive market, which is known as the most optimal method of assigning the value of goods in economics.

The value determined with the use of WTA and WTP is, by definition, neither normative nor realistic. It is subjective, because it mirrors a personal perception of the value of goods. The value of WTA and WTP usually differ significantly. This difference, known as the "endowment effect", produces the lowering of the transaction volume. The number of transactions is smaller than in the situation in which the value of WTA and WTP were similar. However, the deficiency of information usually causes an increase of the difference between the WTA and WTP, which leads to the market decrease. Sometimes the multiplicity of information promotes correct subjective valuing and the increase of transaction number. Thus, the information is an economical catalyst. The increase of its perceived value and the increase of the demand for it should be the aim of each market-oriented organization interested in increasing the demand for its product. It is especially true in case of the supplier of content. The information is often the essential part of the market goods, so if its value is increasing, the value of the goods also increases, what decreases the negative effect of the decrease of the volume of transaction (Raban, 2002).

In an organization, knowledge, information and intangible assets are parts of the human capital, information capital and organizational capital. The human capital is abilities, talents and employees' knowledge, that are at the organisation disposal. The information capital is databases, information systems, network and technical infrastructure. The organizational capital is a culture of organization, leadership and the employees' ability to identify themselves with the organisation aims and their ability to share knowledge.

At first sight the intangible assets can not be assigned the value, but in fact there are indirect methods of doing it. These indirect methods are, for example, the measure of the influence of the intangible assets, which include information, on the organization; and researching the efficiency of the intangible assets management.

One of the best known methods of the intellectual capital valuing in organization is the Stassman ratio. It determines the information productivity PI (Michna, 2008):

$$PI = Z/K,$$

where: Z – refund on the intelectual resources (the difference between the net profit and the capital cost), K – costs of management.

The higher value of this ratio, the better the condition of the organisation.

The Scandia method is also often used. This method is based on Edvison and Malone's model, in which the intellectual capital of the organisation is divided into three elements: human capital, structural capital and consumer capital (relations with the clients); its latest modifications divide the intellectual capital into human and structural capital. The structural capital consists of the consumer and organisation capital; innovation capital is a part of the latter. (Michna, 2008).

Another concept is the balanced scorecard, which is a systematic measurement of the strategic readiness of human capital, information capital and organizational capital. The human capital defines if the employees have qualifications proper for the needs of the organisation internal processes. In general, this method is recognized as a „revolutionary method of strategic management" (Friedag, 2003), but the fast development does not limit it to the measurement and the monitoring of the organisation situation. The measurement consists of following steps: (Olender-Skorek & Wydro, 2007):

1. Singling out strategical process.
2. Distribution of positions in individual processes.
3. Determination of the profile of competence.
4. Assigment of the optimal number of employees to the post.
5. Proportional participation of the existing state in respect to the desirable state (e.g.

If the required number of employees on the post is 100, but in this organization this post is occupied by 40 employees only, then readiness of human capital in this fragment of organization amounts to 40%).

The information capital is measured by adjusting the teleinformatic infrastructure to the advancement of internal processes.

The organisational capital is the most difficult to measure, because it has certain attributes, which should be treated individually. These are: culture, leadership, correspondence of the employees' aims and teamwork.

The balanced scorecard do not convert the value of intangible assets to money. It rather presents their essence in the forming of the value of organization. However, taking into consideration its popularity, this method cannot be overlooked.

One of the often used methods is the Sveiby's method (Sveiby, 2008; Sveiby, 1997). It is the monitoring of intangible assets. The author divides the intangible assets into three types, which account the difference between the market value of organization and its book value. The „surplus", which is not taken into consideration in the book value is attributed to the employees' competence and the internal and external structure of the organization. While in Scandia model the culture and the management are treated as parts of the human capital, the Sveiby's method includes them to the iternal structure. This theorem assumes that people are the only good agents and all of the factors in the organisation result from their operations.

The use of this model has some specific conditions, and all its factors are created by the zero-one method (e.g. good – bad). It is not always proper, because it omits certain specificity of organizations functioning in the market.

In 1997, G. Roos (Pike & Roos, 2000) together with a group of scientists proposed IC (Intelectual Capital) index which joined all individual factors into one comparable value. The same scientists recognized, that the narrow prospect of look on assets with the use of traditional accountancy methods is not very good from the management and strategic point of view. They suggested HVA (Holistic Value Approach) model, which is based on mentioned assumptions.

Other indirect measure of intangible assets is Tobin's Q index, which is the relation between the market value of organization and the cost of restoring its tangible assets. The higher the value, the higher participation of the intangible assets in the value of organisation.

To use presented measures in distributed decision support system, we have to modify them, so that they consider the specificity of these systems.

As it was written before, in the distributed system such phenomena occur as:

1. Out-of-date data. If the system makes use of the data replication, which is significant for the system reliability and efficiency, a situation may occur in which the information stored on some nodes of the system are out-of-date (in a distributed system there are often delays in data updating on different nodes resulting from both the methods of replication used and properties of the hardware, for example delays on network connections).
2. "Information chaos" – presently there is so much information on the Internet, that it is very difficult to manage.
3. Different kinds of node failures – there can always happen a hardware or software failure (e.g. "byzantine" failure).

Because of the presented phenomena the information can be not actual, unreliable and incomprehensible. Therefore, the methods of the measurement of the value of information have to be introduced, which allow to determine the influence of individual nodes on this value of information.

Three basic methods are to be mentioned:

1. the use of the standard deviation and rejection of the information from the nodes of the highest standard deviation, therefore:

$$WI = \frac{\sum_{i=1}^{n} WI_i - \max\left(\sqrt{\frac{\sum_{j-1}^{n}(WI_j - \overline{WI})^2}{n-1}}\right)}{n-1}$$

where:

n - number of system nodes,
WI – value of information in system,
WI_z – value of information in node *z*.

The value of information in the whole system is corrected by the value of information in the node which has the highest deviation from the other nodes. However, the question is: If the value of information in the most of the nodes is on the middle level and the value of information in one of the nodes is high, would it not be better to consider the information of the highest value? Unfortunately, we do not know if this node is damaged and generate false information, so not considering it is a better option. Of course, it is possible to modify this formula (basing on the system size or the problem character) and not taking into consideration the value from several nodes or not taking into consideration the value from a node, which standard deviation is higher than a fixed value.

2. the credibility of a given node can be evaluated on the base of historical data.

Let WI_t be the value of information in moment *t*, *m* – the number of historical measurement, so:

$$WI = \frac{\sum_{i=1}^{n} WI_i - \min\left(\frac{\sum_{j=1}^{m}(WI_{t-j})}{m}\right)}{n-1}$$

The value of information in the node, which value of information was low previously is not taken into consideration.

3. Weight method – modifies the previous method, instead of ignoring the information from some of the nodes, it is possible to attribute weights to the values of information in this node. This weight attribution is based on the standard deviation or the historical results.

The implementation of the above methods in distributed decision making support systems makes it possible for the system to correctly determine the value of the information and in consequence to efficiently support the decision-maker in the decision making process. Of course, other methods of the information value evaluation may be developed for distributed decision support systems but the methods presented here are easy to implement and do not overload processors, which is a significant factor affecting the efficiency of the system.

It must be emphasized that if the system is able to evaluate a given piece of information, it may reject it if it is of little value and retain only such pieces of information that are of uttermost importance for the decision-maker. On the basis of such information the system is able to present solutions that will help the decision-maker to take a proper decision. The measurement of the value of information is a very important element of functioning of the distributed decision support system, however it is necessary to increase the value of information because it affects the quality of the decisions. In next part of the chapter the ways of increasing the value of information in distributed decision support systems will be presented.

WAYS OF INCREASING THE VALUE OF INFORMATION IN DISTRIBUTED DECISION SUPPORT SYSTEMS

One of the main problems that occurs when we assess the value of information is the so-called "information chaos" in the Internet. A distributed decision support system has to select from this "chaos" useful high-quality information. One of the methods of such searching is the technique of Knowledge Discovery in Databases (KDD). It is a field of IT that deals with developing algorithmic tools used for discovering knowledge in data (Ślęzak, Synak, Wieczorkowska & Wroblewski, 2002). The motivation for considering such tools comes from the continuous development of technological means for gathering and analysing data containing amounts of possibly valuable information that could complete human knowledge. The implementation of KDD process is simply necessary in many cases, because of rapid increase of information required for making decisions, for starters. The implementation of KDD is widely recognized, especially in comparably new fields, where the so-called expertise is not complete nor thorough. These are as follows:

- Data mining on Internet traffic,
- e-marketing,
- automatic acquisition of multimedia,
- the identification of image, writing, speech, etc.,
- supporting medical diagnostics,
- genetic experimentation,
- historical analysis of banking operations,
- data warehouse design,
- CRM operations optimisation.

It is worth mentioning, that the essence of the above applications requires executing operations using a large amount of information of various structures. This excludes the use of conventional methods of data analysis, which do not work effectively enough with large databases having a non-uniform formant (e.g. websites). The complexity of data nature as well as the complexity of problems occurring during its analysis is beginning to impede the formation of questions, which the user wants to obtain answers to. For instance, while analysing data on user behaviour on the Web, it is necessary to establish what sort of data we are in possession of and what we would like to find out. In many cases, the actual aim of such analysis becomes clear while working with data. Therefore, the identification of the aim takes place during an interactive process that allows us to consider the knowledge and preferences of the user. Taking Internet data for example, we notice that it can be gathered on the way, in the form of descriptions of so-called sessions made by individual users or nodes of a distributed system. The essence of a problem may require to include information about individual users or nodes in the analysis (information about nodes may not be entirely available), as well as the information about the websites they have visited. When it comes to e-marketing, it may also be necessary to add data on the results of advertising campaigns, etc. Of course, the choice of data sources depends on the questions formed by the user. It is clear at this point, that the variety of information inventories does not always allow to identify their sources. Any analysis must be preceded by a selection of data that seems adequate in our consideration. The chosen sources need to be saved using a more or less uniform formant which will ease the work of data-seeking algorithms, searching for interesting relations or regularities. Even at the point of data selection and preparation for further analysis, we are not able to completely isolate those components of their specification, that turn out to be most useful in providing solution to a problem set beforehand. We should also bear in mind that, for instance, the information about each user or node can be saved with vary many different properties, not all of which may prove useful to the user as practical knowledge. This is the point where we deal with data saved in the form of a table (provided it is possible), where all lines correspond to objects (users, net surfers, DNA chains, audio recordings), and all columns correspond to properties that describe the above. Data mining is the algorithmic detection of relations between the values of these properties. It can be carried out with a number of different methods, based on statistics, artificial intelligence or resulting from mechanical education methods. The next step is the interpretation of relations found – this is a stage where the decision maker, after consulting a panel of analysts, makes his call, whether or not the obtained results are useful to the completion of the task set beforehand. It often turns out, that this is not the end of the project at all, as there may be possible suggestions or criticism from people who ordered the analysis. That may lead to repeated employing of the entire KDD process described above, after considering a number of modifications. It is important not to take this phenomenon the wrong way as something bad. The complexity of contemporary analytical tasks as well as the variety of data mined for the purpose of completing the former, simply goes way beyond human perception. Data mining is defined as a process of detection of "regularities" in data, that are interesting to the user. Those "regularities" bring us information on those properties which are really significant and useful in constructing e.g. an OLAP-server. The knowledge entailed in their form is something significantly new. It is a key to a successful assessment of the entire KDD process. It can also constitute a source of suggestions on necessary modifications of previous stages. The problem is, there is in fact an "infinite number" of such regularities in data, but the user finds only few of them interesting, to a certain degree. What is more, we cannot perfectly define what "interesting" really means. Proper regularities may have the following properties:

- they occur in new data as well,
- they meet the requirements and preferences of the user,
- they are formerly unknown, however intuitive, to the experts,
- they are clear and comprehensible,
- they can be put into practice,
- in fact, only thorough experience with multiple practical applications of KDD enables us to put the customer's expectations into a language of algorithmic data mining methods and, finally, into a desired result.

The described KDD process helps us to increase the value of information through "mining" the information required for a proper decision-making from the "information chaos".

The value of information becomes particularly significant, when the usefulness of the decision is assessed with a large number of criteria. In this case, the value of information must also be assessed with these criteria. In conventional decision support systems, one criterion is identified and then an optimum solution is sought (Trzaskalik, 2006). Since a real number set has a certain order, there is an opportunity to compare different decision variants based on a chosen criterion. If there are many assessment criteria to be considered, each variant is described not by one evaluation (a real number) but by a vector of evaluations with a number of components equal to the number of criteria we have chosen to consider. Making a decision for a number of criteria often comes down to finding a vector with the highest values. It is called vectorial maximization task. We can formulate it when we are certain that the decision maker aims at a simultaneous maximization of all goals set by them. Many publications (e.g. Nowak, 2004; Trzaskalik, 2006) present problems of discreet multiple-criteria decision making. Problems of such kind occur in situations when a single decisive variant is isolated from a certain set o variants, to effectively achieve the goals considered by the decision maker. The ELECTRE methods are often used in this case, which allow to consider the variability and lack of precision in the assessment and preferences of the decision maker. The Bipolar method, introduced by Konarzewska-Gubała (Konarzewska-Gubała, 1989) is also popular. The method is used for sorting and ranking a finite number of decision variants. The comparison of decision variants is not carried out immediately but with the use of a bipolar reference system, specified by the decision maker. The system contains "good" and "bad" objects. The Bipolar method first compares the decision variants with the elements of a reference system, and then specifies the position of each decision variant with reference to a bipolar reference system. In the last phase, the method makes inference about the relations within the set of the tested decision variants, on the basis of results obtained earlier.

In distributed decision support systems for multiple-criteria decisions the value of information can be increased through assigning certain weight to each assessment criterion. In this case one should place special emphasis on obtaining information, that has the highest value for the criteria with the highest weight.

Another way to increase the value of information in distributed decision support systems is to eliminate the contradiction of information within the system. The methods used for this elimination will be presented with an example of a multi-agent distributed decision support system. A multi-agent system can be defined in various ways. To sum up all the definitions from different publications (Dyk, Lenar, 2006; Ferber, 1999, Nguyen 2002, Korczak & Lipiński, 2008), we can say that a multi-agent system is a system characterised by:

- *environment* E, that contains certain boundaries;
- *objects* (that create the O set), that belong to and are located within the environment E, objects can be examined, created, modified and eliminated by the agents;
- *agents* (that create the A set), being active objects of a system ($A \subseteq O$);
- *relations* (that create the R set), that join objects together and assign semantics to the joint;
- *operations* (that create the Op set), that enable the agents from the set A examine, create, use and modify objects from the O set;
- application representation operators for the mentioned operations and the response of the environment for the operations, which we call *rules that govern the environment.*

The main purpose of the system is to help the user make the right decision. The multi-agent system that we are discussing supports making decisions in the event of uncertainty. The system is composed of several agent programs, able to communicate with one another via computer network. Each agent search and retrieves data from the Internet, LAN, employees or other sources and then proceeds with inference-making process, using data mining or artificial intelligence methods. The result is processed information (or decision in special cases). A situation might occur, when each agent presents different information. For this reason, the next phase uses choice or consensus methods (described in detail later on) in order to agree on one single piece of information for all agents, which will be presented to the user. The diagram for a multi-agent distributed decision support system is shown on Figure 1.

The system is composed of the following elements:

1. Information – it can be found on the Internet, LAN, among employees or in other sources. Each agent search and retrieves the information required to make a decision from Internet servers.
2. Agent – an intelligent program, which not only makes inference from the obtained information, but also takes action aimed at achieving the required goal, which in this

case is decision making. Each agent employs a different method (way) of information processing in order to make a decision. An agent can be implemented to any computer with Internet and LAN access.

3. Methods of eliminating the contradiction of information within the system – allow to agree on one decision, which will be presented to the user, on the basis of various items of information (or decisions) from each agent. The system uses choice or consensus methods.
4. Users – people, who use computers with network access to read decisions made through several methods of eliminating the contradiction of information within the system. They can be stock investors, people responsible for making decisions in companies, etc.

The purpose of a multi-agent distributed decision support system is to provide assistance for company managers, institution managers or investors in order to make the right decision. Apart from supporting decisions by proposing particular

Figure 1. Schematic diagram for a multi-agent distributed decision support system. (source: author's own)

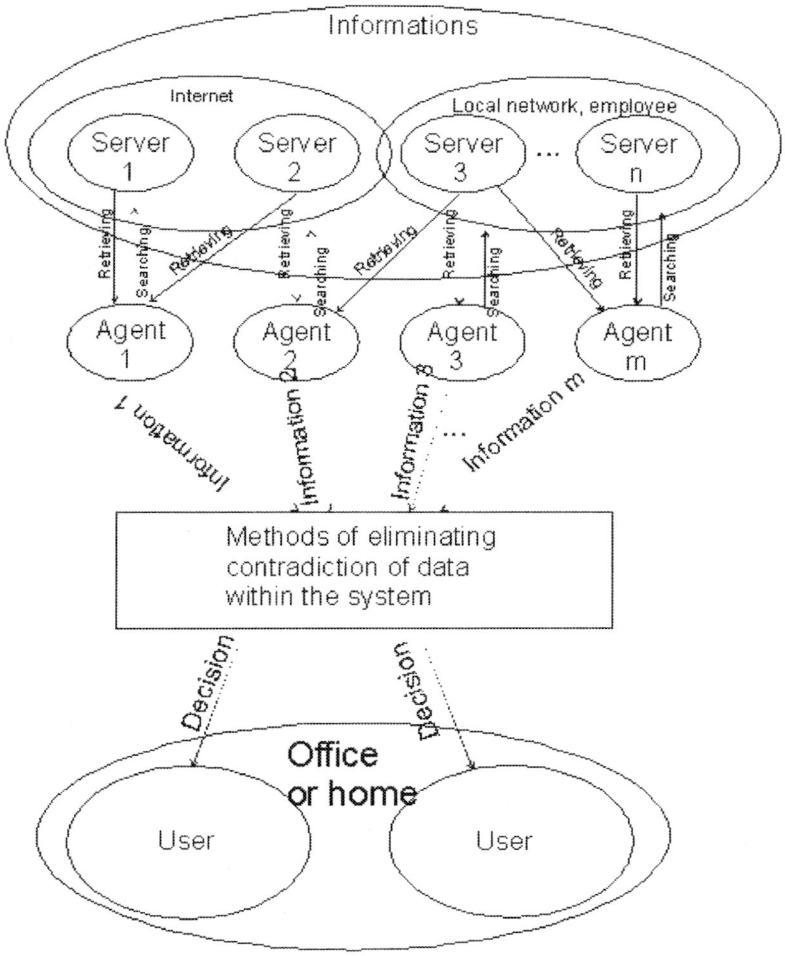

solutions (the system proposes the best solution to its knowledge, it is the person's job to make the final decision), which is the main function of the system, it can also carry out the following additional tasks:

- independent decision making (if we decide, that the decision made by the system is final, the system can make decisions independently, without the user),
- finding the best solution among different alternatives (in special cases we can disable the agent programs and only use the methods of eliminating the contradiction of information within the system for decisions given by the user),
- notifying the user on changes within the environment.

The following part of this chapter will characterize the choice and consensus methods used in a multi-agent decision support system. The choice theory originates from social sciences. It was described e.g. by (Arrow, 1951; Gibbard, 1973; Moulin, 1998, Myerson, 1996). The choice theory deals with the following problem: there is a given Z set (e.g. a set of objects) which is a subset of a set of alternatives X. As for choice, we make a selection on the basis of certain criteria of a certain Y subset of Z set. The set of subsets of Z set is called a profile and is represented by $P(Y)^N$. The choice function is represented as follows:

$F: P(Y)^N \rightarrow Y.$

Therefore, when making our choice, we seek a subset of profile that meets certain criteria. In distributed decision support systems, the criteria for choice are established individually (employing the rules of subjective information value assessment) according to the user's (decision maker's) preferences. The publications for this field place high emphasis on two basic postulates that should act as choice functions: the anonymity postulate and the neutrality postulate. The anonymity postulate requires the choice criteria used by a single user to be unknown to other users of the system without the user's consent. The neutrality postulate states that the criteria set by a user cannot influence the system's choice of an optimum decision based on criteria set by another user.If we employ the choice methods to eliminate the contradiction of information within the system, only one node of the system is taken into consideration while making the final decision. The other nodes do not contribute to the solution to the user and do not have to accept the chosen solution. Therefore, the result of the choice methods represents only one of the system nodes.

The methods of eliminating the contradiction of information within the system that proved to be much better are the consensus methods, therefore they will be explained much more thoroughly in the following part of the chapter. Similarly to the choice theory, the consensus theory deals with the following problem: there is a given Z set (e.g. a set of objects) which is a subset of X set. As for choice, we make a selection on the basis of certain criteria of a certain Y subset which does not have to be a subset of Z set and does not need to have the same structure as the elements of Z set. At the beginning the consensus theory applied only to simple structures, such as linear ordering or partial ordering. Later however, it was employed for more complex structures, such as splitting, hierarchies, n-trees. Therefore the consensus theory deals with problems resulting from data analysis for the purpose of gathering useful information (the same as data mining). However, while the purpose of data mining methods concerns seeking casual relations contained in data, the purpose of consensus methods concerns determining a set of certain data versions in such a way as to best represent the versions or create a compromise, acceptable by the parties that created the versions. The consensus theory helps us resolve all sorts of conflicts that occur on data level. The publication by (Nguyen, 2002) the problems solved with the use of the consensus theory are divided into the following categories:

1. Problems connected with discovering the hidden structure of an object. For instance: there is a given set of elements, and the structure to be discovered is the distance function between the elements.
2. Problems connected with reconciling incoherent or contradictory data concerning the same object. For instance: experts present different data versions and one must find one single version to be presented to the user of the system.

Consensus finding is divided into several stages. Firstly, one must examine the structure of *Z* set thoroughly. Then the distance between each subset of *Z* set must be measured. Consensus finding means choosing a set with minimum distance between the set (consensus) and subsets of Z set (according to various criteria). The results obtained by employing the consensus methods represent a given set very well, because they consider all subsets of a set in question, while the choice methods mainly consider only one subset of a given set and only partially other subsets of a set in question. Generally, we can divide the consensus methods into constructive methods, optimisation methods and methods that employ Boolan reasoning (Nguyen, 2002). Constructive methods consists in solving consensus problems on two levels: microstructure and macrostructure of *U* universe. The microstructure of *U* set is the structure of its elements. The macrostructure of *U* set is the structure of the set itself. Optimisation methods consist in defining a consensus function by means of optimisation rules. In many cases these methods employ quasi-median functions, thanks to which the consensus is closer to all solutions from which it is achieved. At the same time, the distance to each solution is uniform. Methods that employ Boolan reasoning encode the consensus problem as a Boole formula in such a way, that each first implicant of the formula determines the solution to the problem. Boole inference proves useful when the number of variables and their fields are not large. Each type of consensus method is used depending on the data structure to which the consensus is sought. A multi-agent decision support system uses mainly constructive and optimization methods.

If we assume that the decisions are represented by means of certain data structures, then the decision making process consists in choosing a subset from the set of possible solutions. We can therefore define a distance function.

We assume that the macrostructure of *U* universe is a certain function

$$o: U \times U \rightarrow [0,1],$$

that meets the requirements:

a) $(\forall x,y \in U)(o(x,y) \geq 0)$,
b) $(\forall x,y \in U)[o(x,y)=0 \Leftrightarrow x=y)$,
c) $(\forall x,y \in U)[o(x,y)= o(y,x))$.

So the *o* function meets all the conditions of a distance function. Note however, that we do not assume the condition of triangle inequality at this point, so the distance function does not have to be metric. The publication (Nguyen, 2002) states that metric conditions are often imposed on distance functions, but in some cases they are too strong. The pair (*U,o*) constitutes some space, called space *with distance*. In a multi-agent distributed decision support system the most useful functions are EM (expense minimizing) and SD (share determining) distance functions which were thoroughly discussed in (Hernes, 2004; Hernes, Nguyen, 2007; Nguyen 2002; Sobieska-Karpińska, Hernes, 2006). The EM distance function between two sets of elements consists in determining minimum cost of transforming one set into the other. As we assume that decisions are sets of elements, it makes a lot of sense to employ the distance function of this kind in a multi-agent distributed decision support system. Very often, however, apart from a set of certain elements (solutions), the decision also contains a time interval that specifies the boundaries of validity of the decision. In this case one should also employ the SD distance function between two sets of infinitesimal values of a given attribute. The function determines the share of each infinitesimal value in the difference. (Nguyen, 2002). An axiomatic approach is often employed to determine consensus function. The purpose of introducing axioms is to use them to determine the class of consensus function, or, in other words, different methods of consensus finding. Besides, since axioms are intuitive conditions to be met by consensus function, they will allow us to give reasons for putting these functions into practice. In the following part of the chapter, we will use the following symbols:

$\Gamma(U)$ - set of all don't empty subsets of uniwersum U,

$\Gamma'(U)$ - det of all don't empty subsets with repetitions of uniwersum U,

$\cup'$ – sum of set with repetitions.

Let $X, X_1, X_2 \in \Gamma'(U), x \in U$. Let us assume the following parameters:

$$o(x,X)=\sum_{y\in X} o(x,y),$$

$$o^n(x,X)=\sum_{y\in X} [\, o(x,y)]^n \text{ dla } n\in N.$$

Note that the parameter $o(x,X)$ represents the sum of distance from x element of universe U to elements of X profile, and the quantity $o^n(x,X)$ represents the sum of n-powers of the distance. This value can be interpreted as a measure of distance uniformity from x element to elements of X profile. The bigger n value, the more uniformity within the distance. The publication (Nguyen, 2002) provides the following definition of consensus function:

Consensus choice function (or consensus function) in space (U,o) is any function represented by:

$$c: \Gamma'(U) \rightarrow \Gamma(U).$$

For profile $X\in\Gamma'(U)$ each set element $c(X)$ will be called its *consensus* and the entire set of $c(X)$ will be called the *representation* of X profile. Let C denote a set of all consensus functions in space (U, o). The following definition presents the axioms for the consensus function (Nguyen, 2002), that express the basic conditions for consensus function, thus determining different methods of consensus:

Let X be any given profile; we state that the consensus function $c\in C$ meets the following postulates:

1. Reliability (Re), if

$$C(X)\neq\emptyset.$$

The postulate assumes that for each profile one can always find a consensus. It corresponds to an optimistic attitude: *any conflict is resolvable.* Reliability is a common criterion in the choice theory. (Dyk, Lenar, 2006).

2. Coherence (Co), if

$$(x\in C(x)) \Rightarrow (x\in c(X\cup' \{x\})).$$

The postulate of *coherence* requires meeting a condition that if any x element is consensus for the X profile, after extending the profile by x (i.e. $X\cup' \{x\}$), the element should form consensus for the new profile. Coherence is a very important property of consensus function, because it allows the user to predict the behaviour of consensus-finding rules, when the premises of independent choices are connected.

3. Quasi-unanimity (Qu), if

$$(x\notin C(x)) \Rightarrow ((\exists n\in N) x\in c(X\cup' \{n*x\})).$$

According to the postulate of *quasi*-unanimity, if an x element is not consensus for an X profile, then it should be consensus for an X^1 profile that contains X and n number of occurence of x element for a given n. In other words, every element of U universe should be chosen as consensus for such a profile, as long as the number of its occurrence is high enough.

4. Proportionality (Pr), if

$$(X_1 \subseteq X_2 \wedge x \in c(X_1) \wedge y \in c(X_2)) \Rightarrow (o(x,X_1) \leq o(y,X_2).$$

The postulate of *proportionality* is quite a natural property, because the bigger the profile the bigger difference between its elements and consensus chosen for it.

5. 1-Optimality (O_1), if

$$(x \in C(x)) \Rightarrow (o(x,X) = \min_{y \in U} o(y,X)).$$

6. 2-Optimality (O_2), if

$$(x \in C(x)) \Rightarrow (o^2(x,X) = \min_{y \in U} o^2(y,X)).$$

The last two postulates are very peculiar. The first one, the postulate of *1-optimality* requires that the consensus be as close (as similar) to the profile elements as possible. Being very common in publications, this postulate determines a specific function class, called *medians*. On the other hand, The postulate of *2-optimality* requires that the sum of square distance from consensus to profile elements be as small as possible. The reason for introducing this postulate results from a completely natural condition concerning consensus function: the consensus needs to be "just"; it means that its distance to profile elements should be as uniform as possible. Note that the number $o^n(x,X)$ defined above can be treated as a measure of uniformity of distance between an object x and X profile elements. Therefore, the above condition requires that the value o^n (consensus, X) be minimum. The publication (Nguyen, 2002) indicates that those functions that meet the postulate of *2-optimality* are better than the functions that meet the postulate of *1-optimality* because of higher uniformity. The difference between them and other consensus functions is that they are more similar to profile elements. Thus, the postulate of *2-optimality* is a good criterion in finding consensus. In the decision making process when there is a case of uncertainty, it is good to employ consensus which is more uniform, meaning it takes all the possible solutions into consideration to the same degree. If therefore the postulate of *2-optimality* allows to acquire higher uniformity than the postulate of *1-optimality*, one should also define a postulate of *n-optimality* that when $n>2$ will allow us to acquire even higher consensus uniformity than the postulate of *2-optimality*. Therefore, the postulate will have the following definition:

We say that consensus function $c \in C$ meets the postulate of n-optimality, (O_2), if

$$(x \in C(x)) \Rightarrow (o^n(x,X) = \min_{y \in U} o^n(y,X)).$$

The postulate is a generalisation of the two postulates of *1-optimality* and *2-optimality*.

The publication (Nguyen, 2002) proves that it is not possible for consensus function to meet all postulates at the same time. Therefore, specific consensus functions, defined for various structures will differ according to postulates they are to meet. The postulates of consensus function determine each kind of consensus method. In constructive methods we can use all the postulates. Of course, as we mentioned earlier, a specific consensus function (that determines consensus for a specific data structure) cannot meet all the postulates at the same time, however in constructive methods we can define various consensus functions, that is why these methods generally use all the postulates. Optimisation methods use the postulates *Pr*, O_1, O_2, O_n. They allow to define quasi-median functions. Methods that employ Boolean reasoning are used mainly with the postulates *Re,Co, Qu.* The publications often present other postulates of consensus function, however this chapter indicates those postulates which can be used in a multi-agent decision support system. If we use consensus finding methods for the purpose of reconciling a decision for the user, then what we call consensus is a solution which allows to take all system nodes into consideration and helps all nodes indicate the smallest "loss" possible. Each node contributes to the consensus and all nodes accept it.

We can say that consensus is a representation of all the nodes of the system.

The example methods of increasing information value presented here make distributed decision support systems function more properly, thus helping the decision maker (the user) make the right decision.

FUTURE RESEARCH DIRECTIONS

Information has become a factor creating new values which are of great economic importance. Its relevance as a resource has been widely recognized. It can be expected that rigorous rules governing information distribution and protection will be introduced. This involves also the changes of the requirements that information systems need to meet as regards data storage, processing and transfer. The development of information systems is a continuous process, depending mainly on the expectations and demands of decision-makers in different types of organizations and on the ever changing environment. Multi-agent systems are gaining on importance as nowadays decision –makers require the system not only to process information and draw conclusions but also to undertake specific actions depending on socio economic circumstance, both internal and external. It is not enough, for example, for a system to inform the manager that a given piece of information is out-of-date; it ought to be able to find another source providing an up-to-date piece of information so that the manager does not need to bother with this problem. Because only the information that has a given value may constitute the basis of the decision making process, we may expect further intensification of the attempts to determine the value of information, which shall simplify trading in this resource. If the decision –maker in a company does not know the specific value of the information, they are not able to estimate the costs of taking a decision in this particular case. If, however, the value of the information is known (for example if it is expressed in terms of money), the decision –maker is able to estimate the costs of taking a specific decision and in consequence they are aware what kind of benefits the organization may gain.

If the company uses a distributed decision support system, then of course this system needs to suggest solutions that will be useful for the decision-makers in taking the right decisions. As has already been emphasized, the main factor affecting proper functioning of a dispersed decision making support system is the possession of the information that has the value required by the decision-maker. Thus, the value of the information in such systems is gaining on importance because the amount of information is increasing all the time and any piece of information needs to be evaluated more and more precisely in order to take the right decision. Another important aspect is the intensification of the search for ways of increasing the value of the information already possessed, which undoubtedly simplifies making right decisions. Currently, more and more often decision support systems are incorporated in the whole process of knowledge management in the company, that is all actions enabling the creation, dissemination and application of knowledge in the implementation of business processes. Thus, more and more often the discussion concerns not only the value of information but the value of knowledge, that is the information skillfully used to draw proper conclusions.

CONCLUSION

Information value plays a significant role in dispersed decision making support systems. It must be noticed that nowadays there is excess of information and it is extremely important to select the information needed to solve a given problem, or in other words, to make the right decision. Users have ever increasing expectations and the best possible outcome of the system functioning is of paramount importance, which is of course impossible without correct determination of the value of the information constituting the basis of the system functioning. In this paper only selected information measures and ways of increasing information value in distribyted decision support systems have been presented. However, the issues discussed here may be further investigated in subsequent works on this subject..

REFERENCES

Ahituv, N., & Neumann, S. (1986). *Principles of information systems for measurement*. Dubuque: W. C. Brown Publ.

Alexander, T. M. (2003). Measuring the value of geo-spatial information: Critical need or fools errand. In *Proceedings of the 3 Biennial Coastal GeoTools Conference*. Charleston, USA. Retrieved August 2008 from http://www.csc.noaa.gov/geotcols/proceedings/pdf.files/os abs/alexander.pdf

Arrow, K. J. (Ed.). (1963). *Social choice and individual values.* New York: John Wiley.

Drucker, P. F. (1995). *Managing in a time of great change*. New York: Truman Talley Books/Dutton.

Dyk, P., & Lenar, M. (2006). Applying negotiation methods to resolve conflict in multi-agent environments. In C. Daniłowicz (Ed), *Multimedia and network information systems* (pp. 259-269). Wrocław: Wroclaw University of Technology Press.

Ferber, J. (1999). *Multi-agent systems*. New York: Addison Wesley.

Friedag, H. R., & Schmidt, W. (2003). *My balanced scorecard.* Warszawa: Wydawnictwo C. H. Beck.

Gudea, S. W. (2004). Media richness and the valuation of online discussion support systems. In *Proceedings of the Annual Conference of the Southern Association for Information Systems.* Savannah, GA, USA.

Hernes, M. (2004). Coordinate inconsistent of knowledge in a distributed systems using a consensus method. In C. Daniłowicz (Ed.), *Multimedia and network information systems*. Wrocław: Wroclaw University of Technology Press.

Hernes, M., & Nguyen, N. T. (2004). Deriving consensus for incomplete ordered partitions. In N.T. Nguyen (Ed.), *Intelligent technologies for inconsistent knowledge processing. Advanced knowledge international.* Australia: Advanced Knowledge International.

Hernes, M., & Nguyen, N. T. (2007). Deriving consensus for hierarchical incomplete ordered partitions and coverings. *Journal of Universal Computer Science*, *13*(2), 317–328.

Jaworski, M. (2002). Wywiad gospodarczy na wewnętrzny użytek. *EBIB Elektroniczny Biuletyn Informacyjny Bibliotekarzy*, 11. Retrieved August 2008 from http://ebib.oss.wroc.pl/2002/40

Konarzewska-Gubała, E. (1989). *BIPOLAR: Multiple Criteria Decision Aid Using Bipolar Reference System,* (Cashier and Documents no 56). Paris: Dauphine Universite Paris, LAMSADE.

Korczak, J., & Lipiński, P. (2008). Systemy agentowe we wspomaganiu decyzji na rynku paperów wartościowych. In S. Stanek, H. Sroka, M. Paprzycki, & M. Ganzha (Eds.), *Rozwój nformatycznych systemów weloagentowych w środowsach społeczno-gospodarczych*. Warszawa: Placet Press.

Kulikowski, R., Libura, M., & Słomiński, L. (1998). *Investment decision support*. Warszawa: Polish Academy of Science.

McCann, J. M. (1994). *Adding product value through information*. Retrieved May 2007 from http://www.duke.edu/_mccann/infovalu.htm.

Michna, A. (2008). *Przegląd koncepcji kapitału intelektualnego przedsiębiorstw*. Retrieved June 2008 from http://www.paba.org.pl/publikacje/ koncepcje kapitału intelektualnego.pdf.

Morrison, C. T., & Cohen, P. R. (2005). Noisy information value in utility-based decision making. In *Proc. Workshop on Utility-based Data Mining*. Chicago, USA.

Myerson, R. B. (1996). *Fundamentals of social choice theory* (Discusion Paper No. 1214). Center for Mathematical Studies in Economics and Management Science, Nortwestern University.

Nguyen, N. T. (2002). *Methods for consensus choice and their applications in conflict resolving in distributed systems*. Wrocław: Wroclaw University of Technology Press.

Nowak, M. (2004). Preference and veto thresholds in multicriteria analysis based on stochastic dominance. *European Journal of Operational Research, 158*(2), 339–350. doi:10.1016/j.ejor.2003.06.008

Olender-Skorek, M., & Wydro, K.B. (2007). Wartość Informacji. *Telekomunikacja i techniki informacyjne,* 1-2, 72-80.

Pike, S., & Roos, G. (2000). *Intellectual capital measurement and holistic value approach (HVA)*. Works Institute Journal Japan, vol. 42. Retrieved June 2008 from http://www.intcap.com/ICS Article 2000 IC Measurement HVA.pdf

Purczyński, J. (2003). *Using a computer simulation in estimation chosen ekonometric and statistics models*. Szczecin: Szczecin University Science Press.

Ślęzak, D., Synak, P., Wieczorkowska, A., & Wróblewski, J. (2002). KDD-based approach to musical instrument sound recognition. In M.S. Hacid, Z.W. Raś, D.A. Zighed, Y. Kodratoff (Eds.), *Foundations of Intelligent Systems. Proc. of 13th Symposium ISMIS 2002, Lyon, France* (LNAI 2366, pp. 28-36).

Sobieska-Karpińska, J., & Hernes, M. (2006). Consensus methods in hierarchical and weight incomplete ordered partitions. In J. Dziechciarz (Ed.), *Ekonometric. Employment of quantitative methods*. Wrocław: Wroclaw University of Economics Press.

Sobieska-Karpińska, J., & Hernes, M. (2007). Metody consensusu w systemach wspomagających podejmowanie decyzji, In J. Dziechciarz (Ed), *Ekonometria. Zastosowania metod ilościowych*. Wrocław: Wrocław: Wroclaw University of Economics Press.

Stanek, S., Sroka, H., & Twardowski, Z. (2003). *Decision Support Systems and New Information Technologies at the Beginning of Internet Age*. 7th International Conference of the International Society for Decision Support Systems, Ustroń, Poland.

Stefanowicz, B. (2004). *Informacja*, Warszawa: Oficyna Wydawnicza Szkoły Głównej Handlowej w Warszawie.

Sveiby, K. E. (1997). *The new organization wealth*. San Francisco: Berrett-Koehler Publ.

Sveiby, K. E. (2008). *Measuring intangibles and intellectual capital – an emerging first standard.* Retrieved July 2008 from http://www.sveiby.com

Tappenden, P., Chilcott, J., Eggington, S., Oakley, J., & McCabe, C. (2004). Methods for expected value of information analysis in complex health economic models: developments on the health economics models (...). *Health Technology Assessment, 8*(27).

Trzaskalik, T. (Ed.). (2006). *Metody wielokryterialne na polskim rynku finansowym.* Warszawa: Polskie Wydawnictwo Ekonomiczne.

Van Alsyne, M. V. (1999). *A proposal for valuing information and instrumental goods.* International Conference on Information Systems, Charlotte, USA.

Varian, H. R. (2002). *Mikroekonomia. Kurs średni – ujęcie nowoczesne.* Warszawa: PWN.

Wierzbicki, A. P., & Wydro, K. B. (2006) *Informacyjne aspekty negocjacji.* Warszawa: Wydawnictwo Naukowe Obserwacje.

ADDITIONAL READING

Ahituv, N. (1989). *Assessing the value of information: problems and approaches.* In *Proceedings of ICIS-89*, Boston, USA

Bell, D. (1973). *The coming of post-industrial society. A venture in social forecasting.* New York: Basic Books.

Bernknopf, R. L., Brookshire, D. S., McKee, M., & Soller, D. R. (1997). Estimating the social value of geologic map information: A regulatory application. *Journal of Environmental Economics and Management, 32*, 204–218. doi:10.1006/jeem.1996.0963

Bouri, G., Martel, J. M., & Chabchoub, H. (2002). A multicriterion approach for selecting attractive portfolio. *Journal of Multicriteria Decision Analysis, 11*(3), 269–277. doi:10.1002/mcda.334

Horia, D. (2001). *Baze de date.* Oradea: University of Oradea Publishing House.

Kahneman, D., & Lovallo, D. (1993). Timid choices and bold forecasts. A cognitive perspective on risk taking. *Management Science*, 39.

Kaplan, R., & Norton, D. (2004). *Measuring the strategic readiness of intangible assets.* Cambridge: Harvard University, Harvard Business Review.

Krol, D., & Nguyen, N. T. (Eds.). (2008). *Intelligence integration in distributed knowledge management.* Hershey, PA: IGI Global.

Meyer, H. W. J. (2005). *The nature of information and the effective use of information in rural development.* Information Research, *10*(2).

National Research Council, Space Studies Board and Ocean Studies Board. (2001). *Transforming Remote Sensing Data into Information and Applications.* Washington, DC: National Academy Press.

Nguyen, N. T., Kolaczek, G., & Gabrys, B. (Eds.). (2008). *Knowledge processing and reasoning for information society.* Warsaw: EXIT.

Raban, D. R., & Rafaeli, S. (2002). *Subjective value of information: Rhe endowment effect.* Haifa: University of Haifa.

KEY TERMS AND DEFINITIONS

Value of Information: Relative usefulles of informaton for user.

Quality of Information: Property by information definite attributes.

Distributed System: System consist of many computers joined by network assigned for realization definite purpose.

Decision Support Systems: Computer systems aiming decision making process.

Information Structuralizing: Writing information in the form of certain structure.

Knowledge Discovery in Databases: Domain of computer science deal with deployment of algorythmits instruments for discovering knowledge from data.

Agent Program: An intelligent program, which is able to react on change in its environment

Multi-Agent System: Distributed system deal with many program agents.

Multicriterial Decisions: Decisions making base many criterions of estimate.

Conflict in Distributed Systems: Situation in which nodes in distributed systems own different data.

Choice Methods: Metods helping solve conflict in distributed systems rely on choice one of solution present by participant of conflict.

Consensus Methods: Metods helping solve conflict in distributed systems rely on assigment of new sollution base on solutions presente by participant of conflict.

Chapter 10
Accounting and Billing in Computing Environments

Claus-Peter Rückemann
Westfälische Wilhelms-Universität (WWU), Münster, Germany; Gottfried Wilhelm Leibniz Universität Hannover (LUH), Hannover, Germany; North-German Supercomputing Alliance (HLRN), Norddeutscher Verbund für Hoch- und Höchstleistungsrechnen, Germany

ABSTRACT

This chapter gives a comprehensive overview of the current status of accounting and billing for up-to-date computing environments. Accounting is the key for the management of information system resources. At this stage of evolution of accounting systems it is adequate not to separate computing environments into High Performance Computing and Grid Computing environments for allowing a "holistic" view showing the different approaches and the state of the art for integrated accounting and billing in distributed computing environments. Requirements resulting from a public survey within all communities of the German Grid infrastructure, as well as from computing centres and resource providers of High Performance Computing resources like HLRN, and ZIVGrid, within the German e-Science framework, have been considered as well as requirements resulting from various information systems and the virtualisation of organisations and resources. Additionally, conceptual, technical, economical, and legal questions also had to be taken into consideration. After the requirements have been consolidated and implementations have been done over one year ago, now the overall results and conclusions are presented in the following sections showing a case study based on the GISIG framework and the Grid-GIS framework. The focus is on how an integrated architecture can be built and used in heterogeneous environments. A prototypical implementation is outlined that is able to manage and visualise relevant accounting and billing information based on suitable monitoring data in a virtual organisation (VO) specific way regarding basic business, economic, and security issues.

DOI: 10.4018/978-1-60566-890-1.ch010

INTRODUCTION

Computation is based on counting. Making use of computing environments is based on accounting. The meaning of "accounting" has changed over the last decades as new computing paradigms evolved. So in the golden age of computing there was not much use of accounting as human operating could oversee the whole computing installation. With technology developing towards concurring users, multiple processes, many processing units, vast amounts of disk space the relevance of accounting got prominent to those people operating the computing resources. But lastly the triumphal procession of omnipresent computing facility on the average desktop made accounting one of the top issues on the list of challenges for making large and networked installations of resources and services feasible. Currently we are in a stage of development where billing of resources, meaning hardware, software, and services, gets into public interest. Society demands and huge branches of computing and software industry rely on the fact that their efforts remunerate. With this development the pricing and billing aspects form new interests.

The basic work consolidating the available mechanisms and building an integrated solution has been done in the last years (Rückemann, 2006; Rückemann, Göhner, & Baur, 2007). Various groups running computing environments rely on these preparatory work and customise them to their needs (D-Grid, 2008; HLRN, 2008). As systems evolve single or national solutions and fragmentation must be prevented in order to make integrated accounting and billing part of future system management for the next generation of computing environments including resources and services.

The objectives of this chapter are to reveal some "bleading edge" aspects of accounting and billing strategies based on this preparatory work and to demonstrate the current and near future developments in the world of scientific and public computing stepping into broadening of commercial interests. All trademarks and names used in this text copyright their respective owners. As resulting in management of information system resources, this includes load from information systems on these resources. Examples for using information systems based on accountable resources are given in connection with these topics.

BACKGROUND

As the meaning of the terms monitoring, accounting and billing is not sharply delimited, with respect to computing environments the following conventions may be helpful:

- **Monitoring** means metering, gathering, analysing and reporting as well as management of information belonging to the state of computing resources and services.
- **Accounting** means gathering, analysing and reporting as well as management of information belonging to the usage of computing resources and services. The most important objectives are optimisation and journaling of resource usage. With appropriate basic implementations, accounting can extend monitoring for the mentioned purposes.
- **Billing** means pricing and charging, based on the calculation of certain quantities of computing resource usage on various economic foci. With appropriate basic implementations, billing can extend accounting for this purpose.

It must be emphasised that "resources" in this context does cover hardware resources as well as services. The chances for configuring an accounting for your specific information-related services will be shown in the comparison of existing systems and concepts. Services is just a specific type of resource. As services is much more heterogeneous than hardware accounting for any specific purpose metrics will have to be defined. The system chosen should be able to support a flexible concept for metrics. Based on these fundaments, accounting and billing can provide valuable means for steering the resource usage in computing environments. As for steering this is meant to be hardware in most cases, the examples given within the sections describing the integrated architecture, concentrate on the purpose of accounting of information-related services for complementing the view for the end-user.

Due to the fact that in most currently implemented systems, monitoring, accounting, and billing systems often reside as one or more components that implement the necessary functionalities in parallel or redundant ways, a first overall concept for the implementation of an integrated monitoring, accounting, and billing system for computing in heterogeneous environments is needed. This system must be able to span several communities, respect their local policies, and inherit a complex federal state background.

Publicly available systems like APEL (Accounting Processor for Event Logs) (Byrom, Cordenonsi, Cornwall, Craig, Abdeslem, Ducan, Fisher, Gordon, Hicks, Kant, Leake, Middleton, Thorpe, Walk, & Wilson, 2005), DGAS (Distributed Grid Accounting System), GASA (Grid Accounting Services Architecture) (Barmouta & Buyya, 2003), GRASP (Grid Based Application Service Provision) (GRASP Tutorial, 2005), GSAX (Grid Service Accounting Extensions) (Beardsmore, Hartley, Hawkins, Laws, Magowan, & Twigg, 2002), Nimrod/G, and SGAS (SweGrid Accounting System) (Elmroth, Gardfjäll, Mulmo, Sandgren, & Sandholm, 2003; Gardfjäll, 2003) implement a variety of solutions, suitable for distributed computing environments and High Performance Computing (HPC). There is documentation details and illustration for all of these systems available (Göhner & Rückemann, 2006, "Accounting-Ansätze ...").

Well known projects facing developments for accounting are DEISA (Distributed European Infrastructure for Supercomputing Applications, 2007), EGEE (EGEE, 2005), GGF (Global Grid Forum, 2006), OGF (Open Grid Forum, 2007), LCG (Large Hadron Collider Computing Grid), GESA (Grid Economic Services Architecture Working Group, 2006; Newhouse, 2003), MOGAS (Lim, Ho, Zhang, Lee, & Ong, 2005), EcoGrid (Abramson, Buyya, & Giddy, 2001), and DGI (D-Grid Integration project) within the German Grid Initiative (D-Grid, 2008). As for one of the most current activities, D-Grid, the Sections Monitoring, Accounting, Billing (M/A/B) in the DGI recognised SGAS the most suitable framework for the future.

Most future Grid will need support for Virtual Organisations (VO) and secure authentication (Rieger, Gersbeck-Schierholz, Mönnich, & Wiebelitz, 2006). Using adequate management is therefore most important (VOMS). As upcoming standards like GMA and R-GMA (Relational Grid Monitoring Architecture, 2006), MDS (Monitoring and Discovery Service), OGSA (Open Grid Service Architecture), WSRF (WebService-Resource Framework) should be used anyhow, storage, exchange and transfer of accounting data can already be handled using Usage Records (Mach, Lepro-Metz, Booz, Jackson, & McGinnis, 2003) standards like RUR (Resource Usage Records) and RUS (Resource Usage Services). So with this development, aspects like QoS (Quality of Service) are getting immanent for day to day usage. Service provisioning via Cloud Computing is on its way. CSM (Customer Service Management) will round these efforts off.

For an overall example on aspects of measurement and the process of monitoring one should take into consideration the illustrations and descriptions available on the Web (Göhner & Rückemann, 2006, "Konzeption eines Grid Accounting Systems"). For an example of a Mobile Grid scenario you will see additional specific requirements (Morariu, Waldburger, & Stiller, 2006). Many issues have been investigated on the service layer, regarding the integration of multiple and often heterogeneous possibilities to realise an integrated monitoring and accounting system. Important issues have been the investigation and, where applicable, the integration of different schemata for resource descriptions as well as the selection of standardised components that provide suitable access methods to monitoring and accounting services.

This text presents the results of the work that can be seen "on presentation level" as the integration of standardised services in a web-based basic application on top of a Service Management Platform which can be used for the visualisation of monitoring and accounting data of different Virtual Organisations.

HIGH END COMPUTING AND HIGH PERFORMANCE COMPUTING

As far as High End Computing (HEC) being a genus for High Performance Computing and various other ambitioned computing paradigms is an issue of national interest for most countries, reliability and security are the most important factors for operating these services. Science and Research is depending on the results of their computations. Just with this everyone is depending on systems and operating systems used. So problems most imminent arise with

- large number of cores,
- large number of nodes,
- distributed memory usage,
- large number of large hard disks.

Depending on standards like those developed by the Department of Defense, accountability is one of the keys for employing vast computing power. Any system use has to be accountable in order to ensure that access is comprehensible and can be reproduced. Nevertheless this is even more important if billing of resource usage has to be done. The key challenges for the next ten years will be

- integrating new concepts and managing complexity of systems,
- handling huge numbers of hardware and software components,
- preserving industry independent science and research,
- maintaining a strong domestic HEC industry through government funding, as necessary,
- establishing viable national and international technology development strategies to support future HPC and HEC,
- clarifying critical dependencies on HEC in the science, technology, and national security communities,
- building far more effective partnerships between academia, government, industry, and the HEC vendor development and user communities,
- recruiting, training, and developing our successors,
- implementing some cohesive national programs that creatively cement the points above.

The fundamental computer architectural developments like the introduction of vector processing by Cray was one of the major impacts on modern system design. Balanced use of processors, memory, and communication for different applications were the key to more than a decade for optimised use of computers as "tools". Now that scalar and vector processing tended to go on, scalability got to it's saturation and the MPP (Massively Parallel Processing) paradigm provided a new way to more computing power. With developments like Beowulf and "stone soup" installations, "High Performance Computing" got into reach of many research groups that up to that point have had no chance to get hold of own HPC installations. For anyone being serious in the business, there is no such thing like "Distributed HPC". For example with earth sciences and environmental tasks, various national and public interests exist for motivating industry to get into these issues more easily.

As the tool you have must be suited for the kind of problem, today it is still difficult to create specialised applications for solving specific problems with existing architectures, e.g. the massively parallel single instruction architectures.

The cluster computing for the masses displaced the focus though. In the public "institutional" interest the limits of HPC became blurred for years now and the development of more scalable solutions slowed down. The trend is heading for massive MultiCore clusters. This trend will force adaption of many of the current software designs.

ManyCore and MultiCore architectures need a lot of software support to be successful. Today it is clearly predictable that software if the crucial point at this stage, otherwise installations with over one hundred thousand or even millions of cores will not be effectively operable:

- significant parts of operating systems will have to be redesigned,
- management software and operating software will have to reduce the heterogeneity and complexity seen in day to day life,
- compilers will have to be basically and transparently ManyCore and MultiCore aware,
- scheduling and job management will have to consider new strategies,
- a resource sparing monitoring is necessary for handling basic information,
- batch systems will have to be developed to collect the overall system information, maybe even for brokering these vast resources,
- and accounting systems are needed to fulfill the requirements of all of these for delivering a contemporary overview, being an window to the management and to the public.

At this level the usability and operability of computing environments crucially depends on the system software. And the developments for this step must be put into practice in the near future. This is where industry and market forces are setting their marks. The pricing and billing of these resources are beginning to play a driving role. Early vehicles for these bumpy roads will be tuned applications, adapted algorithms used so far, and in the end library sets and standardisation may result. Currently industry hesitates to pursue this way and the isolated development outposts of most institutes and projects are only listened with half an ear.

COMPUTING ENVIRONMENTS: PRESENT SITUATION

Initiatives and alliances for High Performance Computing already do have decades of tradition in the scientific world. Within the last decade several national Cluster and Grid initiatives all over the world tried to enforce a momentum for distributed computing, like in the United Kingdom, Germany, the United States, Greece – just to name a few. Companies gained market readiness with what they call "Utility Computing", "Autonomic Computing" and a lot of different names. Institutions and Organisation that could not afford market solutions tried using their "spare" resources at night hours – sometimes using cheap power during the night time, using heterogeneous architectures and so on.

The D-Grid is a sustainable Grid infrastructure in Germany with the objective to establish methods of e-Science in the German scientific community. Within D-Grid in the year 2009, several so-called Community Grids from various areas of research (e.g., medicine, astronomy, high energy physics, climate research, spatial information sciences, business and financial areas etc.) as well as diverse resource providers (e.g., supercomputing centres, universities, research institutions etc.) jointly offer a broad range of offering complex Grid services and Grid resources which can be used by the German scientific community. In the context of D-Grid, the inter-organisational accounting of Grid resources and Grid services which may be itself supplied by a multiplicity of providers inheres a particular importance and poses new challenging questions to the task of accounting.

The acquisition, determination, administration, supply, and evaluation of usage data determines an essential basis for the provisioning and billing of resources and services within the context of complex computing environments. Thus, the development and specification of an adequate Grid accounting architecture within the e-Science framework is one of the major tasks taking into account specific requirements and characteristics against the background of Virtual Organisations as well as of resource and service provisioning across administrative borders. Even for the European DEISA there is currently no integrated accounting and billing approach available. Existing middlewares like Globus Toolkit (Globus Alliance, 2008) and UNICORE (UNICORE, 2008) can be used on High Performance Computing installations as well as with Grid Computing. Beside that aspect, an accounting system supporting the Grid middleware UNICORE does not yet exist. Moreover, a fundamental difficulty regarding the conceptual development of the proposed accounting system is a result of the varying requirements as well as partly different perceptions of the D-Grid communities respective resource providers with respect to the process of accounting.

So what we need are developments that lead to a sustainable solution, aware of monitoring, accounting, and billing. For the implementation of an integrated monitoring, accounting, and billing architecture for computing environments the existing different and heterogeneous conditions within the science community regarding High Performance Computing and Grid Computing has to be taken into consideration.

Three small examples for present conditions are given in order to illustrate this aspect.

- **Condition 1:** computational compound structure, steering via scientific committee, assignment of contingents, no end-user billing.

Typically for present High Performance Computing and Supercomputing.

- **Condition 2:** commercial participation of economic interests respective branches of trades, in part exclusive use of computing resources, proprietary solutions.

Typically for present High Performance Computing partly financed by economy partners.

- **Condition 3:** federal structures, heterogeneous concepts and applications, scientific research centered, no billing, scientific fair-share idea.

Typically for present Grid Computing.

After having seen the different conditions, we will now show some prominent examples for the different activities present within the commercial, the scientific supercomputing and the Grid Computing areas.

Commercial Activities

With the evolving computing landscape of the last years currently there exist a number of different paradigms for Cluster and Grid Computing. Regarding different companies we see a variety of different "Grid Islands" (Rückemann, 2007) for example Sun uses terms like "Cluster", "Enterprise Grids", "Global Grids", Hewlett Packard promotes "Utility Computing", and IBM is in with "Autonomic Computing", "Resource centred Computing", and promotes "dynamic Virtual Organisations". Accounting solutions are more or less vendor specific.

Cluster Activities

A very nice Grid and Cluster Computing project started years ago within state of Nordrhein-Westfalen with the ZIVGrid (Leweling, 2005) and ZIVcluster (Ost & Leweling, 2005; ZIV der WWU Münster – ZIVcluster, 2006). The ZIVGrid project is using Condor software for providing heterogeneous hardware resources like workstations and personal computer pools (Thain, Tannenbaum, & Livny, 2002) to users while enlarging the average utilisation of existing resources. Computing resources of various ZIVPools being part of a Condor-pool can be used by selecting a specific "Universe" which means a defined hardware and software environment. The standard "Universe" supports checkpointing and and remote system calls so that it easily enables job run times for several weeks and in some cases for more than 120 days. In the year 2006 ZIVcluster has been upgraded, including Cluster System Management (CSM), Portable Batch System (PBS), GPFS, new compiler and MPICH versions. A mix of heterogeneous hardware architecture (32 bit and 64 bit) is supported. ZIVGrid has been combined with the regional Grids of the University of Aachen (NRW-Grid of RWTH Aachen) and the University of Cologne. So with this configuration there exist configurable automatic overflow computing capabilities with several hundred nodes. There is one defined submit host from ZIVGrid and results from any calculation are transferred back to ZIVcluster. Accounting is done via Condor but there are no limitations to academic users regarding use of resources or consumption of computing time.

Scientific Supercomputing: North-German Supercomputing Alliance

HLRN (Norddeutscher Verbund für Hoch- und Höchstleistungsrechnen) is the North-German Supercomputing Alliance (HLRN, 2008). HLRN provides high-end High Performance Computing (HPC) resources jointly used and co-funded by the northern German states of Niedersachsen, Berlin, Bremen, Hamburg, Mecklenburg-Vorpommern, Schleswig-Holstein, and the Federal Government of Germany / German Research Society (DFG).

Those resources include HLRN-II, a system comprised of two identical computing and storage complexes, one located at the RRZN in Hannover and the second in Berlin (HLRN-II Photo Gallery, 2008). By connecting the two systems via the HLRN-Link dedicated optic network, HLRN can operate and administer them as one system. Each complex consists of MPP (Massively Parallel Processing) and SMP (Symmetric Multi-Processing) cluster components (SGI Altix ICE and XE) installed in two phases. The first phase has been installed in the year 2008.

The HLRN-II system (at 312 TFlop/s peak) operated with SLES is used by scientists for HPC applications from a wide range of disciplines, including Geosciences, Environmental Sciences, Physics, CFD, Modeling and Simulation, Chemistry, Biology, and Engineering. All projects are supported by the HLRN service and competence network. The base for accounting in the HLRN is contingents described by the North-German parallel computer performance unit "NPL" (Norddeutsche Parallelrechner-Leistungseinheit). The NPL definition is based on computation time and the number of processors and resources used. Due to the evolution of HLRN resources and hardware configuration over the years this definition is depending on the the specific system used. Therefore the definition has been modified with the transition from HLRN-I to HLRN-II in the year 2008. A new accounting algorithm had to be created for handling the computing resources, differing from those with HLRN-I. For a period of time both algorithms have to exist in parallel on the systems. The causes for different algorithms are dependencies on

- hardware (CPU, memory, disk storage),
- software (operating system, system and management software),

- networks (Input/Output, Message Passing Interface),
- organisational background,
- integration of different resources.

Any of the resource descriptions and algorithms must be comparable. The optimal choice is depending on what is decided to be most suitable for the specific community of users. This is not restricted to computing power. Even more difficult that computing power cannot be defined by one aspect. For example benchmark algorithms like SPEC do lead to different results on different processors, because of the primary issues they address. This forces to use benchmarking suites of different benchmarks and this complicates the valuation. This is where means of brokering of resources can fill the gap for leading to a market concept. This is as well triggered by the fact that resource valuations will have to change over the time, so there is an "aging factor" within brokering of resources.

One essential part of the accounting prerequisites is the batch system. For a lot of High Performance Computing and Grid Computing installations Moab (Moab Admin Manual, 2008; Moab Users Guide, 2008) and Torque (Torque Administrator Manual, 2008) are used. As with large and complex computing environments, nearly all systems worldwide are individually customised from the hardware, networking, and software point of view. So accounting systems in High Performance Computing environments need to stay custom solutions at a certain extent.

Grid Computing: German Grid Initiative

The D-Grid project is part of the national Grid initiative in Germany (D-Grid, 2008) and started in September, 2005 (Heise Newsticker, 2005). The results presented in this text are partially based on the work of the sections "Monitoring", "Accounting", and "Billing" (M/A/B) within the D-Grid Integration project (DGI). The major objective is the design of a substantial D-Grid-wide system for user and resource management and usage compensation. This also involves issues of Customer Service Management (CSM). The overall challenge to achieve this aim is the heterogeneity of the existing organisational structures, hardware, and Grid middlewares. In the years 2006/2007 the first conceptional basis for a suitable prototype system for monitoring, accounting, and billing has been worked out. The concepts and frameworks of the sections M/A/B provided an adequate basis for further discussions with and within the D-Grid communities in order to create a sustainable and coordinated conceptual solution for accounting and cost allocation in D-Grid aiming at an integrated implementation for accounting, billing, and customer services (Rückemann, Müller, & von Voigt, 2007). The work has gone on implementing dynamic, accountable applications on High Performance Computing and Grid Computing resources based on events (Rückemann, 2007).

COMPUTING ENVIRONMENTS: REQUIREMENTS

Designing a prototype for High Performance Computing and Grid Computing while taking into consideration the problems and incorporating the different models for handling computing resources in all cases necessitate a comprehensive requirements analysis. For getting into requirements for resource usage let us just show some scenarios and discuss the overall state of the requirements analysis.

Computing with Linguistics and Thesauri

So for example while using various linguistic algorithms, calculation can easily be done in parallel (Matthies & Rückemann, 2003), calculating various character strings. One will have to wait for the slowest stream within the calculation. After all separate stream calculations are finished they can be combined to build combined character strings. The same procedure would be done for accounting these calculation processes. If there are requirements for using complex thesauri databases with these calculations the algorithms can get very complicated as they get non-linear. It will therefore no longer be possible to do a loosely coupled parallel processing and accounting. So premise is to accept some reduction of complexity for defined day-to-day application purposes. Appropriate algorithms have been successfully tested on HPC and Cluster resources like HLRN and ZIVGrid/ZIVcluster.

Computing and Heterogeneous Encyclopedic Scientific Information

With the lexicographical analysis of large heterogeneous information a lot of challenges arise. Many of which have been studied within the interdisciplinary LX Project over the last years (LX Project, 2008), building categories and parallel processing algorithms as well as selection and reduction of uniformly structured data with pattern support. For the calculation distributed computing resources in the state of Nordrhein-Westfalen have been used. For loosely parallel processing Grid resources have been used, for large single requests High Performance Computing cluster resources were required in order to minimise synchronisation latencies. As with these requirements basic accounting is straight forward. Premise is to bring complexity to clearly defined steps. Appropriate algorithms have been successfully tested on HPC and Grid resources like HLRN and ZIVGrid/ZIVcluster.

Computing and Scientific Geoinformation

Computing of geoinformation for dynamical applications and processing of geoscientific data for supporting e-Science is one of the goals of the GISIG framework (Applications with Active Map Software, 2005; Rückemann, 2001; Rückemann, 2007) for creating components for geoscientific information systems. A lot of applications have been demonstrated with the actmap component, using distributed compute clusters, High Performance Computing and Grid Computing resources for these purposes. Accounting can be done for various parts of the application. Premise is to define a set of application components that can be handled within the configuration of the resources involved. Appropriate algorithms have been successfully tested on HPC, Cluster, and Grid resources like HLRN, ZIVcluster, and ZIVGrid.

State of Requirements Analysis for Computing Environments

Based on a comprehensive requirements analysis (Rückemann, 2006; Rückemann, Müller, Ritter, Reiser, Kunze, Göhner, Falkner, & Mucha, 2005), details for internationally available monitoring, accounting, and billing systems have been discussed. The results presented in these documents have been the fundament for the Globus Toolkit based monitoring infrastructure in the DGI, the conception of the accounting architecture for the D-Grid, the D-Grid billing framework, and the prototype GridCSM.

All documentation from the D-Grid sections mentioned here is publicly available in form of D-Grid documents (D-Grid, 2008), including the requirements analysis, accounting systems and a billing framework. Providing an overall overview for the implementation of the accounting system, this document contains an evaluation of existing accounting and billing approaches which can be used in an integrated monitoring, accounting, and billing system. Foundations for the evaluation are, on the one hand, the requirements derived from the requirements catalogue and, on the other hand, the analysis of the results of the comprehensive survey conducted in the years 2005/2006 with respect to the requirements of the Grid communities and Grid resource providers.

Further work has been done for specifying the conception of an accounting system, as well as deducting an architecture and a prototype for resource and service monitoring in different Virtual Organisations. Many issues have been investigated on the service layer, regarding the integration of multiple and often heterogeneous possibilities to realise an integrated monitoring and accounting system. Important issues have been the investigation and, where applicable, the integration of different schemata for resource descriptions as well as the selection of standardised components that provide suitable access methods to monitoring and accounting services. This text is based the results of the work done in various countries and can be seen on presentation layer as the integration of standardised services in a web-based basic application on top of a Service Management Platform which can be used for the visualisation of monitoring and accounting data of different Virtual Organisations. As for an example at the present time at the end of the year 2008, the German D-Grid is characterised by a high degree of heterogeneity resulting from a multitude of different Grid middleware solutions, diverse hardware platforms, underlying operating systems, as well as various types of heterogeneous Grid resources provided within the German Grid infrastructure providing a variety of organisational, software, legal and security issues (Rückemann, 2008).

In addition, several Grid based accounting systems are currently used and activities going on within the Grid communities (D-Grid, 2008) and resource providers (e.g. Forschungszentrum Jülich (FZJ), Forschungszentrum Karlsruhe (FZK), Gesellschaft für Wissenschaftliche Datenverarbeitung Göttingen (GWDG), Höchstleistungsrechenzentrum Stuttgart (HLRS), Leibniz-Rechenzentrum der Bayerischen Akademie der Wissenschaften (LRZ) München, Regionales Rechenzentrum für Niedersachsen (RRZN) Hannover, MediGRID, Biz2Grid, BISGrid, FinGrid, InGrid) or a deployment is intended in the near future.

Due to the fact, that currently deployed accounting approaches partly represent proprietary developments or do not provide a high degree of interoperability, a horizontal integration of existing systems does not seem to be a reasonable approach as it would result in extensive development works. Beside that aspect, an accounting system supporting the Grid middleware UNICORE does not yet exist.

Moreover, a fundamental difficulty regarding the conceptual development of the proposed accounting system is a result of the varying requirements as well as partly different perceptions of the Grid communities respective resource providers with respect to the process of accounting. Cluster and High Performance Computing issues from the experiences from the computing scenarios described above, have been taken into consideration as well for this analysis.

CONCEPTS AND SYSTEMS COMPARISON OVERVIEW

The following passages give a compact overview of some prominent systems available for accounting and billing for High Performance Computing, Grid Computing, and Cluster Computing. Advantages and disadvantages are stated in order make these systems and their features comparable. These systems are examples for state of the art developments. As must be emphasised that there does not exist an universal implementation one will recognise that while deciding to implement a monitoring, accounting, and billing, it is inevitable to go into existing concepts and to take a look on the existing concepts. The following passages

Table 1. Overview of accounting systems regarding compliance with the criteria categories

Criterion/Category	*System/Tool*						
	APEL	*DGAS*	*GASA*	*GRASP*	*GSAX*	*Nimrod/G*	*SGAS*
Interoperability/portability	(3)	(3)	(3)	n.g.	(3)	3	3
Scalability	3	(3)	–	n.g.	3	3	3
Integrability	(3)	(3)	(3)	n.g.	(3)	3	3
Inter-organisational accounting	3	3	3	n.g.	3	n.g.	3
Flexibility/extendability	3	n.g.	3	n.g.	3	(3)	3
Supporting standards	–	–	(3)	(3)	(3)	n.g.	3
Customer-specific visualisation	3	–	–	n.g.	n.g.	n.g.	–
Transparency	n.g.	n.g.	n.g.	n.g.	n.g.	n.g.	(3)
Accounting heterogeneous res.	(3)	3	3	(3)	n.g.	n.g.	(3)
Accounting virtual resources	n.g.	n.g.	n.g.	n.g.	n.g.	n.g.	(3)
Support for high dynamics	3	(3)	(3)	n.g.	n.g.	3	3
Security	n.g.	3	3	n.g.	3	n.g.	3
Uniform, generic interfaces	–	–	–	n.g.	(3)	3	(3)
Support for various metrics	3	3	3	n.g.	3	n.g.	3
Precision	3	3	3	3	3	n.g.	3
Support for various acc. policies	3	3	n.g.	n.g.	3	n.g.	(3)
Fault tolerance	n.g.	n.g.	(3)	n.g.	n.g.	n.g.	3
Admin./maintainability	n.g.	(3)	n.g.	n.g.	n.g.	n.g.	3
Verification	n.g.	3	3	n.g.	n.g.	3	3

contain the most comprehensive and compact overview of existing concepts that is available today. If you need a more detailed comparison, the documents on study and comparison from within D-Grid can be recommended. Please see the references. As for their relevance for up to date developments, two examples have to be named, SGAS and DGAS. The features of the SweGrid Accounting System (SGAS) go far beyond a conventional hierarchical structure. Accounting information can be stored in the LUTS. In order to minimise complexity different instances of LUTS, in standard installations there is no coordination or transfer between different instances necessary. Due to the latest developments, SGAS delivers a much higher scalability than most other accounting systems. There are high performance bank versions available that scale up to ten thousands of jobs (Gardfjäll, Elmroth, Johnsson, Mulmo, & Sandholm, 2006). A normalisation of CPU and other specific metrics can be used if needed. Due to the modular concept nearly any normalisation, dynamic price setting or accounting algorithm can be implemented via modules. At this base valuation of resource usage is possible for High Performance Computing and even in heterogeneous Grid environments. SGAS may be used independently from the middleware used.

For the other system, less flexible but also widely used, a large number of developers is needed to implement features. The non-modular implementation concept of DGAS is less effective since DGAS has not been considered for future development in large heterogeneous computing environments as they now exist.

Criteria Overview

The following compilation (Table 1) gives a very compact overview of the accounting and billing systems and approaches regarding the different categories and criteria. A check means yes available or if bracketed means conditional, "n.g." means no information given or specified, and a dash means that the feature does not exist.

As mentioned when discussing the background for building services and resource configurations for information purposes, the most important aspects are flexible support for various metrics, support for various accounting policies, and accounting features for virtual resources.

For end-user applications it will be necessary to form composite metrics. These metrics can combine several properties suitable for the specific kind of information. For example regarding geographic information services besides computing resources a composite metric can consider a data quality component, a data enhancement component, and a base pricing of raw data.

The provider of the service will have to specify the appropriate weighting factors within the algorithm. As new service features get introduced, from economic point of view this algorithm might be the most important target for a change.

Classification of Resources

An essential part of implementing a flexible and future-oriented accounting and billing solution is the support for existing standards. At the interoperability point of view a solution must have support for standardised formats and protocols like Grid protocols as suggested by large research groups and organisations.

Architecture specific standards like OGSA, OGSI (Tuecke, Czajkowski, Foster, Frey, Graham, Kesselman, Maquire, Sandholm, Snelling, & Vanderbilt, 2003), and WSRF will have to be part of any implementation as well as standards suggestions from the Global Grid Forum (GGF), regarding storage of accounting and payment data, especially Resource Usage Services (RUS) and Resource Usage Records (RUR) (Göhner & Rückemann, 2006, "Konzeption ..."). These are also to be evaluated with respect to application and modification.

In order to guarantee a high degree of interoperability, in the ideal case a data set of accounting records should contain a minimal amount of information and should be stored and submitted or exchanged in a standard format like RUR.

It is therefore essential to build groups of resources. Table 2 shows different resources groups and sub groups with examples for hardware in these groups. It shows hardware installations used in High Performance Computing, Cluster and Grid Computing and names accounting units that can be used in this context.

Additionally, for example with data acquisition there might be very special hardware. A lot of systems for collecting information presently exist. Information like details on Points of Interest (POI), mobile Web-Cameras, traffic support systems, navigation systems and many more. These systems can consist of mobile units with GPS and navigation support, automated or with local human interaction, with of without on-site support. For these cases one will need special virtual and composite units for fitting these cases into the existing economic models. We should not regard the human part to be human resources but one can as well integrate it into the accounting and billing process that way.

Today most of these components do not get accounted as models are too complex, but for the future it will be necessary to customise accounting systems for these information systems for creating business benefits.

Integrated Architecture

The base of implementing an integrated monitoring, accounting, and billing is how to integrate heterogeneous resources into the market the

Table 2. Overview of resource groups and accounting units for computing environments

Resource group	***Possible sub groups***	***Examples***	***Examples in the context of HPC / Cluster / Grid***	***Possible accounting units***
Computat. elements	Multi processor systems	• Vector computer • Parallel computer • Cluster computer • HPC computer • etc.	• SGI Altix ICE (HLRN-II / RRZN) • SGI Altix XE (HLRN-II / RRZN) • IBM p690 (HLRN-I / RRZN) • SGI Altix 3700 Bx 2 (LRZ) • IBM BlueGene /L (FZJ), etc.	• CPU seconds • CPU hours • Wallclock time • Number of CPUs • Number of nodes • Numb. of comp. / comp. systems • MIPS • etc.
	Single processor systems	• Desktop PCs • etc	• x86, x86_64 (ZIVGrid, heterogen.) • PowerPC • Power4, Power4+, Power6 • IA32, IA640 etc.	
	Hardware elements / emulators	• FFT hardware • Co processors • etc.	• Special hardware emulators • etc.	
Storage resources	Primary storage elements	• Main memory • Caches • etc.	• Special harddisk cache • Primary storage of computational elements, etc.	• Numb. of page acc. • Main mem. (max.) • Main mem (avg.), etc.
	Mass storage elements	• RAID systems • Tape systems • Archive systems • Backup systems etc.	• Data archive with Simulation data • Picture Archiving and Communication System (PACS) • etc.	• Used storage (MB / GB / TB / PB) • Used storage × time • etc.
Databases	Relational Databases	• mySQL • Oracle • IBM DB2 • etc.	• Genom databases (MediGRID) • Databases with medical data (MediGRID) • Datab. with climate data (C3-Grid) • Geoscientific datab. (LX Project) • Geoinformation databases • Event databases (GISIG, actmap) • Environmental databases, etc.	• Number of accesses • Utilisation time • Value of extracted information • etc.
	XML databases	• eXist • Xindice • Tamino etc.		
Network components	–	• Router • Switch • Gateway • etc.	• Communication networks, e.g. LAN, WLAN, WAN • I/O and MPI networks, e.g. IB • etc.	• Bandwidth • Transferred Data (MB / GB / TB / PB) • etc.
Appl./ Libraries	–	• Software licenses • Program libraries • Special SW comp. • etc.	• Medical software (e.g. MediGRID) • Licensed SW libraries • Libraries for the Geosciences • Spatial information libraries, etc.	Costs for: • SW licenses • Applications • Access to libraries • etc.
Resources for data acquisition	–	• Gauging station • Special hardware • Sensors • etc.	• Virtual telescope, e.g. virtual observatory (AstroGrid-D) • Accessible telescopes (e.g. ESO) • Electron microscope • Medical devices, etc.	• Number of accesses • Utilisation time • etc.
Additional resources	–	• Service comp. / • Service elements • Information syst. • QoS parameters (e.g. priorities), etc.	• ISV codes (InGrid) • Special print services • Visualisation • Administration / support • etc.	Due to the heterogeneous characteristics of resources and services very appl. specific accounting units

details described so far naturally can get very complex and technical even with the prototypical implementation presented (Rückemann & Göhner, 2006; Rückemann, Göhner, & Baur, 2007), based on very flexible monitoring, accounting, and billing records databases (Göhner, 2006) and SGAS. This integrated architecture even works with commercial closed source accounting systems

Figure 1. Illustration of the integrated monitoring, accounting, and billing architecture

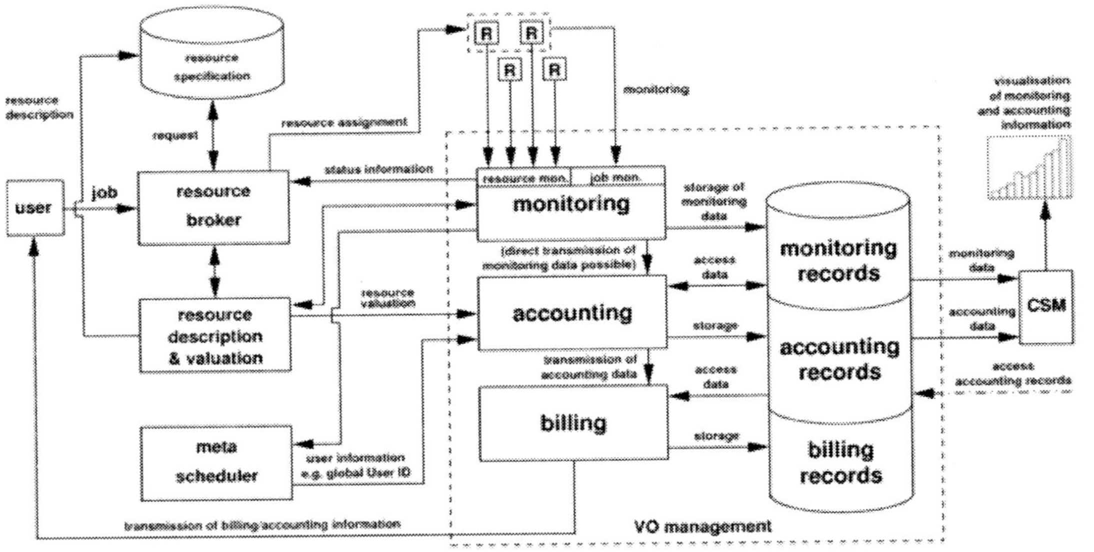

like Tivoli Storage Manager (TSM) and others. The following section concentrates on a detailed overview of an integrated architecture for monitoring, accounting, and billing. Therefore, relevant interfaces of the involved components depicted in Figure 1 (Rückemann, Göhner, & Baur, 2007), as well as existing interactions are specified, and the whole workflow from the submission of a user job to the visualisation of the associated accounting data is outlined. If composite metrics are used then usage data regarding the services provided can be handled, transferred and stored, too.

For showing the essentials of the concept this illustration will concentrate on the architecture and not on the implementation. In this context, the components representing the building blocks of the architecture can be seen as black boxes here as these are meant to be custom tailored components, already existing. Figure 1 gives the essential functional components needed for this concept, as these are:

- job submission and batch system,
- resource broker,
- resource description for the resources participating, resource description framework,
- meta scheduler,
- resource and/or job and/or process monitoring,
- monitoring, accounting, billing database,
- accounting system handling the information for the above components,
- customer service management.

Beside monitoring, accounting, and billing components, the proposed architecture also incorporates other aspects. Examples are the description, specification, and evaluation of resources, the management of Virtual Organisations, resource broker and meta scheduler, as well as tools and platforms for Customer Service Management being responsible for a customer specific visualisation of monitoring as well as accounting relevant data.

So before starting to describe the workflow it can be helpful to give some examples what the custom components could be. Please remember that this concept in itself is independent of an implementation of the components. Anyway the batch system might be Torque, the resource broker might be Calanha, monitoring and accounting can be done via SGAS or in the same installation via DGAS and Perl interface scripts, billing can be done with SGAS modules, records can be stored in a database using RUR/RUS specifications for communication. Components like the database should be suitable for the context of the resources network planned, regarding administrative concepts, brokering requirements, network redundancies and latencies and so on. This will have to be decided when implementing the specific architecture for the specific infrastructure. What is essential is the workflow.

The workflow starts with the request of a user for a specific resource or service in order to execute a specified user job. Fundamental elements of the request expressed by means of a Job Description Language (JDL) comprise a formalised specification of the user job, a list of required Grid resources, as well as possible time and/or budget constraints. Moreover, further optional parameters contain attributes as for example the specification of an user or project account, Quality of Service (QoS) parameters (e.g., duration, response time etc.), Service Level Agreement (SLA) as well as various VO specific attributes (e.g., membership information, authorisation policies). As usual with complex environments in most cases the issues of agreements and policies will have to be handled individually, e.g. regarding requirements and constraints of partners and federal aspects.

The resource allocation should be performed by means of resource brokers as well as service or resource specific schedulers accepting job requests from users and globally searching for appropriate fulfillments by means of a database containing resource specifications in form of XML files. Besides static resource information which is provided by the description language, also highly dynamic monitoring data as for instance the current processor load, availability of resources, and further status information etc. are taken into account by the scheduling algorithms. Based on static as well as dynamic resource information, the resource broker has the ability to dynamically perform an identification and assignment of suitable resources or services matching the user's request. With respect to the creation of accounting records reflecting resource consumption and service usage, in particular information determining job and resource monitoring are of interest. These data are provided by the monitoring component and are stored in a monitoring database in form of monitoring records (e.g., using the Open Grid Forum (OGF) GLUE schema) or may be directly transferred to the accounting component.

In the case that the monitoring data is stored in a local or distributed monitoring database, by means of defined interfaces, relevant data is then extracted by the accounting component in order to perform the so called usage-to-user mapping which means to correlate local monitoring data with global user and job specific information provided by the meta scheduler in order to obtain accounting records. In this context, the meta scheduler can be seen as a central coordinator that interacts with local schedulers of resources and services, reserves resources, and calculates job IDs, etc. After the process of allocation, filtering, aggregation, and conversion of accounting relevant data into a standardised format (at the current state the OGF Usage Records), the acquired accounting data is then stored in form of accounting records in a XML based accounting database as for example eXist, an open source native XML database.

Based on specified interfaces, the accounting information can further be extracted by the billing system in order to calculate the incurred costs of resource and service usage and to forward a bill to the customer based on virtual or monetary units. Besides users, respective user groups, further components as for instance resource brokers (e.g., for optimisation purposes, load balancing) or platforms for analysis or visualisation may be interested in the acquired monitoring and accounting data. The transfer of these data is performed using predefined interfaces and standardised formats for the exchange of the respective information.

If the purpose is accounting and billing of information-centred services, for example for brokering products build from cartographic and satellite data, you will need to define a meta level integrating the broker commonly used for this task with the resource brokering. Both data will go into the resource description and be stored for any access. Standards like the Web Services Resource Framework (WSRF) and the Web Services Description Language (WSDL) can help to implement these meta levels in a modular way. This does contain the integration of storage like with the DataGrid Workload Management System, currently based on DGAS features.

For the economic algorithm this means due to the possibility for controlling all of the parameters within the workflow any part of the tasks of accounting raw information value, creating enriched information, service costs, Quality of Service properties, transaction, storage, and hardware usage can be accounted, priced, and billed.

In order to integrate community and (virtual) organisation specific workflows and policies and to not reveal internal business logic or security relevant data to unauthorised users, implementations and deployments of the components are dependent to the real and virtual organisations they belong to. In order to realise integrated monitoring and accounting workflows in an automated and integrated implementation and deployment, a coordinated use of standardised components and interfaces as well as the definition of service access points is required. In an automated and integrated implementation and deployment of the system, a coupling of the components with a dynamic VO management system should be applied to enable explicit dynamic VO based transactions.

Finally, based on the stored records, the visualisation component allows for the graphical representation of relevant data to the users or customers. With regard to accounting records, the user should have the possibility to inspect accounting data within a specific accounting interval or to view associated information of a particular user job based on an unique job ID. The visualisation components then allows for the graphical representation of filtered or aggregated VO specific monitoring, accounting, and billing data.

We need some abstraction in order to illustrate the requirements of a real scenario. An example for handling this complexity is the "Grid-GIS house" for the Geosciences and Geoinformation Sciences (Rückemann, 2007) incorporating High Performance Computing and Grid Computing resources, being a prototype for customer oriented information management.

The illustration (Figure 2) shows the Grid-GIS framework, the "Grid-GIS house" as it can be used with the GISIG and actmap components. The implementation of an information system presented here as a case study is used for e-Science and decision making in various distributed computing environments.

As the features presented here are already implemented, this is still work in progress as new fields of application for Geoscientific Grid Computing are currently under development. Planning has already begun for using Web Services via the Web Services Resource Framework (WSRF) and Spatial Data Infrastructures (SDI) also known as Geographic Data Infrastructures (GDI), supporting the Open Grid Service Architecture (OGSA) and Open Grid Services Infrastructure (OGSI) with the framework in the future. Interdisciplinary work should be encouraged.

For both Grid and HPC monitoring, accounting, and billing will become just more pragmatic when differing models can be overcome. Some of the basic work (Rückemann, 2001) has been done within the ZIVGrid and D-Grid projects (Rückemann, 2006) with the result of a Grid-GIS framework and a monitoring/accounting/billing concept on which the current prototype for the integrated, solution has been set up. In order to support a working geoinformation market, an

Figure 2. The "Grid-GIS house": GIS and computing resources, including GISIG

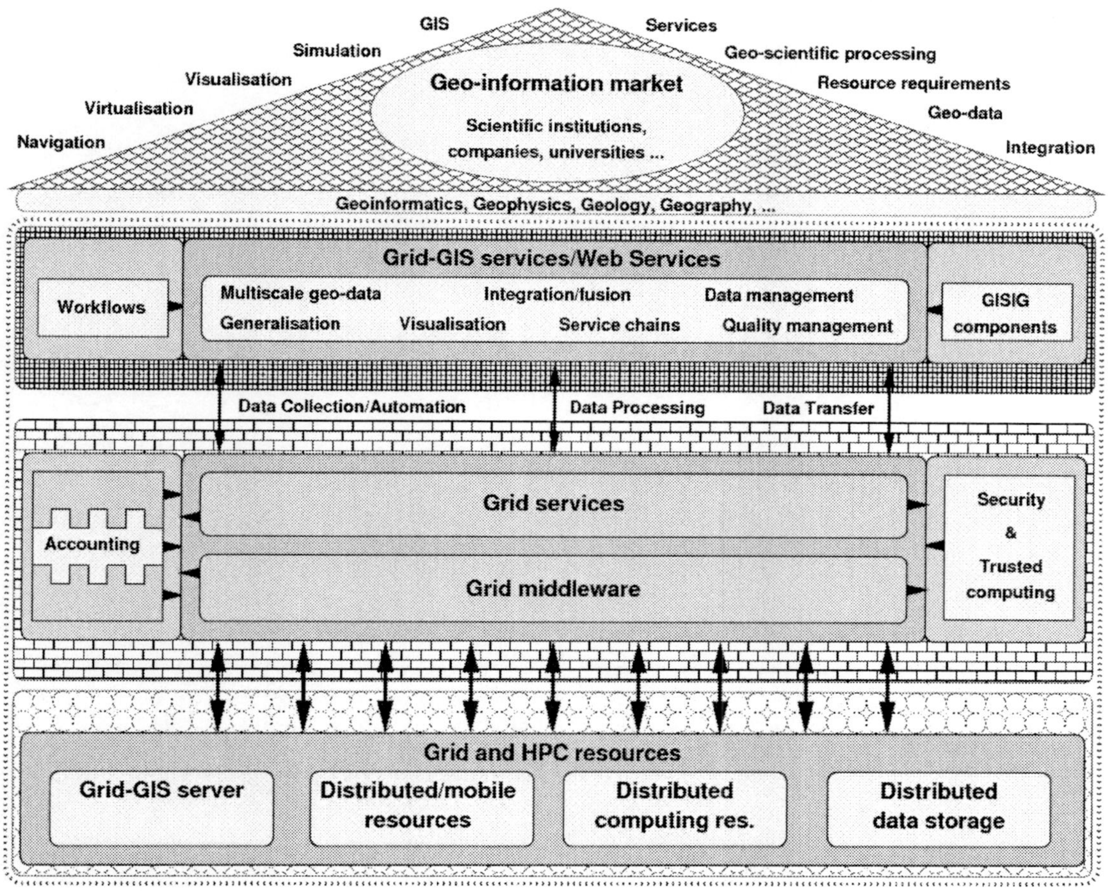

integrated, "holistic", modular solution (Rückemann, Göhner, & Baur, 2007) for monitoring, accounting, and billing is needed.

The GISIG and actmap components used can be configured very flexible and used with any of the HPC, Cluster and Grid resources as for calculating views, points of interest (POI) data, retrieving data and using services (Rückemann, in press). In principle anything used within these components (Figure 3), from interaction and event data, remote sensing data, geoscientific and environmental data, photographic raster images, and POI can as well be monitored and accounted as interactive and batch usage of resources from HPC, Cluster and Grid resources. It is depending on policies and cooperation with the resource partners involved how far a pricing or billing, e.g. using the Web Pricing and Ordering Service (WPOS), will be necessary or suitable.

The framework still has to be upgraded regarding inter-level connectivity and still has to be extended using Web Services and common standards as in cooperation with the Open Geospatial Consortium (OGC) and the Infrastructure for Spatial Information in the European Community (INSPIRE). Therefore with an integrated monitoring, accounting, and billing it will be possible to do accounting for Web Services as well. Basic fundamentals are Grid and HPC resources namely computing and storage resources. Based on this layer Grid middleware and Grid services are installed. Special services can be created for

Figure 3. Example GISIG application using various accountable data and interaction

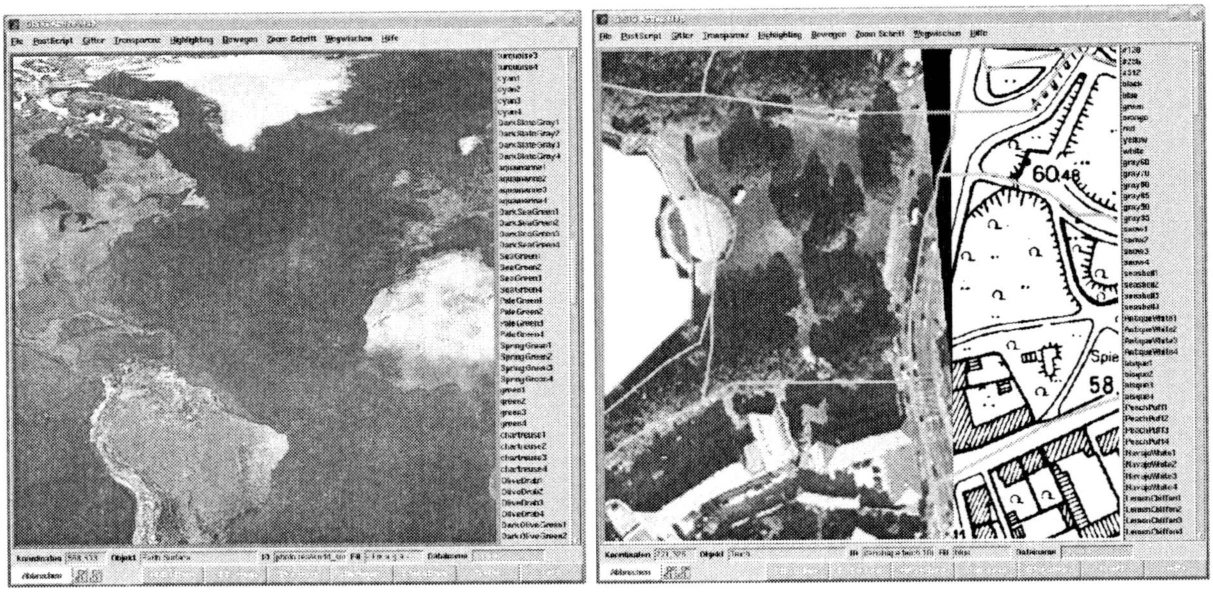

nearly any application needed at this level. Future joint efforts like HET (HPC in Europe Task force) can help to build the necessary meta-organisation background for HPC and Grid Computing.

Main issues for enliving the "Grid-GIS house" under aspects of the geoinformation market are Grid accounting as well as trusted computing and security (Chakrabarti, 2007) at the service level. Grid-GIS services and Web Services interfacing with GISIG namely the actmap component (Rückemann, 2001; Rückemann, 2005) are sitting on top of that layer providing the interface for the geoinformation market while providing usage of Grid services for data collection and automation, data processing, and data transfer (Applications with Active Map Software, 2005).

The Grid-GIS house implementation gave insight into the employment of scripting languages and source code based persistent object data for enabling the use of computing resources for geoscientific information systems (Tcl Developer Site, 2008). The basic concept of object graphics based on Active Source has been developed within the GISIG actmap project. Dynamical, event based cartography and visualisation using event-triggered databases and using distributed computing resources have been very successfully adopted for different use cases.

With the available Tcl features one can configure an accounting interface combined with policies for trusted computing and history features like accounting dynamically started job calls and executing commands from the shell history.

The implementation offers a wide range of applications for dynamical visualisation and to remotely controlled and multimedia cartography and presentation using computational intensive processes. Based on the concept put into practice for Grid Computing, Cluster Computing, and HPC the prototype offers a lot of flexibility for application and steering of resource usage.

What are the main benefits from this architectural concept for business and economy? With common means it is not possible to transparently exploit the vast resources of modern computing installations. Implementation is more heterogeneous today for HPC, Grid Computing, Cluster Computing, Cloud Computing than on any other less high performing architecture. Accounting systems with sophisticated features and a modular concept allowing composite metrics will enable a large variety of economic algorithms and more or less complete business processes.

FUTURE ACCOUNTING AND BILLING ACTIVITIES

As High End Computing environments like HPC, Cluster and Grid Computing merge, in the future even more companies will get into the business of building complex systems that essentially need effective system management solutions. The increasing need for planing and optimising current and future resources has to rely on accounting data for almost every decision making process. Designing a prototype for an integrated accounting and billing implementation for these systems while taking into consideration the problems and incorporating the different models for handling complex and distributed computing resources necessitates a comprehensive requirements analysis and a basically interdisciplinary approach.

The current research activities in building solutions for new information systems is based on the paradigm of integrated developments like integrated accounting and billing. Some obstacles for the use of GIS with High Performance Computing and Grid Computing have been overcome with the present concept, although the conformity with standards will have to go on. Integrability, portability, interfaces, computing framework, availability, extendability, application of methods, and reusability have been concisely demonstrated. Basic work has been done for showing the direction of developments.

Future interdisciplinary developments will more closely combine existing means with the use of Web Services and Geographic Data Infrastructures in order to encourage the ongoing achievements from the interaction of GIS, Grid Computing, and HPC and build the "Grid-GIS house" framework for the geoinformation market.

Managing the problems of system design the liable software designers need to have detailed knowledge about currently existing concepts, standards like OGSA and OGSI, and a precise systems comparison overview.

Resources within the computing environments involved need to be classified. As we have seen there are various mechanisms like brokering supporting dynamic classification. Flexible banking and brokering components are needed for the problems addressed with resource usage.

An integrated monitoring, accounting, and billing architecture is needed for seamless integration. This can be a prototype for customer oriented information (Rückemann, Göhner, & Baur, 2007). Grid initiatives will on long-term be forced to have an integrated accounting solution. The best starting point for this will be SGAS as outlined and demonstrated. A temporary add-on solution via DGAS seems to be viable.

Security issues as with authorisation concepts and protocols need to be addressed (Rückemann, 2008). Additional aspects arise with building large and heterogeneous installations, for example for the specification of an user or project account, Quality of Service (QoS) parameters (e.g., duration, response time etc.), Service Level Agreement (SLA) as well as various VO specific attributes (e.g., membership information, authorisation policies) are important for creating real world environments. Standardised accounting units, resource descriptions, user-friendly resource brokers will be next on the list.

CONCLUSION

For implementing an integrated monitoring, accounting, and billing architecture for complex computing environments a solution as presented from the results of Cluster experiences, ZIVGrid, HLRN and various national Grid activities should be built. The Grid-GIS house framework is one example for a working implementation with up-to-date requirements, considering High Performance Computing and Grid Computing resources being integrated into a working market concept. It shows that information systems using an integrated solution can be deployed with various business and economic strategies as the integrated solution can work with most of the existing accounting systems, even commercial ones based on closed source.

Currently the most widely useful accounting component in this context is SGAS as it is modular, very scalable and extensible for heterogeneous architectures and nearly any form of metrics. But there are other components necessary like components for banking, brokering, and accessing resources. Cloud Computing will help provisioning service components and services on graduated levels. All of these components need extensive development for the next years but the focus will have to be on systems management as society and commercial interests depend on working solutions for the next generations of computing facilities.

Different customised accounting installations for every Grid initiative and HPC installation is by far not enough, this will be contra-productive on long-term. But experience shows that people tend to avoid best practice. Suitable measures must be taken to prevent that fragmentation of systems management is going on. We need coordination not only locally but nationally, and internationally.

For todays generation of researchers and developers it is common to dedicate at least 25 to 30 percent of the time working to learning new and complementary methods and not less important presenting their efforts in national and international context. In a progressive field like complex computing environments we will have to double the efforts for the first years of stepping into the complex matter of understanding High Performance Computing.

We see strong needs for collaborative research and interdisciplinary cooperation in these areas of computing environments, but it is international initiative and coordination what is most important for laying the foundation stone for an operative task force creating the next generation of distributed system management as monitoring and accounting are becoming even more important for growing significance of information systems. And this coordinating council and operative task force can be the base for successful business and billing facilities for future use of resources in computing environments.

As computational sciences is all of natural sciences, technology, basic sciences, and art – regarding accounting and billing it is computational sciences that "counts".

REFERENCES

Abramson, D., Buyya, R., & Giddy, J. (2001). *A case for economy grid architecture for service oriented Grid computing.* Retrieved January 10, 2007, from http://www.csse.monash.edu.au/~davida/papers/ecogrid.pdf

Applications with active map software, screenshots (2005). Retrieved October 21, 2008, from http://wwwmath.uni-muenster.de/cs/u/ruckema/x/sciframe/en/screenshots.html

Barmouta, A., & Buyya, R. (2003). GridBank: *A Grid accounting services architecture (GASA) for distributed systems sharing and integration.* Retrieved February 18, 2007, from http://www.gridbus.org/papers/gridbank.pdf

Beardsmore, A., Hartley, K., Hawkins, S., Laws, S., Magowan, J., & Twigg, A. (2002). *GSAX Grid service accounting extensions.* Retrieved November 18, 2007, from http://www.doc.ic.ac.uk/~sjn5/GGF/ggf-rus-gsax-01.pdf

Byrom, R., Cordenonsi, R., Cornwall, L., Craig, M., Abdeslem, D., Ducan, A., et al. (2005). *APEL: An implementation of Grid accounting using R-GMA.* Retrieved June 18, 2007, from http://www.gridpp.ac.uk/abstracts/allhands2005/apel.pdf

Chakrabarti, A. (2007). *Grid computing security* (1st ed.). Berlin/Heidelberg: Springer.

D-Grid, The German Grid Initiative. (2008). Retrieved October 21, 2008, from http://www.d-grid.de

Distributed European infrastructure for supercomputing applications (DEISA) (2007). Retrieved July 26, 2006, from http://www.deisa.org/

EGEE. (2005). *Review of accounting and monitoring software deliverable: D1.* Retrieved October 10, 2008, from https://www.egee.cesga.es/documents/D1/EGEE-D1-Review-Accounting-Monitoring-v0.8.pdf

Elmroth, E., Gardfjäll, P., Mulmo, O., Sandgren, Å., & Sandholm, T. (2003). *A coordinated accounting solution for SweGrid.* Retrieved November 18, 2007, from http://www.pdc.kth.se/grid/sgas/docs/SGAS-0.1.3.pdf

Gardfjäll, P. (2003). *SweGrid Accounting System bank.* Retrieved June 18, 2007, from http://www.sgas.se/docs/SGAS-BANK-DD-0.1.pdf

Gardfjäll, P., Elmroth, E., Johnsson, L., Mulmo, O., & Sandholm, T. (2006). Scalable Grid-wide capacity allocation with the SweGrid Accounting System (SGAS). *concurrency and computation practice and experience.* John Wiley & Sons, Ltd. (Submitted for Journal Publication, October 2006). Retrieved April 14, 2007, from http://www.cs.umu.se/~elmroth/papers/sgas_submitted_oct2006.pdf

Global Grid Forum. (2006). Retrieved February 18, 2007, from http://www.gridforum.org/

Globus Alliance. (2008). Retrieved October 21, 2008, from http://www.globus.org/

Göhner, M. (2006). *Status quo: Abrechnung im Bereich des Grid Computing (*Bericht Nr. 2006-03). Institut für Informationstechnische Systeme, Universität der Bundeswehr München. Retrieved December 28, 2007, from https://www.unibw.de/rz/dokumente/getFILE?fid=1441518

Göhner, M., & Rückemann, C.-P. (2006). *Accounting-Ansätze im Bereich des Grid-Computing.* D-Grid Integration project, D-Grid document. Retrieved December 28, 2007, http://www.d-grid.de/fileadmin/dgi_document/FG2/koordination_mab/mab_accounting_ansaetze.pdf

Göhner, M., & Rückemann, C.-P. (2006). *Konzeption eines Grid-Accounting-Systems.* D-Grid Integration project, D-Grid document. Retrieved December 28, 2007, http://www.d-grid.de/fileadmin/dgi_document/FG2/koordination_mab/mab_accounting_system.pdf

Grid Economic Services Architecture Working Group. (2006). Retrieved September 5, 2007, from https://forge.gridforum.org/projects/gesa-wg

Heise Newsticker. (2008). *17 Millionen Euro für den Aufbau einer nationalen Grid-Infrastruktur.* Heise Newsticker, (2005,September 8). Retrieved July 10, 2008, from http://www.heise.de/newsticker/meldung/63739

HLRN. North-German Supercomputing Alliance (Norddeutscher Verbund für Hoch- und Höchstleistungsrechnen) (2008). Retrieved October 12, 2008, from http://www.hlrn.de

Leweling, M. (2005). *ZIVGrid – Grid-Computing mit Condor.* Zentrum für Informationsverarbeitung der Universität Münster, inforum, Jahrgang 29, Nr. 3, December (pp. 19-20). Retrieved October 20, 2008, from http://www.uni-muenster.de/ZIV/inforum/2005-3/a12.html

Lim, D., Ho, Q.-T., Zhang, J., Lee, B.-S., & Ong, Y.-S. (2005). *MOGAS. A multi-organizational Grid accounting system.* Retrieved December 18, 2007, from http://ntu-cg.ntu.edu.sg/mogas_pragma/MOGAS.pdf

Mach, R., Lepro-Metz, R., Booz, A. H., Jackson, S., & McGinnis, L. (2003). *Usage record – format recommendation.* Usage Record Working Group, Global Grid Forum. Retrieved September 18, 2007, from http://forge.ggf.org/sf/sfmain/do/downloadAttachment/projects.ggf-editor/tracker.submit_ggf_draft/artf3385?id=atch3485

Matthies, T.-C., & Rückemann, C.-P. (2003). Vom Urwald der Wörter zur strukturierten Suche. In R. Schmidt (Ed.), *Proceedings, 25. Online-Tagung der DGI, Competence in Content, Frankfurt am Main, 3.–5. Juni 2003, Deutsche Gesellschaft für Informationswissenschaft und Informationspraxis e. V.*, (pp. 285–296).

Moab Admin Manual. (2008). Retrieved September 20, 2008, from http://www.clusterresources.com/products/mwm/moabdocs/index.shtml

Moab Users Guide. (2008). Retrieved September 20, 2008, from http://www.clusterresources.com/products/mwm/docs/moabusers.shtml

Morariu, C., Waldburger, M., & Stiller, B. (2006). *An accounting and charging architecture for mobile Grids.* IFI Technical Report, No. ifi-2006.06, April 2006. Retrieved January 14, 2009, from ftp://ftp.ifi.uzh.ch/pub/techreports/TR-2006/ifi-2006.06.pdf

Newhouse, S. (2003). *Grid economic services architecture (GESA).* Grid economic services architecture working group, global Grid forum. Retrieved September 5, 2007, from http://www.doc.ic.ac.uk/~sjn5/GGF/CompEconArch-GGF7.pdf

Open Grid Forum. (2007). Retrieved August 29, 2007, from http://www.ogf.org

Ost, S., & Leweling, M. (2005). *ZIVcluster, Der Linux-HPC-Cluster des Zentrums für Informationsverarbeitung.* Retrieved August 10, 2008, from http://www.uni-muenster.de/ZIV/inforum/2005-1/a11.html

Photo Gallery, H. L. R. N.-I. I. (2008, May 9). RRZN Top-News. Retrieved October 21, 2008, from http://www.rrzn.uni-hannover.de/hlrn_galerie.html

Project, L. X. (2008). Retrieved October 12, 2008, from http://zen.rrzn.uni-hannover.de/cpr/x/rprojs/de/index.html

R-GMA. Relational Grid monitoring architecture (2006). Retrieved August 10, 2008, from http://www.r-gma.org/

Rieger, S., Gersbeck-Schierholz, B., Mönnich, J., & Wiebelitz, J. (2006). Self-Service PKI-Lösungen für eScience. In C. Paulsen (Ed.), *Proceedings 13. DFN Workshop "Sicherheit in vernetzten Systemen", 1.-2. März 2006, Hamburg, Deutschland.* DFN-CERT publications (pp. B-1–B-15).

Rückemann, C.-P. (2001). *Beitrag zur Realisierung portabler Komponenten für Geoinformationssysteme. Ein Konzept zur ereignisgesteuerten und dynamischen Visualisierung und Aufbereitung geowissenschaftlicher Daten.* Dissertation, Westfälische Wilhelms-Universität, Münster, Deutschland, 2001. 161 (xxii + 139) Seiten, Ill., graph. Darst., Kt. Retrieved September 22, 2008, from http://wwwmath.uni-muenster.de/cs/u/ruckema/x/dis/download/dis3acro.pdf

Rückemann, C.-P. (2005). *Active Map Software.* 2001, 2005. Retrieved August 10, 2008, from http://wwwmath.uni-muenster.de/cs/u/ruckema

Rückemann, C.-P. (Ed.). (2006). *Ergebnisse der Studie und Anforderungsanalyse in den Fachgebieten Monitoring, Accounting, Billing bei den Communities und Ressourcenanbietern im D-Grid.* Koordination der Fachgebiete Monitoring, Accounting, Billing im D-Grid-Integrationsprojekt, 1. Juni 2006, D-Grid Document, Deutschland, 141 pp. Retrieved September 22, 2008, from http://www.dgrid.de/fileadmin/dgi_document/FG2/koordination_mab/mab_studie_ergebnisse.pdf

Rückemann, C.-P. (2007). *Security of information systems.* EULISP Lecture Notes, European Legal Informatics Study Programme, Institut für Rechtsinformatik, Leibniz Universität Hannover (IRI/LUH).

Rückemann, C.-P. (2007). Geographic Grid-computing and HPC empowering dynamical visualisation for geoscientific information systems. In R. Kowalczyk (Ed.), *Proceedings of the 4th International Conference on Grid Service Engineering and Management (GSEM), September 25–26, 2007, Leipzig, Deutschland, co-located with Software, Agents and services for Business, Research, and E-sciences (SABRE2007)*, volume 117. GI-Edition, Lecture Notes in Informatics (LNI), Gesellschaft für Informatik e.V. (GI), (pp. 66-80).

Rückemann, C.-P. (2008). *Fundamental aspects of information science and security of information systems.* EULISP Lecture Notes, European Legal Informatics Study Programme, Institut für Rechtsinformatik, Leibniz Universität Hannover (IRI/LUH).

Rückemann, C.-P. (2009). Using parallel MultiCore and HPC systems for dynamical visualisation. In *Proceedings of the International Conference on Advanced Geographic Information Systems & Web Services (GEOWS 2009), DigitalWorld, February 1-7, 2009, Cancún, México, International Academy, Research, and Industry Association (IARIA)*, Best Paper Award, IEEE Computer Society Press, IEEE Xplore Digital Library, (pp. 13-18).

Rückemann, C.-P., & Göhner, M. (2006). *Konzeption einer Grid-Accounting-Architektur.* D-Grid Integration project, D-Grid document. http://www.d-grid.de/fileadmin/dgi_document/FG2/koordination_mab/mab_accounting_konzeption.pdf

Rückemann, C.-P., Göhner, M., & Baur, T. (2007). *Towards integrated Grid accounting/billing for D-Grid.* Grid Working Paper.

Rückemann, C.-P., Müller, W., Ritter, H.-H., Reiser, H., Kunze, M., Göhner, M., et al. (2005). *Erhebung zur Studie und Anforderungsanalyse in den Fachgebieten Monitoring, Accounting und Billing (M/A/B) im D-Grid, Informationen von den Beteiligten (Communities) im D-Grid-Projekt hinsichtlich ihrer D-Grid-Ressourcen.* D-Grid, Fachgebiete Monitoring, Accounting und Billing im D-Grid-Integrationsprojekt, D-Grid Document. 33 Seiten. Retrieved Oktober 12, 2007, from http://www.d-grid.de/fileadmin/dgi_document/FG2/koordination_mab/Erhebung_MAB_CG.pdf

Rückemann, C.-P., Müller, W., & von Voigt, G. (2007). Comparison of Grid accounting concepts for D-Grid. In M. Bubak, M. Turała, & K. Wiatr (Ed.), *Proceedings of the Cracow Grid Workshop, CGW'06*, Cracow, Poland, October 15-18, 2006 (pp. 459-466).

Tcl Developer Site. (2008). Retrieved September 20, 2008, from http://dev.scriptics.com/

Thain, D., Tannenbaum, T., & Livny, M. (2002). Condor and the Grid. In *Grid Computing: Making the Global Infrastructure a Reality.*

Torque Administrator Manual. (2008). Retrieved September 20, 2008, from http://www.clusterresources.com/wiki/doku.php?id=torque:torque_wiki

Tuecke, S., Czajkowski, K., Foster, I., Frey, J., Graham, S., Kesselman, C., et al. (2003). *Open Grid services infrastructure (OGSI), Version 1.0.* Open Grid Services Architecture Working Group, Global Grid Forum. Retrieved September 15, 2007, from http://www.gridforum.org/documents/GFD.15.pdf

Tutorial, G. R. A. S. P. (2005). *First presentation: SLA document, manageability and accounting sub-system.* Retrieved June 18, 2007, from http://eu-grasp.net/english/SalernoMeeting/GRASP%20 Tutorial%20Final%20-%20Verdino.ppt#1

UNICORE. (2008). Retrieved September 25, 2008, from http://www.unicore.eu

ZIV der WWU Münster – ZIVcluster. (2006). Retrieved September 5, 2008, from http://zivcluster.uni-muenster.de/

KEY TERMS AND DEFINITIONS

Accounting: Gathering, analysing and reporting as well as management of information belonging to the usage of computing resources and services. The most important objectives are optimisation and journaling of resource usage. With appropriate basic implementations, accounting can extend monitoring for the mentioned purposes

Billing: Pricing and charging, based on the calculation of certain quantities of computing resource usage on various economic foci. With appropriate basic implementations, billing can extend accounting for this purpose

High End Computing (HEC): Provision and use of high end resources for computing purposes.

High Performance Computing (HPC): Provision and use of highly performing computing resources, the formula one of computing

North-German Supercomputing Alliance (HLRN): The alliance of the northern states of Germany for providing and use of High Performance Computing resources.

Grid Computing: Grid Computing refers to a hardware and software infrastructure that allows service oriented, flexible, and seamless sharing of heterogeneous network resources for compute and data intensive tasks and provides faster throughput and scalability at lower costs

Cluster Computing: Using a computing machinery containing a cluster of compute nodes with a defined number of processor cores and memory.

Security: Security is the characteristic of a safe system to accept only such system states which do not result in unauthorised modification or acquisition of information.

Monitoring: Metering, gathering, analysing and reporting as well as management of information belonging to the state of computing resources and services

Chapter 11
Methodological Aspects of the Evaluation of Individual E-Banking Services for Selected Banks in Poland

Witold Chmielarz
University of Warsaw, Poland

ABSTRACT

The main purpose of this chapter is the comparison of differences between results of three methods used for quality evaluation of individual e-banking services. The comparison has been conducted for selected sixteen banks in Poland. The author uses three types of research: traditional expert scoring method, AHP (Analytic Hierarchy Process) method and conversion method. After a general introduction, a detailed report of the results arising from this research is presented and analyzed. Finally, the author draws general conclusions from the analysis. He also discusses the future research regarding this topic.

INTRODUCTION

The literature concerning problems of websites' evaluation in e-banking is very extensive. Its brief overview shows that websites are analysed from point of view of:

- usability (site map, addresses directory),
- functionality: (global search, navigation, content relevancy),
- visualisation (colours, background, graphics, letters)
- reliability and accessibility (Dinitz et al, 2005, Balachandher et alBalachandher et al: (2003), Saraswat and Katta (2008), Mateos et al (2001), Chiemeke et al (2006), Miranda et al (2006), Achour and Bensedrine (2005), Migdadi (2008).)

The frameworks of the majority of **evaluation methods** (of e-banking) are generally based on e-commerce website evaluation model (Whiteley (2000), Evans and King (1999), Selz and Schubert (1997)). These methods are mainly traditional. They are deriving from management information systems evaluation, supported by sets of criteria and scor-

DOI: 10.4018/978-1-60566-890-1.ch011

ing points with determined scale. It seems that previous scientific approaches have focused on technical and functional factors. Most of them additionally contain plenty of subjective factors, such as: text clearness, attractiveness of colours, pictures or photos, high presentation quality, etc.). Obtaining desired results can often be better achieved using a few, matching criteria for sample evaluation (such as in Web Assessment Index method, which focuses on four categories: speed, accessibility, navigability and content analysis, see Miranda (2006)). The selection of evaluation criteria still requires more theoretical approach, justification, verification and discussion about its scope. On the other hand we have some problems not only with establishing the set of criteria, but also determination of relations between them. There are also problems with setting preferences from the point of view of a final user (customer) or expert who is evaluating this phenomenon. This chapter deals with these issues and it will be useful for researchers and practitioners who look for solutions to these problems.

Its main objective is establishing a reasonable methodology of measuring customer satisfaction with e-services. In this case the author concentrated on individual e-banking sector in selected banks operating in Poland for verifying this problem. The chapter constitutes a continuation and, simultaneously, a development of previous studies dealing with the comparison and evaluation of IT systems implemented in organizations which form the basis of electronic economy. The considerations presented below are a consequence of a second series of analyses – in relation to the one performed in 2007 (as a part of e-commerce research - Chmielarz, 2007) - concerning the evaluation of e-banking, where the author tried to eliminate previously occurring methodological inconvenience and problems connected with obtaining rational expert evaluation. In a sense it is also an extension of the author's study into the transformation of IT banking systems applications, performed since 1999 (Chmielarz, 2005).

The second series of experiments connected with electronic business systems started with presenting applications of traditional methods – a scoring method, with its different variations (with experts' preference scale), and concluded with constructing the author's own method (conversion) which combines the advantages of scoring and relative evaluation methods (Chmielarz, 2008). The applied methods allowed for indicating – the best at a time – banking services for an individual client.

The third series, which includes also this paper, was initiated by the studies which are meant to facilitate the methodologies of websites' evaluation. Therefore, initially, they were applied to a limited number of banks offering services for an individual client, as only internet banks have been considered. The present stage of this series consists in widening the selection to a larger number of banks.

It is difficult to estimate the number of the Internet users using internet banking. Clients having access through internet channel are counted several times for ever increasing number of products e.g. savings accounts and credit cards – possibly a few within one bank. It is worth mentioning that also banks are interested in the most favourable image which reflects their market share in internet banking. It is the reason why the statistics of some banks should be treated more as a potential possibility of all clients using an offered range of services within products available via the Internet. Nevertheless, on the basis of data obtained from Związek Banków Polskich (Polish Banks Association), making a simple forecast with the consideration of the latest preference trends, we can estimate that in Poland the number of personal accounts operated via the Internet will reach over 12m in the end of 2008, and in 2009 it will exceed 13m. (Ref: Figure 1). Even if we assume that the number of active users is about 2m smaller (Macierzyński, 2007), still, we can conclude that in Poland over 45% of personal accounts owners use the internet channel.

Figure 1. The number of users with internet access to accounts ((zbp, 2008), 2008, 2009 – forecast with latest preferences)

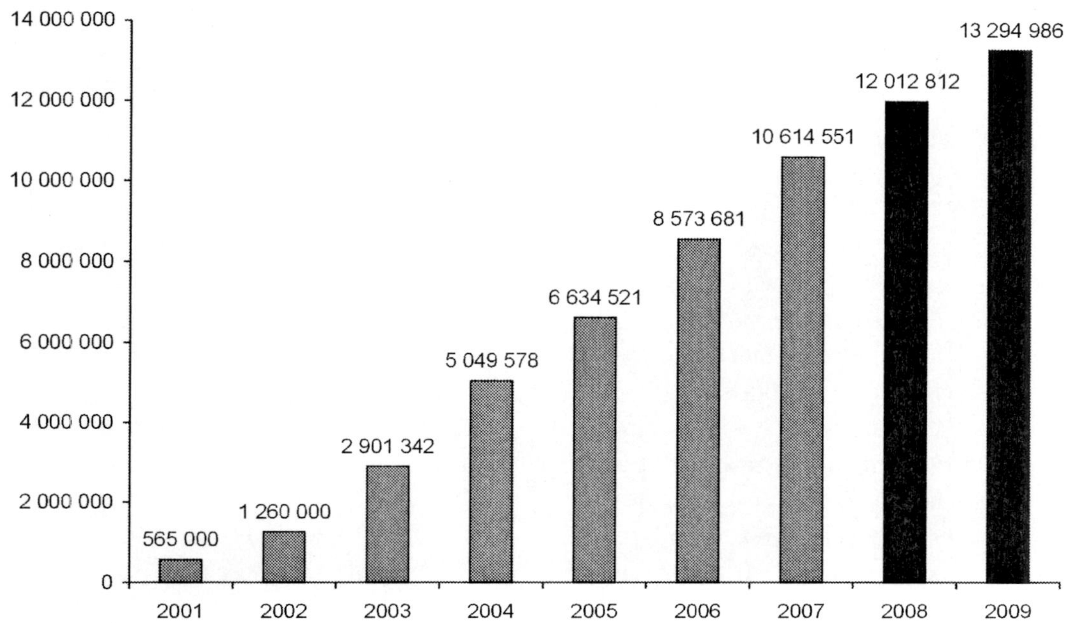

The published data state that over 90% of commercial banks' clients have a potential possibility of using this connection. It is estimated that six banks with the greatest number of internet access accounts at present have 6.5m of active users of Internet accounts (out of 14.5m of their personal accounts). If it was not for clients' fears of having their accounts broken into (47%), taking over a password and login (14%), Internet scams – phishing bank websites (6%), viruses (3%), spying on transactions (3%) and other threats (f-secure, 2008) as well as problems connected with using security tools preventing all the above – the number of individual clients of electronic services would be increasing even at a faster rate.

Electronic banking, which is a modern, 'non-contact' form of providing banking services without the necessity to visit a bank branch, is becoming a very important division of institutional and individual customer service.

Theoretically, with regard to its organization form it can be divided into:

- Virtual branch – access to electronic account – a client who wants to use an internet access account opens a new account, even if the customer already has a traditional account in this bank,
- Electronic account – a client does not have to open a new account, but obtains additional internet access to her or his traditional account together with a number of other services on offer,
- Virtual bank – offering only accounts with network access, not having its own branches – the client has access to his or her account only through electronic access channels, and one can contact the bank by means of a telephone, e-mail or mail.

In the further part of this chapter the author will present and analyse services related to e-banking services offered on the Polish market for all the above forms with regard to individual clients.

The basis for the undertaken research was

a preparatory stage consisting in gathering and establishing an evaluating expert panel. This time they were specialists in the electronic banking field from reputable universities in Poland, already experienced in this kind of research. Next, the selected team identified the evaluation criteria for **e-banking services**. Usually, in similar studies functional, technical, economic, organisational and psychological criteria were applied. Previous studies (see: Chmielarz, 2007) point to the fact that at present psychological criteria and, to a large extent, organisational criteria for electronic services aimed at individual clients are shaped in a very similar way (results of detailed criteria evaluation were almost equal). It seems that we are dealing with an analogous situation in the case of visualisation and navigation of bank websites chosen for this research. Therefore, mainly economic and functional criteria have been taken by experts into consideration, adding, following the example websites' analyses, basic technological criteria, apart from websites' characteristic features (discussion of this problem is in Chmielarz, 2005). In the study the author differentiated the following criteria:

- Economic – annual nominal interest rate, maintaining an account month/PLN, surcharge for access to electronic channels (including a token, if there is one), a fee for transfer to a parent bank, fee for a transfer to another bank, interest rate on deposits –10,000 PLN, fee for issuing a card, monthly fee for a card - month/PLN,
- Functional – with regard to large similarity of basic services we only selected non-standard additional services such as: insurance, investment funds, cross-border transfer or foreign currency account,
- Technological – the number of surcharge-free ATMs, account access channels (branches, the Internet, Call Centre, mobile phone), security (ID and password, token, SSL protocol, a list of single-use passwords, a list of single-use codes).

USING A SCORING METHOD TO ANALYSE E-BANKING SERVICES FOR INDIVIDUAL CLIENTS

In the first step the author applied a traditional **scoring method** together with its mutations and the assumed preference scale. In the scoring method the author collected information on selected criteria; they were assigned values according to the assumed scoring scale and the results were analysed in a combined table. The following scoring scale has been used:

- 1.00 – very good (complete criterion fulfilment, the lowest costs);
- 0.75 – good (almost complete fulfilment of criterion, slightly higher costs);
- 0.50 – medium (partial criterion fulfilment, medium costs);
- 0.25 – sufficient (satisfactory criterion fulfilment, high costs);
- 0.00 – insufficient (no feature, the highest costs).

A scoring method was used in two variations: simple – where criteria were treated equivalently; and one with a preference scale – where sets of criteria were assigned indicator values differentiating their treatment by clients (the total of coefficients = 1).

In a simple scoring method you measure the distance from the maximum value to be obtained (according to the assumed scoring scale). It concerns the value of criterion measure and in the sense of a distance it is the same when we measure the distance from one criterion to another as the other way round. However, we do not define the relations between particular criteria. Assigning a preference scale to particular criteria (or sets of criteria) can be regarded as such a measure. A linear preference scale in a normalized form defines in turn the participation of particular criteria in the final score. It establishes a one-time relation between criteria in relation to the final score, it is also a specific „averaged" measure of criteria in particular cases, without the individualization of the evaluation for any of them. However, it does not specify to what degree one criterion is better/ worse than the other. It is merely a derivative of the normalized distance.

Unfortunately, this commonly used methodology (mentioned in the first part of the chapter) – in different variations - has certain disadvantages such as: subjectivity of experts' evaluations, inadequacy of applied criteria for the evaluation of the situation, also there occur problems with comparability adjustments of various criteria evaluations. Also, this method causes problems connected with doubts as to the need for collective comparisons of various categories of banking services (e.g. cards, internet services, front-line services etc.) in various forms of e-banking (electronic access to a traditional account, electronic branch, virtual bank); or the scoring scale and its calculation from price value into agreed scoring or percentage.

Evaluation subjectivity can be limited by engaging a team of experts and calculating the average/ establishing a modal value from their assessments. Averaging does not eliminate subjectivity, but at least it can be reduced. Experts panel can also establish a set of evaluation criteria, eliminating, or at least limiting, their lack of conformity to the situation, and they can also determine an algorithm to be used for turning the valued indicators into quantitative ones.

The basic advantage of this group of methods is a possibility to present a combined score by means of one indicator for each bank, which is comparable to the score depicting other banks and enables such a comparison. This way we are provided with an unequivocal answer to the question which of the selected banks is the best for a specified category of a client, not going into speculations concerning ranking of particular kinds of banking services. Also, it does not enforce – for the sake of comparison – creating an average banking services package, characterised by valued assessment, which clients perceive as illusory and approach with certain reservations (it is very difficult to establish an average basket of banking services; a case for VWagen Bank was published in Chmielarz, 2005).

To evaluate cost, functional, technological and other criteria the author used a preliminary table presenting bank offers related to internet banking services and fees connected with using bank accounts operated via the Internet. This table has been generated on the basis of data obtained from websites of selected banks. On its basis the author created a simplified and averaged combined table of criteria evaluations generated by experts. The data have been obtained from analyses performed from February to March 2008 which involved websites of selected, the most popular among clients, sixteen banks with electronic access accounts (including four internet banks), using information provided by helpline or other internet sources, if necessary. This time eight experts from academic spheres participated in the research.

Simple adding up scores obtained from the table presents a specified ranking of e-banking services for particular banks. The first place in this ranking was taken by mBank (81.25% of the maximum level services, compared to 68.42% in 2007), next Lucas Bank (76.04% owing to its very well-organized customer service), and in subsequent positions two internet banks: Toyota Bank (73.96% of the maximum score with relation to 77.63% last year – the unquestionable leader of last year) and Volkswagen Bank with e-direct service (72.92%). Inteligo PKO BP ranked next, and its low position is the consequence of the owner's inflexible policy (especially in terms of pricing).

Rating difference in the scores of the best three banks is limited to nearly 9 percentage points (compared to 2.25 points in the previous year), which demonstrates little price differentiation – this time the banks were being examined in the moment of changing mutual relations towards individual customers. Nevertheless, despite 24 points of the rating difference between the best and the worst score, we can notice that banks observe each other carefully and draw conclusions from failures and successes of their competition. In the majority of cases there are no obligatory minimum monthly payments, or they are deliberately minimised (which is not fully visible in the scoring scale), transfers to the bank are usually free of charge, and the level of security can be regarded as satisfactory for clients (2-4 kinds of security). Other elements are subject to competitive bidding on the market, striking a precarious, changing balance between the wish to gain a competitive advantage and the profit of the bank (in Poland still the latter is a dominating factor).

In particular it starts to concern the visualization (its tradition and new fashions and trends) and functional additional services (insurance, investment funds, cross-border transfers, foreign currency account, virtual card, etc.). ING – direct account 57.29%, Millenium – personal account – 58.33% and Nordea Bank – Nordea Spectrum account – 59.38% ranked the lowest. Apart from Millenium, whose low position is surprising (clients emphasise the poor navigation of the website), they are usually new partners in the market and they try to make up for their lack of experience in providing individual electronic services by adopting a good competitive strategy in terms of economic criteria (e.g. interest rates on deposits).

The results of the ranking are presented in Figure 2.

From the chart presented in Figure3 we can conclude that two services: a fee for issuing a card and a fee for transfer to a parent bank reached a level which, at present, satisfies clients' needs in more than 90%. Undoubtedly, the worst indicator is an annual nominal interest rate (evaluated by the majority of users as too low – 31.8% of the maximum scores). Indicators for fees for a transfer to another bank and additional services exceed slightly 50% of maximum values (Ref.: Figure 3.).

From the factors not listed within the criteria clients paid attention to the lack of possibility to make a cross-border transfer or no possibility of fully automatic obtaining a credit – via the Internet.

As stated previously, the first method limiting a specific subjectivity in the expert panel's evaluations is applying unitary preferences with regard to particular criteria or sets of criteria. Four experiments assigning preferences to variants have been carried out (Ref: Figure 4.):

- Economic (60%), technological 20%, functional 20%;
- Technological (60%), economic 20%, functional 20%;
- Functional (60%), economic 20%, technical 20%;
- Non-economic (functional 45%, technical 45%), economic 10%.

In each case mBank has a secure, first position. With decreasing influence of economic factors good positions of Inteligo and Toyota Bank move to individual accounts of BZ WBK and iKonto PKO BP. Lukas Bank is characterized by well-balanced evaluation factors in two out of four cases, and it moves to the second position in the ranking. The order of the last positions does not change significantly – apart from previously mentioned: Millenium and ING, there is also Getin Bank, with the dominance of economic factors changing places with Dominet Bank.

The presented results, obtained by means of a traditional scoring method and a **scoring method with a** different **preference scale**, do not exhaust the possibilities of websites' evaluation. Detailed studies conducted for the last year show that methods eliminating subjective indicators show

Figure 2. Ranking of the usefulness of electronic access to individual accounts of selected banks in Poland in 2008

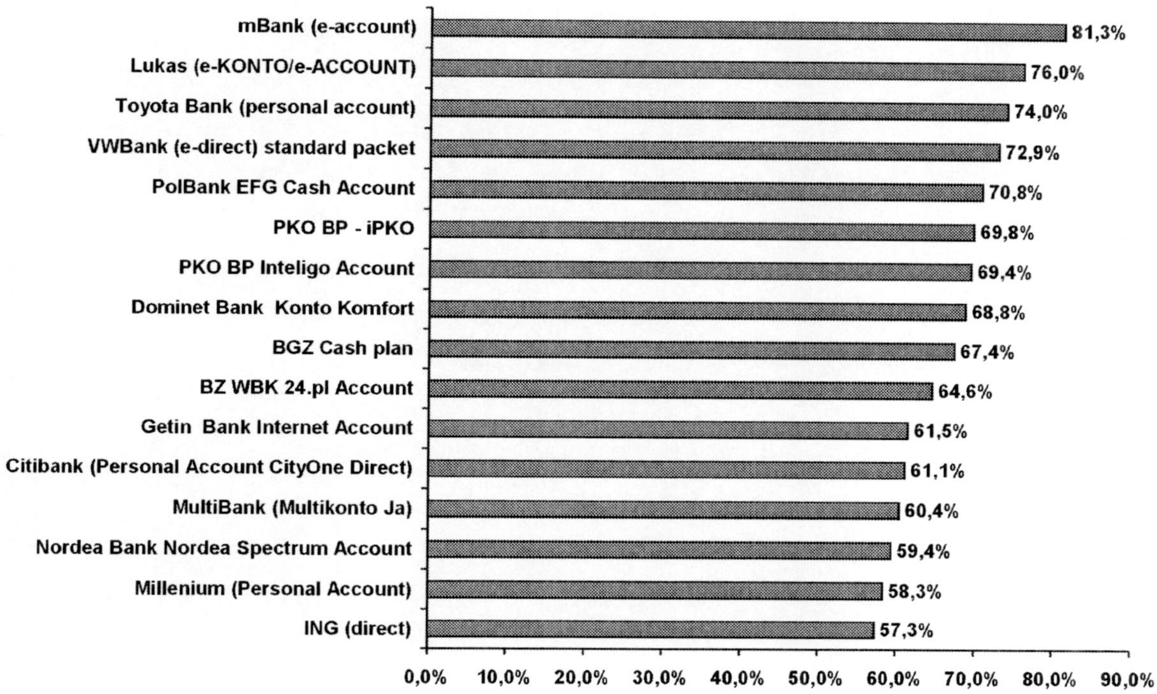

slightly different results than the ones presented in this study. Because the chief aim of this research is obtaining a rational method of the evaluation of websites' usefulness for a client, therefore, the next stage will be testing various preference scales, AHP method and the author's method of minimizing the distance from the maximum possible scores.

USING AHP METHOD TO ANALYSE E-BANKING SERVICES FOR INDIVIDUAL CLIENTS

In **AHP (Analytic Hierarchy Process) method** we apply a completely different procedure. Namely, a comparison for the examined group of banks is performed separately for each criterion. In order to evaluate the degree to which a given criterion has been realised in one bank in relation to every other bank we use a simplified Likert's scale:

- 1 – criteria are realised in an equivalent way;
- 3 – minor advantage of realisation of a subsequent criterion in a particular website over the realisation of the same criterion in another analysed website (respectively 1/3 with inverse relation);
- 5 – major advantage of realisation of a subsequent criterion in a particular website over the realisation of the same criterion in the case of another analysed website (respectively 1/5 with inverse relation);
- 7 – significant advantage of realisation of a subsequent criterion in a particular website over the realisation of the same criterion in

Figure 3. Ranking of evaluation criteria of electronic access to individual accounts in selected banks in Poland in 2008

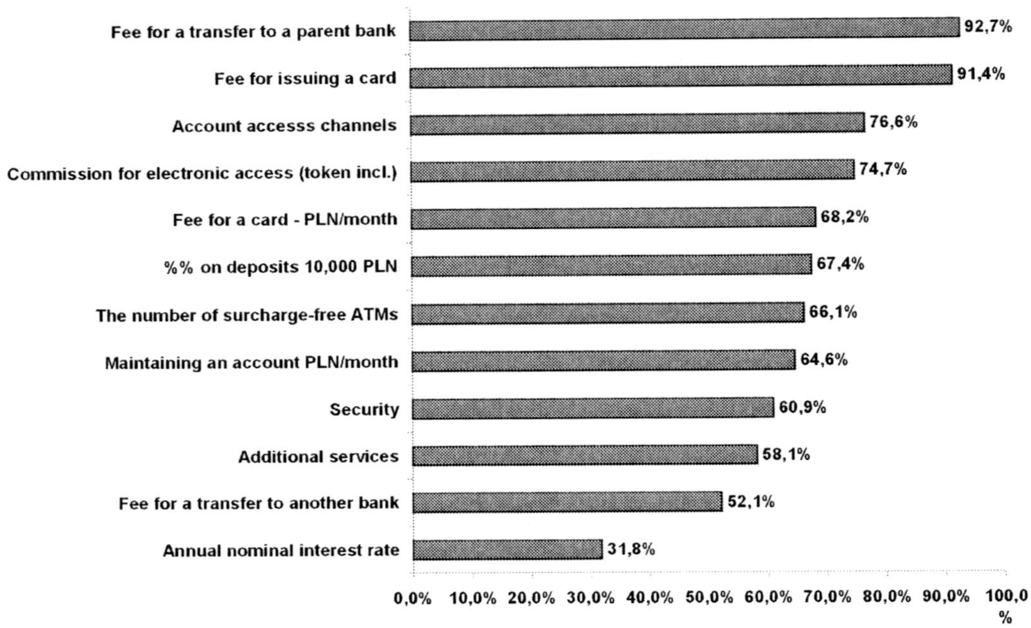

the case of another analysed website (1/7 with inverse relation);

- 9 – absolute advantage of realisation of a subsequent criterion in a particular website over the realisation of the same criterion in the case of another analysed website (1/9 with inverse relation).

Analysing the above compilation we can conclude that the value of the realisation of a criterion in every bank is not evaluated in an absolute way, it is only a relation of the realisation of a particular criterion in one bank to the realisation of the same criterion in other banks. If we treated it in terms of a distance (relative advantage) we would observe that e.g. the distance of realisation of the first criterion in one bank to the realisation of the same criterion in another bank is different than the reverse relation. It allows evading the answer concerning the value of a criterion feature and, simultaneously, defines its relation to others. Nevertheless, if we group total scores for all criteria, we arrive at a combined table of evaluations for each bank. The preference scale for the criteria in this method is obtained in an analogical way. Criteria are compared in pairs according to the same scale, and their total (actually the sum of their squares) after normalization can constitute a specific preference scale and it can show which of them are the most significant for an expert and which can be disregarded.

Roughly, Saaty's AHP method (Saaty, 1990) is a relative, multi-criteria expert evaluation consisting in pair wise comparison of experts' evaluations. Not going into methodological details, the stages of the comparison procedure were the following (Saaty, 1999):

- On the high level (pair wise comparison of evaluation criteria) the author applied a method of averaging experts evaluations, which was turned into a combined matrix,
- According to AHP method the square matrix has been calculated, and subsequently

Figure 4. Ranking of a scoring evaluation according to various kinds of preferences for selected banks in Poland in 2008

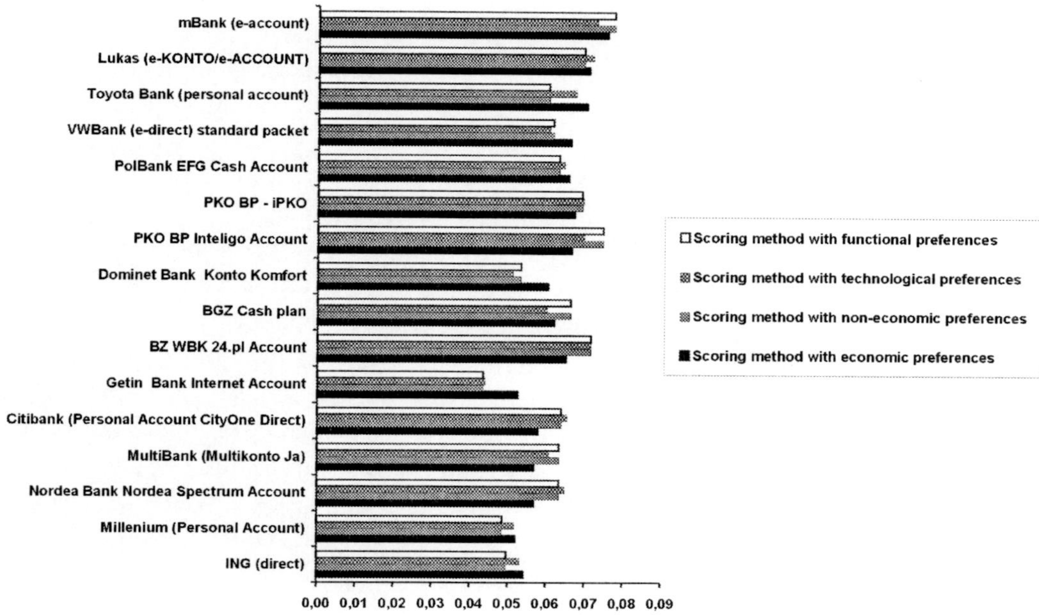

– on the basis of the sum of rows – weight vector, and normalised preference vector with regard to criteria (through referring particular elements to the sum of the preference vector elements),

- For each criterion a low level average preference matrix has been constructed for each pair of compared banks (on the basis of experts' evaluations),
- By collecting scores for each criterion a low level preliminary matrix has been constructed and a preference vector has been calculated with regard to banks; data matrix has been multiplied by preference vector with regard to criteria, and subsequently a preference vector with regard to particular banks (repeating operations analogically as before),
- Obtained findings were analysed.

AHP methodology has caused considerable difficulty for the gathered experts' team. First problems concerned the pair wise comparison of criteria. While within particular sets of criteria it seemed possible and reasonable, in the case of comparing e.g. functional and economic criteria the importance and advantage of ones over the others did not seem that obvious.

The final form of the table was a result of a compromise reached by experts. There was a common view (which did not appear during the scoring method), that there are too many considered criteria and it is sometimes too difficult to decide which of them differ and to what extent (similar situation was described in Sikorski, 2003). It would be definitely easier to evaluate the degree to which the criterion has been fulfilled and its relation to the criteria fulfilment in the case of other banks. Also, the fact that there were as many as twelve tables was an additional problem. Moreover, by way of experiment, we notice that experts – especially inexperienced – pay more attention to these criteria in a pair which appeared in the side-heading of a table than those which are in the heading, assigning better scores to the first ones. Their evaluation – as it was later discovered – is also influenced (though it should not take place) by the order in which criteria are considered. It appears that this method is not objective as well – each expert evaluated both the relations between criteria and their fulfilment in particular banks in a slightly different way. Similarly to a scoring method, during calculations averaged experts evaluations have been applied. Nevertheless, also in this case we can conclude which of the used variants of Internet banking services is optimal.

The obtained results differed considerably from the previous findings. Unexpectedly, Dominet Bank ranked first, though in previous studies it was taking one of the last places. mBank, the best and the only virtual bank near the lead, ranked second and the third one was – again surprisingly – electronic access to Inteligo PKO BP account (currently named iPKO in contrast to Inteligo), which so far has been ranked low. The main decisive factors in this case were relatively high scores for the first and the last crucial criteria, such as a transfer to another bank – which were ranked as the worst in the case of other banks, as well as an extended – in relation to the previous one – scoring scale. The worst positions in this ranking were taken by PolBank and City Bank, which was just behind Polbank. The third in reverse order was VWBank for many periods leading in traditional methods of expert evaluations (results - Ref. Figure 3.).

AHP method can also be used in an indirect way. Namely, the preference vector calculated in the first steps of this method can be used in expanding the simple method instead of preference vectors imposed or agreed collectively by experts. The findings of such operations are shown in Figure 5. The obtained results are closer to traditional methods (without a consideration of relativity in the evaluation of particular criteria fulfilment by subsequent banks). The first and second positions are taken by mBank and Toyota Bank, and the third was PolBank (valuated as the worst in Saaty's method), and just behind them– with equally low scores - VWBank. The last places were taken by ING, Millenium and Dominet Bank.

The results of both methods are given in Figure 5.

An AHP disadvantage which was the most difficult to eliminate – from the experts' point of view – was the work consumption of the method and relativity of criteria comparison. The second – no possibility of direct evaluation of the degree of realizing a given criterion in particular banks.

Therefore, experts suggested creating a method combining the characteristics of both methods. The major problem in constructing it was a conversion of a linear evaluation scale of the scoring method into relative references in Likert's scale. Experts convinced of the possibilities created by the new method, asked – for the sake of comparison – to examine the phenomenon by means of AHP method, treated the latter evaluations in a rather random way.

USING A CONVERSION METHOD TO ANALYSE E-BANKING SERVICES FOR INDIVIDUAL CLIENTS

The assumptions of a **conversion method** were as follows: after experts construct a table of evaluations of particular criteria for each bank – conversion should be started with establishing a preference vector for superior level criteria. The following transformation of a combined scoring table into a preference vector (first converter) is recommended:

- Constructing a matrix of distances from the maximum value for each criterion in each website,
- Calculating the average distance from the maximum value for each criterion,

Figure 5. Ranking of the evaluation of electronic access to individual accounts of selected banks in Poland in 2008 according to AHP and a scoring method multiplied by AHP method preference vector

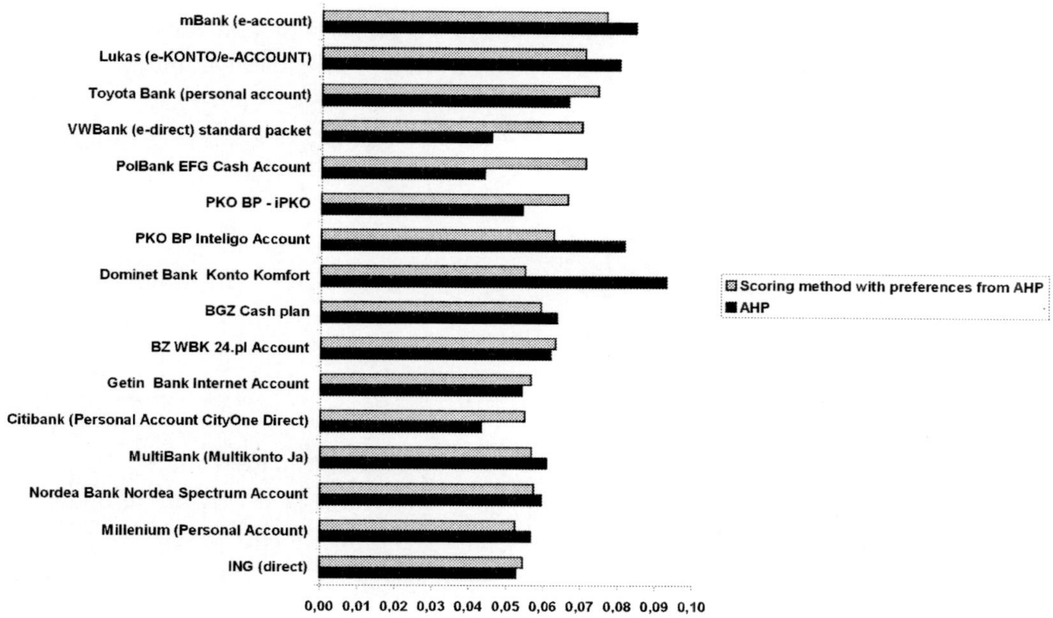

- Constructing a matrix of differences in the distance from the maximum value and the average distance according to criteria,
- For each bank website: constructing conversion matrices (4) - modules of relative distances of particular criteria to remaining criteria (the distance from the same criterion is 0), the obtained distances below the diagonal are the converse of the values over the diagonal,
- Averaging criteria conversion matrices – creating one matrix of average modules of values for all criteria,
- Transforming the matrix of average value modules into a superior preference matrix (calculating squared matrix, adding up rows, standardization of the obtained preference vector; repeated squaring, adding up rows, standardization of preference vector – repeating this iteration until there are minimum differences in subsequent preference vectors).

Subsequently, the author performed a transformation of the scores presented by experts on the level of a matrix specifying expert websites' evaluations for particular criteria (second converter). The results have been obtained in an analogical way:

- Constructing a matrix of distances from the maximum value for each criterion and each website,
- Calculating the average distance from the maximum value for each website,
- Constructing a matrix of differences of deviations from maximum value and the average distance of the features from the maximum value,
- For each criterion: constructing a matrix (12) of transformations (conversions) of the differences of the average distance from the maximum value between the websites, analogically as presented above (the distance for a particular feature in the

same website from the same website is 0), values below the diagonal are the converse of the values over the diagonal,

- Constructing a module matrix of transformations of the differences of average distance from maximum value between the websites, for each criterion,
- For each module transformation matrix of differences of the average distance from the maximum value between the websites, squaring it, adding up rows, standardization of the obtained ranking vector and repeating this operation until the obtained differences between two ranking vectors for each criterion will be minimal,
- Using the obtained vectors to construct a combined ranking matrix – returning to the matrix where in its side-heading there are criteria, in the heading names of bank websites by appropriate transfer of the obtained preference vectors for each criterion,
- Multiplying the matrix obtained in such a way by the previously calculated preference vector,
- Analysing final results and drawing conclusions (Note: the lowest distances in this case are the most favourable, comparability adjustments to other methods can be obtained by subtracting these values from 1 and their repeated standardization).

Conversion method – based on averaged distances from the mean ones – flattened the obtained results. Nonetheless, there occurs greater conformity with the results obtained by means of a scoring method than in AHP method.

In the first three positions – mBank (1) and Toyota Bank (3), confirm the results of the scoring method. A similar relationship occurs in the service of individual accounts in the case of the worst banks. A definite differentiation of scores in comparison to a scoring scale took place after multiplying the results of the scoring method by a preference vector from the conversion method. Here, Toyota Bank and Lukas Bank took first positions, and MultiBank and CityBank ranked the lowest. A similar dependence appeared in a scoring scale with non-economic preferences. The scores for conversion method and the scoring method multiplied by the preference vector from the conversion method are presented in Figure 6.

CONCLUSION

In the findings presented above three groups of methods of IT ventures evaluation have been applied: the scoring method (also called multi-criteria scoring method), AHP method as well as the author's own conversion method, based on measuring average distances obtained from the scoring method. The conversion method was created as a compromise between AHP method and the scoring method, and it seems to take into account all answers to claims made with reference to improving the scoring method (above all, it limits the subjectivity of experts evaluations).

Simultaneously, in this paper the author presents preliminary **methods of preventing evaluation subjectivity**:

- Gathering an expert team, whose average scores were taken into consideration when assessing the measurement,
- Team's establishing various (technical, functional, economic and non-economic) user preference scales and the analysis of results of applying such assumptions,
- Applying preference scales of other methods (here: AHP method and conversion method).

Although the evaluation of the same websites according to various methods in the same period of time was carried out by the same team of experts, the obtained rankings – despite keeping within the main trend (leading in one ranking usually meant

Figure 6. Ranking of electronic access to individual accounts in selected banks in Poland in 2008 acc. to conversion method and a scoring method with preferences from conversion method

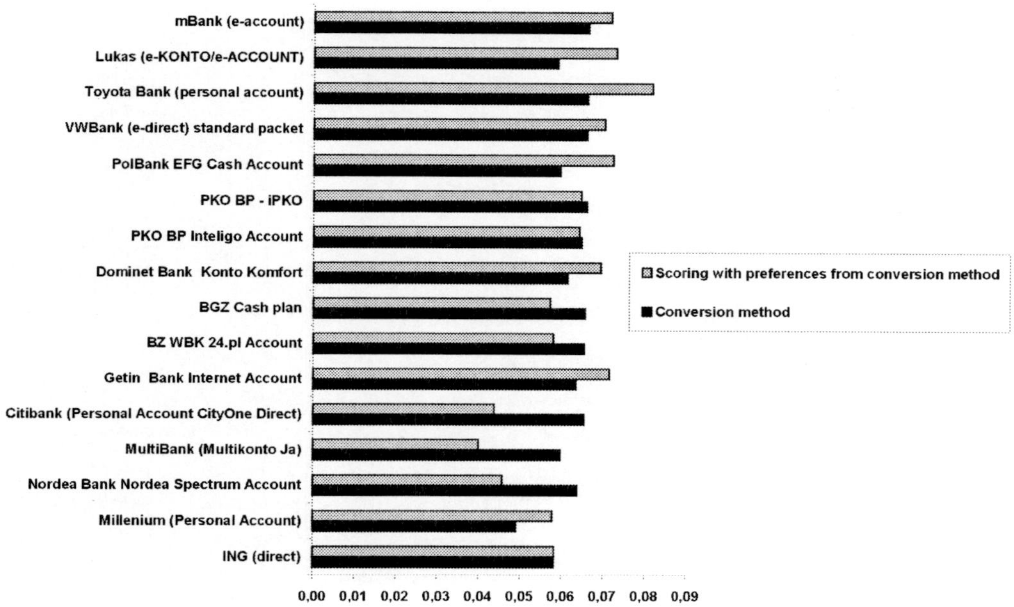

taking first positions in another), differed slightly. Considering the number of applied criteria it is sometimes difficult to point to the actual reasons for these differences.

Generally:

- Scoring method, though regarded as subjective, despite applying a large number of criteria and a traditional linear scoring scale, was evaluated by experts in a positive way, as a rational evaluation method which is easy to acquire. After taking into consideration the preference scale, experts claimed that – in their view – the impression of subjectivity and equivalence of radically different criteria is not as significant as the evaluations of academics suggest.
- In the experts' view, AHP method turned out to be more troublesome in the case of the necessity to compare many websites, by means of a larger number of criteria. Declarative objectivity of this method was

Table 1. Collective evaluation of the possibilities of methodologies applications in the evaluation of websites used for individual client banking services

Characteristic feature	Scoring method	AHP method	Conversion method
Ease of application	High	Low	High
Ease of acquisition	High	Low	n/a
Ease of performing calculations	High	High, with appropriate software	High, with appropriate software
Objectivity	Low	High	Medium
Findings interpretation	High	Medium	Medium

Figure .7. Ranking of electronic access evaluation of individual accounts in selected banks in Poland in 2008 acc. to scoring method, AHP and conversion method

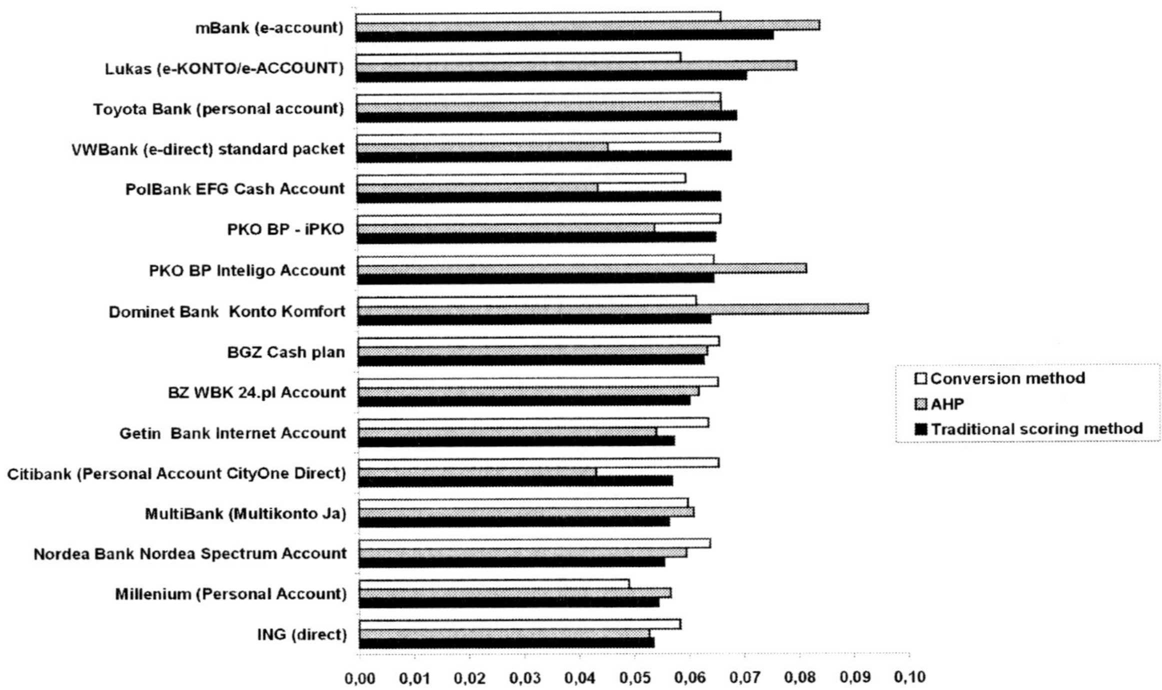

losing out with an expert's fatigue; therefore, frequently the websites which were examined first were evaluated higher than subsequent websites (the change of the order of websites' evaluation produced entirely different results). The presented score was often regarded by experts as ambiguous, owing to its relativity and the extended scale. Work consumption of this method was increasing, in comparison to the scoring method, exponentially in relation to the number of used evaluation criteria and the number of bank websites which were examined.

- Conversion method combining advantages of a scoring method (unequivocal, easy criterion evaluation) and Saaty's method (specifying the relation of one criterion to other criteria), consisting in defining the relation of one criterion with reference to other criteria based on averaged distances from a potential maximum value on the basis of the earlier scoring method, is regarded as a reasonable compromise between these methods.

The final results of the application of these methods for Internet services of e-banking websites for individual clients are presented on Figure 7.

Furthermore, both in the case of bank websites and earlier in the analysis of other e-business websites, experts pointed to a specific substitutability of particular features of evaluated websites. It was represented by attracting clients with economic features or – on the other hand, with technological advantages, with identical (comparable) functional features. Therefore, the best clients' scores were assigned to the websites which on the one hand, were crudely constructed, but offered a wide range of goods or services at reasonable prices, or on the other – those technically sophisticated (search engines, high score for graphics, etc.) but with a limited range of more expensive goods and/or with more sophisticated services offered at higher prices. This phenomenon, which so far has not been analysed in the literature from the point of view of information technologies' evaluation – will be examined in further studies.

REFERENCES

Achour, H., & Bensedrine, N. (2005) An evaluation of Internet banking and online brokerage in Tunisia. Retrieved from http://medforist.grenoble-em.com/Contenus/Conference%20Amman%20EBEL%2005/pdf/25.pdf

Balachandher, K. G., Bala, S., Nafis, A., & Perera, J. C. (2003). An evaluation of Internet banking sites in Islamic countries. [JIBC]. *The Journal of Internet Banking and Commerce, 2*(8).

Chiemeke, S. C., Evwiekpaefe, A. E., & Chete, F. O. (2006). The adoption of Internet banking in Nigeria: An empirical investigation. [JIBC]. *The Journal of Internet Banking and Commerce, 3*(11).

Chmielarz, W. (2005). *Systemy elektronicznej bankowości (Electronic banking systems).* Warsaw, Difin.

Chmielarz, W. (2007). *Systemy biznesu elektronicznego (Electronic business systems).* Warsaw, Difin.

Chmielarz, W. (2008). Metody oceny witryn banków internetowych w zakresie obsługi klienta indywidualnego (Evaluation methods of Internet bank websites with regard to individual client). *Rachunkowość bankowa, 3*(40), 65-77.

Dinitz, E., Porto, R. M., & Adachi, T. (2005) Internet Banking in Brazil: Evaluation of functionality, reliability and usability, *The Electronic Journal of Information System Evaluation,* 1 (8), 41-50; from: http://www.ejise.com.

Evans, J. R., & King, V. E. (1999). Business-to-business marketing and World Wide Web: Planning managing and assesssing web sites. *Industrial Marketing Management, 28,* 343–358. doi:10.1016/S0019-8501(98)00013-3

Macierzyński, M. (2007). *40 procent rachunków obsługiwanych jest przez Internet (40 per cent of accounts are operated via the Internet).* Retrieved from http://www.bankier.pl/wiadomosc/Juz-40-procent-rachunkow-obslugiwanych-jest-przez-internet-1588175.html

Malmari, H. (n.d.). F-Secure Reveals Consumer Attitudes Toward Internet Security Across Europe and North America. Retrieved May 5, 2008 from http://www.f-secure.com/f-secure/pressroom/news/fs_news_20080228_01_eng.html

Mateos, M. B., Mera, A. C., Gonzales, F. J., & Lopez, O. R. (2001). A new Web assessment index: Spanish universities analysis. *Internet Research: Electronic Application and Policy, 11*(3), 226–234. doi:10.1108/10662240110396469

Migdadi, Y. K. (2008). quantitative evaluation of the Internet banking service encounter's quality: Comparative study between Jordan and the UK retail banks. *Journal of Internet Banking and Commerce, 2*(13).

Miranda, F. J., Cortes, R., & Barriuso, C. (2006). Quantitative evaluation of e-banking Web sites: An empirical study of Spanish banks. *The Electronic Journal Information Systems Evaluation, 2*(9), 73-82, from http://www.eiise.com

Saaty, T. L. (1990). How to make a decision: The analytic hierarchy process. *European Journal of Operational Research, 48,* 9–26. doi:10.1016/0377-2217(90)90057-I

Saaty, T. L. (1999). Fundamentals of the analytic network process. In *Proceedings of 5th International Conference on th Analytic Hierarchy Process, Kobe* (pp. 20-33).

Saraswat, A., & Katta, A. (2008). Quantitative evaluation of e-banking websites: A study of Indian banks. *Icfai University Journal of Information Technology*, *3*(4), 32–49.

Selz, D., & Schubert, P. (1997). Web assessment: A model for the evaluation and the assessment of successful electronic commerce applications. *Electronic Markets*, *3*(7), 46–48. doi:10.1080/10196789700000038

Sikorski, M. (2003). Zastosowanie metody AHP do analiz bezpieczeństwa na stanowiskach pracy (Application of AHP Method for Occupational Safety Analysis). In O. Downarowicz (Ed.), *Wybrane metody zarządzania bezpieczeństwem pracy* (pp. 71-96). Wydawnictwo Politechniki Gdańskiej, Gdańsk.

Whiteley, D. (2000). *e-Commerce: Strategies, technologies and applications*. McGraw Hill.

KEY TERMS AND DEFINITIONS

Electronic Banking: A modern, 'non-contact' form of providing banking services without the necessity to visit a bank branch, consist of several distribution channels. PC banking, internet banking, mobile banking and TV-based banking.

Internet Banking: A part of electronic banking, customer access to bank services using a PC or mobile media by web browser.

Retail I-Banking Customer Services: All services for individual clients of a bank accessible in remote-control way using Internet.

Evaluation of the Internet Banking: Measurement of a bank website with a set of criteria including functionality, user-friendliness, usability, efficiency and site reliability.

Methods of I-Banking Evaluation: Bank websites' assessment techniques and procedures.

Comparative Study: A way of measurement of similarities or differences between two or more categories.

Criteria of Evaluation: Set of main features of a bank or principles of bank activities used for judgement or decision-making process.

Chapter 12
Health Infonomics:
Intelligent Applications of Information Technology

Michael Mackert
The University of Texas at Austin, USA

Pamela Whitten
Michigan State University, USA

Bree Holtz
Michigan State University, USA

ABSTRACT

Researchers are currently challenged to document the economic aspects of information across an array of contexts. While some lessons can be applied generally, certain contexts present unique challenges for researchers interested in the acquisition, management, and use of information. Health is one such field currently undergoing a revolution driven by new applications of information-based technologies and services. This chapter provides background on health informatics and current issues as health informatics impacts the provision of health in doctors' offices, shifts the provision of healthcare services into patients' homes, and presents new opportunities to address public health concerns. An outline of a future research agenda in health informatics and a look at the prospect of health informatics applications provides the necessary foundation for focused work on the economic impact of this information-driven transformation in healthcare delivery.

INTRODUCTION

Informatics, the maximization of data use and acquisition through the intersection of information and computer science, is becoming commonplace across a range of applications that interface with everyday life. Currently, researchers are challenged to document economic aspects of information across a vast array of decision-making contexts. There are important general lessons that can be applied across applications from the field of infonomics, but context can also drive the impact and evolution of information use in distributed business environments.

Healthcare is one such context uniquely poised for transformation based on informatics and the economic aspects of information-driven changes

DOI: 10.4018/978-1-60566-890-1.ch012

in the provision of healthcare. The delivery of health services represents one of the more complex examples of distributed decision making as multiple stakeholders - providers, patients, family caregivers, insurance payers, and government regulators - have interests in individuals' health decisions and treatments.

Prompted by rising healthcare costs and concerns over quality, there is significant pressure to reform healthcare in both developed and developing countries. Stakeholders are looking to a wide array of information technologies to address challenges in health delivery, including access to care, medical errors, cost efficiencies, health outcomes, patient and provider satisfaction, demographic challenges such as aging populations, and provider shortages. Such challenges are particularly pressing given the unprecedented strain the health care industry will face due to an aging global population. The United Nations projects that by 2050 the number of older people (60 years or older) will outnumber younger people worldwide, due to people around the world living longer and having fewer children (United Nations, 2002).

While informatics may not present a solution to every problem in healthcare, appropriate applications of new information technology to the provision of health can indeed present promising strategies for addressing shortcomings in the healthcare system or advancing the practice of medicine. The sheer quantity of information necessary to practice medicine and to be an informed patient is rapidly increasing. Health informatics systems can serve as gateways for this vast amount of information to be utilized and managed by both providers and patients.

In line with the recognition that information technology can be used as a tool to address the challenges in healthcare, there is also a growing movement for paradigmatic shifts in the very nature of healthcare provision. For example, the movement toward "patient-centered care" seeks to provide health services that explore a patient's main reason for a health visit, concerns, and need for information; gain an integrated understanding of the patient's emotional needs and life issues, find common understandings of the etiology of the problem, allow the patient and health provider to mutually agree on management; enhance prevention and health promotion; and reinforce the continuing relationship between the patient and health provider (Stewart, 2001). Health informatics can assist in this movement of patient-centered care, empowering patients and their communities so they can make informed decisions regarding their healthcare (Cornford & Klecun-Dabrowska, 2001). Operationalizing this concept calls for employing information technologies to meet the core goals of patient-centered care, namely (Sherer, 1993):

- Locating services as close as possible to patients
- Redefining work by desegregating job tasks and providing health workers with necessary support, skills, and training
- Meeting patient needs, rather than the needs of a department, discipline or field.

This chapter seeks to illustrate the evolution and impact of health informatics, review what research has taught us to date, and comment upon future directions to advance health informatics and infonomics research. The discussion will include the utilization of health informatics systems designed to assist healthcare providers in their work, technology to bring health services into patients' homes, and population-based applications that can advance public health. A greater understanding of health informatics applications - what these systems are and how they could radically transform the healthcare system - can provide the foundation for studies of the economic impact of an information-driven revolution in healthcare delivery. While many of the statistics and examples cited in this chapter are drawn from the U.S., lessons learned and potential applications would be similar in international contexts. Differences between the U.S. and other countries are noted when relevant.

THE UNDERPINNINGS OF HEALTH INFORMATICS

Health informatics has emerged as a rapidly evolving scientific field that studies the interrelationship between information (e.g., computers and communications), science (e.g., engineering and technology) and health (practice, education, and research). Health informatics, by nature, encompasses multiple disciplines, including communication, economics, engineering, computer science, nursing, and medicine. This new academic domain includes multiple applications, such as:

- Development and delivery of public health information
- Design and analysis of electronic medical records and personal health records
- Evaluation of the impact of IT on the clinical processes, outcomes, and resources
- Telemedicine and remote monitoring
- Data management and database construction
- Development of terminology, coding, and classification schemes
- Process re-engineering
- Interactions and interfaces between technology, providers, and patients
- Implications for policy and ethics
- Bioinformatics
- Clinical decision tools and decision support systems
- Geographic Information systems

With its broad array of disciplines it should not be surprising that health informatics also encompasses a variety of terms referring to transferring data to maximize patient care. Terminology commonly used in the literature when discussion heath informatics includes electronic medical records (EMR), electronic health records (EHR), health information technology (HIT), health information network (HIN) and health information exchange (HIE).

Before EMRs, paper records were launched in the 19th century as the standard of recording patient data, treatments, and procedures (Shortliffe, 1999). Generally, EMRs simply refer to an individual record in which a healthcare provider records treatments, drugs, and future recommendations electronically. There are several advantages of an electronic record, including legible orders and the ability for quicker searches through the record (D. Bates, Ebell, Gotlieb, Zapp, & Mullins, 2003). While the terms EMR and EHR are often used synonymously, many consider EHRs to be more comprehensive (Busis & Hier, 2007). EHRs include individual patient information from a variety of sources, such as radiology (films), pharmacy (interaction checks), and specialist information (cardiologist, dermatologist, etc.).

Examining the broader scope of electronic health data management, HIT is defined by the Department of Health and Human Services as a "comprehensive management of medical information and its secure exchange between healthcare consumers and providers" (Department of Health and Human Services, 2008). HIT is being recognized as an extremely important tool for improving healthcare quality and outcomes, reducing costs, and improving access to care. HIEs or HINs are necessary when connecting all of the individual patient records across regions or organizations. Through the years these have also been coined CHINs (Community Health Information Network) or RHIOs (Regional Health Information Organization).

New health informatics applications are often cited in calls to improve the healthcare system, such as in the early 1990s when the Institute of Medicine called for the creation of computerized patient records nationally (Dick, Steen, & Detmer, 1991). While many healthcare professionals and policymakers at that point understood the benefit of sharing patient information among healthcare providers, a decade later it was necessary to produce more calls for the public to recognize the importance of information technology in healthcare as the Institute of Medicine published two additional reports *To Err is Human* (2000) and *Crossing the Quality Chasm* (2001). *To Err is Human* is now considered to be a seminal report on restructuring the healthcare system in order to improve health outcomes. That report declared that up to 98,000 people in the United States were dying due to medical errors each year. The report posited the entire healthcare system must be revised in order to meet six goals - to provide care that is safe, effective, patient-centered, timely, efficient, and equitable (Johnston, Pan, Walker, Bates, & Middleton, 2003; Kohn, Corrigan, & Donaldson, 2000). The report also asserted health informatics would be a key to resolving this crisis in healthcare (Johnston, et al., 2003; Kohn, et al., 2000). In *Crossing the Quality Chasm* a strategic plan was proposed to address the problems highlighted in *To Err is Human*. In it, health informatics is positioned as being able to facilitate in addressing all six goals of improving healthcare.

Three years later, in 2004, President George Bush declared by 2014, most Americans should have a national EHR and created the position of the National Health Information Technology Coordinator (Blumenthal & Glaser, 2007). Still, almost a decade after *Crossing the Quality Chasm*, researchers and practitioners are still no closer to implementing national EHRs (Miller & Sim, 2004). A study conducted through 2005, demonstrated less than twenty-four percent of physicians used EHRs in an ambulatory setting, only five percent of hospitals had a computerized physician order entry (CPOE) system, and less than two percent of the hospitals were actively using CPOE systems (Holbrook, 2006; Jha, et al., 2006). This is despite the fact that HIT has been found to improve patient care and quality (Chaudhry, et al., 2006). The challenges faced by implementation of a nationwide health network were also noted in the IOM's 2001 report, these issue consist of interoperability, standardization, privacy, regulatory, human factors and the large financial investment requires (Institute of Medicine, 2002). Even today these barriers remain as key hurdles facing IT diffusion in healthcare, though progress is being made - 29.2% of office-based physicians were using EMRs in 2006, a 22% increase from 2005 and 60% increase since 2001 (Hing, Burt, & Woodwell, 2007).

Some of the key challenges facing these projects include cost, lack of reimbursement, technical issues, system interoperability, legal and policy issues, and concerns over security, privacy, and confidentiality (Hersh, 2004; Schoenman, Keeler, Moiduddin, & Hamlin, 2006; Whitten, Buis, & Love, 2007). Physicians are often expected to front upwards of $24,000 to install and implement a HIT system with little return on investment (ROI) (Hersh, 2004; Johnston, et al., 2003; Kleinke, 2005). Insurers, laboratories, patients and others generally uninvolved in the payment for electronic systems assume the remainder of the ROI (Hersh, 2004; Whitten, Buis, & Love, 2007). Any type of health information technology application generally involves systems with high complexity that must be customized to a particular clinic or office (Whitten, Buis, & Mackert, 2007). Hersh (2004) suggested that health care facilities, especially those in rural or underserved areas, adopt a simple and inexpensive solution to HIT. System interoperability is also a concern regarding the adoption of HIT in the health field. Most information is inaccessible from one system to the next, making a cohesive record for patients impossible, lowering the incentives for single physician offices or small clinics to implement this type of technology (Hersh, 2004, 2006; Kleinke, 2005; Walker, et al., 2005). Security, privacy, and confidentiality are an important topic when dealing with HIT, as many studies report that electronic data have more security features than traditional paper records (Hersh, 2004). In general, patients do not perceive security issues as a major barrier, whereas clinicians are extremely concerned (Whitten, Buis, & Love, 2007).

Some of the challenges facing the rollout of health technology in the U.S., specifically the fragmented healthcare system, are not present in other countries. Indeed, many other countries, specifically those with more centralized systems of health care – the United Kingdom, Canada, Norway, Singapore, etc. – have been able to advance far ahead of the U.S. (E. Shortliffe, 2005). Overall, the governments of those countries have initiated programs to advance HIT and most are at least six years ahead of the United States (Anderson, Frogner, Johns, & Reinhardt, 2006). While many countries are further along in their implementation, they are still facing a myriad of hurdles to full adoption and diffusion. Many of these countries' programs started with disjointed and unstandardized systems but discovered that such a strategy hindered adoption. Some countries adopted standards set by the eEurope 2002 and eEurope 2005 Action Plans. Many other countries have adopted the Health Level Seven (HL7) standards, including Canada, Germany, the United Kindgom, and the U.S. (Anderson, et al., 2006). HL7 "provides standards for interoperability that improve care delivery, optimize workflow, reduce ambiguity and enhance knowledge transfer among ...healthcare providers, government agencies, the vendor community" (HL7, 2009).

In the past, there has been a fundamental assumption that health informatics will inherently improve the quality of healthcare (Heathfield, Pitty, & Hanka, 1998; Kaplan, 2001). Above and beyond improvements potential improvements in healthcare, health informatics research involves understanding the implementation and utilization of these technologies while also examining the actual use by the healthcare workers in their health specialty (Kaplan, 2001; Lærum, Ellingsen, & Faxvaag, 2001). Many researchers studying health informatics now understand that human factors, organizational institutionalism, and medical specialty contribute in the overall diffusion and success of these tools. The following section provides an overview of recent research in health informatics.

CURRENT ISSUES IN HEALTH INFORMATICS

Health informatics systems span the healthcare system, from hospitals and doctors' offices to patients' homes to the efforts of public health officials to improve population-level health indicators. Informatics in health offers the opportunity to study large scale information systems based on human-centered considerations. As there are multiple types of large scale information systems in the health context, special consideration must be paid to the unique nuances of these information-based services. This section highlights study of US-based applications.

EHRs and Healthcare Quality

Widespread deployment and adoption of EHR systems is one important step toward improving healthcare in the U.S., an important goal given that U.S. adults only receive approximately half of the care they should (McGlynn, et al., 2006). As stated earlier, adoption of EHRs in the U.S. has been quite slow, however, with 25-30% of practices currently making use of such systems (Berner, Detmer, & Simborg, 2005; Burt & Sisk, 2005; Gans, Kralewski, Hammons, & Dowd, 2005).

There are numerous reasons that EHR adoption has been slow, including difficulty in making the business case for EHRs and incentive systems that do not reward healthcare providers for adopting EHRs (Middleton, Hammond, Brennan, & Cooper, 2005; E. Shortliffe, 2005). Additional structural barriers within the healthcare system provide further hurdles to EHR adoption, such as difficulties arriving at technical and administrative standards

(E. Shortliffe, 2005); the U.S.'s relative lack of a national structure could be one reason that health systems that are more centrally coordinated (e.g., Sweden, Australia, and Denmark) have had comparatively greater success adopting EHR systems (Harris Interactive, 2002). Assuming the context within which EHR systems are implemented improves to favor adoption, studying current EHR efforts sheds light on additional issues likely to arise as healthcare organizations seek to install an EHR system. These include a fear among providers that EHRs might depersonalize the delivery of healthcare (Aydin, Rosen, & Felitti, 1994) and reluctance to spend sufficient time learning the actual technology (Overhage, Tierney, McDonald, & Pickett, 1991). It is important to recognize that such barriers are indeed significant and can impact the perceived benefits to widespread EHR adoption.

Providers are certainly aware of the benefits EHRs might offer, including quicker reviews of charts and improved patient privacy and security (Massachusetts Medical Society, 2003; E. H. Shortliffe, 2005). Other advantages to EHR deployment include cost savings for healthcare providers (Ash & Bates, 2005), increased continuity of care (Kibbe, Jr., & Green, 2004), and reduced medical errors (Hillestad, et al., 2005). Recent work has demonstrated that provider acceptance is largely dependent on providers' perceptions regarding the overall benefits of widespread EHR adoption – those providers who perceive the greatest benefits are most likely to endure temporary, personal troubles associated with EHR adoption in their own practices (Whitten, Buis, & Mackert, in press). Even if the current healthcare system is not driving health providers to adopt EHRs, that could change in the coming years as the Institute of Medicine has called for increased transparency, including public reporting of healthcare quality and increased payments to those providers offering superior care (Institute of Medicine, 2002).

In the end, of course, widespread EHR adoption will depend primarily on proving the success of such systems in improving patient outcomes. In providing the rationale for a study of EHR use on the quality of ambulatory care in the U.S., Linder et al. (2007) point to the often-conflicting results regarding impact of EHRs on healthcare quality. This could be due to the fact that many of the studies reporting positive findings come from a relatively small number of institutions that have developed internal EHR systems (Chaudhry, et al., 2006). As such, the basic justification of EHRs could be based on a shaky foundation.

Given the key role that widespread adoption of EHRs will play in a national effort to improve healthcare through the use of new health informatics systems, the current state of affairs leaves significant room for improvement. Continued improvements in design, research into impacts on healthcare quality, and better training projects are needed if EHRs are to fulfill their potential as a core element of healthcare systems.

E-Health and the Provision of Healthcare

Shifting from healthcare providers' use of health informatics to a patient-centered view, the spread of broadband Internet access has made possible two phenomena with particularly important implications for the U.S. healthcare system – widespread use of the Internet to obtain health information and the provision of healthcare services to the home via telemedicine.

One of the more accepted definitions of e-health is supplied by Eysenbach (2001):

e-health is an emerging field in the intersection of medical informatics, public health and business, referring to health services and information delivered or enhanced through the Internet and related technologies. In a broader sense, the term characterizes not only a technical development, but also a state-of-mind, a way of thinking, an attitude, and a commitment for networked, global thinking, to improve healthcare locally, region-

ally, and worldwide by using information and communication technology.

With more than 70% of American adults going online in general, data also indicate that a whopping 80% of these users are specifically looking for health-related information e-health increasingly ubiquitous (Fox, 2006; Pew Internet and American Life Project, 2007). People venturing online can make use of a variety of e-health applications, from systems designed to connect patients and providers via e-mail to online support groups (Arrington, 2004; May, Finch, Mair, & Mort, 2005). For patients interested in maintaining their own Personal Health Record (PHR), e-health applications such as Google Health (Google, 2008) and Microsoft HealthVault (Microsoft, 2008) allow users to organize their health information in one central location. Such systems raise important questions regarding ownership and access to data, as well as the quality and accuracy of patient-entered information. Widespread adoption of PHRs does introduce a variety of patient privacy and data protection issues, though a majority of respondents in one recent survey expressed a willingness to share health information if it meant better healthcare (Ball & Gold, 2006; California HealthCare Foundation, 2005).

Health communication researchers have established significant benefits to these types of e-health applications in providing health interventions. Users benefit from increased access to information from a variety of sources, as well as the anonymity that some patients value when dealing with certain health issues (Willis, Demiris, & Oliver, 2007). Information providers can benefit from the ability to tailor information to better match the cultural values and needs of users (Oenema, Brug, & Lechner, 2001). Indeed, research has demonstrated e-health applications can educate low health literate individuals, and such interventions are useful and appreciated even among more literate audiences (Mackert, Whitten, & Garcia, 2008; Whitten, Love, Buis, & Mackert, in press).

At the same time, e-health applications permit healthcare consumers to reach out in search of effective strategies for managing their own health.. Telemedicine, one of those applications, makes it possible to provide healthcare services directly into patients' homes. Telemedicine, defined broadly, is the provision of healthcare services via telecommunication technology. The earliest work in telemedicine took place in the 1960s (Wittson, Affleck, & Johnson, 1961), and has since grown to the point that it is no longer possible to quantify the number of systems operating in the U.S.(Whitten & Kuwahara, 2003)

Initially, telemedicine typically employed some form of videoconferencing to link a health provider at a hospital to a patient at a remote clinical setting. Such videoconferencing could take place via low-bandwidth phone lines or higher-bandwidth Integrated Services Digital Network (ISDN), though advances in Internet Protocol (IP) networking solutions have dramatically increased the speed, flexibility, and cost-effectiveness of telemedicine systems in recent years.

Today, telemedicine has expanded beyond videoconferencing to include the exploding application of remote monitoring, the home-based monitoring of patients with chronic diseases; related systems let caregivers remotely monitor patients' compliance taking their medications. Telemedicine has demonstrated its efficacy in an assortment of medical applications, including dermatology (Chen, See, & Shumack, 2002), psychiatry (Kuulasmaa, Wahlberg, & Kuusimaki, 2004), and physical therapy (Rizzo, Strickland, & Bouchard, 2004), to name a few. Telemedicine researchers continue to explore innovative and efficacious methods of providing healthcare at a distance, so the capabilities of the technology and range of uses will continue to improve. This is particularly true as advances in information storage and transmission will make it easier, and more cost effective, to use telemedicine technology for store-and-forward imaging systems (e.g., teleradiology). Advances in mobile technology, such as cellular phones with built-in video cameras, will present telemedicine researchers with platforms on which they can build innovative telemedicine systems to meet patients' healthcare needs.

Above and beyond the technological capacity of existing and future e-health and telemedicine systems, the impact of these technologies on the doctor-patient relationship must be considered. Even within a single study, patients' perceptions of the interplay between online sources of information and the doctor-patient interaction can vary significantly (Kahlor & Mackert, in press). The takeaway lesson, as with the introduction of any technology into the healthcare system, appears to be that there is no simple answer; thus the more flexible that e-health and telemedicine systems can be designed, to let providers and patients customize their own experience with the technology, the more likely it is that such systems will achieve sustained usage.

Health Informatics and Public Health

The rationale for implementing new telemedicine and e-health systems in patients' homes often involves the goal of eliminating health disparities resulting from uneven access to healthcare services. There are a variety of reasons such disparities might be present, including significant differences that often exist between urban and rural areas. Improvements in Geographic Information Systems (GIS) tools have made it possible to further investigate the efficacy and equity of the healthcare system and public health efforts, moving beyond urban-rural disparities (Noor, Zurovac, Hay, Ochola, & Snow, 2003).

As an example of the application of GIS to public health, Gordon-Larsen et al. found that inequality in the built environment (e.g., parks and other recreational areas) resulted in disparities in physical activity and increased obesity among lower-income and minority populations (Gordon-Larsen, Nelson, Page, & Popkin, 2006). Such findings from GIS-based research can help public health professionals to design and effectively target interventions designed to reduce the prevalence and impact of health disparities. GIS systems can be used to track the spread of infectious and acute diseases, in addition to the incidence and distribution of chronic conditions (Croner, Sperling, & Broome, 1996).

Some of the more significant benefits to GIS-based research and interventions can only come about by sharing the information contained in databases by various state and national government agencies. Effectively merging the information managed by the Centers for Disease Control and the U.S. Environmental Protection Agency, for example, could make it possible to study the impact of pollution and environmental quality at the population-level.

Widespread deployment of EHRs and patient-controlled PHRs could provide invaluable information to researchers and healthcare agencies using GIS tools to investigate public health. While the benefits to public health are clear, there are indeed potential concerns regarding privacy and how such information might be used. Public health interventions based on GIS data are likely to be welcomed by the public, but concerns over how insurance companies could potentially use such information are valid and likely to counterbalance those benefits for some healthcare professionals and members of the general public for some time to come.

A RESEARCH AGENDA TO ADVANCE HEALTH INFORMATICS AND HEALTH INFONOMICS

As health informatics has the potential to alter the healthcare system in a variety of positive ways, it is imperative that scholars continue to advance research regarding health informatics as nations around the world struggle to improve services while managing costs to both healthcare consumers and national budgets. And while health informatics and practice moves forward, the ability to tease out the economic impact of new health information and strategies for managing that information will become more pronounced.

As EHRs can be viewed as the foundation upon which many other systems can be built, any research agenda to advance health informatics can productively begin with EHRs. Given the fact that many of the positive results from EHR deployments come from leading healthcare institutions and providers, it is important to expand studies of EHRs into a variety of other settings. If the only healthcare providers that can achieve significant economic or quality improvements through the use of EHRs are premier institutions, that could suggest some fundamental issues that need to be addressed as policymakers push for widespread adoption of EHRs. Related to this, comparative studies of different national programs for promoting EHR adoption are needed to codify and improve upon the best policies for promoting EHR adoption across national healthcare systems.

Healthcare providers and consumers are seeking new ways of improving access to health information for all. Some of these efforts are being advanced by healthcare providers (e.g., remote monitoring of patients in the home), while others are driven by consumers' desire to become active participants in their own health (e.g., e-health applications like HealthVault and Google Health). In either case, there is a real need for research into what factors most strongly influence provider and patient acceptance, in addition to elements of system design that might contribute significantly to successful deployment (e.g., interoperability with other e-health applications, perceived usefulness, perceived ease of use). Research from related fields, such as Information Systems can provide a starting point for such investigations. Similarly, work in economics, specifically Transaction Cost Economics, has the potential for direct application to the sharing of information among healthcare institutions (Coles & Hesterly, 1998; Hodgkin, Horgan, & Garnick, 1997; Williamson, 1996). Additionally, policy and ethics researchers could productively explore the privacy and security issues surrounding the widespread adoption of e-health applications, whether such technologies are embraced voluntarily by healthcare consumers or brought to them as standard care without their approval.

As EHRs and e-health systems begin to accumulate more and more data about populations - either nationally or at the local/regional level - the potential for GIS-based public health investigations will continue to grow. But the promise of improved health interventions must be balanced against less acceptable uses of such technology, such as insurers determining coverage based on GIS data and trends. How will healthcare consumers balance the positives and negatives of such technology? It is entirely possible – if not likely – that the average healthcare consumer is unqualified to have an informed opinion on such issues. Policy and ethics researchers must continue to debate the public health benefits that could result from widespread use of GIS-based systems and the potential downside to this information as it might impact individual people. Additionally, more work must be done to assess the public's understanding of health and privacy issues, as well as their willingness to share private health information in exchange for improvements in healthcare services. Of course, this is just one part of the much larger issue of healthcare decisions and responsibility in general being shifted to patients.

Another need, across all kinds of health informatics applications, is to study differences in how larger and smaller institutions adopt these systems, as well as how the economic costs and benefits of implementing informatics applications varies among different institutions. Bates (2009) recently suggested that some kinds of applications – such as order entry and decision support systems – are sufficiently mature to merit widespread adoption among larger healthcare institutions. The benefits of these systems in smaller healthcare institutions, as well as the benefits of other informatics applications, are less clear. As health infonomics research advances it must focus on helping to provide answers to practitioners on when a particular informatics application is likely to provide economic benefits to an institution - with the final answer depending on factors such as size of the institution, the particular application, and the designer of the system (vendor vs. in-house).

Finally, a significant need across all research areas in health is an increased focus on projects that, while perhaps not complete failures, certainly do not represent complete successes or examples of best practices. As important as it is to learn what works, it is equally vital that researchers and professionals have more opportunities to find out what has not worked. The *Journal of Telemedicine and Telecare*, an international journal focusing on telemedicine and e-health, dedicates a supplement each year specifically to successes and failures in this area. Topics covered include elements of projects that if neglected can virtually ensure significant problems (e.g., Mackert & Whitten, 2007) and systematic reviews of the quality of studies investigating both success and failures in telehealth projects (e.g., Bensink, Hailey, & Wootton, 2007). Researchers much continue to share the causes and results of less successful projects if the field is to advance as smoothly and quickly as possible.

As important as it is to pursue a productive research agenda in health informatics and infonomics, it must be recognized that these advances are dependent upon contributions from a variety of fields. Researchers from medicine, nursing, communication, information technology, economics, public health, and computer science are all essential to advancing the design and application of health informatics systems. Thorough studies of health informatics and infonomics almost by definition will be interdisciplinary, thus providing opportunities for collaboration among academics from a variety of specialties.

A LOOK TOWARD HEALTH INFORMATICS AND INFONOMICS OF THE FUTURE

A range of illustrious publications have called for investment and implementation of various health informatics solutions to address health quality, access and cost issues. Even though a host of barriers have impeded diffusion to date, there are few who doubt the inevitable transition to a wide-scale infonomics phenomenon in health. This evolution will not occur in isolation of the contextual factors that drive health services today and tomorrow.

Health infonomics must operate in a setting that serves more patients. In many developed countries, baby boomers are transitioning from middle to old age in record numbers. With this aging population comes increased disease incidence as well as expectations for prolonging life. Along with the increase in patients will come more technologies leading to increased amounts of information from which health providers and patients must manage health events. Electronic technologies offer a solution to improving efficiency for a new continuum of care. The role of the patient will change as we witness increased self-diagnosis and self-care as patients and their family caregivers obtain more information. We will see a shift as hospitals become the site for the extremely ill as more people are able to remain at home. The enhanced availability of data to the public and health providers will cause improvements in processes and outcomes. As a result, we may witness a significant change in the delivery model where care becomes more routinized for more common diseases.

Currently, health informatics systems for the exchange of information are typically designed and deployed with local utilization in mind. Typical exchange interoperability challenges are addressed through tailoring the software to address such issues as differences in the data structures and ambiguous interpretation from implied metadata. However, problems increase exponentially when a new party seeks access to the informatics-based data, the number of users and need for records increases, and when clinical structures evolve over time. All of these challenges will call for generic interfaces that can comply and adapt with these changes, as well as built in mechanisms to find the location of the needed data items. The bottom line is the future informatics solutions will differentiate the users and the data location. This infonomic infrastructure will require communication between the systems to be based on the needs of the healthcare worker and/or patient; however, the actual location of the information will be transparent and less important (van der Linden, Kalra, Hasman, & Talmon, 2008). Such large-scale infrastructure will also make it possible for health infonomics researchers to consider the economic tradeoffs evident in any health policy decision, such as the increased costs associated with a particular medical advance or the ability to maintain a particular level of care at a reduced cost.

Perhaps the most important future shift to be noted concerns the pattern and style of interactions rather then any technology-related detail. Healthcare workers in the early 21st century communicate in ways that parallel human conversation - one person defines and requests information. In fact, current information retrieval from established standards such as HL7 and archetype 13606 is based upon this paradigm. However, expectations and communication patterns are slowly shifting as we employ an Internet that makes it so simple to move from a one-to-one exchange to a one-to-many exchange. In addition, we are now recognizing the unnecessary need to store everything locally. Instead, health infonomics will demonstrate the enhanced efficiencies of retrieving all forms of data only when they are needed from any secure storage location.

CONCLUSION

Few dispute the inevitable shift to adoption and dependence of informatics to a degree that reshapes the very foundation of health infonomics. As presented in this paper, there are a range of specific applications to operationalize this shift such as EHRs, e-health activities, and GIS services to impact public health. Typically, arguments concerning positive impacts on costs and health outcomes dominate the call for adoption and diffusion of these technology-based solutions. We concur, noting the need for ongoing documentation of these important impacts. However, this essay must acknowledge the role and importance of human perceptions that will drive health infonomics. Indeed, attaining a deep understanding of the usage of health informatics systems, as well as challenges these systems face, is necessary before the full economic impact of information-driven healthcare can be pursued and recognized.

Health advocates commonly call for a revised role for the health consumer. For example, Garson and Levin (2001) predict that we are witnessing a shift whereby the patient will eventually be the ultimate consumer and measures of patient satisfaction and other patient-oriented report cards will assume growing importance. With this in mind, we wish to close by acknowledging the potential perceptions of patients who experience healthcare in an environment that makes wide use of information technology applications. Whitten and colleagues (2007) conducted a study where they investigated the relationship between investment in health information technology and patient satisfaction in the hospital context. This study analyzed patient satisfaction data for hospitals that were included in the 2005 *Hospitals & Health Networks* annual list of the "100 most wired hospitals and health systems." Specifically, they assessed the level of satisfaction from multiple angles between patients from the most wired hospitals and patients who had used a hospital not included in this list. Analyses from this study found that patients from the most wired hospital group reported higher levels of global satisfaction than did patients from the other group of hospitals. Patients from the most wired hospitals also reported higher satisfaction related to the admission process, their experiences with physicians, and personal issues such as sensitivity and pain. In addition, higher satisfaction scores were associated with most wired hospital status more so than for any specific demographic variable tested. The results of this study suggest that among the longer-term benefits of IT investment in hospitals may actually be issues related to patient satisfaction. These data imply that IT enhancements affect the way patients receive and perceive their care.

As we move toward a new paradigm of health delivery necessitated by public and private desires to contain health costs and improve health outcomes, we are witnessing a reality where patients will be more knowledgeable about managing healthcare, better informed about the benefits, risks, costs and alternatives for treatments, more technologically savvy, and more engaged in decision-making. The implications for health infonomics are critical. The superhighway for health information exchange will be crowded with multiple stakeholders driving our future course in this crucial area of infonomics.

REFERENCES

Anderson, G. F., Frogner, B. K., Johns, R. A., & Reinhardt, U. E. (2006). Health care spending and use of information technology in OECD countries. *Health Affairs*, *25*(3), 819–831. doi:10.1377/hlthaff.25.3.819

Arrington, M. I. (2004). The role of the Internet in prostate cancer survivors' illness narratives. In P. Whitten & D. Cook (Eds.), Understanding health communication technologies (pp. 181-186). San Francisco, CA: Jossey-Bass.

Ash, J., & Bates, D. (2005). Factors and forces impacting EHR system adoption: Report of a 2004 ACMI discussion. *Journal of the American Medical Informatics Association*, *12*(1), 8–12. doi:10.1197/jamia.M1684

Aydin, C. E., Rosen, P. N., & Felitti, V. J. (1994). Transforming information use in preventive medicine: Learning to balance technology with the art of caring. Paper presented at the Eighteenth Annual Symposium on Computer Applications in Medical Care, Washington, DC.

Ball, M. J., & Gold, J. (2006). Banking on health: Personal records and information exchange. *Journal of Healthcare Information Management*, *20*(2), 71–83.

Bates, D., Ebell, M., Gotlieb, E., Zapp, J., & Mullins, H. (2003). A proposal for electronic medical records in U.S. primary care. *Journal of the American Medical Informatics Association*, *10*, 1–10. doi:10.1197/jamia.M1097

Bates, D. W. (2009). The effects of health information technology on inpatient care. *Archives of Internal Medicine*, *169*(2), 105–107. doi:10.1001/archinternmed.2008.542

Bensink, M., Hailey, D., & Wootton, R. (2007). A systematic review of successes and failures in home telehealth. Part 2: Final quality rating results. *Journal of Telemedicine and Telecare*, *13*(S3), 10–14. doi:10.1258/135763307783247121

Berner, E. S., Detmer, D. E., & Simborg, D. (2005). Will the wave finally break? A brief view of the adoption of electronic medical records in the United States. *Journal of the American Medical Informatics Association*, *12*(1), 3–7. doi:10.1197/jamia.M1664

Blumenthal, D., & Glaser, J. (2007). Information technology comes to medicine. *The New England Journal of Medicine*, *356*, 2527–2534. doi:10.1056/NEJMhpr066212

Burt, C. W., & Sisk, J. E. (2005). Which physicians and practices are using electronic medical records? *Health Affairs*, *24*(5), 1334–1343. doi:10.1377/hlthaff.24.5.1334

Busis, N. A., & Hier, D. (2007). How to get your electronic health records in order. *Neurology Today*, *7*, 16. doi:10.1097/01.NT.0000296515.14653.5f

California HealthCare Foundation (2005). National Consumer Health Privacy Survey 2005.

Chaudhry, B., Wang, J., Maglione, M., Mojica, W., Roth, E., & Morton, S. C. (2006). Systematic Review: Impact of health information technology on quality, efficiency, and costs of medical care. *Archives of Internal Medicine*, *144*(10), 742–752.

Chen, K., See, A., & Shumack, S. (2002). Website discussion forums: Results of an Australian project to promote telecommunication in dermatology. Journal of Telemedicine and Telecare, 8(Suppl 3), S3:5-6.

Coles, J., & Hesterly, W. S. (1998). The impact of firm-specific assets and the interaction of uncertainty: An examination of make or buy decisions in public and private hospitals. *Journal of Economic Behavior & Organization*, *36*, 383–409. doi:10.1016/S0167-2681(98)00102-4

Cornford, T., & Klecun-Dabrowska, E. (2001). Telehealth technology: Consequences for structure through use. *Medinfo*, *10*(pt 2), 1140–1144.

Croner, C. M., Sperling, J., & Broome, F. R. (1996). Geographic information systems (GIS): New perspectives in understanding human health and environmental relationships. *Statistics in Medicine*, *15*(18), 1961–1977. doi:10.1002/(SICI)1097-0258(19960930)15:18<1961::AID-SIM408>3.0.CO;2-L

Department of Health and Human Services. (2008). Health information technology home. Retrieved from http://www.dhhs.gov/healthit/

Dick, R. S., Steen, E. B., & Detmer, D. E. (Eds.). (1991). The computer-based patient record: An essential technology for health care. Washington, DC: National Academy Press.

Eysenbach, G. (2001). What is e-health? *Journal of Medical Internet Research*, *3*(2), e20. doi:10.2196/jmir.3.2.e20

Fox, S. (2006). Online Health Search 2006. Washington, DC: Pew Internet & American Life Project.

Gans, D., Kralewski, J., Hammons, T., & Dowd, B. (2005). Medical groups' adoption of electronic health records and information systems. *Health Affairs*, *24*(5), 1323–1333. doi:10.1377/hlthaff.24.5.1323

Garson, A. Jr, & Levin, S. A. (2001). The 10-year trends for the future of healthcare: Implications for academic health centers. *The Ochsner Journal*, *3*(1), 10–15.

Google (2008). Google Health. Retrieved September 28, 2008, from https://www.google.com/health

Gordon-Larsen, P., Nelson, M. C., Page, P., & Popkin, B. M. (2006). Inequality in the built environment underlies key health disparities in physical activity and obesity. *Pediatrics*, *117*(2), 417–424. doi:10.1542/peds.2005-0058

HL7. (2009). Health Level 7. Retrieved from http://www.hl7.org

Harris Interactive. (2002). European Physicians Especially in Sweden, Netherlands and Denmark, Lead U.S. in Use of Electronic Medical Records. Retrieved February 20, 2006, from http://www.harrisinteractive.com/news/newsletters/healthnews/HI_HealthCareNews2002vol2_Iss16.pdf

Heathfield, H., Pitty, D., & Hanka, R. (1998). Evaluating information technology in health care: Barriers and challenges. *British Medical Journal, 316*, 1959–1961.

Hersh, W. (2004). Health care information technology: Progress and barriers. *Journal of the American Medical Association, 292*(18), 2273–2274. doi:10.1001/jama.292.18.2273

Hersh, W. (2006). Who are the informaticians? What we know and should know. *Journal of the American Medical Informatics Association, 13*(2), 166–169. doi:10.1197/jamia.M1912

Hillestad, R., Bigelow, J., Bower, A., Girosi, F., Meili, R., & Scoville, R. (2005). Can electronic medical record systems transform health care? Potential health benefits, savings, and costs. *Health Affairs, 24*(5), 1103–1117. doi:10.1377/hlthaff.24.5.1103

Hing, E. S., Burt, C. W., & Woodwell, D. A. (2007). Electronic medical record use by office-based physicians and their practices. *Advance Data, 393*, 1–7.

Hodgkin, D., Horgan, C., & Garnick, D. (1997). Make or buy: HMO's contracting arrangement for mental health care. *Administration and Policy in Mental Health, 24*(4), 359–376. doi:10.1007/BF02042519

Holbrook, S. (2006). Clinical portals: A win for providers. *Electronic Healthcare, 4*, 104–106.

Institute of Medicine (2002). Leadership by example: Coordinating government roles in improving health care quality.

Jha, A., Ferris, T., Donelan, K., DesRoches, C., Shields, A., & Rosenbaum, S. (2006). How common are electronic health records in the United States? A summary of evidence. *Health Affairs, 25*, 496–507. doi:10.1377/hlthaff.25.w496

Johnston, D., Pan, E., Walker, J., Bates, D. W., & Middleton, B. (2003). The value of computerized provider order entry in ambulatory settings. Wellesley, MA: Center for IT Leadership.

Kahlor, L., & Mackert, M. (in press). Perceived helpfulness of information and support sources and associated psychosocial outcomes among infertile women. *Fertility and Sterility*.

Kaplan, B. (2001). Evaluating informatics application: Clinical decision support system literature review. *International Journal of Medical Informatics, 64*, 15–37. doi:10.1016/S1386-5056(01)00183-6

Kibbe, D. C. Jr, R. L. P., & Green, L. A. (2004). The continuity of care record. *American Family Physician, 70*(7), 1220–1222.

Kleinke, J. D. (2005). Dot-Gov: Market failure and the creation of a national health information system. *Health Affairs, 24*(5), 1246–1262. doi:10.1377/hlthaff.24.5.1246

Kohn, L., Corrigan, J., & Donaldson, M. (2000). To err is human: Building a safer health system. National Academies Press.

Kuulasmaa, A., Wahlberg, K. E., & Kuusimaki, M. L. (2004). Videoconferencing in family therapy: A review. *Journal of Telemedicine and Telecare, 10*(3), 125–129. doi:10.1258/135763304323070742

Lærum, H., Ellingsen, G., & Faxvaag, A. (2001). Doctors' use of electronic medical records in hospitals: Cross sectional survey. *British Medical Journal, 323*, 1344–1348. doi:10.1136/bmj.323.7325.1344

Linder, J. A., Ma, J., Bates, D. W., Middleton, B., & Stafford, R. S. (2007). Electronic health record use and the quality of ambulatory care in the United States. *Archives of Internal Medicine, 167*(13), 1400–1405. doi:10.1001/archinte.167.13.1400

Mackert, M., & Whitten, P. (2007). The relationship between healthcare organizations and technology vendors: An overlooked key to telemedicine success. *Journal of Telemedicine and Telecare*, *13*(S3), S50–S53. doi:10.1258/135763307783247419

Mackert, M., Whitten, P., & Garcia, A. (2008). Evaluating e-health interventions designed for low health literate audiences. *Journal of Computer-Mediated Communication*, *13*(2), 504–515. doi:10.1111/j.1083-6101.2008.00407.x

Massachusetts Medical Society. (2003). MMS Survey: Most doctors are slow to incorporate technology into practices. Retrieved February 21, 2006, from http://www.massmed.org/AM/Template.cfm?Section=Search&template=/CM/HTMLDisplay.cfm&ContentID=10048

May, C., Finch, T., Mair, F., & Mort, M. (2005). Towards a wireless patient: Chronic illness, scarce care and technological innovation in the United Kingdom. *Social Science & Medicine*, *61*(7), 1485–1494. doi:10.1016/j.socscimed.2005.03.008

McGlynn, E. A., Asch, S. M., Adams, J., Keesey, J., Hicks, J., & DeCristofaro, A. (2006). The quality of health care delivered to adults in the United States. *The New England Journal of Medicine*, *348*(26), 2635–2645. doi:10.1056/NEJMsa022615

Microsoft (2008). HealthVault. Retrieved September 28, 2008, from http://www.healthvault.com/

Middleton, B., Hammond, W. E., Brennan, P. F., & Cooper, G. F. (2005). Accelerating U.S. EHR adoption: How to get there from here. Recommendations Based on the 2004 ACMI Retreat. *Journal of the American Medical Informatics Association*, *12*(1), 13–19. doi:10.1197/jamia.M1669

Miller, R., & Sim, I. (2004). Physicians' use of electronic medical records: Barriers and solutions. *Health Affairs*, *23*, 116–126. doi:10.1377/hlthaff.23.2.116

Noor, A. M., Zurovac, D., Hay, S. I., Ochola, S. A., & Snow, R. W. (2003). Defining equity in physical access to clinical services using geographical information systems as part of malaria planning and monitoring in Kenya. Tropical Medicine and International Health, 8(10), 917-926(910).

Oenema, A., Brug, J., & Lechner, L. (2001). Web-based tailored nutrition education: Results of a randomized controlled trial. *Health Education Research*, *16*(6), 647–660. doi:10.1093/her/16.6.647

Overhage, J., Tierney, W., McDonald, C., & Pickett, K. (1991). Computer-assisted order entry: Impact on intern time use. *Clinical Research*, *39*(3), 794A.

Pew Internet and American Life Project. (2007). E-patients with a disability or chronic disease. Washington, D.C.

Rizzo, A. A., Strickland, D., & Bouchard, S. (2004). The challenge of using virtual reality in telerehabilitation. *Telemedicine Journal and e-Health*, *10*(2), 184–195. doi:10.1089/tmj.2004.10.184

Schoenman, J., Keeler, J., Moiduddin, A., & Hamlin, B. (2006). Roadmap for the adoption of health information technology in rural communities. Washington, DC: Office of Rural Health Policy.

Sherer, J. L. (1993). Putting patients first: Hospitals work to define patient-centered care. *Hospitals*, *67*, 14–19.

Shortliffe, E. (2005). Strategic action in health information technology: Why the obvious has taken so long. *Health Affairs*, *24*(5), 1222–1233. doi:10.1377/hlthaff.24.5.1222

Shortliffe, E. H. (1999). The evolution of electronic medical records. *Academic Medicine*, *74*, 414–419. doi:10.1097/00001888-199904000-00038

Stewart, M. (2001). Towards a global definition of patient centred care. *British Medical Journal, 32*, 444–445. doi:10.1136/bmj.322.7284.444

United Nations. (2002). World Population Ageing: 1950-2050. Retrieved from http://www.un.org/esa/population/publications/worldageing19502050

van der Linden, H., Kalra, D., Hasman, A., & Talmon, J. (2008). Inter-organizational future proof of HER systems: A review of the security and privacy related issues. *International Journal of Medical Informatics, 78*(3), 141–160. doi:10.1016/j.ijmedinf.2008.06.013

Walker, J., Pan, E., Johnston, D., Adler-Milstein, J., Bates, D., & Middleton, B. (2005). The value of health care information exchange and interoperability. *Health Affairs, W5*, 10–18.

Whitten, P., Buis, L., & Love, B. (2007). Physician-Patient e-visit program. *Disease Management & Health Outcomes, 14*(4), 207–214. doi:10.2165/00115677-200715040-00002

Whitten, P., Buis, L., & Mackert, M. (2007). Factors impacting providers' perceptions regarding Midwestern EMR deployment. Telemedicine and e-Health, 13(4), 391-398.

Whitten, P., & Kuwahara, E. (2003). Telemedicine from the payor perspective: Considerations for reimbursement decisions. *Disease Management & Health Outcomes, 11*(5), 291–298. doi:10.2165/00115677-200311050-00002

Whitten, P., Love, B., Buis, L., & Mackert, M. (in press). Health education online for individuals with low health literacy: Evaluation of the diabetes and you website. *Journal of Technology in Human Services*.

Williamson, O. (1996). Transaction cost economics. The Mechanisms of Governance (pp. 54-92). Oxford University Press.

Willis, L., Demiris, G., & Oliver, D. (2007). Internet use by hospice families and providers: A review. *Journal of Medical Systems, 31*(2), 97–101. doi:10.1007/s10916-006-9033-0

Wittson, C., Affleck, D., & Johnson, V. (1961). Two-way television in group therapy. *Mental Hospitals, 12*, 22–23.

KEY TERMS AND DEFINITIONS

E-Health: Health services and information delivered or enhanced by the Internet and related technologies

Electronic Medical Record (EMR): Individual record in which healthcare providers record treatments, drugs, and future recommendations electronically

Electronic Health Record (EHR): Electronic record that includes patient information from a variety of sources, such as radiology (films), pharmacy (interaction checks), and specialist information (cardiologist, dermatologist, etc.)

Healthcare Information Technology (HIT): Technology used to store, manage, and transmit information between healthcare providers and consumers

Informatics: The intelligent management of information to maximize data acquisition and usage

Personal Health Record (PHR): E-health tools that let patients manage all of their health information in one location

Telemedicine: Provision of healthcare services via telecommunication technology

Chapter 13
The Information Sector in the Economy and its Strategic Value

Dariusz T. Dziuba
Warsaw University, Poland

ABSTRACT

This discussion focuses on the idea of an information society studied in view of economic aspects. The subject matter of inquiry is a strategic sector decisive for the situation of economy, society and the state: the so-called information sector in the economy. Its importance and intrinsic value are discussed. Studies on economics of the information sector are brought to light as well as relationships with other disciplines, including economics of information (information systems) and information ecology. Based on the Polish Classification of Activities (PKD), the methodology of classification and categorization of the information sector is developed and used to evaluate its development and, indirectly, the development of the information society in Poland. Research is based on available statistics on the number of employed persons and employment in 1997-2006. It is evidenced that the information sector dominates in Poland today (in the four-sector model of the economy) and the trend of its regular growth is observed.

INTRODUCTION

Man has rarely been far from the information business. Looking back over history it could be said that people have, from early times, been traveling, exchanging ideas, and acquiring information and knowledge. However, radical changes in this field have taken place only recently, together with the development of communication technology, television, radio, and today, the Internet, distributed business environments and information systems implemented in borderless organizations.

Economies have always been "propelled" along their way by information and knowledge (although this was never actually focused on or measured), and by innovation (today recognized as primarily IT). However, changes present in managerial and decision-making environments, resulting especially from the influence of information and technology,

DOI: 10.4018/978-1-60566-890-1.ch013

and process virtualization, are of a spectacular nature, as reflected in numerous statistics.

Economists have only recently tried to estimate the influence of information processes on the economy. Now, given that nearly all types of operations are essential for economic processes, this observation has been applied to information-related business operations. Information is often placed at the centre of economic thinking and studies undertaken.

As stated in one such study: "(...) Information describes land, work and capital. Information reduces the need for land, work and capital, raw materials and energy (...). It is sold in a specific way and constitutes raw material for a new sector of the economy (...) – the information sector" (Stonier, 1984, p. 212).

The subject under consideration is the strategic sector, crucial to the state of the economy, society and the state – known as the information sector of the economy.

In this paper the concept of the fourth sector and its essential role is discussed in the context of a specific economic discipline – economics of the information sector, whose main aim is to assess sections of the national economy – its information sector.

BACKGROUND

Economics literature suggests various categorizations of economic sectors. Usually the three-sector model is adopted as follows:

- the primary sector (I): in statistics, it covers agriculture, hunting, forestry, fishery, fishing, mining; this sector is associated with basic food, mining and quarrying, obtaining raw materials such as coal or wood, etc.;
- the manufacturing sector (II): associated with processing of raw materials into finished goods; in statistical classifications it covers production and construction and, additionally, electricity, gas and water supplies;
- the service sector (III): created by other activities in the area of education, banking and finance, trade, public administration, healthcare, transport, tourism etc.

The theory of the tree-sector model introduced by Kaldor (1967) argues that there is a strong correlation between employment and manufacturing in individual sectors and the level of overall social and economic development, i.e. that sectoral proportions of the economy evidence the level of an economic development of particular countries.

Today this classification needs to be supplemented with a new fourth sector of the economy: the information sector (IV).[1] This need is an outcome of the function of information (and knowledge) in economic processes, a vigorous development of information and communication technologies and an increasing importance of information and IT for economic development. Following Kaldor's train of thought it may be concluded that modern economies of developed countries are dominated by the information sector.

For the purposes of this work, a four sector model was proposed – comprising the primary sector (I), along side the manufacturing sector (II) and service sector (III), and the fourth sector – the information sector, which incorporates elements of the above three sectors including, amongst others, the education and scientific research sphere, computer production, the publishing industry, the postal service and telecommunications, information services and public administration etc. The concept of an information sector was introduced into economic research by M.U. Porat (1974, 1976, 1977).

In the further discussions, we propose the following definition of the information sector: The information sector in the economy is understood as overall business activities that support the production, use, protection, collection, storage, transfer and transmission of information, its control and management or trade. The information sector encompasses all employees in: production, use and transmission of information, as well as those creating the information infrastructure. In other words, the information sector represents the set of business activities and related entities that produce, use, collect, transfer information etc. The list of such functions may be further detailed, it is an open question.

The definition presented appears to reflect the significance and share of the information branches in the economy to a sufficient degree. The information sector encompasses:[2]

- the production of information products, e.g. electronics and precision electronics and paper industries, the production of computers etc.,
- the provision of information services, e.g. information processing, telecommunications services, consulting etc.

Empirical research indicates that there is a strong causal relationship between the development of the information sector of a given country and the state of its economy.

INFORMATION SECTOR ECONOMICS IN THE COURSE OF ECONOMIC ASSESSMENTS

Economics is the science dealing with social management of resources. Various study directions and schools are proposed as part of economics. In addition to mainstream economic researches, some more narrow trends are being explored, usually called "industry" or specific economics.

Many industry economics are subject to scientific researches, including economics of agriculture, forestry, transport, trade, tourism (and recreation), labor, education, healthcare, natural resources, enterprises (including their types, e.g. production, trade, farming enterprises, etc.), real estate or media. "Sectoral economics" are also specified, for example service economics, public sector economics, etc.

As part of specific economic disciplines, *per analogiam* to industry economics, a new branch – information sector economics – may be proposed.[3] The fundamental research objective of the economics of the information sector is the evaluation of a part of the national economy – its information sector.

Information sector economics is a specific economic discipline that uses methods of economics as a science; it investigates economic relationships occurring in one sphere of the national economy – the information sector. We will focus on the information sector in the economy and specific aspects of management in this sector, on selected sections of this sector. Information sector economics gives attention to this sector of the national economy (taken as a whole) as well as individual businesses included in this sector.

At a certain stage of development of society, the information sector emerges and develops into an important element of the economy and its infrastructure, conditioning the performance of other economic sectors and the entire economy. Our purpose is to take a closer look at this sector of the national economy.

It can be assumed that the economics of the information sector is a review of the rules in the area of the functioning of the information sector in the economy, both theoretically, by observance of the laws of economics and descriptively – by observation of the appearance and the course of the processes. Such rules do not need to appear in the other areas of management (and this is frequently how it is), and may be of an autonomous nature.

Information sector economics deals with research, descriptions and analyses of the information sector in the economy as well as with searching for and evaluation of relationships in the information sector and between the information sector and other economic sectors in the process of information production, distribution and consumption.

Information sector economic researches can involve a number of issues. I believe that the most important aspects include:

- Classification of the information sector as a separate (fourth) sector of the economy; relevant segmentation of the economy for that purpose;
- Discovering dependencies and rules appearing in the informaton sector;
- Statistical analyses and evaluations of the information sector;
- Comparative analyses between groups of countries;
- Attempting to forecast the development of the information sector;
- Analysis of the information sector structure, also in view of providing information services versus products;
- Identification of professions and specialties creating the information sector; classification of present professions and potential professions that may appear in the next years[4];
- Evaluation of shortages in specific groups of specialists in the information sector;
- Analysis of the employment structure in the information sector by class, profession, specialty, education, qualification, gender, ethnic group, etc.;
- Estimation of the scale of development of the information economy and the "electronic economy", establishment of the information service level in the economy, in particular with the use of IT;
- Assessment of the scale of applications and the influence of IT on the New Economy, which represent a significant impulse for research, development, technical progress and the distribution and use of new knowledge;
- Separation of information capital[5] inherent in the information sector;
- Definition of the borders[6] between the information sector and the non-information sector.

The proposed list does not exhaust the majority of research problems related to the economics of the information sector. This problem area is a necessary direction for future research. In researching the information sector and the problem area of information in the economy, further appears to be particularly important at a time of creating information societies and information economies.

I believe that at the present stage of development of the specific economics in question, key analyses and researches include those related to or integrated with various, sometimes different, methods of classification, breakdown and measurement of the information sector.[7]

It is also advisable to mention relationships with other fields. Information sector economics is inseparable, for example, with economics of information (information systems). See: (Oleński, 2001). In each of these fields, however, the accent is put on different issues.

The evaluation of information is highlighted in the economics of information, while information and information systems are underlined in the economics of information systems, whereas the evaluation of the part of the national economy – its information sector – is emphasised in the economics of the information sector. The relationship of these research topics indicates that it is possible to use the methods that have been developed in each of them in the remaining approaches. This also applies to infocology (ecology of information)[8]. In addition, research areas of the abovementioned disciplines overlap.

EXAMPLE METHOD OF THE CLASSIFICATION OF THE INFORMATION SECTOR

Subsequent efforts made to adjust the domestic standard statistical base resulted in the introduction of the *Polish Classification of Activities* (PKD). In 1998-1999, it was used in statistic researches together with *Statistical Classification of Economic Activities* in the European Community (NACE) and on January 1, 2000 it replaced NACE and became the only one classification in force. PKD serves as a basis for economic and social classifications. PKD was updated based on NACE rev. 1.1 and its updated version was introduced on the date of Poland's integration with the EU structures.

In PKD, classification is made on five different levels (sections and subsections, divisions, groups, classes and subclasses), an additional middle level is also included. PKD and NACE are integrated and comparable. PKD is compliant with NACE up to the level of a class and the subclass level is a national level introduced with a view to deal with characteristics of Poland's economy.

Out of sixteen sections of PKD, I have assigned to the information sector the two following sections in their entirety: *Education* (Section M) and *Financial intermediation* (Section J). The elements from the remaining sections have been selected as follows:

From Section D - *Manufacturing*:

- manufacture of pulp, paper and paper products (from Division 21);
- entire publishing activities (22);
- manufacture of unrecorded media (24.66.Z);
- manufacture of office machinery and computers (30);
- selected classes from Division 31, e.g. manufacture of fiber-optic cables;
- manufacture of radio, television and communication equipment and apparatus (32)
- and manufacture of precision and optical instruments (33), except for medical and surgical equipment and orthopedic appliances.

Selected classes from Section G – *Trade and repair*, including: wholesale and retail trade of radio and television goods, records, tapes and compact discs; office machinery and equipment (computers and peripherals); as well as repairs of radio and television equipment. Selected divisions and classes from Section I – *Transport, storage and communication*, including: activities of travel agencies (63.30), e.g. tourist assistance activities; selected activities of transport agencies (63.40), e.g. brokerage, preparation of shipping documents; booking intermediary; entire division of post and telecommunications (64).

Selected divisions and classes from Section K – *Real Estate, renting and business activities*, including: real estate activities (70); renting of office machinery and equipment, including computers (71.33); computer and related activities (72)[9] and research and development (73); other business activities (74), for example advertising, photographic activities, secretarial and translation activities.[10] Section L – *Public administration and defense, compulsory social security* is included in its entirety with a few subclass exceptions. Under Section N – *Health and social work* some classes are selected such as medical practice activities. Section O – *Other community, social and personal service activities* is covered with respect to activities of membership organizations (91); selected recreational, cultural and sporting activities (92), for example activities related to motion picture and video production, radio and television, artistic creations and interpretations, entertainment, news agencies, libraries, archives and museums.

From Section P – *Activities of households and employers of domestic staff*, private tutors are selected (95.00). Under Section Q – *Extra-territorial organizations and bodies*, information

Table 1. Share of the information sector in total number of employed persons in Poland (1997-2006)

Years	1997	1998	1999	2000	2001	2002	2003	2004	2005	2006
%	19.76	20.24	21.35	23.51	24.47	28.75	30.04	30.39	30.60	30.62

Source: own elaborate

activities of international organizations is covered (99.00.Z).

The information sector is formed on the basis of existing economic sectors (three-sector model), mainly from the manufacturing sector (II), the service sector (III), and also selected elements of the primary sector (I), i.e. subclasses from Section A – *Agriculture, hunting and forestry.*[11] No divisions, classes or subclasses are included from the following sections: *Fishing* (B), *Mining and quarrying* (C), *Construction* (F), and *Hotels and restaurants* (H). The methodology is discussed in detail in the author's paper such as (Dziuba, 2007).

The proposed methodology reflects the entire information activities in the economy. The methodology is, furthermore, based on available statistical data; such data exist, while the issue of access to them remains.

THE SIZE OF THE INFORMATION SECTOR IN THE POLISH ECONOMY

Data costs, however, made it impossible to purchase detailed statistics aggregated according to this methodology. Therefore, a simplified approach was adopted, based on aggregated data published in generally available Statistical Yearbooks and Bulletins. Thus, I suppose that the obtained results are underestimated by some percentage points but they still give a general picture of the sector and its development.

The analysis covered the size of the information sector in 1998-2006 (according to PKD) and also for 1997 (NACE was the only classification available at that time). The following structure of data aggregation was adopted:

A. Manufacture of pulp and paper;
B. Publishing activities; printing and reproduction of recorded media;
C. Manufacture of office machinery and computers;
D. Manufacture of electrical machinery and apparatus;
E. Manufacture of radio, television and communication equipment and apparatus;
F. Manufacture of medical, precision and optical instruments, watches and clocks;
G. Transport supporting activities, activities of travel agencies;
H. Post and telecommunications;
I. Financial intermediation;
J. Real estate and business activities;
K. Public administration and defense; compulsory social security;
L. Education;
M. Activities of membership organizations;
N. Activities connected with culture, recreation and sports.

Results are illustrated in Table 1. See also: Table 2 and Table 3.[12]

A consistent growth of the information sector was observed both in terms of the number of the employed (from 3,149,800 to 4,047,900.) and percentage share (from 19.76% to 30.62%).

Total average employment in the information sector in subsequent years was as follows (figures

Table 2. Employed persons in four sectors of the Polish economy (1997-2006), percentage shares

Sectors / years	I	II	III	IV	Total
1997	29.51	25.31	25.42	19.76	100
1998	29.23	24.77	25.76	20.24	100
1999	29.25	23.89	25.51	21.35	100
2000	29.30	22.00	25.19	23.51	100
2001	30.10	21.13	24.30	24.47	100
2002	18.56	23.85	28.84	28.75	100
2003	18.50	23.56	28.00	30.04	100
2004	18.35	23.69	27.57	30.39	100
2005	18.06	23.48	27.86	30.60	100
2006	17.60	24.00	27.78	30.62	100

Source: own elaborate

in thousands): 2720.9 (1997), 2819.5 (1998), 2950.0 (1999), 2948.0 (2000), 2976.9 (2001), 2988.9 (2002), 3115.3 (2003), 3090.9 (2004), 3161.9 (2005), 3251.6 (2006). Thus employment figures evidence a growing size of the information sector, both in absolute numbers[13] and constantly increasing percentage shares. The information sector increased sizably (in terms of employment) in 2006 (up to 40.55%).

THE INFORMATION SECTOR IN THE FOUR-SECTOR MODEL OF THE POLISH ECONOMY

The presented methodology also enable to demonstrate relationships in the four-sector model of the Polish economy. See: Table 2 and Table 3.

The primary sector includes agriculture, hunting and forestry, fishery and (separated from manufacturing) mining and quarrying. Sector II includes production and construction (reduced by

Table 3. Employed persons in four sectors of the Polish economy (1997-2006), figures in thousands

Sectors / years	I	II	III	IV	Total
1997	4,703.8	4,035.1	4,052.1	3,149.8	15,940.8
1998	4,653.1	3,943.6	4,101.9	3,222.5	15,921.1
1999	4,590.7	3,747.9	4,002.2	3,350.9	15,691.7
2000	4,538.1	3,407.4	3,901.8	3,641.5	15,488.8
2001	4,513.3	3,168.5	3,644.4	3,669.4	14,995.6
2002	2,376.4	3,052.4	3,692.9	3,681.6	12,803.3
2003	2,344.6	2,977.1	3,540.0	3,796.8	12,640.7
2004	2,334.9	3,011.9	3,507.4	3,866.2	12,720.2
2005	2,328.9	3,025.6	3,591.2	3,945.0	12,890.7
2006	2,326.7	3,172.6	3,672.8	4,047.9	13,220.0

Source: own elaborate

the share of the information sector). The number of employees in the service sector (III) is calculated as the difference between the total number of the employed and employees of the remaining sectors (I, II and IV).

The structure of the Polish economy is different than in other most developed countries. In 1997-2001 a dominant share of the primary sector was observed. It reached as much as 30.10% (2001). Agriculture with over 90 percentage points has the strongest presence in this sector while mining accounts for a few percent. A significant decline in the share of the primary sector in total employment was observed in 2002-2006 and formed a general downward trend (to 17.60% in 2006), which evidences positive developments in the economy. This decline favors changes in structures of other sectors, in particular services and information. In line with transformation processes, the size of the primary sector (and its dominance) has reduced in favor of other sectors. The share of the service sector fluctuated, initially it increased, in 1999-2001 it dropped to nearly 24%, then increased by 4.5 percentage points and stabilized below 28%. The share of the manufacturing sector declined until 2001 (to approx. 21%) and stabilized in the 23-24% range.

In the years 2003-2006 dominance of the information sector in the Polish economy was confirmed. It is the only assessed sector which, in the years analyzed, showed an ongoing growth tendency. Attention should be given to high dynamics of changes in the information sector, for example in relation to 1997. It grew from 2.4% to as much as 55% (2006), i.e. in 1997-2006 the size of the information sector (versus other sectors of the economy) increased by over a half.

This indicates an enduring growth trend for the information sector. It also illustrates the gradual development of the information society in Poland.

INFORMATION SECTOR IN ECONOMIES OF OTHER COUNTRIES

The current global crisis clearly shows how much we depend on sales and other markets in nearly all sectors of the economy, in particular the sectors connected with information. Globalization has a huge influence on the organization of work and development of the information sector. Globalization processes in today economies require a more in-depth look at the issues in question, also from an international perspective.

Researches on the information sectors were carried out in many countries, including Great Britain (Wall, 1977), Singapore (Jussawalla, & Cheah, 1983), Japan (Morikawa, 1988), South Africa (Boon, et al, 1994), Australia (Engelbrecht, 1985; Jones, 1996), India (Lal, 2005), Brazil (Bueno, 2005), etc. Nonetheless, a major part of these researches were fragmentary and referred to individual countries and various periods of time.

M. Jussawalla adopted Porat's method to determine the share of the information sector in economies of the selected countries in the Pacific region (see: Jussawalla, Dworak, 1988). R.L. Katz (1986) analyzed the structure of employment, including the information sector, for six developing countries: Brazil, Egypt, India, South Korea, Philippines and Venezuela. The OECD (1981) estimated the size of the information sector for nine member states in 1950 to 1970.

The table below presents the results of some recently available researches for the selected countries.

The information sector has a sizeable share in the number of employees (employment) or the GNP (GDP) in highly developed economies such as the United States, Great Britain, Germany, Canada, Japan, Australia, etc. Lower values are correlated with less developed economies.

Poland with its average GDP is situated in the group of countries with medium percentage shares of employment in the information sector.

Table 4. Size of the information sector in economies of the selected countries

Country	Size of the information sector (years)	Researches by
USA	share in the total average employment: 52.5% (years: 1980 to 1990), 54.8% (1990 - 2000)	Wolff (2005)
USA	share in the GNP: 46.3% (1967), 55.9% (1992), 63.0% (1997)	Apte, & Nath (2007)
South Korea	share in the GDP: 51.92% (1990), 56.54% (1995), 59.03% (2001)	Choi, Rhim, & Park (2006)
Canada	share in the total employment: 55.5% (1990), 54.8% (1995)	Benyahia (2000)
Australia	share in the total employment: 37.7% (1991), 39.2% (1996)	Bredt (2001)
Australia	share in the total employment: approx. 40.0% (1994)	Jones (1996)
New Zealand	share in the total full-time employment: 44.6% (1991), 45.4% (1996), 47.7% (2001)	Engelbrecht, & Mahon (2003)
Finland	share in the total employment: 44.0% (1995), 45.5% (2000)	Pyöriä (2005)
India	share in the total number of employees: 13.78% (1991)	Lal (2005)
Thailand	share in the total number of employees: 8.0 – 13.0% (years: 1991 to 2000)	Aswalap (2005)

Source: Prepared based on the sources cited

On average, these shares are lower by more than 27 percentage points in relation to the US or by 8.5 percentage points in relation to Australia. Based on the author's estimates, today the share of the information sector in the GNP of the Polish economy is below 30%, i.e. by 25 to 30 percentage points less than in the economy of the United States and other developed countries.

To sum up, various methods are proposed to separate and analyze the information sector. In addition, such researches, if any, often assume different purposes, measurement methods and other indices (e.g. the number of employees or employment; the GDP or the GNP), are based on various (often) different sources of statistical data, refer to different countries or regions and, what is the most important, various periods of time, often completely different. Therefore, there are few country comparisons available, in particular for a larger group of countries, including countries at a different level of development.

Such researches are usually expensive taking into account the need to access (purchase) specific data from the resources of statistical offices. In addition, some information activities are still hard to measure and represent a bottleneck in the work of national statistical offices and international groups as well.

Despite various methods of separation and examination of the information sector and, in turn, different results obtained, such researches are extremely important and forward-looking.

The importance of these researches stems from an important strategic role of the information sector, in particular in contemporary economies. This role is called the "value of the information sector". This term is understood as the importance of the information sector for the economic development and transformation processes.

THE VALUE OF THE INFORMATION SECTOR IN THE ECONOMY

The importance of studies on the information sector determines its growth prospects and implications for economic development.

The information sector has major development perspectives and has a significant influence on economic growth:

- It is strictly related to the development of new information technologies and their use in the economy,
- It is an integral element of the concept of the information society.

New information and communications technologies have now created different capabilities of accessing information, changing the conditions of the economic decision making processes and leading to the phonomenon known as the reduction in the economic time. The reduction in the economic time allows for a significant acceleration in the economic processes. Economic decisions, particularly on the financial market, may be made in a very short time (in fractions of a second), in groups, as well as automatically (based on models implemented by the computer) without the participation of a person. The speed of implementation of the processes points to a significant reduction in costs. This is illustrated by e.g. (see: Dziuba, 1996) the functioning of electronic markets.

The sector under review includes, *inter alia*, R&D, education, post and telecommunications, manufacturing of computers and software, various IT services, banking and finance etc. An economic surplus, necessary for economic development, is being created in the information sector.[14]

In highly developed countries this sector is the dominant sector (accounting for approx. 50% of employment, 50-60% of GDP). In addition, the information sector in these countries grows at higher rate than the entire economy and other sectors; based on ITU's data, in 1994 the global information sector increased by over 5% while the global economy increased by a mere 3% annually.

This sector conditions effective performance of other sectors and industries in the economy (i.e. agriculture, manufacturing and services). It facilitates decision-making, in particular in an electronic, dispersed or virtual environment. It creates new jobs, professions and areas of specialization in the economy. It is a distinctive "flywheel of the economy". It is required for the diffusion of IT; it makes it possible to spread information technology[15] and innovation.

The sector „cuts across" existing classifications – this is both an advantage and a disadvantage (it is difficult to distinguish it within the framework of the classification). The information sector determines competitiveness, as well as technical and economic leadership.

The information sector is decisive as to economic potential and the possibility of economic development – as much in global, national and regional categories as in individual economic entities, especially in a virtual environment.

Today, this sector serves as a carrier of technical progress (similarly to the processing industry some time ago) because of a structural and overwhelming role of IT in the economy.

It has been already mentioned in one paper:[16] "since information is the carrier of each innovation and an in-between link for each application of science, the development of information technologies is one of base pillars of a scientific and technical revolution".

The information sector development depends on a proactive policy of the state (it is both its prospect and limitation).

These result in recommendations for statistical methodologies, as well as the development strategy and policy. The information sector includes:

- R&D sector – this is where scientific and technical progress and innovation are fuelled; R&D creates new information and generates an economic surplus;
- Information on innovations and technologies.

Therefore, the information sector is a strategic sector determining the state of the economy, society and the country. How to translate this information revolution into its noticeable influence on economic development is the task of the politicians and decision-makers.

The information sector creates a very specific type of value for the economy. It is necessary to manage this value and capital in, amongst others, the context of ecology of information and also information recycling. This relates in particular to the implementation of new categories of information systems allowing the acquisition of valuable information.

The strategic role of the information sector is prominent especially in the face of globalization of economies. Today, the information sector can and should be considered in global terms. Its individual segments are involved in the international electronic market. This is true in particular in case of the financial and banking sector and the IT sector *per se*.

The Internet is an inherent element of the information sector that enable an effective transfer of information and knowledge both on a transnational scale and within national economies (between segments of the information sector and other traditional sectors). The Internet is a key information infrastructure, backbone of the contemporary economy and its information sector. In fact, the global computer network is an accelerator of economic developments and transformations observed today.

CONCLUSION

Based on available statistical data, the information sector of the Polish economy was selected and its key attributes were specified showing that the share of the information sector in the Polish economy is much lower than in other most developed countries. In the process of Poland's economic transformation, it is observed, however, that the employment structure of the information sector tends to mimic the typical structure of developed market economies. As evidenced, at present it is a dominant sector (in the four-sector model of the Polish economy).

To determine the share of the information sector in the economy, I also suggest other approaches[17] connected with:

- working time related to information activities;
- labor costs associated with specific activities of employees/positions;
- costs of specific activities and business processes, in particular related with information processing;
- specific researches on kinds of activities and businesses are also recommended.

These issues require standardization in the area of new classifications and other aspects of the standard statistical base. Such a stage of work is necessary although relatively time-consuming. The following example shows how lengthy it may be (see: Castells, p. 114): statisticians of the US Labor Department still classified expenditures on computer software under consumption instead of investments until 1998. I believe that work on the standardization of international and national classifications commenced recently under the auspices of the United Nations (called "Operation 2007")[18] will facilitate the separation of the information sector from existing traditional economic sectors as well as international comparisons.

REFERENCES

Apte, U. M., & Nath, H. K. (2007). Size, structure and growth of the U.S. information economy. In U. Apte, & U. Karmarkar (Eds.), *Managing in the information economy. Current research issues. Annals of information systems* (Vol.1). New York: Springer.

Aswalap, J. (2005). "Information society" development in Thailand: Information workforce and information and communication technology perspectives. *First Monday, 10*(10).

Benyahia, H. (2000). Trends in the productivity of the information sector in Canada. *IEEE Canadian Review*, Fall/Automne.

Boon, J. A., Britz, J. J., & Harmse, C. (1994). The information economy in South Africa: Definition and measurement. *Journal of Information Science*, *5*(20).

Bredt, J. C. (2001). An occupational view of the Australian labor force patterns of job growth and decline. *International Journal of Manpower*, *5*(22).

Bueno, M. F. (2005). *A Economia da Informacão no Brasil*. Retrieved Oktober 17, 2007, from http://www.ie.ufu.br/ix_enep_mesas/

Castells, M. (2003). *Galaktyka Internetu*. Poznan, Poland: Rebis.

Choi, M., Rhim, H., & Park, K. (2006). *New business models in the information economy: GDP and case studies in Korea*. Korea University Business School, June 2. Retrieved June 10, 2007, from http://www.bit.unisi.ch/abstracts-presentations/presentation-choi_rhim_park.pdf

Działalności, P. K. *(PKD). Nomenclature des Activités de Communauté Européenne – NACE rev. 1.1.* (2004). Warsaw, Poland: Central Statistical Office.

Dziuba, D. T. (1992). Analiza zatrudnienia w sektorze informacyjnym gospodarki. *Wiadomości Statystyczne 11*. Warsaw, Poland: Central Statistical Office.

Dziuba, D. T. (1996). *Toward electronization of the economic market. Global trends and Polish experience* (Economic Discussion Papers No. 22). Warsaw, Poland: University of Warsaw, Faculty of Economic Sciences.

Dziuba, D. T. (1998). *Analiza możliwości wyodrębniania i diagnozowania sektora informacyjnego w gospodarce Polski*. Warsaw, Poland: Univeristy of Warsaw.

Dziuba, D. T. (2000). *Gospodarki nasycone informacją i wiedzą. Podstawy ekonomiki sektora informacyjnego*. Warsaw, Poland: Nowy Dziennik.

Dziuba, D. T. (2003). Information sector in the new economy. In *The "New Economy" and Postsocialist Transition. V International Conference Papers*. Leon Kozminski Academy of Entrepreneurship and Management. Warsaw, Poland: Tiger.

Dziuba, D. T. (2005). Kilka rozważań o informacji i kapitale informacyjnym. In M. Rószkiewicz, & E. Wędrowska (Eds.), *Informacja w społeczeństwie XXI wieku* (pp. 21-36). Warsaw, Poland: Szkoła Główna Handlowa.

Dziuba, D. T. (2007). *Metody ekonomiki sektora informacyjnego*. Warsaw, Poland: Difin.

Engelbrecht, H. J. (1985). An exposition of the information sector approach with special reference to Australia. *Prometheus*, *3*(2). doi:10.1080/08109028508629004

Engelbrecht, H. J., & Mahon, A. (2003). Information workforce in New Zealand, 1991-2001. *New Zealand Population Review*, *29*(2).

Jones, B. (1996). *Sleepers Wake!* Oxford: Oxford University Press.

Jussawalla, M., & Cheah, C. W. (1983). Towards an information economy - The case of Singapore. *Information Economics and Policy*, 1.

Jussawalla, M., & Dworak, S. (1988). The primary information sector of the Philippines. In M. Jussawalla, D. M. Lamberton, & N. D. Karunaratne (Eds.), *The cost of thinking: Information economies of ten pacific countries*. Norwood, New Jersey: Ablex Publishing Corporation.

Kaldor, N. (1967). *Strategic factors in economic development*. New York: Cornel University.

Katz, R. L. (1986). Explaining information sector growth in developing countries. *Telecommunications Policy*, 10.

Lal, K. (2005). In quest of the information sector: Measuring information workers for India. *Malaysian Journal of Library & Information Science, 2*(10).

Machlup, F. (1962). *The production and distribution of knowledge in the United States*. Princeton, NJ: Princeton University Press.

Morikawa, M. (1988). Future outlook for JAPAN`s information industry. *Japan Computer Quarterly*, 72.

OECD, Organization for Economic Cooperation and Development (1981). *Information activities, electronics and telecommunication technologies. Impact on employment, growth and trade*, vol. 1- 2, ICCP Series (61). Paris: OECD.

Oleński, J. (2001). *Ekonomika informacji*. Warsaw, Poland: PWE.

Pańkowska, M. (1999). Infokologia – ekologia informacji. Zakres i specyfika środków. *Firma i rynek,* 1.

Porat, M. U. (1974). Defining an information sector in the U.S. economy. *Information Reports and Bibliographies, 5*(5).

Porat, M. U. (1976). *The information economy.* Center for Interdisciplinary Research, Stanford University.

Porat, M. U. (1977). *The information economy. OT Special Publication (77-12),* Vol. 1-9. U.S. Washington D.C.: Department of Commerce, Office of Telecommunications.

Pyöriä, P. (2005). *A growing trend towards knowledge work in Finland*. Retrieved June 10, 2007, from http://www.etla.fi/files/1373_FES_05_2_a_growing_trend/...pdf

Stonier, T. (1984). The knowledge industry. In R. Forsyth (Ed.), *Expert systems. Principles and case studies*. London: Chapman & Hall.

Wall, S. D. (1977). *Four sector time-series of the U.K. labour force, 1941-1971*. London: UK Post Office, Long Range Studies Division.

Wolff, E. N. (2005). The growth of information workers in the U.S. economy. *Communications of the ACM, 10*(48).

Zacher, L. W. (Ed.). (1997). *Rewolucja informacyjna i społeczeństwo. Niektóre trendy, zjawiska i kontrowersje*. Warsaw, Poland: Educational Foundation "Transformations".

ADDITIONAL READING

Arrow, K. J. (1971). *The value of and demand for information. Essays in the theory of risk-bearing.* Chicago: Markham.

Arrow, K. J. (1979). *The economics of information*. In M. L., Dertouzos, & J., Moses (Eds.), *The computer age: A twenty-year view*. Cambridge, MA: MIT Press.

Bateson, G. (1972). *Steps to an ecology of mind.* New York: Ballantine Books.

Belkin, N. J., & Robertson, S. E. (1976). Information science and the phenomenon of information. *Journal of the American Society for Information Science American Society for Information Science, 4*(27).

Boisot, M. H. (1995). *Information space, A framework for learning in organizations. Institutions and culture*. London: Routledge.

Boisot, M. H. (1998). *Knowledge assets, securing competitive advantage in the information economy*. Oxford: Oxford University Press.

Castells, M. (1997). *The rise of the network society. The information age: Economy, society and culture*, Volume 1. Oxford: Blackwell Publishers.

Cooper, M. D. (1983). The structure and future of the information economy. *Information Processing & Management, 1*(19).

Dordick, H. S., & Wang, G. (1993). *The information society; A retrospective view*. London: Sage.

Machlup, F. (1980). *Knowledge - It's creation, distribution and economic significance. Vol. I: Knowledge and knowledge production*. Princeton, NJ: Princeton University Press.

Machlup, F. (1982). *Knowledge - It's creation, distribution and economic significance. Vol. II: The branches of learning*. Princeton, NJ: Princeton University Press.

Machlup, F. (1984). *Knowledge - It's creation, distribution and economic significance. Vol. III: The economics of information and human capital*. Princeton, NJ: Princeton University Press.

Marchand, D. A. (2000). *Competing with information*. Chichester: J.Wiley & Sons.

Marchand, D. A., & Horton, F. (1986). *Infotrends – Profiting from your information resources*. New York: John Wiley.

Porat, M. U. (1978). Global implications of the information society. *The Journal of Communication, 1*(28).

Shapiro, C., & Varian, H. R. (1999). *Information rules. A strategic guide to the network economy*. Boston, MA: Harvard Business School Press.

Turner, C. (2000). *The information e-economy. Business strategies for competing in the digital age*. London: Kogan Page.

KEY TERMS AND DEFINITIONS

Economics of the Information Sector: Economics of the information sector is a specific economic discipline that investigates economic relationships occurring in one sphere of the national (or international) economy – the information sector.

Information: Bateson (1972) defines information as "a difference which makes a difference" (pp. 448-466).

Information Economy: The information economy is defined as an economy where more than half of the employment (number of employees) is generated in the information sector, the information sector has become more dominant than other sectors of the economy.

Information Sector: The information sector in the economy is understood as overall business activities that support the production, use, protection, collection, storage, transfer and transmission of information, its control and management or trade.

Information Society: The information society is defined as a society in which the production, distribution, processing and consumption of information are regarded as crucial socio-economic activities.

ENDNOTES

1 I suggested the information sector as a separate sector of the Polish economy in my papers (Dziuba, 1992, 1998, 2003).

2 The information sector integrates entities and activities both in the public and private spheres.

3 I used this term for the first time in my paper (Dziuba, 1998), and its idea was outlined in (Dziuba, 2000).

4 Within the frameworks of this sector, new specialties appear (e.g. call center opera-

tors, web masters etc.) and existing ones are modified.

5 The paper (Dziuba, 2005) explains the conceptual relationship between different forms of capital and relations between information capital and the information sector.

6 The economics of the information sector does not apply (directly) to the non-information sector of the economy. On the other hand, attention should also be drawn to the fact that the scope of the information sector is expanded; non-information areas may in the near future become information areas, e.g. as a result of the introduction of automation and IT into human activities.

7 List of researches on the information sector in the economy and proposals of new methods included in the author's paper (Dziuba, 2007).

8 Several researches have been already commenced with respect to the application of an ecological approach to the information society. The ecological approach requires the integration of researches and different view of such separate disciplines as ecology, entropy, evolution, culture, society, organization and technology. According to Pańkowska (1999), only then it is possible to see the scale of an information revolution and how quickly it progresses.

9 E.g. hardware and software advisory, data processing, databases, repairs and maintenance of office and accounting equipment as well as computer hardware.

10 Also services such as specialized cleaning services (e.g. for processing centers). See: (Machlup, 1962).

11 PKD also groups: architectural and engineering activities etc., including subsoil water engineering (activities of agronomists), urban planning and landscaping (e.g. forest landscaping, projects for agriculture and forestry); organization of exhibitions, fairs, trades (e.g. in agriculture).

12 Due to organizational aspects of this paper, detailed data tables are not included. This issue is discussed in more detail in the author's papers (Dziuba 2000, 2007).

13 A small drop in 2004, connected with a decrease in overall employment from 8,661,700 in 2003 to 8,640,200 in 2004.

14 To date, the manufacturing sector was considered to be a driving force of economic development both at the country and regional levels.

15 An analogy is noticeable between the information sector in the economy and the information system in the company. The information system is very important – it supplies all (almost all) of the company`s departments. And we study the IT system itself.

16 Views of R. Richta quoted from (Zacher, 1997, p. 16).

17 I suggested the set of various methods to measure, research and analyze the information sector (in the Polish economy versus other countries) from the perspective of the information sector economics in the paper (Dziuba, 2007).

18 Here, the particular attention should be given to intensive standardization efforts carried out in the United States, Canada and Mexico with respect to the NAICS, work of the OECD, the Voorburg Group, integration of statistical researches in Europe (NACE), Japan, Australia and New Zealand.

Section 4
Collaboration in Networks

Chapter 14
Designing Collaborative Infrastructures to get Business Value from Collaboration in Large Scale Networks

Igor Hawryszkiewycz
School of Systems, Management and Leadership University of Technology, Sydney, Australia

ABSTRACT

Collaboration is playing an increasing role in business especially given an increase in business networking. Such networks are formed to gain business advantage by combining expertise from many businesses or organizational units to quickly create new and competitive products and services. Most processes in business networks now consist of a number of activities whose processes must be coordinated to reach enterprises goals. This chapter addresses ways of supporting such activities using technology and proposes a collaboration infrastructure that encourages collaboration and sharing of knowledge across the activities.

INTRODUCTION

Collaboration and use of technology are now generally recognized as necessary to improve business processes. For example (Hansen, Nohria, Tierney, 1999) described a system, which reduced the preparation of response documents from 4 to 2 months in consulting organizations. Another case quoted as an example was where a supplier could quickly respond by supplying valves to a car manufacturer (Evans and Wolf, 2005). This occurred when a Toyota plant supplying components burnt down, arrangements where quickly made with other suppliers to supply the parts and restore operations within 4 days of the fire. Kodama (2005) also describes the role of strategic communities in strategic planning. Another obvious example here is emergency response systems (Jacobs, 1998) that must quickly respond to rapidly emerging situations. In business processes there are also situations that require response. Examples can be falling market share, a new competitor or opportunity provided by a new technology.

The general consensus is that enterprises must become agile and quickly respond to emerging situations in creative and innovative ways. The emphasis

DOI: 10.4018/978-1-60566-890-1.ch014

on collaboration is also expounded in research such as that of Evans and Wolf, who in their 2005 article to the Harvard Business Review describe the kinds of results that can be achieved by teams working together on focused goals. Although not commonly found in business the idea of bringing people together quickly to address problems is gaining attention. It sees evolving collaboration between organizational units that were sometimes seen as silos to collaboration across firms to form a business web. Agility and innovation in turn require ways to support knowledge workers (Davenport, 2005) within the organization to use their collective knowledge to quickly provide innovative solutions. Knowledge workers develop ideas, make plans, negotiate arrangements and do a myriad of other things to create innovative solutions. All these activities are collaborative in nature. Collaboration is essential to facilitate knowledge sharing and improve the quality of any solutions, as well as reducing the time to produce these solutions. The goal here is to bring all the necessary information to groups of people who can then make the necessary decisions.

Benefits from collaboration are particularly possible in processes that are knowledge intensive (Grant, 1996). Such processes require people to deal with increasingly complex situations that require a quick response. There is also a general view that technology can support and facilitate collaboration. However, at the same time using technology for collaboration is still quite challenging. Most technical support systems are based on preprogrammed activities whereas collaboration is often emergent and requires support systems that can evolve as collaboration evolves. Furthermore, such emergence is initiated by knowledge workers themselves rather than by information technology professionals. Process emergence characterizes what is known as Enterprise 2.0 (McAfee, 2006). It is perhaps fair to say that Enterprise 2.0 sets a direction rather than a concrete structure. Enterprise 2.0 was introduced by McAfee (2006) in his article in the Sloan Management Review as a natural trend towards obtaining additional competitive advantage by using the new technologies available through Web 2.0. It sees a business environment where collaboration extends from groups and individuals to organizational units and whole enterprises and uses Web 2.0 technologies as facilitating such growth.

The question, however, is how collaboration can leverage technology in ways that adds business value and leads to competitive advantage. This applies especially when we go beyond small teams working on well defined projects, such as preparing a document to support enterprise wide collaboration. Large scale collaboration requires planning of work processes and maintaining context and awareness between such units. It also requires the sharing on any created knowledge during the process. This paper proposes that enterprises need to consider the development of what are called here collaborative infrastructures to get the benefits of collaboration.

COLLABORATIVE INFRASTRUCTURES

The kind of architectures increasingly required to support knowledge workers is shown in Figure 1. The major components in Figure 1 are:

Knowledge workers, who carry out analytic work through workspaces that provide the information and communication needed in collaboration;

Corporate transaction systems that are repositories of everyday transactions. These are usually structures and follow well-defined processes and use the software is provided by vendors.

Workspaces for analytic work that are flexible in the sense that they can be reconfigured to solve emerging problems;

A collaborative infrastructure that allows knowledge workers to collaborate and create new knowledge. It is made up of collaboration software and a collaborative database, which

Figure 1. An Integrated Enterprise (reproduced with permission of Palgrave Macmillan)

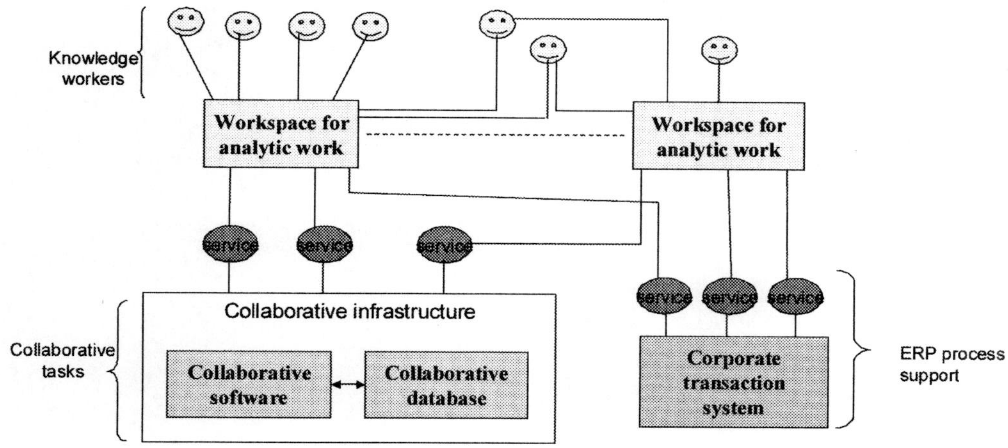

is the new knowledge created by the work of knowledge workers. The collaboration software is based on Web 2.0 technologies. However, often such technologies are used in an ad-hoc manner and knowledge is not widely shared.

Figure 1 introduces two emerging trends in the development of new systems and integrates them into the architecture. One is greater integration between dual structure of knowledge and ERP processes so that knowledge workers can both access corporate transaction information and collaborate while carrying out the necessary analytic work to develop ideas for new products and services. The other is the ability to capture knowledge that is created during this collaboration for later use across the enterprise. The paper proposes to develop a collaborative infrastructure for this latter purpose.

The idea of a collaborative infrastructure is illustrated in Figure 2. It sees business enterprises as made up of a number of activities whose processes are coordinated to reach organizational goals. Workspaces are provided to integrate people's interactions and capture the created knowledge. The workspaces provide the services for collaboration for sharing knowledge. This paper will define ways to model processes that characterize such collaboration and develop architectures that integrate social connectivity into the process, rather than relying on individual workers to select individual services such as e-mail for each interaction.

Collaborative technologies are already widely used in industry but in most cases in an ad-hoc manner. What is needed is a more systematic approach where such knowledge can be managed across the different activities. This paper proposes such a systematic approach to developing such infrastructures. It develops a blueprint that defines the major elements and then discusses their effect on design processes. The major effect is to provide greater focus on people relationships in an enterprise with a view of supporting such relationships with a collaborative infrastructure.

USING A SYSTEMATIC APPROACH TO DEVELOP REQUIREMENTS

The systematic approach gets away from the most common approach of simply to providing the technologies and allow people to use them as new projects or issues arise. One drawback here is that knowledge developed as part of individual projects is often difficult to share. The alternative is to use a systematic approach to identify an infrastructure that can provide both the tools and

Figure 2. Collaborative Infrastructure

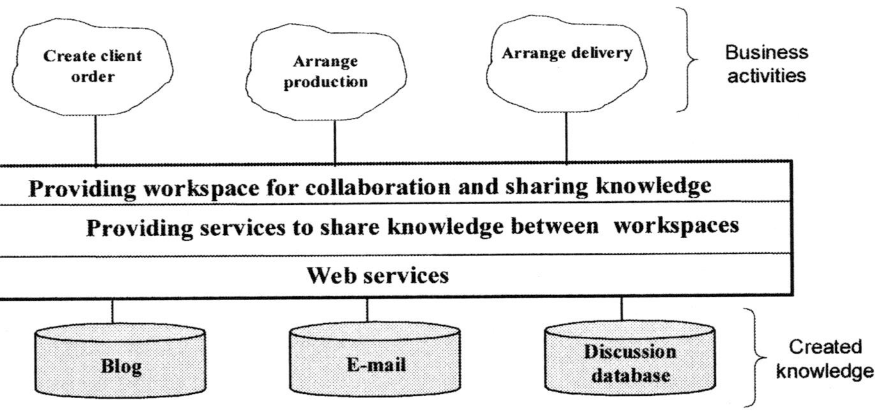

services to manage knowledge processes and to facility enterprise wide sharing. This approach is described here. It starts with developing an enterprise wide vision.

Develop a Vision

A vision as developed by stakeholders is essential in any systematic approach. This may often depend on an industry, as for example, managing mold changes better (Ni, 2007), or improving outsource management. It can also be applied across organizations within a given industry. For example in health there are visions such as developing transferable patient record systems or facilitating aged care among others. Metaphors (Morgan, 1996) have sometimes been suggested as a useful theoretical framework for developing visions especially at a broad enterprise level. For example, Morgan's metaphors describe organizations as working as machines, organisms adapting to their environment, tribes of people, or political systems.

Some of these metaphors, for example organizations as living organisms, which continually evolve or continually transform, correctly reflect the dynamics of the more agile and knowledge based systems today. The working as machines

Figure 3. The blueprint for modelling adaptive information systems (reproduced with permission of Palgrave Macmillan.)

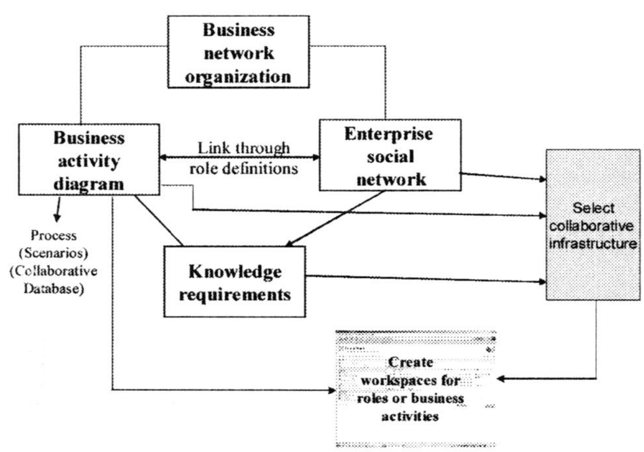

metaphor more closely reflects the more Oates and Fitzgerald (2007) go further and recommend a multi-metaphor approach be adopted in the design of systems where designers choose metaphors as needed to combine ideas or serve as a communication tool. They can use these techniques to simplify the complexity and in this way assist in the understanding of ways to resolve complexities. To do this the paper suggests a blueprint that identifies the major design components.

A Blueprint for Designing Collaborative Infrastructures

The blueprint, which is shown in Figure 3, combines the business network organization, the business activities, collaboration networks, and knowledge as the basic constructs for any model. They can also be seen as different perspectives of networking. One sees the network from an organizational perspective, the other from an activity perspective and a third from the people networking perspective.

Firstly the business activities are seen as loosely connected and the connections can change over time. We combine the business activities with enterprise social networking as an integral part of the systems and seeing it as a link between the different activities. Similarly knowledge requirements are often the explicit databases found in most business systems. The knowledge requirements go beyond simple transaction databases but include records of social interactions integrated into the activities. They will be focused on the knowledge needs of roles within the social structure. Collaboration patterns will provide a strong guideline for defining such social knowledge. For example, a leadership structure needs different knowledge to that in providing expert service or for brokering within a business network. Such enterprise social networks will provide useful patterns both for linking to business activities and for defining the knowledge requirements.

The goal of modelling is to develop a better idea of how a business network operates from the three perspectives and how to integrate these into a model and eventually use the model to identify the requirements of a collaborative infrastructure. The paper describes the modelling in terms of an example with details found in Hawryszkiewycz (2009).

AN EXAMPLE – DEVELOPING AN INFRASTRUCTURE FOR OUTSOURCING

The analysis of requirements must consider the four perspectives of the blueprint. The analysis develops models which are then converted to a technical specification. Outsourcing is one example that requires collaboration between business enterprises. Outsourcing arrangements of entire processes are quire complex and can be viewed as alliances of multiple organizations. An example of the organizational perspective is shown in Figure 4, which is a simplified form of an ongoing case study. It shows four organizations involved in an outsourcing process. It also shows the interactions between the organizations.

- The client who requires a service provider to manage a selected process,
- The process service provider who provides a service (which may include a number of applications) and subcontracts the provision of application programs for a third party, the application vendor.
- The network provider, who supplies the network and any operating systems to support the outsourcing arrangement.
- The software vendor, who provides the software to run the application.

Different roles are associated with each of these organizations and they must collaborate to

Figure 4. Business network organization for outsourcing business arrangement

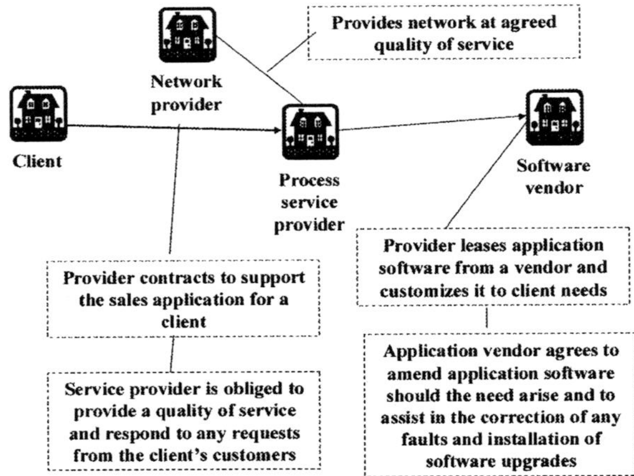

resolve any issues. In this case the initial analysis indicates a business requirement to maintain a quality of service to the client through response to queries and general maintenance of a level of client satisfaction. These roles are shown on the business activity diagram.

The Business Activity Diagram

Figure 5 is an example of a business activity diagram showing typical activities in an outsourcing arrangement. It reflects the general structure of contemporary business networks where each unit follows its own process but these processes must be coordinated to reach a global goal. Each activity is one such process. The diagram also shows a description for each activity in terms of the kind of work carried out in the activity. For example:

- "Receive service report" and "Sales recording" are both operational with a task focus,
- "Resolving a service report" can be classified as at the operational management level, often of a collaborative nature.
- "Arrange program change" has a mix of different work kinds and hence should probably be decomposed into two activities, one to decide what change is needed and the other to coordinate the change implementation.

Each of these activities has its own process.

Transient activities may be constructed to resolve an urgent issue. Thus a virtual team is created to solve an issue. The project leader 'o1' becomes the coordinator of this team and members are assigned from the provider and vendor teams.

The next step is now to create the enterprise social network by looking at each activity and matching it to a standard collaboration patterns.

The Enterprise Network Model for Process Outsourcing

The enterprise social network is now constructed by looking at the activity description and matching a social pattern to the activity. A different pattern is constructed for each of the teams, which are primarily collaborative at the operational management level and focus on task execution.

Figure 6 shows:

- The roles and role participants. The roles are shown as dots whereas the participants

Figure 5. A business activity diagram also showing the activity descriptions

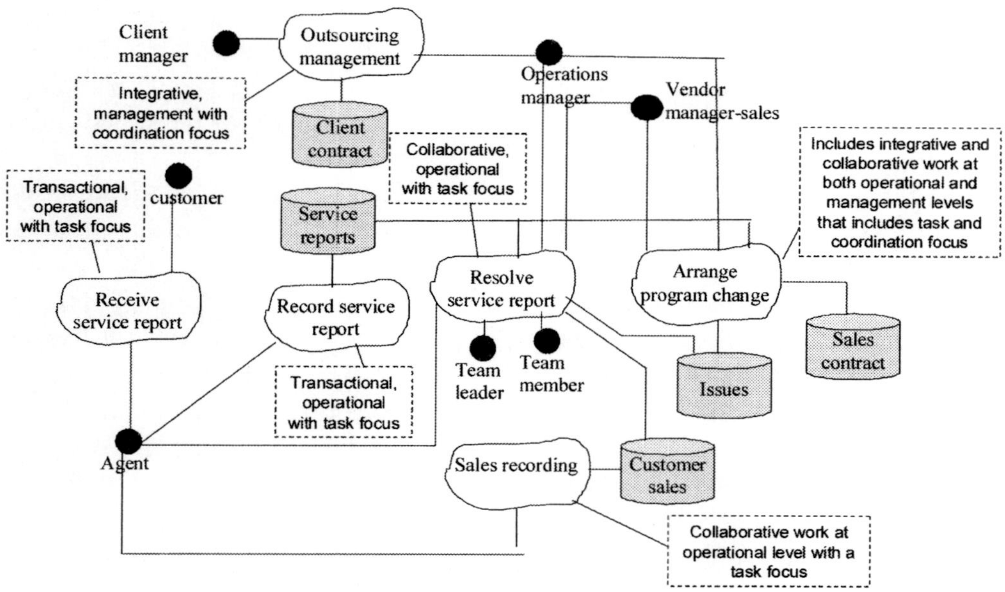

are shown as faces. For example 'a1' is the team leader in the provider team,

- The collaboration within activities shown by the circles,
- The role responsibilities shown by the dotted boxes linked to the roles,
- The interactions between the roles shown in dotted boxes linked by dotted lines to the interaction.

Here we show the responsibilities and interactions on the diagram. These tend to be brief for illustrative purposes. Actual documentation

Figure 6. The Social Network Diagram for process outsourcing (reproduced with permission of Palgrave Macmillan)

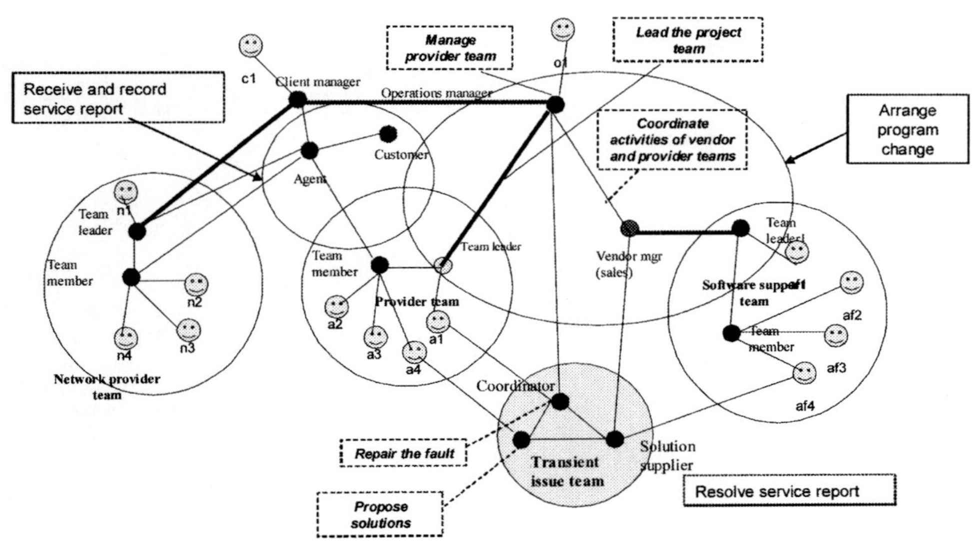

is more complete and can be provided separate from the diagram.

DEFINING TECHNOLOGY SUPPORT

The eventual goal is to develop a collaboration infrastructure that supports knowledge workers within an enterprise. This support is provided by workspaces, which can be of many forms including web portals, middleware or workflow systems. A number of options exist for providing workspaces for people in the enterprise network. These are illustrated in Figure 7. The two dimensions here are:

- The degree of specialization of interfaces to user ranging from a web portal used by everyone to each person having their own specially designed workface,
- Responsibility for developing the workspace,

Although a specially customized workspace is ideal for knowledge workers, it is costly to realize using current technologies. In most cases it would require information technology specialists to construct an interface for each individual. Figure 7 shows a number of compromise alternatives:

- Developing a special interface for different roles as for example a client interface, a salesperson interface and so on,
- Providing a lightweight platform made up of a range of services that can be placed into workspaces,
- Providing platforms where users themselves can mashup their own workspace.

The remainder of the paper focuses on the lightweight approach as this s increasingly seen as matching the requirements of knowledge work. The goal here is to provide individuals with the flexibility to select the best services for their work and assemble them in the one workspace.

Developing Customizable Lightweight Workspaces

Lightweight workspaces are those that primarily allow users to select services as they need them rather than requiring particular processes to be followed. Ease of use is one of the driving factors and the ability to change the interface itself is an important factor. They have three major characteristics. They are:

Figure 7. Who to support? (reproduced with permission of Palgrave Macmillan)

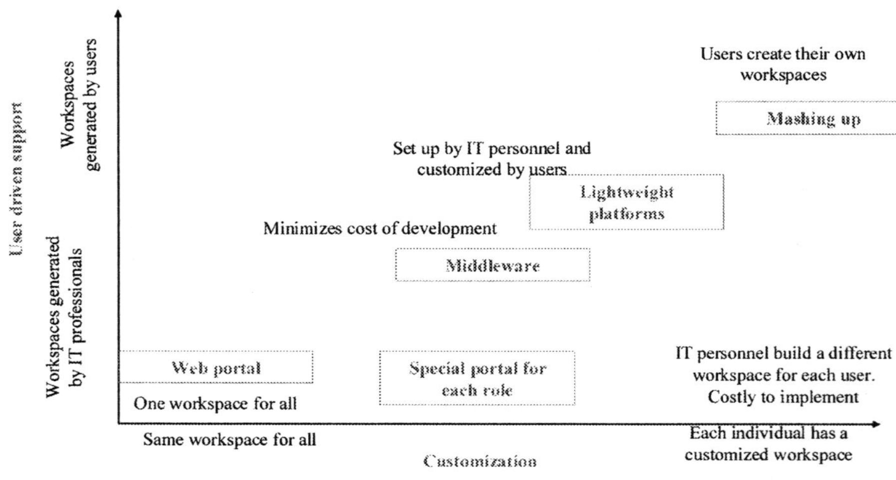

Figure 8. A lightweight platform

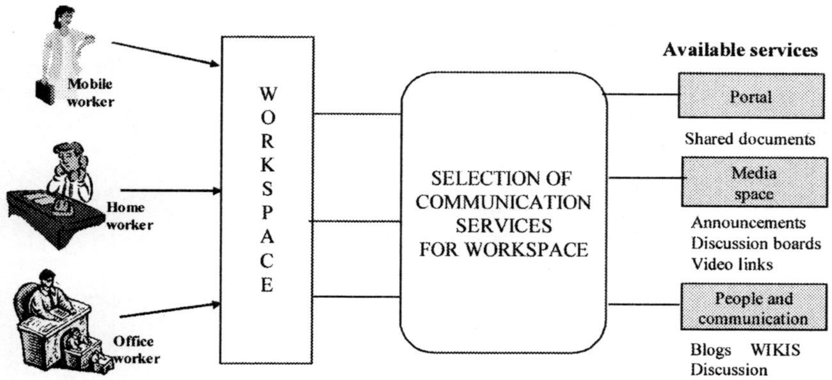

Low cost entry,
Flexible in that they can be easily changed by their users, and
Web based to support distributed teams.

Lightweight platforms can vary in the kind of services provided and can support different kinds of collaboration. The paper describes three levels of platform – lightweight exchange, lightweight collaboration and lightweight workflow.

Lightweight Exchange

A lightweight exchange platform provides services to support the kind of communication generally found in offices. The idea of lightweight platforms is illustrated in Figure 8.

The platform provides a set of services. These services include portals, media spaces as well as people in the organization. The platform provides ways to select and assemble services into a workspace. Such a platform raises social awareness of what people in a community are doing.

The discourses found here are those generally found in normal office work. Here people know by experience how to collaborate and use the basic facilities as needed. The kinds of interactions in lightweight exchange usually focus on communication and maintaining shared objects. Typical communication services include:

Conversational task threading, intermittent communication tasks with different individuals. System must keep track of the interactions

Quick connection such as phone, video conference and one way drop leaving brief messages asynchronously as for example using e-mail or pagers.

Sharing objects that are used to mediate conversation, such as shared portal.

This kind of platform is typified by a web portal or a simple workspace system. Examples include recreational systems such as Facebook, workspace systems such as BCSW or specially designed web portals.

Lightweight Collaboration

This now includes many additional services that are often needed to in joint work. In particular it should use collaborative databases such as e-portfolios or program boards to maintain the quality and effectiveness of collaboration.

Lightweight collaboration provides additional services to allow people in communities to make arrangements of who does what. The kinds of services here on team management and joint document development. The workspace focuses on the assignment of tasks to people, agreement and description of tasks. They also include maintaining awareness of progress and more advanced

Figure 9. Collaborative Lightweight Services

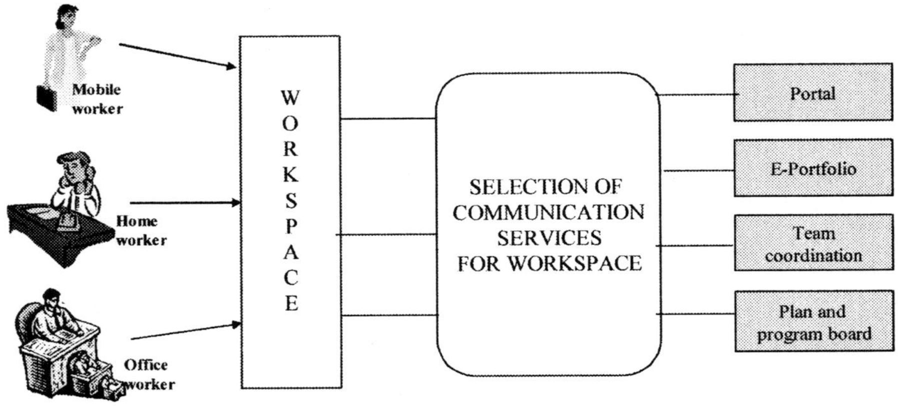

communication tools such as blogs, discussion boards, program boards, or e-portfolios. The main difference from lightweight exchange is that it is often necessary to keep records of the collaboration – that is to maintain a collaborative database. An example of a typical scenario is shown in the use case shown in Figure 10.

Lightweight Workflow

Lightweight platforms are user driven and usually based on the InterNet. They support the kind of communication often found in offices. People exchange notes and documents, makes comments and observations, and suggest courses of action. The platform may also support a limited amount of collaboration, such as for example preparing a document or assessing an emerging situation.

Lightweight workflow requires community members to monitor the progress of processes. They agree on the process steps, and their completion times, monitor task completions and decide on next task. It often also includes reviewing progress and changing the process.

Choosing Lightweight Platforms Strategies

The kind of work and group size provide the following guidelines for choosing the kinds of platform.

Task execution, small group -→ lightweight exchange
Coordination, small group → lightweight exchange
Coordination, integrative work, large group -→ lightweight coordination

Figure 10. Use case illustrating lightweight collaboration

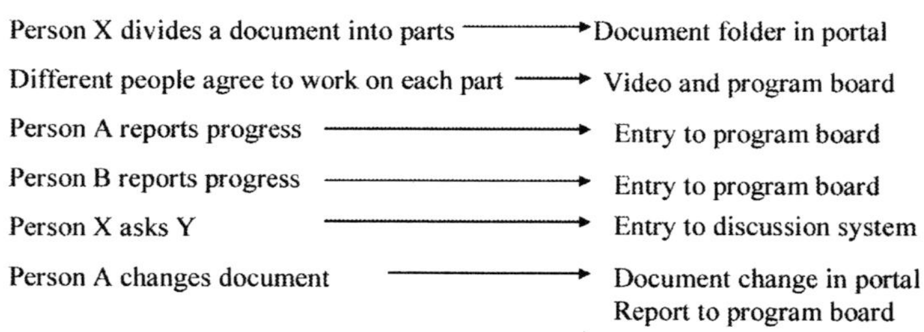

Figure 11. Illustrating the complexity

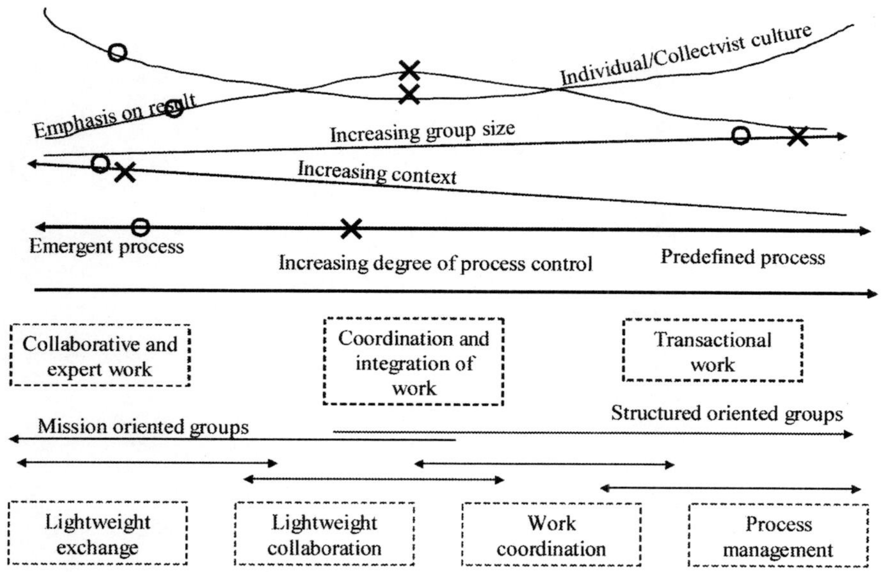

Coordination, integrative work, small group -→ lightweight coordination

Figure 11 defines some guidelines for choosing the appropriate technical strategy. It combines various organizational aspects particularly the kind of process and scope of the work. Figure 6 contains a number of lines. The way to read the Figure 11 is to look along the horizontal axis, select a platform and then look vertically to see the kind of activity that best characterizes that platform. For example for lightweight collaboration we see that it is best suited for the following kind of activity – relatively wide context, smallish group sizes, emphasis on results.

Typical guidelines are:

- Increasing group size usually calls for more structured support,
- The bigger the project the more emphasis on workflow,
- Wider contexts usually call for increasing communication and hence platforms with greater emphasis on exchange and collaboration.

To use the guidelines we go in the opposite way. Basically plot the characteristics of the community on the top lines and then select the appropriate platform. Choices however often require compromises to be made. For example suppose in Figure 11 analysis has identified an organization characterized by the circles in Figure 11. The collectivist characteristic, large context and emergent process suggest lightweight exchange. However it is a large group which calls for a more structured support perhaps lightweight workflow. Hence some compromise must be made.

For example in Figure 5, arrange program change is best supported by a lightweight collaboration where people make arrangements to carry out a program change, whereas ‘resolve service report’ requires lightweight exchange as it is seeking opinions from a number of people.

Identifying the infrastructure

The other component is to choose the technology to provide the services needed in collaboration and the functionality to compose workspaces that use a selection of the services. Commercially the kinds

Figure 12. A role based interface

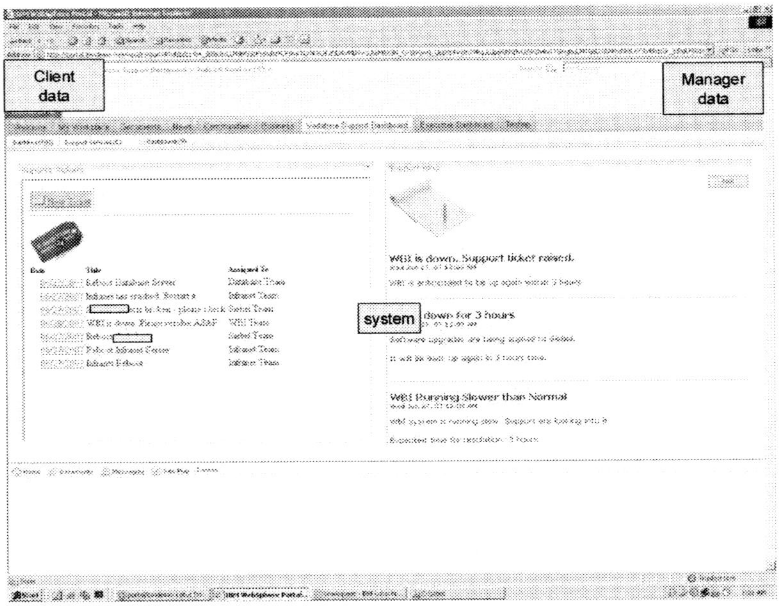

of systems include available workspace systems or middleware. Workspace management systems provide the services but often require some training to be used by non-technical users. Hence at best in reference to Figure 8 they are somewhere up the half way mark of user driven support. A typical system here is Microsoft Sharepoint which in this context provides a platform for lightweight collaboration.

Middleware systems are typified by systems such as websphere. These usually require some intervention by IT professionals and often lead to either role based or activity based workspaces.

The goal is to provide a workspace for each role with access to a common context. The role responsibilities are identified from the business activity diagram. These activities are included in the role interface. The interface also includes access to all roles connected to the role in the work network to encourage informal interaction. The goal is to allow each role to have a role specific interface, as for example shown in Figure 12, (with some sensitive information blocked) with access to a common context. This context includes all the documents accessible to the project manager. The role responsibilities are identified from the social network analysis by identifying the activities of the role and presenting them in the role interface.

CONCLUSION

The chapter has identifies the importance of collaboration in contemporary firms. It suggested the need for enterprise wide collaborative infrastructures rather than collaboration evolving in individual groups. It then proposed a systematic approach to developing such infrastructures. The approach focuses on integrating social structures into business application. A blueprint for a method of designing such systems was described and an example given.

REFERENCES

Davenport, T. (2005). *Thinking for a living*. Harvard Business School Press.

Evans, P., & Wolf, B. (2005). Collaboration rules. *Harvard Business Review*, July-August.

Grant, R. M. (1996). Prospering in dynamically-competitive environments: Organizational capability as knowledge integration. *Organization Science*, *7*(4), 375–387. doi:10.1287/orsc.7.4.375

Hansen, M. T., Nohria, N., & Tierney, T. (1999). What's your strategy for managing knowledge. *Harvard Business Review*, (March-April): 106–116.

Hawryszkiewycz, I. T. (1996). Support services for business networking. In E. Altman & N. Terashima (Eds.), *Proceedings IFIP96*, Canberra. London: Chapman and Hall.

Hawryszkiewycz, I. T. (1997). A framework for strategic planning for communications support. In *Proceedings of The inaugural Conference of Informatics in Multinational Enterprises*, Washington, October, 1997 (pp. 141-151).

Hawryszkiewycz, I. T. (2005). A Metamodel for collaborative systems. *Journal of Computer Information Systems*, 131–146.

Hawryszkiewycz, I.T. (in press). Knowledge management: Organizing for business value through collaboration. Palgrave Macmillan, Basingstoke.

Hawryszkiewycz, I. T., & Lin, A. (2003). Process knowledge support for emergent processes. In *Proceedings of the Second IASTED International Conference on Information and Knowledge Management, Scottsdale, Arizona, November, 2003* (pp. 83-87).

Jacobs, J. L., Dorneich, C. P., & Jones, P. M. (1998). Activity representation and management for crisis action planning. *IEEE International Conference on Systems, Management and Cybernetics, October 1998* (pp. 961-966).

Kodama, M. (2005). New knowledge creation through leadership-based strategic community – a case of new product development in IT and multimedia business fields. [Elsevier Press]. *Technovation*, *25*, 895–908. doi:10.1016/j.technovation.2004.02.016

McAfee, A. P. (2006). Enterprise 2.0: The dawn of emergent collaboration. *MIT Sloan Management Review* (pp. 21-28).

Ni, Q., Lu, W. F., Yarlagadda, K. D. V., & Mimg, X. (2007). Business information modeling for process integration in the mold making industry. *Robotics and Computer-integrated Manufacturing*, *23*, 195–205. doi:10.1016/j.rcim.2005.12.006

KEY TERMS AND DEFINITIONS

Collaboration: A process, where two or more people or organizations work together to achieve a common goal by sharing knowledge and material resources, by joint learning and building consensus

Social Networking: The grouping of individuals into specific groups, like small rural communities or a neighborhood division. Social networking is possible in person, especially in the workplace, at universities and high schools. Traditionally social networking required face-to-face communication, but now it is very popular online.

Lightweight Technologies: Software technologies enabling a software creation using only the basic components provided by software vendors, avoiding additional tools that can be expensive as well as too complicated for the end users.

Chapter 15
Governance of Virtual Networks:
Case of Living and Virtual Laboratories

Brane Semolic
Project & Technology Management Institute Faculty of Logistics, University of Maribor, Slovenia

Jure Kovac
Faculty of Organizational Sciences University of Maribor, Slovenia

ABSTRACT

Technological and organizational excellence is the key element for business success in a modern business environment. In contemporary business environments, companies will restore and keep their competition capability not only by optimizing their own potentials, but mainly by utilizing capability of foreign resources and their connection to complete business process in the so called network organizations. Virtual organizations are a special form of network organizations. Among virtual organizations the so called Living Laboratory takes place. This chapter presents the findings of the research regarding the state of development and application of laser living laboratory management and governance system in Toolmakers Cluster of Slovenia.

INTRODUCTION

Modern companies are permanently analyzing their business activities and the global market, and are searching for business opportunities to improve the competitive capacities of their own company. New forms of network organization of companies' business activities are coming to the fore, which organize individual business activities in the regions that from the business viewpoint seem favourable with respect to the prices of manpower, special know-how, raw materials etc.

Trans-national research, development and production networks are being formed. Their formation and development is influenced by the scope of business environment development of the involved countries, regions, national and regional government rules and regulations, social and cultural conditions etc. The world is becoming a more and more intertwined network consisting of a series of different trans-national networks and specialized economic entities, working in different parts of the world.

DOI: 10.4018/978-1-60566-890-1.ch015

The urge for the concentration of resources resulted in the creation of network-structured integrations as one of the most appropriate solutions. One of the major features of creating network organizational structures is the integration based on rather loose and temporary association of particular resources in order to obtain the objective of competitive advantage. Virtual network organizations are a special form of network organizations based on the use of modern information and communication technologies and collaboration between different organizations that has similar research and development interests.

The mission and concern of the proposed chapter is to present the concepts of the living and virtual laboratories design. Within this framework the problems and theoretical solutions will be presented:

- How to design governance and management model for the specific needs of living and virtual laboratories clients;
- How to start architecture design of living and virtual laboratories.

Described theories are partly illustrated using the case studies from Toolmakers Cluster of Slovenia.

VIRTUAL ORGANIZATION, VIRTUAL LABORATORIES AND LIVING LAB?

Most of the existing studies point out that virtual organizations are a temporary consortium of partners from different organizations establishes to fulfill a value-adding task, for example a product or service to a customer (Duin, 2008, p.26). According to Rabelo and Pereira-Klen (2004) virtual organizations are temporary alliances between organizations to share skills or core competencies and resources in order to better respond to new collaboration opportunities (Loss et al., 2008, p.77). This way, virtual organizations represent cooperation between formally non-connected organizations or persons who establish vertical or horizontal links and present themselves to the customers of their products or services as a single association. Apart from the professional literature concerning virtual organizations emphasis is also given to the information and communication technology as well as to the absence of the central control functions. (Mohrman, Galbraith & Lawler III., 1998, p.77; Dessler, 2001, p. 230; Pettigrew et al., 2003, p. 8; Vahs, 2005, p. 507).

As indispensable precondition for the functioning of the above mentioned organizational connectedness the authors quote timely adjusted cooperative processes, organizational development, space dispersion and use of modern communication technology to master the processes of cooperation (Rohde, Rittenbuch, & Wulf, 2001. p. 2).

In the literature, the companies are often described as a network of companies (i.e. organizations – boundary-less firms or boundless organizations). These are dynamic, i.e. virtual companies, linked together at the base of the inter-organizational information systems, pursuing the aim to be successful in the area of given projects.

Virtual laboratories are a special form of network organizations. A virtual laboratory is an interactive online environment established so as to create and channel simulations and experiments in a certain science field. It is an environment designed for working in teams from different locations and creates opportunities for cooperation in research and development. One of its important tasks is also the remote access to expensive laboratory and other equipment. Virtual laboratories further include the so called living labs.

The basic concept of the living lab was developed at the American MIT Institute in Boston, USA. It was first used for designing and planning urban area architecture. A living lab is an R&D methodology for identifying, validating and finding solutions to complex problems by including a real-life environment. In such an environment, product and service innovation is carried out, tested and introduced.

GOVERNANCE OF VIRTUAL ORGANIZATIONS AND LIVING LABORATORIES

Recent years have seen an increased interest in corporate governance. There are several reasons for that, resulting from individual business scandals to increasingly complex environments that require close cooperation between owners and management. Corporate governance can be defined as a system by which companies are directed and controlled. Boards of directors are responsible for the governance of their companies. The stockholders' role in governance is to appoint directors and auditors and to make sure that an appropriate governance structure is in place. The responsibilities of the board include setting the company's strategic goals, providing the leadership to put them into effect, supervising the management of the business, and reporting to stockholders on their stewardship. The board's actions are subject to laws, regulations, and the wishes of the stockholders in the general meeting (Bnet Business Dictionary, Mallin, 2007, p.12).

The area of governance and that of management are closely connected. In the area of network organizations with special focus on virtual organizations, the connection of the processes of governance and management is even more expressive. For this purpose, we will ensue from the term governance as explained by the author Hilb, when we present the models of governance and management in a virtual organization and living laboratories. Hilb defines corporate governance as s system "by which companies are strategically directed, integratively managed and holistically controlled in an entrepreneurial and ethical way in a manner appropriate to each particular context" (Hilb, 2006, p. 9-10) .

Processes of governance take place at virtual connections on the level of connection and in individual associations. The complexity of governance processes demands a clear distinction and mutual adjustment. For the purpose of easier recognition and understanding of governance processes, we can divide them in:

- Governance processes of forming inter-organizational virtual connections and
- Governance processes of ensuring development and operations of inter-organizational virtual connections.

The key aspects of governance processes in forming inter-organizational virtual network organizations are:

- Goals and
- Forms of virtual network organization.

Definition of the strategy behind virtual network organizations must stem from the organization's strategy (Mohrman, Galbraith & Lawler III., 1998, p.79). The other set of governance processes embodies:

- Forms of virtual network organization
- Assignment of the role that individual organizations assume.

The form of virtual network organizations is closely related to the goal definition of virtual network organizations. When joining into a virtual network organization the owners and management must ask themselves the following questions:

- What are the primary goals, purposes, and strategy of forming a virtual network organization?
- What advantages and dangers does it imply to the company?
- What are the advantages of a virtual network as a whole?

- What place will our company have in a virtual network (specialist or integrating of the entire network)?
- What are the alternatives?

When forming a virtual network special attention must be paid to the selection of partners. The first step in this process is to know and understand the strategic goals of partners. Good knowledge and understanding of partner's reasons for the involvement in virtual networking can spare us from future unpleasant surprises. In practice, we have cases where certain organizations are closely connected in a network for the sole reason of acquiring information on its partners. This enables them greater control, price pressure, etc. That is why the key to partner selection is to know their strategic implications for joining (Mohrman, Galbraith & Lawler III., 1998, p. 86).

Having chosen the partner, the company must then select forms of virtual network organizations and reach an agreement on the role of the organizations (conclusion of a contract). The role that an organization assumes depends on the ability, purpose, and goals for joining a network. Primarily, we speak of the decision on the form of the legal status and ways of implementing an integrative role as well as a definition of the place and role of other companies in the network. Basic criteria for the selection of a coordinating role in a virtual network are (Mohrman, Galbraith & Lawler III., 1998, p.101):

- Knowledge of the entire process or the chain of added value
- Experience
- Ability to gain the necessary resources for the operation of a virtual network.
- Disposable resources
- Credibility of the organization
- Key factors or abilities of individual organizations
- Management resources with the required expertise and experience.
- Readiness to assume the role.

It is appropriate to stress that many times the required managerial effort for the implementation of integrative processes is underestimated (Schräder, 1996, p.83). Therefore, the selection of managers and other personnel that work in inter-organizational virtual networks is especially important.

Managers, who control, organize and guide integrative processes in virtual networks must posses the following expertise and skills (Krystek, Rede & Reppegather, 1997, p.174):

- Integrative abilities
- Goal-oriented management control
- Sensitivity to various organizational cultures
- Expertise in the field of virtual networking
- Participation
- Ability to motivate
- Restriction of constructive conflict management
- Communicative and representative skills
- Controlling of information management

In addition, it is crucial that individuals that assume key positions in virtual network organizations have the following expertise and skills (Krystek, Rede & Reppegather, 1997, p. 178, Reiß, 2000, p. 30):

- Professional and functional knowledge
- Communication skills
- Cultural adaptability
- Adaptable and constructive conflict management
- A desire to participate
- A need for horizontal and lateral professional and personal development
- Entrepreneurship
- Independence and a sense of responsibility

Selection of individuals that hold key positions in a virtual network reduces conflicts, which are one of the most sensitive areas of management. There are many conflicting areas in virtual networking. This is why one of the most important managerial goals is to lay the principles, means, and instruments to resolve any possible future conflicts while forming a virtual network. One must clearly set the procedures and levels of conflict solving.

MANAGERIAL PROCESSES INSIDE VIRTUAL ORGANIZATIONS AND LIVING LABORATORIES

Every virtual network organization must establish a management system that assumes the coordinating role within a network. Managerial system of coordination involves management at a classical level. Without a doubt, there are differences between the implementation of managerial tasks in a classical organization and the operation of management with a coordinating role in a virtual network organization. The differences are as follows:

- Management system for the needs of coordination within a virtual network exists for the time that the network is operational.
- Management jurisdictions responsible for coordination in a virtual network are not comparable with management jurisdictions in a classical organization.
- Management processes for coordination purposes within a virtual network can be distributed among several institutions.

Despite the noted aspects, we must emphasize that management processes are linked to a certain form of organization that must form itself for the operational needs of a virtual network as a whole. In principle, we differentiate three forms of a management system in coordination (Mohrman, Galbraith & Lawler III., 1998, p. 88-91):

- One partner carries out coordinating processes
- There is a division of coordinating processes among partners and
- Self-sustaining model of coordination.

Without a doubt, the first form is most common in implementing coordinating processes. The latter, self-sustaining, is appropriate in the first stage of forming a virtual network organization.

The central place at ensuring development and virtual networking belongs to strategy. Strategy is the starting point for management operations as all individual management activities derive from it. Up to a certain point strategy of a virtual network can stem from strategies of individual organizations included in a network. Figure 1 clearly shows that it is the strategy at the level of virtual networking which represents the key connection between strategies of organizations and their business strategies.

The making of key strategic starting points is by no means simple. We must first look for common ground and points and then form the key strategic goals. The common strategy is guidance for management operation in a network at key tasks such as:

- Allocation of resources within a virtual network and
- Evaluation of the achieved business results.

In classical companies, the role of the managers is to – among other tasks – allocate the financial, material resources and personnel abilities. One of the primary management tasks lies also in virtual network organizations. The difference is that management in virtual network organizations predominantly deals with personnel abilities, tech-

Figure 1. Strategic levels in a virtual network organization (Krystek, Rede & Reppegather, 1997, p. 304)

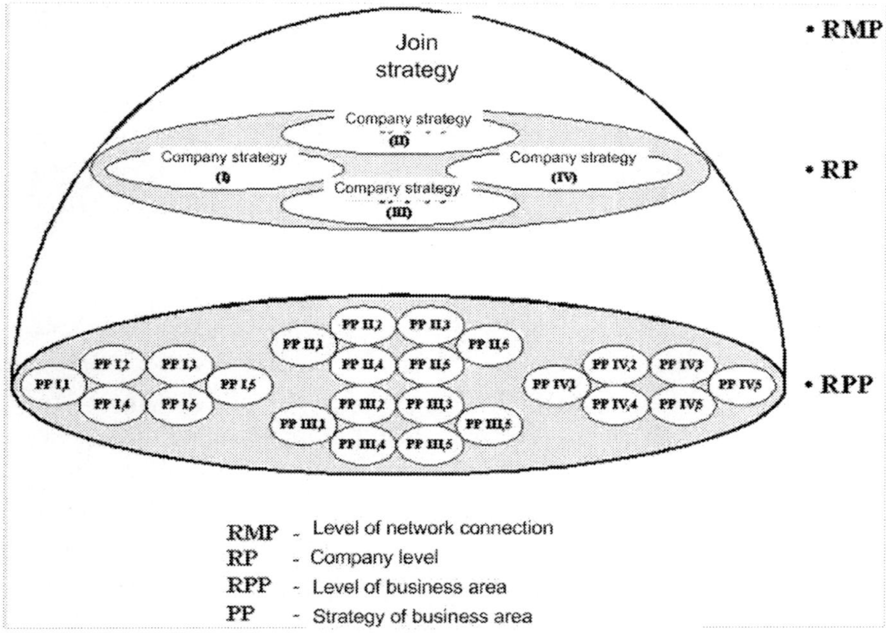

nology, self-sustainment and support to individual tasks (Schräder, 1996, p.80).

One particularly sensitive area of management activity in virtual network organizations is the area of forming unified elements or organizational culture. The process of forming a virtual network organizational culture is different from that of the classical organizations. Virtual network organizations have a high degree of differentiation of organizational culture with explicit presence of individual subcultures (Krystek, Rede & Reppegather, 1997, p.159).

This implies that we cannot expect a formation of a unified virtual network organizational culture that all organizations in the network will embrace. We can speak only of common elements of organizational culture. The basis for identification and strengthening of common elements of organizational culture are the joint starting points of organizations, where unification can be achieved. In most cases, these are openness and customer orientation.

Virtual network organizations form basic outlines of a common organizational culture only through joint projects, products, or services. The common elements of organizational culture can greatly contribute to achieving set goals of the network, and above all facilitate conflict resolution, which is one of the most sensitive areas of management activities. There are many conflict areas in virtual networks; therefore, the foundation of principles, means, and instruments of their resolution is one of the important tasks of management when forming a virtual network.

HOW TO START ARCHITECTURE DESIGN OF LIVING LABORATORIES

The value chain links of the organization are represented by the individual business functions which the organization needs to perform its activity. The individual business function defines the logical frame of professional tasks the organization has

Figure 2. The organization's management is responsible to identify and define all necessary business functions (Semolic, 2004, p. 136)

to perform. It relates to research, development, marketing, supply, procurement, production, sales, finances etc. The organization's management is responsible to identify and define all business functions, which the organization needs, and to ensure their proper performance (Figure 2). The contents, organizing and organization of functioning of the individual function and related tasks must be subject of constant innovation, just like the organization's products and related technologies.

The sole problem is not only to set forth correct contents, organization and organizing of functioning of individual business functions, but also to set forth the interconnecting of the individual function (e.g. connection between research, development, production, finances etc.). Primary and supporting business areas are distinguished. Primary business functions represent the elements of the basic business process ranging from research and development of the product to its sale on the market. On the other hand, the supporting businesses areas actually make that happen. The supporting business activities include business planning, organizing, financing, managing and supervising.

In any organization two simultaneous, closely connected processes are going on (Figure 3):

- Technical process,
- Entrepreneurial process.

Figure 3. In any organization two simultaneous, closely connected processes taking place (Semolic, 2004, p. 137)

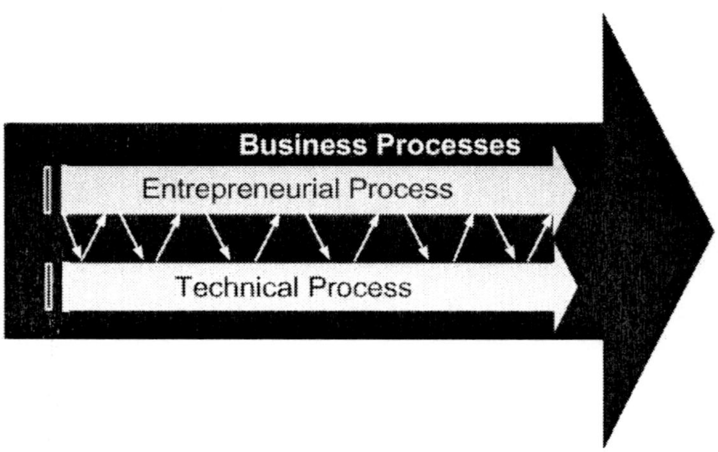

The technical process comprises of the sequence of all tasks which have to be performed in order to make the product. The result of the technical process is the "finished product". The entrepreneurial process makes the first process possible; its result is the sold product and realized profit or other organization's business benefits. The first process represents the technical part, whereas the second process represents the business part of the organization's value chain.

MATRIX OF VALUE CHAIN OF LIVING LABORATORY

The value chain of the living laboratory refers to defining the interconnected specialized activities with which the organizations enter into business connections with other virtual laboratory entities taking part in completion of the product. Figure 3 illustrates the example of an organization without external business connections (Classical approach to make a business), performing all research, development and testing activities inside an own organization, and a highly specialized organization performing only certain business activities at home, while the others are performed through outsourcing with the living laboratory organizations. Figure 4 shows the types and content of business connections between the partners of living laboratory.

Also in living laboratory the following connections are distinguished:

- primary and
- supporting connections.

Presentation of practical example of the links of chain of primary connections in LENS Living Laboratory:

Figure 4. Classic and outsourcing approach to the company's value chain set-up (Semolic, 2004, p. 139)

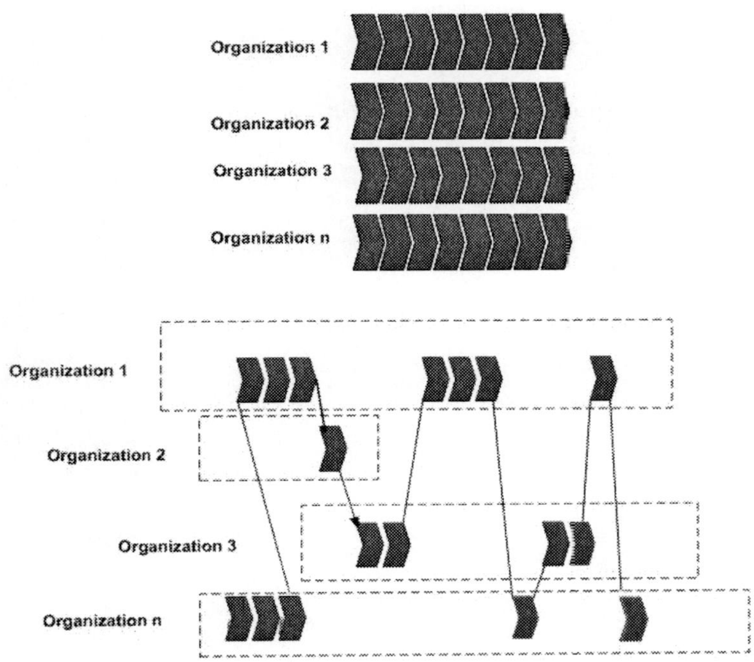

Figure 5. Organizations outsourcing and clustering cube (Semolic, 2004, p. 139)

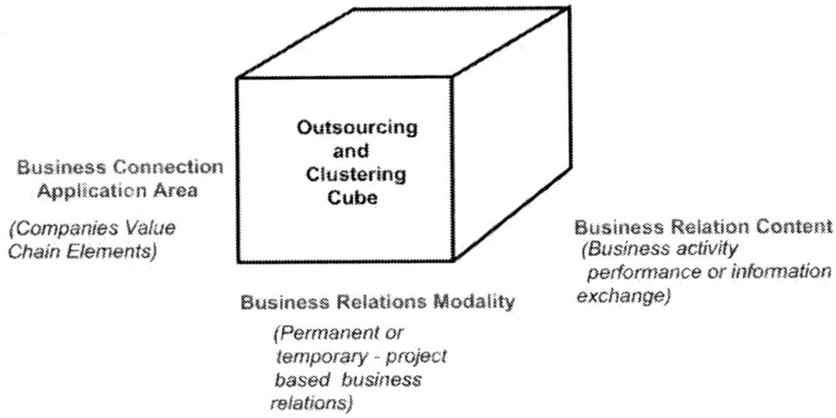

- development of new materials and alloys,
- material surface treatment,
- conceiving and designing,
- computer analyses and simulations,
- special testing or production services,
- etc.

The individual link of the primary value chain represents specialization of involved organizations.

The value chains of primary connections between the organizations of the living laboratory are formed in accordance with the living laboratory development strategy.

The support and orientation of the development of living laboratories value chains are assured by supporting value chain links, thus creating conditions for successful connecting of business companies and organizations, by orienting the value chain primary links formed by companies and organizations of the living laboratory. The supporting value chain links consist of the following business activities:

- living lab digital eco-system development and maintenance,
- living lab e-collaboration platform development and maintenance,
- living lab professional virtual communities social networking support,
- living lab governance and management systems development maintenance,
- living lab e-program and project management,
- living lab marketing etc.

In conjunction with the participating organizations, the leading companies – organizers of business networks within the living laboratory organize the business chains, hence assuring optimum value of products and services offered to the clients and their end users.

The organization of Living Laboratory's (virtual organization) Breeding Environment (ECOLEAD, 2004) represents the living laboratory management. The living laboratory management must take care of orienting, stimulating and supporting the business cooperation and connecting. Accordingly, they must provide and develop a suitable supporting value chain of specialized services, required for this purpose.

The basic driving force of each work in any participating organizations of the living laboratory must be "client's value".

Figure 6. Examples of metal products for automotive industry with example of progressive tool for production of parts from metal plates (EMO, 2002)

TOOL MAKING INDUSTRY CASE STUDY

Tool and Die Industrial Sector

Tool and Die-making workshops (Figure 14) are facing the challenges how to enhance performance of project-oriented production in multi-project and multi-organizational environment. Each customer order presents the project charter (see Figure 6) for the project of development and construction of a unique new tool. As illustration of the size of its market we can say that automotive producer needs more that 1000 tools and dies for production of a new car. In the project of a new tool development and construction companies outsourcing capacities from different partners and creating a different modalities of production network organizations.

In this context in project we developed reference business model. It provides a framework, including all relevant main business process applications.

Next, the practical example of the technical and entrepreneurial value chain in tool-making industry will be presented. Tool-making industry consists of SMEs, producing special purposed (unique) machines and tools for clients from manufacturing industries (ex. automotive etc.).

Elements of the technical value chain of a tool-making company:

- researches and development of new technical knowledge,
- development of new production technologies,
- design of tools,
- tool manufacturing technology development,
- tool manufacture,
- tool tests,
- start-up of tools,
- tool maintenance,
- tool recycling (after expiration of the tool service life).

Figure 7. The basic concept of LENS technology and examples of products (OPTOMEC, 2006, p.15)

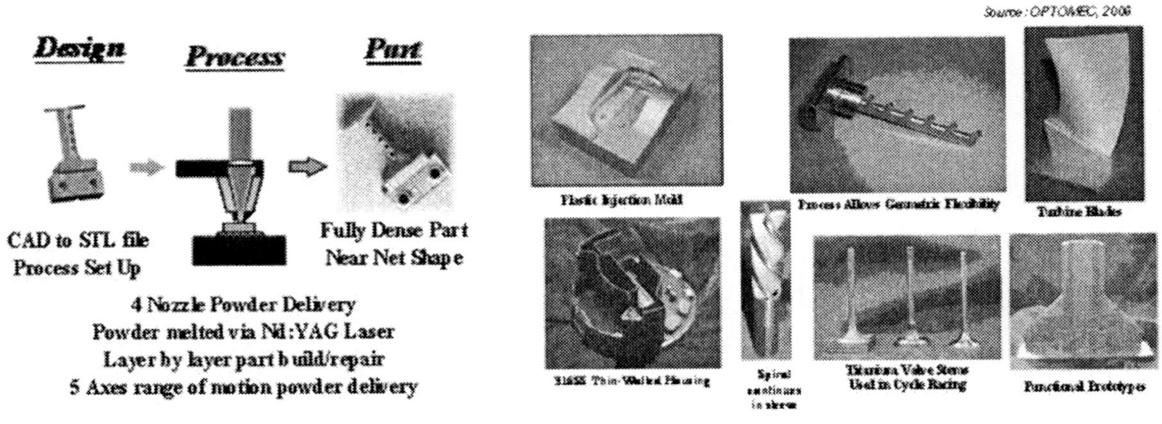

Elements of the entrepreneurial value chain of a tool-making company:

- researches and development of new business knowledge,
- development of new business technologies,
- marketing and sales,
- supplies for production,,
- production,
- client's taking-over of tool,
- after-sales activities.

The technical and entrepreneurial value chain must be coordinated and subject to constant introducing of novelties and innovative solutions which are a prerequisite for maintaining or increasing the company's competitiveness

What is LENS Living Lab?

LENS Living Lab is organized by coordination of Slovenian Toolmakers Cluster (TCS). Laser Engineered Net Shaping (LENS) Living Laboratory (LENS Living lab) is a real-life research and operational laboratory with the focus on a LENS new technology applications development and operational use (Figure 7). The LENS Living Lab creates a base for inventing, testing, prototyping and marketing of new LENS technology applications. The major advantage of virtual organization is the creation of pools of innovative organizations and experts from different research and end user areas who are collaborating and cooperating in this virtual environment.

The LENS Living Lab core members are business partners (users, researchers, developers etc.) who have long-term interest in such cooperation and collaboration. Those organizations and individuals are from research and industrial sector. LENS living lab creates open "value space" for researchers, developers and end users who have professional interest in collaboration in this field. They can be innovators, researchers, developers or advanced users. Figure 8 shows phases in the process of a technology life cycle (TLC) and LENS Living lab areas of support.

LENS Living Lab supports three major TLC phases: new design and manufacturing concepts development; testing of new developed technologies and connected "early birds" and support to phase of new technologies implementation and its operations support. The horizontal supporting services are related to functionalities of LENS Living Lab project office and LENS Living Lab general collaboration platform (Tool East Platform).

Figure 8. TLC phases and LENS Living Lab areas of support (Semolic, 2009)

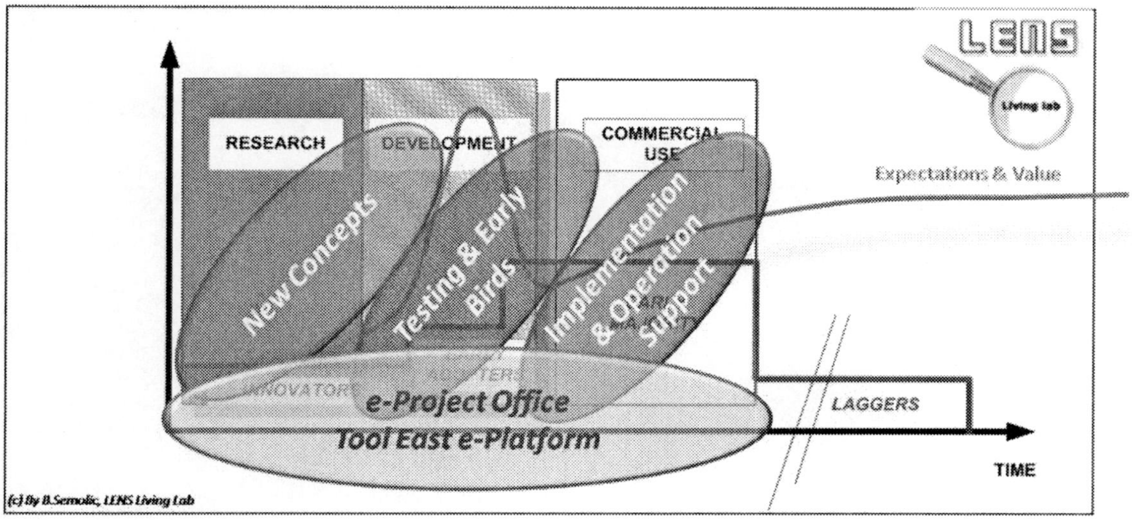

The customers of LENS Living Lab application research and operations are SMEs who are working in different industries, like tool-making and niche machines production, automotive, aeronautics, medicine etc.

The participating organizations are divided in different open research groups like material scientists, mechanical engineers, laser and electronics experts, end users, ICT experts, business design developers etc. They have been involving in three operational and research frameworks as follows:

- Technological and Innovative Centre,
- LENS Living Lab and
- Open Laser Collaboration Platform

Governance and Management in LENS Living Lab

The LENS Living Lab is an open network organization with three levels of inter-organizational governance and coordination (see Figure 9). The first level deals with strategic business issues. At this level, the participating partners sign a long-term cooperation agreement. This agreement defines areas of cooperation and management of LENS Living Lab. The second level deals with the inter-organizational issues (joint and support operation and project management). This level is related to the coordination of agreed business activities and connected organizational processes. The third level of coordination is related to the definition of IT and telecommunication platform of cooperation.

The organizational architecture of the second level which deals with the inter-organizational issues is based on the principles of open project based matrix organization (see Figure 10). One side of this matrix organization is composed by independent open international R&D groups (R&D organizations, SMEs, independent researchers and developers etc.) which represent LENS Living lab research and development capacities. Another side comprises of a list of agreed R&D programs and projects. In the cross-sections of this matrix we are identifying demanded R&D resources and creating temporary collaborative virtual project teams.

Strategic level of LENS Living lab governance is performed by the support of strategic annual conferences, by collaboration between

Figure 9. Levels of coordination in LENS Living Lab (Semolic & Kovac, 2008, p. 413)

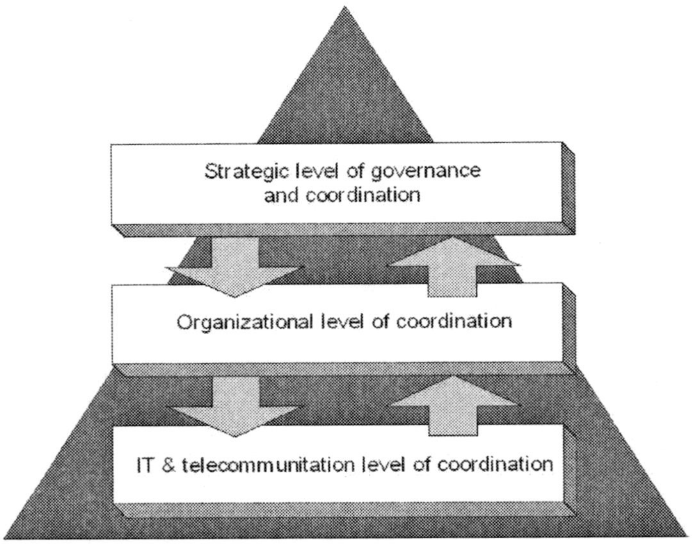

Figure 10. LENS Living lab – open project based matrix organization (Semolic, 2009)

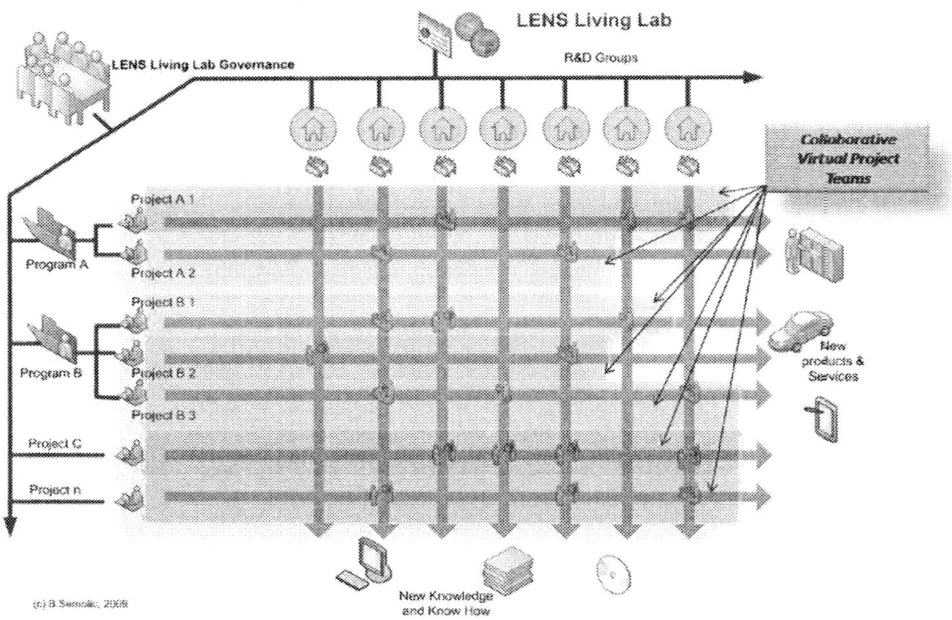

coordinators of open international R&D groups, by collaborative program management, by collaborative project management, by management of collaborative virtual project teams etc.

CONCLUSION

If we want to develop a competitive strength of our company, it often turns out that despite using our knowledge, capacities and other resources we are still not able to reach the desired goal. In the modern business environment, the companies will establish and maintain their competitiveness not solely by optimizing their own potentials, but more often by being able to use the resources of others and by interconnecting them into an overall process of creating new value. New forms of network organization appear which organize individual business activities in the regions favorable from the business viewpoint with respect to the prices of manpower, special know-how, raw materials etc. Methods and forms of organizing network virtual organizations are based on modern and flexible business models.

Living Laboratory represents one of many forms of virtual network organizations. The article presents some basic theories related to this subject. A Living Lab is an environment in which researchers, developers and users cooperate with the common objective of delivering a tested product, solution or service respecting users' requirements and in a shortest time possible.

We illustrated the creation of virtual organizations and living laboratories on the case study of tool and die making industry. By illustrating the governance and coordination of LENS Living lab we presented the discussed theories in praxis.

REFERENCES

Dessler, G. (2001). *Management*. NJ: Prentice Hall, Inc.

Dictionary, B. B. (n.d.). Retrieved October 10, 2008, from http://www.bnet.com

Duin, H. (2008). *Systemic strategic management for VBEs in the manufacturing sector*. In L.M. Camarinba-Matos, & W. Picard (Eds.), *Pervasive Collaborative Networks, IFIP TC 5 WG 5.5. Ninth Working Conference on Virtual Enterprises, Sept. 2008, Poznan, Poland*. NewYork: Springer.

EMO (2000). *Internal project documentation*. Celje: EMO Orodjarna.

Hilb, M. (2006). *New corporate governance*. New York: Springer Verlag.

Knez, M., Cedilnik, M., & Semolic, B. (2007). *Logistika in poslovanje logističnih podjetij*. Celje: Fakulteta za logistiko UM

Krystek, U., Redel, W., & Reppegather, S. (1997). *Grundzüge virtueller organisation*. Wiesbaden: Gabler.

Loss, L., Pereira-Klen, A. A., & Rabelo, R. J. (2008). *Value creation elements in learning collaborative networked organizations*. In L.M. Camarinba-Matos, & W. Picard (Eds.), *Pervasive Collaborative Networks, IFIP TC 5 WG 5.5. Ninth Working Conference on Virtual Enterprises, Sept. 2008, Poznan, Poland*. NewYork: Springer

Mallin, C. A. (2007). *Corporate governance*. Oxford: Oxford University Press.

Mohrman, A. S., Galbraith, J. R., & Lawler, E., III. (1998). *Tomorrow's Organization*, San Francisco: Jossey-Bass.

Pettigrew, A., Whittington, R., Melin, L., Runde, C. S., & Bosch, F. A. J. den, Ruigrok, W., & Numagami, T. (2003). *Innovative forms of organizing*, London: Sage Publications.

Peyton, R. (2004). *Toolmakers cluster of Slovenia, feasibility study*. Los Alamos, World Tech, Inc.

Rohde, M., Rittenbuch, M., & Wulf, V. (2001). *Auf dem Weg zur virtuellen Organisation*. Heidelberg: Physica-Verlag.

Schraeder, A. (1996). *Management virtueller Unternehmungen*. Frankfurt/Main: Campus Verlag.

Semolic, B., & Dworatschek (2004). *Project management in the new geo-economy and the power of project organization*. Maribor: IPMA Expert Seminar Series, University of Maribor.

Semolic, B. (2007). *LENS Living Laboratory – Project documentation*. Celje: INOVA Consulting; Project & Technology Management Institute, Faculty of Logistics, University of Maribor.

Semolic, B. (2009). TA Platform, LENS Living Lab. Vojnik, INOVA Consulting, TCS.

Semolic, B., & Kovac, J. (2008). *Strategic information system of virtual organization*. Pervasive Collaborative Networks. Poznan: IFIP, Springer.

Vahs, D. (2005). *Organisation*. Stuttgart: Schaffer-Poeschel Verlag.

KEY TERMS AND DEFINITIONS

Network Organizations: Network organizations (i.e. organizations – boundary-less firms or boundless organizations). These are dynamic, i.e. virtual companies, linked together at the base of the inter-organizational information systems, pursuing the aim to be successful in the area of given projects.

Virtual Organizations: Virtual organizations are a temporary consortium of partners from different organizations establishes to fulfill a value-adding task, for example a product or service to a customer

Virtual Laboratory: A virtual laboratory is an interactive online environment established so as to create and channel simulations and experiments in a certain science field. It is an environment designed for working in teams from different locations and creates opportunities for cooperation in research and development.

Living Lab: A living lab is an R&D methodology for identifying, validating and finding solutions to complex problems by including a real-life environment. In such an environment, product and service innovation is carried out, tested and introduced.

Corporate Governance: Corporate governance can be defined as s system by which companies are strategically directed, integratively managed and holistically controlled in an entrepreneurial and ethical way in a manner appropriate to each particular context.

Chapter 16
New Forms of Work in the Light of Globalization in Software Development

Darja Smite
Blekinge Institute of Technology, Sweden; University of Latvia and Riga Information Technology Institute, Latvia

Juris Borzovs
University of Latvia and Riga Information Technology Institute, Latvia

ABSTRACT

Globalization in software development introduced significant changes in the way organizations operate today. Software is now produced by team members from geographically, temporally and culturally remote sites. Organizations seek benefits that global markets offer and face new challenges. Naturally resistant to change, these organizations often do not realize the necessity for tailoring existing methods for distributed collaboration. Our empirical investigation shows a great variety in the ways organizations distribute responsibilities across remote sites and conclude that these can be divided into two main categories: joint collaboration that requires investments in team building and independent collaboration that requires investments in knowledge management and transfer. Finally, we discuss practices that are applied in industry to overcome these challenges and emphasize necessity to fully understand the pros and cons of different ways to organize distributed software projects before starting a project in this new environment.

INTRODUCTION

Recognized as the phenomenon of the 21st century (Friedman, 2005), globalization of the world economies brought significant changes to nearly all industries, including information technology (IT) and, in particular, software development. Global software work originates from IT outsourcing that is recognized as a natural evolution of how the global market operates today (Minevich et al, 2005).

Tight budgets, shortage in resources and time has motivated many companies to start looking for partners outside. Accordingly, outsourcing and especially offshoring (relocation of business processes to a lower cost country) have become components of a new global paradigm that is based on the selection

DOI: 10.4018/978-1-60566-890-1.ch016

of appropriate and strategic technologies, skills and resources with the strongest potential and the lowest cost within the global marketplace.

The decision to source software development to an overseas firm is looked at frequently in simple economic terms - it's cheaper, and skilled labor is easier to find (Carmel et al, 2005). The list of assumed benefits of global software engineering (GSE) also includes the necessity of reaching mobility in resources, obtaining extra knowledge through deploying the most talented people around the world, speeding time-to-market, increasing operational efficiency, improving quality, expanding through acquisitions, reaching proximity to market and many more. However, a recent empirical investigation shows that these benefits are neither clear-cut nor can their realization be taken for-granted as the GSE literature may lead one to believe (Conchúir et al, 2006). After a decade of experimentations companies come to realize that blind cost reduction strategies tend to fail. And the reason for this is distinction between manufacturing of goods and intellectual work.

It is not a secret that manufacturing has spread globally, and even branded products are nowadays developed by emerging nations. Software industry follows this trend and leads towards mass-production of software components following standardized product-line approaches. India and China became well known phenomenally growing software development centers. Smaller nations are also competing with each other for their best deals from the world leading contractors.

However, in contradiction to manufacturing, distribution of intellectual work is not as easy as it may seem. No matter how much companies try to industrialize software development processes by developing small pieces that would be integrated into a product at the end, the process of software development significantly depend on human interaction. In contrast to other engineering disciplines, where actual development is based on stable plans and technical designs, software engineering is suffering from rapid changes in requirements throughout the development life cycle. And if a co-located team can cope with uncertainty and changes more effectively, distribution of software life cycle activities among team members separated by contextual, organizational, cultural, temporal, and geographical boundaries introduces significant difficulties in managing interdependencies. Virtual and often asynchronous environment that characterize globally distributed projects affect the way team members interact and communicate and form an iceberg of problems that are often hidden to an unfamiliar eye.

BACKGROUND

The main challenges of global software engineering are caused by the uniqueness of working environment and are not related to technical challenges that project managers are used to overcome. These challenges are brought by geographic, temporal and cultural distance between the global software team members. Related studies recognize that the key areas of concern and major sources of overhead caused by these barriers are concentrated around communication, coordination and control activities (Ågerfalk et al, 2005).

Communication in globally distributed projects is troubled by temporal and geographic distance. A lack of working hour overlap leads to asynchronous interaction and sequential delays in information turnaround. Geographic distance affects the ways of interaction. Computer-mediated communication is much poorer than personal contact or even a phone conversation. However the later are costly and thus often not considered in global projects. Distance between the remote sites affects the amount of interaction too. Frequency of communication decreases with the distance among the team members (Carmel, 1999). Issues that are easily discussed and resolved at a cup of coffee in the corporate kitchen often hang in inbox for several days. Poor socialization, lack of frequent feedback, and unpredictability in communication often leads to lacking trust among the team members (Moe et al, 2008). Empirical study of speed and communication in globally distributed software development suggests that distributed work items appear to take about 2.5 times as long to complete as similar items where all the work is colocated due to interdependencies between the people involved in the project (Herbsleb et al, 2003). Moreover, empirical studies indicate an exponential decrease in productivity as dispersion increases. Thus, global environment is a challenge for developing an effectively performing software team.

Coordination of work between the remote sites is also challenged by separation. Task deconstruction and allocation becomes more complex due to lacking proximity and increasing complexity of maintaining interdependencies between the remote sites working together. Research agenda demand exploring whether product decoupling can successfully reduce coordination challenges at the same time without sacrificing the essence of teamwork (Powell et al, 2004). On one hand, related research suggests that coordination and performance will improve, if distributed team members are decoupled, which will automatically decrease the necessity to synchronize efforts and minimize the amount of communication needed to perform the tasks (Ramesh et al, 2002). This can be achieved through e.g. task decomposition using feature-oriented task allocation strategies and thus introducing coordination through standardization of low-level work processes as suggested by McChesney and Gallagher (McChesney et al, 2004). On the other hand, Conchúir et al (2006) found that, while the modularization of work can be effective in reducing the required level of cross-site communications, it might also be an obstacle to the creation of a sense of cross-site teamness. Moreover, their empirical investigation shows that there are different approaches to task modularization and these may lead to advantages as well as disadvantages (Conchúir et al 2006). Another emerging trend to address coordination and communication challenges is introduction of agile methods in distributed software teams to encouraging coordination based on mutual adjustment. Empirical studies show that agile practices are found to be useful for reducing communication, coordination, and control problems that have been associated with distributed work (Holmström et al, 2006).

Control of the remote sites in globally distributed software development projects can be characterized by lack of transparency and computer-mediation of the processes. Computer-mediated, geographic and temporal separation leads to breakdown in control and can easily paralyze managers in their daily supervision. Thus global project managers often feel insecure and tend to overly supervise the remote team members. However, lack of trust and direct supervision as a result of this insecurity is found to have a negative effect on team performance (Moe et al, 2008).

These are only few examples of challenges that are brought by various aspects of distance and diversity – challenges that are inherited in global software engineering environment. Though co-located or in-house software development life cycle management has already achieved certain maturity, globalization requires new processes, methods, and tools to be implemented. Solutions that have been applied in co-located teams to overcome similar problems, do not have expected outcome when team members work in separation. Thus, achieving global project success is not an easy task. Furthermore, a high increase in required resources is often caused by untimely or inadequate reaction to problems such as too overhead of coordination and communication, rigorous documentation and standardization of the processes, as well as extra travel and training of the team members that tend do grow along with an increasing attrition. Moreover, projects that face a productivity decrease caused by incapable developers from overseas are actually fewer than projects run by unprepared managers. Problems associated with distribution may jeopardize a project and thus have to be monitored on a regular basis. Managers have to be aware that different ways of organizing distributed software work can lead to more effective or less effective performance. Thus a deep understanding of alternative ways of collaboration is very important.

FORMS OF WORK IN DISTRIBUTED PROJECTS: CASE STUDY

Empirical Background

In this chapter we share experience and reflections from empirical investigation of different forms of work practiced by an international software house that provides software development outsourcing services. The investigated entity of the software house is located in Latvia and was established in the late 80s and changed its owners and structure several times. It has been oriented towards the international market and achieved ISO 9001:2000 certified quality management. At the time of our empirical investigation the organization had successfully accomplished more than 200 projects both in Latvia, Western Europe and Scandinavia, and employed over 380 employees. For confidentiality reasons we do not disclose the name of the company.

Our conclusions discussed in this chapter are based on a survey of 38 distributed projects, field observations and interviews conducted with project managers and team members involved in distributed projects. In this chapter we illustrate different work-partitioning approaches used by the studied projects and discuss factors that affect alternatives and the effect of each form of work. At the end we share recommendations gained from practitioners.

Collaboration Models

We analyze different form of work based on investigation of remote site involvement in software development activities. In particular, our aim was to understand whether the remote sites were engaged in independent activities or worked jointly on completion of software development activities. We differentiate two major sites involved in collaboration – the investigated organization, which we call supplier, and its customers that engage outsourcing service suppliers in distributed collaboration.

By the means of a survey we received data from 38 distributed projects indicating different collaboration models. We have identified 19 different models out of 38 investigated projects. In addition, we have also gathered qualitative measurements of success and failure of each model; however, our conclusions cannot be generalized due to statistical insignificance. Nonetheless, investigation of different collaboration models supports conclusions on different forms of work and their variations based on the level of remote site involvement (see Table 1).

The investigated collaboration models can be divided into four different forms of work:

- Involvement of supplier in joint activities (M1-M4);
- Outsourcing of selected activities with some level of joint performance (M5-M11);
- Outsourcing without joint performance (M12-M17);
- Independent remote development (M18-M19).

Motivated by market pressures, cost saving strategies and lack of awareness of global threats, the most frequently met collaboration type is outsourcing without joint performance. Accordingly, the most frequent collaboration model is sending coding activities to a remote supplier (followed by 5 projects – M5, M6, M7) or sending one or several other activities to a remote supplier (followed by 5 projects – M8, M9, M10, M11).

There are many projects with mixed distribu-

Table 1. Different Forms of Work

Nr.	Involvement of remote sites in software development activities				No of Projects
	System Analysis	Design	Implementation	Testing	
M1	jointly	jointly	jointly	jointly	3
M2	customer	customer	jointly	jointly	1
M3	customer	jointly	jointly	customer	2
M4	customer	customer	jointly	customer	1
M5	[no information]	[no information]	supplier	[no information]	2
M6	[no information]	[no information]	supplier	customer	1
M7	customer	customer	supplier	customer	5
M8	customer	customer	customer	supplier	1
M9	customer	customer	supplier	supplier	3
M10	customer	supplier	supplier	supplier	1
M11	customer	supplier	supplier	customer	5
M12	customer	customer	supplier	jointly	1
M13	customer	supplier	supplier	jointly	2
M14	jointly	jointly	supplier	supplier	3
M15	customer	jointly	supplier	jointly	2
M16	customer	jointly	supplier	customer	1
M17	customer	jointly	supplier	supplier	1
M18	jointly	supplier	supplier	supplier	1
M19	supplier	supplier	supplier	jointly	1

tion of activities – joint and independent performance. There are 6 projects with dominance of the customer independence (M2, M3, M4, M12, and M16) and 8 projects with supplier independence dominating (M13, M14, M17, M18, and M19). Full outsourcing projects, especially the most extreme representatives of this type of collaboration, don't appear among the investigated projects, because there is no process distribution. Accordingly these projects do not fit the phenomenon under study. However, variations of independent remote development appear (followed by only 2 projects).

And finally, joint performance between the partners is experienced by 3 projects (M1).

Factors Affecting Lifecycle Distribution

Empirical observations and interviews with practitioners help to derive the following list of factors affecting lifecycle distribution in global projects.

- Motives for going global. The main motives for organizations to switch to remote software service supplier often determine the selection of lifecycle distribution. Accordingly, organizations aiming to decrease costs usually send independent pieces of work to remote suppliers, whereas organizations aiming to gain extra knowledge or workforce usually engage remote sites in joint performance to fill the competence gaps.

Table 2. Problems Associated with Different Forms of Work

Teamwork Challenges	Knowledge Transfer Challenges
• Lack of teamness • Uncooperative behavior • Lack of trust • Inability of synchronous work and communication due to temporal distance • Lack of specific tool support that facilitates distributed work	• Unwillingness to share knowledge and experience due to fear of job loss • Lack of trust • Insufficient detail of requirements specification and task descriptions • Lack of tools that support remote access and information exchange

- Level of experience with outsourcing. Our investigation shows that forms of work may change over time within one project or from project to project conducted among the collaborating partners. Organizations are also resistant to allocate responsibility for a large piece of work to a remote partner, when collaboration in new.

Teamwork Challenges vs. Knowledge Transfer Challenges

By the nature of each of the forms of work, we can conclude that projects managers have to balance between distributed teamwork challenges and distributed knowledge transfer challenges dependent on the chosen collaboration model. We have gathered experience from projects and discuss different problems associated with each of these approaches in the following table.

Lack of proximity and next-door closeness between the developers involved in the project makes it difficult to expect the remote developers acting as a joint co-located team without additional team building activities. Moe and Smite (2008) report the results of a multi-case study conducted in the same organization as described in this book. The study points out that although remote team members ought to form a joint team they often consider distribution as team separator that hinders distributed members to form a joint team. Similarly, Casey and Richardson (2006) discuss un-cooperative behavior of remote team members who use e-mail as a weapon to publicly attack fellow team members. Treinen and Miller-Frost (2007) describe how remote teams exhausted by the asynchronous work over multiple temporal zones lay blame for overall project problems on each other. At the same time, team-building activities are often withdrawn due to limited budgets and thus building trust without "touch" becomes a challenge (Moe et al., 2008). In result, as previously discussed, empirical studies show that distributed teams are far much less productive than co-located teams (Herbsleb et al, 2003).

On the other hand, independent performance requires far much more effort and, subsequently, the cost of documenting requirements than practiced in co-located projects (Herbsleb et al, 2005). This shall be done to avoid inconsistency, misunderstandings, and rough transfer between the phases. Computer-mediated communication troubles clarification of inconsistent requirements over the distance (Smite, 2006). Empirical studies show that remote teams experience knowledge sharing barriers, such as unwillingness to share knowledge due to fear of job loss caused by outsourcing (Casey et al, 2006). Knowledge management is also challenged by technical infrastructure and inability to access information from remote locations (Oshri et al, 2007).

RECOMMENDATIONS TO PRACTITIONERS

Areas of Improvement

Despite the popularity of global software engineering, no research could determine the exact recipe for effective outsourcing performance (Loh et al, 1995). The results of our investigation indicate that there is a great variety of ways to organize distributed work. Process distribution and remote partner involvement decisions are related to different factors such as previous experience and reasons for outsourcing. Thus there might be no silver bullet or "one-fits-all" solutions to address the needs of every organization that is engaged in distributed software development. Moreover, the two alternative approaches – reliance on distributed teamwork and reliance on distributed knowledge transfer – have both their pros and cons. Hence, every organization shall consider the strengths and weaknesses of their distributed teams, and invest either in team building activities or knowledge management processes.

Analysis of global software engineering improvement areas leads to a conclusion that in both cases, whether it is necessity for team building or better knowledge management, improvements shall be developed and implemented across borders. This means that distributed project members shall put joint effort into process improvement initiatives. This however becomes an issue if collaboration involves team members from different organizations. Empirical studies show that supplier initiatives may face indifference from the customer site (Moe, 2008), but improvements focused only in one site may have a limited impact on overall project performance. Thus, joint effort into problem resolution is required.

Considerations

Our empirical investigation emphasizes the necessity of deliberate planning and analysis of alternatives for organizations engaging in global software engineering. Besides considering the two options of process distribution, we also recommend to consider the following issues:

- Don't underestimate the effect of diversity. Evaluate the risks associated with knowledge transition between remote locations taking into account diversity in background, education and work habits of the team members. Our experience shows that even organizations from the seemingly close locations, such as countries around Europe, may have different approaches to software engineering activities and thus, may lead to misaligned expectations and requirements of the remote sites. Thus, getting to know each other's ways of working are essential for successful collaboration.
- Pay attention to flexibility and adaptability. Diversity and inconsistency, in other words heterogeneity of the remote sites and their backgrounds may lead to various problems regarding collaboration. Despite the fact that organizations are naturally resistant to change, those that involve subcontractors should experiment and adjust the global product delivery models by decreasing the processes and interaction layers that "steal" time and consider changes focusing on improvements that would enable effective cooperation of distributed team members.

Corrective Actions

Interviews with experienced project managers and field observations form a set of practices that proved to be effective in an industrial context of the Latvian software house under study. Supplemented by related literature, our recommendations for organizing the work across remote sites are as follows.

- *Establish common philosophy and approach.* To mitigate diversity between the collaborating sites, project managers shall establish common philosophy and approach. This is related to work practices, as well as perception of certain aspects of lifecycle management, such as quality, process inputs, outputs and entry/exit criteria etc., and is essential for both types of collaboration whether it will be independent or joint performance. However, organizations shall not take this recommendation formally. Establishing common project standards is not the main challenge. The most important thing is to achieve a common understanding and commitment from the remote team members on how they will collaborate together.

- *Plan and perform small increments.* Pessimistic project managers often lack belief in ability to perform from a far-off location. This may negatively affect sites working in a globally distributed environment. Planning and performing small increments with frequent deliverables will provide supplier a chance to demonstrate ability to perform and assure project success. This shall contribute to establishment of cognition, mutual respect and trust.
- *Effective information- and knowledge-sharing mechanisms* are recognized as one of the key factors determining the ability to achieve benefits of global software enrineering (Holmström et al, 2006). Experienced project managers suggest temporal or permanent relocation of team members during critical project phases in order to bridge the remote sites more effectively. Our observations show that it is recommended and practiced to encourage systems analysts to travel to remote sites for more efficient requirements clarification. This recommendation is also supported by many related studies, which also call these 'liaisons' bridgeheads (Lings et al, 2007) or knowledge scouts (Dutoit et al, 2001).
- *Improve performance during the project, if it is lower than expected.* Ineffective global projects and remote team members performing below the expected productivity level is more than just a headache. Yet practice shows that productivity problems can be caused not only by poor performance and lack of knowledge of the supplier. Root of many problems may come from inappropriate project lifecycle management or infrastructure. Explore the actual sources of problems and mitigate them on a continuous basis.

FUTURE RESEARCH DIRECTIONS

It has been noted that communication, coordination and control are the three major challenges in distributed software development (Ågerfalk et al, 2005). It is important to understand the impact of different approaches to software project life cycle organization. In the light of empirical findings we see the need for investigating the advantages and disadvantages of the two studied approaches for organizing the work across remote sites, namely involvement of remote sites in independent or joint performance. Future research shall deepen our understanding of investments necessary to build an effective team from one hand, and the context of applicability for independent performance on the other hand. Moreover, we support Powell at al. (2004) and encourage to explore whether product decoupling can successfully reduce coordination challenges at the same time without sacrificing the essence of teamwork.

CONCLUSION

Global software engineering is certainly more than a temporary trend. It is a part of today's market with a stable growth in future. It requires new skills and will drive organizations to significant changes not only in respect to business forms, but also forms of work, habits, skill portfolios and corporate culture.

In this chapter we discuss results of our empirical investigation that uncovered a great variety of different ways to organize collaboration across remote locations. These collaboration types vary between full outsourcing and full partnership categorized into 4 major groups: involvement of supplier in joint activities; outsourcing of certain activities with some level of joint performance; outsourcing without joint performance; independent remote development. The major difference between different approaches is rooted in the level of supplier involvement in either independent or joint software development activities. It has been observed that joint collaboration require investments into team building and independent collaboration stresses necessity for knowledge transfer and proper work decoupling.

Due to market pressures, cost saving strategies and lack of awareness of global threats organizations often try to organize outsourcing software projects similarly to co-located projects, which inevitably leads to inconsiderate decisions regarding process distribution and failure. Moreover, naturally resistant to change, organizations involved in distributed work often do not realize the unique challenges of distributed projects till it is already too late to improve and save the project from failure. However, facing unmet expectations and hindered benefits, managers come to realize the need for process reengineering. In the study conducted by Casey and Richardson processes effective for single site development proved inadequate for a virtual software team environment (Casey et.al, 2006). Thus we emphasize necessity to fully understand the pros and cons of different ways to organize distributed software projects and timely preparations for new working environment.

REFERENCES

Ågerfalk, P. J., Fitzgerald, B., Holmström, H., Lings, B., Lundell, B., & Conchúir, E. Ó. (2005). A framework for considering opportunities and threats in distributed software development. In: *International Workshop on Distributed Software Development (DiSD)* (pp. 47-61), Austrian Computer Society

Carmel, E. (1999). *Global software teams: Collaborating across borders and time zones.* Upper Saddle River, NJ: Prentice-Hall

Carmel, E., & Tjia, P. (2005). *Offshoring information technology: Sourcing and outsourcing to a global workforce*. Cambridge University Press

Casey, V., & Richardson, I. (2006). Uncovering the reality within virtual software teams. In P. Kruchten et al. (Eds.), *International workshop on global software development for the practitioner* (pp. 66-72). New York: ACM.

Conchúir, E. Ó., Holmström, H., Ågerfalk, P. J., & Fitzgerald, B. (2006). Exploring the assumed benefits of global software development. In P. Fernandes et al. (Ed.), *IEEE International Conference on Global Software Engineering* (pp.159-168). Los Alamitos, CA: IEEE Computer Society.

Dutoit, A. H., Johnstone, J., & Bruegge, B. (2001). Knowledge scouts: Reducing communication barriers in a distributed software development project. In H. Jifeng et al. (Eds.), *Asia-Pacific Software Engineering Conference (APSEC)* (pp. 427-430). Los Alamitos, CA: IEEE Computer Society.

Friedman, T. L. (2005). *The world is flat: Brief history of the 21st Century*. New York: Farrar, Straus and Giroux.

Herbsleb, J., Paulish, D. J., & Bass, M. (2005). Global software development at Siemens: Experience from nine projects. In W. Griswold et al. (Eds.), *International Conference on Software Engineering (ICSE)* (pp. 524-533). New York: ACM.

Herbsleb, J. D., & Mockus, A. (2003). An empirical study of speed and communication in globally distributed software development. *IEEE Transactions on Software Engineering, 29*(6), 481–494. doi:10.1109/TSE.2003.1205177

Holmström, H., Fitzgerald, B., Ågerfalk, P. J., & Conchúir, E. Ó. (2006). Agile practices reduce distance in global software development. *Information Systems Management, 23*(3), 7–18. doi:10.1201/1078.10580530/46108.23.3.20060601/93703.2

Lings, B., & Lundell, B. Agerfalk, P. J., & Fitzgerald, B. (2007). A reference model for successful distributed development of software systems. In F. Paulisch et al. (Eds.), *International Conference on Global Software Engineering* (pp.130-139). Los Alamitos, CA: IEEE Computer Society.

Loh, L., & Venkatraman, N. (1995). An empirical study of information technology outsourcing: Benefits, risks, and performance implications. In *International Conference on Information Systems* (pp.277-288)

McChesney, I. R., & Gallagher, S. (2004). Communication and co-ordination Practices in Software Engineering Projects. *Information and Software Technology, 46*(7), 473–489. doi:10.1016/j.infsof.2003.10.001

Minevich, M., & Richter, F. J. (2005). *Global Outsourcing Report 2005*. New York: Going Global Ventures Inc.

Moe, N. B., & Smite, D. (2008). Understanding a lack of trust in global software teams: A multiple-case study. *Software Process Improvement and Practice, 13*(3), 217–231. doi:10.1002/spip.378

Oshri, I., Kotlarsky, J., & Willcocks, L. P. (2007). Global software development: Exploring socialization and face-to-face meetings in distributed strategic projects. *The Journal of Strategic Information Systems, 16*(1), 25–49. doi:10.1016/j.jsis.2007.01.001

Powell, A., Piccoli, G., & Ives, B. (2004). Virtual teams: A review of current literature and directions for future research. *The Data Base for Advances in Information Systems, 35*(1), 6–36.

Ramesh, V., & Dennis, A. (2002). The object-oriented team: Lessons for virtual team from global software development. In J. F. Nunamaker Jr. et al. (Eds.), *Annual Hawaii International Conference on System Sciences* (pp. 212-221). Los Alamitos, CA: IEEE Computer Society.

Smite, D. (2006). Global software development projects in one of the biggest companies in latvia: Is geographical distribution a problem. *Software Process Improvement and Practice, 11*(1), 61–76. doi:10.1002/spip.252

Treinen, J. J., & Miller-Frost, S. L. (2006). Following the sun: Case studies in global software development. *IBM Systems Journal, 45*(4), 773–783.

ADDITIONAL READING

Carmel, E. (1999). *Global software teams: Collaborating across borders and time zones.* Upper Saddle River, NJ: Prentice-Hall

Carmel, E., & Tjia, P. (2005). *Offshoring information technology: Sourcing and outsourcing to a global workforce.* Cambridge University Press

Friedman, T. L. (2005). *The world is flat: Brief history of the 21st Century.* New York: Farrar, Straus and Giroux

KEY TERMS AND DEFINITIONS

Outsourcing: Subcontracting one or more software development processes to an external supplier.

Offshoring: Relocation of one or more software development processes to a lower cost country within the same organization.

Global Software Engineering: Transition of common co-located software engineering to more complex software life cycle activities distributed among teams separated by various boundaries, such as contextual, organizational, cultural, temporal, geographical, and political.

Globally Distributed Software Engineering: See Global software engineering.

Forms of Work: Collaboration models that outline process distribution and partner involvement in global software engineering projects.

Teamwork: Joint involvement of remote partners in globally distributed software engineering project activities.

Knowledge Transfer: Explicit and implicit knowledge sharing among remote partners necessary for transition between activities in a software engineering project.

Chapter 17
Digital Confidence in Business: A Perspective of Information Ethics

Lichun Chiang
National Cheng Kung University, Taiwan

ABSTRACT

This chapter aims to understand the perceptions of employee information ethics using a company within the Environmental Protection Science Park in the southern part of Taiwan. The two purposes of this research are (1) to understand the environments of employees who understand information ethics, and (2) to clarify variables regarding information ethics which could provide a framework for policy controlling information ethics for businesses related to information technology (IT). The findings of this study show respondents understand the concept of unethical or illegal use of IT. All respondents perceived unauthorized behaviors, such as illegal downloads and reading other IT accounts without permission as unethical behaviors.

INTRODUCTION

In the last two decades, Information Technology (IT) has been applied in organizations, including public and private sectors. Researchers Hauptman (1988), Carr (2003) and Kostrewski and Oppenheim (1980) wrote articles on ethical issues for an information age. Kostrewski and Oppenheim (1980) pointed out user ethical issues, such as confidentiality of information and the many aspects of social responsibility of an information scientist. Hauptman (1988) and Carr (2003) showed ethical challenges in the context of trust in librarianship, and addressed user ethical problems related to privacy, information access, copyright and codes of ethics. The ethical problems in information work span the unauthorized use of work facilities, confidentiality of inquiries, bias in presented results and many aspects of social responsibility for an information scientist.

Information ethics has developed as a discipline in information science. It has evolved with many other disciplines as a confluence of the ethical concerns of media, journalism, library and information science, computer ethics (including cyberethics),

DOI: 10.4018/978-1-60566-890-1.ch017

management information systems, business and the internet. Certain IT ethical problems are intertwined with organization interests such as copyright and privacy (Schultz, 2006). Mathiesen (2004) addressed informational ethics and the value that information has in human life, and that information access via information technology is related to individual privacy, secrecy, censorship, and the rights enjoyed by owners of intellectual property (which involve restricting access to information.) Information ethics can provide an important conceptual framework to understand a multitude of ethical issues arising from new information technologies, such as privacy, intellectual property, filtering, censorship, and the digital divide (which is about who should have access to information and under what conditions.) Thus, information ethics is required to specify the relationship between people and information within an information society.

This study aims to examine the perceptions of employee information ethics by studying a company in the Environment Protection Science Park, Kaoshiung County, Taiwan. The two purposes of this research are (1) to understand those employees who understand information ethics in the workplace, and (2) to clarify variables in information ethics which could provide a framework for policy controlling information ethics on high-tech businesses. The questionnaires were designed after review of literature regarding information ethics, and sent to workers in the Epoch Energy Technology Corporation within the Science Park to help us better understand employee intentions for observing information ethics in the business field.

The study is divided into four parts. First is a review of the theoretical literature on ethics and information technology and a discussion of some supporting experimental evidence. Second is a presentation of the research method used in this paper, including the methodological approach, analysis variables, case sampling, and questionnaire design. The third section analyzes the research results and attempts to identify the influential factors and properties of information in the Science Park. The last section contains a discussion of the implications of these results and identifies future work that should be done in this area.

BACKGROUND

Information is intrinsically important and valuable (Van den Hoven, 1995; Floridi, 2006). Information Technologies have revolutionized information delivery in business, from its production and management to its consumption, thus deeply affecting our moral behaviors. As Cowton and Thomspon (2000:165) stated, "codes of conduct are one of the most visible features of business practice associated with business ethics." Ethics is concerned about what people should do and also referred to by 'morality,' 'value,' and 'justice, and it is associated with the value or goodness of things and situations and with the justness of institutions (Schultz, 2006) Ethics are related to particular professions often requiring a high level of education, skill, and intelligence, such as doctors in hospitals and computer experts in high tech companies. These professionals receive trust from society and have a responsibility to act in an ethical manner. Therefore, ethical rules follow from the existence of professions (Parker, 1968). User incentives to follow ethics are bookended between two moral attitudes: (1) the moralistic attitude according to which the quality of character of the member of society ought to be a central public concern and (2) the economic attitude means private vices come from public benefits; that is, the incentives are the aggregate outcomes of individual choices and not their motivation or moral quality (Grant, 2006). Ethical problems arise because they involve conflicts between different interests that cannot be resolved on the level of interests alone. Wu and Tsang (2008) studied factors of participant trust and institutional trust in the virtual communities, and found beneficial attraction and shared value as significant positive effects on building participant trust, and a significant positive effect on building institutional trust. Trust building influences commitment to virtual communities and willingness to share information.

When information technology has been created and applied in business organizations, businesses have increasingly relied on IT for their survival. Because business organizations use IT for office automation and accounting tasks, IT users in small businesses have been trained as sophisticated users of this new technology (Phukan & Dhillon, 2000; Capurro, 2008). When IT applications are more pervasive in organizations, many studies have questioned whether today's IT user is a responsible and ethical one (Maner, 1996; Phukan & Dhillon, 2000; Suter, et. al, 2004; Calluzzo & Cante, 2004; Kuo, et. al, 2006; Kaptein & Schwartz, 2008). In the mid 1970s, Maner created the term 'computer ethics' to discuss ethical problems transformed by information technology. Maner (1996) stated that "information ethics is an academic field in its own right with unique ethical issues that would not have existed if computer technology had not been invented" (p.137). Computers bring qualities of cost effectiveness, fast retrieval, and ease of manipulation. The information stored in computers may also have special characteristics such as malleability, coded, clonability, discreteness, and complexity. Maner (1996) provided three of main reasons for the study of information ethics: (1) to make us behave like responsible professionals, (2) to teach us how to avoid computer abuse and catastrophes, (3) to deal with the policy vacuums caused by the advance of computer technology. Accordingly, information ethics required two parts: (1) the analysis of the nature and social impact of information technology, and (2) the corresponding formulation and justification of policies for the ethical use of such technology (Moor, 1985). Moor used "information technology" as the subject matter to broadly include computers and associated technology, including software, hardware, and networks. Following Moor's viewpoints, Bynum and Rogerson (1989) identified computer ethics and analyzed the impacts of information technology on social and human values, such as freedom, democracy, knowledge, privacy, security and self-fulfillment. Therefore, computers involved in human conduct could create new ethical issues such as computer abuse or other catastrophes (Maner, 1996). Parker (1968:200) postulated that the code of information ethics was a helpful guide to the members of the profession and that the public expected competence, trustworthiness, and expeditious action, and their unethical actions were condemned and punished.

As a consequence of rapid IT growth, IT ethical standards are still evolving, creating a problematic situation. IT increases the capabilities of computers with easy and widely available Internet access which presents new ethical challenges (Molnar, Kletke & Chongwatpol, 2008). Parker et al. (1990) offered several reasons why ethical problems involving IT pose a special challenge: (1) using computers and data communications alters the relationship among people, for example, decreasing face-to-face interactions. (2) Information in electronic form is more 'fragile' than when it is on paper. The questions of property rights, plagiarism, piracy and privacy arising from use of the internet have become new ethical and legal issues. (3) Efforts to protect information integrity, confidentiality and availability often conflict with the benefits of information sharing. (4) The lack of widespread means of authorization and authentication exposes IT to unethical practices. The above challenges become new ethical issues. In 2003, the WSIS Executive Secretariat announced the Geneva Declaration concerning the "Ethical Dimensions of the Information Society (B10) as follows:

1. The Information Society should respect peace and uphold the fundamental values of freedom, equality, solidarity, tolerance, shared responsibility, and respect for nature.

2. We acknowledge the importance of ethics for the Information Society, which should foster justice, and the dignity and worth of the human person. The widest possible protection should be accorded to the family and to enable it to play its crucial role in society.
3. The use of Information Communication Technologies (ICTs) and content creation should respect human rights and fundamental freedoms of others, including personal privacy, and the right to freedom of thought, conscience, and religion in conformity with relevant international instruments.
4. All actors in the Information Society should take appropriate actions and preventive measures, as determined by law, against abusive uses of ICTs, such as illegal and other acts motivated by racism, racial discrimination, xenophobia, and related intolerance, hatred, violence, all forms of child abuse, including pedophilia and child pornography, and trafficking in, and exploitation of, human beings.

According to the above, information ethics involve fundamental ethical values, human rights and moral behaviors. Phukan and Dhillon (2000) studied the beliefs and attitudes of small- and medium-sized enterprises (SMEs) regarding the ethical use of information technology, and found a clear lack of awareness of basic ethical issues in US SMEs, such as software piracy and confidentiality of data. The participants did not seem to understand the importance of their moral and ethical responsibilities in the use of IT. Thus, the rules of information ethics are ineffective unless respected by the vast majority or all computer users (Bynum & Rogerson, 1996:134). Calluzzo and Cante (2004) discussed Ethics in Information Technology and Software Use among college students, and found that respondents thought "stealing computer software" to be highly unethical. Roma´n (2007) studied ethics of online retailing from the consumer's perspective and found security, privacy, non-deception and fulfillment/reliability as four factors strongly to influence online consumer satisfaction and trust.

Per the above mentioned illustrations, information ethics in this study are related to user confidence involved in ethical perceptions in the use of software, the internet, files/data download and so on. The ethical levels users perceive will influence user digital confidence in the cyber world.

USERS' PERCEPTIONS OF INFORMATION ETHICS IN THE WORKPLACES RESEARCH ISSUES

Ethics is a general term for concerns about what people should do. Based on the Geneva Declaration, Molnar, et. al, (2008), Maner (1996) and relative literature, information ethics is user confidence, moral values, behaviors and perceptions in using information technology, including computer equipment (hardware and software), documents, the Internet, email, and chat. The main question in this research is to explore employee perceptions of ethical behaviors and values in using IT related to equipment (including software and hardware) and relative business information in their workplace.

Accordingly, the questionnaire focused on demographic information of the respondents, such as education and working experience, and respondent perceptions regarding IT ethics. The bulk of the questions center on user attitude toward the usage of software, piracy, chat and the internet involving respondent awareness of information unethical issues, such as copying of software for others and confidentiality of data. Employee perceptions regarding information ethics possibly influence business secrecy, security and monitoring in the workplace, especially in high technology companies (Phukan and Dhillon, 2000). The study selected an international high tech company as the research object, the Epoch Energy

Table 1. Questionnaire Questions

A. How do you think your colleagues feel about the following question?	B. How do you feel about the following question?
Q1 Using MSN or Email for personal correspondence at the job	Q1 Using MSN or Email for personal correspondence at the job
Q2 Downloading database from the Internet for personal use	Q2 Downloading database from the Internet for personal use
Q3 Surfing data at the Internet at the job for personal demands	Q3 Surfing data at the Internet at the job for personal demands
Q4 Printing personal documents on the job	Q4 Printing personal documents on the job
Q5 Copying software from the job for personal use	Q5 Copying software from the job for personal use
Q6 Copying software from the job for a friends use	Q6 Copying software from the job for a friends use
Q7 Reading other's business e-mail	Q7 Reading other's business e-mail
Q8 Reading other's private e-mail	Q8 Reading other's private e-mail
Q9 Reading other's job files	Q9 Reading other's job files
Q10 Reading other's private files	Q10 Reading other's private files

Note: Each question is measured using a 5-item scale (+1: highly unethical, +2: unethical, +3: neutral, +4: ethical, and +5: highly ethical) in terms of individual perceptions of ethical behaviors in the workplace

Technology Corporation in the Science Park in Tainan. Epoch has developed a fuel generator for non-polluting, safe and economic application to protect our environment.

Research Method

Based in part on questionnaires designed by Calluzzo and Cante (2004) and Phukan and Dhillon (2000), the questionnaire in this study included demographic data, and 20 questions used to describe highly ethical or unethical behaviors in the working environments such as using software, chat, reading other's files and download data. (See Table 1) Each respondent is asked to evaluate each term twice: once for "colleague" and once for "self" in the workplace; that is, "How do you think your colleagues feel about the following question?" and second, "How do you feel about the following question?" The questionnaire's two-part structure was designed to assure of respondent confidence and honest answers. Each question is measured using a 5-item scale (+1: highly unethical, +3: neutral, and +5: highly ethical) in terms of individual perceptions related to ethical behaviors in the workplace (see Table 1). When answering the questionnaire, the respondents were assured that their individual responses would be held in confidence and used solely for academic purposes.

Employees using personal computers in Epoch were asked to participate in the study. In September 2008, the pilot questionnaire was sent to 8 IT related experts (Non-Epoch employees) to test its reliability. The composite reliability values of the two parts (for self and for colleague) are ranged from 0.60 to 0.69 (Cronbach $\alpha \geq .60$). In discussing the reliability of the measures, .60 is considered acceptable in an exploratory study (Hu & Bentler, 1995).

60 questionnaires were sent to participants working in Epoch (including China and Taiwan) from October 15 to November 5 in 2008. 48 valid questionnaires were returned (81.67%). This consisted of 31 employees working in Taiwan and 17 employees in China. The composite reliability values of the two parts (for self and for colleagues) are ranged from 0.83 to 0.86 (Cronbach $\alpha \geq .80$). The research analyses by gender and working place were performed using employee *t*-test to test the significance of the difference between two sample means on each of the 10 questions for "colleague" and for "self".

Table 2. Demographic Data (N=48)

Terms Frequency % Terms Frequency %
Sex Education
Male 27 56.30 High School 11 22.90
Female 21 43.70 University 31 64.60
Age (Years Old) Graduate School 6 12.50 21-25 14 29.20 Years of Employment
26-30 13 27.10 Less than 1 yr 22 45.80
31-35 11 22.90 1-3 yrs 14 29.20
36-40 4 8.30 4-6 yrs 3 10.40
41-45 4 8.30 7-9 yrs 2 6.30
46-50 1 2.10 10-12 yrs 1 4.20
51-55 0 0 13-15 yrs 0 0
56+ 1 2.10 16-18 yrs 1 2.10
Working Places 19+ yrs 1 2.10
China 16 33.30
Taiwan 32 66.70

RESEARCH ANALYSIS

From the demographic data shown in Table 2, 27 of respondents are males (56.30%) and 21 of them females (43.70%). For age, most ranged from 21 to 35 years old and 56.30% were 21 to 30 years old. 64.60% of respondents possessed a college degree. 11 Employees in China had high school degrees, and 5 employees had university degrees. In Taiwan, 26 employees had a bachelor degree, and 6 respondents had earned their master degrees. Regarding working experiences, 70% of respondents had been with the Epoch Company for less than 3 years.

Analysis by Gender

The results presented in Tables 3 and Table 4 will be discussed on the basis of the responses of (1) gender and (2) work place: China or Taiwan. Overall, the respondents perceived as 'unethical' concerning the nature of "Using MSN or Email for personal correspondence at the job" for both their colleagues and themselves. (question 1).

By gender, there was a significant difference between male and female responses for both locales in the direction of it being unethical (for colleagues, t=-1.39; for self, t=-1.80). Therefore, there are gender differences regarding ethical perceptions in using MSN or Email while working in the company. See Table 3.

Likewise, the overall sample felt unethical about the nature of "Downloading database from the Internet for personal use" (question 2). There is a significant difference between male and female respondents perceived unethical behaviors on the issue. There is no significant difference from the colleague's perspective (for colleagues, t = 0.11; for self, t = -1.12). On the behavior of "Surfing data at the Internet at the job for personal demands" (question 3), there was a difference between male and female responses where the behavior attained an unethical score from their self viewpoint (for colleagues, t = 0.03; for self, t = -0.66). Female employees seem to have higher ethical perceptions for themselves than males do.

On the behavior of "Printing personal documents on the job" (question 4), there was no significant difference at the 2% and 5% level between male and female responses in analyzing

Table 3. Results Analyzed by Gender

Q Mean Score Significance Mean Score Significance (N= 48)
For Colleague t-Value $t_{-0.05} t_{-0.02}$ For Self t-Value $t_{-0.05} t_{-0.02}$
Male Female 1.96 2.33 Male Female 1.96 2.33
1 1.93 2.43 -1.39 D ND 1.70 2.33 -1.80 D D
2 2.19 2.14 0.11 ND ND 1.93 2.33 -1.12 D ND
3 2.30 2.29 0.03 ND ND 2.04 2.29 -0.66 D ND
4 1.63 1.67 -0.15 ND ND 1.78 1.95 -0.52 ND ND
5 1.59 1.62 -0.10 ND ND 1.89 1.57 1.07 ND ND
6 1.41 1.43 -0.10 ND ND 1.37 1.52 -0.71 ND ND
7 1.33 1.62 -0.97 ND ND 1.37 1.67 -1.05 D ND
8 1.19 1.14 0.32 ND ND 1.26 1.19 0.32 ND ND
9 1.59 1.67 -0.26 ND ND 1.70 1.71 -0.36 ND ND
10 1.26 1.19 0.40 ND ND 1.22 1.14 0.45 ND ND

Note: D = Difference; ND = No Difference. The total number of male is 27; that of female is 21.

ethical behaviors of question 4 (for colleagues, t = -0.15; for self, t = -0.52). An "unethical" score was attained by gender on the behavior of "Copying software from the job for personal use" (question 5) and "Copying software from the job for a friends use" (question 6). There was no significant difference between male and female responses in discussing both issues (for colleagues, t = -0.10; for self, t = 1.07; respectively for colleagues, t = -0.10; for self, t = -0.71).

Table 4. Results by Working Places

Q Mean Score Significance Mean Score Significance (N = 48)
For Colleague t-Value $t_{-0.05} t_{-0.02}$ For Self t-Value $t_{-0.05} t_{-0.02}$
China Taiwan 1.96 2.33 China Taiwan 1.96 2.33
1 1.69 2.38 -1.84 D D 1.38 2.28 -2.55 D D
2 2.38 2.06 0.78 ND ND 2.19 2.06 0.32 ND ND
3 2.63 2.13 1.29 ND ND 2.19 2.13 0.16 ND ND
4 1.44 1.75 -1.23 D D 1.88 1.84 0.89 ND ND
5 1.81 1.50 1.09 D ND 1.94 1.66 0.90 ND ND
6 1.25 1.50 -1.16 D ND 1.31 1.50 -0.82 D ND
7. 1.25 1.56 -1.01 ND ND 1.25 1.63 -1.27 D ND
8 1.13 1.19 -0.43 ND ND 1.31 1.16 0.56 ND ND
9 1.63 1.63 0 ND ND 1.81 1.66 0.51 ND ND
10 1.25 1.22 0.17 ND ND 1.25 1.16 0.50 ND ND

Note: D = Diffidence; ND = No Difference. The total number of China is 16; that of Taiwan is 32.

In discussing the ethical behavior of "Reading other's business e-mail" (question 7), there is a significant effect on male female perceptions from the individual perspective, but insignificant effect on gender from colleague's perspective (for colleagues, t = -1.39; for self, t = -1.80). On the behavior of "Reading other's private e-mail" (question 8), "Reading other's job files" (question 9) and "Reading other's private files" (question 10), there are no significant effect on gender either from colleague's perspective or from the individual perspective. (See Table3)

Analysis by Work Place

As the results shown in Table 4, the respondents perceived self and their colleagues as 'unethical' regarding the ethical nature of "Using MSN or Email for personal correspondence at the job" (question 1). By working place, there was a significant difference of ethical behaviors between employees working in China and Taiwan in using MSN for personal correspondence (for colleagues, t = -1.84; for self, t = -2.55). Likewise, the overall sample thought it unethical to "Download database from the Internet for personal usage" (question 2). According to this issue, there is no difference between IT ethical perceptions in China and Taiwan (for colleagues, t = 0.78; for self, t = 0.32).

In discussing the behavior of "Surfing data at the Internet at the job for personal demands" (question 3), there are no significant differences between employees working in China and in Taiwan in that both were in the direction of it being unethical (for colleagues, t = 1.29; for self, t = 0.16). On the behavior of "Printing personal documents on the job" (question 4), for the colleague's perspective, there is significant difference at the 2% and 5% level between China and Taiwan. There is no significant difference from the individual viewpoint in analyzing ethical behaviors of question 4 (for colleagues, t = -1.23; for self, t = -0.89). An "unethical" score was attained by working place on the behavior of "Copying software from the job for personal use" (question 5). For colleagues, there is significantly different ethical perceptions between China and Taiwan (for colleagues, t = 1.09; for self, t = 0.90). In discussing "Copying software from the job for a friends use" (question 6), there are significantly different IT ethical perceptions between employees working in China from the colleague's and individual viewpoints (for colleagues, t = -1.16; for self, t = -0.82). .

A shift in response towards "highly unethical" was noted for both "Reading other's business" (question 7) and for "Reading other's private e-mail" (question 8) for both the overall sample and by gender. There are differences on question 7 from colleague's perspective but no difference from individual viewpoint (for colleagues, t = -1.01; for self, t = -1.27). For question 8, there is no significant difference between employees working in China and Taiwan in the direction of it being unethical (for colleagues, t = -1.39; for self, t = -1.80). Upon working places, respondents in China and Taiwan have significant different insights about ethical behaviors in discussing reading other's emails. For the behaviors of "Reading other's job files" (question 9) and "Reading other's private files" (question 10), there were no differences between employees working in China and Taiwan. (See Table 4)

As the results shown, there were differences between male and female employee responses on downloading database (Q1), surfing data (Q2), reading other's working emails (Q7). Likewise, male respondents have higher insights into what IT ethics is than females do. Employees working in Taiwan generally have different information ethical judgments from those who do in China in discussing issues related to downloading database (Q1), printing personal documents on the job (Q 4), and copying software from the job for personal use or for a friends use (Q 5 & Q 6). Generally, employees in Epoch were quite ethical in those behaviors associated with personal privacy, the Internet or data access.

Solutions and Recommendations

The findings of this study show respondents understand what the unethical or illegal use of IT is. All respondents perceived unauthorized behaviors, such as illegal downloads and read other's IT accounts or email on the job as the unethical behaviors, as Calluzzo and Cante (2004) studies. There is a noticeable finding that all respondents pay more attention for self-discipline of ethical behaviors than for other colleagues. That is, they are willing to control their own behavior of IT use instead of criticizing a colleague's behaviors concerning IT use. Further, by gender, male respondents show lower personal ethical values than females in using information technology, such as access to the Internet, data download or surfing, coinciding with Kuo, Lin, and Hsu's (2007) study. Conversely, regarding colleagues, female employees have lower ethical expectations than males in the working place. Female employees may have more lenient ethics than males do when their colleagues do actions such as download and read IT accounts belonging to others.

For working place, there are different information ethical concepts between employees working in China and in Taiwan, especially in the issues related to downloading database, printing personal documents, copying software and reading other's email. From the colleague's perspective, employees in Taiwan have higher ethical perceptions to judge their colleagues than those who work in china. The reasons for this may include factors such as the educational level and the years of employment. As the above mentioned results, those workers in China have lower education than those who work in Taiwan. Therefore, an educational background, the working environment and training program may be influential factors to establish IT ethical codes of conduct, as Bynum and Rogerson (1989), Lozano, Folguera and Arenas (2003) and Roma´n (2007) suggested.

In sum, participants have confidence in self-discipline when asking their viewpoint about their own ethical behaviors of IT personal use. Employees view their colleagues' ethical behaviors less strict than their own behavior. It is possible that employees may allow their colleagues to use IT in unethical ways.

FUTURE RESEARCH DIRECTIONS

This paper focused on describing information ethics in business especially on ethical behaviors of employees regarding IT use on the job. This study was to help understand the effects of gender, education and workplace difference on information ethics. In taking this research forward, the author hopes to extend and use the initial findings presented in this study conduct focused in-depth interviews with some of the survey participants to explore the relationship between digital confidence and information ethics in business. In a subsequent stage, the author wishes to conduct a similar research for large IT or non-IT enterprises in China and Taiwan to compare and contrast the extent of IT related ethical practices based on gender, education, specialty and workplace in different businesses.

CONCLUSION

In the era of the internet, digital confidence in the virtual community has become an integral part of information ethics. Without confidence or trust in using IT, users cannot believe reliability or truthfulness of data accessed from the cyber world. IT ethics involves ethical problems for users to avoid doing something they feel is unethical. Moreover, information ethics is required to specify the relationship between users and information technology in an information society.

According to the results shown in this study, a high tech company may need to take notice of individual male ethical behaviors. For female employees, the company has to remind them of legal rules for instances such as downloading documents for their colleagues and reading other's IT accounts or copying software in the workplace. The company has to promote information to elevate ethical perceptions of employees working in China both from individual and colleague's viewpoints. Therefore, the training programs related to information ethics for employees are important in the improvement of information ethics in the high tech companies.

In order to avoid unethical situations, an ethical education is particularly useful in the workplace where employees can have a positive influence in each other. Ethical education will be more effective if it can factor the self-efficacy of the Internet users into account and provide some stimulus to those employees abiding by information ethics.

REFERENCES

Bynum, T. W., & Rogerson, S. (1996). Introduction and overview: Global information ethics. *Science and Engineering Ethics*, *2*(2), 131–136. doi:10.1007/BF02583548

Calluzzo, V. J., & Cante, C. J. (2004). Ethics in information technology and software use. *Journal of Business Ethics*, *51*, 301–312. doi:10.1023/B:BUSI.0000032658.12032.4e

Capurro, R. (2008). Information ethics for and from Africa. *Journal of the American Society for Information Science and Technology*, *59*(7), 1162–1170. doi:10.1002/asi.20850

Carr, D. W. (2003). An ethos of trust in information service. In B. Rockenbach, & T. Mendina. *Ethics and electronic information: A festschrift for Stephen Almagno* (pp.45-52). Jefferson, North Carolina: McFarland & Company, Inc.

Cowton, C., & Thomspon, P. (2000). Do codes make a difference? The case of bank lending and the environment. *Journal of Business Ethics*, *24*, 165–178. doi:10.1023/A:1006029327264

Floridi, L. (2006). Information technologies and the tragedy of good will. *Ethics and Information Technology*, *8*(4), 253–262. doi:10.1007/s10676-006-9110-6

Grant, R. W. (2006). Ethics and incentives: A political approach. *The American Political Science Review*, *100*(1), 29–39. doi:10.1017/S0003055406061983

Hu, L. T., & Bentler, P. M. (1995). Evaluating model fit. In R. H. Hoyle (ed.), *Structural equation modeling: Concepts, issues, and applications* (pp.76-99). Thousand Oaks, CA.: Sage.

Kaptein, M., & Schwartz, M. S. (2008). The effectiveness of business codes: A critical examination of existing studies and the development of an integrated research model. *Journal of Business Ethics*, *77*, 111–127. doi:10.1007/s10551-006-9305-0

Kuo, F. Y., Lin, C. S., & Hsu, M. H. (2007). Assessing gender differences in computer professionals' self-regulatory efficacy concerning information privacy practices. *Journal of Business Ethics*, *73*, 145–160. doi:10.1007/s10551-006-9179-1

Lozano, J. M., Folguera, C., & Arenas, D. (2003). Setting the context: The role information technology in a business ethics course based on face-to-face dialogue. *Journal of Business Ethics*, *48*, 99–111. doi:10.1023/B:BUSI.0000004381.51505.67

Maner, W. (1996). Unique ethical problems in information technology. *Science and Engineering Ethics*, *2*(2), 137–154. doi:10.1007/BF02583549

Mathiesen, K. (2004). What is Information Ethics? *ACM SIGCAS Computers and Society, 34*(1).

Molnar, K. K., Kletke, M. G., & Chongwatpol, J. (2008). Ethics vs. IT Ethics: Do undergraduate students perceive a difference? *Journal of Business Ethics*, *83*, 657–671. doi:10.1007/s10551-007-9646-3

Moor, J. H. (1985). What is computer ethics? *Metaphilosophy*, *16*(4), 266–275. doi:10.1111/j.1467-9973.1985.tb00173.x

Parker, D. B. (1968). Rules of ethics in information processing. *Communications of the ACM, 11*(3), 198–201. doi:10.1145/362929.362987

Parker, D. B., Swope, S., & Baker, B. (1990). Ethical conflicts in information and computer science, technology, and business. Wellesley, MA: QED Information Sciences, Inc.

Phukan, S., & Dhillon, G. (2000). Ethics and information technology use: A survey of US based SMEs. *Information Management & Computer Security*, *8*(5), 239–243. doi:10.1108/09685220010353907

Roma'n, S. (2007). The ethics of online retailing: A scale development and validation from the consumers' perspective. *Journal of Business Ethics*, *72*, 131–148. doi:10.1007/s10551-006-9161-y

Schultz, R. A. (2006). *Contemporary issues in ethics and information technology*. Hershey, PA: IRM Press.

Suter, T. A., Kopp, S. W., & Hardesty, D. M. (2004). The relationship between general ethical judgments and copying behavior at work. *Journal of Business Ethics*, *55*, 61–70. doi:10.1007/s10551-004-1779-z

van den Hoven, M. J. (1995). Equal access and social justice: Information as a primary good. *ETHICOMP*, *95*, 1–17.

World Summit on the Information Society. (2003). The Geneva declaration of principles and plan of action. Geneva: WSIS Executive Secretariat. Retrieved from http://www.itu.int/wsis/docs/geneva/official/dop.html

Wu, J. J., & Tsang, A. S. L. (2008). Factors affecting members' trust belief and behaviour intention in virtual communities. *Behaviour & Information Technology*, *27*(2), 115–125. doi:10.1080/01449290600961910

ADDITIONAL READING

Bahry, D., Kosolapov, M., Kozyreva, P., & Wilson, R. K. (2005). Ethnicity and trust: Evidence from Russia. *American Politics Research*, *99*(4), 521–532.

Berg, J., Dickhaut, J., & Mccabe, K. (1995). Trust, reciprocity, and social history. *Games and Economic Behavior*, *10*, 122–142. doi:10.1006/game.1995.1027

Briggs, P., Burford, B., De Angeli, A., & Lynch, P. (2002). Trust in online advice. *Social Science Computer Review*, *20*, 321–332.

Capurro, R. (2008). Hermeneutics facing the Information Enframing . *ACM Ubiquity*, *9*(8), 79–85.

Chaiken, S., & Maheswaran, D. (1994). Heuristic processing can bias systematic processing: effects of source credibility, argument ambiguity, and task importance on attitude judgment. *Journal of Personality and Social Psychology*, *66*, 460–473. doi:10.1037/0022-3514.66.3.460

Clear, T., Gotterbarn, D., & Kwan, C. (2006). Managing software requirements risks with software development impact statements. *New Zealand Journal of Applied Computing*, 70-77. Retrieved from http://www.naccq.ac.nz/conference05/proceedings_04/gotterbarn.pdf

Cooper, T. L. (Ed.). (2001). *Handbook of administrative ethics*. New York: Marcel Dekker, Inc.

Corritore, C. L., Kracher, B., & Wiedenbeck, S. (2003). Online trust: concepts, evolving themes, a model. *International Journal of Human-Computer Studies*, *58*, 737–758. doi:10.1016/S1071-5819(03)00041-7

Davis, D. L., & Vitell, S. J. (1992). The ethical problems, conflicts and beliefs of small business information personnel. *Journal of Computer Information Systems*, *22*(4), 53–57.

Dutton, W. H. (2004). *Social transformation in the information society*. Paris: UNESCO Publications for the WSIS.

Dyer, J. H., & Chu, W. (2003). The role of trustworthiness in reducing transaction costs and improving performance: Empirical evidence from the United States, Japan, and Korea.

Earle, T. C., Siegrist, M., & Gutscher, H. (2002). *Trust and confidence: A Dual-Mode model of cooperation*. Western Washington University, WA, USA. Unpublished Manuscript.

Fritzsche, D. J. (2005). Business ethics: A global and managerial perspective (2nd ed.). New York: McGraw-Hill Higher Education.

Gambetta, D. (Ed.). (1988). *Trust: Making and breaking cooperative relations*. New York: Basil Blackwell.

Glover, S. H. (2002). Gender differences in ethical decision making. *Women in Management Review*, *17*(5/6), 217–227. doi:10.1108/09649420210433175

Hardin, R. (2002). *Trust and trustworthiness*. New York: Russell Sage Foundation.

Jones, T. (1987). Ethical decision making by individuals in organizations: An issue-contingent Model. *Academy of Management Review*, *16*(2), 231–248.

Klang, M. (2001). Who do you trust? Beyond encryption, secure e-business. *Decision Support Systems*, *31*, 293–301. doi:10.1016/S0167-9236(00)00140-8

Marshall, K. P. (1999). Has technology introduced new ethical problems? *Journal of Business Ethics*, *19*(1), 81–90. doi:10.1023/A:1006154023743

Mcknight, D. H., Cummings, L. L., & Chervany, N. L. (1998). Initial trust formation in new organizational relationships. *Academy of Management Review*, *23*, 473–490. doi:10.2307/259290

... *Organization Science*, *14*(1), 57–68. doi:10.1287/orsc.14.1.57.12806

Peslak, A. R. (2007). A review of the impact of ACM code of conduct on information technology moral judgment and intent. *Journal of Computer Information Systems*, *47*(3), 1–10.

Reid, R. A., Thompson, J. K., & Logsdon, J. L. (1992). Knowledge and attitudes of management students toward software piracy. *Journal of Computer Information Systems*, *23*(1), 46–51.

Wang, Y. D., & Emurian, H. H. (2005). An overview of online trust: Concepts, elements, and implications. *Computers in Human Behavior*, *21*, 105–125. doi:10.1016/j.chb.2003.11.008

Yamgishi, T., & Yamagishi, M. (1994). Trust and commitment in the United States and Japan. *Motivation and Emotion*, *18*, 130–166.

KEY TERMS AND DEFINITIONS

Business Ethics: A form of applied ethics that examines ethical principles and moral or ethical problems that arise in a business environment.

Gender Differences: A distinction of biological and/or physiological characteristics typically associated with either males or females of a species in general.

Information Technology: As defined by the Information (ITAA), IT is the study, design, development, implementation, support or management of computer-based information systems, particularly software applications and computer hardware. IT deals with the use of electronic computers and computer software to convert, store, protect, process, transmit, and securely retrieve information.

Information Society: A society in which the creation, distribution, diffusion, use, integration and manipulation of information is a significant economic, political, and cultural activity.

Information Ethics: The field that investigates the ethical issues arising from the development and application of information technologies. It provides a critical framework for considering moral issues concerning informational privacy, moral agency (e.g. whether artificial agents may be moral), new environmental issues (especially how agents should one behave in the infosphere), problems arising from the life-cycle (creation, collection, recording, distribution, processing, etc.) of information (especially ownership and copyright, digital divide). Information Ethics is therefore strictly related to the fields of computer ethics and the philosophy of information.

Software Piracy: The unauthorized copying of software. Most retail programs are licensed for use at just one computer site or for use by only one user at any time. By buying the software, you become a *licensed user* rather than an owner (see End-User License Agreement). You are allowed to make copies of the program for backup purposes, but it is against the law to give copies to friends and colleagues.

Trust: Relationship of reliance. It allows us to form relationships with others and to depend on others.

For Love: For advice, for help with our plumbing, or what have you. Trust always involves the risk that the trusted person will not pull through for the trusting person.

ENDNOTE

1 (Sources from Wikipedia, the free encyclopedia)

Chapter 18
Ethics of Information in Distributed Business Environment

Adriana Schiopoiu Burlea
University of Craiova, Romania

ABSTRACT

The aim of this chapter is to examine some of the issues of ethics related to information in DBE. The ethical issue of what is moral to do in order to optimize the use of information in DBE is dealt with. The varied ways of integrating and putting into the practice information in DBE is discussed as well as the great variety of ethical approaches. In the field of ethics of information in DBE we are no longer confronted with "policy vacuum"; we are facing dissipation of ethical responsibility (DER) and this phenomenon leads to difficult and usually late localisation and solving of ethical dilemmas within the system.

INTRODUCTION

Current ethics is limited by the antagonistic attitude of researchers and practitioners in information in *DBE,* and the use of information raises new ethical dilemmas in the making of ethical decisions. The ethical approach may signal the need for a new code of ethics and new values that should be better suited to our times. We present the state-of-the-art and discuss the importance of ethics in *DBE* and its emerging developments.

DOI: 10.4018/978-1-60566-890-1.ch018

Yan, Wang and Chand (2004, p. 42) consider that "the enterprise usually collects information from spread sub-companies. This kind of the enterprise is called as distributed business environment".

A *DBE* is more complex than "an enterprise that collects information" and can be described as an environment in which two worlds live together, the real world in which the human factor is the most important resource, and the virtual world in which the basic resource is information. In this environment the former boundaries of organisations disappear because of modern information technology reasons distributed all over the world.

The permanent goal of the real world is survival and success. In order to attain these targets, the real world requires permanent changes which, in turn, impose improvements of the systems that function in the virtual world. Therefore, the human factor must adapt its behaviour to the permanent changes that occur in the real world, and solve the ethical dilemmas in a responsible way, accountable by the use of information that exists in the relation between the affordances of the virtual world and these changes. For instance, more recently, the INTERNET has changed the business style of organisations, while modern information systems (e.g. Web or grid services) have made the business environment react more quickly.

This chapter aims to emphasize the relevance of the ethics of information in *DBE* and to discuss the main issues related to this subject.

Consequently, we demonstrate that it is possible for a variety of ethical approaches to be integrated and put into the practice of information in *DBE* and we seek the answer to the following questions:

- How should ethics of information in *DBE* be defined and applied?
- How to solve any ethical dilemma that may arise?
- What are the economic, social, cultural and ethical implications these may create?
- What are the specific ethical responsibilities of professionals that take action in this domain?

This chapter is organized as follows: Section 1 offers some ethical historical approaches useful to localize our subject in the computer ethics field. In section 2 we provide a detailed presentation of the aspects of the ethics of information in *DBE*. In section 3 we discuss some solutions and recommendations to solve the ethical dilemmas of information in *DBE*. In the next section future research directions are given, which represent a real opportunity to develop ethical guidance specific to information in *DBE* based on practical situations the actors and organisations are confronted with. Finally, we draw some brief conclusions regarding *dissipation of ethical responsibility* which is the most important phenomenon that influences ethical decisions and creates most of the ethical dilemmas in a DBE.

SHORT HISTORICAL PERSPECTIVE ON ETHICS IN LITERATURE

Economic, social and technological progresses have broadened the range and comprehensiveness ethical issues, both from the perspective of the individual and society. This may explain the interest of philosophers, sociologists, psychologists and other professionals in ethical dilemmas, irrespective of their nature

Like any issue with deep philosophical roots, debates on ethical issues have stirred controversies synchronically and diachronically. The more ethical problems are surrounded by unknown elements, the more controversial and heated the debates are. After more than two thousand years, Aristotle's ethical theory, with its individualistic perceptions of life, based on virtues and vices, remains one of the most important achievements in ethics (Aristotle, 2000).

Major ethical theories, e.g. *universalism and relativism*, using specific arguments, which justify man's actions and their consequences, are in continual competition in the difficult process of tracing the line between right and wrong. *Ethical universalism* proclaims that right and wrong should be viewed from the perspective of the consequences of an action. *Ethical relativism* considers that there are no universal moral norms, and right and wrong are relative notions, depending on the cultural, temporal, social and local context characteristics in which the action is carried out (Bowie, 1999). Consequently, rational ethical judgments based on logic are incompatible with ethical relativism, because each society has its own values and moral code

As a consequence of the ethical debate, a distinction between morals and ethics has been established; Cicero used the term "moralist" to translate the Greek "èthikos", and the French "moral" may be translated into English by "ethical" or "moral" (Lalande, 1996). Thus, morals has been attributed to individual experiences, meant to guide man's behaviour, while ethics was assigned to collective experience and is expected to play a role in working out the problems appeared in the field of morality when people live together. Thus, the role of ethics—whether it refers to the *ethics of responsibility, discussion, convictions, business, strategy, or to descriptive, computer, or information ethic*—is constructive and enables the solving of real problems generated by individual or collective decisions or actions by means of imperative moral rules and principles.

Computers in the everyday life of individuals, organisations and society have led to upspring of a new kind of ethics, i.e. the computer ethics, whose pioneer was Norbert Wiener (1948). He believed that three "great principles of justice"—the Principle of Freedom, the Principle of Equality and the Principle of Benevolence (Wiener, 1954, pp. 105-106) there can be ethically elicited. Computers' use and work in the virtual space have laid their print on the autonomy and solidarity of the person, generating conditions for the selfish development of the individual and the promotion of subjective ethical principles that might be used to obtain welfare, happiness or satisfaction by person but not by a community. Thus, the individual conscience is founded on the imperatives of 'individual good' and not on those of a 'general good'.

Paradoxically, computer ethics is the 'offspring' of the harmful consequences that can result from computing and involves the analysis of the "badness" of consequences (Friedman & Kahn, 1997; Parker, Swope, & Baker, 1990; Weizenbaum, 1976). Individuals act according to what right and wrong mean in their own ethical, cultural, religious value systems, paying more attention to their rights than their duties. Moor (1985) argues that computer ethics is a special field of study that analyses both problems generated by general ethics, as well as problems specific to the field of computer technology. James Moor is among the most aggressive promoters of the independent ethical approach, sustaining that the problems that appear at a certain moment in computer ethics cannot be solved through the already existing policies, as, at the moment, they are no longer apt to guide the action that has generated the ethical problem, because of the changes that have occurred in the field meanwhile.

The alternating attitude of specialists between "western" and "nonwestern" notions of ethics has led to a multi-level, interdisciplinary approach to computer ethics: the disclosure level, the theoretical level, and that of applications (Brey, 2000). Within the same range, and in context with elements of relativism and antirealism, Floridi and Sanders (2004) analyse three levels of abstraction: *ontological levels of organisation; methodological levels of explanation and conceptual schemes.* Floridi (2006b) makes a clear distinction between informational ethics and computer ethics, considering informational ethics both as macroethics and the result of researchers' activity in various fields: computer ethics, business ethics, medical ethics, computer science, the philosophy of information, social epistemology and library, and science of information. Mathiesen (2004) considers that informational ethics is a conceptual framework which ethical issues generate through a new information technology. Informational ethics seen as macroethics can no longer be considered applied ethics useful in helping to cram the policy vacuums and conceptual muddles that exist in computer ethics field (Moor, 1985).

Whether it refers to computer or informational ethics, any definition is based on technology, computer technology, minimizing, thus, the part played by the human factor in the creation, promotion and use of ethical instruments.

AN OPTIMISTIC APPROACH TO THE ETHICS OF INFORMATION IN DBE

Ethics of information in DBE is the result of conjoining several complementary fields of applied ethics, e.g. computer, informational and business ethics; it is an object of study with multiple antecedents in business ethics in which the key thinkers are: Confucius, Plato, Aristotle, Hume, Kant, Bentham, Nietzsche (Aristotle, 2000; Martinsons & So, 2000), computer ethics (Wiener, 1948, 1954, Maner, 1996), and informational ethics (Floridi, 1999, 2006a, 2006b).

The DBEs cross boundaries, transforming the specific workplace into a global one, and these transformations:

- impose their print on employees, employers, shareholders, and stakeholders who need to develop specific expertise in order to communicate successfully in such environments; to build and share individual cultures and principles of professional ethics with colleagues and stakeholders (Brown, & Humphreys, 2006; Richman, Noble, & Johnson, 2002; Sapp, 2004),
- bring to the front new ethical issues related to accuracy, accessibility, authentication, scalability, accountability, security, privacy and systems reliability.

The ethical approach of information in *DBE* combines the analysis of traditional ethical theories (e.g. utilitarianism, Kantianism) with modern ones that assemble principles and standards of professional practice, codes of ethics in social responsibility. Therefore, the core of the informational ethical discourse in *DBE* is a Confucian version of the Golden Rule—"do not do unto others that which you would not want done to you" (Martinsons & So, 2000).

The principles of informational ethics in *DBE* are based both on the general principles of ethics and on the particular characteristics of the domain, and are:

1. freedom of information, and consistency,
2. integrity and respect for people's rights, dignity, privacy and confidentiality,
3. professional responsibility and accountability,
4. social responsibility.

The most frequently quoted principle is that of *freedom of information, and consistency*. This principle, associated with that regarding the finality of action, can generate ethical dilemmas. The relationship between privacy and freedom of information becomes antagonistic whether it is about physical, mental, decisional or informational privacy. In *DBE*, privacy is not only an individual's problem, but a general one, based on the global information that is circulated in the system at a given moment, and on the accessing or manipulation of information, that can be the source of wrongness. An informational entity becomes a dilemma when privacy and confidentiality are destroyed, legally or ethically.

Integrity and confidentiality assume pecuniary aspects, because in *DBE* technical, economic and social information important to organisations is circulated and cheating and divulging may immensely prejudice these organisations. Consequently, it is necessary to explain to actors the ethical delimitations between private information and global information, in order to avoid misunderstandings and reduce the tension between actors within the same system. This domain is one of logical and professional relationships and involves a variety of actors (i.e. employees, employers, stakeholders and shareholders), who are interconnected by creativity, as a modulation point between them (Mason, 1986).

Professional responsibility involves the colleagues' assistance in their professional development, but the complexity of the domain makes the relationship between academics and practitioners very difficult. For example, the academics devise certain ethical principles which cannot be used in *DBE*, or their use requires special training or knowledge. The ACM code of ethics (ACM, 1992) includes, in chapter 2, entitled—More Specific Professional Responsibilities—, some general recommendations referring to the acquiring, maintaining and developing professional competence, but does not mention anything about the way(s) to eliminate tensions between actors. Unfortunately, some professional organisations might not care to acknowledge the professional development of their employees, thus removing the impact of the code on the individual's ethical decision-making. In *DBE* it is very important for the employees to express themselves in this medium and to find a way to deal with ethical problems by themselves. Consequently, the employer' demand needs to be motivated by the application of standards that highlight the relationships between the employee's competence and professional recognition.

Social responsibility is the principle of ownership and respect for personal rights in social context. Professional organisations in computer sciences minimize this principle. Elements of social responsibility are only included in the organisations' code of conduct. Social responsibility in *DBE* may have an important impact on business relations. In general, people expect the triple bottom-line of the social responsibility (social-economic-environmental issues) to act in consensus with personal development, and this action is governed by principles of justice that receive the endorsement of all stakeholders. This principle mostly produces moral benefits based on moral awareness, and establishes a bridge between human action and the stakeholder's status in the global context.

Ethical principles are viable only when the actors accept full responsibility for their decisions, even if they are aware that they can translate the responsibility to other actors, depending on when their decisions' results appear. Every actor's actions must be evaluated in terms of their consequences, and all consequences must be comparable according to quantitative indicators and in relation with the outcome in the system which they affect. This means that the actors are not in competition with each other, they co-operate.

Based on an ethical framework, *reactive analysis* leads to the improvement of the moral quality of an action while *the proactive analysis* imposes the course of action (figure 1). Because decision effects in DBE are social and economic, a decision made by an actor in a *DBE* at a given moment – moment t—can generate the following consequences:

- it can produce effects at a moment t+n, after it has several stages and has taken over the action course from other actors in the system;
- if moment t+n is relatively close, the decision effects are felt only within the system, without affecting external users;
- if moment t+n is distant, the decision effects are felt by external users.

Changes in the business system are taken up by actors—the latter re-playing the ethical flow, depending on their place in the system at the moment (figure 2). It is important to mention that, irrespective of the decision made at times t and t+n, the system operates, and in this status of the system it is necessary to repeat the ethical flow in order to identify the ethical consequences of the situational factors and to construct another sequence of individual actions. The *DER* can generate contrary effects on stakeholders, the former leading to the success or failure of the business. We cannot isolate the factors that generate ethical dilemmas because we are in a *DBE*, but we can impose behavioural discipline that requires the actors' professionalism and responsibility.

Ethical dilemmas are caused by cultural differences, lack of time and trust, and unwilling-

Figure 1. The ethical process at the moment t

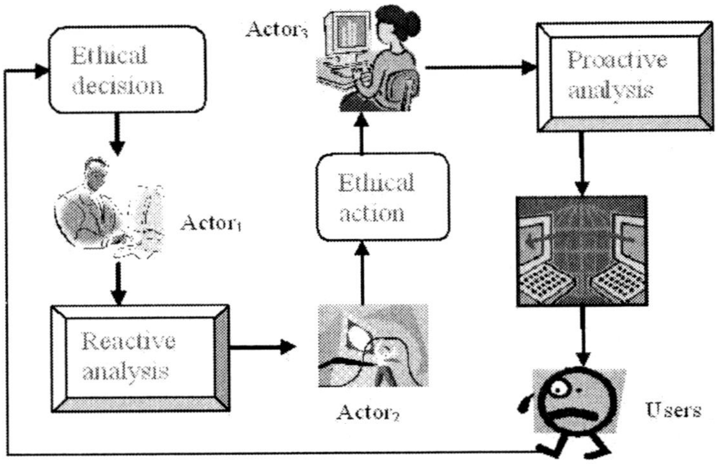

Figure 2. The ethical process at the moment t + n

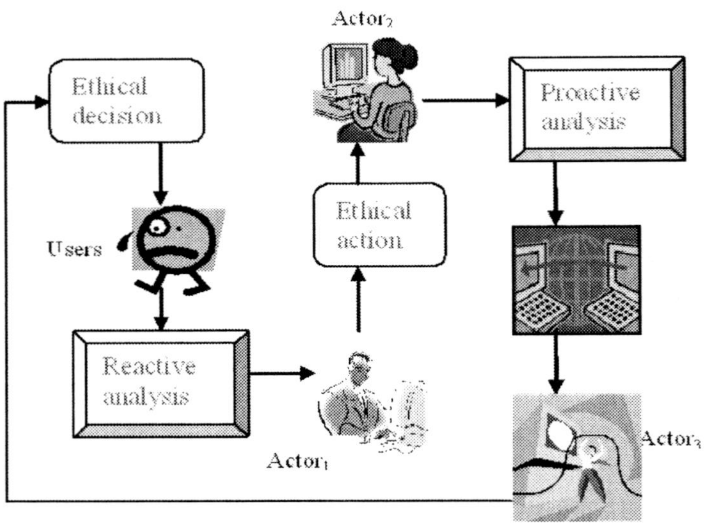

ness to use applications due distrust or lack of knowledge.

Dilemma 1: Unfair competition

Mark has been working with the company for over 5 years and he is expecting a very good evaluation this year. Unfortunately, the best evaluation has been attributed to a colleague working in another subsidiary of the company, who, for a merger of two banks, has used a Grid computing technology that provided a stable, scalable, and high-performing environment. Mark was frustrated because he also had a contribution in the project – he had tested each part of the system and had made some suggestions to his colleague. The latter, however, had not mentioned Mark's contribution in the final report and the superiors attributed the merits of the successful solution to a single person. The new project Mark was working on was the merger of two multinational companies affected by the international crisis. Mark's dilemma was whether he should get involved in this project as much as he had done in the previous one or to treat everything more superficially. He reasoned that the eventual failure of the project was a sweet revenge for unfair competition, but on the other hand he feared a diminution of his salary or, worse, the loss of his place of work. What will Mark do? Will he disregard the ethical principle of professional responsibility and accountability, or will he continue to work with his colleague hoping that this time it will not be an unfair competition but open cooperation?

Dilemma 2: Unreasonable pressure for results, and limited resources

The deadline for the finalisation of the project was only two weeks ahead and John was calm as he thought he had enough time to test the final improvements of the system.

His superiors, however, called an urgent work meeting to announce the fact that because of the tight competition the team was to finish the project in 4 days max. John is in a big dilemma – either to give up the testing of the latest improvements and risk the failure of the project and, consequently, the computing grid would not allow to run applications 600 times faster than previously by putting to work the power of disaster recovery servers and other under-utilized resources, or to do extra hours and test the system to make sure that the project will be a success?

It is obvious that the remaining time is too short for John to run a complete test of the suggested solutions. John counts on the fact that it will be difficult to prove that the project has failed because of a weakness generated by insufficient testing or lack of information.

How will John come out of this situation?

Dilemma 3: Dissipation of ethical responsibility

Karl is a member in the team that conceives and implements an identity management system for accounting management designed to enhance the authentication, authorisation and accountability of a person. In the latest test he has found a programming error that facilitated the modification of the facial image of the user. Karl was aware that this error could become an inspiration source for hackers and thus, produce financial damage to its user. Unfortunately, he could not find a solution and time is pressing him, as he needs to finish in a week. If they did not deliver the system on time, they were likely to lose the contract in favour of a rival company. Karl said to himself that he was not the only member of the team who was qualified to notice the existing disadvantage and was waiting to see his colleagues' reaction, but nobody seemed to have noticed it. What will Karl do? Will he tell his colleagues about the problem he has noticed, but for which he had no solution or will he keep it to himself in the hope that the weakness of the system will not be seen by the hackers?

We have identified a number of dilemmas which a distributed business system might face when undertaking a system development activity. These dilemmas are:

- What analysis should the actor use if the other actor in the system considers that the initial decision was unethical (Dilemma 1)?
- Whose ethical decisions will dominate the development of the system (Dilemma 2)?
- How can *DER* within the system be prevented (Dilemma 3)?
- Is the code of ethics an efficient instrument in promoting ethical principles in *DBE* (Dilemma 1)?

How can professional accountability be assessed? How can subjectivity in assessment systems be removed? How can responsibility be socially promoted (Dilemma 1 and Dilemma 3)?

SOLVING ETHICAL DILEMMAS OF INFORMATION IN DBE - SOLUTIONS AND RECOMMENDATIONS

The above-mentioned examples reveal the fact that DBE dilemmas entwine the principles of business ethics with those of informational ethics, and the individual oscillates between self-interest and the interests of the organisation. If in the field of business ethics, ethical or unethical behaviour can be easily seen on the basis of financial and accounting documents or other documents; in the field of informational ethics non-innocence are more difficult to prove because of the *DER*.

A process or an action may by right or wrong irrespective of its consequences, or depending on the way it positively or negatively affects its user and the organisations which are involved in a *DBE*. From this angle, the following situations can be encountered:

- if finality *is positive* for the actor, without causing important *disruptions* to organisations, stakeholders, clients. For instance, Mark cannot justify himself through unfair competition for the failure of the new project but he can use *DER* to report on the weakness of the team and start a process of evaluation. Had Mark been correctly evaluated, it would have made him more responsible and more willing to get involved in the completion of the project.
- if finality *is positive* for organisations, stakeholders, clients – the actor as a member of the organisation *benefits* from the effects of his actions. For example, John should work on the project with the same responsibility and professionalism to its conclusion. If he cannot test all the improvements of the system, he should report the likely risks to his colleagues and superiors and the decision will have to be a collective one.
- if finality *is positive* for the actor and *is negative* for organisations, stakeholders, and clients, because the actor promotes his interest at the expense of profession, client, or employer. For instance, Karl believes that it is more advantageous for him do disregard the deficiency in the system and hope that no other colleague will notice it. If somebody did see it and himself had no solution for it, he was risking to be thought incompetent. The system would be delivered on time even if there was a strong risk of generating financial damage to its user and, implicitly to Karl's company.
- if finality *is positive* for organisations, stakeholders, clients and generates *negative* results for the actor as a member of the organization. For example, Karl believes that he is morally obliged to report the deficiency existing in the system, risking to be penalised because he is not able to find a solution. In this situation the final decision belongs to the company.
- if finality *is negative* for actor, organisations, stakeholders, and clients, because of associations of businesses and organisations which are in conflict with ethical

principles. For instance, Mark decides to treat the new project superficially. The project does not meet the same success as the former, and the company meets financial losses.

If one wants to get out of these ethical dilemmas, one needs to interweave reactive and proactive analyses, because theory and practice in *DBE* involve two sets of problems: *the conceptual problems* and *the technical ones* by which the concepts of ethics can be put into practice in order to obtain a successful application of the ethical principles. Localisation of ethical dilemmas within the system is a difficult and usually late process. Ethical decisions need to be evaluated with respect to the antagonistic relationship between short-term or long-term risks and benefits.

The quick evolution of information systems makes the ethical-unethical behaviour acquire other values and meanings. For instance, not reporting the security deficiency at time t, may no longer represent an ethical dilemma for Karl at time t+1, if it did not produce losses to its user till that moment or, if a solution for another system can be applied to his system as well. The human factor uses the information as an instrument to promote ethical or unethical behaviour.

Thus, reactive analysis is required in designing a business distributed system, and proactive in the stage of using a business distributed system. The perspective of goodness and badness changes according to the actor's position within the system and his justification at the moment of action. The ethical paradox of information in *DBE* is represented by the permanent change of the individual's status in the system, the complexity of activities and the individual's responsibilities. This paradox leads to the translation of responsibilities between actors within the same system (i.e. from information sender to the information receiver). In *DBE* the consequences of the actors' actions are difficult to predict, and they usually affect more persons. Ethical principles have to be incorporated into a control procedure that could be applied without pressure and constraint. In this case, we have to reconsider the principle of equality – what is moral for a pair of information sender-receiver should remain moral when the two actors swap places. The moral context of a new situation changes and the rules or values are not applicable because this ethical paradox involves a diversity of interests, and sometimes these interests can become conflictual, because each actor avoids to disclose enough information to expose his identity. Therefore, the ethical discourse and responsibilities are dissipated within the system, preventing the objective and normative evaluation of systems and practices.

According to each situation it is very important to clearly establish what is moral and what is not, regardless of the finality of the action – right versus wrong, wrong versus right, wrong versus wrong and right versus right. Non-conflictual situations - right versus wrong and right versus right – rise different problems for the actors, e.g. the situation right versus wrong in a DBE could have *positive consequences* for organisations, stakeholders, clients, and the actor as a member of the organisation *benefits* from the effects of his actions, unlike the situation of right versus right, which could be *negative* for an actor, because of the personal ethical values which come into conflict with the ethical principles of organisation. In this second situation the actor could be forced to choose between freedom against security, truth against loyalty, and personal values against community values.

At this moment we are no longer confronted with "policy vacuum", but with *DER*. One of the *DER* causes is that in *DBE*, individuals are often unknown to each other, and access control based on identity may be ineffective. The solution of *DER* is the creation of networks of ethical principles that take over the dilemma and treat it as a human error.

The *DER* is due to a misunderstanding of autonomy and self-governance in this field. The specificity of *DBE* imposes a global interpretation of justice and freedom in the context of business and of the consequences that result from an unethical behaviour on a free market. The ethical questions that arise in *DBE* come from computer ethics and, up to a point, need common interpretation. The modulation point in solving ethical dilemma is situated at the intersection between computer and business ethics where the debate might be focused upon real ethical dilemma. In *DBE* we cannot ignore the constructive relationship between the moral role of technology and the political, economic and legal institutions that make the rules in the system. The five-step process of ethical analysis (Rahanu, Davies & Rogerson, 1996) cannot be applied because, in this field, formal guidelines and ethical theories are very general and it is extremely difficult for the actors to distinguish between ethical and non-ethical values.

Demanding access to information with fraudulent intentions leads to the loss of organisational and individual identity, which, in turn, is a sure way to chaos, bankruptcy and crisis. Decision-making must always belong to actor – responsibility should be human, and definitely placed within the network. Chaos in *DBE* is omnipresent and can be controlled through the development of healthy ethical principles which should work simultaneously, both at individual (i.e. motivational factors – professional accountability and salary, code of ethics) and organisational levels (i.e. social responsibility based on code of conducts).

Codes of ethics are always decorative and purely illustrative, because they contain common themes as: personal integrity, privacy of information, conflict of interest, public safety, and participation in professional societies (AAPOR, 1977; ACM, 1973; ACM, 1992: Anderson, 1992; IEEE, 1990; Johnson, 1985; Oz 1992, 1993). The actor will not observe ethical principles as long as those around him (i.e. colleagues, stakeholders, clients) ignore them. Therefore, legislation in the field should be strict, while punishment for disregarding ethical principles should never be symbolical, either for the individual or for the organisation. Both informal and formal codes of ethics should contain a mixture of practical information related to business ethics and computer ethics literature. Furthermore, the organisation must foster the development of ethical standards of individual performance, which has the role to restrict the *DER* and avoid ethically ambiguous situations. Sometimes, the actor ignores the ethical issues because he believes that his basic moral principles are enough to protect him, and because the ethical principles in many codes of professional ethics are very difficult to understand and apply.

In *DBE* the problem is not to identify the existence of a moral dilemma but to evaluate the effects that the moral decision may have on the individual himself, and, secondly, on the organisation. The line between right and wrong is displaced by the individual, depending on individual characteristics, risk inherent to the decision, and social context. Ethical dilemmas in *DBE* are influenced by the specific characteristics of the environment and can influence the lives and well-being of other stakeholders.

FUTURE RESEARCH DIRECTIONS IN ETHICS OF INFORMATION IN DBE

The new financial crisis poses some questions concerning the ethical behaviour and decision-making in computer ethics and business ethics in general, and in *DBE,* in particular. The ethical decision- support process in *DBE* can be based on the reconsideration of the actor-network theory achieved through the perspective of ethical dilemmas. There is a real opportunity to develop ethical guidance specific to information in *DBE,* based on practical situations the actors and organisations are confronted with. By using the actor-network theory we intend to identify the best alternative action in a critical situation. In this context, it is necessary for the actor to have a basic understanding of the nature of ethical principles in computer and business fields. The theoretical foundations of *DBE* need re-evaluation in terms of legal consequences, and in consensus with isomorphic ethical behaviour. Therefore, we must reconsider the theory of neo-institutionalism from the perspectives of ethical dilemmas.

The degree of ethical structural isomorphism is higher in a *DBE*, especially the ethico-mimetic isomorphism, because of the cultural schemes and conventions that shape the activity. The ethico-mimetic isomorphism is a process through which the ethical behaviour of an organisation is adapted to an uncertain environment characterized by a great degree of uncertainty, by imitating the ethical behaviour of the organisations perceived as successful. The ethical discourse commences without the user's understanding of the ethical ideal or, even worse, without the existence of a previous ethical ideal—out of inertness – because of the external pressure of the business environment. This is why organisations' bankruptcy may appear as a result of the pressure, as well as of the misunderstanding of isomorphism, which is a mechanism of adjustment. As a result, the organisation' ethical action is based on a set of rationalized patterns, models and cultural schemes that lead to the definition of a social entity. Logically, there is one more question: Why do organisations not simply adopt and use an efficient set of ethical *ideals, ethical discourses, and ethical control techniques*?

The answer is relatively simple, but difficult to put into practice. It is so, because ethical ***ideals*** are not accompanied by efficient ethical ***discourses*** that should present them, and ethical ***control techniques*** do not make possible the expression and the implementation of the fragile relations based on discourse.

CONCLUSION

The factors that differentiate behaviour and thinking of individuals belonging to various societies, to one organisation or other, are dictated by the social and legal environment the individuals live in and carry out their activity. Therefore, there are no universal standards of ethics, and moral responsibility is relative to cultural practices. Traditional ethical considerations must be carefully adapted to the new challenges in order not to translate the weight from highlighting the individual's value to the worshipping of technology because neglecting a person may stimulate and motivate unethical decisions.

Ethical dilemmas of information in *DBE* are generated by the circulation of information and transfer of responsibility. The unpleasant consequences can be foreseen neither by individuals nor by other actors, because these consequences occur in real time. Because of the *DER*, ethical dilemmas have a delayed effect and, for this reason, in *DBE* we are not dealing with a "conceptual vacuum", but rather with the difficulty of classifying problems as ethical or unethical. Therefore, no single approach to ethics can be implemented, because the effect of the action can no longer be evaluated from an ethical point of view, and the future ethical decisions will be marked by a high level of uncertainty.

Research must be based on real life, taking into account:

- the dissipation of responsibility and the set of roles of an actor in *DBE*, and
- the protection of the identity and physical safety of the actors.

Because human nature is the same, irrespective of time or geographical place, *the individual responsibility and accountability need to be based on strong, palpable extrinsic motivation.*

In *DBE* the human factor is the most important resource, and information represents the value of this environment. Thus, ethics of information in *DBE* has the role of detecting the factors that negatively influence the individuals' behaviour. In *DBE*, the application of the principles of general ethics should be avoided, because it is very difficult to predict the consequences of the actors' actions in an environment of dissipated responsibilities.

To conclude, in *DBE*, the *DER* is the most important phenomenon that influences ethical decisions and creates most of the ethical dilemmas, even if information is available for the whole group of actors involved in the system at the same time (i.e. employees – employer– stakeholders).

REFERENCES

AAPOR - American Association for Public Opinion Research. (1977). *Code of professional ethics and practices*. Bylaws of the AAPOR. POB 17, Princeton, NJ 08542.

ACM - Association for Computing Machinery. (1973). Proposed ACM code of professional conduct. *Communications of the ACM, 16*(4), 265–269.

ACM - Association for Computing Machinery. (1992). ACM code of ethics and professional conduct. *Communications of the ACM, 35*(5), 94–99. doi:10.1145/129875.129885

Adam, A. (2001). Computer ethics in a different voice. *Information and Organization, 11*, 235–261. doi:10.1016/S1471-7727(01)00006-9

Anderson, R. E. (1992). Social impacts of computing: Codes of professional ethics. *Social Science Computer Review*, 463–469.

Aristotle. (2000). *Nicomachean ethics*. Cambridge: Cambridge University Press (Trans. R. Crisp).

Bowie, N. E. (1999). Relativism, cultural and moral. In T. Donaldson & P. Werhane (Eds.), *Ethical issues in business: A philosophical approach* (6th ed.). Upper Saddle River, NJ: Prentice Hall.

Brey, Ph. (2000, December). Disclosive computer ethics. *Computers & Society*, 10–16. doi:10.1145/572260.572264

Brown, A. D., & Humphreys, M. (2006). Organizational identity and place: A discursive exploration of hegemony and resistance. *Journal of Management Studies, 43*(2), 231–257. doi:10.1111/j.1467-6486.2006.00589.x

Capurro, R. (2008). Hermeneutics facing the information enframing, *ACM Ubiquity,* 9(8).

Floridi, L. (1999). Information ethics: on the theoretical foundations of computer ethics. *Ethics and Information Technology, 1*(1), 37–56. doi:10.1023/A:1010018611096

Floridi, L. (2006a). Information technologies and the tragedy of good will. *Ethics and Information Technology, 8*(4), 253–262. doi:10.1007/s10676-006-9110-6

Floridi, L. (2006b). Information ethics, its nature and scope. *SIGCAS Computers and Society, 36*(3), 21–36. doi:10.1145/1195716.1195719

Floridi, L., & Sanders, J. W. (2004). Levellism and the method of abstraction, *IEG – RESEARCH REPORT* 22.11.04. Retrieved June 11, 2008, from http://web.comlab.ox.ac.uk/oucl/research/areas/ieg.

Friedman, B., & Kahn, P. (1997). People are responsible, computers are not. In M. Erman, M.Williams & M. Shauf (Eds.), *Computers, Ethics and Society* (pp. 303–12). Oxford: Oxford University Press.

IEEE - Institute of Electical and Electronics Engineers. (1990). *IEEE Code of Ethics*. IEEE, 345 E. 47th St., New York, NY 10017-2394.

Johnson, D. G. (1985). *Computer ethics.* Englewood Cliffs, NJ: Prentice Hall.

Lalande, A. (1996). *Vocabulaire technique et critique de la Philosophie*. Dix-huitième édition reliée, Presses Universitaires de France.

Maner, W. (1996). Unique ethical problems in information technology. In T.W. Bynum & S. Rogerson (Eds.), *Global Information Ethics* (pp. 137-154). Opragen Publications.

Martinsons, M. G., & So, S. K. K. (2000). *The information ethics of American and Chinese managers*, Pacific Rim Institute for Studies of Management Report 2000-02.

Mason, R. (1986). Four ethical issues of the information age. *MIS Quarterly*, *10*(1), 5–12. doi:10.2307/248873

Mathiesen, K. (2004). What Is information ethics? *Computers and Society, 32*(8). Retrieved April 15, 2008, from http://www.computersandsociety.org/sigcas_ofthefuture2/sigcas/subpage/sub_page.cfm? article=909&page_number_nb=901.

Moor, J. (1985). What is computer ethics? *Metaphilosophy*, *16*, 266–275. doi:10.1111/j.1467-9973.1985.tb00173.x

Oz, E. (1992, December). Ethical standards for information systems professionals: A case for a unified code. *MIS Quarterly*, 423–433. doi:10.2307/249729

Oz, E. (1993). Ethical standards for computer professionals: A comparative analysis of four major codes. *Journal of Business Ethics*, *12*(9), 709–726. doi:10.1007/BF00881385

Parker, D., Swope, S., & Baker, B. N. (1990). *Ethical conflicts in information & computer science*. Technology & Business, QED Information Sciences.

Rahanu, H., Davies, J., & Rogerson, S. (1996). Ethical analysis of software failure cases. In P. Barroso, T.W. Bynum, S. Rogerson, & L. Joyanes (Eds.), *Proceedings of ETHICOMP 96* (pp. 364-383). Madrid: Complutense University.

Richman, A., Noble, K., & Johnson, A. (2002). *When the workplace is many places: The extent and nature of off-site work today*. Watertown, MA: WFD Consulting. Executive Summary. Retrieved June 12, 2008, from http://www.abcdependentcare.com/docs/ABC_Executive_Summary_final.pdf

Sapp, D. (2004). Global partnerships in business communication. *Business Communication Quarterly*, *67*, 267–280. doi:10.1177/1080569904268051

Weizenbaum, J. (1976). *Computer power and human reason: From judgment to calculation*. Freeman.

Wiener, N. (1948). *Cybernetics: Or control and communication in the animal and the machine*. Technology Press.

Wiener, N. (1954). *The human use of human beings: Cybernetics and society* (2nd ed.). Boston: Houghton Mifflin.

Yan, K. Q., Wang, S. C., & Chiang, M. L. (2004). New application of reliable agreement: Underlying an unsecured business environment . *ACM SIGOPS Operating Systems Review*, *38*(3), 42–57. doi:10.1145/1035834.1035840

ADDITIONAL READING

Barker, J. R., & Sewell, G. (2001). Neither good, nor bad, but dangerous: Surveillance as an ethical paradox. *Ethics and Information Technology*, *3*, 183–196.

Baron, D. P. (2000). *Business and its environment* (3rd ed.). Upper Saddler River, NJ: Prentice Hall.

Barry, N. P. (2000). *Business ethics*. West Lafayette, IN: Purdue University Press.

Bohlman, H. M., & Dundas, M. J. (2002). *The legal, ethical and international environment of business* (5th ed.). Cincinnati, OH: West/Thomson Learning.

Bynum, T., & Rogerson, S. (2004). *Computer ethics and professional responsibility* (pp. 60-85) Blackwell Publishing.

Chadwick, R. F., & Schroeder, D. (2002). *Applied ethics: Critical concepts in philosophy; v. 5: business and economics*. New York: Routledge.

Clear, T., Gotterbarn, D., & Kwan, C. (2006). Managing software requirements risks with software development impact statements. *New Zealand Journal of Applied Computing.*

Cole, E., & Ring, S. (2006). *Insider threat: Protecting the enterprise from sabotage, spying, and theft*. Rockland, MA: Syngress.

Contos, B. T. (2006). *Enemy at the water cooler: Real-life stories of insider threats and enterprise security management countermeasures*. Rockland, MA: Syngress.

Cramton, C. D., & Hinds, P. (2005). Subgroup dynamics in internationally distributed teams: Ethnocentrism or cross-national learning? In B. M. Staw & R. M. Kramer (Eds.), *Research in organizational behavior* (Vol. 26, pp. 231-263). Greenwich, CT: JAI.

Frank, R. H. (2004). *What price the moral high ground? Ethical dilemmas in competitive environments*. Princeton, NJ: Princeton University Press.

Fuhua, O. L. (2005). *Designing distributed learning environments with intelligent software agents*. Hershey, PA: Idea Group Inc.

Gotterbarn, D. (2007). Enhancing ethical decision support methods: Clarifying the solution space with line drawing. *SIGCAS Computers and Society*, *37*(2), 53–63. doi:10.1145/1327325.1327329

Gotterbarn, D., & Rogerson, S. (2005). Responsible risk analysis for software development: Creating the software development impact statement. *Communications of the Association for Information Systems*.

Harris, C. E., Jr., Pritchard, M. S., & Rabins, M. J. (2004). *Engineering ethics: Concepts and cases* (3rd ed.). Wadsworth.

Hasselbladh, H., & Kallinikos, J. (2000). The project of rationalization: A critique and reappraisal of neo-institutionalism. *Organization Studies*, *21*(4), 697–720. doi:10.1177/0170840600214002

Hooker, J. (2003) Working across cultures. Stanford, CA: Stanford Business Books.

Johnson, R. A. (2002). *Whistleblowing: When it works-and why*. Boulder, CO: Lynne Rienner Publishers.

Machan, T. R. (2000). *Morality and work*. Stanford, CA: Hoover Institution Press.

Maner, W. (2002). Heuristic methods for computer ethics. [from http://csweb.cs.bgsu.edu/maner/heuristics/maner.pdf]. *Metaphilosophy*, *33*(3), 339–365. Retrieved August 18, 2008. doi:10.1111/1467-9973.00231

McGraw, G. (2006). *Software security: Building security in*. Boston, MA: Addison-Wesley.

Meyer, J. W., & Rowan, B. (1977). Insitutionalized organizations: Formal structure as myth and ceremony. *American Journal of Sociology*, *83*, 340–363. doi:10.1086/226550

Pagano, B. (2004). *The transparency edge: How credibility can make or break you in business*. New York: McGraw-Hill.

Peltier, T. R. (2001). *Information security policies, procedures, and standards: Guidelines for effective information security management*. Boca Raton, FL: Auerbach.

Phillips, R. (2003). *Stakeholder theory and organizational ethics*. San Francisco, CA: Berrett-Koehler.

Powell, W. W., & DiMaggio, P. J. (1991). The new institutionalism. *Organizational analysis*. Chicago: University of Chicago Press.

Quinn, M. J. (2006). *Ethics for the information age* (2nd ed.). Reading, MA: Addison-Wesley.

Ramamoorti, S., & Olsen, W. (2007). Fraud: The human factor. *Financial executive,* July/August, 53-55.

Schneier, B. (2003). *Beyond fear: Thinking sensibly about security in an uncertain world*. New York: Copernicus Books.

Schoorman, F. D., Mayer, R. C., & Davis, J. H. (2007). An integrative model of organizational trust: Past, present, and future. *Academy of Management Review*, *32*(2), 344–354.

Starke-Meyerring, D. (2005). Meeting the challenges of globalization: A framework for global literacies in professional communication programs. *Journal of Business and Technical Communication*, *19*, 468–499. doi:10.1177/1050651905278033

Tavani, H. M. (2004). *Ethics and technology: Ethical issues in an age of information and communication technology*. Hoboken, NJ: John Wiley and Sons.

Treviño, L. K., & Weaver, G. R. (2003). *Managing ethics in business organizations: Social scientific perspective*. Stanford, CA: Stanford Business Books.

KEY TERMS AND DEFINITIONS

Distributed Business Environment (DBE): A *DBE* can be described as an environment in which two worlds live together, the real world, in which the human factor is the most important resource, and the virtual world, in which the basic resource is information. In this environment the former boundaries of organisations disappear because of modern information technology existing all over the world

Ethical Universalism: It states that right and wrong are judged according to the consequences of an action.

Ethical Relativism: It says that there are no universal moral norms, and right and wrong are relative notions depending on the local, cultural, temporal and social contexts in which actions are carried out

Ethics of Information in *DBE***:** It is the result of conjoining several complementary fields of applied ethics, like computer ethics, informational ethics and business ethics, and is an object of study with multiple antecedents in business ethics

Social Responsibility: It is the principle of ownership and respect for personal rights in social context.

Dissipation of Ethical Responsibility (*DER***):** The *DER* is due to a misunderstanding of autonomy and self-governance in this field. One of the *DER* causes is that in *DBE* the individuals are often unknown to each other, and access control based on identity may be ineffective. The solution for solving *DER* is the creation of networks of ethics that take over the dilemma and treat it as a human error

Compilation of References

6P., Goodwin, N., Peck, E, & Freeman, T. (2006). *Managing networks of twenty-first century organizations.* London: Palgrave Macmillan.

AAPOR - American Association for Public Opinion Research. (1977). *Code of professional ethics and practices.* Bylaws of the AAPOR. POB 17, Princeton, NJ 08542.

Abecker, A. (2000). Information supply for business processes: Coupling workflow with document analysis and information retrieval. *Knowledge-Based Systems, 13,* 271–284. doi:10.1016/S0950-7051(00)00087-3

Abramson, D., Buyya, R., & Giddy, J. (2001). *A case for economy grid architecture for service oriented Grid computing.* Retrieved January 10, 2007, from http://www.csse.monash.edu.au/~davida/papers/ecogrid.pdf

Achour, H., & Bensedrine, N. (2005) An evaluation of Internet banking and online brokerage in Tunisia. Retrieved from http://medforist.grenoble-em.com/Contenus/Conference%20Amman%20EBEL%2005/pdf/25.pdf

ACM - Association for Computing Machinery. (1973). Proposed ACM code of professional conduct. *Communications of the ACM, 16*(4), 265–269.

Adam, A. (2001). Computer ethics in a different voice. *Information and Organization, 11,* 235–261. doi:10.1016/S1471-7727(01)00006-9

Ågerfalk, P. J., Fitzgerald, B., Holmström, H., Lings, B., Lundell, B., & Conchúir, E. Ó. (2005). A framework for considering opportunities and threats in distributed software development. In: *International Workshop on Distributed Software Development (DiSD)* (pp. 47-61), Austrian Computer Society

Ahituv, N., & Neumann, S. (1986). *Principles of information systems for measurement.* Dubuque: W. C. Brown Publ.

Alexander, T. M. (2003). Measuring the value of geospatial information: Critical need or fools errand. In *Proceedings of the 3 Biennial Coastal GeoTools Conference.* Charleston, USA. Retrieved August 2008 from http://www.csc.noaa.gov/geotools/proceedings/pdf.files/os abs/alexander.pdf

Allen, D. (2007). Cost/benefit analysis for implementing ECM, BPM systems. *The Information Management Journal,* May-June, 34-41.

Anderson, G. F., Frogner, B. K., Johns, R. A., & Reinhardt, U. E. (2006). Health care spending and use of information technology in OECD countries. *Health Affairs, 25*(3), 819–831. doi:10.1377/hlthaff.25.3.819

Anderson, R. E. (1992). Social impacts of computing: Codes of professional ethics. *Social Science Computer Review,* 463–469.

Apel, K. O. (1972). The priori of communication and the foundation of the humanities. *Man and World/an international philosophical review, 5*(1), 3-37.

Applications with active map software, screenshots (2005). Retrieved October 21, 2008, from http://wwwmath.uni-muenster.de/cs/u/ruckema/x/sciframe/en/screenshots.html

Apte, U. M., & Nath, H. K. (2007). Size, structure and growth of the U.S. information economy. In U. Apte, & U. Karmarkar (Eds.), *Managing in the information economy. Current research issues. Annals of information systems* (Vol.1). New York: Springer.

Aristotle. (2000). *Nicomachean ethics.* Cambridge: Cambridge University Press (Trans. R. Crisp).

Arrington, M. I. (2004). The role of the Internet in prostate cancer survivors' illness narratives. In P. Whitten & D. Cook (Eds.), Understanding health communication technologies (pp. 181-186). San Francisco, CA: Jossey-Bass.

Arrow, K. J. (Ed.). (1963). *Social choice and individual values.* New York: John Wiley.

Ash, J., & Bates, D. (2005). Factors and forces impacting EHR system adoption: Report of a 2004 ACMI discussion. *Journal of the American Medical Informatics Association, 12*(1), 8–12. doi:10.1197/jamia.M1684

AspectJ website. (n.d.). Retrieved from http://www.eclipse.org/aspectj/

Astley, W. G., & Fombrun, C. J. (1983). Collective strategy, social ecology for organizational environments. *Academy of Management Review, 8*(4), 476–587. doi:10.2307/258259

Aswalap, J. (2005). "Information society" development in Thailand: Information workforce and information and communication technology perspectives. *First Monday, 10*(10).

Avison, D., & Fitzgerald, G. (2006). *Information system development: Methodologies, techniques and tools* (4th ed.). McGraw-Hill Education.

Aydin, C. E., Rosen, P. N., & Felitti, V. J. (1994). Transforming information use in preventive medicine: Learning to balance technology with the art of caring. Paper presented at the Eighteenth Annual Symposium on Computer Applications in Medical Care, Washington, DC.

Balachandher, K. G., Bala, S., Nafis, A., & Perera, J. C. (2003). An evaluation of Internet banking sites in Islamic countries. [JIBC]. *The Journal of Internet Banking and Commerce, 2*(8).

Ball, M. J., & Gold, J. (2006). Banking on health: Personal records and information exchange. *Journal of Healthcare Information Management, 20*(2), 71–83.

Banisar, D. (2000). *Privacy and human rights: An international survey on privacy laws and developments.* Washington: Electronic Privacy Information Centre.

Barker, J. R., & Sewell, G. (2001). Neither good, nor bad, but dangerous: Surveillance as an ethical paradox. *Ethics and Information Technology, 3,* 183–196.

Barmouta, A., & Buyya, R. (2003). GridBank: *A Grid accounting services architecture (GASA) for distributed systems sharing and integration.* Retrieved February 18, 2007, from http://www.gridbus.org/papers/gridbank.pdf

Baron, D. P. (2000). *Business and its environment* (3rd ed.). Upper Saddler River, NJ: Prentice Hall.

Barry, N. P. (2000). *Business ethics.* West Lafayette, IN: Purdue University Press.

Bates, D. W. (2009). The effects of health information technology on inpatient care. *Archives of Internal Medicine, 169*(2), 105–107. doi:10.1001/archinternmed.2008.542

Bates, D., Ebell, M., Gotlieb, E., Zapp, J., & Mullins, H. (2003). A proposal for electronic medical records in U.S. primary care. *Journal of the American Medical Informatics Association, 10,* 1–10. doi:10.1197/jamia.M1097

Bauer, B., Müller, J. P., & Odell, J. (2001). Agent UML: A formalism for specifying multiagent software systems. In *Proceedings of the first international workshop on agent-oriented software engineering (AOSE-2000), Limerick, Ireland* (LNCS 1957, 91-104).

Beardsmore, A., Hartley, K., Hawkins, S., Laws, S., Magowan, J., & Twigg, A. (2002). *GSAX Grid service accounting extensions.* Retrieved November 18, 2007, from http://www.doc.ic.ac.uk/~sjn5/GGF/ggf-rus-gsax-01.pdf

Belecheanu, R. A., et al. (2006). Commercial applications of agents: Lessons, experiences and challenges. In *Proceedings of the 5th international conference on autonomous agents and multiagent systems (AAMAS 06)* (pp. 1549-1555). ACM Press.

Belkin, N. J. (1995). Cases, scripts, and information-seeking strategies: On the design of interactive information retrieval systems. *Expert Systems with Applications, 9*(3), 379–395. doi:10.1016/0957-4174(95)00011-W

Bensink, M., Hailey, D., & Wootton, R. (2007). A systematic review of successes and failures in home telehealth. Part 2: Final quality rating results. *Journal of Telemedicine and Telecare, 13*(S3), 10–14. doi:10.1258/135763307783247121

Benyahia, H. (2000). Trends in the productivity of the information sector in Canada. *IEEE Canadian Review*, Fall/Automne.

Bergenti, F. (2001). Deploying FIPA-compliant systems on handheld devices. *IEEE Internet Computing, 5*(4), 20–25. doi:10.1109/4236.939446

Bergenti, F., Gleizes, M. P., & Zambonelli, F. (Eds.). (2004). *Methodologies and software engineering for agent systems: The agent-oriented software engineering handbook* (Vol. 11). Springer-Verlag.

Berner, E. S., Detmer, D. E., & Simborg, D. (2005). Will the wave finally break? A brief view of the adoption of electronic medical records in the United States. *Journal of the American Medical Informatics Association, 12*(1), 3–7. doi:10.1197/jamia.M1664

Bezzazi, E.-H. (2007). On some inferences based on stratified forward chaining: An application to e-Government. *Advances in Information Systems Development* (Vol. 1). Springer Verlag.

Bezzazi, E.-H. (2007, November). *Identité numérique et anonymat: concepts et mise en oeuvre*. Paper presented at the Colloque International sur la sécurité de l'individu numérisé, Paris, France.

Bicocchi, N., & Zambonelli, F. (2007). Autonomic communication learns from nature. *IEEE Potentials, 26*(6), 42–46. doi:10.1109/MPOT.2007.906119

Blaha, M., & Rumbaugh, J. (2005). *Object-oriented modeling and design with UML* (Second ed.). Pearson Education Inc.

Bloem, J., Van Doorn, M., & Mittal, P. (2006). *Making IT governance work in a Sarbanes-Oxley World*. Hoboken, NJ: John Wiley & Sons.

Blumenthal, D., & Glaser, J. (2007). Information technology comes to medicine. *The New England Journal of Medicine, 356*, 2527–2534. doi:10.1056/NEJMhpr066212

Bohlman, H. M., & Dundas, M. J. (2002). *The legal, ethical and international environment of business* (5th ed.). Cincinnati, OH: West/Thomson Learning.

Boisot, M. H. (1995). *Information space, A framework for learning in organizations, institutions and culture*. New York: Routledge.

Booch, G., Rumbaugh, J., & Jacobsson, I. (1999). *The Unified Modelling Language user guide*. MA: Addison Wesley Longman, Inc.

Boon, J. A., Britz, J. J., & Harmse, C. (1994). The information economy in South Africa: Definition and measurement. *Journal of Information Science, 5*(20).

Bordini, R., et al. (Eds.). (2005). *Multiagent programming languages, platforms and applications*. New York: Springer.

Bowie, N. E. (1999). Relativism, cultural and moral. In T. Donaldson & P. Werhane (Eds.), *Ethical issues in business: A philosophical approach* (6th ed.). Upper Saddle River, NJ: Prentice Hall.

Bradshaw, J. (1997). *An introduction to software agents* (pp. 1-46). AAAI Press/The MIT Press. Retrieved from http://www.cs.umbc.edu/agents/introduction/01-Bradshaw.pdf

Brancheau, J. C., & Wetherbe, J. C. (1986). Information architecture: Methods and practice. *Information Processing & Management, 22*(6), 453–463. doi:10.1016/0306-4573(86)90096-8

Brancheau, J. C., & Wetherbe, J. C. (1986). Information architecture: Methods and practices. *Information Processing & Management, 22*(6), 45–463. doi:10.1016/0306-4573(86)90096-8

Brazier, F. M. T. (1997). DESIRE: Modelling multi-agent systems in a compositional formal framework. *International Journal of Cooperative Information Systems, 6*(1), 67–94. doi:10.1142/S0218843097000069

Bredt, J. C. (2001). An occupational view of the Australian labor force patterns of job growth and decline. *International Journal of Manpower, 5*(22).

Bresciani, P., et al. (2002). *TROPOS: An agent-oriented software development methodology* (Technical report

DIT-02-015). Informatica e Telecomunicazioni, University of Trento, Italy.

Brewster, C., O'Hara, K., Fuller, S., Wilks, Y., Franconi, E., & Musen, M. A. (2004). Knowledge representation with ontologies: The present and future. *IEEE Intelligent Systems, 19*(1), 72–81. doi:10.1109/MIS.2004.1265889

Brey, Ph. (2000, December). Disclosive computer ethics. *Computers & Society*, 10–16. doi:10.1145/572260.572264

Brier, S. (2004). Cybersemiotics and the problems of the information-processing paradigm as a candidate for a unified science of information behind library information science. *Library Trends, 52*(3), 629–657.

Brown, A. D., & Humphreys, M. (2006). Organizational identity and place: A discursive exploration of hegemony and resistance. *Journal of Management Studies, 43*(2), 231–257. doi:10.1111/j.1467-6486.2006.00589.x

Bruszt, L. (2002). Market making as state making: Constitutions and economic development in post-communist eastern Europe. *Constitutional Political Economy, 13*, 53–72. doi:10.1023/A:1013687107792

Buchanan, S., & Gibb, F. (2007). The information audit: Role and scope. *International Journal of Information Management, 27*, 159–172. doi:10.1016/j.ijinfomgt.2007.01.002

Bueno, M. F. (2005). *A Economia da Informacão no Brasil.* Retrieved Oktober 17, 2007, from http://www.ie.ufu.br/ix_enep_mesas/

Bürckert, H.-J., & Vierke, G. (1999). Simulated trading mechanismen für speditionsübergreifende transportplanung. In H. Kopfer & C. Bierwirth (Eds.), *Logistic management – intelligente I+K technologien.*Springer-Verlag.

Bürckert, H.-J., Fischer, K., & Vierke, G. (1998). Transportation scheduling with holonic MAS – The TELETRUCK approach. In H.S. Nwama & D.T. Ndumu (Eds.), *Proceedings of the third international conference on practical application of intelligent agents and multi-agent technology (PAAM'98).*

Bürckert, H.-J., Fischer, K., & Vierke, G. (1999). Holonic fleet scheduling with TELETRUCK. In *Proceedings of the second international conference on computing anticipatory systems (CASYS'98).*

Bunge, M. (1979). *Treatise on basic philosophy: A world of systems* (Vol. 4, Ontology II). Dordrecht, Holland: D.Reidel Publishing Company.

Burrafato, P., & Cossentino, M. (2002). Designing a multi-agent solution for a bookstore with the PASSI methodology. In *Proceedings of the fourth international bi-conference workshop on agent-oriented information systems (AOIS-2002) at CAiSE'02, Toronto, Ontario, Canada.* Retrieved from http://www.pa.icar.cnr.it/cossentino/paper/AOIS02.pdf

Burt, C. W., & Sisk, J. E. (2005). Which physicians and practices are using electronic medical records? *Health Affairs, 24*(5), 1334–1343. doi:10.1377/hlthaff.24.5.1334

Burton, R. M., Eriksen, B. H., & Hakonsson, D. D. Knudsen, T., & Snow, C.C. (2008). *Designing Organizations, 21st Century Approaches.* New York: Springer.

Bush, G., Cranefield, S., & Purvis, M. (2001). *The Styx agent methodology.* The information science discussion papers series 2001/02. Department of Information Science, University of Otago, Otago, New Zealand. Retrieved from http://waitaki.otago.ac.nz/~martin/Documents/dp2001-02.pdf

Busis, N. A., & Hier, D. (2007). How to get your electronic health records in order. *Neurology Today, 7*, 16. doi:10.1097/01.NT.0000296515.14653.5f

Buxmann, P., Wietzel, T., Westarp, F., & Konig, W. (1999). The standardization problem – An economic analysis of standards in information systems. In *Proceedings of the 1st IEEE Conference on Standardization and Innovation in Information Technology* (pp.157-162). SIIT'99, Aachen, Germany, Retrieved October 13, 2008, from http://www.nets.rwth-aachen.de/~jakobs/siit99/Proceedings.html

Bynum, T. W., & Rogerson, S. (1996). Introduction and overview: Global information ethics. *Science and Engineering Ethics, 2*(2), 131–136. doi:10.1007/BF02583548

Bynum, T., & Rogerson, S. (2004). *Computer ethics and professional responsibility* (pp. 60-85) Blackwell Publishing.

Byrom, R., Cordenonsi, R., Cornwall, L., Craig, M., Abdeslem, D., Ducan, A., et al. (2005). *APEL: An implementation of Grid accounting using R-GMA*. Retrieved June 18, 2007, from http://www.gridpp.ac.uk/abstracts/allhands2005/apel.pdf

Caire, G., et al. (2002). Agent oriented analysis using MESSAGE/UML. In *Proceedings of the agent-oriented software engineering II second international workshop (AOSE 2001), Montreal, Canada* (LNCS 2222, pp. 101-108).

Calder, A., & Watkins, S. (2006) *International IT Governance: An executive guide to ISO17799/ISO 27001*. London: Kogan Page.

California HealthCare Foundation (2005). National Consumer Health Privacy Survey 2005.

Calluzzo, V. J., & Cante, C. J. (2004). Ethics in information technology and software use. *Journal of Business Ethics, 51*, 301–312. doi:10.1023/B:BUSI.0000032658.12032.4e

Capurro, R. (2008). Hermeneutics facing the information enframing, *ACM Ubiquity*, 9(8).

Capurro, R. (2008). Information ethics for and from Africa. *Journal of the American Society for Information Science and Technology, 59*(7), 1162–1170. doi:10.1002/asi.20850

Carmel, E. (1999). *Global software teams: Collaborating across borders and time zones*. Upper Saddle River, NJ: Prentice-Hall

Carmel, E., & Tjia, P. (2005). *Offshoring information technology: Sourcing and outsourcing to a global workforce*. Cambridge University Press

Carr, D. W. (2003). An ethos of trust in information service. In B. Rockenbach, & T. Mendina. *Ethics and electronic information: A festschrift for Stephen Almagno* (pp.45-52). Jefferson, North Carolina: McFarland & Company, Inc.

Casey, V., & Richardson, I. (2006). Uncovering the reality within virtual software teams. In P. Kruchten et al. (Eds.), *International workshop on global software development for the practitioner* (pp. 66-72). New York: ACM.

Castells, M. (2003). *Galaktyka Internetu*. Poznan, Poland: Rebis.

Catarci, T. (2000). What happened when database researchers met usability. *Information Systems, 25*(3), 177–212. doi:10.1016/S0306-4379(00)00015-6

Chadwick, R. F., & Schroeder, D. (2002). *Applied ethics: Critical concepts in philosophy; v. 5: business and economics*. New York: Routledge.

Chaim, Z. (2007). Conceptual approaches for defining data, information, and knowledge. *Journal of the American Society for Information Science and Technology, 58*, 335–350. doi:10.1002/asi.20507

Chakrabarti, A. (2007). *Grid computing security* (1st ed.). Berlin/Heidelberg: Springer.

Chakrabarti, A., Damodaran, A., & Sengupta, S. (2008). Grid computing security: A taxonomy. *IEEE Security and Privacy, 6*(1), 44–51. doi:10.1109/MSP.2008.12

Chandrasekaran, B., Johnson, T.R., & Benjamins, V.R. (1999). Ontologies: What are they? Why do we need them?. *IEEE Intelligent Systems and their Applications, 14*(1), 20-26.

Chang, J. F. (2005). *Business process management systems, strategy and implementation*. Boca Raton, FL: Auerbach Publications.

Chatterjee, S., & Harrison, J. S. (2005). Corporate governance. In M.A. Hitt, R.E. Freeman, & J.S. Harrison (Eds.), *The Blackwell handbook of strategic management* (pp.543-564). Blackwell Publishing.

Chaudhry, B., Wang, J., Maglione, M., Mojica, W., Roth, E., & Morton, S. C. (2006). Systematic Review: Impact of health information technology on quality, efficiency, and costs of medical care. *Archives of Internal Medicine, 144*(10), 742–752.

Chen, D., & Doumeingts, G. (2004). Basic concepts and approaches to develop interoperability of enterprise applications. In L.M. Camarinha-Matos & H., Afsarmanesh (Eds.), *Processes and foundations for virtual organizations* (pp. 323-330). Boston: Kluwer Academic Publishers.

Chen, H., Finin, T., & Joshi, A. (2005). The SOUPA ontology for pervasive computing. *Whitestein Series in Software Agent Technologies* (pp. 233-254).

Chen, K., See, A., & Shumack, S. (2002). Website discussion forums: Results of an Australian project to promote telecommunication in dermatology. Journal of Telemedicine and Telecare, 8(Suppl 3), S3:5-6.

Chen, Y.-J., & Chen, Y.-M. (2008). On technology for functional requirement-based reference design retrieval in engineering knowledge management. *Decision Support Systems*, *44*, 798–816.

Cheng, Y., Farha, R., Kim, M. S., Leon-Garcia, A., & Won-Ki Hong, J. (2006). A generic architecture for autonomic service and network management. *Computer Communications*, *29*(18), 3691–3709. doi:10.1016/j.comcom.2006.06.017

Chervenak, A., Foster, I., Kesselman, C., Salisbury, C., & Tuecke, S. (2001). The data grid: Towards an architecture for the distributed management and analysis of large scientific datasets. *Journal of Network and Computer Applications*, *23*, 187–200. doi:10.1006/jnca.2000.0110

Chess, D. M., Palmer, C. C., & White, S. R. (2003). Security in an autonomic computing environment. *IBM Systems Journal*, *42*(1), 107–118.

Chiemeke, S. C., Evwiekpaefe, A. E., & Chete, F. O. (2006). The adoption of Internet banking in Nigeria: An empirical investigation. [JIBC]. *The Journal of Internet Banking and Commerce*, *3*(11).

Chmielarz, W. (2007). *Systemy biznesu elektronicznego (Electronic business systems).* Warsaw, Difin.

Chmielarz, W. (2008). Metody oceny witryn banków internetowych w zakresie obsługi klienta indywidualnego (Evaluation methods of Internet bank websites with regard to individual client). *Rachunkowość bankowa*, *3*(40), 65-77.

Choi, M., Rhim, H., & Park, K. (2006). *New business models in the information economy: GDP and case studies in Korea.* Korea University Business School, June 2. Retrieved June 10, 2007, from http://www.bit.unisi.ch/abstracts-presentations/presentation-choi_rhim_park.pdf

Clear, T., Gotterbarn, D., & Kwan, C. (2006). Managing software requirements risks with software development impact statements. *New Zealand Journal of Applied Computing.*

Cliquet, G., Hendrikse, G., Tuunanen, M., & Windsperger, J. (Eds.). (2007). *Economics and management of networks, franchising, strategic alliances, and cooperatives.* Berlin: Springer.

Coad, A. (2005). Strategy and control. In A.J. Berry, J. Broadbent, & D. Otley (Eds.), *Management control, theories, issues and performance* (pp. 167-191). New York: Palgrave Macmillan.

Coad, P., & Yourdon, E. (1991). *Object-oriented analysis.* London: Prentice-Hall, Inc.

Cole, E., & Ring, S. (2006). *Insider threat: Protecting the enterprise from sabotage, spying, and theft.* Rockland, MA: Syngress.

Coles, J., & Hesterly, W. S. (1998). The impact of firm-specific assets and the interaction of uncertainty: An examination of make or buy decisions in public and private hospitals. *Journal of Economic Behavior & Organization*, *36*, 383–409. doi:10.1016/S0167-2681(98)00102-4

Conchúir, E. Ó., Holmström, H., Ågerfalk, P. J., & Fitzgerald, B. (2006). Exploring the assumed benefits of global software development. In P. Fernandes et al. (Ed.), *IEEE International Conference on Global Software Engineering* (pp.159-168). Los Alamitos, CA: IEEE Computer Society.

Contos, B. T. (2006). *Enemy at the water cooler: Real-life stories of insider threats and enterprise security management countermeasures.* Rockland, MA: Syngress.

Cool, C., & Spink, A. (2002). Issues of context in information retrieval. (IR): An introduction to the special issue. *Information Processing & Management*, *38*, 605–611. doi:10.1016/S0306-4573(01)00054-1

Cornford, T., & Klecun-Dabrowska, E. (2001). Telehealth technology: Consequences for structure through use. *Medinfo*, *10*(pt 2), 1140–1144.

Cossentino, M., & Potts, M. (2002). A CASE tool supported methodology for the design of multi-agent systems. In *Proceedings of the 2002 international conference on software engineering research and practice (SERP'02), Las Vegas, USA*. Retrieved from http://www.pa.icar.cnr.it/cossentino/paper/SERP02.pdf

Coutaz, J., Crowley, J., Dobson, S., & Garlan, D. (2005). Context is key. *Communications of the ACM*, *48*(3), 49–53. doi:10.1145/1047671.1047703

Cowton, C., & Thomspon, P. (2000). Do codes make a difference? The case of bank lending and the environment. *Journal of Business Ethics*, *24*, 165–178. doi:10.1023/A:1006029327264

Cramton, C. D., & Hinds, P. (2005). Subgroup dynamics in internationally distributed teams: Ethnocentrism or cross-national learning? In B. M. Staw & R. M. Kramer (Eds.), *Research in organizational behavior* (Vol. 26, pp. 231-263). Greenwich, CT: JAI.

Croner, C. M., Sperling, J., & Broome, F. R. (1996). Geographic information systems (GIS): New perspectives in understanding human health and environmental relationships. *Statistics in Medicine*, *15*(18), 1961–1977. doi:10.1002/(SICI)1097-0258(19960930)15:18<1961::AID-SIM408>3.0.CO;2-L

Curran, K., Mulvenna, M., Nugant, C., & Galis, A. (2007). Challenges and research directions in autonomic communications. *Int. J. Internet Protocol Technology*, *2*(1), 3–17. doi:10.1504/IJIPT.2007.011593

d'Inverno, M. (1997). A formal specification of dMARS. *Intelligent Agents IV* (. *LNAI*, *1365*, 155–176.

d'Inverno, M., & Luck, M. (2001). *Understanding agent systems*. Berlin: Springer.

Daily, C. M., Dalton, D. R., & Cannella, A. A. (2003). Corporate governance: Decades of dialogue and data. *Academy of Management Review*, *28*(3), 371–382.

Davenport, T. (2005). *Thinking for a living*. Harvard Business School Press.

Dean, M., & Schreiber, G. (Eds.). (2004). *OWL Web ontology language reference* (W3C recommendation).

Debenham, J., & Henderson-Sellers, B. (2002). Full lifecycle methodologies for agent-oriented systems – The extended OPEN process framework. In *Proceedings of the workshop on agent oriented information systems (AOIS-2002) at CAiSE'02, Toronto, Canada.*

Dejong, P. (2006). Going with the flow. *ACM Queue; Tomorrow's Computing Today*, *4*(2), 24–32. doi:10.1145/1122674.1122686

DeLoach, S. (2001). Analysis and design using MaSE and agentTool. In *Proceedings of the 12th Midwest artificial intelligence and cognitive science conference (MAICS 2001), Oxford, OH, March 31-April 1, 2001* (pp. 1-7).

Department of Health and Human Services. (2008). Health information technology home. Retrieved from http://www.dhhs.gov/healthit/

Derbel, A., Agoulmine, N., & Salaun, M. (2009). ANEMA: Autonomic network management architecture to support self-configuration and self-optimization in IP networks. *Computer Networks*, *53*, 418–530. doi:10.1016/j.comnet.2008.10.022

Desouza, K. C. (2007). Preface. In K. C. Desouza (Ed.), *Agile information systems, conceptualization, construction, and management* (pp. 11-18). Amsterdam: Elsevier.

Dessler, G. (2001). *Management*. NJ: Prentice Hall, Inc.

D-Grid, The German Grid Initiative. (2008). Retrieved October 21, 2008, from http://www.d-grid.de

Diaz, c., Seys, S., Claessens, J., & Preneel, B. (2002). Towards measuring anonymity (LNCS 2482).

Dick, R. S., Steen, E. B., & Detmer, D. E. (Eds.). (1991). The computer-based patient record: An essential technology for health care. Washington, DC: National Academy Press.

Dictionary, B. B. (n.d.). Retrieved October 10, 2008, from http://www.bnet.com

Dietz, J. L. G. (2001). DEMO: Towards a discipline of organisation engineering. *European Journal of Operational Research*, *128*, 351–363. doi:10.1016/S0377-2217(00)00077-1

Dietz, J. L. G. (2006). *Enterprise ontology theory and methodology.* Berlin/Heidelberg: Springer-Verlag.

Dignum, F. (2007). The challenges of finding intelligent agents. *IEEE Intelligent Systems*, *22*(4), 3–7. doi:10.1109/MIS.2007.78

Dinitz, E., Porto, R. M., & Adachi, T. (2005) Internet Banking in Brazil: Evaluation of functionality, reliability and usability, *The Electronic Journal of Information System Evaluation*, 1 (8), 41-50; from: http://www.ejise.com.

Distributed European infrastructure for supercomputing applications (DEISA) (2007). Retrieved July 26, 2006, from http://www.deisa.org/

Dobson, S., Denazis, S., Fernandez, A., Gaiti, D., Gelenbe, E., & Massacci, F. (2006). A survey of autonomic communications. *ACM Transactions on Autonomous and Adaptive Systems*, *1*(2), 223–259. doi:10.1145/1186778.1186782

Dolenc, M., Kurowski, K., Kulczewski, M., & Gehre, A. (2007). InteliGrid document management System: An overview. In M. Bubak, M. Turała, K. Wiatr (Eds.), *Cracow'06 Grid Workshop* (pp. 21-28), Cyfronet AGH Cracow.

Dori, D. (2002). *Object-process methodology.* Berlin/Heidelberg: Springer-Verlag.

Dou, D., McDermott, D., & Qi, P. (2004). Ontology translation on the Semantic Web. *Journal on Data Semantics II*, (. *LNCS*, *3360*, 35–57.

Drogoul, A., & Zucker, J.-D. (1998). *Methodological issues for designing multi-agent systems with machine learning techniques: Capitalizing experiences from the Robocup challenge* (Technical report LIP6 1998/041). Laboratoire d'Informatique de Paris 6.

Drucker, P. F. (1995). *Managing in a time of great change.* New York: Truman Talley Books/Dutton.

Dubray, J. J. (2007). The Seven fallacies of business process execution [Electronic Version]. Retrieved September 23, 2008, from http://www.infoq.com/articles/seven-fallacies-of-bpmhttp://www.infoq.com/articles/seven-fallacies-of-bpm

Duin, H. (2008). *Systemic strategic management for VBEs in the manufacturing sector.* In L.M. Camarinba-Matos, & W. Picard (Eds.), *Pervasive Collaborative Networks, IFIP TC 5 WG 5.5. Ninth Working Conference on Virtual Enterprises, Sept. 2008, Poznan, Poland.* NewYork: Springer.

Dutoit, A. H., Johnstone, J., & Bruegge, B. (2001). Knowledge scouts: Reducing communication barriers in a distributed software development project. In H. Jifeng et al. (Eds.), *Asia-Pacific Software Engineering Conference (APSEC)* (pp. 427-430). Los Alamitos, CA: IEEE Computer Society.

Dyk, P., & Lenar, M. (2006). Applying negotiation methods to resolve conflict in multi-agent environments. In C. Daniłowicz (Ed), *Multimedia and network information systems* (pp. 259-269). Wrocław: Wroclaw University of Technology Press.

Działalności, P. K. *(PKD). Nomenclature des Activités de Communauté Européenne – NACE rev. 1.1.* (2004). Warsaw, Poland: Central Statistical Office.

Dziuba, D. T. (1992). Analiza zatrudnienia w sektorze informacyjnym gospodarki. *Wiadomości Statystyczne 11.* Warsaw, Poland: Central Statistical Office.

Dziuba, D. T. (1996). *Toward electronization of the economic market. Global trends and Polish experience* (Economic Discussion Papers No. 22). Warsaw, Poland: University of Warsaw, Faculty of Economic Sciences.

Dziuba, D. T. (1998). *Analiza możliwości wyodrębniania i diagnozowania sektora informacyjnego w gospodarce Polski.* Warsaw, Poland: Univeristy of Warsaw.

Dziuba, D. T. (2000). *Gospodarki nasycone informacją i wiedzą. Podstawy ekonomiki sektora informacyjnego.* Warsaw, Poland: Nowy Dziennik.

Dziuba, D. T. (2003). Information sector in the new economy. In *The "New Economy" and Postsocialist Transition. V International Conference Papers.* Leon Kozminski Academy of Entrepreneurship and Management. Warsaw, Poland: Tiger.

Dziuba, D. T. (2005). Kilka rozważań o informacji i kapitale informacyjnym. In M. Rószkiewicz, & E. Wędrowska (Eds.), *Informacja w społeczeństwie XXI wieku* (pp. 21-36). Warsaw, Poland: Szkoła Główna Handlowa.

Dziuba, D. T. (2007). *Metody ekonomiki sektora informacyjnego*. Warsaw, Poland: Difin.

EGEE. (2005). *Review of accounting and monitoring software deliverable: D1.* Retrieved October 10, 2008, from https://www.egee.cesga.es/documents/D1/EGEE-D1-Review-Accounting-Monitoring-v0.8.pdf

Eggleston, B. (1996). *The new engineering contract.* London: Blackwell Science.

Elammari, M., & Lalonde, W. (1999). An agent-oriented methodology: High-level and intermediate models. In *Proceedings of the 1st international workshop on agent-oriented information systems.*

Electronic Privacy Information Center. (2002). *Privacy and human rights: An international survey of privacy laws and developments.* EPIC.org.

Elmroth, E., Gardfjäll, P., Mulmo, O., Sandgren, Å., & Sandholm, T. (2003). *A coordinated accounting solution for SweGrid.* Retrieved November 18, 2007, from http://www.pdc.kth.se/grid/sgas/docs/SGAS-0.1.3.pdf

EMO (2000). *Internal project documentation.*Celje: EMO Orodjarna.

Engelbrecht, H. J. (1985). An exposition of the information sector approach with special reference to Australia. *Prometheus, 3*(2). doi:10.1080/08109028508629004

Engelbrecht, H. J., & Mahon, A. (2003). Information workforce in New Zealand, 1991-2001. *New Zealand Population Review, 29*(2).

Etzioni, O., & Weld, D. (1995). Intelligent agents on the Internet: Fact, fiction, and forecast. *IEEE Expert, 10*(4), 44–49. doi:10.1109/64.403956

Evans, J. R., & King, V. E. (1999). Business-to-business marketing and World Wide Web: Planning managing and assesssing web sites. *Industrial Marketing Management, 28*, 343–358. doi:10.1016/S0019-8501(98)00013-3

Evans, P., & Wolf, B. (2005). Collaboration rules. *Harvard Business Review*, July-August.

Eysenbach, G. (2001). What is e-health? *Journal of Medical Internet Research, 3*(2), e20. doi:10.2196/jmir.3.2.e20

Fahy, M., Roche, J., & Weiner, A. (2005). *A beyond governance, creating corporate value through performance, conformance and responsibility.* Chichester: John Wiley & Sons.

Fan, Y., & Lai, J. (2002). An architecture for cross-organization business process integration. In *Proceedings of the 5th international conference on managing innovations in manufacturing (MIM), Milwaukee, Wisconsin, USA, September 9-11, 2002* (pp. 125-134).

Ferber, J. (1999). *Multi-agent systems.* New York: Addison Wesley.

Feuerlicht, G. (2006). *System development life-cycle support for service-oriented applications.* Quebec, Ont., Canada.

Fidel, R. (2004). A multidimensional approach to the study of human information interaction: A case study of collaborative information retrieval. *Journal of the American Society for Information Science American Society for Information Science, 55*(11), 939–953.

Flakiewicz, W. (1990). *Informacyjne systemy zarządzania* (*Management Information Systems*). Warsaw, Poland: Polskie Wydawnictwo Ekonomiczne.

Floridi, L. (1999). Information ethics: on the theoretical foundations of computer ethics. *Ethics and Information Technology, 1*(1), 37–56. doi:10.1023/A:1010018611096

Floridi, L. (2006). Information technologies and the tragedy of good will. *Ethics and Information Technology, 8*(4), 253–262. doi:10.1007/s10676-006-9110-6

Floridi, L. (2006b). Information ethics, its nature and scope. *SIGCAS Computers and Society, 36*(3), 21–36. doi:10.1145/1195716.1195719

Floridi, L., & Sanders, J. W. (2004). Levellism and the method of abstraction, *IEG – RESEARCH REPORT* 22.11.04. Retrieved June 11, 2008, from http://web.comlab.ox.ac.uk/oucl/research/areas/ieg.

Food Quality and Safety in Europe, Project Catalogue, European Commission, Brussels, December 2007, http://ec.europa.eu/research/biosociety/food_quality/download_en.html

Foster, I. (2002). What is the Grid? A three point checklist. *GRID Today.*

Fowler, M. (1997). *Analysis patterns: Reusable object models.* Addison-Westley Longman, Inc.

Fox, M. S., Barbuceanu, M., & Teigen, R. (2000). Agent-oriented supply-chain management. *International Journal of Flexible Manufacturing Systems, 12*, 165–188. doi:10.1023/A:1008195614074

Fox, S. (2006). Online Health Search 2006. Washington, DC: Pew Internet & American Life Project.

Frank, R. H. (2004). *What price the moral high ground? Ethical dilemmas in competitive environments.* Princeton, NJ: Princeton University Press.

Frey, D., et al. (2003). Integrated multi-agent-based supply chain management. *Proceedings of the 1st international workshop on agent-based computing for enterprise collaboration.* Gambardella, L. M., Rizzoli, E., & Funk, P. (n.d.). Agent-based planning and simulation of combined rail/road transport. Retrieved from http://www.idsia.ch/~luca/simulation02.pdf

Friedag, H. R., & Schmidt, W. (2003). *My balanced scorecard.* Warszawa: Wydawnictwo C. H. Beck.

Friedman, B., & Kahn, P. (1997). People are responsible, computers are not. In M. Erman, M.Williams & M. Shauf (Eds.), *Computers, Ethics and Society* (pp. 303–12). Oxford: Oxford University Press.

Friedman, T. L. (2005). *The world is flat: Brief history of the 21st Century.* New York: Farrar, Straus and Giroux.

Fuhua, O. L. (2005). *Designing distributed learning environments with intelligent software agents.* Hershey, PA: Idea Group Inc.

Ganek, A. G., & Corbi, T. A. (2003). The dawning of the autonomic computing era. *IBM Systems Journal, 42*(1), 5–18.

Gans, D., Kralewski, J., Hammons, T., & Dowd, B. (2005). Medical groups' adoption of electronic health records and information systems. *Health Affairs, 24*(5), 1323–1333. doi:10.1377/hlthaff.24.5.1323

Garcia, A., & Lucena, C. (2008). Taming heterogeneous agent architectures. *Communications of the ACM, 51*(5), 75–81. doi:10.1145/1342327.1342341

Garcia, A., Lucena, G., & Cowan, D. (2004). Agents in object-oriented software engineering. *Software, Practice & Experience, 34*(5), 489–521. doi:10.1002/spe.578

Gardfjäll, P. (2003). *SweGrid Accounting System bank.* Retrieved June 18, 2007, from http://www.sgas.se/docs/SGAS-BANK-DD-0.1.pdf

Gardfjäll, P., Elmroth, E., Johnsson, L., Mulmo, O., & Sandholm, T. (2006). Scalable Grid-wide capacity allocation with the SweGrid Accounting System (SGAS). *concurrency and computation practice and experience.* John Wiley & Sons, Ltd. (Submitted for Journal Publication, October 2006). Retrieved April 14, 2007, from http://www.cs.umu.se/~elmroth/papers/sgas_submitted_oct2006.pdf

Garson, A. Jr, & Levin, S. A. (2001). The 10-year trends for the future of healthcare: Implications for academic health centers. *The Ochsner Journal, 3*(1), 10–15.

Genesereth, M. R. (1995). Interoperability: An agent based framework. *AI Expert, March 1995*, 34-40.

Genesereth, M. R., & Ketchpel, S. P. (1994). Software agents. *Communications of the ACM, 37*(7), 48–53. doi:10.1145/176789.176794

Gerber, A., & Klusch, M. (2002). Agent-based integrated services for timber production and sales. *IEEE Intelligent Systems, 17*(1), 33–39. doi:10.1109/5254.988446

Gibb, F., Buchanan, S., & Shah, S. (2006). An integrated approach to process and service management. *International Journal of Information Management, 26*, 44–58. doi:10.1016/j.ijinfomgt.2005.10.007

Giunchiglia, F., Mylopoulos, J., & Perini, A. (2002). The Tropos software development methodology: Processes, models and diagrams. In *Proceedings of the third international workshop on agent-oriented software engineering (*LNCS 2585, pp. 162-173).

Glasser, N. (1996). The CoMoMAS methodology and environment for multi-agent system development. *Multi-agent systems, methodologies and applications, Second*

Australian workshop on distributed artificial intelligence (. *LNAI, 1286*, 1–16.

Glassey, O. (2008). A case study on process modelling – Three questions and three techniques. *Decision Support Systems, 44*, 842–853. doi:10.1016/j.dss.2007.10.004

Glushko, R. J., & McGrtah, T. (2005). Document engineering: analyzing and designing the semantics of business service networks. In *Proceedings of the IEEE EEE05 International Workshop on Business Services Networks*.

Göhner, M. (2006). *Status quo: Abrechnung im Bereich des Grid Computing (*Bericht Nr. 2006-03). Institut für Informationstechnische Systeme, Universität der Bundeswehr München. Retrieved December 28, 2007, from https://www.unibw.de/rz/dokumente/getFILE?fid=1441518

Göhner, M., & Rückemann, C.-P. (2006). *Accounting-Ansätze im Bereich des Grid-Computing.* D-Grid Integration project, D-Grid document. Retrieved December 28, 2007, http://www.d-grid.de/fileadmin/dgi_document/FG2/koordination_mab/mab_accounting_ansaetze.pdf

Göhner, M., & Rückemann, C.-P. (2006). *Konzeption eines Grid-Accounting-Systems.* D-Grid Integration project, D-Grid document. Retrieved December 28, 2007, http://www.d-grid.de/fileadmin/dgi_document/FG2/koordination_mab/mab_accounting_system.pdf

Google (2008). Google Health. Retrieved September 28, 2008, from https://www.google.com/health

Gordon-Larsen, P., Nelson, M. C., Page, P., & Popkin, B. M. (2006). Inequality in the built environment underlies key health disparities in physical activity and obesity. *Pediatrics, 117*(2), 417–424. doi:10.1542/peds.2005-0058

Goser, K., et al. (2006). Next-generation process management with ADEPT2. In M. Adams & S. Sadiq (Eds.), *Proceedings of the BPM demonstration program at the fifth international conference on business process management (BPM'07) Brisbane, Australia, 24-27 September 2007.*

Gotterbarn, D. (2007). Enhancing ethical decision support methods: Clarifying the solution space with line drawing. *SIGCAS Computers and Society, 37*(2), 53–63. doi:10.1145/1327325.1327329

Gotterbarn, D., & Rogerson, S. (2005). Responsible risk analysis for software development: Creating the software development impact statement. *Communications of the Association for Information Systems.*

Grant, R. M. (1996). Prospering in dynamically-competitive environments: Organizational capability as knowledge integration. *Organization Science, 7*(4), 375–387. doi:10.1287/orsc.7.4.375

Grant, R. W. (2006). Ethics and incentives: A political approach. *The American Political Science Review, 100*(1), 29–39. doi:10.1017/S0003055406061983

Graudina, V., & Grundspenkis, J. (2006). Agent-based systems, their architecture and technologies from logistics perspective. *Scientific proceedings of Riga Technical University, Computer science, Applied computer systems, 5th Series, Vol. 26* (pp. 159-173). Riga: RTU Publishing House.

GRIA. (2009). *GRIA - PBAC 2 Manual.* Retrieved February 10, 2009, from http://www.gria.org/documentation/5.1/manual/pbac-2-manual

Grid Economic Services Architecture Working Group. (2006). Retrieved September 5, 2007, from https://forge.gridforum.org/projects/gesa-wg

Griethuisen, J. J. (1982). *Concepts and terminology for the conceptual schema and information base* (No. 695).

Grundspenkis, J. (2008). Intelligent agents in logistics: Some trends and solutions. In *Proceedings of the 11th international workshop on harbor maritime multimodal logistics modelling & simulation, September 17-19, 2008, Campora S. Giovanni, Italy, DIPTEM University of Genoa* (pp. 174-179).

Grundspenkis, J., & Kirikova, M. (2005). Impact of the intelligent agent paradigm on knowledge management. In C.T. Leondes (Ed.), *Intelligent knowledge-based systems: Business and technology in the new millennium* (Vol. 1, pp. 164-206). Boston: Kluwer Academic Publishers.

Grundspenkis, J., & Lavendelis, E. (2006). Multiagent based simulation tool for transportation and logistics decision support. In *Proceedings of the 3rd international workshop on computer supported activity coordination (CSAC 2006)* (pp. 45-54). Portugal: INSTICC Press.

Grundspenkis, J., & Pozdnyakov, D. (2006). An overview of the agent based systems for the business process management. In *Proceedings of the international conference on computer systems and technologies (CompSysTech'06), June 15-16, 2006, Veliko Tarnovo, Bulgaria*, II.13-1 - II.13-6.

Gudea, S. W. (2004). Media richness and the valuation of online discussion support systems. In *Proceedings of the Annual Conference of the Southern Association for Information Systems*. Savannah, GA, USA.

Guerrero, A., Villagrá, V.A., López de Vergara, J.E., & Berrocal. J. (2005). Ontology-based integration of management behaviour and information definitions using SWRL and OWL. *DSOM'2005* (LNCS 3775, pp.12-23).

Gustas, R. (2000). Integrated approach for information system analysis at the enterprise level. In J. Filipe (Ed.), *Enterprise information systems* (pp. 81-88). Kluwer Academic Publishers.

Gustas, R., & Gustiené, P. (2002). Extending Lyee methodology using the enterprise modelling approach. In H. Fujita & P. Johannesson (Eds.), *New trends in software methodologies, tools and techniques. Proceedings of Lyee_Wo2* (Vol. 1, pp. p. 273-288). Frontiers in Artificial Intelligence and Applications. Amsterdam: IOS Press.

Gustas, R., & Gustiené, P. (2004). Towards the enterprise engineering approach for information system modelling across organisational and technical boundaries. In *Enterprise Information Systems* (pp. 235-252). Netherlands: Kluwer Academic Publisher.

Gustas, R., & Gustiené, P. (2008). *A New method for conceptual modelling of information systems.* Paper presented at the the 17th International Conference on Information System Development (ISD2008), Paphos, Cyprus.

Gustas, R., & Gustiene, P. (2008). Pragmatic-driven approach for service-oriented analysis and design. In P. Johannesson & E. Söderström (Eds.), *Information systems engineering: From data analysis to process networks* (pp. 97-128). Hershey, PA: IGI Global.

Gustas, R., & Gustiené, P. (2009). Service-oriented foundation and analysis patterns for conceptual modellling of information systems. In C. Barry, K. Conboy, M. Lang, G. Wojtkowski & W. Wojtkowski (Eds.), *Information system development: Challenges in practice, theory and education. Proceedings of the 16th International Conference on Information System Development (ISD2007)* (Vol. 1, pp. 249-265). Springer Science+Business Media, LLC.

Gustiené, P. (2003). On desirable qualities of information system specifications. In J. Cha, R. Jardim-Goncalves & A. Steiger-Garcao (Eds.), *Concurrent Engineering: The Vision for the Future Generation in Research and Applications. Proceedings of the 10th ISPE International conference on concurrent engineering: Research and applications* (Vol. 1, pp. 1279-1287). The Netherlands: Swets & Zeitlinger B.V.

Gustiene, P., & Gustas, R. (2008). Introducing service-orientation into system analysis and design. In J. Cordeiro & J. Filipe (Eds.), *ICEIS 2008 Proceedings of the Tenth International Conference on Enterprise Information Systems* (Vol. ISAS-2, pp. 189-194). Barcelona, Spain-June 12-16 INSTICC-Institute for Systems and Technologies of Information, Control and Communication.

Haas, R., Droz, P., & Stiller, B. (2003). Autonomic service deployment in networks. *IBM Systems Journal, 42*(1), 150–165.

Hamilton, S. (2000) Controlling risks. In D.A. Marchand (Ed.), *Competing with information, A Manager's guide to creating business value with information content* (pp. 209-230). Chichester: John Wiley & Sons.

Hammer, M., & Champy, J. (2001). *Reengineering the corporation: A manifesto for business revolution.* New York: Harper Business.

Hansen, M. T., Nohria, N., & Tierney, T. (1999). What's your strategy for managing knowledge. *Harvard Business Review*, (March-April): 106–116.

Harmon, G. (1984). The measurement of information. *Information Processing & Management, 1-2*, 193–198. doi:10.1016/0306-4573(84)90049-9

Harris Interactive. (2002). European Physicians Especially in Sweden, Netherlands and Denmark, Lead

U.S. in Use of Electronic Medical Records. Retrieved February 20, 2006, from http://www.harrisinteractive.com/news/newsletters/healthnews/HI_HealthCare-News2002vol2_Iss16.pdf

Harris, C. E., Jr., Pritchard, M. S., & Rabins, M. J. (2004). *Engineering ethics: Concepts and cases* (3rd ed.). Wadsworth.

Hartley, R. W. L. (1928). Transmission of Information. *The Bell System Technical Journal*, *7*(3), 535–563.

Hasselbladh, H., & Kallinikos, J. (2000). The project of rationalization: A critique and reappraisal of neo-institutionalism. *Organization Studies*, *21*(4), 697–720. doi:10.1177/0170840600214002

Hawryszkiewycz, I. T. (1996). Support services for business networking. In E. Altman & N. Terashima (Eds.), *Proceedings IFIP96*, Canberra. London: Chapman and Hall.

Hawryszkiewycz, I. T. (1997). A framework for strategic planning for communications support. In *Proceedings of The inaugural Conference of Informatics in Multinational Enterprises*, Washington, October, 1997 (pp. 141-151).

Hawryszkiewycz, I. T. (2005). A Metamodel for collaborative systems. *Journal of Computer Information Systems*, 131–146.

Hawryszkiewycz, I. T., & Lin, A. (2003). Process knowledge support for emergent processes. In *Proceedings of the Second IASTED International Conference on Information and Knowledge Management, Scottsdale, Arizona, November, 2003* (pp. 83-87).

Hawryszkiewycz, I.T. (in press). Knowledge management: Organizing for business value through collaboration. Palgrave Macmillan, Basingstoke.

Hayes, R., Pisano, G., Upton, D., & Wheelwright, S. (2005). *Operations, strategy, and technology: Pursuing the competitive edge*. Hoboken, NJ: John Wiley & Sons.

Heathfield, H., Pitty, D., & Hanka, R. (1998). Evaluating information technology in health care: Barriers and challenges. *British Medical Journal*, *316*, 1959–1961.

Heidegger, M. (1962). *Being and time*. New York: Harper and Row.

Heise Newsticker. (2008). *17 Millionen Euro für den Aufbau einer nationalen Grid-Infrastruktur*. Heise Newsticker, (2005, September 8). Retrieved July 10, 2008, from http://www.heise.de/newsticker/meldung/63739

Helaakoski, H., Iskanius, P., & Peltomaa, I. (2007). Agent-based architecture for virtual enterprise to support agility. In L. Camarinha-Matos, H. Afsarmanesh, P. Novais, & C. Analide (Eds.), *Establishing the foundation of collaborative networks* (pp. 299-306). Berlin: Springer.

Hendler, J. (2001). Agents and the semantic Web. *IEEE Intelligent Systems*, *16*(2), 30–37. doi:10.1109/5254.920597

Henoch, J., & Ulrich, H. (2000). Agent-based management systems in logistics. In I.J. Timm et al. (Eds.), *14th European conference on artificial intelligence, Workshop notes, Agent technologies and their application scenarios in logistics* (pp. 11-15).

Herbsleb, J. D., & Mockus, A. (2003). An empirical study of speed and communication in globally distributed software development. *IEEE Transactions on Software Engineering*, *29*(6), 481–494. doi:10.1109/TSE.2003.1205177

Herbsleb, J., Paulish, D. J., & Bass, M. (2005). Global software development at Siemens: Experience from nine projects. In W. Griswold et al. (Eds.), *International Conference on Software Engineering (ICSE)* (pp. 524-533). New York: ACM.

Hernes, M. (2004). Coordinate inconsistent of knowledge in a distributed systems using a consensus method. In C. Daniłowicz (Ed.), *Multimedia and network information systems*. Wrocław: Wroclaw University of Technology Press.

Hernes, M., & Nguyen, N. T. (2004). Deriving consensus for incomplete ordered partitions. In N.T. Nguyen (Ed.), *Intelligent technologies for inconsistent knowledge processing. Advanced knowledge international*. Australia: Advanced Knowledge International.

Hersh, W. (2004). Health care information technology: Progress and barriers. *Journal of the American*

Medical Association, 292(18), 2273–2274. doi:10.1001/jama.292.18.2273

Hersh, W. (2006). Who are the informaticians? What we know and should know. *Journal of the American Medical Informatics Association, 13*(2), 166–169. doi:10.1197/jamia.M1912

Hilb, M. (2006). *New corporate governance.* New York: Springer Verlag.

Hillestad, R., Bigelow, J., Bower, A., Girosi, F., Meili, R., & Scoville, R. (2005). Can electronic medical record systems transform health care? Potential health benefits, savings, and costs. *Health Affairs, 24*(5), 1103–1117. doi:10.1377/hlthaff.24.5.1103

Hinds, P. J., & Weisband, S. P. (2003). Knowledge sharing and shared understanding in virtual teams. In C.B. Gibson & S.G. Cohen (Eds.), *Virtual teams that work, creating conditions for virtual team effectiveness* (pp. 21-36). San Francisco: Jossey-Bass.

Hing, E. S., Burt, C. W., & Woodwell, D. A. (2007). Electronic medical record use by office-based physicians and their practices. *Advance Data, 393,* 1–7.

HL7 Organisation. (2009). *Health Level 7.* Retrieved Februart 10, 2009, from http://www.hl7.org

HL7. (2009). Health Level 7. Retrieved from http://www.hl7.org

HL7Australia. (2009). HL7 Affiliates Links. Retrieved February 10, 2009, from http://www.hl7.org.au/HL7-Links.htm

HLRN. North-German Supercomputing Alliance (Norddeutscher Verbund für Hoch- und Höchstleistungsrechnen) (2008). Retrieved October 12, 2008, from http://www.hlrn.de

Hodgkin, D., Horgan, C., & Garnick, D. (1997). Make or buy: HMO's contracting arrangement for mental health care. *Administration and Policy in Mental Health, 24*(4), 359–376. doi:10.1007/BF02042519

Hogben, G., Wilikens, M., & Vakalis, I. (2003). On the ontology of digital identification (LNCS 2889).

Holbrook, S. (2006). Clinical portals: A win for providers. *Electronic Healthcare, 4,* 104–106.

Holmström, H., Fitzgerald, B., Ågerfalk, P. J., & Conchúir, E. Ó. (2006). Agile practices reduce distance in global software development. *Information Systems Management, 23*(3), 7–18. doi:10.1201/1078.10580530/46108.23.3.20060601/93703.2

Hooker, J. (2003) Working across cultures. Stanford, CA: Stanford Business Books.

Horrocks, I., Patel-Schneider, P.F., Boley, H., Tabet, S., Grosof, B., & Dean, M. (2004). *SWRL: A Semantic Web rule language combining OWL and RuleML.* W3C Member submission (21 May 2004).

Hu, L. T., & Bentler, P. M. (1995). Evaluating model fit. In R. H. Hoyle (ed.), S*tructural equation modeling: Concepts, issues, and applications* (pp.76-99). Thousand Oaks, CA.: Sage.

Hugoson, M.-A., Magoulas, T., & Pessi, K. (2008). Interoperability strategies for business agility. In J.L.G. Dietz, A. Albani & J. Barjis (Eds.), *Advances in enterprise engineering I* (pp.108-121). Berlin: Springer.

Huhns, M. N., & Singh, M. P. (1998). Agents and multiagent systems: Themes, approaches and challenges. In M.N. Huhns & M.P. Singh (Eds.), *Readings in agents* (pp. 1-23), San Francisco, CA: Morgan Kaufman.

IBM (2001). *Autonomic computing concepts* [IBM White paper].

IBM (2003). *An architectural blueprint for autonomic computing.* April, revised October.

IEEE - Institute of Electical and Electronics Engineers. (1990). *IEEE Code of Ethics.* IEEE, 345 E. 47th St., New York, NY 10017-2394.

Iglesias, C., et al. (1997). Analysis and design of multiagent systems using MAS-CommonKADS. In *Proceedings of the agent theories, architectures and languages workshop (ATAL 97).* Java agent development framework. (n.d.). Retrieved from http://jade.cselt.it/

Ihnatowicz, I. (1989). *Człowiek. Informacja. Społeczeństwo (Man, Information, Society).* Warsaw, Poland: Czytelnik.

Ingwersen, P. (1996). Cognitive perspectives of information retrieval interaction: Elements of a cognitive IR theory. *The Journal of Documentation*, *52*(1), 3–50. doi:10.1108/eb026960

Institute of Electrical and Electronics Engineers. (1990). *IEEE standard computer dictionary: A compilation of IEEE standard computer glossaries*. New York.

Institute of Medicine (2002). Leadership by example: Coordinating government roles in improving health care quality.

IT Governance Institute (2003, October). *Board Briefing on IT Governance* (2nd ed.). Rolling Meadows: Author..

ITU-T (2000). *M.3010 principles for a telecommunications management network*. ITU-T Recommendations, February.

Jackobson, G., & Weissman, M. D. (1993). Alarm correlation. *IEEE Network*, *7*(6), 52–59. doi:10.1109/65.244794

Jackson, P., & Klobas, J. (2008). Transactive memory systems in organizations: Implications for knowledge directories. *Decision Support Systems*, *44*, 409–424. doi:10.1016/j.dss.2007.05.001

Jacobs, J. L., Dorneich, C. P., & Jones, P. M. (1998). Activity representation and management for crisis action planning. *IEEE International Conference on Systems, Management and Cybernetics, October 1998* (pp. 961-966).

Jaworski, M. (2002). Wywiad gospodarczy na wewnętrzny użytek. *EBIB Elektroniczny Biuletyn Informacyjny Bibliotekarzy*, 11. Retrieved August 2008 from http://ebib.oss.wroc.pl/2002/40

Jennings, B., van der Meer, S., Balasubramaniam, S., Botvich, D., & Foghlú, Ó, M., & Donnelly, W. (2007). Towards autonomic management of communications networks. *IEEE Communications Magazine*, *45*(10), 112–121. doi:10.1109/MCOM.2007.4342833

Jennings, N. R. (2000). Autonomous agents for business process management. *Applied Artificial Intelligence*, *14*, 145189.

Jennings, N. R. (2001). An agent-based approach for building complex software systems. *Communications of the ACM*, *44*(4), 35–41. doi:10.1145/367211.367250

Jennings, N. R., Norman, T. J., & Faratin, P. (1998). ADEPT: An agent-based approach to business process management. *SIGMOD Record*, *27*, 32–39. doi:10.1145/306101.306112

Jennings, N. R., Sycara, K., & Wooldridge, M. (1998). A roadmap of agent research and development. *Autonomous Agents and Multi-Agent Systems*, *1*(1), 7–38. doi:10.1023/A:1010090405266

Jessop, B. (1999). The dynamics of partnership and governance failure. *The new politics of local governance in Britain* (pp.11-32). Basingstoke: Macmillan.

Jha, A., Ferris, T., Donelan, K., DesRoches, C., Shields, A., & Rosenbaum, S. (2006). How common are electronic health records in the United States? A summary of evidence. *Health Affairs*, *25*, 496–507. doi:10.1377/hlthaff.25.w496

Jin, H., Sun, A., Zhang, Q., Zheng, R., & He, R. (2006). MIGP: Medical Image Grid Platform based on HL7 Grid middleware. In *Advances in Information Systems* (pp. 254-263). Berlin/Heidelberg: Springer.

Johnson, D. G. (1985). *Computer ethics*. Englewood Cliffs, NJ: Prentice Hall.

Johnson, R. A. (2002). *Whistleblowing: When it works-and why*. Boulder, CO: Lynne Rienner Publishers.

Johnston, D., Pan, E., Walker, J., Bates, D. W., & Middleton, B. (2003). The value of computerized provider order entry in ambulatory settings. Wellesley, MA: Center for IT Leadership.

Jones, B. (1996). *Sleepers Wake!* Oxford: Oxford University Press.

Jussawalla, M., & Cheah, C. W. (1983). Towards an information economy - The case of Singapore. *Information Economics and Policy*, 1.

Jussawalla, M., & Dworak, S. (1988). The primary information sector of the Philippines. In M. Jussawalla, D. M. Lamberton, & N. D. Karunaratne (Eds.), *The cost of thinking: Information economies of ten pacific countries*. Norwood, New Jersey: Ablex Publishing Corporation.

Kaen, F. R. (2003). *A blueprint for corporate governance strategy, accountability and the preservation of shareholder value*. New York: Amacom American Management Association.

Kagal, L., Finin, T., & Joshi, A. (2003). A policy language for a pervasive computing environment. *IEEE 4th International Workshop on Policies for Distributed Systems and Networks* (pp.63-74).

Kahlor, L., & Mackert, M. (in press). Perceived helpfulness of information and support sources and associated psychosocial outcomes among infertile women. *Fertility and Sterility*.

Kaldor, N. (1967). *Strategic factors in economic development*. New York: Cornel University.

Kanellopoulos, D. (2009). Adaptive multimedia systems based on intelligent context management. *Int. J. Adaptive and Innovative Systems*, *1*(1), 30–43. doi:10.1504/IJAIS.2009.022001

Kaplan, B. (2001). Evaluating informatics application: Clinical decision support system literature review. *International Journal of Medical Informatics*, *64*, 15–37. doi:10.1016/S1386-5056(01)00183-6

Kaptein, M., & Schwartz, M. S. (2008). The effectiveness of business codes: A critical examination of existing studies and the development of an integrated research model. *Journal of Business Ethics*, *77*, 111–127. doi:10.1007/s10551-006-9305-0

Katz, R. L. (1986). Explaining information sector growth in developing countries. *Telecommunications Policy*, 10.

Keeney, J., & Lewis, D. O'Sullivan, D., Roelens, A., Boran, A., & Richardson, R. (2006, April). Runtime semantic interoperability for gathering ontology-based network context. In *Proc. 10th IFIP/IEEE Network Operations and Management Symposium (NOMS'2006)*, Vancouver, Canada.

Kelly, D. (2006). Measuring online information seeking context, Part 1: Background and method. *Journal of the American Society for Information Science American Society for Information Science*, *57*(13), 1729–1939.

Kelly, D. (2006). Measuring online information seeking context, Part 2: Findings and discussion. *Journal of the American Society for Information Science American Society for Information Science*, *57*(14), 1862–1874.

Kendall, E. A., Malkoun, M. T., & Jiang, C. H. (1996). A methodology for developing agent based systems. *Distributed artificial intelligence: Architecture and modelling, First Australian workshop on DAI, Canberra, ACT, Australia, November 13, 1995* (LNCS 1083).

Kephart, J. O., & Chess, D. M. (2003). The vision of autonomic computing. *IEEE Computer*, *36*(1), 41–50.

Kibbe, D. C. Jr, R. L. P., & Green, L. A. (2004). The continuity of care record. *American Family Physician*, *70*(7), 1220–1222.

Kiczales, G., et al. (1997). Aspect-oriented programming. In *Proceedings of the European conference on object-oriented programming (ECOOP'97)* (LNCS 1241, pp. 220-242).

Kinny, D., & Georgeff, M. (1997). Modeling and design of multi-agent systems. In *Proceedings of the agent theories, architectures, and languages workshop (ATAL 06)* (LNCS 1193).

Kinny, D., Georgeff, M., & Rao, A. (1996). A methodology and modelling technique for systems of BDI agents. *Agents breaking away, 7th European workshop on modelling autonomous agents in a multi-agent world, Eindhoven, The Netherlands* (. *LNCS*, *1038*, 56–71.

Kleinke, J. D. (2005). Dot-Gov: Market failure and the creation of a national health information system. *Health Affairs*, *24*(5), 1246–1262. doi:10.1377/hlthaff.24.5.1246

Kloppmann, M., Koenig, D., Leymann, F., Pfau, G., Rickayzen, A., von Riegen, C., et al. (2005, July). *WS-BPEL Extention for people-BPEL4People* [Electronic Version, *A* Joint White Paper by IBM and SAP].

Knapik, M., & Johnson, J. (1998). *Developing intelligent agents for distributed systems*. New York: McGraw-Hill.

Knez, M., Cedilnik, M., & Semolic, B. (2007). *Logistika in poslovanje logističnih podjetij.* Celje: Fakulteta za logistiko UM

Kodama, M. (2005). New knowledge creation through leadership-based strategic community – a case of new product development in IT and multimedia business fields. [Elsevier Press]. *Technovation, 25,* 895–908. doi:10.1016/j.technovation.2004.02.016

Kohn, L., Corrigan, J., & Donaldson, M. (2000). To err is human: Building a safer health system. National Academies Press.

Kolmogorov, A. N. (1969). K logiczeskim osnovam teorii informacii i tieorii vierojatnosti (On the Logical Principles of the Theory of Information and the Theory of Probability). *Problemy Peredaczi informacii* (Problems of information transmission).

Konarzewska-Gubała, E. (1989). *BIPOLAR: Multiple Criteria Decision Aid Using Bipolar Reference System,* (Cashier and Documents no 56). Paris: Dauphine Universite Paris, LAMSADE.

Korczak, J., & Lipiński, P. (2008). Systemy agentowe we wspomaganiu decyzji na rynku paperów wartościowych. In S. Stanek, H. Sroka, M. Paprzycki, & M. Ganzha (Eds.), *Rozwój nformatycznych systemów weloagentowych w środowsach społeczno-gospodarczych.* Warszawa: Placet Press.

Kotz, D., & Gray, R. (1999). Mobile agents and the future of the Internet. *ACM Operating Systems Review, 33*(3), 7–13. doi:10.1145/311124.311130

Kotz, D., Gray, R., & Rus, D. (2002). Future directions for mobile agent research. *IEEE Distributed Systems Online, 3*(8), 1-6. Retrieved from http://dsonline.computer.org/

Koubarakis, M., & Plexousakis, D. (2001). A formal framework for business process modeling and design. *Information Systems, 27,* 299–319. doi:10.1016/S0306-4379(01)00055-2

Kroksmark, T., & Marton, F. (1987). Läran om undervisning. *Forskning om utbildning,* 3, 14-26.

Krystek, U., Redel, W., & Reppegather, S. (1997). *Grundzüge virtueller organisation.* Wiesbaden: Gabler.

Kulikowski, R., Libura, M., & Słomiński, L. (1998). *Investment decision support.* Warszawa: Polish Academy of Science.

Kuo, F. Y., Lin, C. S., & Hsu, M. H. (2007). Assessing gender differences in computer professionals' self-regulatory efficacy concerning information privacy practices. *Journal of Business Ethics, 73,* 145–160. doi:10.1007/s10551-006-9179-1

Kuulasmaa, A., Wahlberg, K. E., & Kuusimaki, M. L. (2004). Videoconferencing in family therapy: A review. *Journal of Telemedicine and Telecare, 10*(3), 125–129. doi:10.1258/135763304323070742

Lærum, H., Ellingsen, G., & Faxvaag, A. (2001). Doctors' use of electronic medical records in hospitals: Cross sectional survey. *British Medical Journal, 323,* 1344–1348. doi:10.1136/bmj.323.7325.1344

Lal, K. (2005). In quest of the information sector: Measuring information workers for India. *Malaysian Journal of Library & Information Science, 2*(10).

Lalande, A. (1996). *Vocabulaire technique et critique de la Philosophie.* Dix-huitième édition reliée, Presses Universitaires de France.

Lanfranchi, G., Della Peruta, P., Perrone, A., & Calvanese, D. (2003). Toward a new landscape of system management in an autonomic computing environment. *IBM Systems Journal, 42*(1), 119–129.

Lange, D., & Oshima, M. (1999). Seven good reasons for mobile agents. *Communications of the ACM, 42*(3), 88–89. doi:10.1145/295685.298136

Langefors, B. (1980). Infological models and information users view. *Information Systems, 5,* 17–32. doi:10.1016/0306-4379(80)90065-4

Langefors, B. (1995). *Essays on infology – Summing up and planning for the future.* Lund, Studentlitteratur.

Lankhorst, M. (2004). *ArchiMate Language Primer*: Telematica Institute/Archimate Consortium.

Lankhorst, M. (2005). *Enterprise architecture at work, modelling, communication and analysis.* Berlin: Springer.

Lenz, H., & James, M. L. (2007). International audit firms as strategic networks – The evolution of global professional service firms. In G. Cliquet, G. Hendrikse, M. Tuunanen & J. Windsperger (Eds.), *Economics and management of networks* (pp. 367-392). Heidelberg: Springer.

Leweling, M. (2005). *ZIVGrid – Grid-Computing mit Condor.* Zentrum für Informationsverarbeitung der Universität Münster, inforum, Jahrgang 29, Nr. 3, December (pp. 19-20). Retrieved October 20, 2008, from http://www.uni-muenster.de/ZIV/inforum/2005-3/a12.html

Lewis, D., O'Sullivan, D., Feeney, K., Keeney, J., & Power, R. (2006). Ontology-based engineering for self-managing communications. *1st IEEE International Workshop on Modeling Autonomic Communications.*

Lewis, J. D., & Weigert, A. (1985). Trust as a social reality. *Social Forces, 63*(4), 967–985. doi:10.2307/2578601

Lim, D., Ho, Q.-T., Zhang, J., Lee, B.-S., & Ong, Y.-S. (2005). *MOGAS. A multi-organizational Grid accounting system.* Retrieved December 18, 2007, from http://ntu-cg.ntu.edu.sg/mogas_pragma/MOGAS.pdf

Lind, J. (2000). A development method for multiagent systems. *Cybernetics and systems: Proceedings of the 15th European meeting on cybernetics and systems research, Symposium: from agent theory to agent implementation.*

Linder, J. A., Ma, J., Bates, D. W., Middleton, B., & Stafford, R. S. (2007). Electronic health record use and the quality of ambulatory care in the United States. *Archives of Internal Medicine, 167*(13), 1400–1405. doi:10.1001/archinte.167.13.1400

Lindstrom, L., & Jeffries, R. (2003). Extreme programming and agile software development methodologies. In C.V. Brown & H. Topi (Eds.), *IS management handbook* (pp. 511-530). London: Auerbach Publications.

Linell, P. (1989). *Computer technology and human projects: Theoretical aspects and empirical studies of socio-cultural practices of cognition and communication.* Linköping: Universitet.

Linell, P. (1994). *Approaching dialogue: On monological and dialogical models of talk and interaction.* University of Linköping: Department of Communication Studies

Lings, B., & Lundell, B. Agerfalk, P. J., & Fitzgerald, B. (2007). A reference model for successful distributed development of software systems. In F. Paulisch et al. (Eds.), *International Conference on Global Software Engineering* (pp.130-139). Los Alamitos, CA: IEEE Computer Society.

Litke, A., Skoutas, D., & Varvarigou, T. (2004). *Mobile Grid computing: Changes and challenges of resource management in a mobile Grid environment.* Access to Knowledge through Grid in a Mobile World, PAKM 2004 Conference. Vienna.

Liu, H., & Parashar, M. (2006). Acoord: A programming framework for autonomic applications. *IEEE Transactions on Systems, Man and Cybernetics. Part C, Applications and Reviews, 36*, 341–352. doi:10.1109/TSMCC.2006.871577

Loh, L., & Venkatraman, N. (1995). An empirical study of information technology outsourcing: Benefits, risks, and performance implications. In *International Conference on Information Systems* (pp.277-288)

López de Vergara, J. E., Villagrá, V. A., & Berrocal, J. (2004a). Applying the Web ontology language to management information definitions. *IEEE Communications Magazine, 42*(7), 68–74. doi:10.1109/MCOM.2004.1316535

López de Vergara, J. E., Villagrá, V. A., Asensio, J. I., & Berrocal, J. (2003). Ontologies: Giving semantics to network management models. *IEEE Network, 17*(3), 15–21. doi:10.1109/MNET.2003.1201472

López de Vergara, J.E., Villagrá, V.A, & Berrocal J. (2004b). Benefits of using ontologies in the management of high speed networks (LNCS 3079, pp.1007-1018).

Loss, L., Pereira-Klen, A. A., & Rabelo, R. J. (2008). *Value creation elements in learning collaborative networked organizations.* In L.M. Camarinba-Matos, & W. Picard (Eds.), *Pervasive Collaborative Networks, IFIP TC 5 WG 5.5. Ninth Working Conference on Virtual Enterprises, Sept. 2008, Poznan, Poland.* NewYork: Springer

Lozano, J. M., Folguera, C., & Arenas, D. (2003). Setting the context: The role information technology in a business ethics course based on face-to-face dialogue.

Journal of Business Ethics, *48*, 99–111. doi:10.1023/B:BUSI.0000004381.51505.67

Luck, M., Griffiths, N., & d'Inverno, M. (1997). From agent theory to agent construction: A case study. *Intelligent agents III* (. *LNAI*, *1193*, 49–64.

Mach, R., Lepro-Metz, R., Booz, A. H., Jackson, S., & McGinnis, L. (2003). *Usage record – format recommendation.* Usage Record Working Group, Global Grid Forum. Retrieved September 18, 2007, from http://forge.ggf.org/sf/sfmain/do/downloadAttachment/projects.ggf-editor/tracker.submit_ggf_draft/artf3385?id=atch3485

Machan, T. R. (2000). *Morality and work.* Stanford, CA: Hoover Institution Press.

Machlup, F. (1962). *The production and distribution of knowledge in the United States.* Princeton, NJ: Princeton University Press.

Maciaszek, L. (2001). *Requirements analysis and system design: Developing information systems with UML*: Pearson Education Limited.

Macierzyński, M. (2007). *40 procent rachunków obsługiwanych jest przez Internet (40 per cent of accounts are operated via the Internet).* Retrieved from http://www.bankier.pl/wiadomosc/Juz-40-procent-rachunkow-obslugiwanych-jest-przez-internet-1588175.html

Mackert, M., & Whitten, P. (2007). The relationship between healthcare organizations and technology vendors: An overlooked key to telemedicine success. *Journal of Telemedicine and Telecare*, *13*(S3), S50–S53. doi:10.1258/135763307783247419

Mackert, M., Whitten, P., & Garcia, A. (2008). Evaluating e-health interventions designed for low health literate audiences. *Journal of Computer-Mediated Communication*, *13*(2), 504–515. doi:10.1111/j.1083-6101.2008.00407.x

Maedche, A., Motik, B., Silva, N., & Volz, R. (2002). MAFRA — A MApping FRAmework for Distributed Ontologies. *Knowledge engineering and knowledge management: Ontologies and the Semantic Web* (LNCS 2473, pp. 69-75).

Maedche, A., Motik, B., Stojanovic, L., Studer, R., & Volz, R. (2003). Ontologies for enterprise knowledge management. *IEEE Intelligent Systems*, *18*(2), 26–33. doi:10.1109/MIS.2003.1193654

Makinson, D., & Van Der Torre, L. (2000). Input-output logics. *Journal of Philosophical Logic*, *29*, 383–408. doi:10.1023/A:1004748624537

Mallin, C. A. (2007). *Corporate governance.* Oxford: Oxford University Press.

Malmari, H. (n.d.). F-Secure Reveals Consumer Attitudes Toward Internet Security Across Europe and North America. Retrieved May 5, 2008 from http://www.f-secure.com/f-secure/pressroom/news/fs_news_20080228_01_eng.html

Maner, W. (1996). Unique ethical problems in information technology. In T.W. Bynum & S. Rogerson (Eds.), *Global Information Ethics* (pp. 137-154). Opragen Publications.

Maner, W. (1996). Unique ethical problems in information technology. *Science and Engineering Ethics*, *2*(2), 137–154. doi:10.1007/BF02583549

Maner, W. (2002). Heuristic methods for computer ethics. [from http://csweb.cs.bgsu.edu/maner/heuristics/maner.pdf]. *Metaphilosophy*, *33*(3), 339–365. Retrieved August 18, 2008. doi:10.1111/1467-9973.00231

Marcolin, B. L. (2006). Spiraling effects of IS outsourcing contract interpretations. In R. Hirschheim, A. Heinzl, & J. Dibbern (Eds.), *Information systems outsourcing* (pp. 223-256). Heidelberg/Berlin: Springer.

Martinsons, M. G., & So, S. K. K. (2000). *The information ethics of American and Chinese managers*, Pacific Rim Institute for Studies of Management Report 2000-02.

Marton, F. (Ed.). (1986). *Vad är fackdidaktik?* (Vol. 1). Lund: Studentlitteratur.

Marton, F., & Booth, S. (1997). *Learning and awareness.* New Jersey: Lawrence Erlbaum Association.

Mason, R. (1986). Four ethical issues of the information age. *MIS Quarterly*, *10*(1), 5–12. doi:10.2307/248873

Massachusetts Medical Society. (2003). MMS Survey: Most doctors are slow to incorporate technology into practices. Retrieved February 21,

2006, from http://www.massmed.org/AM/Template.cfm?Section=Search&template=/CM/HTMLDisplay.cfm&ContentID=10048

Massonet, P., Deville, Y., & Neve, C. (2002). From AOSE methodology to agent implementation. In *Proceedings of the first international joint conference on autonomous agents and multiagent systems, Bologna, Italy* (pp. 27-34).

Mateos, M. B., Mera, A. C., Gonzales, F. J., & Lopez, O. R. (2001). A new Web assessment index: Spanish universities analysis. *Internet Research: Electronic Application and Policy, 11*(3), 226–234. doi:10.1108/10662240110396469

Mathiesen, K. (2004). What Is information ethics? *Computers and Society, 32*(8). Retrieved April 15, 2008, from http://www.computersandsociety.org/sigcas_ofthefuture2/sigcas/subpage/sub_page.cfm?article=909&page_number_nb=901.

Mathiesen, K. (2004). What is Information Ethics? *ACM SIGCAS Computers and Society, 34*(1).

Matthies, T.-C., & Rückemann, C.-P. (2003). Vom Urwald der Wörter zur strukturierten Suche. In R. Schmidt (Ed.), *Proceedings, 25. Online-Tagung der DGI, Competence in Content, Frankfurt am Main, 3.5. Juni 2003, Deutsche Gesellschaft für Informationswissenschaft und Informationspraxis e.V.*, (pp. 285–296).

May, C., Finch, T., Mair, F., & Mort, M. (2005). Towards a wireless patient: Chronic illness, scarce care and technological innovation in the United Kingdom. *Social Science & Medicine, 61*(7), 1485–1494. doi:10.1016/j.socscimed.2005.03.008

Mazur, M. (1970). *Jakościowa teoria informacji* (*A Quality Theory of Information*). Warsaw, Poland: Wydawnictwo Naukowo-Techniczne.

McAfee, A. P. (2006). Enterprise 2.0: The dawn of emergent collaboration. *MIT Sloan Management Review* (pp. 21-28).

McArthur, T. (1981). *Longman lexicon of contemporary English*. Longman Group Limited.

McBurney, P., & Luck, M. (2007). The agents are all busy doing stuff. *IEEE Intelligent Systems, 22*(4), 6–7. doi:10.1109/MIS.2007.77

McCann, J. M. (1994). *Adding product value through information*. Retrieved May 2007 from http://www.duke.edu/_mccann/infovalu.htm.

McChesney, I. R., & Gallagher, S. (2004). Communication and co-ordination Practices in Software Engineering Projects. *Information and Software Technology, 46*(7), 473–489. doi:10.1016/j.infsof.2003.10.001

McGlynn, E. A., Asch, S. M., Adams, J., Keesey, J., Hicks, J., & DeCristofaro, A. (2006). The quality of health care delivered to adults in the United States. *The New England Journal of Medicine, 348*(26), 2635–2645. doi:10.1056/NEJMsa022615

McGraw, G. (2006). *Software security: Building security in*. Boston, MA: Addison-Wesley.

Meltz, R. (2009). Marc L***. *Le tigre, 28* (nov.-déc. 2008). Retrieved February 15, 2009, from http://www.le-tigre.net/Marc-L.html

Mette, K. A. (2004). *Governance*. Cambridge: Polity.

Meyer, J. W., & Rowan, B. (1977). Insitutionalized organizations: Formal structure as myth and ceremony. *American Journal of Sociology, 83*, 340–363. doi:10.1086/226550

Michna, A. (2008). *Przegląd koncepcji kapitału intelektualnego przedsiębiorstw*. Retrieved June 2008 from http://www.paba.org.pl/publikacje/koncepcje kapitału intelektualnego.pdf.

Microsoft (2008). HealthVault. Retrieved September 28, 2008, from http://www.healthvault.com/

Middleton, B., Hammond, W. E., Brennan, P. F., & Cooper, G. F. (2005). Accelerating U.S. EHR adoption: How to get there from here. Recommendations Based on the 2004 ACMI Retreat. *Journal of the American Medical Informatics Association, 12*(1), 13–19. doi:10.1197/jamia.M1669

Migdadi, Y. K. (2008). quantitative evaluation of the Internet banking service encounter's quality: Comparative study between Jordan and the UK retail banks. *Journal of Internet Banking and Commerce, 2*(13).

Miller, J., & Mukerji, J. (2003). MDA Guide, version 1.0.1, [Electronic Version]. *OMG Architectural Board.* Retrieved March 12, 2007 from http://www.omg.org/docs/omg/03-06-01.pdf

Miller, R., & Sim, I. (2004). Physicians' use of electronic medical records: Barriers and solutions. *Health Affairs, 23*, 116–126. doi:10.1377/hlthaff.23.2.116

Minevich, M., & Richter, F. J. (2005). *Global Outsourcing Report 2005.* New York: Going Global Ventures Inc.

Mintzberg, H., & Quinn, J. B. (1991). *The strategy process, concepts, contexts, cases.* Englewood Cliffs, NJ: Prentice Hall.

Miranda, F. J., Cortes, R., & Barriuso, C. (2006). Quantitative evaluation of e-banking Web sites: An empirical study of Spanish banks. *The Electronic Journal Information Systems Evaluation, 2*(9), 73-82, from http://www.eiise.com

Moab Admin Manual. (2008). Retrieved September 20, 2008, from http://www.clusterresources.com/products/mwm/moabdocs/index.shtml

Moab Users Guide. (2008). Retrieved September 20, 2008, from http://www.clusterresources.com/products/mwm/docs/moabusers.shtml

Moe, N. B., & Smite, D. (2008). Understanding a lack of trust in global software teams: A multiple-case study. *Software Process Improvement and Practice, 13*(3), 217–231. doi:10.1002/spip.378

Mohrman, A. S., Galbraith, J. R., & Lawler, E., III. (1998). *Tomorrow's Organization*, San Francisco: Jossey-Bass.

Molnar, K. K., Kletke, M. G., & Chongwatpol, J. (2008). Ethics vs. IT Ethics: Do undergraduate students perceive a difference? *Journal of Business Ethics, 83*, 657–671. doi:10.1007/s10551-007-9646-3

Moor, A. (2005). *Patterns for the pragmatic Web.* Paper presented at the 13th International Conference on Conceptual Structures (ICCS), Kassel, Germany.

Moor, J. (1985). What is computer ethics? *Metaphilosophy, 16*, 266–275. doi:10.1111/j.1467-9973.1985.tb00173.x

Moor, J. H. (1985). What is computer ethics? *Metaphilosophy, 16*(4), 266–275. doi:10.1111/j.1467-9973.1985.tb00173.x

Morariu, C., Waldburger, M., & Stiller, B. (2006). *An accounting and charging architecture for mobile Grids.* IFI Technical Report, No. ifi-2006.06, April 2006. Retrieved January 14, 2009, from ftp://ftp.ifi.uzh.ch/pub/techreports/TR-2006/ifi-2006.06.pdf

Morikawa, M. (1988). Future outlook for JAPAN's information industry. *Japan Computer Quarterly*, 72.

Morris, C. W. (1938). *Foundations of the theory of signs.* Chicago, IL: University of Chicago Press.

Morrison, C. T., & Cohen, P. R. (2005). Noisy information value in utility-based decision making. In *Proc. Workshop on Utility-based Data Mining.* Chicago, USA.

Munroe, S. (2006). Crossing the agent technologies chasm: Experiences and challenges in commercial applications of agents. *The Knowledge Engineering Review, 21*(4), 345–392. doi:10.1017/S0269888906001020

Murch, R., & Johnson, T. (1999). *Intelligent software agents.* NJ: Prentice Hall PTR.

Myerson, R. B. (1996). *Fundamentals of social choice theory* (Discusion Paper No. 1214). Center for Mathematical Studies in Economics and Management Science, Nortwestern University.

Newhouse, S. (2003). *Grid economic services architecture (GESA).* Grid economic services architecture working group, global Grid forum. Retrieved September 5, 2007, from http://www.doc.ic.ac.uk/~sjn5/GGF/CompEconArch-GGF7.pdf

NEXUM Insurance Technologies. (2005). *Business process management (BPM) for insurance industry.*

Nguyen, N. T. (2002). *Methods for consensus choice and their applications in conflict resolving in distributed systems.* Wrocław: Wroclaw University of Technology Press.

Ni, Q., Lu, W. F., Yarlagadda, K. D. V., & Mimg, X. (2007). Business information modeling for process integration in the mold making industry. *Robotics and Computer-integrated Manufacturing, 23*, 195–205. doi:10.1016/j.rcim.2005.12.006

Nimis, J., & Stockheim, T. (2004). The Agent.Enterprise multi-multi-agent system. *Special track on agent technology in business applications (ATeBa 04) at multi-conference on business information systems (MKWI 2004).*

Noor, A. M., Zurovac, D., Hay, S. I., Ochola, S. A., & Snow, R. W. (2003). Defining equity in physical access to clinical services using geographical information systems as part of malaria planning and monitoring in Kenya. Tropical Medicine and International Health, 8(10), 917-926(910).

Nowak, M. (2004). Preference and veto thresholds in multicriteria analysis based on stochastic dominance. *European Journal of Operational Research, 158*(2), 339–350. doi:10.1016/j.ejor.2003.06.008

Noy, N., & Musen, M. (1999, July). An algorithm for merging and aligning ontologies: Automation and tool support. In *Proceedings of the Workshop on Ontology Management. Sixteen National Conference on Artificial Intelligence*. Orlando, Florida, USA.

Nwana, H. (1996). Software agents: An overview. [Retrieved from http://agents.umbc.edu/introduction/ao/]. *The Knowledge Engineering Review, 11*(3), 1–40. doi:10.1017/S026988890000789X

O'Brien, P. D., & Wiegand, M. E. (1998). Agent based process management: Applying intelligent agents to workflow. *The Knowledge Engineering Review, 13*(2), 161–174. doi:10.1017/S0269888998002070

Odell, J., Parunak, H. V. D., & Bauer, B. (2000). Extending UML for agents. In *Proceedings of the agent-oriented information systems workshop at the 17th national conference on artificial intelligence* (pp. 3-17).

OECD, Organization for Economic Cooperation and Development (1981). *Information activities, electronics and telecommunication technologies. Impact on employment, growth and trade*, vol. 1- 2, ICCP Series (61). Paris: OECD.

Oenema, A., Brug, J., & Lechner, L. (2001). Web-based tailored nutrition education: Results of a randomized controlled trial. *Health Education Research, 16*(6), 647–660. doi:10.1093/her/16.6.647

Olender-Skorek, M., & Wydro, K.B. (2007). Wartość Informacji. *Telekomunikacja i techniki informacyjne,* 1-2, 72-80.

Olenski, J. (2001). *Ekonomika informacji* (*Information Economics*). Warsaw, Poland: Polskie Wydawnictwo Ekonomiczne.

Oleński, J. (2001). *Ekonomika informacji.* Warsaw, Poland: PWE.

Omrichi, A. (2001). SODA: Societies and infrastructure in the analysis and design of agent-based systems. In *Proceedings of the first international workshop of agent oriented software engineering (AOSE-2000)* (LNCS 1957, pp. 185-194).

Open Grid Forum. (2007). Retrieved August 29, 2007, from http://www.ogf.org

Oshri, I., Kotlarsky, J., & Willcocks, L. P. (2007). Global software development: Exploring socialization and face-to-face meetings in distributed strategic projects. *The Journal of Strategic Information Systems, 16*(1), 25–49. doi:10.1016/j.jsis.2007.01.001

Ost, S., & Leweling, M. (2005). *ZIVcluster, Der Linux-HPC-Cluster des Zentrums für Informationsverarbeitung.* Retrieved August 10, 2008, from http://www.uni-muenster.de/ZIV/inforum/2005-1/a11.html

Overhage, J., Tierney, W., McDonald, C., & Pickett, K. (1991). Computer-assisted order entry: Impact on intern time use. *Clinical Research, 39*(3), 794A.

Oz, E. (1992, December). Ethical standards for information systems professionals: A case for a unified code. *MIS Quarterly*, 423–433. doi:10.2307/249729

Oz, E. (1993). Ethical standards for computer professionals: A comparative analysis of four major codes. *Journal of Business Ethics, 12*(9), 709–726. doi:10.1007/BF00881385

Padgham, L., & Winikoff, M. (2002). Prometheus: A methodology for developing intelligent agents. In *Proceedings of the third international workshop on agent oriented software engineering at AAMAS 2002, Bologna, Italy.*

Padgham, L., & Winikoff, M. (2004). *Developing intelligent agent systems. A practical guide*. Chichester: John Wiley & Sons.

Pagano, B. (2004). *The transparency edge: How credibility can make or break you in business*. New York: McGraw-Hill.

Palmer, E. R. (1969). *Hermeneutics*. Evanston: Northwestern University Press.

Pang, G. (2000). *Implementation of an agent-based business process* [Diploma thesis]. Institut für Informatik der Universität Zürich.

Pańkowska, M. (1999). Infokologia – ekologia informacji. Zakres i specyfika środków. *Firma i rynek,* 1.

Parker, D. B. (1968). Rules of ethics in information processing. *Communications of the ACM, 11*(3), 198–201. doi:10.1145/362929.362987

Parker, D. B., Swope, S., & Baker, B. (1990). Ethical conflicts in information and computer science, technology, and business. Wellesley, MA: QED Information Sciences, Inc.

Patterson, D.A., Brown, A., Broadwell, P., Candea, G., Chen, M., Cutler, J., Enriquez, P., Fox, A., Kiciman, E., Merzbacher, M., Oppenhiemer, D., Sastry, N., Tetzlaff, W., Traupman, J., & Treuhaft, N. (2002, 15 March). *Recovery-oriented computing (ROC): Motivation, definition, techniques, and case studies* (UC Berkeley Computer Science Technical Report, UCB//CSD-02-1175). University of California, Berkeley.

Peltier, T. R. (2001). *Information security policies, procedures, and standards: Guidelines for effective information security management.* Boca Raton, FL: Auerbach.

Periasamy, K. P., & Feeny, D. F. (1997). Information architecture practice: Research–based recommendations for the practitioner. In L.Willcocks, D. Feeny, G.Islei (Eds.). *Managing IT as a strategic resource* (pp. 339-359). London: The McGraw-Hill Companies.

Perotti, V. J., & Pray, T. F. (2002). Integrating visualization into the modeling of business simulations. *Simulation & Gaming, 33*(4), 409–424. doi:10.1177/1046878102238605

Petrelli, D. (2008). On the role of user-centred evaluation in the advancement of interactive information retrieval. *Information Processing & Management, 44*, 23–38. doi:10.1016/j.ipm.2007.01.024

Pettigrew, A., Whittington, R., Melin, L., Runde, C. S., & Bosch, F. A. J. den, Ruigrok, W., & Numagami, T. (2003). *Innovative forms of organizing*, London: Sage Publications.

Pew Internet and American Life Project. (2007). E-patients with a disability or chronic disease. Washington, D.C.

Peyton, R. (2004). *Toolmakers cluster of Slovenia, feasibility study.* Los Alamos, World Tech, Inc.

Phillips, R. (2003). *Stakeholder theory and organizational ethics.* San Francisco, CA: Berrett-Koehler.

Photo Gallery, H. L. R. N.-I. I. (2008, May 9). RRZN Top-News. Retrieved October 21, 2008, from http://www.rrzn.uni-hannover.de/hlrn_galerie.html

Phukan, S., & Dhillon, G. (2000). Ethics and information technology use: A survey of US based SMEs. *Information Management & Computer Security, 8*(5), 239–243. doi:10.1108/09685220010353907

Pike, S., & Roos, G. (2000). *Intellectual capital measurement and holistic value approach (HVA).* Works Institute Journal Japan, vol. 42. Retrieved June 2008 from http://www.intcap.com/ICS Article 2000 IC Measurement HVA.pdf

Porat, M. U. (1974). Defining an information sector in the U.S. economy. *Information Reports and Bibliographies, 5*(5).

Porat, M. U. (1976). *The information economy.* Center for Interdisciplinary Research, Stanford University.

Powell, A., Piccoli, G., & Ives, B. (2004). Virtual teams: A review of current literature and directions for future research. *The Data Base for Advances in Information Systems, 35*(1), 6–36.

Powell, W. (1990). Neither market nor hierarchy: Network forms of organization. *Research in Organizational Behavior, 12*, 295–336.

Powell, W. W., & DiMaggio, P. J. (1991). The new institutionalism. *Organizational analysis*. Chicago: University of Chicago Press.

Power, M. (2007). *Organized uncertainty: Designing a world of risk management*. Oxford University Press, Oxford.

Power, M. J., Desouza, K. C., & Bonifazi, C. (2006). *The Outsourcing handbook, how to implement a successful outsourcing process*. London: Kogan Page.

Project, L. X. (2008). Retrieved October 12, 2008, from http://zen.rrzn.uni-hannover.de/cpr/x/rprojs/de/index.html

Purczyński, J. (2003). *Using a computer simulation in estimation chosen ekonometric and statistics models*. Szczecin: Szczecin University Science Press.

Pyöriä, P. (2005). *A growing trend towards knowledge work in Finland*. Retrieved June 10, 2007, from http://www.etla.fi/files/1373_FES_05_2_a_growing_trend/...pdf

Quigley, E. J., & Debons, A. (1999). Interrogative theory of information and knowledge. In [ACM Press.]. *Proceedings of SIGCPR, 99*, 4–10. doi:10.1145/299513.299602

Quinn, M. J. (2006). *Ethics for the information age* (2nd ed.). Reading, MA: Addison-Wesley.

Quirolgico, S., Assis, P., Westerinen, A., Baskey, M., & Stokes, E. (2004). Toward a formal Common Information Model ontology. *WISE'2004* (. *LNCS, 3307*, 11–21.

Quitadamo, R., & Zambonelli, F. (2007). Autonomic communication services: A new challenge for software agents. *Autonomous Agents and Multi-Agent Systems, 17*(3), 457–475. doi:10.1007/s10458-008-9054-9

Rabaey, M., Vandijck, E., & Tromp, H. (2003). Business intelligent agents for enterprise application integration: The link between business process management and Web services. In *Proceedings of the 16th international conference on software & systems engineering and their applications, Paris, December 2-4, 2003.*

Rahanu, H., Davies, J., & Rogerson, S. (1996). Ethical analysis of software failure cases. In P. Barroso, T.W. Bynum, S. Rogerson, & L. Joyanes (Eds.), *Proceedings of ETHICOMP 96* (pp. 364-383). Madrid: Complutense University.

Ramamoorti, S., & Olsen, W. (2007). Fraud: The human factor. *Financial executive,* July/August, 53-55.

Ramesh, V., & Dennis, A. (2002). The object-oriented team: Lessons for virtual team from global software development. In J. F. Nunamaker Jr. et al. (Eds.), *Annual Hawaii International Conference on System Sciences* (pp. 212-221). Los Alamitos, CA: IEEE Computer Society.

Razzaque, M. A., Dobson, S., & Nixon, P. (2007). Cross-layer architectures for autonomic communications. *Journal of Network and Systems Management, 15*(1), 13–27. doi:10.1007/s10922-006-9051-8

Reichert, M., Bauer, T., & Dadam, P. (1999). Enterprise-wide and cross-enterprise workflow management: Challenges and research issues for adaptive workflows. In *Proceedings of the Informatik'99 workshop: Enterprise-wide and cross-enterprise workflow management: concepts, systems, applications, Paderborn, Germany, 1999.*

Reichert, M., et al. (2005). Adaptive process management with ADEPT2. In *Proceedings of the 21st international conference on data engineering (ICDE 2005).*

Reihlen, M. (1996). *The logic of heterarchies, making organizations competitive for knowledge-based competition.* Arbeitsbericht nr 91/ Working Paper No 91, Seminars fur Allgemeine Betruebswirtschaftslehre, Betriebswirtchaftliche Planung und Logistik, der Universitat zu Koln, University of Cologne, Germany. Retrieved October 13, 2008, from http://www.spl.uni-koeln.de/fileadmin/documents/arbeitsberichte/arbb-91.pdf

Report, K. D. H. P. Coverage & Access (2008, September 22). *U.S. residents cut back on health care spending as economy worsens*. Available at http://www.kaisernetwork.org/daily_reports/rep_index.cfm?DR_ID=54579

Revere, D. (2007). Understanding the information needs of public health practitioners: A literature review to inform design of an interactive digital knowledge management system. *Journal of Biomedical Informatics, 40*, 410–421. doi:10.1016/j.jbi.2006.12.008

R-GMA. Relational Grid monitoring architecture (2006). Retrieved August 10, 2008, from http://www.r-gma.org/

Richman, A., Noble, K., & Johnson, A. (2002). *When the workplace is many places: The extent and nature of off-site work today.* Watertown, MA: WFD Consulting. Executive Summary. Retrieved June 12, 2008, from http://www.abcdependentcare.com/docs/ABC_Executive_Summary_final.pdf

Ricoeur, P. (1976). *Interpretation theory: Discourse and the surplus of meaning.* Texas: Texas Christian University Press.

Rieger, S., Gersbeck-Schierholz, B., Mönnich, J., & Wiebelitz, J. (2006). Self-Service PKI-Lösungen für eScience. In C. Paulsen (Ed.), *Proceedings 13. DFN Workshop Sicherheit in vernetzten Systemen, 1.-2. März 2006, Hamburg, Deutschland.* DFN-CERT publications (pp. B-1–B-15).

Riemer, K., & Klein, S. (2006). Network management framework. In S. Klein, & A. Poulymenakou (Eds.), *Managing dynamic networks* (pp. 17-68). Berlin: Springer.

Rizzo, A. A., Strickland, D., & Bouchard, S. (2004). The challenge of using virtual reality in telerehabilitation. *Telemedicine Journal and e-Health, 10*(2), 184–195. doi:10.1089/tmj.2004.10.184

Rocha, L. M. (2001). *Adaptive Webs for heterarchies with diverse communities of users.* Paper prepared for the Workshop from Intelligent Networks to the Global Brain: Evolutionary Social Organization through Knowledge Technology, Brussels, July, 3-5. Retrieved October 13, 2008, from http://www.ehealthstrategies.com/files/heterarchies_rocha.pdf

Rohde, M., Rittenbuch, M., & Wulf, V. (2001). *Auf dem Weg zur virtuellen Organisation.* Heidelberg: Physica-Verlag.

Roma'n, S. (2007). The ethics of online retailing: A scale development and validation from the consumers' perspective. *Journal of Business Ethics, 72*, 131–148. doi:10.1007/s10551-006-9161-y

Romero, D., Giraldo, J., Galeano, N., & Molina, A. (2007). Towards governance rules and bylaws for virtual breeding environments. In L. Camarinha-Matos, H. Afsarmanesh, P. Novais, C. Analide, *Establishing the Foundation of Collaborative Networks* (pp. 93-102). Berlin: Springer.

Rosenau, J. N. (2004). Governing the ungovernable: The challenge of a global disaggregation of authority. In *Regulation & Governance* (pp. 88-97). Retrieved October 13, 2008, from http://www3.interscience.wiley.com/cgi-bin/fulltext/117994572/PDFSTART

Rosenberg, I., & Juan, A. (2009). *Integrating an SLA architecture based on components* [BEinGRID White Paper].

Rowlands, D. (2007). *Report on the HL7 Working Group Meeting held in Cologne, Germany.* Retrieved February 10, 2009, from http://www.hl7.org.au/docs/HL7%20Mtg.%202007-04%20Koln%20-%20Combined%20WGM%20Report.pdf

Rückemann, C.-P. (2001). *Beitrag zur Realisierung portabler Komponenten für Geoinformationssysteme. Ein Konzept zur ereignisgesteuerten und dynamischen Visualisierung und Aufbereitung geowissenschaftlicher Daten.* Dissertation, Westfälische Wilhelms-Universität, Münster, Deutschland, 2001. 161 (xxii + 139) Seiten, Ill., graph. Darst., Kt. Retrieved September 22, 2008, from http://wwwmath.uni-muenster.de/cs/u/ruckema/x/dis/download/dis3acro.pdf

Rückemann, C.-P. (2005). *Active Map Software.* 2001, 2005. Retrieved August 10, 2008, from http://wwwmath.uni-muenster.de/cs/u/ruckema

Rückemann, C.-P. (2007). Geographic Grid-computing and HPC empowering dynamical visualisation for geoscientific information systems. In R. Kowalczyk (Ed.), *Proceedings of the 4th International Conference on Grid Service Engineering and Management (GSEM), September 25–26, 2007, Leipzig, Deutschland, co-located with Software, Agents and services for Business, Research, and E-sciences (SABRE2007)*, volume 117. GI-Edition, Lecture Notes in Informatics (LNI), Gesellschaft für Informatik e.V. (GI), (pp. 66-80).

Rückemann, C.-P. (2007). *Security of information systems.* EULISP Lecture Notes, European Legal Informatics Study Programme, Institut für Rechtsinformatik, Leibniz Universität Hannover (IRI/LUH).

Rückemann, C.-P. (2008). *Fundamental aspects of information science and security of information systems.* EULISP Lecture Notes, European Legal Informatics Study Programme, Institut für Rechtsinformatik, Leibniz Universität Hannover (IRI/LUH).

Rückemann, C.-P. (2009). Using parallel MultiCore and HPC systems for dynamical visualisation. In *Proceedings of the International Conference on Advanced Geographic Information Systems & Web Services (GEOWS 2009), DigitalWorld, February 1-7, 2009, Cancún, México, International Academy, Research, and Industry Association (IARIA)*, Best Paper Award, IEEE Computer Society Press, IEEE Xplore Digital Library, (pp. 13-18).

Rückemann, C.-P. (Ed.). (2006). *Ergebnisse der Studie und Anforderungsanalyse in den Fachgebieten Monitoring, Accounting, Billing bei den Communities und Ressourcenanbietern im D-Grid.* Koordination der Fachgebiete Monitoring, Accounting, Billing im D-Grid-Integrationsprojekt, 1. Juni 2006, D-Grid Document, Deutschland, 141 pp. Retrieved September 22, 2008, from http://www.dgrid.de/fileadmin/dgi_document/FG2/koordination_mab/mab_studie_ergebnisse.pdf

Rückemann, C.-P., & Göhner, M. (2006). *Konzeption einer Grid-Accounting-Architektur.* D-Grid Integration project, D-Grid document. http://www.d-grid.de/fileadmin/dgi_document/FG2/koordination_mab/mab_accounting_konzeption.pdf

Rückemann, C.-P., Göhner, M., & Baur, T. (2007). *Towards integrated Grid accounting/billing for D-Grid.* Grid Working Paper.

Rückemann, C.-P., Müller, W., & von Voigt, G. (2007). Comparison of Grid accounting concepts for D-Grid. In M. Bubak, M. Turała, & K. Wiatr (Ed.), *Proceedings of the Cracow Grid Workshop, CGW'06*, Cracow, Poland, October 15-18, 2006 (pp. 459-466).

Rückemann, C.-P., Müller, W., Ritter, H.-H., Reiser, H., Kunze, M., Göhner, M., et al. (2005). *Erhebung zur Studie und Anforderungsanalyse in den Fachgebieten Monitoring, Accounting und Billing (M/A/B) im D-Grid, Informationen von den Beteiligten (Communities) im D-Grid-Projekt hinsichtlich ihrer D-Grid-Ressourcen.* D-Grid, Fachgebiete Monitoring, Accounting und Billing im D-Grid-Integrationsprojekt, D-Grid Document. 33 Seiten. Retrieved Oktober 12, 2007, from http://www.d-grid.de/fileadmin/dgi_document/FG2/koordination_mab/Erhebung_MAB_CG.pdf

Russell, S., & Norvig, P. (2003). *Artificial intelligence. A modern approach* (2nd ed.). NJ: Prentice Hall.

Saaty, T. L. (1990). How to make a decision: The analytic hierarchy process. *European Journal of Operational Research, 48*, 9–26. doi:10.1016/0377-2217(90)90057-I

Saaty, T. L. (1999). Fundamentals of the analytic network process. In *Proceedings of 5th International Conference on th Analytic Hierarchy Process, Kobe* (pp. 20-33).

Sapp, D. (2004). Global partnerships in business communication. *Business Communication Quarterly, 67*, 267–280. doi:10.1177/1080569904268051

Saracevic, T. (1996). Interactive models in information retrieval (IR): A review and proposal. In *Proceedings of the 59th Annual Meeting of the American Society for Information Science,* 33, 3-9.

Saraswat, A., & Katta, A. (2008). Quantitative evaluation of e-banking websites: A study of Indian banks. *Icfai University Journal of Information Technology, 3*(4), 32–49.

Satapathy, G., Kumara, S. R. T., & Moore, L. M. (1998). Distributed intelligent agents for logistics (DIAL). *Expert Systems with Applications, 14*(4), 409–424. doi:10.1016/S0957-4174(98)00001-3

Saxton, G. (2004). *The rise of participatory society: Challenges for the nonprofit sector.* 33rd Annual Conference of the Association for Research on Nonprofit Organizations and Voluntary Action, November 18-20, Los Angeles CA. Retrieved October 13, 2008, from http://www.itss.brockport.edu/~gsaxton/ participatorysociety_research.htm

Schelp, J., & Winter, R. (2007). Integration management for heterogeneous information systems. In K.C. Desouza (Ed.), *Agile information systems, conceptualization, construction, and management* (pp. 134-150). Amsterdam: Elsevier.

Schneier, B. (2003). *Beyond fear: Thinking sensibly about security in an uncertain world.* New York: Copernicus Books.

Schoenman, J., Keeler, J., Moiduddin, A., & Hamlin, B. (2006). Roadmap for the adoption of health information technology in rural communities. Washington, DC: Office of Rural Health Policy.

Schoorman, F. D., Mayer, R. C., & Davis, J. H. (2007). An integrative model of organizational trust: Past, present, and future. *Academy of Management Review, 32*(2), 344–354.

Schraeder, A. (1996). *Management virtueller Unternehmungen.* Frankfurt/Main: Campus Verlag.

Schultz, R. A. (2006). *Contemporary issues in ethics and information technology.* Hershey, PA: IRM Press.

Schutz, A., & Luckmann, T. (1974). *The structures of the life-world.* London: Heinemann.

Seidler, J. (1983). *Nauka o informacji (Science of Information).* Warsaw, Poland: Wydawnictwo Naukowo-Techniczne.

Selz, D., & Schubert, P. (1997). Web assessment: A model for the evaluation and the assessment of successful electronic commerce applications. *Electronic Markets, 3*(7), 46–48. doi:10.1080/10196789700000038

Semolic, B. (2007). *LENS Living Laboratory – Project documentation.* Celje: INOVA Consulting; Project & Technology Management Institute, Faculty of Logistics, University of Maribor.

Semolic, B. (2009). TA Platform, LENS Living Lab. Vojnik, INOVA Consulting, TCS.

Semolic, B., & Dworatschek (2004). *Project management in the new geo-economy and the power of project organization.* Maribor: IPMA Expert Seminar Series, University of Maribor.

Semolic, B., & Kovac, J. (2008). *Strategic information system of virtual organization.* Pervasive Collaborative Networks. Poznan: IFIP, Springer.

Shannon, C. E. (1948). A mathematical theory of communication. *Bell System Techn. Journal, 27*(3-4).

Sherer, J. L. (1993). Putting patients first: Hospitals work to define patient-centered care. *Hospitals, 67,* 14–19.

Shortliffe, E. (2005). Strategic action in health information technology: Why the obvious has taken so long. *Health Affairs, 24*(5), 1222–1233. doi:10.1377/hlthaff.24.5.1222

Shortliffe, E. H. (1999). The evolution of electronic medical records. *Academic Medicine, 74,* 414–419. doi:10.1097/00001888-199904000-00038

Shoval, P., & Kabeli-Shani, J. (2008). *Designing class methods from dataflow diagrams.* Paper presented at the 17th International Conference on Information System Development (ISD), Paphos, Cyprus.

Sikorski, M. (2003). Zastosowanie metody AHP do analiz bezpieczeństwa na stanowiskach pracy (Application of AHP Method for Occupational Safety Analysis). In O. Downarowicz (Ed.), *Wybrane metody zarządzania bezpieczeństwem pracy* (pp. 71-96). Wydawnictwo Politechniki Gdańskiej, Gdańsk.

Singh, M. P. (2002). *The pragmatic Web: Preliminary thoughts.* Paper presented at the NSF-EU Workshop on Database and Information Systems Research for Semantic Web and Enterprises, Amicalolo Falls and State Park, Georgia.

Ślęzak, D., Synak, P., Wieczorkowska, A., & Wróblewski, J. (2002). KDD-based approach to musical instrument sound recognition. In M.S. Hacid, Z.W. Raś, D.A. Zighed, Y. Kodratoff (Eds.), *Foundations of Intelligent Systems. Proc. of 13th Symposium ISMIS 2002, Lyon, France* (LNAI 2366, pp. 28-36).

Smite, D. (2006). Global software development projects in one of the biggest companies in latvia: Is geographical distribution a problem. *Software Process Improvement and Practice, 11*(1), 61–76. doi:10.1002/spip.252

Smith, H. (2003). *The third wave of business process management.* CSC Europe.

Smits, M. T., van der Poel, K. G., & Ribbers, P. M. A. (1999). Information strategy. In R.D. Galliers, D.E. Leidner & B.S.H. Baker (Eds.), *Strategic information management, challenges and strategies in managing information systems* (pp.61-85). Butteworth-Heinemann, Oxford.

Sobieska-Karpińska, J., & Hernes, M. (2006). Consensus methods in hierarchical and weight incomplete ordered partitions. In J. Dziechciarz (Ed.), *Ekonometric. Employment of quantitative methods*. Wrocław: Wroclaw University of Economics Press.

Sobieska-Karpińska, J., & Hernes, M. (2007). Metody consensusu w systemach wspomagających podejmowanie decyzji, In J. Dziechciarz (Ed), *Ekonometria. Zastosowania metod ilościowych*. Wrocław: Wrocław: Wroclaw University of Economics Press.

Spronk, R. (2008, August 21). *HL7 ADT Messages*. Retrieved October 28, 2008, from http://www.ringholm.de/docs/00210_en_HL7_ADT_messages.htm

Sroka, H. (Ed.). (2006). *Strategie i metodyka przekształcania organizacji w kierunku e-biznesu na podstawie technologii informacyjnej*. Wydawnictwo Akademii Ekonomicznej, Katowice.

Sroka, H. (Ed.). (2007). *Zarys koncepcji nowej teorii organizacji i zarzadzania dla przedsiebiorstw e-gospodarki*. Wydawnictwo Akademii Ekonomicznej, Katowice.

Stanek, S., Sroka, H., & Twardowski, Z. (2003). *Decision Support Systems and New Information Technologies at the Beginning of Internet Age*. 7th International Conference of the International Society for Decision Support Systems, Ustroń, Poland.

Stark, D. (2001). Ambiguous assets for uncertain environments: Heterarchy in postsocialist firms. In P. DiMaggio (Ed.), *The twenty-first-century firm: Changing economic organization in international perspective* (pp. 69-104). Princeton, NJ: Princeton University Press. Retrieved October 13, 2008, from http://www.colbud.hu/main/PubArchive/PL/PLo8-Stark.pdf

Starke-Meyerring, D. (2005). Meeting the challenges of globalization: A framework for global literacies in professional communication programs. *Journal of Business and Technical Communication, 19*, 468–499. doi:10.1177/1050651905278033

Stefanowicz, B. (2004). *Informacja*,Warszawa: Oficyna Wydawnicza Szkoły Głównej Handlowej w Warszawie.

Steinmueller, W. E. (2007). The economics of ICTs: Building blocks and implications. In R. Mansell, Ch. Avgerou, D. Quanh, R. Silverstone (Eds.), *The Oxford handbook of information and communication technologies* (pp. 196-224). Oxford: Oxford University Press.

Stenmark, D. (2002). Information vs. knowledge: The role of intranets in knowledge management. In *Proceedings of HICSS-35*. Hawaii, January 7-10, 2002.

Sterritt, R. (2002). Facing fault management as it is, aiming for what you would like it to be. In D.W. Bustard, W. Liu, R. Sterritt Ceds (Eds.), *Soft Ware: First International Conference on Computing in an Imperfect World* (LNCS 2311, pp. 31-45).

Sterritt, R. (2004). Autonomic networks: engineering the self-healing property. *Engineering Applications of Artificial Intelligence, 17*, 727–739. doi:10.1016/S0952-1976(04)00111-3

Sterritt, R., Parashar, M., Tianfield, H., & Unland, R. (2005). A concise introduction to autonomic computing. *Advanced Engineering Informatics, 19*, 181–187. doi:10.1016/j.aei.2005.05.012

Stewart, M. (2001). Towards a global definition of patient centred care. *British Medical Journal, 32*, 444–445. doi:10.1136/bmj.322.7284.444

Stockheim, T., et al. (2004). How to build a multi-multi-agent system: The Agent.Enterprise approach. In *Proceedings of the 6th international conference on enterprise information systems (ICEIS 2004)* (pp.1-8).

Stojanovic, L., Abecker, A., Stojanovic, N., & Studer, R. (2004b). Ontology-based correlation engines. *International Conference on Autonomic Computing* (pp. 304-305).

Stojanovic, L., Schneider, J., Maedche, A., Libischer, S., Studer, R., & Lumpp, T. (2004a). The role of ontologies in autonomic computing systems. *IBM Systems Journal, 43*(3), 598–616.

Stojanovic, N., Studer, R., & Stojanovic, L. (2003). An approach for the ranking of query results in the Semantic Web. In *Proceedings of the 2nd International Semantic Web Conference (ISWC2003)* (LNCS 2870, pp. 500-516).

Stonier, T. (1984). The knowledge industry. In R. Forsyth (Ed.), *Expert systems. Principles and case studies.* London: Chapman & Hall.

Sturm, A., & Shehory, O. (2002). Towards industrially applicable modelling technique for agent-based systems. In *Proceedings of the first international joint conference on autonomous agents and multiagent systems (ADMAS 2002), Bologna, Italy* (pp. 39-40). ACM Press.

Sundaramurthy, Ch., & Lewis, M. (2003). Control and collaboration: paradoxes of governance. *Academy of Management Review, 28*(3), 397–415.

Sundgren, B. (1973). *An infological approach to data bases.* Stockholm: Skriftserie Statistika Centralbyran.

Suter, T. A., Kopp, S. W., & Hardesty, D. M. (2004). The relationship between general ethical judgments and copying behavior at work. *Journal of Business Ethics, 55,* 61–70. doi:10.1007/s10551-004-1779-z

Sveiby, K. E. (1997). *The new organization wealth.* San Francisco: Berrett-Koehler Publ.

Sveiby, K. E. (2008). *Measuring intangibles and intellectual capital – an emerging first standard.* Retrieved July 2008 from http://www.sveiby.com

Szaniawski, K. (1971). Pragmatyczna wartość informacji (Pragmatic Theory of Information). In: J. Kozielecki (Ed.), *Problemy psychologii matematycznej* (*Problems of the Mathematical Psychology*) (pp. 325-347). Warsaw, Poland: Polish Scientific Publishing House.

Tappenden, P., Chilcott, J., Eggington, S., Oakley, J., & McCabe, C. (2004). Methods for expected value of information analysis in complex health economic models: developments on the health economics models (...). *Health Technology Assessment, 8*(27).

Tavani, H. M. (2004). *Ethics and technology: Ethical issues in an age of information and communication technology.* Hoboken, NJ: John Wiley and Sons.

Tcl Developer Site. (2008). Retrieved September 20, 2008, from http://dev.scriptics.com/

Teng, J. T. C., & Kettinger, W. J. (1995). Business process redesign and information architecture: Exploring the relationships. *Data Base Advances, 26*(1), 30–42.

Thain, D., Tannenbaum, T., & Livny, M. (2002). Condor and the Grid. In *Grid Computing: Making the Global Infrastructure a Reality.*

Torque Administrator Manual. (2008). Retrieved September 20, 2008, from http://www.clusterresources.com/wiki/doku.php?id=torque:torque_wiki

Trammel, K. (1996). Workflow without fear. *Byte, April 1996.*

Treinen, J. J., & Miller-Frost, S. L. (2006). Following the sun: Case studies in global software development. *IBM Systems Journal, 45*(4), 773–783.

Treviño, L. K., & Weaver, G. R. (2003). *Managing ethics in business organizations: Social scientific perspective.* Stanford, CA: Stanford Business Books.

Trzaskalik, T. (Ed.). (2006). *Metody wielokryterialne na polskim rynku finansowym.* Warszawa: Polskie Wydawnictwo Ekonomiczne.

Tsalgatidou, A. (1996). Multilevel Petri Nets for modeling and simulating organizational dynamic behavior. *Simulation & Gaming, 27*(2), 484–506. doi:10.1177/1046878196274005

Tuecke, S., Czajkowski, K., Foster, I., Frey, J., Graham, S., Kesselman, C., et al. (2003). *Open Grid services infrastructure (OGSI), Version 1.0.* Open Grid Services Architecture Working Group, Global Grid Forum. Retrieved September 15, 2007, from http://www.gridforum.org/documents/GFD.15.pdf

Tutorial, G. R. A. S. P. (2005). *First presentation: SLA document, manageability and accounting subsystem.* Retrieved June 18, 2007, from http://eu-grasp.net/english/SalernoMeeting/GRASP%20Tutorial%20Final%20-%20Verdino.ppt#1

Tveit, A. (2001). A survey of agent-oriented software engineering. In *Proceedings of the first NTNU computer science graduate student conference, Norwegian University of Science and Technology, May 2001.* Retrieved from http://amundtveit.info/publications/2001/aose.pdf

Ubayashi, N., & Tamai, T. (2001). Separation of concerns in mobile agent applications. In *Proceedings of the 3rd international conference Reflection 2001* (LNCS 2192, pp. 89-109).

UNICORE. (2008). Retrieved September 25, 2008, from http://www.unicore.eu

United Nations. (2002). World Population Ageing: 1950-2050. Retrieved from http://www.un.org/esa/population/publications/worldageing19502050

Ursul, A. D. (1971). *Informacija*. Moscow: Nauka.

Vaast, E. (2007). What goes online comes offline: Knowledge management system use in a soft bureaucracy. *Organization Studies*, *28*(3), 283–306. doi:10.1177/0170840607075997

Vahs, D. (2005). *Organisation*. Stuttgart: Schaffer-Poeschel Verlag.

Van Alsyne, M. V. (1999). *A proposal for valuing information and instrumental goods*. International Conference on Information Systems, Charlotte, USA.

van den Hoven, M. J. (1995). Equal access and social justice: Information as a primary good. *ETHICOMP*, *95*, 1–17.

van der Linden, H., Kalra, D., Hasman, A., & Talmon, J. (2008). Inter-organizational future proof of HER systems: A review of the security and privacy related issues. *International Journal of Medical Informatics*, *78*(3), 141–160. doi:10.1016/j.ijmedinf.2008.06.013

Van Grembergen, W. (2004). *Strategies for information technology governance*. Hershey, PA: IGI Global.

Varga, L. Z., Jennings, N. R., & Cockburn, D. (1994). Integrating intelligent systems into a cooperating community for electricity distribution management. *International Journal of Expert Systems with Applications*, *7*(4), 563–579. doi:10.1016/0957-4174(94)90080-9

Varian, H. R. (2002). *Mikroekonomia. Kurs średni – ujęcie nowoczesne*. Warszawa: PWN.

Venugopal, S., Buyya, R., & Ramamohanarao, K. (2006). A taxonomy of data Grids for distributed data sharing, management, and processing. *ACM Computing Surveys*, *38*(1). doi:10.1145/1132952.1132955

Veronneau, S., & Cimon, Y. (2007). Maintaining robust decision capabilities: An integrative human-systems approach. *Decision Support Systems*, *43*, 127–140. doi:10.1016/j.dss.2006.08.003

Von Goldammer, E., Paul, J., & Newbury, J. (2003). *Heterarchy – Hierarchy, Two complementary categories of description*. Retrieved October 13, 2007, from http://www.vordenker.de /heterarchy/het_into_en.htm

Wagner, G. (2001). Agent-oriented analysis and design of organizational information systems. In J. Barzdins & A. Caplinskas (Eds.), *Databases and information systems* (pp. 111-124). Kluwer Academic Publishers.

Wagner, G. (2002). A UML profile for external AOR models. In *Proceedings of the international workshop on agent-oriented software engineering (AOSE-2002), held at Autonomous agents & multi-agent systems (AAMAS 2002), Palazzo, Re Enzo, Bologna, Italy, July 15, 2002* (LNAI 2585).

Wagner, G. (2003). The agent-object-relationship metamodel: Towards a unified view of state and behaviour. [Retrieved from http://www.informatik.tu-cottbus.de/~gwagner/AORML/AOR.pdf]. *Information Systems*, *28*(5), 475–504. doi:10.1016/S0306-4379(02)00027-3

Walker, J., Pan, E., Johnston, D., Adler-Milstein, J., Bates, D., & Middleton, B. (2005). The value of health care information exchange and interoperability. *Health Affairs*, *W5*, 10–18.

Wall, S. D. (1977). *Four sector time-series of the U.K. labour force, 1941-1971*. London: UK Post Office, Long Range Studies Division.

Walsh, C. (2002). *Key management ratios*. London: Financial Times/Prentice Hall.

Wang, M., & Wang, H. (2006). From process logic to business logic – A cognitive approach to business process management. *Information & Management*, *43*, 179–193. doi:10.1016/j.im.2005.06.001

Weiss, G. (1995). Adaptation and learning in multi-agent systems: Some remarks and a bibliography. *Proceedings of the IJCAI'95 workshop on adaptation and learning in multi-agent systems* (LNAI 1042, 1-22).

Weiss, G. (Ed.). (2000). *Multiagent systems. A modern approach to distributed artificial intelligence*. Massachusetts: The MIT Press.

Weizenbaum, J. (1976). *Computer power and human reason: From judgment to calculation.* Freeman.

White, S. A. (2004). Process modelling notations and workflow patterns. *IBM Corp.* Retrieved June 9, 2005 from http://www.bpmn.org

Whiteley, D. (2000). *e-Commerce: Strategies, technologies and applications.* McGraw Hill.

Whitten, P., & Kuwahara, E. (2003). Telemedicine from the payor perspective: Considerations for reimbursement decisions. *Disease Management & Health Outcomes, 11*(5), 291–298. doi:10.2165/00115677-200311050-00002

Whitten, P., Buis, L., & Love, B. (2007). Physician-Patient e-visit program. *Disease Management & Health Outcomes, 14*(4), 207–214. doi:10.2165/00115677-200715040-00002

Whitten, P., Buis, L., & Mackert, M. (2007). Factors impacting providers' perceptions regarding Midwestern EMR deployment. Telemedicine and e-Health, 13(4), 391-398.

Whitten, P., Love, B., Buis, L., & Mackert, M. (in press). Health education online for individuals with low health literacy: Evaluation of the diabetes and you website. *Journal of Technology in Human Services.*

Wiener, N. (1948). *Cybernetics: Or control and communication in the animal and the machine.* Technology Press.

Wiener, N. (1954). *The human use of human beings – Cybernetics and society* (2nd ed). New York: Doubleday Anchor Books, Doubleday & Company, Inc.

Wiener, N. (1954). *The human use of human beings: Cybernetics and society* (2nd ed.). Boston: Houghton Mifflin.

Wierzbicki, A. P. (2007). Modeling as a way of organizing knowledge. *European Journal of Operational Research, 176,* 610–635. doi:10.1016/j.ejor.2005.08.018

Wierzbicki, A. P., & Wydro, K. B. (2006) *Informacyjne aspekty negocjacji.* Warszawa: Wydawnictwo Naukowe Obserwacje.

Williamson, O. (1996). Transaction cost economics. The Mechanisms of Governance (pp. 54-92). Oxford University Press.

Willis, L., Demiris, G., & Oliver, D. (2007). Internet use by hospice families and providers: A review. *Journal of Medical Systems, 31*(2), 97–101. doi:10.1007/s10916-006-9033-0

Winograd, T., & Flores, F. (1986). *Understanding computers and cognition: A new foundation for design.* Norwood: Ablex Publishing Corporation.

Wittson, C., Affleck, D., & Johnson, V. (1961). Two-way television in group therapy. *Mental Hospitals, 12,* 22–23.

Wolff, E. N. (2005). The growth of information workers in the U.S. economy. *Communications of the ACM, 10*(48).

Wong, A. K. Y., Ray, P., Parameswaran, N., & Strassner, J. (2005). Ontology mapping for the interoperability problem in network management. *IEEE Journal on Selected Areas in Communications, 23*(10), 2058–2068. doi:10.1109/JSAC.2005.854130

Wooldridge, M. (1999). *Intelligent agents* (pp. 1-51). The MIT Press. Retrieved from http://www.csc.liv.ac.uk/~mjw/pubs/mas99.pdf

Wooldridge, M. (2002). *An introduction to multi agent systems.* Chichester, UK: John Wiley & Sons. Retrieved from http://www.csc.liv.ac.uk/~mjw/pubs/imas/

Wooldridge, M., & Jennings, N. (1995). Intelligent agents: Theory and practice. *The Knowledge Engineering Review, 10*(2), 1–46. doi:10.1017/S0269888900008122

Wooldridge, M., Jennings, N., & Kinny, D. (2000). The Gaia methodology for agent-oriented analysis and design. *Journal of Autonomous Agents and Multi-Agent Systems, 3*(3), 285–312. doi:10.1023/A:1010071910869

World Summit on the Information Society. (2003). The Geneva declaration of principles and plan of action. Geneva: WSIS Executive Secretariat. Retrieved from http://www.itu.int/wsis/docs/geneva/official/dop.html

Wu, J. J., & Tsang, A. S. L. (2008). Factors affecting members' trust belief and behaviour intention in virtual communities. *Behaviour & Information Technology*, *27*(2), 115–125. doi:10.1080/01449290600961910

Wustenhoff, E. (2002). *Service level agreement in the data center*. Retrieved February 10, 2009, from http://www.sun.com/blueprints/0402/sla.pdf

Xie, H. (2006). Understanding human-work domain interaction: Implications for the design of a corporate digital library. *Journal of the American Society for Information Science and Technology*, *57*(1), 128–143. doi:10.1002/asi.20261

Xilin, J., & Jianxin, W. (2007). Applying semantic knowledge for event correlation in network fault management. *2007 Int. Conf. on Convergence Information Technology* (pp.715-720).

Yan, K. Q., Wang, S. C., & Chiang, M. L. (2004). New application of reliable agreement: Underlying an unsecured business environment. *ACM SIGOPS Operating Systems Review*, *38*(3), 42–57. doi:10.1145/1035834.1035840

Yoo, J., Catanio, J., Paul, R., & Bieber, M. (2004). Relationship analysis in requirements engineering [Electronic Version]. *Requirements Engineering*, 1–19.

Yuhong, Y., Zakaria, M., & Weiming, S. (2001). Integration of workflow and agent technology for business process management. *The sixth international conference on CSCW in design, July 12-14, 2001, London, Ontario, Canada* (pp. 420-426).

Zacher, L. W. (Ed.). (1997). *Rewolucja informacyjna i społeczeństwo. Niektóre trendy, zjawiska i kontrowersje*. Warsaw, Poland: Educational Foundation "Transformations".

Zack, M. H. (1999). Developing a knowledge strategy. *California Management Review*, *41*(3), 125–145.

Zeng, Z., Meng, B., & Zeng, Y. (2005). An intelligent agent-based system in Internet commerce. *Proceedings of the fourth international conference on machine learning and cybernetics, Guangzhou, China, August 2005*, 18-21.

Zheng, R., Jin, H., Zhang, Q., Liu, Y., & Chu, P. (2008). Heterogeneous medical data share and integration on Grid. *International Conference on BioMedical Engineering and Informatics. 1* (pp. 905-909). Sanya: IEEE.

Zhengping, L., Low, M. Y. H., & Kumar, A. A. (2003). A framework for multi-agent system-based dynamic supply chain coordination. In *Proceedings of the workshop at the second international joint conference of autonomous agents and multiagent systems (AAMAS 2003)*.

Zhong, N., Liu, J., & Yao, Y. (Eds.). (2003). *Web intelligence*. Berlin: Springer.

Zimmermann, H.-J. (2006). Knowledge management, knowledge discovery, and intelligent data mining. *Cybernetics and Systems: An International Journal*, *37*, 509–531. doi:10.1080/01969720600734412

ZIV der WWU Münster ZIVcluster. (2006). Retrieved September 5, 2008, from http://zivcluster.uni-muenster.de/

About the Contributors

Malgorzata Pankowska is an Assistant Professor of the Department of Informatics at the Karol Adamiecki University of Economics in Katowice, Poland. She received the qualification in econometrics and statistics from the Karol Adamiecki University of Economics in Katowice in 1981, the Ph.D. degree in 1988 and the Doctor Habilitatus degree in 2009, both from the Karol Adamiecki University of Economics in Katowice. She participated in EU Leonardo da Vinci Programme projects as well as gave lectures within the Socrates Program Teaching Staff Exchange in Braganca, Portugal, Trier, Germany, Brussels, Belgium, and in Vilnius, Lithuania. She is a member of ISACA and the Secretary in the Board of the Polish Scientific Society of Business Informatics. Her research interests include Virtual Organization development, ICT project management, IT outsourcing, information governance, and business information systems design and implementation.

* * *

Vassiliki Andronikou obtained her diploma from the Electrical and Computer Engineering Department of the National Technical University of Athens in 2004. She has worked in the National Bank of Greece and the Organization of Telecommunications of Greece, and since 2004 she has been a research associate and Ph.D. candidate in the Telecommunications Laboratory of the NTUA. In 2005 she was given the Ericsson award for her Thesis on Mobile IPv6 with Fast Handovers. Her research has involved her participation in many European projects, with her interests focusing on the fields of the security and privacy aspects of biometrics and data management in Grid.

Ole Axvig developed an interest in information management over years spent as a project manager and operations manager for small consulting firms. He currently works as an independent management consultant.

Hassan Bezzazi is a lecturer at law faculty of University de Lille 2 where he is currently Project Manager for the Internet and Informatics Certificate, Legal Professions (C2I-LP). He has a doctorate in Computer Science from University de Lille 1. He led educational activities for nine years in Athens. His main research areas are Information Systems and Law, Artificial Intelligence and e-learning. He is member of a number of conference and project evaluation committees. He designed and developed a number of tools related to expert systems and education. He participated in interdisciplinary projects with lawyers on as various subjects as security, data protection and e-government. His current research activities focus on the design and development of distributed e-learning platforms for interdisciplinary training as well as appropriate training and assessment methods for informal knowledge and competence transfer.

Doctor **Habilitatus Juris Borzovs** is a Professor and the Head of Computing Department at University of Latvia, Director and Chairman of the Board at Riga Information Technology Institute (RITI), and Deputy President in Quality Affairs at a/s Exigen Services Latvia. He is also the founder and first president of Latvian Information and Communications Technology Association (LIKTA) and the founder and first president of Latvia Chapter of Information Systems Audit and Control Association (ISACA). Borzovs is a member of IEEE Computer Society and IEEE-Standards Association. His research interests include software engineering methods and standards, quality management, terminology, information technology education and training. Borzovs received a habilitation qualification (Doctor habilitatus) in Computer Science from University of Latvia in 1999. Contact him at University of Latvia, Computing Department; Raina bulv. 19, LV-1586, Riga, Latvia; Juris.Borzovs@lu.lv

Adriana Schiopoiu Burlea is a Professor of human resources management at the University of Craiova, Faculty of Economics and Business Administration, Romania. Her research interests include computer ethics, corporate social responsibility, online education, human behavior in designing, implementing, and applying IT. She continues to focus on research that explores innovation processes using knowledge, organizational networking perspectives, management skills, competence and capability. Her research emphasizes a critical, practice-based understanding of the social aspects of knowledge management, and organizations networked relations. She has published more than 75 journal articles and conference papers, as well as numerous books and book chapters in the areas of human resource management, information systems, corporate social responsibility, human capital and intellectual capital.

Sten Carlsson has a Ph.D. in Information Systems from Karlstad University (2000). His research focus is on communication and learning in systems development. As senior lecturer at the department of Information Systems at Karlstad University, Sweden, he is a supervisor for doctoral students. He is involved in the Life World Group at Gothenburg University where his research interest concerns phenomenological and philosophical questions about what understanding of computers and system development means as ontological questions. His publication of research articles has concerned different contexts like electronic commerce, system development and models, using computers at school in a didactical perspective, the problem of interpretation of the usability of computers and prototyping.

Lichun Chiang is an Associate Professor at the Department of Political Science in the National Cheng Kung University, Tainan, Taiwan. Her interest research topics are e-government, public administration and information technology. She may be reached at e-mail: lcchiang@mail.ncku.edu.tw.

Prof. Doctor **Habilitatus Witold Stefan Chmielarz** is a lecturer and researcher at Faculty of Management of University of Warsaw. He studied economy at Faculty of Economy, University of Warsaw, where he obtained his M.Sc. for the thesis "*Effectiveness of IT using in Polish Airlines*". Next he worked at Institute of Systems Research of Polish Academy of Science. In 1984 he received his Ph.D. degree in management science from University of Warsaw for the thesis "*Information Problems of Region Economy Modeling*". From this time he worked at University of Warsaw. He completed his habilitation in 1997. His habilitation work was on "*Decision Support Systems: Model Aspects in Systems Construct-*

ing". He is Full Professor in economy from 2006 for the research work on "*e-Banking Systems*". His practical experience includes three years in several computer firms, as a designer and advisor. He also has consulting experience for banks and small and medium enterprises. His major research interests include e-commerce and e-banking. He has published over 100 articles, papers and books.

Prof. Doctor **Habilitatus Dariusz Dziuba** is working at Economics Faculty, Warsaw University (WU), as Chair of Information Systems and Economic Analysis Department. He studied at WU, and graduated from the Economics Faculty (1982). Since 1982 he has worked at WU. He received Ph.D. degree in economics for the thesis "*Economic semiotics*" at WU in 1989. He was habilitated in economics for the thesis "*Economics of the information sector*" at WU in 1999. He took part in the fellowships at Glasgow University, Scotland (1991/92) and at Universitat des Saarlandes, Saarbrucken (1993/95). He was the visiting professor at Aalborg University, Denmark (1988) and at Humboldt University (1990), Fachhochschule Heidelberg, Germany (1995). In 1992/93 he was the Director of the Department of Statistical Training and Foreign Cooperation in the Central Statistical Office of Poland. He was the Professor at Skarbek Graduate School of Business Economics, Department of Business Informatics, Warsaw (2003/04). He has numerous publications in the following areas: information economy, information society, economics of the information sector, business informatics, artificial intelligence and semiotics methods for analysis and synthesis of economic information systems, economics information, banking information systems, history of exchanges, auctions.

Michael Firopoulos is Project Manager in Intracom, a Greek information and communication technology solutions provider. As a specialist in the analysis and design of hospital information systems, he has worked as Hospital Information System Consultant and has led many national projects related to the provision of healthcare solutions for Greek hospitals. His most recent activities involved the development of an advanced system enabling the interoperability among the Greek hospitals and the public insurance organizations.

Janis Grundspenkis is a Professor of the Department of Systems Theory and Design and the Dean of the Faculty of Computer Science and Information Technology at Riga Technical University, Latvia. He received a qualification in electrical engineering from Riga Polytechnical Institute in 1965, a Dr.sc.ing. degree in 1972 and a Dr.habil.sc.ing. degree in 1993, both from Riga Technical University. His research interests are: integration of intelligent agent and multiagent techniques with knowledge management approach for the development of intelligent tutoring, business process management and logistics systems, and mathematical methods for the analysis of complex system structure. He has about 200 publications in these and related areas. In 2006 he received the award as "RTU scientist 2006". He teaches several courses of Systems Theory and Artificial Intelligence. He is an affiliate member of IEEE Computing Society and a professional member of Association for Computing Machinery.

Prima Gustiené is a lecturer at the department of Information Systems at Karlstad University, Sweden. She holds a high education diploma in Information Systems from Karlstad University. She is a member of the research group at Karlstad University on Enterprise System Architecture. Her research interests include the Pragmatic and Semantic aspects of Information System Development, Enterprise Modeling and Graphical Representations of business processes. She is involved in the development of the Pragmatic-driven method for service-oriented modeling of information systems. Prima Gustiené participated in several research projects such as Models and Methods of Electronic Commerce and in the international project on new software technologies that was sponsored by the Japanese industry agency. Prima Gustienė is the author/co-author of more than dozen research publications. She is teaching Object-Oriented System Design and System Development courses.

Dr. **Dimitrios Halkos** is Research Associate in the Telecommunication Laboratory of the Institute of Communication and Computer Systems (ICCS), Athens, Greece. He graduated from the Dept. of Electrical and Computer Engineering of the National Technical University of Athens, Greece in 2001. In 2008 he acquired, from the same university, his Ph.D. in the area of Maritime Operational Research with a focus on cargo ships routing and scheduling. He has been involved in several EU and national funded projects and his research interests include implementation of routing and scheduling algorithms and multi-criteria decision support systems. He has also worked as technical manager, consultant and software engineer in private sector.

Prof. **Igor Hawryszkiewycz** completed a BE and ME degrees in Electrical Engineering at the University of Adelaide, and a PhD degree at the Massachusetts Institute of Technology. He has developed methods for the design of systems emphasizes which over time covered database design, information systems design and currently focuses on developing requirements for collaborative systems and supporting them with technology that integrates collaboration into the business process. His work has included both research as well as industrial applications and has been reported in over 150 publications and 3 text books.

Marcin Hernes is a Ph.D. student of Management, Computer Science and Finance Department of Wroclaw University of Economics, a university teacher of Academy of Management in Lodz (Poland). He is the author and co-author of many articles published in national and international publishing houses. Moreover, he is a participant of scientific national and international conferences, a lecturer of the issues that concern distributed decision support systems, conflicts in multi-agent systems, the methods of consensus, negotiation and cooperation, the systems of deductive and temporary data bases, and the systems of coordination and visualization. Marcin Hernes is a practitioner (of many years) in the scope of management systems, coordination and automation of production processes, digital systems of measurement, systems of distributed data bases, and multi-agent decision support systems. Apart from that, he is the author of several dozen computer applications that function in industrial enterprises or state-owned institutions.

Ms. **Bree E. Holtz** holds a Master of Science degree in Analysis, Design, and Management of Information Systems from the London School of Economics (London, UK), along with a Bachelor's degree in Telecommunications from Michigan State University. She is currently a doctoral candidate in the Media and Information Studies program at Michigan State University where she studies technology in healthcare as well as peoples' perceptions and adoption of technology in the health setting. Currently, Ms. Holtz is a Site Coordinator and researcher for Midwest Alliance for Telehealth and Technology Resource Center (MATTeR). She also is a research assistant for many e-Health initiatives through the Telehealth Research Lab at Michigan State University. Previously, Ms. Holtz worked for CoreComm as a Project Manager and Business Analyst in the development of new products and formation of external partnerships.

Dimitris Kanellopoulos holds a Ph.D. in multimedia communications from the Department of Electrical and Computer Engineering of the University of Patras, Greece. He is a member of the Educational Software Development Laboratory (ESDLab) in the Department of Mathematics at the University of Patras. His research interests include multimedia communications, intelligent information systems, knowledge representation and web-based education. He has authored many papers in international journals and conferences at these areas. He serves as an Editor in ten scientific journals.

Dr. **Jure Kovač** is the Associate Professor of organization and management at the Faculty of Organizational Sciences, University of Maribor. His teaching and research interest are: organization theory, organization design, management and project management.

Dr. **Michael Mackert**'s current research focus is on health literacy, with a particular interest in the best ways to design health messages to reach low health literate populations. This work applies to both new digital media (e.g., e-health interventions designed specifically for low literate and low health literate audiences) and traditional media (e.g., health literacy issues in direct-to-consumer pharmaceutical advertising). Other research interests include telemedicine implementations to provide healthcare services at a distance, the role of trust in communication and advertising, and mass media/interpersonal impacts on healthy behaviors.

Antons Mislevics is a research assistant and Ph.D. student of the Department of Systems Theory and Design of the Faculty of Computer Science and Information Technology at Riga Technical University. He received an M.Sc. degree in computer systems from Riga Technical University in 2007. His research interests are intelligent agents and business process management. He has participated in several projects in the area of multiagent systems development, and also is developing a software tool for plagiarism detection in students' individual works. He is working for Microsoft Latvia as a Development Consultant, specializing in collaboration platforms and solutions for business process management.

Judit Olah has been a researcher and a practitioner in the area of interactive information retrieval and information management. She graduated from Rutgers University, School of Information, Library and Communication Studies in 2003; her dissertation focused on modeling user behavior in interactive information retrieval. Since then she continued to focus on the role and efficiency of information interactions and access to information sources in a variety of user environments: educational, corporate and non-profit settings.

Dr. rer. nat. **Claus-Peter Rückemann** studied geophysics, computer science, geosciences, and archaeology with strong interests in scientific information systems and distributed and High Performance Computing. He received his university diploma in geophysics and his doctorate diploma in geosciences, informatics, and geoinformatics from the Westfälische Wilhelms-Universität (WWU) Münster, Germany. Dr. Rückemann teaches information systems and security in the European Legal Informatics Study Programme at the institute for legal informatics, Leibniz Universität Hannover (LUH), Germany. He is leading scientific advisor for national and international projects. For the last fifteen years he worked for scientific institutes and computing centers as lecturer, project manager, scientific author, coordinator and project leader of interdisciplinary research projects and as initial coordinator of the sections Monitoring, Accounting, and Billing, for establishing the German D-Grid in the German e-Science Initiative. As scientific member of the WWU and LUH he currently works for the North-German Supercomputing Alliance (HLRN) and the Computing Centre of the LUH.

Dr. **Brane Semolic** is the head of Project & Technology Management Institute, he is the International Project Management Association, IPMA assessor for Project Management, PM competences, and the assessor for IPMA project award, as well as the International Cost Engineering Council ICEC Distinguished International Fellow, and Professor of project and program management, technology management, management of virtual network organizations on graduate and postgraduate level at the University of Maribor, Cranefield College and visiting professor in many international programmes.

Gabriel Sideras received his diploma from the Informatics department of the Athens University of Economics and Business (AUEB) in 2006. He has worked in the private sector as software developer and consultant, while currently he is a Research Associate in the Telecommunications Laboratory of the National Technical University of Athens. His research interests include e-health and system interoperability within the healthcare sector.

Dr. **Darja Smite** is an Assistant Professor and a Senior Researcher in Software Engineering at Blekinge Institute of Technology, and an Assistant Professor at University of Latvia. She also works as an IT consultant at Riga Information Technology Institute in Latvia. Her research interests include global software engineering, benefits and challenges of outsourcing and offshoring software work, team coordination and software process improvement. Smite received a Ph.D. in Computer Science from University of Latvia in 2007. Contact her at Blekinge Institute of Technology; School of Engineering (APS), SE-37225, Ronneby, Sweden; Darja.Smite@bth.se, or University of Latvia, Computing Department; Raina bulv. 19, LV-1869, Riga, Latvia; Darja.Smite@lu.lv

Jadwiga Sobieska-Karpińska is a Professor of Wroclaw University of Economics, a head of Economic Communication Department; she has been a deputy dean of Management, Computer Science and Finance Department twice, a member of the senate, a chairwoman of Curriculum Council of Scientific Works in the domain of economic computer science. Moreover, she is the editor of the book series: "Computer Science in Management" , a Professor of the Academy of Management in Lodz (Poland), a dean of the non-resident department. She has been a former head of Silesian International Business School; a Doctor Habilitatus in economic sciences in the scope of economics and computer science. Apart from that, Jadwiga Sobieska-Karpińska specializes in the domains of economic computer science, economic communication, e-business, computer decision support systems, and information society. Furthermore, she is a member and a founder of the Polish Scientific Society of Business Informatics, the author and co-author of 209 scientific works, inter alia, books and reports on international conferences.

Prof. Doctor **Habilitatus Henryk Sroka** is the Director of the Department of Informatics at the Karol Adamiecki University of Economics in Katowice, Poland. His research interests cover Decision Support Systems, methodologies of information systems development, expert Systems and integrated information systems implementation. He focuses on business process reengineering and information systems strategy development for business organizations. In his publications he considers the problems of information society and global information economics as well as e-business models. He teaches several courses of Decision Support Systems and e-Business Strategy and Models. He is the President of the Polish Scientific Society of Business Informatics.

Prof. Doctor **Habilitatus Bogdan Stefanowicz** (1937) received university degree in mathematical statistics at the Warsaw University. He is a scientific researcher at the Warsaw School of Economics, Department of Business Informatics. He is a member of several scientific societies in Poland. He is the author of over 120 publications on information, information processing and systems, programming, and the related issues. The main areas of his interest are as follows: infological interpretation of information (its properties, variety, functions, quality); information processes; business information systems; Artificial Intelligence methods in business.

Prof. **Theodora A. Varvarigou** received the B. Tech degree from the National Technical University of Athens, Athens, Greece in 1988, the Ma.E. degrees in Electrical Engineering (1989) and in Computer Science (1991) from Stanford University, Stanford, California in 1989 and the Ph.D. degree from Stanford University as well in 1991. She worked at AT&T Bell Labs, Holmdel, New Jersey between 1991 and 1995. Between 1995 and 1997 she worked as an Assistant Professor at the Technical University of Crete, Chania, Greece. In 1997 she was elected an Assistant Professor and since 2007 she is a Professor at the National Technical University of Athens, and Director of the Postgraduate Course "Engineering Economics Systems". Prof. Varvarigou has great experience in the area of semantic web technologies, scheduling over distributed platforms, embedded systems and grid computing. In this area, she has published more than 150 papers in leading journals and conferences. She has participated and coordinated several EU funded projects.

Pamela Whitten, Ph.D., is a Professor in the Department of Telecommunications and an Associate Dean in the College of Communication Arts & Sciences and at Michigan State University. In her faculty position, Dr. Whitten is responsible for conducting technology and health-related research, as well as teaching graduate and undergraduate courses. Dr. Whitten's research focuses on the use of technology in health care with a specific interest in telehealth and its impact on the delivery of health care services and education. Prior research projects range from telepsychiatry to telehospice and telehome care for COPD and CHF patients. In addition to her work assessing outcomes and impacts of telemedicine, she also conducts research that examines innovative uses of mediated communication to reach underserved populations, such as the creation of health websites for low literate adults.

Index

B

C

D

E

H

I

J

K

L

M

N

O

P

T

U

V

W

X

Z